The Individual, Society, and Education

The Individual, Society, and Education

A History of American Educational Ideas

Second Edition

Clarence J. Karier

UNIVERSITY OF ILLINOIS PRESS
Urbana and Chicago

Illini Books edition, 1986

© 1967, 1986 by the Board of Trustees of the University of Illinois
Manufactured in the United States of America
P 5 4 3 2

This book is printed on acid-free paper.

Library of Congress Cataloging-in-Publication Data

Karier, Clarence J.
The individual, society, and education.

Rev. ed. of: Man, society, and education. 1967.
Includes bibliographies and index.
1. Education—United States—History.   2. Education—
Philosophy—History.   I. Karier, Clarence J.   Man,
society, and education.   II. Title.
LA205.K3   1986   370'.973   85-24547
ISBN 0-252-01309-3

To Norma

Contents

Preface

When first approached on whether I would like to reissue *Man, Society, and Education* (1967), my reaction was that it needed to be brought up-to-date and that I could do so by adding a major chapter on the post-World War II period and a follow-up chapter on the Supreme Court. I was, it seems, overly optimistic. In researching and writing these chapters, I was reminded of the perceptiveness of John Dewey when he said:

The slightest reflection shows that the conceptual material employed in writing history is that of the period in which a history is written. There is no material available for leading principles and hypotheses save that of the historic present. As a culture changes, the conceptions that are dominant in a culture change. Of necessity new standpoints for viewing, appraising, and ordering data arise, history is then rewritten.[1]

In the twenty years since *Man, Society, and Education* was first developed, American society has undergone extremely rapid change along certain cultural dimensions. These changes, as Dewey pointed out, "of necessity" create "new standpoints for viewing, appraising, and ordering data." As these new standpoints emerge as part of one's perceptual vision of the world and a reordering is required, one becomes self-consciously aware of the process. In the past twenty years I have become increasingly sensitized to the many ways in which racism and sexism pervade our social life and, as a consequence, I have become increasingly uncomfortable with the title *Man, Society, and Education*. While one can recognize that in the earlier work the term *man* was used in the generic sense and was not intended to mean man as male, as opposed to female, nevertheless the offensive nature of that usage exists. I have, therefore, changed the title of the book to *The Individual, Society, and Education*, even though the term *individual* does not

---

1. John Dewey, *Logic: The Theory of Inquiry* (New York: Henry Holt and Company, 1938), p. 253.

quite capture the full meaning of the generic term *man*. It does come close.

The problem, however, does not end there. As one proceeds through the text, one is struck by the extent to which such phrases as the "nature of man," "broad as man," etc., permeate the content and very structure of the book. Over the years I have not only become conscious of the sexist language I had been using, but I also have come to agree with the arguments against the use of such language. Therefore, if I were to rewrite this book in its entirety, I would eliminate the offending language altogether. Sad to say, the problem extends further than language. Reading through the text, one finds a lack of material on the women's struggle for equity in the pre- and post-Civil War period, as well as any serious reflection on their struggle in the twentieth century. Once again, if the text were to be rewritten, it would have to include not only the women's movement as a separate section, but would also have to incorporate much of the excellent history that has been done on women as an integrated part of a more complete picture of the American history of education. In the new chapter on the cold war period, I have incorporated a section on the women's movement, but this in no way makes up for the lack of materials elsewhere in the text.

Much of the same kind of criticism can be leveled at my treatment of minorities and the problem of racism which permeates our history. Certainly, my failure to treat Jefferson's racism would require correcting,[2] as would my lack of treatment of that issue in Lester Frank Ward's ideas, as well as in much of the liberal ideology at the turn of the century. Also lacking in the 1967 material is any analysis by which many liberals incorporated their racial and sexist ideologies into the eugenics movement and the mental hygiene movement, as part of the broader progressive reform movement at the turn of the century. Here, too, I would like to correct the offending language. My frequent use of "Negro" would change to "black."

The material on pragmatism as expressed in the neo-Enlightenment thought of Peirce, James, and Dewey, and the new liberalism as expressed by Dewey, Mead, and others, fairly depicted the optimistic philosophy which dominated American thought for the first half of the twentieth century. It does not, however, treat critically enough the reasons why liberalism in both thought and practice in the second half of the twentieth century has failed to be reconstructed, and therefore has tended to go down to defeat at the hands of neo-conservative forces. Part of this failure, no doubt, can be tied to the emergence of the cold war and the failure to achieve the necessary social dialog required for such a reconstruction.

On the other hand, part of the problem might be found in the uncritical way in which the younger generation of educational philosophers learned to practice their philosophy. As that generation joined the "John Dewey" society, they tended to become imitators rather than critics of the great man. John Dewey, as *the* American philosopher, cast a shadow over the

---

2. See, for example, Winthrop D. Jordan, *White over Black: American Attitudes Toward the Negro 1550–1812* (Baltimore, Md.: Penguin Books, Inc., 1968), pp. 429–481.

next generation, a shadow which seemed to inhibit "growth." It is ironic that the philosopher who so emphasized growth had, in the end, produced so little growth around him. Thirty years after his death, one could not name a single American educational philosopher anywhere near the stature of Dewey. The torch had failed to pass. Perhaps the age of "great" men and women had passed, too. Nevertheless, the need for reconstruction of the American liberal philosophy and the liberal philosophy of education lives on in the existential circumstances of daily events.

It is perhaps unfair to place too much emphasis for the demise of the new liberalism in the last two decades on the leaders who so successfully reconstructed nineteenth-century classical liberalism into twentieth-century new liberal ideology. After all, they did their job, even if their influence in later years tended to stifle rather than liberate dialog. Here, of course, historical context is most important. The effects of the cold war on American education and society in the second half of this century have been profound in every respect. The fear of Communism, both without and within, has affected liberal and conservative alike. "Willing to go anywhere and pay any price," Americans sacrificed much in their forty-year anti-Communist crusade. The inescapable fact is that liberals, more so than conservatives, were the architects of that era. Sidney Hook, student, follower, and heir apparent to John Dewey, spent much of his life in the service of that cause. The cold war is, no doubt, a major reason why American liberal social and educational philosophy has never been reconstructed in any meaningful sense in the postwar period.

Therefore, in Chapter Eleven, I have tried to show the struggle to reform American social and educational institutions within the context of the ever-present influence of the cold war conditions. While the overall picture portrayed is not very optimistic, one must recognize that in spite of the stilted dialog and failed opportunities resulting from cold war activities, the nation is still undergoing a major social struggle of women, minorities, and blacks for social justice and equity, the future for whom is yet undetermined. Much of this struggle is taking place in the courtroom, and is reflected in the inordinate numbers of United States Supreme Court cases involving education which I develop in Chapter Thirteen.

Thus, the social and educational challenge for the future remains. Whether that future will be more humane than our past can be determined only by our future efforts. Hayden V. White once said, "The contemporary historian has to establish the value of the study of the past, not as 'an end in itself' but as a way of providing perspective on the present that contributes to the solution of problems peculiar to our own times."[3] It is hoped that *The Individual, Society, and Education* may prove useful for those who struggle to find solutions to our problems.

In bringing this volume up-to-date, I have incurred a debt to the many students, faculty, secretaries, typists, and research assistants it has been my good fortune to know, to learn from, and to dialog with, while at the

---

3. Hayden V. White, "The Burden of History," *History and Theory*, V, 2 (1966), 111–134.

University of Illinois. While I share with them the responsibility for whatever strengths are to be found in this material, I take full responsibility for its shortcomings. Lastly, to Norma Karier, my wife, goes my very deepest gratitude for her continued encouragement and constant support.

Clarence J. Karier

Preface to the first edition

Although men like Emerson and Dewey often spoke of education as being as "broad as man," seldom has the history of education been pursued from that point of view. Most often it has been pursued as if education were as "broad as the school." Indeed, the field of history of education has usually been confined to the development of the school as an institution and of pedagogy as a science. This book differs from many other textbooks on the history of education in that its chief focus is on men and ideas, with somewhat less emphasis on what took place in the schools. Rather than using the school as the center of our discussion, I have deliberately focused attention on concepts of *human nature* and *community,* on the assumption that the way men defined themselves and their ideal society has had important implications for educational thought as well as practice. We are thus concerned with religious, social, and political thought as well as with the purely pedagogical. The school emerges in this context as only one among a number of social agencies that educate man. Therefore, those who are looking for the complete history of the American school or the complete history of American educational thought will not find it here. This book presents but one perspective of the American educational experience.

Out of the vast and varied panorama of the history of American thought, I have chosen to emphasize the last one hundred years. The century from 1865 to 1965 was one of great transformation in American society, thought, and education. By 1865, Marx and Engels had issued their *Communist Manifesto;* Charles Darwin had published *The Origin of Species;* and Sigmund Freud and John Dewey had been born. By 1965, our conceptions of man and society had been radically altered by developments in the new social science fields of psychology, sociology, and anthropology, as well as by astounding advances in human knowledge in the theoretical and technical sciences and by an increasing concern with human rights.

We cannot, however, ignore or discount all that went before; history is cumulative, and the present must be built on the past. The first three chapters, therefore, are devoted to the period prior to 1865. The first chapter deals with Puritan New England and its conception of man and society. This conception is a useful and important point of departure for viewing American education in the seventeenth and eighteenth centuries. This is not to imply that nothing of educational significance occurred in the South or in the Middle Atlantic colonies. However, it may certainly be argued that New England was the most significant region of the country in this era, and it is clear that the Puritan left a distinctive mark on New England, just as New England left its educational trademark on the nation.

Chapter Two deals with the eighteenth- and nineteenth-century Enlightenment conception of human nature and the good society. Thomas Jefferson and Benjamin Franklin are identified as exemplars of the Enlightenment view of man and society and as precursors of much that took place in nineteenth-century educational practice.

Chapter Three focuses attention on the social and intellectual conditions related to Horace Mann's sense of community and his role in the development of the common school. Again, this is a selective account. There were other leaders involved in the common school, such as Henry Barnard in Connecticut and Caleb Mills in Indiana; nevertheless, if one person most reflects the sense of community which motivated the development of the common school, that person is Horace Mann.

Chapter Four deals with the development of the academy into the modern high school and the transformation of institutions of higher learning into our modern colleges and universities. Involved in these changes were the growing realization of the impact of education on society and the concomitant feeling of public responsibility; the decline of the classical curriculum; and the new idea of state universities.

The next four chapters deal with different views of human nature, the good society, and education. In Chapter Five neo-Enlightenment views are discussed, including those of Herbert Spencer, William Graham Sumner, and Lester Frank Ward. Pragmatism is examined in Chapter Six, including a discussion of the ideas of Charles S. Peirce, William James, and John Dewey. Chapter Seven deals with psychological conceptions of man and the good society, including the primitivistic, neoclassical, social behavioristic, and connectionist. The views of the humanists—rhetorical, philosophic, religious—are discussed in Chapter Eight.

Nineteenth- and twentieth-century educators have been faced with a dilemma of focus: Should the schools educate the "man" or the "citizen"? Should they be most interested in the nature of the child or in the good of society? Chapter Nine discusses various views on the subject, including those of Heinrich Pestalozzi, Johann Friedrich Herbart, and James B. Conant.

Chapter Ten discusses Communist and Fascist views of the nature of man and the good society, both in the past and in the present. Finally, Chapter Eleven presents a brief history of the relationship between the United States Supreme Court and education. Landmark cases are discussed as well as overall problems, both those that have been solved and those still unsolved.

With the increased availability of excellent primary sources in paperbacks, it is apparent that one could teach the history of American education through the use of primary sources alone. Yet students often seem to need a model which gives some sense of continuity and perspective without presuming to tell the whole story. In this sense, *Man, Society, and Education* was conceived as a stimulant for further reading in the primary sources in history of education. Indeed, if this book achieves its purpose, it should leave the student with more questions than answers, a conscious awareness of his incomplete knowledge of the American educational tradition, and some sense of the vast, uncharted, intellectually rich and exciting aspects of the tradition. The student who has all the answers has not seriously faced the right questions, just as a book that has all the answers has failed to raise the significant questions.

In writing this book, I have incurred a debt to many people. While I take sole responsibility for the weaknesses in this work, I share with many the responsibility for its strengths.

To the students at the University of Rochester, I am indebted for their responsive challenge to many of the ideas expressed in this book. To Dean William A. Fullagar of the College of Education, University of Rochester, I am indebted for the clerical and financial support which helped make the book possible, and to the Faculty he represents, I am deeply grateful for many hours of fruitful discussion. My appreciation also goes to Henry E. Butler, Jr., and Robert L. Osborn, who read, criticized, and constructively challenged the ideas in this book when it was in the early draft stage. Their assistance in providing a critical dialog through which many of the concepts in this book could be sifted and winnowed has been of immeasurable value. To Merle Borrowman, Catherine J. Sullivan, and Effie L. Riley, who sensitively read and criticized the manuscript in its final form, goes my appreciation. I am further indebted to Margaret M. Mattern, Education Librarian, University of Rochester, for her expert and willing assistance in obtaining necessary documentary materials. To Norma Karier, my wife, goes my deepest gratitude not only for her tireless efforts in typing the original manuscript but for her constant support and encouragement.

Clarence J. Karier

.

Introduction

*It is open to every man to choose the direction of his strivings;
and also, every man may draw comfort from Lessing's fine
saying, that the search for truth is more precious than its
possession.* ALBERT EINSTEIN

History is not the story of man's past but rather that which certain
men have come to think of as their past. One may read a particular
interpretation of a historic period but never *the* history of that period.
Historians, as human beings, can neither live in the past, which is dead,
nor divorce themselves from their own subjective values acquired in
the present. While Leopold von Ranke's idea of objective history served
a useful function in removing history from the realm of literary fiction,
his work nonetheless suffered from the same problem of subjective
value judgment that marks all historical study. One can agree with Carl
L. Becker that "All historical writing, even the most honest, is unconsciously subjective, since every age is bound, in spite of itself, to make
the dead perform whatever tricks it finds necessary for its own peace
of mind," and with Frederick Jackson Turner that "Each age writes the
history of the past anew with reference to the conditions uppermost in
its own time." Such frank recognition of the subjective and tentative
nature of historical study need not destroy the value of historical inquiry. It should, however, sharpen our awareness of those subjective
factors which give meaning to a sequence of events and ideas, as well
as redirect our attention to the uses of history.

If it is true that the past is dead, that history does not repeat itself,
and that history cannot prove anything, it is equally true that men persist in trying to prove things with history. There are few current debates
which do not begin with a historical interpretation. Nikita Khrushchev

appreciated the function of the historian when he said, "Historians are dangerous people. They are capable of upsetting everything. They must be directed." History can be and is used to support or discredit every social institution created by men. The student of the past is inevitably involved with the issues of the present.

History can also have a more personal, individualized utility. For some, historical inquiry provides a sense of continuity, a sense of space and time which seems to lighten the burden of an existential loneliness; for others, it offers new insight into current phenomena; and for still others, it affords an escape from reality.[1] But while it might be pleasing to conclude that every man is his own historian and every function of history a legitimate function, there does exist an objective world to which men must reconcile their subjective values. In one sense, the clinical psychologist is faced with a historical problem when he attempts to reconstruct the history of his patient. He must rely on empirical data while interpreting the subjective perception of the patient as well as keeping check on his own selective perception. From such complex patterns, he draws meaning for the current situation. The historian must also rely on empirical data, already subjectively screened by another age he cannot experience, to which he adds his own structure to develop meaning. Subjective judgments are made in this process, but they cannot remain private judgments. In the final analysis, historical knowledge must be public knowledge,[2] open to critical review and subject to acceptance or rejection on the basis of various criteria. Beyond the individual inquiry, historical truth is that upon which the best-informed observers can reach substantial agreement.

A student of history of education invariably finds that his inquiry takes him through at least a three-dimensional view of education. First, he is concerned with the major ideas and values which seem to predominate in any given period; second, he is concerned with the material conditions of life which seem to influence educational practice as well as ideology;[3] and third, he is concerned with actual practices in both formal and informal education of the young.

FOCUS ON IDEOLOGY

This book is not a definitive history of education; it is rather an interpretive study of certain American educational ideas. The focus of the book, therefore, is limited to those systems of ideas which have given form and purpose to educational practice in the United States. This does not mean, however, that major social forces and actual practice

---

1. For differing views of the uses of history, see Herbert J. Muller, *The Uses of the Past* (New York: Oxford University Press, 1952). Also see Erich Kahler, *The Meaning of History* (New York: George Braziller, Inc., 1964).

2. *Public knowledge* is defined as that knowledge which all men can obtain if they follow the same stated canons of inquiry.

3. *Ideology* is used in this text to mean that system of ideas and values by which men profess to live.

can be ignored. On the contrary, the expressed ideology may at any one time be as much a rationalization for economic and social forces as a controlling agent. The major emphasis of this book, then, is on ideology, which is used here as only one factor in a possible constellation of factors at work in any process of educational change.

Continuity and change occur simultaneously, and ideology is a part of both processes. In this respect one can agree with Butts and Cremin, who said, "The history of education must record the history of ideas as instruments of educational change as well as social conditions that serve to accelerate or thwart educational change."[4] Modern man, living in what has been described as a post-Christian era and an age of technological determinism, tends to underestimate the importance that religion, philosophy, literature, and general ideology have had in determining educational practice. While a strong case can be made for economic determinism in American formal educational institutions, the thesis breaks down when applied to individuals. The ideology one holds seems related to personality, and personality undoubtedly is markedly affected by child-rearing practices, which, in turn, seem as much related to ideological factors as to economic forces. Any single determinant can render only partial truth and partial insight.

FOCUS ON THE LAST CENTURY

Because of the rapid changes wrought in ideology and institutional education in the century from 1865 to 1965, those hundred years are overwhelmingly important in the history of American educational thought. As both the philosopher and the theologian were asked to take a lower seat at the table of culture, it became apparent that man's concept of man and society had shifted from a sectarian, supernatural view to a more secular, naturalistic position. Increasingly, men placed their faith in a science controlled by men rather than in a theology controlled by God.

This was the era when America passed from a rural to an urban to a "rurbanized" society; from a basically agrarian society to a laissez-faire industrial economy to an affluent industrial economy; and from a rather insignificant nation to an unsure-of-itself isolationist world power to an international leader. Such a massive cultural transformation had an inevitable impact on educational institutions as well as on educational ideology. With the closing of the Western frontier came the opening of the educational frontier. In advising a young man about his future, it might have been customary in 1865 to suggest that he "Go West," but by 1965 he was more often advised, "Go to college!"

Most of the present American educational system, from the standpoint of institutional structure, was completed during this period. The education of the American young passed from an informal, face-to-face, community kind of instruction to a formal, bureaucratic educational

---

4. Freeman Butts and Lawrence Cremin, *A History of Education in American Culture* (New York: Henry Holt and Company, 1953), p. 66.

establishment. Such an establishment tended to reflect the virtues and vices of the culture at large as well as the most critical intellectual, moral, and social issues of that culture. As the informal educational agencies, such as the neighborhood and family, decreased in importance, the school increased in significance. Viewed as the single most important vehicle of social mobility and as the single most important educational agency, the American school inevitably became the center of social and ideological conflict. If the geographical frontier was fraught with physical conflict, the educational frontier was scarred by ideological conflict.

FUNDAMENTAL IDEOLOGICAL QUESTIONS

In spite of vast economic, social, and ideological change, men have persisted in asking certain significant questions that lend themselves to a broader, more meaningful interpretation of the process of education in a cultural setting. While these questions are not assumed to have any metaphysical or transcendental reality, the persistence with which men have been concerned with them may be accounted for by the fact that man is a social animal with a need to define himself, his society, and what he accepts as truth. Since education begins and ends with man, one of the most basic questions is "What is the nature of man?" Going from the microcosm to the macrocosm, an equally revelant question is "What is the nature of the good society?" In defining himself and his society, man usually asks what criterion provides a basis for truth? The criterion he comes to accept often influences his answers to the prior questions. Men, movements, and periods may be generally classified with reference to these questions, and within this context continuity and change may be detected. These are the questions through which American educational thought will be considered in this book.

Concepts of human nature

How men conceive human nature usually influences educational practice. If one assumes that men are inherently good, as Rousseau proclaimed, as Walt Whitman, Thoreau, and Emerson envisioned, and as Earl Kelley, Carl Rogers, and Ashley Montagu have assumed, then one advocates a child-centered curriculum. Since nature is good and the child of nature is good, educators must look to the child for clues to his natural development. What the child needs is freedom to develop his natural self to become that which he is naturally capable of becoming. Emerson advised teachers:

It is not for you to choose what he shall know, what he shall do. It is chosen and foreordained, and he only holds the key to his own secret. Wait and see the new product of nature. Respect the child. Be not too much his parent. Trespass not on his solitude.[5]

---

5. Ralph Waldo Emerson, *The Complete Writings of Ralph Waldo Emerson* (New York: Wm. H. Wise and Company, 1929), p. 993.

His counsel has been reaffirmed throughout the history of American educational thought by men who have premised their own thinking on the assumption that human nature is essentially good.

On the other hand, there have been those who viewed nature as evil and natural man as depraved. Just as John Cotton referred to men as "vipers" and the Reverend John White referred to the first settlers as "the very scum of the land," so, too, Cotton Mather in *A Family Well-Ordered* advised parents that "your Children are the Children of Death and the Children of Hell, and the Children of Wrath, by Nature; and that from you, this Nature is derived and conveyed unto them!" The Puritan, in attempting to amplify the importance of God, weakened the significance of man. In so doing, he automatically increased man's dependency on revealed supernatural religion. The problem of supernaturalism, with God the measure, versus naturalism, with man the measure, has continued throughout the history of Western education. How this issue is temporarily resolved for any given historical period is usually reflected in the educational system of that period.

Concepts of the ideal society

While education begins and ends with man, it always functions through a social system. Thinkers from Aristotle to George H. Mead have proclaimed the obvious; i.e., that man is a social animal who achieves his humanity through a social system. Formal education becomes the vehicle through which the young are inducted into the social system. Conflict arises not only around the most efficient techniques for achieving the purpose but, more significantly, around the nature of the purpose itself. At first glance, it might seem relatively easy to define what "is" and proceed to "consensus" from there. But this approach proves illusory because of at least two factors. First, the social system existing at any one time is seldom viewed as altogether desirable, except in a very static society; and, second, the judgment about what does exist within the social system is distorted by the selective perceptions of the individual or group making the analysis. These selective perceptions are usually conditioned by what the individual or group considers to be the ideal social order; and what men consider a desirable social system or a "good" society is a highly effective tool in the analysis of American educational thought. It would be neater and easier to assume that informal and formal education of the young historically proceeded in a social vacuum. This would force us, however, to ignore not only considerable educational history but much of American social and intellectual thought. The history of the idea of progress, for example, and of its corollary, social meliorism, cannot be adequately treated without consideration of education as a vehicle of social reform.

The good society, to the Puritans, was the theocratic community, which unquestionably influenced the course of educational development for colonial New England. So, too, the good society for the Enlightenment, which was a society free from religious sanctions in the civil domain, had its effect on the institutionalizing of the principle of separation of Church and State. Horace Mann's conception of a good society as one being held together with a common set of values, welded in a common set of experiences in a common school, no doubt influenced his conception of the function of public education in America, just as John Dewey's conception of a pluralistic society conditioned what he advocated in American education.

The educational ideas of the social reconstructionist in the twentieth century, from Albion Small and George S. Counts to Theodore Brameld, cannot be appraised without careful consideration of what these men deem the desirable or "good" society. Nor does it seem possible to examine realistically the ideas of other major participants in the twentieth-century educational dialog—without concern for what they consider the desirable social order. Behind much of the educational conflict in the twentieth century has been disagreement not only on what human nature is and what is an acceptable criterion of truth but also on what is to be considered the good society toward which education must strive.

Bases of truth

Throughout the history of the West, men not only have defined human nature differently and viewed society differently but have also devised different criteria or bases for truth. Of these, at least five can be clearly identified and are used as an analytic guide in this book. Within the realm of public knowledge, the criteria are those of the rationalist, the empiricist, and the esthetic. Within the realm of private knowledge, our concern will center on the criteria of the mystic and the romantic.

Public knowledge

The rationalist relies on reason and assumed universal rules of logic as the basis for truth. He usually asserts that rules of logic are discovered rather than invented and that what can be proved logical can be accepted as true. The rationalist most often operates from *a priori* assumptions and arrives at truth deductively. Much of Western thought, from Plato to Hegel, has been within a rationalistic tradition.

Still within the field of public knowledge, but at a polar position from the rationalist, is the empiricist, who relies on sense observation and a sense-experience test for the basis of his truth. The empiricist views logic as a human invention, a tool which is useful in organizing his data. Much scientific inquiry from Francis Bacon to Albert Einstein is represented by this point of view. While the work of Bacon tended to be heavy in sense observation and that of Einstein in theoretical models, the chief characteristic of these men which permits us to place them in the same tradition is that both would profess that the ultimate test of truth is the empirical test. Rationalism and empiricism are intimately related through the history of mathematics. Both the rationalist and the empiricist tend to have similar views of social reality and are inclined toward building social systems.

While some men arrive at truth through logic and others through empirical test, another group finds truth through a disciplined esthetic taste, disciplined by the ideas of the great thinkers of antiquity, or what Paul Elmer More referred to as the "noble dead." This group of men knows the truth not through a cold logic or an emotionalized intuition but through an "educated" intuition which appreciates the balance and subtle nuances of classical thought. This is the tradition of the belles-lettres, more accurately labeled classical humanism. The classical humanists, from Isocrates to Cicero, from Quintilian to Petrarch, and from Vittorino da Feltre to Erasmus, deserve the title of Schoolmasters of Western Culture. It was this tradition which defined for centuries the meaning of an educated man and of a liberal education. It was also this tradition which fought the battle against the rationalistic mind of the scholastics during the Renaissance and proved to be the most serious obstacle to the advancement of empirical science in institutions of higher learning in the seventeenth and eighteenth centuries. With some modifications, it was this tradition, embodying an esthetic approach to truth, which came to life again in the twentieth century in the form of neo-humanism as expressed by Irving Babbitt, Paul Elmer More, and Norman Foerster.

Private knowledge

In direct conflict with the rationalist, the empiricist, and the esthetic are the mystic and the romantic. To these men, ultimate truth is always a private experience. Truth is discovered by using one's intuition to commune with the source of truth, which may be either God or nature. The mystic, who is a supernaturalist, has direct experience with God, whereas the romantic communes with a transcendental nature or a pantheistic God in nature. In this tradition, ultimate truth is always subjective and private and needs no confirmation by way of a logical or empirical test. Emerson said, "A foolish consistency is the hobgoblin of little minds"; and Pascal asserted that "The heart has its reasons which the reason does not know." It is the mystic and the romantic who emphasize the individual's importance over the needs of the social organization. In a very real sense, the mystic and the romantic have been the rebels of Western social systems, whether the system was an institutionalized church or a nationalized state. Having direct relations with the source of truth, these thinkers are usually impatient with organized bureaucracy. The history of the Roman Church is replete with cases reflecting the difficulty of keeping the mystic within the organized church. In the American tradition, it was a romantic who developed the doctrine of civil disobedience that Mahatma Gandhi found so significant. It was that same romantic, Henry David Thoreau, who cautioned his countrymen that "They are to be men first, and Americans only at a late and convenient hour."

THE IMPORTANCE OF IDEOLOGY

By identifying the rational, the empirical, the classical esthetic, the mystic, and the romantic bases of truth, we have by no means exhausted the field. Nevertheless, these selected concepts are useful in analyzing American educational thought. There is the danger, however, of adhering too strictly to these classifications. In practice, it is difficult to find a pure mystic, a pure rationalist, or a pure empiricist. Most men tend to be some of each, depending on the kinds of questions they are facing; but significant thinkers who tend to dominate an intellectual climate of opinion for any given period are usually not eclectic in these matters but rather tend to rely predominantly on one of these criteria as a basis of their thought. Why some men have been more attracted to one tradition than to another seems to be a condition less of the forcefulness of the argument than the personal temperament of a particular individual in a particular environment. William James may very well have been correct when he assumed that the psychology of the individual and the philosophy of the individual are really two sides of the same coin. When, however, men accept diametrically opposed criteria of truth within any formal institution, such as the school system, the educational dialog becomes laden with conflict. Behind much of the discord in twentieth-century American education lie not only conflicting concepts of human nature but also conflicting bases for truth.

Sometimes the major ideas of a particular period have reached such a consensus that the answers to the questions about human nature and society are merely assumed, or taken for granted. At other times, when a current ideology is threatened, conflicting answers to these questions can usually be found behind the dust and smoke of battle. Indeed, when education becomes a battleground, it often does so for reasons far deeper than the usual problem of determining the most efficient method of educating children. Almost in an orchestral fashion, different positions come to the fore, are heard, and then fade into the background, only to return again in a different context. What causes these changes will probably remain an unanswered question. From one perspective, the ideology of one period can be viewed as a reaction to another; but from another perspective, the same ideology may be viewed as a consequence of economic and social conditions.

Perhaps the dilemma lies fundamentally in man's unique existence, which allows him to be tomorrow that which he is not today. Man is the creator who makes over not only his physical and social environment but also himself. Man the creator is a restless being who always dies a little when he fails to create and nothing inhibits his creating more than *the* truth. In this context one can agree with Lessing that "the search for truth is more precious than its possession."

CHAPTER 1

The European impact
on the educational thought
of Puritan New England

. . . men shall say of succeeding plantacions: the lord make it like that of New England: for wee must Consider that wee shall be as a Citty upon a Hill, the eies of all people are uppon us. . . .[1] JOHN WINTHROP

The Puritan was a man with a sense of purpose and mission directed by God. That mission was to live in the world, engage it, destroy the anti-Christ, and build a city of God in the wilderness. He saw himself not so much pioneering a new world as establishing a base of operation from which he and his fellows could lead the chosen children of God to attack Old World corruptions. In this way he usually viewed his own migration from the Old World as only a tactical retreat from Old World forces. New England, he thought, would be a place where Puritanism could flower according to its basic tenets, and not according to the will of an unsympathetic king or parliament. There on the rocky shores of New England the "Bay Saints" would establish that "Citty upon a Hill," with "the eies of all people . . . uppon us."[2]

Although many other religious groups, such as Quakers, Anglicans, Lutherans, Moravians, Dutch Reformed, and Catholics, came to the New World to escape the Old World restrictions on their religious expression, few saw themselves as having the mission of establishing a base from which they would reform the rest of the world. Perhaps

1. Stewart Mitchell, ed., *Winthrop Papers*, 1498-1630 (The Massachusetts Historical Society, 1931), II, 295.
2. For a comprehensive view of Puritan thought, see Perry Miller, *The New England Mind: From Colony to Province* (Cambridge, Mass.: Harvard University Press, 1953). For an interesting but narrower perspective, see Loren Baritz, *City on a Hill* (New York: John Wiley & Sons, Inc., 1964).

it was their grandiose sense of purpose which enabled the Puritans to cast an influence over American cultural life far out of proportion to their limited numbers. For example, wherever one goes in the history of American fundamentalist theology, one usually meets a Puritan coming back. The Puritan from John Cotton to Jonathan Edwards explored most of the Christian fundamentalist landscape.

Perhaps the key to the Puritan's success lies not so much in his rationalized theology or his militancy as in his ability to institutionalize his values in education. Whatever the case, the Puritan influenced New England's educational thought, and New England, in turn, significantly influenced the educational history of America. Although the Puritan conception of man, community, and education provides an excellent example of the relationship between thought and practice with respect to an important part of the American educational tradition, the influence of the Anglicans in Virginia, the Dutch Reformed Church in New York, the Quakers and Lutherans in Pennsylvania, and the Catholics in Maryland must be recognized (though not emphasized here) as a vital part of the complex colonial educational history.

American educational history is indissolubly bound up with the ideal of culture and learning that the Puritan carried into the wilderness. In general, the Puritans who settled New England were well-educated men. By 1646 no other region in the New World could boast of having at least one university graduate for every forty families, and no other region moved so quickly to establish a college under trying frontier conditions.[3] Relatively poor in physical possessions but rich in cultural values and ideas, the Puritan labored to construct his "city of God" in the wilderness. In these labors he reflected the values of his European origins. His religious intolerance, oligarchic social views, and distrust of majority rule, as well as his conceptions of human nature, the ideal society, and the function of education, were all part of his European heritage. He was, after all, a European and not an American.

EUROPEAN ORIGINS

To a considerable extent, Puritan thought was a product of both the resolved and the unresolved issues of medieval, Renaissance, and Reformation cultures. From his medieval past, the Puritan drew his Christian theology, as well as his faith in institutionalized education; from the Renaissance came his ideas about the meaning of a liberal education; and from the Reformation, he drew his militant theological views, as well as his willingness to sacrifice worldly pleasures. His faith in institutionalized literary education for all believers was very much a function of the Reformation and was shared by most Protestant groups and certain Catholic groups as well.[4] In many ways, the Puritan rep-

---

3. See Samuel Eliot Morison, *The Intellectual Life of Colonial New England* (New York: New York University Press, 1956), p. 18.
4. For example, this attitude was expressed by the seventeenth-century Brothers of the Common Life as well as by the Brothers of the Christian Schools.

resented the end of one age and the beginning of another. As a participant in one of the major transformations of Western religious and social values, he stood between an earlier God-centered feudal social order and a later man-centered bourgeois capitalism.

The medieval legacy

The spirit of medieval Christianity has its beginning and ending with the thought of St. Augustine. It was St. Augustine's *City of God* (c. 426) which intellectually marked the opening of the Middle Ages, and it was the revived interest in Augustine's thought that brought Luther, Calvin, Zwingli, and others into a confrontation with the medieval Church.

Christian theology has forever been confronted with the problem of finding the proper relationship between a self-conscious man and an inscrutable God. This problem involves not only the question of reality but also the question of how man comes to know. It should not seem strange, then, that some of the most significant Judeo-Christian theological tracts involve some of the most profound psychological and philosophical insights of Western thought. Throughout the history of the West, men have persisted in rationalizing their relationship to a God they could not understand and emotionalizing their relationship to a God they could not feel. Reason and emotion represent the human vehicle through which the rationalist and the mystic have sought to establish their relationship to God. When carried to the extreme, the mystic and the rationalist represent a threat to established Christianity. The private religious experience of Tertullian or Anne Hutchinson talking directly to God leaves little need for the church as a functioning intermediary. On the other hand, the rationalist who assumes men can independently reason their way to salvation also threatens the established religious system. St. Augustine and St. Thomas Aquinas attempted to incorporate both reason and emotion into a unified, organic theology. St. Augustine, however, emphasized more the emotional faith of St. Paul, while Aquinas emphasized the rational judgments of Aristotle.

Augustine in his *City of God* had emphasized the omnipotence of God by de-emphasizing the power and significance of man. It was this extreme emphasis on the omnipotence of God that led men down the rough road of predestination. When Augustine's thought was revived in seventeenth-century New England, the question of predestination again became a major theological issue. It was also St. Augustine who, in emphasizing the power of God, demolished the fifth-century Pelagian heresy—that heresy which assumed men were capable of self-regeneration. In seventeenth- and eighteenth-century New England the essentials of the Pelagian position were revived in the form of Arminianism.[5] Although the names had changed, the argument re-

---

5. Much of Puritan covenant theology can be seen as an attempt to cut between the rationalism of Arminianism and the emotional approach of antinomianism. See Baritz, *City on a Hill,* pp. 52-53. Also see Ralph Barton Perry, *Puritanism and Democracy* (New York: The Vanguard Press, 1944), pp. 100-111.

mained the same. The road through fifth-century Pelagianism, seventeenth- and eighteenth-century Arminianism, eighteenth-century Deism, and nineteenth-century Unitarianism is long in time and rough in spots but relatively short in intellectual differences. The common idea is that man has the rational capacity to save his own soul. St. Augustine fought the Pelagians and Jonathan Edwards fought the Arminians along that road, rightly suspecting all the time that somewhere at its end was the death of God. Jonathan Edwards, like St. Augustine before him, based his theology on the emotional psychology of conversion. Ultimately, both great theologians placed reason at the service of faith.

Although New England had its Augustinian philosophy, psychology, and theology in the person of Jonathan Edwards, there was no Puritan counterpart for thirteenth-century St. Thomas Aquinas. Most of the Puritan divines, however, were well aware of Aquinas' masterful adaptation of Aristotle's pagan thought to medieval Christian theology. They respected the quest for unity, the technique of argument, and many of the basic Christian doctrines inherent in the *Summa Theologica,* but they also recognized that the overall effect of the *Summa* was to justify the established Church.

Under the pressure of Aristotelian naturalistic arguments, St. Thomas Aquinas struggled to develop a theology to include both the faith of the theologian and the reason of the philosopher.[6] As a mystic, Aquinas could accept revealed truth, and as a rationalist, he could, with modification, accept most of Aristotle's reasoning. Reason and faith, he argued, could not ultimately be in conflict. What appears as conflict occurs when the theologian or philosopher wanders outside his own legitimate sphere of knowledge. Who, then, determines the legitimate sphere of each? In the final analysis, the Church would make this decision, thus safely controlling all conflicting questions of faith and reason. There was, therefore, within a unified theology, a place for the faith of the theologian and a place for the reason of the philosopher.

In some respects, it was upon this unified system of theology of St. Thomas Aquinas that the Puritan constructed his city of God in the New World. The Puritan was in far greater agreement with the major medieval tenets than most moderns who consider themselves medievalists. As Ralph Barton Perry put it:

A denizen of the modern world who would recover the essential spirit of Christian medievalism would do well to saturate himself with the orthodox protestantism of the seventeenth century. He will find more of its authentic presence there than in the contemporary cult of neo-medievalism, with its fancy for Gothic architecture or Thomistic philosophy.[7]

Most of the fundamental tenets of medieval theology were strictly espoused by the Puritan. Contrary to the suspicions of those who re-

---

6. See Etienne Gilson, *History of Christian Philosophy in the Middle Ages* (New York: Random House, Inc., 1955). See also Etienne Gilson, *Reason and Revelation in the Middle Ages* (New York: Charles Scribner's Sons, 1938).

7. Perry, *Puritanism and Democracy,* p. 83.

mained in the Roman Church, the Puritan's purpose was to rebuild Christendom, not to destroy it. He fully accepted the Biblical account of creation, the doctrine of original sin, the need of grace for salvation, and the unity of Christian theology. Because the Puritan accepted the unity of medieval theology, he also held in high esteem the attempts of the thirteenth-century scholastics to maintain unity of faith and reason. This was reflected in the early history of Harvard College. Samuel Eliot Morison pointed out that "John Harvard had more volumes in his library by St. Thomas Aquinas than by St. John of Geneva."[8] In spite of this esteem, however, the Puritan went back to the early rather than the late Middle Ages for his theology. The patron saint of the Reformation leaders as well as of the Harvard men was not St. Thomas Aquinas, but St. Augustine. Although most Puritan divines used Aquinas' scholastic techniques for debating theological questions, they seemed most interested in debating those questions raised by St. Augustine.

Harvard College was founded and directed by men who were educated at either Oxford or Cambridge, both institutional progeny of the medieval University of Paris.[9] In this respect, the Puritan's notion of formal, organized, institutional education was medieval. In practical education, the colleges of Harvard and Yale clearly reflected the medieval ritualistic practice of granting degrees as well as the medieval organization of knowledge and curriculum along the lines of the seven liberal arts[10] and natural, moral, and mental philosophy. This curriculum, however, was enriched with the belles-lettres and put into the service of Renaissance humanistic ideals.

The Renaissance tradition

While medieval culture had considerable influence on Puritan educational practice, a more significant and sustained impact on American education can be found in the rebirth of classical humanism that characterized the Renaissance. With the development of the Italian Renaissance, there emerged a new interest and respect for the "natural" world; i.e., for human passions, for material rewards, and for secular studies. This tendency appeared to conflict with an earlier medieval tendency to focus more strongly on the things of the spirit. Hence, Petrarch, a leader of the fifteenth-century Italian Renaissance, developed his thoughts in *Secretum Meum* (The Soul's Conflict with Passion)[11] in the context of a debate between himself and St. Augustine. The selection of Augustine rather than Aquinas reflects a shift in emphasis from philosophy to humane letters, from logical to esthetic criteria.

8. Morison, *Intellectual Life of Colonial New England*, p. 11. Also see Samuel Eliot Morison, *The Founding of Harvard College* (Cambridge, Mass.: Harvard University Press, 1935).

9. For the history of the medieval university, see Hastings Rashdall, *Universities of Europe in the Middle Ages* (New York: Oxford University Press, 1936). Also see Charles Homer Haskins, *The Rise of Universities* (Ithaca, N.Y.: Great Seal Books, 1957).

10. The seven liberal arts were grammar, rhetoric, dialectics, arithmetic, geometry, astronomy, and music.

11. See Harold Hooper Blanchard, ed., *Prose and Poetry of the Continental Renaissance in Translation,* 2nd ed. (New York: Longmans, Green & Company, 1955), p. 31.

In some cases, the enthusiasm for classical ideas led Renaissance thinkers perilously close to paganism. This tendency, in turn, brought from the northern humanistic leader Desiderius Erasmus the same recommendation of censorship that earlier Christian humanists had made. Erasmus, in *The Education of a Christian Prince* (1515) and elsewhere, recommended that all belles-lettres offensive to Christian education be censored and those not readily censored be allegorically interpreted in the interest of Christian piety.[12] Although some colonists, like the Anglican William Byrd of Virginia, tended to be more exuberant in their humanism and more playful and more abandoned in their pursuit of clearly secular goals, most New England Puritans followed in the footsteps of Erasmus. When the classics were brought into the service of Christian education, they were usually censored by either Protestant or Catholic clergy.[13] The unending tribute that the Puritan divines, from John Cotton to Cotton Mather, paid to the value of the classics was a testimony to the success with which the clergy had effectively censored out offensive segments of the classics.

Though humanism can be broadly conceived to include all of the classical and some of the Christian tradition, it is important to recognize that educational humanism, insofar as it is literary, poetic, and esthetic, bears the mark of the rhetorical strain of classical humanism.[14] To the extent that one conceives the humanists' interests as man-centered rather than God-centered, literary rather than philosophical, and artistic rather than metaphysical, one finds the roots of educational humanism not among the philosophers or theologians of antiquity but rather among the classical teachers of rhetoric.[15]

The rhetorical humanists from Isocrates and Cicero to Vittorino da Feltre and Erasmus consistently conceived human nature as fixed and dualistic, the good society as aristocratic, and the basic criterion of truth as a disciplined intuitive taste.[16] The relationship between a dual concept of human nature and an aristocratic social ideal is probably nowhere more clearly expressed than in the words of Aristotle:

---

12. See William Harrison Woodward, *Desiderius Erasmus Concerning the Aim and Method of Education,* Classics in Education, No. 19 (New York: Bureau of Publications, Teachers College, Columbia University, 1964).

13. For an example of this kind of censorship by the Roman Catholics, read the Jesuit *Ratio Studiorum* of 1599.

14. "The word 'humanism' itself is not very old. It was coined by historical scholars of the 19th century who were interested in the so-called 'humanists' of the 15th and 16th centuries. The latter received their name from the fact that their learned efforts to revitalize the rediscovered literature and culture of Greece and Rome centered about an ideology which was expressed in one word *humanitas.* They took that concept from one of their greatest ancient authorites in cultural matters, Cicero. . . . The Latin *humanitas* in this sense corresponds to the Greek *paideia."* Werner Jaeger, *Humanism and Theology* (Milwaukee: Marquette University Press, 1943), pp. 20-21.

15. For the contrast between the orator and philosopher, see H. I. Marrou, *History of Education in Antiquity* (New York: Mentor Books, 1964).

16. The classical naturalistic concept of human nature as being divided between man's reason and his passion was usually the intellectual grounds for rapprochement with the Christian supernaturalistic concept of human nature which asserted that man's nature was divided between his spiritual soul and his physical body.

Where then there is such a difference as that between soul and body, or between men and animals (as in the case of those whose business it is to use their body, and who can do nothing better), the lower sort are by nature slaves, and it is better for them as for all inferiors that they should be under the rule of a master.[17]

The social ideal of classical humanism, whether in the philosophical or the rhetorical tradition, was usually based on the principle of rule by an aristocracy of virtue and talent.[18] Since the classical mind could conceive of just political action only in terms of just and virtuous leaders, the central question which concerned most educational theorists was: What kind of education will produce the good ruler, the good statesman? This statesman would be the agent through which culture would be joined with action; it was, therefore, of utmost concern that he be educated to receive the vision of the good life, behave justly in all action, and exemplify the ideal of virtue. When the Puritan and, indeed, his non-Puritan compatriots turned to their revered classical authorities, they found such stalwarts as the classical Greek, Isocrates; the Roman republican, Cicero; and the English Renaissance humanist, Elyot, placing constant stress on the education of the prince, the courtier, and the governor.[19] The virtues of the classical orator and the Renaissance prince or courtier were to become in England those of the "cultured gentleman" and in America those of the "liberally educated man." However, neither in England nor in America in the seventeenth century was it believed that all men were educable by these criteria.

The educational discipline of this strain of classical culture was rhetoric. This subject was concerned with the education of the well-rounded man who could think on his feet, join theory with practice, engage successfully in the human dialog, and, in a sense, be a midwife to that truth which makes a difference in decisions determining action.[20] This ideal of the orator and the importance of the subject of rhetoric were reborn in Italian Renaissance education. The new education of the courtly academies broke with scholastic education as men like Vittorino da Feltre and Guarino da Verona came to grips with the task of educating a well-rounded man. The first concern of the Renaissance academy was to educate the whole child—morally, intellectually, physically, and

---

17. Benjamin Jowett, ed., *Aristotle's Politics* (New York: The Modern Library, 1943), p. 59.

18. Consider Plato's *Republic* and *The Laws,* Aristotle's *Politics,* and Isocrates' *Letter to Nicocles.*

19. Consider, for example, Isocrates' *Letter to Nicocles,* Cicero's *Orator,* Quintilian's *Institutes,* Erasmus' *The Education of a Christian Prince,* and Elyot's *The Boke Named the Governour.*

20. This concept of rhetoric was Isocrates' and was perpetuated in Cicero's and Quintilian's work. It was not Aristotle's conception of the subject. To Aristotle, truth was arrived at through philosophy, and rhetoric was only the art of persuasion. When rhetoric declined, Aristotle's conception usually won out. For the disappearance of rhetoric in the medieval civilization and its revival in the Renaissance, see Louis John Paetow, *The Arts Course at Medieval Universities with Special Reference to Grammar and Rhetoric* (Urbana: University of Illinois Press, 1910).

emotionally—for effective leadership. The "Joyful House"[21] at Mantua and the playing fields of Rugby, Eton, and Harrow were all the progeny of the classical ideal of "well-roundedness." Prolonged exertion, enforced games, and exposure to cold were required in the interest of fortitude, whereas dancing, painting, music, riding, fencing, and swimming were included in the curriculum in the interest of producing the well-balanced, liberally educated, complete man. One finds this ideal restated in Sir Humphrey Gilbert's *Queen Elizabeth's Academy* and in Cleveland's *Institution of a Nobleman.* John Milton, a Puritan renegade, was also within this tradition when he called a complete education "that which fits a man to perform justly, skillfully, and magnanimously all the offices both private and public, of peace and war."[22]

The Americans could choose between an austere, serious humanism like that of Erasmus, which minimized the value of art, athletics, useful knowledge, and play, or a more exuberant strand like that of the fifteenth-century Vittorino da Feltre. In many respects, the education of the Southern gentleman followed in the footsteps of Vittorino,[23] while the education which evolved in Puritan New England tended to follow the leadership of Erasmus. Throughout American colonial education, the classical tradition exerted a dominant influence in the Latin grammar schools, the academies, and the colleges. Such influence often fell far short of either the practical curriculum of Vittorino's "Joyful House" or Milton's ideal of a well-educated man. The lower schools sometimes became submerged in a rote memorization of Cicero's works, while the colleges at times lowered their sights from a well-rounded man to a well-rounded mind, well stocked with classical furniture.[24]

Nevertheless, in spite of these failings, the Latin grammar schools and colleges, alongside the churches, served as the major channels through which flowed the lifeblood of Western culture. That lifeblood was classical as well as Christian. At first glance, the classical tradition might seem peculiarly inappropriate for a new frontier nation, but a closer examination reveals that for all of the seventeenth century and most of the eighteenth, the Latin curriculum not only served as a common bond of the educated class but was also useful as a source of considerable practical knowledge. For much of the colonial era, classical knowledge was far more practical than ornamental. By the beginning of the nineteenth century, however, more and more voices were critical of the

---

21. The Renaissance courtly academies were, in general, child-centered, progressive schools where learning took place in a pleasant, exciting environment. A few generations later these schools became noted for their rote Ciceronianism. It is interesting that this has been the course of virtually all progressive reform movements in education. This happened to Pestalozzian education in the nineteenth century and also to the progressive education movement in the twentieth century. Progressive educational reform movements usually have not been able to sustain themselves beyond the first or at most the second generation.

22. "Milton's Tractate on Education" in *Harvard Classics,* ed. Charles W. Eliot (New York: P. F. Collier and Son, 1909), III, 251.

23. See Louis B. Wright, *The First Gentlemen of Virginia: Intellectual Qualities of the Early Colonial Ruling Class* (San Marino, Calif.: The Huntington Library, 1940).

24. For a view of the classical tradition in American higher education, see R. Freeman Butts, *The College Charts Its Course* (New York: McGraw-Hill Book Company, 1939).

classics as embodying more ornamental than useful knowledge, and by the end of that century, the tradition was increasingly viewed as anachronistic.

The impact of the Reformation

Another and even more pervasive influence in shaping colonial educational thought was the Reformation. Both Lutheranism and Calvinism —indeed, Protestantism in general—turned out to be the religious complements of an emerging nationalism. Given the diffuse pattern of migration to America, this tendency yielded a pattern of strong local autonomy in educational and religious matters, an autonomy particularly marked in such colonies as Virginia and Pennsylvania. In New England, which became largely Calvinist-Congregational, it led to an emphasis on religious and ideological cohesiveness within the community. Largely in reaction to the Reformation, even Catholicism came to be associated with emerging national states, and the colony of Maryland was established originally as a haven for Catholics.

In many ways, the impact of the Reformation on Western education appears paradoxical. Even though few Reformation leaders favored it, religious toleration was one long-range consequence of the Reformation. Neither Luther nor Calvin believed that each man should read and interpret the Bible as he saw fit, but the Reformation gave strong impetus to individualistic religious commitment and a corollary impetus toward greater literacy. To be sure, the Reformation was a return to the theology of St. Augustine, if not to the Hebraism of the Old Testament; however, Protestantism in general and Calvinism in particular proved to be the religious complement of the materialistic spirit of capitalism. On the one side, Calvinism carried with it the thought of predestination, a determinism which, one would logically think, would inhibit human action; but on the other side, Calvinism also seemed to unleash a pervasive confidence and desire for action. These apparent contradictions result from interpreting the Reformation in general and Puritanism in particular by their *unintended* consequences.

The Puritans have been hymned as the pioneers of religious liberty, though nothing was ever farther from their designs; they have been hailed as the forerunners of democracy, though if they were, it was quite beside their intention; they have been invoked in justification for an economic philosophy of free competition and laissez-faire, though they themselves believed in government regulation of business. . . .[25]

With respect to the Puritans' coming to the New World in the cause of religious freedom, it would have seemed strange, indeed, to the many who died because of their religious beliefs at the hands of the Puritans that some centuries later those same Puritans would be hailed as cham-

---

25. Perry Miller, *Puritanism in Early America,* ed. George M. Waller, Problems in American Civilization: Amherst Series (Boston: D. C. Heath and Company, 1950), p. 7.

pions of religious freedom. Religious freedom developed not because of the Puritan influence on American culture but in spite of that influence. To expect the Puritan to believe that one should have the freedom to be wrong in religious matters would be like asking the modern American community to permit the Communist to have the freedom to teach the overthrow of the United States government. At a time when community core values were explicitly religious, as in the case of Puritan New England, men could go to the gallows in the name of "heresy"; since then, the core values have shifted from religion to nationalism, and the modern American goes to the gallows in the name of "treason."[26] This shift in major American core values was a result of a gradual transformation of American society from colonial status to national independence, from communities of relatively uniform religious persuasion to considerable religious pluralism, and in general from a sectarian to a secular view of life. To the devout believer, all this meant a decline of religion in American life, but it also meant freedom of religion. As long as sectarian religion represented the central, most important core values of a community, freedom of choice in religion could not be tolerated.[27]

THE PURITAN VIEW OF THE
GOOD SOCIETY AND EDUCATION

To the seventeenth-century Puritan, the good community was the community of believers, a city of God in the wilderness where religious treason could not be tolerated. The good society of believers was to be ruled not by majorities, which lacked biblical justification, but by the oligarchy of the elect as stewards of God, which was justified by Scripture. As John Cotton put it:

It is better that the commonwealth be fashioned to the setting forth of God's house, which is his church: than to accommodate the church frame to the civill state. Democracy, I do not conceyve that ever God did ordeyne as a fit government eyther for church or commonwealth. If the people be governors, who shall be governed? As for monarchy, and aristocracy, they are both of them clearly approved, and directed in scripture, yet so as referreth the soveraigntie to himselfe, and setteth up Theocracy in both, as the best forme of government in the commonwealth, as well as in the church.[28]

---

26. *Core values* is used throughout this book to mean those values to which the community demands strict adherence, as opposed to those values to which the community does not demand strict adherence, leaving individuals within the community free to choose between competing alternatives. It is clear that religion in modern American society is no longer a core value. For a discussion of core and alternate values, see Ralph Linton, *The Cultural Background of Personality* (New York: Appleton-Century-Crofts, Inc., 1961).

27. For a good treatment of the problem of freedom and religion, see Herbert J. Muller, *Religion and Freedom in the Modern World* (Chicago: University of Chicago Press, 1964).

28. "Letter to Lord Say and Sele," quoted in Vernon Louis Parrington, *Main Currents in American Thought* (New York: Harcourt, Brace and Company, 1930), p. 31.

From its origin, Massachusetts effectively joined State and Church into a unified theocracy. It was no historical accident that Massachusetts was the first colony to accept the idea of public education as being publicly controlled and supported and was the last of the original thirteen states to write into its constitution the principle of separation of Church and State.[29] The theocratic society of Massachusetts which fused the functions of Church and State also, almost from its inception, accepted the idea that education was a public responsibility. This attitude was a by-product of the theocratic society which assumed strict social controls over the lives of adults as well as of the young. The Massachusetts School Law of 1642, which put responsibility for education of the young on the shoulders of the individual householders, and the Law of 1647, which broadened that responsibility to the larger community, reflected, in general, the Puritan's fundamental concern with education.

Although the Act of 1647 was designed to prevent "that old deluder Satan" from keeping from any man a "knowledge of the Scriptures," it is a mistake to consider the Puritan's interest in education to be solely religious. The Puritan society of Massachusetts effectively fused the political, economic, and social realms of life with the religious. In the context of the times, most of the early Massachusetts school legislation was motivated by a conscious attempt to create formal schools for the thoughtful objectives of citizenship and economic competency, as well as that of piety.[30] Even though these laws were not always rigorously enforced, the laws themselves and the community attitudes that lay behind them represent the germ of the idea of public education.

The roots of the idea of public responsibility for education lay deeply embedded in both the theocratic nature of early New England society and the English Poor Laws of 1601. Modeled after the English Poor Law, the Massachusetts School Law of 1642 embodied an apprenticeship provision which required that the selectmen of the towns make sure that all parents and guardians teach their charges not only basic literacy and religion but also a trade or occupation. The selectmen were further empowered, with the approval of a court, to apprentice those children whose parents were incapable of fulfilling their duties. This act reflected the communities' concern not only with indigent children but with all children. Out of this early school legislation there eventually evolved the district school so characteristic of New England in the seventeenth and eighteenth centuries.

Whether it was citizenship training, economic competency, or piety the Puritan sought, the Puritan theocratic sense of community enhanced and facilitated the establishment of formal schools. By the nineteenth century, the theocratic state had all but disappeared, but the idea of public responsibility remained a functioning legal and social attitude. Thus Massachusetts in the nineteenth century was in the vanguard in the establishment of public schools.

---

29. R. Freeman Butts, *The American Tradition in Religion and Education* (Boston: The Beacon Press, 1950).
30. See Morison, *Intellectual Life of Colonial New England.*

A theocratic state

Much of the seventeenth-century political history of Massachusetts is a history of the oligarchy's attempts to maintain theocratic control of the colony. Limiting the franchise to church members, freemen, and property holders kept the control of the theocracy in the hands of the select few.[31] This oligarchy, however, carried within itself the seed of inevitable failure. The granting of land to non-freemen, the adoption of the Plymouth model of congregational church organization by the Massachusetts Bay churches, and the financial prosperity of the elect were all factors contributing to the failure of John Cotton's ideal society. Steps were taken to head off congregational individualism. Under the guise of the principle of consociation, the Cambridge Platform of 1646-1647 stated:

If any church one or more shall grow schismaticall, rending it self from the communion of other churches, or shall walke incorrigibly or obstinately in any corrupt way of their own, contrary to the rule of the word; in such case, the Magistrate is to put forth his coercive power, as the matter shall require.[32]

Though the principle of consociation often passed from brotherly per-suasion to the use of coercive power, congregational individualism con-tinued to develop. The ideal of a religiously homogeneous society could be maintained only at the cost of considerable coercion, expulsion, and bloodshed. The practice of ostracism, however, inevitably led to a greater pluralism, if not in the particular community, at least within the larger geographic region. The more religiously pluralistic New England became, the more impossible became the theocratic ideal.

The theocratic ideal, however, was more than just the elect attempting to maintain power or a particular sect attempting to dominate a particu-lar community; in a broader perspective, it was a logical and necessary corollary to Calvin's social and economic values. Like the medieval Church, Calvin believed that the nature of man was sinful and easily corrupted by worldly goods. The medieval Church, however, tended to put restrictions on the production of wealth, whereas Calvin chose to put restrictions on the consumption of wealth.[33] Having unleashed men's drives for gainful production, Calvin logically concluded that these drives had to be controlled and directed for the greater honor and glory of God. The theocratic society would then regiment the personal lives of men in the right direction.

One of the more significant transformations of values in the history of the West occurred during the Reformation, when the virtue of poverty was transformed into the sin of poverty. Work, diligence, sobriety,

---

31. See James Truslow Adams, *The Founding of New England* (Boston: Little, Brown and Company, 1963), chap. VI.
32. Quoted in Parrington, *Main Currents in American Thought*, p. 25.
33. See Max Weber, *The Protestant Ethic and the Spirit of Capitalism* (New York: Charles Scribner's Sons, 1958). Also R. H. Tawney, *Religion and the Rise of Capitalism* (New York: Harcourt, Brace and Company, 1926).

thrift, and prudence became the important virtues of the Calvinist Puritan who stood in the *avant-garde* of bourgeois capitalism. These were the virtues that the theocratic society revered in New England. When monastic asceticism was carried into the world, it was embodied in a sober, thrifty, prudent Puritan.

The doctrine of the elect and the doctrine of work

Eminently rational, accepting the depravity of man and the omnipotence of God, the Puritan attempted a solution to the problem of predestination by developing "covenant theology."[34] According to this system, God, although still supreme, becomes a constitutional ruler. God sets the rules of salvation and freely binds Himself to abide by such rules. Man can then play the game of salvation according to the rules. Nevertheless, not man but God is the author of salvation, and He alone holds the secret of predestination. Covenant theology made men morally responsible in the face of considerable uncertainty. This uncertainty could be partially relieved, however, when God showered worldly gifts on His elect. Thus, through work, thrift, and diligence, one could prosper; and this prosperity could be taken as reassurance that one was among the elect. This prosperity, though not an absolute guarantee of salvation, could be taken as a favorable clue that the force of the universe was on one's side. In Puritan New England, neither prosperity nor salvation was ever a certainty. But when the doctrine of the elect was combined with the doctrine of work, the economic life of the entrepreneur was religiously justified.

But if the elect were to protect the general community from licentious and ostentatious living, the question of who protected the elect from such living remained. With prosperity came an increase in the interest of the elect in secular affairs and a corresponding distaste for the strict regulation of either their own lives or their neighbors'. John Wesley, speaking of English society, put his finger on the problem when he said:

I fear, wherever riches have increased, the essence of religion has decreased in the same proportion. Therefore I do not see how it is possible, in the nature of things, for any revival of true religion to continue long. For religion must necessarily produce both industry and frugality, and these cannot but produce riches. But as riches increase, so will pride, anger, and love of the world in all its branches.[35]

Although the Puritan theocracy eventually failed in a sustained regulation of the spirit of capitalism, it was eminently successful in justifying it. By the time Benjamin Franklin wrote his *Poor Richard's Almanack,* the virtues of work, thrift, and prudence no longer needed religious justification but were able to stand alone. Franklin well personified the secularization of the Puritan economic virtues in American culture.

---

34. See Miller, *New England Mind.*
35. Quoted in Weber, *Protestant Ethic and the Spirit of Capitalism*, p. 175.

Puritan values in children's literature

American education throughout the colonial period and the nineteenth century consistently transmitted Puritan economic and social values to each new generation. These values regularly reappeared in children's primers, spelling books, and literature. From the *New England Primer* and Noah Webster's *The American Spelling Book* to the McGuffey *Readers,* the virtues of work, frugality, sobriety, and diligence were repeatedly emphasized.[36] Children's literature usually reflected major social events; for example, the content of the *New England Primer* was radically altered by the Great Awakening of the eighteenth century and by the American Revolution.[37] In the nearly two centuries of the primer's history, almost every couplet underwent some change,[38] but the doctrine of original sin remained a constant theme as generation after generation received their first reading experience with "In Adam's fall we sinned all." With this doctrine, fear, obedience, discipline, and absolute authority could be justified as appropriate characteristics of sound child-rearing practices.

THE PURITAN'S CONCEPTION OF MAN AND EDUCATION

Certain that "There is a corrupt nature in thy children, which is a fountain of all wickedness and confusion," Cotton Mather counseled parents to "Charge them to carry their poor, guilty, ignorant and polluted and Enslaved Souls, unto the lord Jesus Christ, that he may Save them from their Sins and Save them from the Wrath to come."[39] Under this charge the whipping post became an important educational facility for Puritan New England. In educational practice, there can be little doubt that the doctrine of original sin was the religious justification for literally beating the devil out of children and also for the passage of the Massachusetts Act of 1641 and Connecticut's Act of 1672, which imposed the death penalty on unruly children. Nevertheless, just how many children died under such laws and just how many children got the devil beaten out of them remain unanswered questions. Historians disagree as to the harshness of the Puritans. While Samuel Eliot Morison and Perry Miller tend to portray the Puritan with considerable sweetness and light, Vernon Parrington and others seem to follow more in

---

36. One wonders to what extent these values are reflected in children's literature today and how appropriate these values may be for an affluent society.

37. See Monica Kiefer, *American Children Through Their Books, 1700-1835* (Philadelphia: University of Pennsylvania Press, 1948). Also Sandford Fleming, *Children and Puritanism: The Place of Children in the Life and Thought of the New England Churches, 1620-1847* (New Haven: Yale University Press, 1933). Also Richard de Charms and Gerald H. Moeller, "Values Expressed in American Children's Readers," *Journal of Abnormal and Social Psychology,* LXIV, 2 (1962), 136-142.

38. See Paul Leicester Ford, ed., *The New-England Primer,* Classics in Education, No. 13 (New York: Bureau of Publications, Teachers College, Columbia University, 1962).

39. Cotton Mather, *A Family Well-Ordered* (Boston: B. Green and F. Allen, 1699), pp. 25-26.

the tradition of H. L. Mencken, who once defined Puritanism as "that haunting fear that somehow, somewhere, someone is happy."

If it was necessary to provide such extreme measures as the death penalty, one wonders just how pure was the Puritan. Paul Leicester Ford suggests:

There was far more living up to total depravity in early New England than most people suspect, and when one reads the charges brought against them by their own ministers, it is not difficult to realize why the New England clergy dwelt so much on the terrors of hell.[40]

Perhaps Bernard Bailyn's thesis—that the New England family unit was severely disrupted as a result of frontier conditions, thus necessitating stricter community regulation—is correct.[41] The question, however, still remains: To what extent was it the Puritan's concept of man and to what extent was it frontier conditions which brought forth the harsher treatment of children? While future historical research in the direction of Bailyn's thesis may develop a more accurate picture of Puritan life, it is nevertheless well established that the Puritan divines who emphasized total depravity, from John Cotton to Jonathan Edwards, also recommended and condoned harsh treatment of children. It also seems evident that the leaders of those religious sects which took a more optimistic view of human nature, such as the Quakers and Mennonites, who faced similar frontier conditions, consistently recommended a more humane approach to child-rearing.[42]

EDWARDS AND THE GREAT AWAKENING

Throughout most of the seventeenth century and part of the eighteenth, the Puritan divines managed to hold in check the rationalistic mind, which by the nineteenth century took the Arminian road to Unitarianism, and the mind of the antinomians, which took the emotional path toward evangelical frontier religion.[43] The last of the Puritan divines, in what one might consider the last stand of Puritan theology, did attempt to merge the mind of the mystic and the mind of the rationalist in the service of orthodox Calvinism. Jonathan Edwards (1703-1758), a brilliant American theologian, was eminently suited for such a formi-

---

40. Ford, *New-England Primer,* p. 53. Ford relates the story that "A newly installed New England pastor said to a spinster parishioner 'I hope, madam, you believe in total depravity,' and received the prompt response: 'Oh, parson, what a fine doctrine it would be, if folks only lived up to it,'" p. 52.

41. See Bernard Bailyn, *Education in the Forming of American Society* (Chapel Hill: University of North Carolina Press, 1960), pp. 22-23.

42. Consider the work of William Penn, John Woolman, Anthony Benezet, and Christopher Dock. See John Woolman, *A Journal* (Philadelphia: Association of Friends for the Diffusion of Religious and Useful Knowledge, 1860), pp. 329-332.

43. For a history of the anti-intellectualism implicit in the evangelical frontier religions, see Richard Hofstadter, *Anti-Intellectualism in American Life* (New York: Alfred A. Knopf, Inc., 1963).

dable task. As a young man, he had passed from religious mysticism to a philosophical idealism. Called to defend the Calvinistic conception of man and the universe against the Arminian heresy and the rising tide of enlightened rationalism, Edwards applied his brilliant intellect to shoring up the rapidly sinking pillars of Calvinist orthodoxy.[44] His logic was cold, harsh, and relentless as he reconfirmed all the consequences implicit in the doctrines that God was all-powerful, all-knowing, and all-just. Original sin, predestination, and the elect were all brought back in living color. Edwards vividly painted the picture of hell across the colonial landscape of pre-Enlightenment America with his sermons on "The Torments of the Wicked in Hell" and the plight of "Sinners in the Hands of an Angry God."

Edwards' rationalism, however, was premised not on the legalism of Calvin nor the metaphysics of Aquinas but on the emotional religious experience of Augustine; thus, in the end, his thought, like that of Augustine, centered on the psychological experience of conversion, as illustrated by the case of Phebe Bartlet, of which Edwards gave the following account:

But I now proceed to the other instance that I would give an account of, which is of the little child forementioned. Her name is Phebe Bartlet, daughter of William Bartlet. I shall give the account as I took it from the mouths of her parents, whose veracity, none that know them doubt.

She was born in March, in the year 1731. About the latter end of April, or beginning of May, 1735, she was greatly affected by the talk of her brother, who had been hopefully converted a little before, at about eleven years of age, and then seriously talked to her about the great things of religion . . . she was observed very constantly to retire, several times in a day, as was concluded for secret prayer, and grew more and more engaged in religion, and was more frequent in her closet, till at last she was wont to visit it five or six times in a day, and was so engaged in it, that nothing would, at any time, divert her from her stated closet exercises. . . .

She once, of her own accord, spake of her unsuccessfulness, in that she could not find God, or to that purpose. But on Thursday, the last day of July about one middle of the day, the child being in the closet, where it used to retire, its mother heard it speaking aloud, which was unusual and never had been observed before, and her voice seemed to be as of one exceeding importunate and engaged, but her mother could distinctly hear only these words, (spoken in her childish manner, but seemed to be spoken with extraordinary earnestness, and out of distress of soul) PRAY BLESSED LORD give me salvation! I PRAY, BEG pardon all my sins! When the child had done prayer, she came out of the closet, and came and sat down by her mother, and cried aloud. Her mother very earnestly asked her several times, what the matter was, before she would make any answer, but she continued exceedingly crying, and wreathing her body to and fro like one in anguish of spirit. Her mother then asked her if she was afraid that God would not give her salvation. She then answered yes, I am afraid I shall go to hell!

---

44. See Edwards, "On the Freedom of the Will." Also see Baritz, *City on a Hill*, pp. 47-89.

After much such carrying on the child suddenly became radiant and proclaimed that the kingdom of heaven had come to her, whereupon she returned to the closet to pray. After this she loudly and constantly proclaimed her love of God as exceeding her love for anyone else and wept for the welfare of her brothers and sisters. She continued to have great interest in attending church, giving the most mature sort of attention to preaching and to scriptures and constantly admonished her brothers and sisters to prepare to die. When questioned by Edwards she showed the confidence that her soul was prepared for death although there were occasional moments of doubt. On one occasion when she fell in with her contemporaries in the theft of some plums and later discovered the sinful nature of the act she was for a long time inconsolable.[45]

In the era of Jonathan Edwards, less than a century after the Salem witchcraft trials, when miracles were vividly portrayed and devils walked the streets of Northampton, Phebe's experience was accepted by many as the "surprising work of God." The fact that Edwards used such a case to verify his position reveals as much about the era in which he lived as it does about Edwards himself. To the modern eye, Phebe appears to be an emotionally disturbed child or, perhaps at best considering her environment, merely engaged in pathological role playing. Was the case of Phebe Bartlet a case for the theologian or the psychologist? Was Phebe's experience the work of God or the work of an emotional disturbance? The age in which empirical psychology vied with religion for a creditable explanation of the mystic's experience had not yet dawned. (When this age did dawn, however, William James, vitally concerned with these fundamental questions, was moved to write one of the truly great classics of American letters, *Varieties of Religious Experience.*)

In many ways, Edwards was a symbol of the past as the last stand of Calvinistic orthodoxy; in other ways, he was a precursor of frontier evangelism. Nevertheless, by the last quarter of the eighteenth century, in the face of the rising tide of enlightened humanitarianism, his rationalism and mysticism appeared increasingly anachronistic. Humanitarianism embodied a new rationalism, premised not on revealed supernatural faith but on empirical science and a new romantic emotionalism which found God in nature. In contrast to Edwards, the romantic humanitarians asserted that man's nature was basically good. As Edwards painted vivid pictures of the torments of hell and damnation, some Americans and many Europeans had already embraced the central Enlightenment doctrine of "man the measure of all things."

While colonial education differed in thought and practice from region to region and from sect to sect, the Puritan who settled in New England played a major role in shaping the course of American educational thought. The Puritan's educational ideas, which represented a syncretization and integration of his medieval, Renaissance, and Reformation

---

45. Carl Van Doren, ed., *Benjamin Franklin and Jonathan Edwards, Selections from Their Writings* (New York: Charles Scribner's Sons, 1920). First three paragraphs are quoted from pp. 332-333; last paragraph is a paraphrase by R. Freeman Butts (not available in published form) of further passages.

past made applicable to the demands of the New World, were eminently rational and proceeded logically from his conceptions of human nature and the nature of the good society.[46] The Puritan's faith in rationality, as well as his faith in the power of public education to develop that rationality, marks him as both a precursor of the Enlightenment and a forerunner of the public education movement. His doctrine of the elect and his doctrine of work, once stripped of their religious connotations, also mark him as the father of the American spirit of capitalism.

In spite of the strange vicissitudes that Puritan values have undergone in American cultural history, elements of this tradition are still reflected in the complex repertoire of values of the modern American. By the beginning of the nineteenth century, however, many of the most cherished Puritan ideals and values were challenged, and by the end of that century, men were still attempting to free themselves of Puritan values. Perhaps the greatness of the Puritan lies in that self-confidence which could assert that "men shall say of succeeding plantacions: the lord make it like that of New England for wee must Consider that wee shall be as a Citty upon a Hill, the eies of all people are uppon us."

SUGGESTED READINGS

Adams, James Truslow. *The Founding of New England.* Boston, Little, Brown and Company, 1963.

Bailyn, Bernard. *Education in the Forming of American Society.* Chapel Hill, University of North Carolina Press, 1960.

Baritz, Loren. *City on a Hill.* New York, John Wiley & Sons, Inc., 1964.

Butts, R. Freeman, and Lawrence Cremin. *A History of Education in American Culture.* New York, Henry Holt and Company, 1953.

Cassirer, Ernst, Paul O. Kristeller, and John A. Randall, Jr. *The Renaissance Philosophy of Man.* Chicago, Phoenix Books, 1961.

Edwards, Jonathan. "A Faithful Narrative of the Surprising Work of God in the Conversion of Many Hundred Souls in Northampton, and the Neighboring Towns and Villages. . . . In a Letter to the Reverend Dr. Benjamin Colman of Boston," *Benjamin Franklin and Jonathan Edwards, Selections from Their Writings,* ed. Carl Van Doren. New York, Charles Scribner's Sons, 1920.

Edwards, Newton, and Herman G. Richey. *The School in the American Social Order,* 2nd ed. Boston, Houghton Mifflin Company, 1963.

Fleming, Sandford. *Children and Puritanism: The Place of Children in the Life and Thought of the New England Churches, 1620-1847.* New Haven, Yale University Press, 1933.

Ford, Paul Leicester, ed. *The New-England Primer,* Classics in Education, No. 13.

46. The reader is reminded that this discussion has been limited to certain aspects of Puritan educational thought. For a detailed coverage of thought and practice for the Middle Atlantic states and the South, read R. Freeman Butts and Lawrence Cremin, *A History of Education in American Culture* (New York: Henry Holt and Company, 1953). Also see Newton Edwards and Herman G. Richey, *The School in the American Social Order,* 2nd ed. (Boston: Houghton Mifflin Company, 1963).

New York, Bureau of Publications, Teachers College, Columbia University, 1962.

Gilson, Etienne. *History of Christian Philosophy in the Middle Ages.* New York, Random House, Inc., 1955.

————. *Reason and Revelation in the Middle Ages.* New York, Charles Scribner's Sons, 1938.

Jernegan, Marcus W. *Laboring and Dependent Classes in Colonial America, 1607-1783.* Chicago, University of Chicago Press, 1931.

Kiefer, Monica. *American Children Through Their Books, 1700-1835.* Philadelphia, University of Pennsylvania Press, 1948.

Mather, Cotton. *A Family Well-Ordered.* Boston, B. Green and F. Allen, 1699.

Miller, Perry. *The New England Mind: The Seventeenth Century.* New York, The Macmillan Company, 1939.

————. *Puritanism in Early America,* ed. George M. Waller, Problems in American Civilization: Amherst Series. Boston, D. C. Heath and Company, 1950.

Morison, Samuel Eliot. *The Founding of Harvard College.* Cambridge, Mass., Harvard University Press, 1935.

————. *The Intellectual Life of Colonial New England.* New York, New York University Press, 1956.

Muller, Herbert J. *Religion and Freedom in the Modern World.* Chicago, University of Chicago Press, 1964.

Paetow, Louis John. *The Arts Course at Medieval Universities with Special Reference to Grammar and Rhetoric.* Urbana, University of Illinois Press, 1910.

Parrington, Vernon Louis. *Main Currents in American Thought.* New York, Harcourt, Brace and Company, 1930.

Perry, Ralph Barton. *Puritanism and Democracy.* New York, The Vanguard Press, 1944.

Weber, Max. *The Protestant Ethic and the Spirit of Capitalism.* New York, Charles Scribner's Sons, 1958.

Woolman, John. *A Journal.* Philadelphia, Association of Friends for the Diffusion of Religious and Useful Knowledge, 1860.

CHAPTER 2

The eighteenth-century
age of Enlightenment

The golden age is not behind us, but in front of us. It is the perfection of social order. Our fathers have not seen it; our children will arrive there one day, and it is for us to clear the way for them.[1] SAINT-SIMON

While Jonathan Edwards was verbally depicting the plight of "sinners in the hands of an angry God," many European and American thinkers were already engrossed in that constellation of ideas and spirit which historians have aptly labeled the Age of Enlightenment. Exactly where this age begins and ends, however, is difficult to discern; the selection of exact boundaries for any historical era involves an exercise of somewhat arbitrary judgment. For example, equally good arguments have been advanced for considering the Enlightenment as beginning with the life of Francis Bacon (1561-1626) or with the publication of Sir Isaac Newton's *Mathematical Principles of Natural Philosophy* (1687). The same difficulty occurs when one attempts to be precise about the end of an era. Certain Enlightenment ideas persist today, just as certain ideas of the medieval, Renaissance, and Reformation periods are still writ large in modern American culture. Most scholars, however, agree that the European Enlightenment was well under way by the beginning of the eighteenth century and fairly well eclipsed by the end of the century by German idealism in philosophy and the Romantic movement in literature. Even though the ideas of Bacon, Newton, Locke, Voltaire, and others did influence American thought during the first half of the eighteenth century, it was not until the second half of the century that the

---

1. Quoted in J. B. Bury, *The Idea of Progress* (New York: Dover Publications, Inc., 1955), p. 282.

American Enlightenment bore revolutionary fruit. In general, the American Enlightenment was later getting started, ideologically influential longer, and less radical than its European counterpart.

While most colonists remained safely within a Christian world view, the influence of European naturalistic thought contributed significantly to the growing liberalism of much eighteenth- and nineteenth-century congregational theology.[2] To what extent the average eighteenth-century colonist was affected by Enlightenment ideas from Europe remains an unresolved historical problem. Nevertheless, the leaders of the Revolutionary and constitutional eras, from Benjamin Franklin to James Madison, consistently reflected Enlightenment ideas and values in much of their thought and action. This leadership not only guided a political revolution but also inspired an ideological revolution which was to have profound consequences on the way future generations of Americans would view human nature, the good society, and the purposes of education.

THE IDEOLOGY OF THE ENLIGHTENMENT

A Newtonian universe

If the central focus of Reformation thought was to work out the meaning of a universe with God at the center, Enlightenment thought focused attention on working out the meaning of a universe with man at the center. Basic medieval cosmology, which held that God was personal and immediately involved in a unified universe, had remained relatively untouched by Reformation thought. With the development of mathematics and science, and the freeing of thought from religious control, came the evolution of an empiricism and a rationalism premised not on faith but on reason, relying for truth not on revelation but on mathematical reasoning and empirical sense experience.

Sir Isaac Newton's *Mathematical Principles of Natural Philosophy* (1687) epitomizes seventeenth-century development in the newer mathematical rationalism and scientific empiricism.[3] Although Newton was a "good" Christian, it was his view of the machinelike character of the universe which basically undercut the medieval Christian cosmology that had survived the Reformation. Science, from Newton on, became the germinator of most new conceptions of man and his universe. Just as Darwinian evolution profoundly influenced nineteenth-century social thought and Einstein's relativism markedly affected the modern social scientist's view of his environment, so Newton's conception of the universe as a mechanism governed by mathematical laws shaped eighteenth-century man's view of himself and his world.

2. See Merle Curti, *The Growth of American Thought*, 3rd ed. (New York: Harper & Row, 1964), pp. 105-108.

3. Behind Newton stands a host of scientific thinkers such as Galileo, Bacon, Kepler, Harvey, Brahe, Copernicus, and others.

The Newtonian system of empirically verified mathematical laws was impressive evidence that nature functioned as a machine. Usually reasoning by analogy, most Enlightenment social thinkers were readily convinced that if the physical universe consists of precise physical laws which govern it, then there must also exist precise natural laws with concomitant natural rights which govern men's social behavior. Thus, there emerged not only a physical but a social world governed, it would seem, by natural laws and natural rights.

Materialism versus idealism

The universe that Newton visualized resembled a watch ticking off celestial time. The place of God in such a world scheme seemed most uncertain. Materialists like Holbach and Helvétius were quick to point out the irrelevance of a God in La Mettrie's world of *L'homme machine.* In this perspective, human nature governed by mechanistic laws was self-sufficient. In the opposite direction, Bishop George Berkeley argued, as an idealist, that the essence of human nature was the spiritual soul, which, in fact, gave life to the body. With the spiritual nature of man thus reaffirmed, Berkeley and others went on to reassert the significance of God. Cutting a middle path between extreme idealism and extreme materialism was the deist, who found a place for God, not as an active watch repairman, but at least as the original watchmaker. God had, indeed, created the universe, but He had created it so well that He did not have to interfere with it.

Deists, such as Jefferson, Paine, Franklin, Condorcet, and Voltaire, did not rely on divine intervention for the solution to human problems. The rational mind of the deist had rejected Christianity. The case for the deist was perhaps best stated by Thomas Paine in an article which appeared in *The Prospect,* February 18, 1804, in which he argued:

The point between Deists and Christians is not about doctrine, but about fact —for if the things believed by the Christians to be facts are not facts, the doctrine founded thereon falls of itself. There is such a book as the Bible, but is it a fact that the Bible is *revealed religion?* The Christians cannot prove it is. They put tradition in place of evidence, and tradition is not proof. If it were, the reality of witches could be proved by the same kind of evidence. . . .

Is it a fact that Jesus Christ died for the sins of the world, and how is it proved? If a God, he could not die, and as a man he could not redeem. How then is this redemption proved to be fact? It is said that Adam ate of the forbidden fruit, commonly called an apple, and thereby subjected himself and all his posterity forever to eternal damnation.

This is worse than visiting the sins of the fathers upon the children unto the *third and fourth generations.* But how was the death of Jesus Christ to affect or alter the case? Did God thirst for blood? If so, would it not have been better to have crucified Adam at once upon the forbidden tree, and made a new man? Would not this have been more creator-like than repairing the old one?

Or did God, when He made Adam, supposing the story to be true, exclude Himself from the right of making another? or impose on Himself the necessity of breeding from the old stock? Priests should first prove facts, and deduce doctrines from them afterwards. But instead of this they assume everything and prove nothing. . . .

The story of the redemption will not stand examination. That man should redeem himself from the sin of eating an apple by committing a murder on Jesus Christ, is the strangest system of religion ever set up. Deism is perfect purity compared with this.

It is an established principle with the Quakers not to shed blood: suppose then all Jerusalem had been Quakers when Christ lived, there would have been nobody to crucify him, and in that case, if man is redeemed by his blood, which is the belief of the Church, there could have been no redemption; and the people of Jerusalem must all have been damned because they were too good to commit murder. The Christian system of religion is an outrage on common sense. Why is man afraid to think?[4]

Humanitarianism

The hard-hitting deistic attack on miracle, mystery, and revealed authority effectively cleared the way for the religion of humanitarianism. The humanitarian took for his supreme objective the improvability, if not the perfectibility, of humanity in this world. Human nature might be selfish, as Thomas Hobbes asserted, or good, as Rousseau claimed, but it was certainly not evil, as the Puritan had preached. Humanitarians agreed that if man's nature was not inherently good, it was at least improvable. Man, if allowed the freedom to inquire, would develop his reason, live according to natural law, preserve his natural rights, and selflessly contribute to the progress of humanity. Men were to be redeemed not for another world but for the future enlightened society, not by Christian grace but by natural reason.

Romantic humanitarians from Rousseau on who proclaimed the goodness of man's nature were usually at a loss to explain the prevalence of evil. The dilemma of evil could not be escaped merely by blaming society, which had itself been created by men who were by nature good. Just how could men who came from the hand of nature's God in such purity become so wretched? The romantic humanitarians constantly proclaimed the goodness in man's nature, but they never adequately accounted for evil. For the most part, the more hard-headed humanitarians were willing to accept the idea that sin was ignorance, and once humanity was enlightened by education, sin would disappear. Almost as the Church had been viewed as a vehicle to help man achieve God's grace in order to overcome the stain of original sin, so most humanitarians viewed education as a vehicle to help man develop his reason in order to overcome ignorance and, therefore, vice.

The Enlightenment ideology, which was based on Newton's concept of the universe, a set of assumed natural laws and natural rights, a deistic God, and a humanitarian faith in the improvability if not the perfectibility of man, culminated in the idea of progress. The central pillar in

---

4. Philip S. Foner, ed., *The Complete Writings of Thomas Paine* (New York: The Citadel Press, 1945), pp. 789-791.

the Enlightenment temple of humanity was a theory of progress which itself was based on education.

THE THEORY OF PROGRESS

Historical roots

The idea of progress was perhaps the single most important contribution of the Enlightenment era to Western thought.[5] This idea, conceived in the Renaissance, was born in the Enlightenment. Neither the classical world nor the medieval or Reformation culture could conceive of human history as a continuous march toward perfection. The deep sense of tragedy which pervaded classical thought cut short the development of any naïve optimistic thinking and thereby inhibited any possible evolution of the idea of progress in classical antiquity.

The classical mind was attracted to a cyclical theory of history which the Latin Church fathers quickly rejected. To the early Christians, the idea that perhaps Christianity would have its rise and fall was clearly unpalatable. Surely one could find little solace in the cyclical theory, especially when one happened to be on the downward side of the cycle. In its place, Christian theologians usually proposed a linear theory in which the city of man continued along the same path of tears with no real possibility of amelioration. The hope of humanity was to be realized in the "city of God." The swift success of the Christian religion in the decadent civilization of Rome can be attributed in large part to this hope that Christianity offered a suffering humanity.

Medieval Christianity, then, developed a theory of progress, which included "hope" in an afterlife and "faith" in the church as a concrete instrument of salvation. Building on the scholarship of medieval thinkers, Enlightenment leaders secularized these Christian virtues and developed a theory of progress which dominated most American thought until the twentieth century.[6]

Secularization of Christian virtues

If a theory of progress results from having hope in the future and faith in an instrument through which amelioration can be achieved, it should be clear that the medieval Church had developed such a theory. Medieval man repeatedly demonstrated a hope in future salvation and a faith in a concrete instrument, the Church and its sacraments, for achieving his aspirations. Enlightenment leaders, however, secularized the medieval virtues of faith, hope, and charity in the cause of humanitarianism. Medieval thinkers believed in the perfectibility of man in

---

5. For a thoughtful treatment of the idea, see Bury, *Idea of Progress.*

6. It should be noted that as European and American cultures became less and less enamored of Enlightenment values, they tended to return to cyclical theories of history. The popularity of the Toynbee and Spengler interpretations of history is an example of this phenomenon.

future salvation, while Enlightenment thinkers thought of improvability of man in this life. On the medieval side, the Church was the practical instrument in which men would invest their faith to work for the amelioration of man's sinful nature; and on the Enlightenment side, the state and the arm of the state, a system of public education, would be the concrete instruments in which men would invest their faith to banish ignorance and usher in the perfection of humanity. In this way, the medieval Church offered hope in an afterlife, whereas the humanitarians offered hope in this life.[7]

The meaning of progress

What is progress, and what are its chief characteristics? A theory of progress inevitably assumes that tomorrow will be better than today and that today is considerably better than yesterday. Firmly believing this proposition, Enlightenment thinkers were quick to label the age from which they derived many of their more fruitful constructs the Dark Age. A fundamental part of any belief in progress is a reluctance to resign oneself to "what is" and an eagerness to invest one's hopes and efforts in "what ought to be." If, however, these hopes are to be anything more than mere flights of fancy, one must also have faith in a practical instrument through which aspirations can be achieved. The intimate transactional relationship between one's aspiration level and one's faith in the practical instrument through which the future is to be controlled sets up the dynamics of the change process. To a considerable extent, Enlightenment thinkers had great hopes in the future progress of humanity because they firmly believed that through the manipulation of such social institutions as the national state and education they could achieve their aspirations.

Revolutionary and evolutionary change

This faith in possibility can be revolutionary. When human beings suffered disease and starvation in the Middle Ages and truly believed nothing could be done to improve their fate, they aspired to very little and starved to death without protest. When, however, human beings suffered starvation prior to the French Revolution but believed that something could be done about their condition, a revolution was born! A similar example can be drawn from the experience of the underdeveloped nations of the world today. For centuries, the people of these nations were willing to endure considerable privation, accepting their condition as inevitable. However, with the growing belief that through political and educational action something could be done to improve their condition, they now actively seek such improvement. Closer to home, and another example of this construct at work, is the Negro revo-

---

7. For an analysis of the secularization of medieval virtues by Enlightenment thinkers, see Carl Becker, *The Heavenly City of the Eighteenth-Century Philosophers* (New Haven: Yale University Press, 1932). For a critical review of Becker's thesis, see Peter Gay, "Carl Becker's Heavenly City," *Political Science Quarterly*, LXXII, 2 (June 1957), 182-199.

lution in American culture today. As long as the Negro lacked a faith in any instrument to ameliorate his condition, he remained docile, but once the Negro in America realized that something could be done through legal and organized effort to better his condition, he no longer remained docile but adopted revolutionary aspirations. Thus a revolution in aspiration often precedes a revolution in politics. The theory of progress carries with it the potential of evolutionary or revolutionary change, depending to a considerable extent on how far the aspiration level of any group has managed to pass beyond the practical limits of evolutionary achievements.

Christianity had always maintained that although the Church could assist the individual along the road to salvation, each individual went to hell or to heaven on his own merits. The humanitarians, on the other hand, approached most problems from a collective environmental standpoint and insisted that their heaven on earth could be entered collectively. Organized, institutional effort was the key to unlock the door of progress through which all men would pass. In this respect, most Enlightenment leaders were social meliorists; i.e., they approached the amelioration of human problems by placing their faith and energy in the organization and construction of social institutions designed to resolve social problems rather than investing their faith and support in charismatic personal leadership.[8] An enlightened humanity, educated to develop its reason, would thus participate collectively in directing its own future progress. Humanitarians endeavored to free humanity from its chains of miracle and mystery with the searing fire of reason. In 1794, Condorcet passionately argued:

The time will therefore come when the sun will shine only on free men who know no other master but their reason; when tyrants and slaves, priests and their stupid or hypocritical instruments will exist only in works of history and on the stage; and when we shall think of them only to pity their victims, and their dupes; to maintain ourselves in a state of vigilance by thinking on their excesses, and to learn how to recognize and so to destroy, by force of reason, the first seeds of tyranny and superstition should they even dare to reappear amongst us.[9]

Impact on America

Even though few American Enlightenment leaders went as far as Condorcet in his optimistic faith in the future progress of human reason, most accepted the basic constructs implicit in a theory of progress. Reinforced by frontier opportunities and a land heavily endowed with rich natural resources, the American also repeatedly demonstrated his faith in a theory of progress. Indeed, throughout most American political and social history, from the formation of the Constitution at the end

---

8. It is important to recognize that when men in the twentieth century lost their faith in their ability to manipulate social institutions to resolve human problems, they often turned to charismatic leadership for solutions. The fascist is the classic case in point.

9. Antoine Nicolas de Condorcet, *Sketch for a Historical Picture of the Progress of the Human Mind,* trans. June Barraclough (New York: The Noonday Press, 1955), p. 179.

of the eighteenth century to the progressive reform movements at the end of the nineteenth to the New Deal in the twentieth, runs an implicit faith in social meliorism. When faced with critical social problems, American culture typically turned to manipulating its social institutions in order to solve its most pressing problems. In this way the American faith in the ability of the social institution of education to solve every major social and moral problem of the last century reflects both the optimism and the naïveté of the Enlightenment tradition in American cultural history. Although many, from Herman Melville to T. S. Eliot, questioned whether this process of social meliorism would lead to progress, most Americans have consistently seen their "golden age" in the future rather than in the past.

TWO EXEMPLARS OF THE AMERICAN ENLIGHTENMENT

Two excellent examples of the educational ideas of the American Enlightenment are found in the versatile and creative thought and action of Benjamin Franklin and Thomas Jefferson. While these two men came from distinctly different educational and social backgrounds, both thoroughly accepted and made part of themselves the basic values of enlightened ideology. Representing a new middle class, Franklin converted the religiously sanctioned Puritan values of hard work, frugality, and investment into values justified by the secular notion that "they pay off." He thus encouraged the emerging merchant and industrial classes in a vigorous and unembarrassed pursuit of capital for its own sake or for the sake of national "progress." At the same time he made more respectable an educational program composed of "useful knowledge" and aimed at turning out productive citizens. Thus, he bridged the Puritan and the nineteenth-century capitalistic ethos.

In contrast, Jefferson's major contribution to the educational tradition tended more in the direction of working ideals for education in an emerging democratic society. Both men, at various times, served as president of the American Philosophical Society for Promoting Useful Knowledge, an organization which undertook to persuade the literate population of the new nation that the future destiny of the nation was intimately tied to the development of a public system of education.[10] These Enlightenment leaders, along with many others, put a kind of special burden on educational systems which made the century 1750-1850 the great century of formal school establishment.

Thomas Jefferson: The well-rounded man

When Jefferson spoke of Bacon, Locke, and Newton as "the three greatest men that have ever lived, without any exception,"[11] he was

---

10. See Allen Oscar Hansen, *Liberalism and American Education in the Eighteenth Century* (New York: The Macmillan Company, 1926).

11. "Letter to John Trumbull," Feb. 15, 1788, in *The Papers of Thomas Jefferson,* ed. Julian P. Boyd (Princeton, N.J.: Princeton University Press, 1958), XIV, 561.

only expressing in another way his <u>Enlightenment faith in an empirical</u> <u>science, human reason, freedom of inquiry, and the progress of humanity.</u> Although this faith tended to guide his thought, it did not by any means encompass the scope of his thinking. Any sampling of Jefferson's fifty thousand letters will reveal a man of broad vision who was equally at home in the worlds of classical humanism and humanitarianism. He was one of the few Americans who successfully integrated the conflicting values of classical humanism and enlightened humanitarianism, of aristocracy and democracy, within a single working philosophy. Unlike Condorcet, Jefferson did not believe in the inevitable perfectibility of human nature but rather in the possibility of improving human nature. Jefferson's idealism tended to be tempered with a pragmatic realism which permeated his thought. Since he constantly tested his ideas against their consequences in action, both Jefferson's thought and his action were receptive to change.

Jeffersonian radicalism

It is a misrepresentation to call Jefferson a political conservative. One who could say, "The tree of liberty must be refreshed from time to time with the blood of patriots and tyrants,"[12] or could agree with Thomas Paine that the earth belongs to the living and that the dead should have neither rights nor power over it, was certainly no conservative for his day or, for that matter, for any day. To be sure, he did believe in states' rights, but he did so at a time when the center of radicalism was in the state government, not in the federal government. One might also consider that Jefferson stood for state authority when state government was, in fact, geographically and psychologically closest to the people.

In the same vein, another misleading stereotype is the Jefferson ideal of government versus that of Jackson. From Jefferson's letters, it is clear that in the last two decades of his life he advocated the extension of suffrage and popular control of government, even to the point of suggesting the direct election of judges. A Jefferson-Jackson view of government, taken together, is better contrasted with a Hamilton-Burke concept. Irving Babbitt, a twentieth-century conservative neohumanist, in examining the problem of democracy and leadership, could only conclude that the real enemy of the conservatively ordered society was, indeed, the author of the Declaration of Independence. It was Jefferson, Babbitt surmised, who emphasized men's rights over their responsibilities and thus "corrupted" the American mind.[13]

Freedom in a democratic society

The kind of liberty that an individual or a group is usually willing to tolerate is contingent on the security and confidence that individual or group has in its own ideals. Because Jefferson believed deeply in the rationality of the common man and his ability to progress toward free

---

12. Quoted in Boyd, *Papers of Thomas Jefferson*, XII, 356.
13. See Irving Babbitt, *Democracy and Leadership* (Boston: Houghton Mifflin Company, 1924).

inquiry, his view of freedom appears radical to some twentieth-century Americans. Confident that men can rationally know the truth and act accordingly, Jefferson, in his bill for establishing religious freedom in Virginia, said:

. . . that truth is great and will prevail if left to herself; that she is the proper and sufficient antagonist to error, and has nothing to fear from the conflict unless by human interposition disarmed of her natural weapons, free argument and debate; errors ceasing to be dangerous when it is permitted freely to contradict them.[14]

At his first presidential inauguration, it was the same confident Jefferson who said, "If there be any among us who would wish to dissolve this Union or to change its republican form, let them stand undisturbed as monuments of the safety with which error of opinion may be tolerated where reason is left to combat it."[15] To Jefferson, the freedom to be wrong as well as right, where reason is left free to combat error, was the keystone in the arch of freedom in a democratic society. In the cause of this kind of freedom, Jefferson argued persistently for freedom of speech and press and against censorship of books. In regard to the latter, he wrote:

I am really mortified to be told that, *in the United States of America,* a fact like this can become a subject of inquiry, and of criminal inquiry too, as an offence against religion; that a question about the sale of a book can be carried before the civil magistrate. Is this then our freedom of religion? and are we to have a censor whose imprimatur shall say what books may be sold and what we may buy? And who is thus to dogmatize religious opinions for our citizens? Whose foot is to be the measure to which ours are all to be cut or stretched? Is a priest to be our inquisitor, or shall a layman, simple as ourselves, set up his reason as the rule for what we are to read, and what we must believe? It is an insult to our citizens to question whether they are rational beings or not, and blasphemy against religion to suppose it cannot stand the test of truth and reason. If M. de Becourt's book be false in its facts, disprove them; if false in its reasoning, refute it. But for God's sake, let us freely hear both sides, if we choose.[16]

The Jeffersonian ideal of free use of reason in the crusade against ignorance was a noble ideal and, like most noble ideals, was difficult to achieve. Jefferson himself was not always supremely confident that truth would prevail if reason was left free. In his Bill for the More General Diffusion of Knowledge, Jefferson required a loyalty oath of teachers: "The said masters and ushers, before they enter on the execution of

---

14. Gordon C. Lee, ed., *Crusade Against Ignorance: Thomas Jefferson on Education,* Classics in Education, No. 6 (New York: Bureau of Publications, Teachers College, Columbia University, 1961), p. 68.

15. Lee, *Crusade Against Ignorance,* p. 28.

16. "Letter to Monsieur N. G. Dufief," April 19, 1814, in *The Writings of Thomas Jefferson,* ed. Andrew A. Lipscomb (Washington, D.C.: The Jefferson Memorial Association of the United States, 1904), XIV, 127.

their office, shall give assurance of fidelity to the commonwealth."[17] It was the same Jefferson, concerned with the teachers and the kinds of texts used in the study of government, who wrote that a new teacher:

... may be a Richmond lawyer, or one of that school of quondam federalism, now consolidation. It is our duty to guard against such principles being disseminated among our youth, and the diffusion of that poison, by a previous prescription of the texts to be followed in their discourses.[18]

In spite of these contradictions, it was Jefferson's ideal which served as the mainstay of academic freedom for generations.

Education of the common man

Jefferson was not satisfied with simply stating the ideals of the Enlightenment. Throughout his life, he was vitally concerned with implementing these ideals in practical action. Firmly believing that popular government ultimately rested on popular enlightenment, Jefferson proposed a bill for a system of public education for Virginia, once in 1779 and again in 1817.[19] In both cases he tied the future of the Republic to the cause of public education. Public liberty rested on public enlightenment, which in turn necessitated public education. This is most apparent in a letter to Washington in which he said, "It is an axiom in my mind that our liberty can never be safe but in the hands of the people themselves, and that, too, of the people with a certain degree of instruction. This is the business of the state to effect, and on a general plan."[20]

On a number of occasions Jefferson pointed out that if he had to make a choice between educating the common man and educating the natural aristocracy, he would choose education for the common man. Nevertheless, he was unsuccessful in his attempts to establish free public education for the common man and successful in establishing the University of Virginia. His proposed Bill for the More General Diffusion of Knowledge went against the grain of too many long-standing traditions and practical realities. The tradition of private and tutorial education, which had for a century dominated the education of the landed gentry in Virginia, could not at that time accommodate itself to the idea of a public system of education. On the practical side, the opposition was quick to point out the difficulty of maintaining a small district system in areas where the plantation system predominated and the cost of maintaining such a system would be prohibitive.

Close scrutiny of the bill, however, reveals that it provided for a minimum of public education. The common man could attend school at public expense for three years to learn to read, write, cipher, and study

---

17. Quoted in Saul K. Padover, ed., *The Complete Jefferson* (New York: Duell, Sloan & Pearce, Inc., 1943), pp. 1052-1053.
18. "Letter to Joseph C. Cabell," Feb. 3, 1825, in *The Writings of Thomas Jefferson,* ed. Henry A. Washington (New York: Riker, Thorne Company, 1854), VII, 397.
19. See "A Bill for the More General Diffusion of Knowledge," 1779, and "A Bill Establishing a System of Public Education," 1817, in Roy J. Honeywell, *The Educational Work of Thomas Jefferson* (Cambridge, Mass.: Harvard University Press, 1931).
20. Quoted in Honeywell, *Educational Work of Thomas Jefferson,* p. 13.

history.[21] Jefferson assumed that this, along with a free press, was enough education to enable the people to recognize tyranny and revolt against it. From that group which could not afford to go on to further schooling, Jefferson would "rake from the rubbish annually" and send the best scholars among the poor to a secondary school where the curriculum would be Latin, Greek, geography, history, and mathematics. Here, he would again rake from the rubbish to get the very best virtue and talent to be sent at public expense to the private College of William and Mary. While the poor were to be carefully screened, and only the best qualified sent on to higher education at public expense, the rich traveled at their own expense to whatever level they chose.[22] Parrington once said that Jefferson had an aristocratic head set on a plebeian frame. In this bill, Jefferson's aristocratic head was dominant. The natural aristocracy of virtue and talent were, however, to be educated to be of responsible service to a community in which the common people would hold the ultimate authority. With this in mind, Jefferson said:

I know of no safe depository of the ultimate powers of the society but the people themselves; and if we think them not enlightened enough to exercise their control with a wholesome discretion, the remedy is not to take it from them, but to inform their discretion by education.[23]

As a son of the Enlightenment, Jefferson was secure in his Newtonian universe, believing firmly in the rationality of man and the efficacy of education to develop that rationality in a society allowing freedom of religion as well as freedom of thought. As a deist, Jefferson saw God as a creator and Jesus Christ as a great human teacher.[24] Unlike Rousseau, who believed that all men were born naturally good, Jefferson believed that while the great bulk of men were born with a good moral sense, some were born moral defectives and various kinds of educational methods were needed to correct the defects.[25]

I sincerely, then, believe with you in the general existence of a moral instinct. I think it the brightest gem with which the human character is studded, and the want of it as more degrading than the most hideous of the bodily deformities.[26]

Jefferson rejected the Puritan concept of original sin as well as that of human nature as being fixed at birth.[27] The progress of humanity, while not infinite and inevitable, was possible and open-ended.

---

21. It should be noted that Jefferson purposely left the Bible and Bible reading out of every educational proposal he made, reflecting his secular views.

22. Here one could argue that the net effect of Jefferson's proposed bill would have been to deprive the lower classes of their talented and most effective leaders.

23. "Letter to William C. Jarvis," Sept. 28, 1820, in *The Writings of Thomas Jefferson,* ed. Paul L. Ford (New York: G. P. Putnam's Sons, 1899), X, 161.

24. Padover, *Complete Jefferson,* pp. 931-957.

25. Lipscomb, *Writings of Thomas Jefferson,* XV, 142-143.

26. Lipscomb, *Writings of Thomas Jefferson,* XV, 143.

27. Padover, *Complete Jefferson,* p. 1099.

Education, in like manner, engrafts a new man on the native stock, and improves what in his nature was vicious and perverse into qualities of virtue and social worth. And it cannot be but that each generation succeeding to the knowledge acquired by all those who preceded it, adding to it their own acquisitions and discoveries, and handing the mass down for successive and constant accumulation, must advance the knowledge and well-being of mankind, not *infinitely*, as some have said, but *indefinitely*, and to a term which no one can fix and foresee.[28]

In the area of educational psychology and methodology, Jefferson was distinctly uncreative. For the most part, he followed John Locke's psychology as well as his specific educational recommendations.[29] Like Locke, Jefferson believed that *all* knowledge was derived from sensory experience, which was shaped by certain functional faculties of mind.[30] Therefore, both men rejected the age-old Platonic notion of innate ideas. Jefferson further recommended the same methods of teaching languages, the same books to be used in educating the gentleman, and the same order in which the books were to be read as John Locke.[31] In much the same way that Jefferson's political ideas expressed in the Declaration of Independence were similar to Locke's *Of Civil Government, Second Treatise,* Jefferson's psychology appears strikingly similar to Locke's *Essay Concerning Human Understanding* and his educational views to Locke's *Some Thoughts Concerning Education.*

Jefferson's educational legacy

As an exemplar of the Enlightenment, Jefferson was successful in implementing his ideas in the development of the principle of separation of Church and State and in the establishment of the University of Virginia. He was also successful in popularizing the idea that the future of a republican society rested on an enlightened populace with the state responsible for education of the common man, but he was only partially successful in popularizing his ideal of academic freedom—i.e., that the mind must be free to be wrong as well as right, so long as reason is left free to combat error.

Even though Jefferson had suggested a semipublic ladder system of education in 1779, it was not until a century later that a complete ladder system of free public education was accomplished. As a representative of the landed aristocracy, Jefferson could find virtue only in the free landholder. He feared the age of industrialization and what he termed "mobs of the great cities." His ideal society was the free, agrarian, secular society. It is ironic, indeed, that Jefferson's cherished system of education should be rejected by a society based on an agrarian economy unable, if

---

28. "Rockfish Gap Report" in Padover, *Complete Jefferson,* p. 1099.

29. In maintaining a faculty psychology of mind, John Locke was true to his medieval past. For his ideas on the faculties of the mind, read his "Essay Concerning Human Understanding." Also see Peter Gay, ed., *John Locke on Education,* Classics in Education, No. 20 (New York: Bureau of Publications, Teachers College, Columbia University, 1964).

30. Padover, *Complete Jefferson,* p. 1093. In "A Catalogue of Books Forming the Body of a Library for the Univ. of Virginia," Jefferson deals with books addressed to the three faculties of memory, reason, and imagination.

31. Honeywell, *Educational Work of Thomas Jefferson,* pp. 171-172.

not unwilling, to carry the economic burden, only to be implemented and far surpassed by an industrial culture which Jefferson truly feared and rejected.

Benjamin Franklin: Prophet of the middle class

If Jefferson was the enlightened natural aristocrat of the landed gentry, it was Benjamin Franklin who best epitomized the virtues by which the lower class rose to respectable middle-class status. Franklin, like Jefferson, held strong physiocratic beliefs, but he did not allow such ideas as "manufactures are founded in poverty" and agriculture is "the only honest way" to acquire wealth[32] to stand in the way of his own efforts to amass his fortune in manufactures and commerce. In his *Principles of Trade,* Franklin advocated the theory of laissez-faire two years before Adam Smith published his *Wealth of Nations.*[33] As a representative of the rising middle class, born in Puritan New England, Franklin, more than any other single American, secularized the Puritan values of industry, frugality, and temperance. Franklin was the prototype for the legendary rags-to-riches success story, which reappeared in various forms in the McGuffey literature and the Horatio Alger myths. With his "Poor Richard Says" aphorisms, Franklin touched the materialistic heart of untold millions. He offered the common man not only the hope of riches but the formula for their attainment. As the apostle of practicality, utility, ingenuity, and versatility, he personified what became the American materialistic dream. Success for the sake of wealth, and wealth for the sake of more wealth, however, were not Franklin's dream.

Franklin's educational proposals

As a son of the Enlightenment, Franklin was a humanitarian who believed in progress, empirical science, the improvability of human nature and the human condition. In a letter to Joseph Priestley, he said:

It is impossible to imagine the Height to which may be carried, in a thousand years, the Power of Man over Matter. . . . O that moral Science were in as fair a way of Improvement, that Men would cease to be Wolves to one another, and that human Beings would at length learn what they now improperly call Humanity![34]

Concerned about the improvement of the human condition, Franklin, in his *Proposals Relating to the Educating of Youth in Pennsylvania* (1744), called for an academy which might supply "the succeeding age with

---

32. Parrington, *Main Currents in American Thought,* pp. 172-173.

33. Parrington, *Main Currents in American Thought,* p. 173. The relationship between a Newtonian universe governed by physical law and a laissez-faire capitalistic system governed by the natural economic law of free competition is a functional relationship. For discussion of this idea, see O. H. Taylor, "Economics and the Idea of Natural Law," *Quarterly Journal of Economics,* XLIV (November 1929), 1-39.

34. "Letter to Joseph Priestley," Feb. 8, 1780, in Chester E. Jorgenson and Frank Luther Mott, eds., *Benjamin Franklin: Representative Selections* (New York: American Book Company, 1936), pp. 420-421.

Men qualified to serve the Publick with Honour to themselves, and to their country." The academy, as he proposed it, was to provide a secular, practical education which would include agriculture, mechanics, and the study of the English language on a par with the classical studies. Just as Jefferson failed to establish popular education but his ideas on education were realized in the nineteenth century, Franklin failed to overcome the strength of the classical tradition in the eighteenth century but many of his proposals for a practical education were realized in the utilitarian nineteenth-century academy.

The schools in Franklin's lifetime did not meet the needs of the middle class he understood so well.[35] To the self-educated Franklin, the classics were ornamental knowledge with only slight utility. In 1789, the year the Constitution went into effect, he wrote:

The still prevailing custom of having schools for teaching generally our children, in these days, the Latin and Greek languages, I consider therefore, in no other light than as the *Chapeau bras*[36] of modern Literature. Thus the Time spent in that Study might, it seems, be much better employ'd in the Education for such a Country as ours.[37]

Franklin's attack on the classical curriculum was premature. It was not until the twentieth century that the classics lost their pre-eminent position in the American secondary school curriculum. It is interesting to note, however, that Jefferson held the classics in far greater esteem. Even though the educational ideas of both Franklin and Jefferson were drawn from a common source, Locke's psychology and methodology of instruction,[38] the major temper of Franklin's educational proposals reflected a more practical and utilitarian kind of education than either Jefferson or Locke ever envisioned.

Franklin and Edwards: Beginning and end of an era

In a broad perspective, Franklin symbolized the dawn of a new era which at times would descend into a crass materialism and at other times would ascend to the Franklin spirit of humanitarianism, offering a suffering humanity hope for its future. In contrast, the mind of Jonathan Edwards symbolized the end of the Puritan era, offering a suffering humanity only the wrath of a just God in another world. One man preached the gospel of practicality, and the other the gospel of Calvin; Franklin died fully acclaimed by his countrymen, and Edwards died

---

35. In contrast, the modern American school is so thoroughly middle class that it fails to accord with the needs of the lower classes.

36. Franklin defined the *chapeau bras* as a hat not worn but customarily carried in one's arm at the French court. Its use was clearly ornamental. Both Jefferson and Franklin conceived of "useful knowledge" as scientific knowledge which provides a base for technology and politics.

37. John Hardin Best, ed., *Benjamin Franklin on Education*, Classics in Education, No. 14 (New York: Bureau of Publications, Teachers College, Columbia University, 1962), p. 174.

38. For a detailed analysis of Franklin's educational ideas, see Best, *Benjamin Franklin on Education*, and Thomas Woody, ed., *Educational Views of Benjamin Franklin* (New York: McGraw-Hill Book Company, 1931).

rejected even by his own congregation. Man the measure and God the measure were the principles at work in these two lives as well as the eras they represented. In 1758, Franklin completed work on *The Way to Wealth* and Edwards, "standing with his back to the world," published *The Great Christian Doctrine of Original Sin Defended.*[39]

TOWARD SEPARATION OF CHURCH AND STATE

By the end of the eighteenth century, American core values had begun to shift from a religious to a secular base. This seems most evident in the acceptance by the Virginia Assembly in 1786 of Jefferson's Bill for Establishing Religious Freedom, which stated in part "that our civil rights have no dependence on our religious opinions, any more than our opinions in physics or geometry."[40] It is also reflected in Benjamin Franklin's statement in 1780:

When a Religion is good, I conceive that it will support itself; and, when it cannot support itself, and God does not take care to support, so that its Professors are oblig'd to call for the help of the Civil Power, it is a sign, I apprehend, of its being a bad one.[41]

Enlightenment leadership had successfully attacked the use of legal sanctions as well as the tax power of the state in support of religion and thus paved the way for the development of the principle of separation of Church and State.

Development of this principle was a unique American cultural accomplishment.[42] It was, in some respects, a consequence of the American Enlightenment, but it was also a consequence of the breakdown of the Puritan theocracy in the face of a middle class whose interests were more secular, as well as of the growth of religious pluralism resulting from the Great Awakening of the eighteenth century. Religious pluralism produced practical difficulties in maintaining an established religion; the secular interests of the new middle class lessened any zeal in maintaining it; and the Enlightenment leadership provided the thought and action for getting rid of it. The secular values of the Enlightenment institutionalized in the First Amendment were to have a profound effect on the course of American educational history.

Typical patterns of Church-State relations

Essentially three patterns of Church-State relations had existed in Europe during the American colonial period. First, there was the pat-

39. For an excellent comparison, see Carl Van Doren, ed., *Benjamin Franklin and Jonathan Edwards, Selections from Their Writings* (New York: Charles Scribner's Sons, 1920).

40. Lee, *Crusade Against Ignorance*, p. 67.

41. "Letter to Richard Price," Oct. 9, 1780, in Jorgenson and Mott, *Benjamin Franklin: Representative Selections*, p. 424.

42. Most European nations still have some kind of established church or churches; in this respect, the American development is still unique.

tern found in many Catholic countries, in which the Church took precedence over the State; second, there was the pattern found in England and in Lutheran Germany, in which the State exercised considerable authority over the Church; and third, there was the theocratic state pattern characteristic of most Calvinistic countries, in which the civil and religious functions were thoroughly fused in one authority. Colonial New England developed the theocratic idea; Virginia and other southern colonies followed the English pattern of State supremacy over the Church; and since the Roman Catholic population remained a small minority, the Catholic pattern in which the Church took precedence over the State never developed in colonial America.[43]

Meaning of one established church

What, then, did the seventeenth-century colonist mean by an established church? He meant, first, that the tax power of the state would be used to support a religion and, second, that the coercive power of the state would be used to support a religion. By the beginning of the eighteenth century, Massachusetts, Connecticut, and New Hampshire had established the Congregational Church; and Virginia, South Carolina, and North Carolina had established the Church of England. While Rhode Island, Pennsylvania, and Delaware were from their origin free from establishment, other colonies like New York, New Jersey, Maryland, and Georgia seemed to fluctuate, depending on which religion was strong enough to prevail over the others.[44]

From single establishment to complete separation

At the time of the Great Awakening of 1740-1760, American society became more religiously pluralistic. This religious pluralism resulted in two major trends which were crucial in the historical development of separation of Church and State. First, it became difficult, if not impossible, to employ the coercive power of the state for a single sectarian purpose, and as a consequence, this aspect of establishment was gradually dropped from practice. Establishment then came to mean only the

---

43. The most clear-cut enunciation of the Catholic doctrine of Church over State was made by Pope Boniface VIII in his famous Bull *Unam Sanctam* of 1302. In this document, he pointed out that there were two swords, one to be wielded by the Church and the other by the hand of the king. The latter sword, moreover, must be wielded at the will and sufferance of the Church, for the spiritual power must ultimately exceed the temporal authority. The case for the theocratic society was best presented by Calvin in his *Institutes of the Christian Religion* (1536), where he argued that the functions of State and Church were one. For the historical root of the idea of State over Church, one must turn to the Peace of Augsburg, where, in 1555, was stated the principle of *cuius regio eius religio* [Whosoever rules the territory, his religion shall prevail], which set the State-Church pattern for Germany. See Raymond P. Stearns, ed., *Pageant of Europe*, rev. ed. (New York: Harcourt, Brace and Company, 1947), p. 118. For a similar State-over-Church relationship in the English Church, one need only turn to the English monarchs' break with Rome for evidence.

44. R. Freeman Butts, *The American Tradition in Religion and Education* (Boston: The Beacon Press, 1950), p. 23.

use of the tax power to support religion. The second major trend was a shift from recognizing only one religion as the established religion, and therefore the recipient of the tax dollar, to recognizing many religions as established religions, and therefore making many religions the beneficiaries of the taxing power of the community. During the Great Awakening, most colonies rapidly shifted from a single to a multiple establishment of religion.[45] By the time the First Amendment was adopted in 1791, none of the original thirteen colonies maintained single establishment, only four maintained multiple establishment, and nine had moved to complete separation.[46] In 1833, Massachusetts was the last of the original thirteen states to give up multiple establishment of religion.[47] The movement of the colonies from multiple establishment to complete separation was a result of the bitter sectarian rivalries for the tax dollar, the inability of the state to define religion to the satisfaction of all concerned, the growing secular views of the American middle class, and the spirited drive of Enlightenment leaders for religious freedom.

The struggle for religious freedom in Virginia

The best case study of this kind of transition under the direction of enlightened leadership is the campaign for the passage of Jefferson's Bill for Establishing Religious Freedom in Virginia. Jefferson himself ranked this bill as one of his most important accomplishments.[48] First introduced in the Virginia Assembly on June 13, 1779, the bill did not become law until January 1786.

The battle over multiple establishment came to a head in the summer of 1785, when James Madison fought the battle against religious assessment to its successful conclusion with the adoption of Jefferson's bill. To arouse the people in this fight, Madison wrote his classic *Memorial and Remonstrance Against Religious Assessments.*[49] In this document, Madison argued, as Jefferson and Franklin before him had argued, that the essence of religion is destroyed when it relies on the civil authority for support and that civil authority does not have the right to intrude into the realm of religious opinion.

---

45. A single establishment occurs when only one religion is the recipient of the tax dollar, whereas multiple establishment occurs when more than one religion is designated as the recipient. In late eighteenth-century America, many statutes designated Christian religions as the recipients of the tax dollar. This, however, excluded any payment to Roman Catholic Churches on the grounds that the Roman Catholic Church was anti-Christ!

46. Butts, *American Tradition in Religion and Education,* p. 42.

47. It should be recognized that the kind of cooperation between Church and State advocated by some today is essentially a multiple establishment of religion which was rejected by the American nation by the end of the eighteenth century.

48. Lipscomb, *Writings of Thomas Jefferson,* XIII, p. 56. In a private memorandum, found among Jefferson's papers, was the statement that in case a memorial over him should ever be erected, he would like the following inscription: "Here was buried Thomas Jefferson, Author of the Declaration of American Independence, of The Statute of Virginia for Religious Freedom and Father of the University of Virginia."

49. See Gaillard Hunt, ed., *The Writings of James Madison* (New York: G. P. Putnam's Sons, 1900-1910), II, 183-191.

Who does not see that the same authority which can establish Christianity, in exclusion of all other Religions, may establish with the same ease any particular sect of Christians, in exclusion of all other Sects? That the same authority which can force a citizen to contribute three pence only of his property for the support of any one establishment, may force him to conform to any other establishment in all cases whatsoever?[50]

To Madison, the freedom to be wrong in religion was as important as the freedom to be right. At considerable intellectual distance from the biting intolerance of the Puritan, Madison argued:

Whilst we assert for ourselves a freedom to embrace, to profess and to observe the Religion which we believe to be of divine origin, we cannot deny an equal freedom to those whose minds have not yet yielded to the evidence which has convinced us.[51]

After struggling so hard and so successfully for religious freedom in Virginia, Madison was subsequently called upon to father the First Amendment to the new Constitution of the United States.

Madison and the First Amendment

While the First Amendment underwent many complex changes before it reached its completed form, it is significant that Madison, in the first draft of the amendment, proposed that it should bind the states as well as the federal government. Failing in this attempt, Madison had to be satisfied with prohibiting only the federal government from establishing religion.[52] It was not until the twentieth century that the U. S. Supreme Court interpreted the Fourteenth Amendment in such a way as to make the First Amendment applicable to the states, thus protecting the citizen from a state's establishing religion.[53] If it was clear to Madison in 1791 that only the federal government was prohibited from using its tax power and its legal and coercive power in support of one religion, many religions, or all religions, it was equally clear to him, upon his retirement from public office, that the federal government had already violated the ban on establishment of religion by allowing tax exemptions for church property, by using public money for the support of chaplains for Congress and the armed forces, and by allowing the Chief Executive to issue religious proclamations.[54] In spite of Madison's misgivings, that constitutional principle of separation of Church and State,

---

50. Hunt, *Writings of James Madison,* p. 186.
51. Hunt, *Writings of James Madison,* p. 186.
52. Butts, *American Tradition in Religion and Education,* pp. 78-92.
53. Virtually all U.S. Supreme Court decisions involving education and religion are based on the citizen's rights guaranteed by the First Amendment, made applicable to the states by the Fourteenth Amendment. The U.S. Supreme Court, however, up to the present moment, has not made all of the first ten amendments applicable to the states.
54. Butts, *American Tradition in Religion and Education,* pp. 97-102.

which has had profound implications for educational practice in both the nineteenth and twentieth centuries, had been launched.[55]

Although the word *education* does not appear in the original Constitution, the federal government's relationship to education has been structured by three crucial amendments—the First, Tenth, and Fourteenth. While the function of education is legally reserved to the states by virtue of the Tenth Amendment, education cases involving freedom of speech and religion come under the provision of the First Amendment, made applicable to the states by the Fourteenth Amendment. The equal-protection clause of the latter amendment also provides the grounds for declaring unconstitutional state educational practices which segregate public school children on the basis of race. The function of education, then, evolved as a state function, but it is important to recognize that the leaders of the newly formed federal government, although evidently convinced that the states could and should maintain and regulate schools, clearly believed that a republican government places such demands on its citizens that formal public education was a necessary condition of successful republicanism at both the state and federal level.

Separation of Church and State and the idea of public schools

Because Enlightenment leadership had popularized the idea that the state has a responsibility to provide public education and at the same time had been successful in separating Church and State, one could surmise that the leaders of the Enlightenment had laid the cornerstone of a secular public school system. In theory this was true, but in practice, American schools were a long way from being either secular or public. The idea of a public school, defined as a school publicly controlled and financed, was an idea which evolved slowly in the first half of the nineteenth century.[56] The line between the public and the private school was often blurred by those who defined a public school as one which kept its doors open to all those who could meet its requirements. Such a school, it was argued, was "public" because it carried on a public service—like the English public schools, for example.[57] The history of the Free School Society of New York from 1807 to 1826 and of the Public School Society of New York from 1826 to 1842 represents a case history of the evolution of the idea of a public school as a school

---

55. Consider such pertinent twentieth-century educational questions as textbooks, bus transportation, medical services, psychological services, guidance services, Federal aid, state aid for parochial schools, as well as the problem of released time, shared time, Bible reading, prayers, and religious exercises in the public schools. The exact meaning of the principle of separation of Church and State, at any one time, is a complex series of social as well as legal traditions reflected in court decisions. For the meaning of separation of Church and State today, one must turn to Supreme Court decisions, which we shall consider in Chapter Twelve.

56. The one exception was Massachusetts, which, by the beginning of the nineteenth century, had essentially developed the concept of public education.

57. This kind of definition of "public school" is employed today by the "Citizens for Educational Freedom" Committee which aggressively argues for federal and state funds for private schools.

publicly controlled and publicly supported.[58] It was not until this concept was fully put into practice that the principle of separation of Church and State had any meaning for education at the state level.

If, in general, the movement to restrict the use of public funds to schools publicly controlled gained headway in the first half of the nineteenth century, the movement to eliminate religious instruction from the public schools did not make much headway until the twentieth.[59] For the most part, nineteenth-century elementary and secondary education remained white and Protestant.

THE AMERICAN ENLIGHTENMENT IN PERSPECTIVE

The American Enlightenment, in general, represented a transformation of ideology and values. Although few Americans conceived man's nature as good, most accepted the milder Lockean notion that his nature was improvable to an indefinite extent. The good society was no longer a religiously homogeneous community ruled by God but a secular community ruled by men in such a way as to guarantee men their natural rights and freedoms. While all Enlightenment leaders were humanitarians, believing firmly in the progress of humanity through education, most expressed a rationalism no longer premised on revealed truth but rather on either self-evident truths or empirical evidence.

In a larger view, the idealism of Jefferson and the practicality of Franklin were most fitting and applicable to a frontier society. Enlightenment optimism reinforced by frontier opportunities provided a fertile seedbed which could nourish the vital Enlightenment concept of a rational humanity charting the course of its own progress through institutional and educational reform. One tragedy of the human condition is that few significant thinkers live to see the fruition of their most significant ideas. In this respect, the American Enlightenment leaders were no exception. Many of the ideas of Franklin, Jefferson, Paine, Madison, and others were seminal ideas. They took a century to come to practical fruition. To be sure, Jefferson had failed to establish a mass system of public education for the common people, Franklin had failed to create a practical academy, and Madison had failed in his quest for complete separation of Church and State; but all had succeeded in directing the course of American thought and action toward these goals. As good sons of the Enlightenment, all these men, in unison, would have agreed with Saint-Simon when he said:

The golden age is not behind us, but in front of us. It is the perfection of social order. Our fathers have not seen it; our children will arrive there one day, and it is for us to clear the way for them.

---

58. See Lawrence A. Cremin, *The American Common School* (New York: Bureau of Publications, Teachers College, Columbia University, 1951), pp. 151-175.

59. In this regard, the practice recommended by Horace Mann of teaching the common elements of all religions by reading the Bible without comment was a Protestant practice. In a broader view, the common-elements approach was a transitional one which occupied a position midway between the American school as a sectarian institution and as a secular institution.

SUGGESTED READINGS

Becker, Carl. *The Heavenly City of the Eighteenth-Century Philosophers.* New Haven, Yale University Press, 1932.

Best, John Hardin, ed. *Benjamin Franklin on Education,* Classics in Education, No. 14. New York, Bureau of Publications, Teachers College, Columbia University, 1962.

Boyd, Julian P., ed. *The Papers of Thomas Jefferson.* Princeton, N.J., Princeton University Press, 1958.

Bury, J. B. *The Idea of Progress.* New York, Dover Publications, Inc., 1955.

Butts, R. Freeman. *The American Tradition in Religion and Education.* Boston, The Beacon Press, 1950.

Condorcet, Antoine Nicolas de. *Sketch for a Historical Picture of the Progress of the Human Mind,* trans. June Barraclough. New York, The Noonday Press, 1955.

Cremin, Lawrence A. *The American Common School.* New York, Bureau of Publications, Teachers College, Columbia University, 1951.

Curti, Merle. *The Growth of American Thought,* 3rd ed. New York, Harper & Row, 1964.

Foner, Philip S., ed. *The Complete Writings of Thomas Paine.* New York, The Citadel Press, 1945.

Ford, Paul L., ed. *The Writings of Thomas Jefferson.* New York, G. P. Putnam's Sons, 1899.

Gay, Peter, ed. *John Locke on Education,* Classics in Education, No. 20. New York, Bureau of Publications, Teachers College, Columbia University, 1964.

————. "Carl Becker's Heavenly City," *Political Science Quarterly,* LXXII, 2 (June 1957), 182-199.

Hansen, Allen Oscar. *Liberalism and American Education in the Eighteenth Century.* New York, The Macmillan Company, 1926.

Honeywell, Roy J. *The Educational Work of Thomas Jefferson,* "A Bill for the More General Diffusion of Knowledge," 1799, and "A Bill Establishing a System of Public Education," 1817. Cambridge, Mass., Harvard University Press, 1931.

Hunt, Gaillard, ed. *The Writings of James Madison.* New York, G. P. Putnam's Sons, 1900-1910.

Jorgenson, Chester E., and Frank Luther Mott, eds. *Benjamin Franklin: Representative Selections.* New York, American Book Company, 1936.

Lee, Gordon C., ed. *Crusade Against Ignorance: Thomas Jefferson on Education,* Classics in Education, No. 6. New York, Bureau of Publications, Teachers College, Columbia University, 1961.

Lipscomb, Andrew A., ed. *The Writings of Thomas Jefferson.* Washington, D.C., The Jefferson Memorial Association of the United States, 1904.

Padover, Saul K., ed. *The Complete Jefferson.* New York, Duell, Sloan & Pearce, Inc., 1943.

Reisner, E. H. *Nationalism and Education Since 1789.* New York, The Macmillan Company, 1922.

Schneider, Herbert W. *A History of American Philosophy,* 2nd ed. New York, Columbia University Press, 1963.

Smyth, Albert H., ed. *The Writings of Benjamin Franklin.* London, The Macmillan Company, 1906.

Van Doren, Carl, ed. *Benjamin Franklin and Jonathan Edwards, Selections from Their Writings.* New York, Charles Scribner's Sons, 1920.

Washington, Henry A., ed. *The Writings of Thomas Jefferson.* New York, Ricker, Thorne Company, 1854.

Woody, Thomas, ed. *Educational Views of Benjamin Franklin.* New York, McGraw-Hill Book Company, 1931.

CHAPTER 3

The common school era

We can not have Puritan common schools—these are gone already—we can not have Protestant common schools, or those which are distinctly so; but we can have common schools, and these we must agree to have and maintain, till the last or latest day of our liberties.[1] HORACE BUSHNELL (1853)

The nineteenth century was a century of transformation of American educational thought and practice. During this period the structural characteristics of American education took concrete form. At the beginning of the century, no state could boast of having a state-wide free system of public elementary schools, just as no state could lay claim to a free public secondary school system or state university. The ladder system of education so typical of modern American education—beginning with a free public elementary school and ending with a free public graduate school—did not exist at the opening of the century. By the end of that century, however, most states had developed such a system.[2]

The status of public educational institutions at the dawn of the nineteenth century can best be characterized by geographic region. In the South, the English tradition of private education held sway. In most Southern states, the educational commitment took the form of private colleges, private academies, and private tutors, with the state responsible only for pauper schools. In general, emphasis on private responsibility

1. Quoted in Rush Welter, *Popular Education and Democratic Thought in America* (New York: Columbia University Press, 1962), p. 108.
2. While the educational ladder was completed by the end of the nineteenth century, it was not until the twentieth century that universal compulsory education became a reality. Mass education was a twentieth-century phenomenon.

remained a chief characteristic of Southern education until well after the Civil War.

In New England, with Massachusetts in the lead, public elementary schools existed in considerable number together with many private academies and colleges.[3] The New England tradition of public responsibility and control of education did not usually extend beyond the elementary school, though public funds were generally used to support certain Latin grammar schools, private academies, and colleges.

While the public school tradition was strongest in New England and the private school tradition strongest in the South, the Middle States, such as New York and Pennsylvania, represented a mixture of both traditions. This mixture was usually reflected in the form of public financial support of private schools.[4]

In the newer Western states, the direction education took was largely influenced by the Ordinance of 1785, which provided federal land grants for public schools, and by the regional origins of the first settlers. The areas settled by New Englanders exhibited strong sentiment for public elementary schools. By the Civil War, all of New England, the Middle States, and most of the newer Western states had moved to establish state systems of elementary schools which were publicly controlled and supported. Although the historic roots of both the public high school and the state university existed in the pre-Civil War era, the major development of both institutions occurred after the Civil War.[5] Just as these institutions were the product of a complex series of evolving forces in the last half of the nineteenth century, the common school,[6] the first major rung on the public educational ladder, was the product of complex economic, social, and intellectual forces of the first half of the century.

CULTURAL CONFLICT AND EDUCATIONAL REFORM

The new American nation was plagued from the very start by fundamental economic and social contrasts; and during its formative years from 1800 to 1850, these contrasts became sharper and deeper. During this period, the North witnessed a rapidly developing industrial economy, a sizable influx of immigrants to man the new industrial machinery, a swift development of labor unions and workingmen's parties, and considerable social unrest and conflict. During this same period, the South solidified an aristocratic social class system based on a slave economy which tended to be free of social unrest. In the North, the new

3. Although the Massachusetts School Laws of 1789 and 1800 did provide for legal public control and support of the elementary school, it was not until 1837 that a state school board was organized and state authority was effectively used in the creation of a state-wide, organized system of common schools.

4. For an analysis of these traditions at work in representative states, see Lawrence A. Cremin, *The American Common School* (New York: Bureau of Publications, Teachers College, Columbia University, 1951).

5. These developments will be considered in the following chapter.

6. The term *common school* does not mean a school for commoners but rather a school which represents all classes and embodies the common elements of American culture.

immigrant from Europe provided a welcome supply of cheap labor for the new industries, whereas in the South, the new immigrant from Africa provided a supply of cheap labor for a vastly expanded plantation system where cotton was king. The difference between these two kinds of manpower had profound effects on the future political, social, and educational history of the nation.

Social mobility and social stability

Although the European immigrant's economic position usually restricted him to the bottom rungs of the socio-economic ladder, the ladder could still be climbed in the North. With economic mobility came the struggle for social mobility, which, in turn, repeatedly shook the social class system of most Northern communities. With each wave of new immigrants came new threats to the established classes, new anxieties, new fears, and often new violence. The open society of the North was not without its problems of integrating new immigrants into the social system. Repeatedly, public education was viewed and used as a vehicle to solve these problems.[7]

In contrast, the slave labor of the South was not economically or socially mobile and thus was not a threat to the established classes. Under these circumstances, Southern society in the first half of the century remained internally secure, static, and aristocratic. It was, then, no historical accident that the South remained politically, socially, economically, and educationally a section apart. Although many reasons can be given for the failure of the South to move toward a common school system in the pre-Civil War era, one of the most important was the absence of the social conflict that engenders a need for such a system.

Where the common school flourished in the North, it did so because many diverse groups of people supported it for decidedly different reasons.[8] To the individual who feared the effect of universal suffrage on the politics of the new republic, the common school was a useful vehicle for educating the new masters. To the property owner, the school was a protective insurance policy against the threat of mob violence. To the entrepreneur, the school was a means of producing more effective workers as well as a greater number of consumers. To the laborer, the school was a device for social mobility; and to the equalitarian social reformer, the school was a means to equalize knowledge, which in turn would presumably have the effect of equalizing wealth and power. To the nativist, the school provided a way to Americanize the immigrant; and to the extreme anti-Catholic, the school was a vehicle to Protestantize the Catholic immigrant's children. To be sure, the common school

---

7. For the relationship between immigrant problems and the progressive education movement in the twentieth century, see Lawrence A. Cremin, *The Transformation of the School* (New York: Alfred A. Knopf, Inc., 1961).

8. This is still very much a common occurrence in American education. School administrators and boards often find themselves supported on a single issue by normally conflicting groups for markedly different reasons.

could not fulfill all these functions and be all things to all people; nevertheless, the motivations for support of the common school movement were many and varied.

These motivations arose out of the complex milieu of a fluid Northern society; most of the social forces which nourished such motivations were absent from Southern society. The Northern cultural milieu was distinguished not only by the immigrant's impact on the American social class system but also by the rise of industrial capitalism with its ensuing class consciousness and the development of extreme nationalism. These trends were further complicated by a virulent anti-Catholicism, a warring sectarianism, and a rapid extension of the suffrage, all of which tended to threaten the position of the established social order.

Jeffersonian-Jacksonian democracy

Jefferson's dream of the good society made up of sturdy, free landholders was, by the time of his death, becoming more and more a dream and less a reality. Missing the significance of industrialization and urbanization to the future of American society, Jefferson could only conclude, "The mobs of great cities add just so much to the support of pure government, as sores do to the strength of the human body."[9] In addition to missing the single most significant economic and social factor in the development of the North, Jefferson also failed to detect the direction Southern agrarianism was taking. With the militant political and economic regionalism of John C. Calhoun, the South became more and more a section apart. "The spirited equality of Jefferson's freehold farmer had changed into the caste-like, benevolent oligarchy of a plantation aristocracy."[10] John Randolph of Roanoke best expressed the temper of the new South when he cried, "I am an aristocrat, I love liberty, I hate equality." However, not all of Jefferson's dreams turned to ash. His statement in the Declaration of Independence that "all men are created equal" became the battle cry of the rising lower classes in their struggle for economic and social mobility. Many of Jefferson's political ideals, including universal suffrage and a faith in weak central government, were carried over and reached fulfillment in Jacksonian democracy.

It is estimated that at the time the Constitution was adopted in 1788, one out of every seven white male citizens could vote; by the time Jackson was elected president in 1828, four out of every seven white male citizens were eligible to vote. With the extension of the suffrage, Jefferson's argument that the survival of a democratic republic depended on an educated citizenry took on new meaning. Throughout the next three decades, this theme was echoed and re-echoed in political campaigns, party platforms, social reform conventions, newspaper editorials, periodicals, and lyceum speeches. There can be little doubt that the extension of the suffrage and "Jacksonian mob rule" spurred the more conservative classes to move rapidly toward the support of a public educational system. In a backhanded way, the "quiet revolution" of

---

9. "Notes on the State of Virginia," quoted in Cremin, *American Common School*, p. 8.
10. Cremin, *American Common School*, p. 27.

Jackson provided the Whig, Horace Mann, with one of his strongest arguments for the common school.

Nativism and anti-Catholicism

The new American nation, undergoing the trauma of a Jacksonian revolution, confident in its own future but at the same time threatened with inundation by foreign immigrants, rapidly developed a spirit of extreme nationalism. Within a matter of decades, all the necessary ritualistic symbols of a nationalistic spirit, from the flag to the Bunker Hill Monument, and from the caricature of Uncle Sam to the George Washington myth, became common lore. As is true of most nationalistic movements, the new American nationalism assumed that the American nation had a mission to perform as the last great hope of humanity.

Such "manifest destiny" found international expression in the Mexican War (1848) and internal expression in the organized efforts of nativist groups to keep America American. By the 1840's, with the large migration of Irish and German Catholics to American shores, anti-Catholic hatred combined with a chauvinistic spirit produced such organizations as "The Sons of the Sires," "The Supreme Order of the Star-Spangled Banner," and "The Order of United Americans." This movement culminated in the organization of the Native American Party of 1850, which limited its membership to Americans who had descended from at least two generations of white Protestant American ancestry.[11] Protestant America, already divided and weakened by a warring sectarianism of its own, was acutely threatened by the presence of growing numbers of Roman Catholics, who aspired to move up the economic ladder and assert social and political power. Nativism, combined with anti-Catholic hatreds, at times burst forth in rioting and the burning of Catholic Church property.[12] With such conflict an immediate social reality, Horace Mann argued that public common schools had to be improved where they existed and established where they did not exist, so that the next generation would learn to preserve and protect our republican institutions. His argument carried significant meaning for the people of Massachusetts and the nation.

SOCIAL RECONSTRUCTION

One of the great beliefs Enlightenment leaders carried into the nineteenth century was that society as a whole could be reconstructed and that education might be so directed as to lead the way. Again and again we shall call attention to educational leaders who reflected this theme. The school as an instrument of social reform captured the vision and channeled the efforts of many men. Robert Owen and William Maclure

---

11. For an analysis of these groups and their relationship to the common school movement, see Cremin, *American Common School.*

12. Horace Mann himself headed a committee to investigate the burning of a Catholic convent by mob violence in Charleston, Massachusetts, on the night of August 11, 1834.

in the first half of the nineteenth century and John Dewey and George S. Counts in the first half of the twentieth century each in his own way reflected this theme. Perhaps the best example of an attempt to use the schools as a major vehicle to reconstruct society in the early nineteenth century is found in the work of William Maclure and Robert Owen at New Harmony, Indiana.

New Harmony: A Utopian experiment

To the wealthy businessmen and philanthropists William Maclure and Robert Owen, both sons of the Scottish Enlightenment and both sensitive to the social problems resulting from industrialization, the new American nation appeared a fertile testing ground for their radical social and educational ideas. It was William Maclure who brought Joseph Neef, the first Pestalozzian teacher, to America in 1806, and it was his patronage that helped Neef set up his school near Philadelphia, thus establishing Pestalozzian education in the United States.[13] In 1825, fresh from a recent attempt at social regeneration in Spain using Pestalozzian methods, William Maclure joined Robert Owen, of New Lanark fame, to form the New Harmony Experimental Communitarian Society in Indiana.[14]

While both men believed in social reconstruction and in the power of education to equalize knowledge, which, in turn, would equalize power and wealth, and both viewed evil as a consequence of ignorance, differences between them as to the function of the individual in the good society proved irreconcilable. When the abstract differences of Maclure and Owen were put to the practical educational test, *one* of the major sources of contention which led, within a matter of a few years, to the breakup of the New Harmony partnership was set in motion.

Maclure, who had been instrumental in encouraging Pestalozzian teachers to join the New Harmony experiment, firmly believed in the efficacy of individual critical intelligence to break all the bonds of miracle, mystery, and authority. He was convinced that the primary function of education was to develop critical understanding and critical intelligence based on empirical facts, and that this could be accomplished only through a flexible curriculum and methodology in which each individual actively pursued his own interests. Robert Owen, on the other hand, was concerned with social cohesion, fulfilling the specifications of the social blueprint, and achieving commitments to the new social order —all of which were to be accomplished by a uniform curriculum using a learning process that was essentially receptive and passive.[15] It is interesting to note that the differences which split Owen and Maclure so

---

13. For an analysis of Pestalozzi's educational ideas, see Chapter Nine; see also the unpublished dissertation (University of Wisconsin, 1962) by Charles Burgess, "The Educational State in America—Selected Views on Learning as the Key to Utopia, 1800-1924."

14. For the history of this community, see Arthur E. Bestor, *Backwoods Utopias: The Sectarian and Owenite Phases of Communitarian Socialism in America, 1663-1829* (Philadelphia: University of Pennsylvania Press, 1950).

15. For an excellent analysis of this issue, see Burgess' dissertation.

early in the nineteenth century also seemed to divide those in the twentieth century who wished to use the schools to reconstruct society.[16] While Maclure and Owen failed to reconcile their differences and implement their ideas completely—by 1828 both patrons had left the experiment—they did significantly influence education. New Harmony had developed a kindergarten, a public library, and a public system of education which did not discriminate against sect or sex. This experimental community also served as a mecca for those interested in Pestalozzian methods and practices.[17]

Robert Dale Owen and equal educational opportunity

By the time Robert Owen left America in 1829, his son, Robert Dale Owen, was already actively involved in the labor movement in New York and Pennsylvania. Labor class consciousness had gradually evolved and was beginning to find organizational expression in the union movement and the development of workingmen's parties.[18] Labor literature represented a social protest against the growing strength of the rich factory owners as opposed to the weakening position of the unorganized independent artisan. One major concern reflected in this literature was the lack of public education. In Philadelphia in 1829, a workingmen's committee investigating the conditions of education in Pennsylvania found that the means of education were not generally available to the laboring class and that where public schools were operating, they were essentially pauper schools. The committee then put forth a series of proposals which, as Cremin has summarized them:

. . . involved *first,* the extension of public education to all districts of the state; *second,* the placing of the management of such public facilities "under the control and suffrage of the people"; *third,* the extension of educational privileges not as an act of charity to the poor but as the equal right of all classes supported, therefore, at the expense of all; and *fourth,* the establishment of infant schools for younger children.[19]

Reacting to these proposals and the general interest in education in New York City, Robert Dale Owen published his six now-famous essays

---

16. The impasse which Maclure and Owen reached was remarkably similar in many ways to the twentieth-century social reconstructionist's dilemma. For example, John Dewey's central educational concern was with developing understanding and individual growth, while G. S. Counts and Theodore Brameld took as their central concern the blueprinting of the new social order and the educating of the young to be committed to that order. Charged disagreement within the social reconstructionist tradition has continued around the subtle but significant differences between these two positions—education for individual understanding and education for social commitment. See Chapter Nine.

17. For the educational influence of New Harmony, see Emma Farrell, "The New Harmony Experiment: An Origin of Progressive Education," *The Peabody Journal of Education,* XV (May 1938), 357-361.

18. By 1836, there were fifty-three unions in Philadelphia, fifty-two in New York, twenty-three in Baltimore, and sixteen in Boston. Workingmen's parties were developed in Philadelphia in 1828, in New York in 1829, and throughout New England during the decade of the thirties. See Cremin, *American Common School,* p. 9.

19. Cremin, *American Common School,* p. 36.

on public education. The thought of Condorcet and William Maclure rings throughout these essays. Reminiscent of Maclure's acute awareness of class conflict,[20] Owen argued:

We have yet to learn, that the world can go on without two classes, one to ride and the other to be ridden; one to roll in the luxuries of life, and the other to struggle with its hardships. We have yet to learn how to amalgamate these classes; to make of men, not fractions of human beings, sometimes mere producing machines, sometimes mere consuming drones, but integral republicans, at once the creators and the employers of riches, at once masters and servants, governors and governed.[21]

Such an amalgamation of classes could not occur where educational opportunity remained unequal. Arguing against public common day schools and for public boarding schools, Owen said:

If state schools are to be, as now in New England, common day schools only, we do not perceive how either of these requisitions are to be fulfilled. In republican schools, there must be no temptation to the growth of aristocratical prejudices. The pupils must learn to consider themselves as fellow citizens, as equals. Respect ought to be paid, and will always be paid, to virtue and to talent; but it ought not to be paid to riches, or withheld from poverty. Yet, if the children from these state schools are to go every evening, the one to his wealthy parent's soft carpeted drawing room, and the other to its poor father's or widowed mother's comfortless cabin, will they return the next day as friends and equals? He knows little of human nature who thinks they will.[22]

To the present-day teachers, school administrators, and social workers who labor so strenuously for some semblance of equality of educational opportunity in modern American urban ghettos, the truth implicit in Owen's latter statement is self-evident. Owen had directed attention to the problem of equalizing educational opportunity for children living in a society of unequal economic and social privilege. In a way, Owen was prophetic, for the problem he clearly foresaw in 1830 became by mid-twentieth century, once reinforced by race prejudice, a cancerous sore on the American body politic. What, then, was Owen's solution to the problem of social inequities which create educational inequities?

The system of Public Education, then, which we consider capable, and only capable, of regenerating this nation, and of establishing practical virtue and republican equality among us, is one which provides for all children at all times; receiving them at the earliest age their parents chose to entrust them to the

---

20. For an examination of Maclure's ideas, see William Maclure, *Opinions on Various Subjects, Dedicated to the Industrious Producers*, 2 vols. (New-Harmony, Indiana: The School Press, 1831).
21. *The Working Man's Advocate*, I (New York, April 24, 1830), 4. Quoted by Cremin, *American Common School*, p. 40.
22. *Working Man's Advocate* (April 24, 1830), 4. Quoted in Cremin, *American Common School*, p. 39.

national care, feeding, clothing, and educating them, until the age of majority. We propose that all the children so adopted should receive the same food; should be dressed in the same simple clothing; should experience the same kind treatment; should be taught (until their professional education commences) the same branches; in a word, that nothing savoring of inequality, nothing reminding them of the pride of riches or the contempt of poverty, should be suffered to enter these republican safeguards of a young nation of equals. We propose that the destitute widow's child or the orphan boy should share the public care equally with the heir to a princely estate; so that all may become, not in word but in deed and in feeling, free and equal.[23]

While radical in orientation, Owen's proposals did not fall on deaf ears. Republished in some sixteen newspapers, these proposals received such support in the ensuing debates that the New York City Workingmen's Party was split and literally wrecked. The opposition effectively pointed to the fact that such a system would break up the family institution by relieving parents of the responsibility of caring for their children. Furthermore, laborers more often did not want the same education for all, as Owen had proposed, but merely educational and social mobility for their own children. In general, labor did not accept Owen's radical proposals but were more inclined to accept the more conservative Philadelphia committee's call for free, public common day schools. However, by staking out the radical position and creating the controversy which followed, Owen clearly stirred organized labor to identify its interest with a public educational system.

In spite of the fact that by 1850 Orestes A. Brownson and others found Owenism lurking in every nook and cranny of the American social scene, radical Enlightenment social reconstructionism had failed, whether it was the communitarianism of Robert Owen and William Maclure or the labor leadership of Robert Dale Owen. Inadvertently, however, Owenism helped make the more conservative middle and upper classes aware that if a free public common school could be used to reconstruct the social order, that same system could also be used to preserve the social order. Daniel Webster reflected this awareness when he defined public education as a "wise and liberal system of police, by which property, and life, and the peace of society are secured."[24] The later Whigs had learned a good deal about supporting public education from the radical educational reformers, just as in politics they had discovered from the Jacksonians "that business has little to fear from a skillfully guided electorate; that quite the safest way, indeed, to reach into the public purse is to do it in the sacred name of the majority will."[25] Pre-eminent among these educational and political Whigs was Horace Mann, one of the founders of the common school.

---

23. *Working Man's Advocate* (April 24, 1830), 4. Quoted in Cremin, *American Common School,* p. 41.

24. Quoted in Burgess, "The Educational State in America," p. 146.

25. Vernon Louis Parrington, *Main Currents in American Thought* (New York: Harcourt, Brace and Company, 1930), p. 152.

EMERSONIAN TRANSCENDENTALISM
AND THE COMMON SCHOOL

Although the social, economic, and political conditions were conducive to the development of the common school, it remained for the
New England Renaissance to set the intellectual climate in which the
common school movement might flourish. Although Emerson's transcendentalism as part of this New England Renaissance had a limited direct
effect on the establishment of common schools per se, the movement
does reflect part of the intellectual ferment of the period which influenced educational theorists well into the twentieth century.

Religion and humanitarianism

If the radical Enlightenment social ideas of Maclure and Owen found
rather barren soil in which to grow in the new American nation, the
radical religion of Deism found no more favorable conditions. Instead
of the deists, it was the representatives of the new emerging religion of
Unitarianism that preached the gospel of humanitarian reform in the
first half of the nineteenth century. Unitarians stayed within the Christian
fold by accepting some revelations and miracles. At the same time they
rejected the Puritan doctrine of depravity and election, espousing in
its stead liberal Enlightenment thought with respect to human nature.
When one moved from the God of Jonathan Edwards to the God of
William Ellery Channing, one moved from an angry, just God to a loving,
redeeming God, and from a view of man as essentially depraved to a
view of man as essentially good. In addition, the Unitarian embraced
the doctrine of progress and its corollary, freedom of inquiry. Eager to
implement their ideas, Unitarians in general were actively involved in
most social reform movements. Careful examination of the leadership
of many of the social reform movements of the period[26] usually reveals
that a Unitarian or a group of Unitarians was in the fore. In this sense,
it was a liberalized Christianity that fired the engines of humanitarian
progress in the first half of the century.

By 1822, in a letter to Benjamin Waterhouse, Jefferson rejoiced in
the growth of Unitarianism but cautioned against "fabricating formulas
of creed and confessions of faith" as well as substituting "Plato for
Jesus."[27] Only two decades later, however, Unitarianism took on the
color of a fixed creed, and Plato was embraced by many in the form of
transcendentalism.

Transcendentalism and a spiritual unity

As the unified Puritan edifice broke into diverse creeds and sects
as a result of the religious individualism of the Great Awakening as

---

26. Such as universal peace, prison reform, temperance, antislavery, anti-imprisonment
for debt, anti-capital punishment, better care for the insane, better working conditions,
women's rights, and educational reform.

27. Andrew A. Lipscomb, ed., *The Writings of Thomas Jefferson* (Washington, D.C.: The
Thomas Jefferson Memorial Association of the United States, 1904), XV, 385.

well as the pressure of Enlightenment thought, the contradiction between the splintering of American culture along sectarian lines and the apparent need for some sense of ideological unity within the new nation became explicit. The American house of intellect was rapidly becoming a house divided along sectarian lines. Transcendentalism tended, superficially at least, to unify American culture just at that point where sectarian religion in a pluralistic society failed. The philosophy of Platonic idealism, if romanticized and tempered to American needs, could be used to save the spiritual essence of man from the fires of materialism, to promote national and spiritual unity in a discordant society, to reinforce Enlightenment faith in the dignity of man, and at the same time to reject the Enlightenment faith in reason, empirical science, and the Newtonian concept of a mechanistic universe. This, indeed, was a large order, but not impossible for the transcendentalist poet-philosopher, Ralph Waldo Emerson.

When Emerson addressed the Harvard Divinity School in 1838, he had already broken with his Unitarian past, which placed so much faith in reason, and had embraced intuition as the chief way of arriving at truth. With this basic shift in thought, Emerson and others were instrumental in ushering in the major American romantic movement of the nineteenth century.

Americanization of Plato

Although Emerson had doubts at times, his faith in the divine spirit of nature prevented any need for drinking from the cup of despair, just as his faith in intuition led him to reject Kantian and Hegelian metaphysics. Emerson romanticized and Americanized Plato at the same time. By freely wandering through the world of Platonic ideas with intuition as his guide, Emerson transformed the neo-Platonic celestial hierarchy of the absolute one, divine reason or *Nous*, and world soul into a single, romanticized Oversoul. It was, then, not necessary to concern oneself with the abstract metaphysical problems implicit in a great chain of being, and thus Platonic thought was adapted to fit the practical temperament of an American nation.[28] To Emerson, the idea of an oversoul served as a source of meaning, unity, and optimism. The divine purpose of the oversoul sketching its meaning through the divine spark in all men gave Emerson's thought a romanticized unity as well as an optimistic fatalism. In spite of Emerson's reflection that "Goethe was the cow from whom their [the transcendentalists] milk was drawn,"[29] considerable intellectual sustenance was also drawn from such English romantics as Coleridge and Wordsworth. These romantics reconfirmed Emerson's faith in the divine in nature as well as in human nature.

---

28. It should be noted that German idealism in America, in its metaphysical form, did not develop until later in the century. It was William T. Harris and Henry Brokmeyer of the St. Louis Hegelian Movement who led the nation in this development. For a comparison of the two movements, see Henry A. Pochmann, *New England Transcendentalism and St. Louis Hegelianism* (Philadelphia: Carl Schurz Memorial Foundation, 1948).

29. As quoted by Parrington, *Main Currents in American Thought*, p. 389.

Transcendental rejection of Enlightenment values

The conflict between the Enlightenment thought of Jefferson and the transcendental thought of Emerson is best symbolized by each man's attitude toward Plato. To Jefferson, Plato was a sophist guilty of foggy mysticism, whose ideas were sheer "nonsense," indeed, a "dunghill of metaphysics"; but to Emerson, Plato was "an American genius."[30] Jefferson's faith in empirical science and social meliorism and Emerson's faith in a romanticized intuition and a Platonic oversoul reflect a basic conflict between the Enlightenment and transcendental movements. To be sure, both men were optimists and both found dignity in human nature, but they did so for decidedly different reasons.

The curse of science was its sole dependence upon intellect. "Pure intellect," remarked Emerson, paying his respects to the eighteenth century Enlightenment, "is the pure devil when you have got off all the masks of Mephistopheles." Reason, he observed, when men depend solely upon it, leads only to science. Feeling, to him, was as important as intellectual analyses in the apprehensions of nature, and, significant though science is, nature can teach man more than Newton's materialism.[31]

The search for oneness—the individual or the state

Platonic idealism, whether it took the form and distinctive direction of Hegelian rationalism or of Emersonian romanticism, is, in essence, a search for oneness, that ultimate unifying purpose which presumably exists behind the facade of a materialistic, changing universe. Crucial, here, is how this purpose manifests itself. To Hegel, this purpose manifested itself not in the individual but in a "folk spirit" involving a single, unified German culture. The individual was thus lost in the concept of the "folk spirit." For generations of Germans this concept was translated into the idea of a "national State." This abstraction, then, was invested with more reality, more purpose, and more meaning than any individual or group of individuals.[32]

In contrast, American transcendentalism found this unifying purpose in the self of the individual. The American scholar, Emerson argued, must learn "that in going down into the secrets of his mind he has descended into the secrets of all minds."[33] Here he would find the arcana of the universe. The most important knowledge was that of self and "beings." The study of nature outside of man was worthwhile because

---

30. Compare Jefferson's letter to John Adams, Lipscomb, *Writings of Thomas Jefferson,* XIV, 148, with Emerson's essay "Plato, or the Philosopher."

31. Ralph Henry Gabriel, *The Course of American Democratic Thought,* 2nd ed. (New York: The Ronald Press Company, 1956), p. 44.

32. This concept had obvious ramifications for the future political and social history of the German nation. In the field of psychology it was no accident that Germany developed the *Gestalt* branch of psychology which assumed the "whole is greater than the sum of its parts."

33. Brooks Atkinson and Tremaine McDowell, eds., *The Complete Essays and Other Writings of Ralph Waldo Emerson* (New York: The Modern Library, 1940), p. 56.

it was a reflection of man's inner soul, and so Emerson could say, "'Know thyself,' and the modern precept, 'Study nature,' become at last one maxim."[34]

The direction that Platonic idealism took in America as opposed to Germany can be appreciated, of course, from the historic conditions of each nation. To a nation which had not yet achieved either unity or national independence, the Hegelian state had significance; but to a nation which had achieved independence and faced other kinds of problems, Emerson's individualism made more sense. One wonders just how many of the thousands and thousands of people who flocked to hear Emerson speak really understood his transcendental abstractions, but they must have felt a soothing balm in his reconciliation of opposites. The new nation was beset by sectional political strife, problems of integrating the immigrant, and warring religious sectarianism, and its faith in the individual was clearly threatened by industrial developments as well as by the stark necessity of frontier life for communal rather than individual action. Emerson's message—if only one is true to one's spiritual self, one will automatically be true to the good society—seemed to preserve individualism and unity at the same time.[35]

As long as Emerson's good society remained not in existing institutions nor even as an Owenlike blueprint toward which men could strive but rather as the inscrutable will of the divine oversoul working its will through individuals, the paradoxical problem of the one and the many, the individual and the society, could be held indefinitely in suspended animation. This could be done by periodically finding some semblance of worth in some social institutions and at the same time critically attacking society as a joint-stock company dedicated to the destruction of human liberty. Unable to stand the tension of such ambivalence, Emerson's friend and transcendentalist colleague, Henry Thoreau, withdrew from the brutish institutions of men to commune with true nature at Walden Pond. Thoreau carried into action Emerson's famous dictum, "Whoso would be a man, must be a nonconformist."

The rejected concept of progress and social meliorism

From his retreat, Thoreau warned the coming generations not only that they must fear the age of the organization man but that "Nothing is so much to be feared as fear."[36] Transcendental individualism culminated in Thoreau's escape to nature and his corollary doctrine of civil disobedience, which became a central doctrine for social revolutionaries in the twentieth century. In many ways, Thoreau's protests against what America was rapidly becoming were prophetic; nevertheless, his individualistic retreat to nature was more of an escape than a solution.

What, then, was the solution? Could men through conscious thought

---

34. Atkinson and McDowell, *Complete Essays,* p. 48.

35. With regard to spiritual unity, Emerson himself remarked that while people would not listen to him on Sundays, they would listen to him every other day of the week.

36. *The Journal of Henry D. Thoreau,* ed. Bradford Torrey and Francis H. Allen (Cambridge, Mass.: Riverside Press, 1949), II, 468.

and effort collectively control their economic and social institutions so as to meliorate social conditions and control the future progress of humanity? The answer was, of course, a resounding "no!" The individual can, at best, only resign himself to the fate that the oversoul has designed for him. The individual can choose between being true to this self or becoming an unauthentic, shallow resemblance of a man. Emerson and Thoreau found no solace in the Enlightenment concept of progress, which rested on social meliorism, nor could they look to institutional reform to usher in the golden age. As Emerson said:

Society never advances. It recedes as fast on one side as it gains on the other. It undergoes continual changes; it is barbarous, it is civilized, it is christianized, it is rich, it is scientific; but this change is not amelioration. For everything that is given something is taken.[37]

Although Emerson could not help taking sides on certain pressing issues of his day, such as antislavery in the 1850's, in general he stayed clear of active involvement in organized social reform movements and thus remained true to his assertion that "The relation of men of thought to society is always the same; they refuse that necessity of mediocre men, to take sides."[38] Emerson's optimism did not rest on the hope that men could resolve the paradox of freedom and conformity, or change human nature, or significantly control and direct human institutions, but rather on a faith in a divine force in nature which foreordained these conditions.[39] In Emerson's view, nature has foreordained a hierarchy of talent and virtue which cannot be changed.

The young adventurer finds that the relations of society, the position of classes, irk and sting him, and he lends himself to each malignant party that assails what is eminent. He will one day know that this is not removable, but a distinction in the nature of things; that neither the caucus, nor the newspaper, nor the congress, nor the mob, nor the guillotine, nor fire, nor all together: can avail to outlaw, cut out, burn or destroy the offense of superiority in persons.[40]

Early in life, Emerson had concluded that the world is made up of two kinds of people at birth, those of talent and those of none, and to these people education could not really make much difference.

Education makes useful men of the dull, and more useful men of the gifted; but it neither gives the first the keys and command of character and society nor

---

37. "Self-Reliance," available in Atkinson and McDowell, *Complete Essays and Writings of Emerson,* p. 166. One may detect here almost a Platonic cyclical approach to human history.

38. "Essay on Aristocracy," quoted in Perry Miller, *The American Transcendentalists: Their Prose and Poetry* (New York: Doubleday and Company, Inc., 1957), p. 287.

39. Here the difference between the nineteenth-century transcendentalist and the twentieth-century existentialist is most clear. To the transcendentalist, the human condition is paradoxical and tragic, but God still lives in nature, while the existentialist, who does not see the hand of God in nature, steps beyond tragedy and assesses the human condition as absurd.

40. Quoted in Miller, *American Transcendentalists,* p. 289.

does its absence take them from the second; Nature establishes her yoke over the kingdom of men in defiance of their petty opposition of books, laws, institutions.[41]

Child-centered educational ideas

While Emerson's views on the social function of education are far from radical, both Emerson's and Thoreau's ideas[42] on educational practice fall well within the radical child-centered wing of the progressive education tradition.[43] Emerson imbibed that intoxicating romantic nectar distilled and aged in the Platonic vessel so familiar to Jean-Jacques Rousseau. Emerson, Rousseau, and Plato advocated the play method in education, the disparagement of the printed page,[44] the need to imitate nature, and the use of sense experience to trigger the unfolding of the child's natural potential. Emerson and Rousseau, of course, did not accept the emphasis on system and dialectics implicit in Plato.

The similarity between Emerson's and Rousseau's thoughts on education is rooted in their romantic naturalism. Both men considered nature intrinsically good and worthy of imitation. Thus Emerson could say, "But this function of opening and feeding the human mind is not to be fulfilled by any mechanical or military method; is not to be trusted to any skill less large than Nature itself,"[45] and Rousseau could advise, "Fix your eyes on nature, follow the path traced by her."[46] The nature of the child would determine not only the learning experience but also the age at which a given experience should occur. The learning tasks proposed by the tutor had to be consistent with the natural development of the child, and so Emerson cautioned, "Leave this military hurry and adopt the pace of Nature. Her secret is patience. . . ."[47] And Rousseau insisted, "Do not save time, but lose it."[48] Emerson was well within that romantic wing of progressive education which emphasized the child-centered curriculum when he said, "Respect the child. Wait and see the new product of Nature. Nature loves analogies, but not repetitions. Respect the child. Be not too much his parent. Trespass not on his soli-

---

41. William H. Gilman, Alfred A. Ferguson, and Merrell R. Davis, eds., *The Journals and Miscellaneous Notebooks of Ralph Waldo Emerson* (Cambridge, Mass.: The Belknap Press, 1964), II, 68.

42. For Thoreau's views on education see Lawrence Willson, "Thoreau on Education," *History of Education Quarterly,* II, 1 (March 1962), 19-29.

43. This child-centered wing of the progressive educational tradition, which was embodied in the thought of Rousseau, Pestalozzi, Froebel, Emerson, Thoreau, and Francis W. Parker, tended also to dominate one whole side of the twentieth-century Progressive Education Association.

44. Within this tradition persists a theme which prefers direct sense-experience learning over vicarious learning through books. This theme, when exploited to its extreme by twentieth-century child-centered progressives, bore the fruit of an anti-intellectualism which John Dewey bitterly protested.

45. *The Complete Works of Ralph Waldo Emerson,* ed. Edward Waldo Emerson (Cambridge, Mass.: Riverside Press, 1904), Vol. X, *Lectures and Biographical Sketches,* p. 148.

46. Jean-Jacques Rousseau, *Émile,* trans. Barbara Foxley (London: J. M. Dent and Sons, Ltd., 1950), p. 14.

47. *Complete Works of Emerson,* X, 155.

48. Rousseau, *Émile,* p. 57.

tude."[49] Such sage advice was repeated over and over in progressive educational literature for the next century.

What, then, were the immediate effects of Emerson's transcendental thought on the development of the common school movement? As the high priest of the transcendental movement, Emerson remained true to himself and did not become actively involved in institutional reform.[50] Nevertheless, Emerson's transcendentalism indirectly helped pave the way for the common school movement. Transcendentalism, as part of the greater New England intellectual renaissance, no doubt spurred interest in and concern about education. More precisely, Emerson's humanitarian views about a natural education which advocated a more humane treatment of children strengthened the hand of most educational reformers of the period. In the same way, Emerson's emphasis on the common spiritual unity of all men in nature helped produce the favorable religious climate which allowed Horace Mann temporarily to solve the thorny problem of teaching religion in the public schools by advocating the teaching of the common elements of all religions. While Emerson influenced educational thought in general, his direct influence on school practice remains highly questionable. While he may have been a radical individualist, he was not a radical or even a conservative social meliorist. After hearing Horace Mann speak one evening, Emerson recorded in his journal that Mann was "full of the modern gloomy view of our democratical institutions, and hence the inference to the importance of schools."[51] Emerson's transcendental individualism had colored his perceptions of even the conservative social meliorists' position.

HORACE MANN AND THE COMMON SCHOOL

The ink was barely dry on Emerson's "Concord Hymn" when Horace Mann, railroad lawyer and eminently successful Whig politician, penned his letter of acceptance for the position of Secretary of the Massachusetts Board of Education. Mann's friends called him a fool for going into education and thereby giving up a promising political future. Mann, however, viewed himself as an apostle of humanity. "Faith is the only sustainer I have," he wrote, "faith in the improvability of the race."[52] Mann was a crusader who, with missionary zeal, championed such diverse causes as the development of public institutions for the care of the insane, temperance, religious liberty, antislavery, public support of railroad interests, and the common school movement.[53] Mann was the kind

---

49. *Complete Works of Emerson,* X, 143.

50. It should be noted, however, that not all transcendentalists took the path of individualism. Those who participated in the Brook Farm experiment moved decidedly toward collective action. Even Emerson and Thoreau participated in a detached manner as observers.

51. Quoted in Welter, *Popular Education and Democratic Thought in America,* pp. 97-98.

52. Quoted in Louise Hall Tharp, *Until Victory, Horace Mann and Mary Peabody* (Boston: Little, Brown and Company, 1953), p. 136.

53. For the definitive work on the early life of Horace Mann, see the unpublished dissertation (Harvard, 1963) by Jonathan C. Messerli, "Horace Mann: The Early Years, 1796-1837."

of person who could be happy only if he could dedicate his life to a cause. His zealous commitment to humanitarian crusading is best expressed in his advice to the graduating class at Antioch College in 1859, shortly before he died: "Be ashamed to die until you have won some victory for humanity." Mann went to his final resting place secure in the knowledge that he had won such a victory.

Of the many leaders who fought the battle for the common school, such as Henry Barnard in Connecticut, Calvin Stowe in Ohio, Caleb Mills in Indiana, John D. Pierce in Michigan, Horace Mann in Massachusetts, and many others, Mann was perhaps the leading spokesman. It was not leadership alone, however, that brought the common schools into existence but rather the combination of leadership and the right social, economic, and political conditions.[54]

Educational conditions

When Mann took office in 1837, Massachusetts had already developed the concept of the public school as publicly controlled and supported and supposedly free from sectarian religious indoctrination.[55] Lacking, however, was any state supervision, control, or influence over the system of decentralized schools. Glaring inequities appeared in the back country. In a socially and politically stable society, poor educational conditions might have been overlooked; such, however, was not the case in Massachusetts. The Jacksonian Democrats, already successful at the national level of government, were threatening to take over the Massachusetts Statehouse. The rapid growth of the Jacksonian party combined with the swift rise of workingmen's parties gave men of property serious cause for concern. As early as 1834, Horace Mann, in a letter to Mary Peabody in Cuba, reported on a new Trades Union party which seemed to have sprung into existence. After watching their procession one evening, he concluded:

The bond of association among these men is mutual support and defence against what they denominate aristocratic institutions and manners. This principle is rapidly extending itself in this country and if something be not done to check it, the advantages of possessing wealth will find what to me would be more than a counterpoise in the envy and dis-social feelings which it will occasion.[56]

Something *was* done to check it. Only three years later the Whig party came to the conclusion that a state board of education, with a prominent Whig politician such as Horace Mann at its head, might have a salutary effect on such dissocial feelings.

While the die-hard conservatives might now and then make a plea for private schools for the rich and state pauper schools for the poor,

---

54. It should be remembered that Jefferson's proposed system of common schools for Virginia fell on deaf ears when neither the social nor economic conditions supported such a development.

55. Important, here, is the Massachusetts School Law of 1827.

56. Quoted in Tharp, *Until Victory,* p. 117.

and the radical Owenites might enter a plea for state boarding schools, the middle position of public common day schools drew support both from the laboring groups, who saw in such schools the possibility of social mobility, and from the wealthier upper classes, who saw the possibility of tempering social radicalism. To ensure the latter possibility, however, the Whigs pushed for state influence in the development of common schools, whereas Jacksonian Democrats struggled to keep local control of the schools. This was essentially the issue at stake when Governor Marcus Morton, a Jacksonian, moved against Mann and the Massachusetts Board of Education in the early 1840's. The defeat of the Jacksonian alternative of local control attests not only the strength of the Whig party but also the political influence of Horace Mann.

The fear of social conflict

To Horace Mann, one of the major functions of the common school was to head off a social revolution before it could get started. When lecturing to a lyceum audience in Salem in 1837, he argued that the French Revolution would never have occurred if there had been free schools. Turning to his own society, he said:

The mobs, the riots, the burnings, the lynchings, perpetrated by the men of the present day, are perpetrated because of their vicious and defective education. We see and feel the ravages of their tiger passions now, when they are full grown; but it was years ago when they were whelped and suckled. And so too, if we are derelict in our duty in this matter, our children in their turn will suffer. If we permit the vulture's eggs to be hatched, it will then be too late to take care of the lambs.[57]

To Mann, class conflict was not inevitable, as Maclure had supposed and Karl Marx had theorized. In the same year that Marx and Engels published the *Communist Manifesto* (1848), Mann completed his twelfth and last *Annual Report* to the Massachusetts Board of Education, in which he argued that the European social and economic theory which assumed that "men are divided into classes,—some to toil and earn, others to seize and enjoy" ran contrary to the Massachusetts theory that "all are to have an equal chance for earning, and equal security in the enjoyment of what they earn."[58] The solution to the problem of extremes of wealth was not to steal from the rich to help the poor but to educate the poor so that they could become more productive and also own property. Social class conflict could thus be reduced. Along these lines of thought, Mann argued:

Property and labor, in different classes, are essentially antagonistic; but property and labor, in the same class, are essentially fraternal. . . . Education, then, be-

---

57. Quoted in Tharp, *Until Victory*, p. 143.
58. Lawrence A. Cremin, ed., *The Republic and the School: Horace Mann on the Education of Free Men,* Classics in Education, No. 1 (New York: Bureau of Publications, Teachers College, Columbia University, 1957), p. 84.

yond all other devices of human origin, is the great equalizer of the conditions of men—the balance-wheel of the social machinery. . . . It does better than to disarm the poor of their hostility towards the rich; it prevents being poor.[59]

Mann firmly believed that education could reconstruct the conflict-torn society of his day by educating the next generation, not toward an Owenite radicalism, but toward the harmony and conservative temper of the great middle class which, in the next century, did become the "balance wheel" of the American social class system. In many ways, Horace Mann was both the prophet and the spokesman of that class, and the common school was its creation.

The function of the common school

If the common school was to be truly common and usher in the harmonious society, all classes, creeds, and sects must be represented. The private school, while clearly a threat to Mann's ideal, was not to be outlawed, however. Mann surmised that through free competition the public school would so excel in quality of education that parents would prefer to send their youngsters to the public school. The common school could attract all the children of the community and then proceed to teach the common elements of American culture. These common elements were represented in the curriculum as reading, writing, spelling, arithmetic, English grammar, geography, and Bible reading, along with history, which was usually taught as part of reading. Mann also vigorously argued for specific instruction in the laws of health and vocal music.[60] Such attempts at broadening the curriculum, however, met with only a limited degree of success.

Methodology and teacher training

To Horace Mann, the common school "victory" depended not only on the broad range of its student body and the nature of its curriculum but also on the *quality* of instruction. The common schools would have to employ well-trained teachers who would use the best methods of instruction. Highly impressed with the effectiveness of the Prussian schools he visited in the spring of 1843, Mann expressed, in his seventh *Annual Report,* his enthusiasm for the Pestalozzian methods which were then being employed. "I heard no child ridiculed, sneered at, or scolded, for making a mistake. . . . No child was disconcerted, disabled, or bereft of his senses, through fear."[61] He could not resist comparing the Prussian schools with the Massachusetts schools, and in so doing he brought down the wrath of the Boston school masters. In the public controversy which followed, Mann took the position that the Pestalozzian methods

---

59. *Republic and the School,* p. 87.
60. The areas of health and vocal music were of particular concern to Mann, primarily because of his personal contact with the tragic loss of life from tuberculosis. Vocal music was considered a healthful way to exercise the lungs.
61. *Republic and the School,* p. 55.

of instruction were socially neutral; i.e., they could be used for a society governed by the people as well as for a society governed by a monarch. Impressed not only with the effectiveness of such methodology, Mann was equally awed by the ability of the German normal schools to train such expert teachers. This confirmed his own thinking that Massachusetts, with its three recently established state normal schools, was on the right educational track.[62]

What Mann missed, however, was the fact that the German normal school was purposely designed to produce teachers who were highly skilled in methodology but extremely weak in academic content beyond the actual level at which they were going to teach. Such teachers would be expert technicians in *how* to teach but could be easily controlled as to *what* to teach. Thus, the teacher in the *Volkschule* would be a "safe" teacher. Isolated from the intellectual ferment of the German university, the graduates of the normal schools would theoretically be immobilized as social revolutionaries or even social critics. That this was the clear intent of the power groups in Prussian society is confirmed by examination of the Prussian Ministry of Education reports through the first half of the nineteenth century.[63] While this may not have been Mann's intention, the effect was similar. The American normal schools did stress methodology over any advanced studies, and they did have the effect of producing a large cadre of teachers for the American common schools, reasonably trained in how to teach but highly dependent on social and political groups for the determination of what to teach.

The normal school mentality

In the long run, the effects of the normal school on American teacher education were many,[64] not the least of which was the development of the "normal school mentality" which persists in many teacher education institutions to the present day. Such a mentality is usually reflected in the demand for an inordinate amount of time to be spent on methodology and a lessening of the time spent on the more academic studies in the preparation program of the elementary school teacher. This point of view can be traced back to the thought of the founders of the early normal schools. Even though many colleges and academies in New England were preparing teachers for the common schools,[65] Mann rejected this more academic approach to teacher education and gave his support to the establishment of separate state normal schools which emphasized the technical aspects of teacher training.

62. Mann was instrumental in establishing these normal schools. The first state normal school to be established in the United States was at Lexington, Massachusetts, in 1839.

63. For an analysis of this subject, see E. H. Reisner, *Nationalism and Education Since 1789* (New York: The Macmillan Company, 1922).

64. For a historical perspective of teacher education in America, see Merle Borrowman, *The Liberal and Technical in Teacher Education* (New York: Bureau of Publications, Teachers College, Columbia University, 1956). Also see Merle Borrowman, ed., *Teacher Education in America*, Classics in Education, No. 24 (New York: Bureau of Publications, Teachers College, Columbia University, 1965).

65. For further development of these issues in teacher education see Borrowman, *Teacher Education in America*.

In a way, it is ironic that in Mann's haste to gain professional status for the common school teacher by establishing separate normal schools, he at the same time closed the door to one of the major avenues of gaining professional status, namely, developing teacher education as a responsibility of the colleges. The effect of Mann's position on teacher education was to hasten the development of the teacher's position in American life as a technician but not as a professional. The two problems encountered in the early normal school development—creating a profession and determining the proper relationship between the academic and technical studies—have continued to plague teacher education.[66]

The history of the normal school in American teacher education in the nineteenth and twentieth centuries is marked by a slow evolution toward college status. In some cases, this progress has been made in name only, whereas in other cases true college status has been achieved.[67] In spite of its deficiencies today, the normal school was the major teacher preparation institution for the nineteenth-century elementary school, and as such it filled a vital need. In a very real sense, this institution served as a major adjunct to the success of the common school movement.

Religion in the schools

Of all the issues that Mann faced in his twelve years as Secretary of the Massachusetts Board of Education, none proved more threatening and emotionally charged than the question of religion in the schools. How could the state provide a moral education in a religiously pluralistic society? Mann's solution again was the common-elements approach. The schools would teach the common elements of all religions and thus produce a moral basis upon which the home and church could build their sectarian creeds. What kind of moral syllabus, then, would embody all the common elements, and what kind of practice would prevent sectarian conflict in the classroom? The answer was that the Bible was to be read periodically without comment by either teacher or pupil.[68]

The facts that the King James version of the Bible might be objectionable to Roman Catholics, that Bible reading itself was particularly a Protestant practice, that the New Testament might offend some Jews, and that the practice of Bible reading was very much in line with his own Unitarian commitments did not seem to trouble him. Mann had on his side not only strong legal arguments[69] as well as the more liberal Protestant groups but also the long tradition of Protestantism which placed

---

66. For a study of the main trends in the American college at this time, see R. Freeman Butts, *The College Charts Its Course* (New York: McGraw-Hill Book Company, 1939).

67. While the upgrading of the normal schools has been the major trend in the twentieth century, extreme variations occur from state to state and even within states at the present time. See James B. Conant, *The Education of American Teachers* (New York: McGraw-Hill Book Company, 1963).

68. As early as 1820, New York State, in its southern district, had employed a common-elements catechism. This catechism, however, met with vigorous doctrinal and sectarian resistance and was eventually dropped from school practice.

69. Massachusetts had just effectively separated Church and State.

great faith in Bible reading. Since Catholics and Jews were in a weak minority, the only serious opposition could come from the orthodox Protestant faiths. These religions were so busy jealously guarding their own doctrinal differences that no realistic alternatives were forthcoming. In the face of bitter sectarian conflict on the one hand and Emerson's message that all men shared a common spark of the Divine on the other, Horace Mann's approach to the problem of religion in the schools found ready acceptance. Within a short time, most states adopted the practice of Bible reading without comment in their public schools.[70] The charge frequently made by Roman Catholics that the common schools were in spirit and practice Protestant schools, as well as the charge that Mann was, in fact, creating a new Protestant religion, usually seemed to fall on deaf ears in an America that was predominantly Protestant.[71]

Discussion of controversial issues

Mann's approach to the religious issue was the same approach he took on all controversial issues. Political, social, and economic issues were also to be ruled out of classroom practice. Only those values, creeds, and beliefs upon which the society had reached consensus should be taught:

> . . . those articles in the creed of republicanism, which are accepted by all, be-lieved in by all, and which form the common basis of our political faith, shall be taught to all. But when the teacher, in the course of his lessons or lectures on the fundamental law, arrives at a controverted text, he is either to read it without comment or remark; or, at most, he is only to say that the passage is the subject of disputation, and that the schoolroom is neither the tribunal to adjudicate, nor the forum to discuss it.[72]

Horace Mann's consistent stand against controversial issues in the class-room stems directly from his conviction that the function of the school is to build into the coming generation a common set of beliefs and atti-tudes. This function logically follows from his conception of the good society wherein all men adhere to the same basic moral, economic, political, and social values. Mann's good society, in this respect, was dis-tinctively a secularized Puritan society. To be sure, this was a society in which middle-class values had replaced religious values; nonetheless, this ideal society was still held together by a large set of common core values.[73]

---

70. It was not until 1963 that the U.S. Supreme Court ruled this practice an "establish-ment of religion" and thus a violation of the First Amendment to the U.S. Constitution.

71. Thus, there evolved within American Catholicism a strong movement to establish parochial schools. The history of this development was influenced by repeated legal and political attempts by various Catholic groups to change the Protestant orientation of the common schools.

72. *Republic and the School*, p. 97.

73. One can well question why the elementary school teacher should allow discussion of controversial issues in the classroom. Do such practices in the long run lessen social conflict or merely tend to increase social conflict, as Mann suspected? One might further

Mann and the public high school

To Horace Mann, the common school, if functioning properly, would be enough to weld the new nation together. Academies and colleges would then "stand ready to receive, at private cost, all whose path to any ultimate destination may lie through their halls."[74] Mann's position on private higher education may have been a result of his own private school experience or conditioned by the fact that private academies and colleges were already flourishing, or perhaps by the fact that some of his most powerful political supporters for the common school also had vested interests in higher education. Why Mann did not push as vigorously for free public high schools as he did for common schools remains an open question. Nevertheless, in spite of Mann's failure to espouse the cause for public high schools with equal vigor and to implement the Massachusetts Law of 1827 which required each town of over five hundred families to maintain a public high school, Massachusetts by 1860 had created some one hundred public high schools, many of which came into existence while Mann was in office.[75] In contrast, other leaders of the period, such as John D. Pierce in Michigan, advocated a complete public ladder system of public education.

Mann, however, was a man of one purpose, and that purpose was the common school. Through public meetings, teacher's institutes, annual reports to the Board of Education, and the *Common School Journal,* he carried on a political campaign for the improvement of public elementary education. Across the nation his name quickly became legend as his writings were used in state after state to persuade legislators to create state boards of education and to persuade these boards to press vigorously for free public common schools. When he died in 1859, the public common school was an accomplished fact for most of the country, except the South and the Far West.

COMMON SCHOOL BOOKS

The common school victory was a victory not for social radicalism but rather for the more conservative temper of a growing middle class.

---

wonder if it is wise to confuse children with the staggering problems of the adult world. Certainly the child cannot solve the problems. Or is the use of controversial issues in the classroom only a motivational device to overcome otherwise dull subject matter? Contrary to Horace Mann's position on controversial issues, John Dewey insisted that such issues had a legitimate place in the elementary classroom. However, Dewey's "good society" was not, like Mann's, a society of homogeneous values but a pluralistic society which encouraged and respected differences. The school would be the place where, through the analysis of controversial issues, children would learn to understand and respect differences in others. At the very heart of the question of teaching controversial issues in the classroom is the broader but more fundamental question of what is the good society toward which education must strive.

74. *Republic and the School,* p. 33.

75. Nelson M. Blake, *A History of American Life and Thought* (New York: McGraw-Hill Book Company, 1963), p. 231.

In practice, the common school was used to integrate the immigrant into American society, curb social radicalism, protect republican institutions, and teach those necessary social skills, attitudes, and values so necessary for a growing bourgeois culture. While the Jacksonians thundered about the rich being in control of the schools and the Owenites dreamed of equal educational opportunity, men of more conservative mind usually wrote the textbooks for the common schools of the nineteenth century. Typical of this trend was Noah Webster's *American Spelling Book,* in which he admonished children to "Envy not the rich, but be content with thy fortune,"[76] and William Holmes McGuffey's advice to children that the revolutionary principles embodied in the Declaration of Independence were really no more than rhetorical flourishes used "to strengthen our position abroad, to raise mere civil war to national war, and to encourage our forces in their endeavor."[77] Politically, socially, and economically conservative, the *McGuffey Readers* also embodied those secularized Puritan virtues of Franklin's *Almanac,* such as thrift, diligence, prudence, and work, so vital for an expanding capitalistic society.

Conservative in purpose as well as in textbooks and curriculum, the common school was conceived and implemented as an institution designed to reconstruct the society from a condition which appeared to many as one of dangerous social dissolution to one of social mobility and social harmony.[78] Such a program ultimately received the support of conservatives, liberals, and radicals for decidedly different reasons. By mid-nineteenth century, farmers, laborers, immigrants, merchants, industrialists, and virtually every political, economic, and social group could agree with the conservative Horace Bushnell that common schools "we must agree to have and maintain, till the last or latest day of our liberties."

SUGGESTED READINGS

Atkinson, Brooks, and Tremaine McDowell. *The Complete Essays and Other Writings of Ralph Waldo Emerson.* New York, The Modern Library, 1940.

Bestor, Arthur E. *Backwoods Utopias: The Sectarian and Owenite Phases of Communitarian Socialism in America, 1663-1829.* Philadelphia, University of Pennsylvania Press, 1950.

Blake, Nelson M. *A History of American Life and Thought.* New York, McGraw-Hill Book Company, 1963.

Borrowman, Merle. *The Liberal and Technical in Teacher Education.* New York, Bureau of Publications, Teachers College, Columbia University, 1956.

---

76. Quoted in Burgess, "The Educational State in America," p. 147.

77. Burgess, p. 146. See Richard D. Mosier, *Making the American Mind: Social and Moral Ideas in the McGuffey Readers* (New York: King's Crown Press, 1947), p. 13.

78. While this was clearly the intent of many who supported the common school, just how much social mobility and social harmony existed in the last half of the century is open to debate, and exactly how much the common school really contributed to what social mobility and social harmony did exist is again an unanswered question.

————, ed. *Teacher Education in America,* Classics in Education, No. 24. New York, Bureau of Publications, Teachers College, Columbia University, 1965.

Cremin, Lawrence A. *The American Common School.* New York, Bureau of Publications, Teachers College, Columbia University, 1951.

————, ed. *The Republic and the School: Horace Mann on the Education of Free Men,* Classics in Education, No. 1. New York, Bureau of Publications, Teachers College, Columbia University, 1957.

Curti, Merle. *The Social Ideas of American Educators,* rev. ed. Paterson, N.J., Littlefield, Adams and Company, 1960.

Emerson, Edward Waldo, ed. *The Complete Works of Ralph Waldo Emerson,* Vol. X. Cambridge, Mass., Riverside Press, 1904.

Farrell, Emma. "The New Harmony Experiment: An Origin of Progressive Education," *The Peabody Journal of Education,* XV, 6 (May 1938).

Gilman, William H., Alfred A. Ferguson, and Merrell R. Davis, eds. *The Journals and Miscellaneous Notebooks of Ralph Waldo Emerson,* Vol. II. Cambridge, Mass., The Belknap Press, 1964.

Grossman, Mordecai. *The Philosophy of Helvetius: With Special Emphasis on the Educational Implications of Sensationalism.* New York, Bureau of Publications, Teachers College, Columbia University, 1926.

Horowitz, Irving L. *Claude Helvetius: Philosopher of Democracy and Enlightenment.* New York, Paine-Whitman Publishers, 1954.

Maclure, William. *Opinions on Various Subjects, Dedicated to the Industrious Producers,* 2 vols. New-Harmony, Indiana, The School Press, 1831.

Miller, Perry. *The American Transcendentalists: Their Prose and Poetry.* New York, Doubleday and Company, Inc., 1957.

Mosier, Richard D. *Making the American Mind: Social and Moral Ideas in the McGuffey Readers.* New York, King's Crown Press, 1947.

Pochmann, Henry A. *New England Transcendentalism and St. Louis Hegelianism.* Philadelphia, Carl Schurz Memorial Foundation, 1948.

Reisner, E. H. *Nationalism and Education Since 1789.* New York, The Macmillan Company, 1922.

Rousseau, Jean-Jacques. *Émile,* trans. Barbara Foxley. London, J. M. Dent and Sons, Ltd., 1955.

Schlesinger, Arthur M., Jr. *The Age of Jackson.* Boston, Little, Brown and Company, 1945.

Tharp, Louise Hall. *Until Victory, Horace Mann and Mary Peabody.* Boston, Little, Brown and Company, 1953.

Thoreau, Henry D. *The Journal of Henry D. Thoreau,* ed. Bradford Torrey and Francis H. Allen. Cambridge, Mass., Riverside Press, 1949.

Tocqueville, Alexis de. *Democracy in America,* ed. Richard D. Heffner. New York, Mentor Books, 1946.

Welter, Rush. *Popular Education and Democratic Thought in America.* New York, Columbia University Press, 1962.

Wilson, Lawrence. "Thoreau on Education," *History of Education Quarterly,* II (1962).

Wish, Harvey. *Society and Thought in America,* Vol. I. New York, Longmans, Green & Company, 1952.

CHAPTER 4

Nineteenth-century transformation of secondary and higher education

There is already a path blazed thru the thicket and jungle of conservatism and tradition, and before the twentieth century dawns in its glory there will be a broad highway thru which a pupil may walk unfettered, amid attractive associations, from the kindergarten to a degree at the end of the postgraduate course of the university and still will the people of the future be able to say, 'There were giants in those days.'[1]

A. F. NIGHTINGALE

The new American nation which emerged in the first half of the nineteenth century was not only a great melting pot of diverse cultures but also a great boiling pot of economic, political, social, and religious conflict. Out of this conflict-laden social milieu evolved, on the one hand, a public common school movement, and on the other, a dramatic increase in the number of private denominational colleges and private academies. Literally hundreds of denominational colleges and thousands of academies were founded during this period.[2] The era of the common school was also the age of the academy and the denominational

---

1. Committee on College Entrance Requirements, 1897 Report, quoted in Edward A. Krug, *The Shaping of the American High School* (New York: Harper & Row, 1964), pp. 140-141.

2. For an analysis of the colleges founded during this period, see Donald Tewksbury, *The Founding of American Colleges and Universities Before the Civil War* (New York: Bureau of Publications, Teachers College, Columbia University, 1932). Also see Henry Barnard, *American Journal of Education*, I (1855).

college.[3] In a frontier society, the Enlightenment faith of Jefferson and Franklin in the idea of progress and the use of education to implement that progress found practical expression in the creation of educational institutions.

College-founding in the nineteenth century was undertaken in the same spirit as canal-building, cotton-ginning, farming and gold-mining. In none of these activities did completely rational procedures prevail. All were touched by the American faith in tomorrow, in the unquestionable capacity of Americans to achieve a better world. In the founding of colleges, reason could not combat the romantic belief in endless progress.[4]

Ironically, it was the competition between religious sects to found colleges that made possible the secular Enlightenment faith in tomorrow that was expressed in higher education. Presbyterians, Methodists, Baptists, Congregationalists, and Catholics did their best to outdo one another.[5] The primary aim of most of these college founders was to perpetuate their own sectarian religious values. However, as these institutions developed and, in many cases grudgingly, responded to the secular and utilitarian demands of American society, the original intent of the college founders was lost. The transformation of American institutions of higher education in the nineteenth century, from narrow, classical seminaries permeated with religious purposes to more secular universities including many colleges, professional and graduate schools, constituted a revolution. Feeding the fires of this revolution were the state universities attuned to the practical needs of society, the German universities pointing the way to the creation of new knowledge, and Harvard College leading the way toward a radical departure in the collegiate curriculum. Although rumblings of the impending revolution could be heard in the first half of the century, it was not until the second half that it materialized. Concurrent with this revolution, and vitally affected by it, was the development of the secondary schools. In general, it was the academy rather than the college that expressed the utilitarian needs of the American people in the ante-bellum period.

SECONDARY EDUCATION

The academy

Although Franklin's idea of a system of education embodying the "most useful and most ornamental" knowledge had met with determined

---

3. In part, at least, the private college growth was given impetus by the U.S. Supreme Court decision in the Dartmouth Case, 1819, which protected private school endowments from state confiscation. Public funds in many states were still being used for private academies and colleges.

4. Frederick Rudolph, *The American College and University* (New York: Alfred A. Knopf, Inc., 1962), pp. 48-49.

5. The sects mentioned here were those which proved most successful in establishing permanent colleges. See Tewksbury, *Founding of American Colleges and Universities*, p. 70.

resistance in the eighteenth century, this same idea came to fruition in the academy movement of the nineteenth century. The academy was a privately controlled, multipurpose educational institution supported in part by public funds. For half a century, the academy served Americans in a diversified and flexible manner. Although some academies confined their function to collegiate preparation in the vein of the Latin grammar schools, other academies such as West Point developed respectable courses at a collegiate level. Still other academies offered courses ranging from a full year of work to a six-week course in acoustics, optics, navigation, surveying, or bookkeeping, as well as moral and natural philosophy.[6]

Since the Latin grammar school graduate could go directly to any college, the academy cannot be considered a secondary school link between the Latin grammar school and the college. It is more accurate to consider the academy, at least until the mid-nineteenth century, as an alternative to, rather than a preparation for, college. Often referred to as people's colleges, the academies were more easily distinguished from colleges by the nature of the curriculum than by the age of the students. Since both the colleges and the academies accepted students at the age of fourteen or fifteen, they were parallel institutions, but they served decidedly different functions. As an example, the Yale faculty, in reviewing its curricula in 1828, assumed that the college would draw students from the same age group as the academies but offer a basically different kind of education. With this in mind, the members of the faculty concluded that modern foreign languages might have a place in the academies but not in the colleges, whose function they believed was to offer a classical course.[7]

The relative position of the academy and college, however, shifted radically between 1840 and 1870, when the colleges began to admit youths at age seventeen or eighteen and the academies held their entrance requirement to youths of fourteen or fifteen years of age. By the last three decades of the century, both the academy and the high school were truly secondary schools, serving as links between the elementary school and the college.

Private academies versus public high schools

A number of characteristics differentiated the high school from the academy. During the pre-Civil War period, the curriculum of the academy was broader. In general, the academy tended to be a privately controlled boarding school, the high school a publicly controlled day school. The academy was peculiarly suited to a rural society, the high school to an urban society. It is not surprising, then, that in the last half of the

---

6. See Elmer Brown, *The Making of Our Middle Schools,* 3rd. ed. (New York: Longmans, Green and Company, 1907). See also Theodore R. Sizer, ed., *The Age of the Academies,* Classics in Education, No. 22 (New York: Bureau of Publications, Teachers College, Columbia University, 1964).

7. See Benjamin Silliman, *The American Journal of Science and Arts* (New Haven: Hezekia Howe, 1829), p. 300.

nineteenth century, when America moved to the cities, the public high school replaced the academy as the leading secondary institution. The growth of the public high school was intimately tied to the growth of urban centers.[8] In those centers the public high school usually originated as an extension of the public elementary school.

> The high school is a city institution. It evolved most frequently as the outgrowth of a common school and was started in response to local pressure, so that students might stay on for higher studies. The addition of Latin to the curriculum usually marked the arrival of the "high-school" department. Most "high schools" in the nineteenth century remained in the same buildings as the elementary schools.[9]

In a few decades, the public high school clearly outdistanced the private academy as the chief secondary institution. By 1890, 61 per cent of all secondary schools were under public control, and by 1918, the figure had risen to 87 per cent.[10] At the dawn of the twentieth century, the major secondary educational institution was the public high school.

Legalizing public financial support of the high school

By 1850, American society had generally accepted the idea of public control and public financial support of the common school. This was not true, however, for the high school. Even though some state legislatures had passed laws permitting the use of public funds for public high schools, this practice was severely questioned.

Some argued that since the general public did not use the high school and only a small percentage of youths could ever be expected to attend such schools, the general public should not be required to carry the financial burden for the few. It was further argued that since the curriculum of the high school was largely classical, dealing with ornamental knowledge, and since such knowledge might be of benefit to the individual but not to society, the general public should not be expected to support this kind of education.

Such debate reached its crest by 1874, when the State Supreme Court of Michigan heard a case brought by active citizen groups in Kalamazoo questioning the legal authority of School District No. 1 to tax citizens for the support of public high schools. In this case, Judge Thomas M. Cooley, in giving the majority opinion, pointed out that it would be highly inconsistent for the state to establish public common schools and a public university and not at the same time furnish public education at the secondary level. The state, he asserted, has the legal right to establish a complete ladder system of public education. In the aftermath of the Kalamazoo decision, courts of other states followed with similar

---

8. Sizer, *Age of the Academies,* p. 41.
9. Sizer, *Age of the Academies,* p. 42.
10. R. Freeman Butts and Lawrence Cremin, *A History of Education in American Culture* (New York: Henry Holt and Company, 1953), p. 421.

decisions, and legislatures gave the public high school firm legal grounding (Wisconsin in 1875 and Minnesota in 1878).

Developing a uniform curriculum

During the closing decades of the nineteenth century, both private academies and public high schools evolved at a rapid pace, developing courses and programs based on a combination of traditional practices and current social needs. While classical studies tended to occupy the central core of the curriculum, modern foreign languages, science, history, English, and mathematics occupied an ever greater share of the student's time. Difficulties developed because of lack of uniformity in courses, programs, and standards. The problem was particularly acute for those few students who expected to go on to higher education and faced conflicting college entrance requirements. In many instances, colleges and universities ran their own preparatory schools in order to ensure a supply of qualified applicants, while in other cases, universities and colleges provided active leadership in developing regional accrediting associations designed to encourage the development of uniform curricula and standards.[11] In some cases, the state universities brought needed pressure to bear on public officials to establish more high schools in their states.

By July 1892, the youthful and vigorous National Education Association[12] undertook to consider the problem of uniform high school curriculum, and for this purpose established the Committee of Ten.[13] The committee was made up of five college presidents, one college professor, three secondary school principals, and the U.S. Commissioner of Education, William T. Harris. Charles W. Eliot, president of Harvard, was chairman. The committee set to work to establish programs of study for the secondary schools. Well into the twentieth century this committee symbolized for many educators the domination of the secondary school by the colleges and universities. From a contemporary standpoint, the programs this committee recommended—Classical, Latin-Scientific, Modern Languages, and English—certainly seem college preparatory; however, from the perspective of 1894, when the committee delivered its report, these programs were not usually so considered. The committee argued that "the secondary schools of the United States, taken as a whole, do not exist for the purpose of preparing boys and girls for colleges. Only an insignificant percentage of the graduates of these schools go to colleges or scientific schools."[14] This being the case, the committee

---

11. For example, the College Entrance Examination Board was the creation of the Middle States Regional Accrediting Association in 1899-1900.

12. This association, first organized as the National Teachers' Association in 1857 and later reorganized as the National Education Association in 1870, provided the platform upon which some of the most crucial and spirited debates about educational practice at the turn of the century took place. See *National Education Association Proceedings,* 1890-1910.

13. For a detailed analysis of the working operation of this committee, see Krug, *Shaping of the American High School,* p. 38.

14. Quoted in Krug, *Shaping of the American High School,* p. 64.

considered all their proposed programs as equally sound terminal education programs.

When finally issued, the committee's report touched off a storm of criticism resounding through most secondary educational gatherings well into the twentieth century. On the one side, Greek scholars echoed cries of "barbarians at the gates" because only two years of Greek were required in the classical program, while on the other side, manual training devotees found themselves outside the gates entirely. Other public secondary school men generally voiced protests of college domination. Although the committee's blueprint for secondary education was not generally accepted in practice, it did serve as a catalytic agent which set off intense, serious analysis of secondary educational programs by educators. It was out of the discussion of school men rather than the specific recommendations of the committee that a working uniformity in secondary school curriculum evolved.

A comprehensive high school

The Committee of Ten report also reflected the persistent tendency in American secondary education to incorporate within the same institution different programs of study rather than to build separate institutions for each new program, as so often occurred in nineteenth-century German, French, and English education. In part, at least, the comprehensive high school resulted from the fact that the high school grew out of the common school, serving the common interest of the community. While many have assumed that the comprehensive high school grew out of a conscious American commitment toward a democratic society, a stronger case can be made for other historical determinants. There can be little doubt that the competitive, multipurpose academy served as a model to influence the growth of the American comprehensive high school. In addition, the economic determinants should not be overlooked. Within a lifetime, secondary education took on a radically different social function, which was reflected in a massive expansion in enrollments and facilities. Most communities could ill afford to create separate secondary institutions for each new proposed program. The pressures of practical economics were a powerful factor in the development of the comprehensive high school. Even here, however, had the classicists held a stronger position in higher education at the turn of the nineteenth century (the period of rapid high school expansion), they might have forced a fractionalized development of the American secondary school, and America might have developed a college preparatory school along the more narrow classical lines of the German *Gymnasium*.

At a time when the high school was serving a very small percentage of American youth, the Committee of Ten asserted that no distinctions in course content or method should be made between those students bound for college and those bound for the world of work. As secondary education evolved in the twentieth century, the comprehensive high school curriculum developed a multitrack system making clear, if sometimes subtle, distinctions in content and method between programs designed for students bound for work and those headed for college. Sixty-five years after Eliot issued his report, another influential former president of Harvard, James B. Conant, issued his report on *The American High School Today,* which depicted the high school as far more track-oriented than had previously been the case.[15] In general, however, it was the comprehensive high school that became the backbone of American twentieth-century secondary education.

Decline of the classics in the secondary school

By 1900, the classicists in the colleges had received a deadly blow from which they never recovered. The man who delivered this blow and led higher education toward the dismantling of the classical curriculum was the same man who chaired the Committee of Ten, Charles W. Eliot, President of Harvard. The method used to break the classicist's control of the college curriculum was the elective system. The practice of permitting students to elect their own courses of study revolutionized the college curriculum. It is important to recognize, however, that Eliot did not push the complete elective system for the high schools but allowed election of programs, two of which—modern language and English—required neither Latin nor Greek; both were acceptable for college entrance. By 1900, classicists in secondary education no longer held the sole key to college entrance. They did, however, manage to hold their influential position in the secondary school curriculum longer than their fellow classicists in the American college.

Although the adoption of the elective system in many American colleges during the last half of the nineteenth century ensured the eventual decline of the classics in American public education, determined classicists fought a spirited but losing battle to hold their place in the secondary schools. As one eminent classicist after another took to the rostrum, organized classical associations, pamphleteered, and generally argued for the preservation of the classical languages, it became increasingly apparent that this defense of classicism was little more than a delaying action of a declining educational tradition. In a society that was massively moving toward the education of the common man, fewer and fewer men agreed with Greek scholar Paul Shorey when he said, "'There is one great society alone on earth, the noble living and the noble dead.' That society is and always will be an aristocracy."[16]

If the classical ideal of the good society seemed less than appropriate for twentieth-century America, the psychology of learning that was advocated by classicists seemed equally unfit. Hard-pressed by the psychological research of Edward L. Thorndike and others, classicists such as Paul Shorey and Andrew F. West increasingly defended the classical, disciplinarian, faculty psychology. In one of his more unguarded moments, West carried the disciplinarian argument to the point of saying, "When we have to learn a thing which does not seem

---

15. See Chapter Nine.
16. Clark S. Northup, ed., *Representative Phi Beta Kappa Orations* (Boston: Houghton Mifflin Company, 1915), p. 498.

worth a great deal practically, we learn at least the noble lesson of disinterestedness."[17] Paul Shorey carried the argument to an even greater extreme. In ridiculing the modern pseudo-scientific educationists' emphasis on "voluntary attention" and "sugar coating of knowledge," as well as their reluctance to "break the will of the child," Shorey clearly implied that knowledge, to be educational, must be not only difficult but distasteful.[18] Shorey's ideal school had drifted a great distance from Vittorino da Feltre's "Joyful House" at Mantua in the fifteenth-century humanistic Renaissance.

While the classicists' ideal social order and learning theories appeared out of step with the main currents of American society, their basic conception of human nature as dualistic was also seriously attacked by pragmatic naturalists,[19] just as their educational ideal of the "well-rounded gentleman" was rendered obsolete by the explosion in human knowledge. Matthew Arnold's fears of a frozen classicism, unable to adjust to the circumstances of a modern world and therefore doomed to inevitable decline, came to pass in American education.[20] At the turn of the century, 50.6 per cent of the total high school population (ninth to twelfth grade) were taking Latin; by 1922 it was 27.5 per cent, and by 1960 it was 7.6 per cent.[21] In 1917, when Andrew F. West called the Conference on Classical Studies in Liberal Education at Princeton, the decline in percentage of Latin enrollment had already begun. In many respects, the statements in support of the classics quoted at this conference, which were contributed by such influential people as Grover Cleveland, Oliver Wendell Holmes, Herbert Hoover, Henry Cabot Lodge, Alexander Meiklejohn, Theodore Roosevelt, William Howard Taft, and Woodrow Wilson, were a fitting tribute to the final passing of what was once a great educational tradition.[22]

Changing social and economic function

While one can discuss the end of the classical tradition's predominant place in American secondary education, one should not assume that Latin had all but disappeared from the American secondary school. As high school enrollments increased from a half million in 1900 to eight

---

17. Andrew F. West, "A Review of President Eliot's Report on Elective Studies," *The Independent* (May 6 and 13, 1886), p. 5.

18. See Paul Shorey, "Discipline in Modern Education," *The Bookman*, 23 (1906), 96; see also Paul Shorey, "Discipline vs. Dissipation in Secondary Education," *School Review*, 5 (1897), 217.

19. For the pragmatists' attack on dualism, see Chapter Six.

20. See essays by Matthew Arnold, "Culture and Anarchy" and "Democracy" in *The Portable Matthew Arnold*, ed. Lionel Trilling (New York: The Viking Press, 1949).

21. See J. Wesley Childers, *Foreign Language Teaching* (New York: The Center for Applied Research in Education, Inc., 1964), pp. 3-4. It is interesting to note that when the first great surge in secondary school enrollments occurred from 1890 to 1900, Latin percentage went from 34.7 per cent to 50.6 per cent. Many have accounted for this increase as a result of "Latin" being viewed by the general public as a social prestige symbol. Greek, never very popular in American education, had all but disappeared from the public high school in 1960; only 222 students were enrolled.

22. See West, *Value of the Classics*.

and a half million in 1960, the relative strength of Latin as a field of study rapidly declined, but the number of students taking Latin increased from 262,752 to 661,563.[23] However, by the early decades of the twentieth century, America was practically answering the Spencerian question, "What knowledge is of the most worth?" As the classics declined, the more practical useful sciences were selected as being of greater worth for a people living in the throes of a technological revolution.[24]

This phenomenon was related, of course, to the rapid change in the function of secondary education in the twentieth century. By midcentury, secondary education was the chief vehicle through which the young gained entrance to the world of work. In 1900, the private academies and the public high schools together enrolled only 10.2 per cent of the youth in the fourteen to seventeen age group, or about one out of ten.[25] Sixty years later, the percentage for the same age group in secondary schools was approximately 90 per cent.[26] As late as 1900, then, at least 90 per cent of American youth, fourteen to seventeen, found avenues other than secondary education to gain entrance into the world of work, economic independence, and some degree of social mobility; sixty years later the situation was reversed. Basic economic changes in American society had an immediate and profound impact on American secondary schools in the twentieth century. The effect of these changes could be seen in the rapid growth of manual training, vocational and technical high schools, and a vastly expanded curriculum for the comprehensive high schools.[27] Formal educational institutions adopted radically different curricula, and at the same time, the public image of youth in this age group changed appreciably.

Creation of an adolescent culture

Prior to 1850, it is difficult to find any evidence of an adolescent culture or a teen-age group clearly distinguishable from the adult population by modes of dress, behavior, attitudes, and values, such as had come to exist by 1950 in American society. Economic factors significantly shaped this cultural phenomenon. To be sure, earlier philosopher-psychologists thought and wrote seriously of an adolescent period of life as a distinctive period of natural growth, but American frontier society, short on labor, moved youth on to the labor market as rapidly as possible by minimizing distinctions between adolescents and adults. In contrast, modern American society keeps adolescents off the labor market by maximizing the differences between these age groups. The

23. See Childers, *Foreign Language Teaching,* p. 4.

24. See E. L. Youmans, *The Culture Demanded by Modern Life* (New York: Appleton and Company, 1867).

25. Krug, *Shaping of the American High School,* p. 173.

26. See U.S. Department of Health, Education, and Welfare, *Digest of Educational Statistics, 1963* (Office of Education, Division of Educational Statistics, 1963), p. 11.

27. For an interesting study of the American high school during this early formative period, see Krug, *Shaping of the American High School.* Also see Theodore R. Sizer, *Secondary Schools at the Turn of the Century* (New Haven: Yale University Press, 1964).

most important milestone in the life of the young is the age at which they can expect to achieve economic independence from the primary educational unit, the family. This age of economic independence and responsibility has been increasingly delayed, so that a large segment of American youth can no longer expect to achieve economic independence until their early twenties. Thus, although many complex psychological, sociological, and historical factors should be considered part of the evolution of the American adolescent,[28] the economic factor looms large as a propelling and compelling force.

In the main, psychologists and sociologists are themselves culture-bound. They produce descriptive studies of adolescent behavior which in itself is a response to a set of social conditions and forces.[29] When one adds to this the practice of using these studies to increase adolescent distinctiveness for the sake of commercial gain,[30] the idea of a distinctive adolescent culture becomes so thoroughly reinforced in the public mind as to appear more natural than artificial.

While many would dispute the exact causal factors which led to the development of a distinctive adolescent culture, few would disagree that such a culture did evolve sometime between 1850 and 1950. No doubt related to this evolution was the fact that this was also the period during which America passed from a rural-agrarian to an urban-industrial society, a period when child labor laws were enacted and compulsory education laws enforced, and a period when the Western frontier closed and the educational frontier opened.

The educational frontier

The definitive description of a major historical period is usually made after the era has passed. Such was the case when Frederick Jackson Turner stepped to the speaker's platform at the American Historical Association meeting in Chicago on July 12, 1893, to deliver his epoch-making paper, "The Significance of the Frontier in American History." Thus, just as the era closed, Turner propounded his thesis that the Western frontier had played a major role in shaping American democratic social institutions.

With this paper, Turner set off a debate among historical scholars that lasted for half a century. Such questions as whether Western state governments were really constitutionally different from Eastern state governments and whether there was, in fact, social mobility on the frontier were rigorously debated as carefully documented statements appeared to support each side of the issue. By mid-twentieth century, as the smoke of battle drifted away, it was clear that many aspects of

---

28. Such as the increase in human knowledge, the increase in life expectancy, changes in means of production and social services, youth's reactions and society's reactions to economic dependence, changes in child-rearing practices, changes in family living, etc.

29. A good example, here, is the sociological and psychological descriptive studies on which Robert J. Havighurst and others based their idea of "developmental tasks."

30. This, indeed, has become a multibillion-dollar business. For a good treatment of the problem, see Jules Henry, *Culture Against Man* (New York: Random House, Inc., 1963).

Turner's thesis had been adequately refuted.[31] However, what was not refuted was the fact that the idea of the Western frontier as the great promoter of social mobility had functioned as a purposeful myth in American history and that people took up stakes and moved westward, thus acting as if the myth were true.[32]

Similarly, the idea that education will make a significant difference in solving social issues, contribute to the development of a democratic society, provide an avenue of social mobility, and thus contribute to social progress is a functioning myth of twentieth-century American society.[33] In this respect, the idea that education can do all these things is believed by many people who willingly invest a large share of their wealth and energy in a mass system of education. The roots of this myth lie buried deep in the Enlightenment idea of progress. As a son of the Enlightenment, Turner in 1910 asserted that the pioneer ideas must be transformed to meet the demands of a new society. "The test tube and the microscope are needed rather than ax and rifle in this new ideal of conquest."[34] Sensitive to both past and present, Turner reflected an awareness of perhaps the single most significant educational transformation in American history.

Just as the controlling myth for the nineteenth century was the Western frontier, the controlling myth of the twentieth century is the educational frontier. In the seventy years between 1870 and 1940, the American population trebled while the American high school population increased ninety times, and the college and the university population increased thirty times.[35] As this educational frontier dawned, a young man would be best advised to go to college rather than to go West. Once fixed in the public mind as the chief arena in which opportunities are gained, education would inevitably become the battleground upon which the most significant social conflict would take place in the twentieth century.

In this context, the high school and college were given new functions and far greater social significance. No longer could the high school or the college be considered the private preserve of the genteel few, nor

---

31. By mid-twentieth century, most social historians lost interest in the frontier studies and increasingly directed their attention to the theme of "the cities in American history." The influence of the current social scene on historical scholarship is unmistakable.

32. Myth is being used here as a sociological term. A *myth* in this sense is defined as any idea or cluster of ideas which people believe in enough to use as a rationale for action. The critical question, then, is not whether the myth is true or false but whether or not it works in shaping human behavior. In this sense, the Western frontier idea might have been a false myth which functioned effectively in shaping the westward movement. Similarly, racism in Germany in the 1930's and in Mississippi in the 1960's was an effective functioning myth in both societies.

33. C. Wright Mills in *The Power Elite* (New York: Oxford University Press, 1956) argues that in spite of increasing opportunities for education of the masses of people, the rate of social mobility has declined in the twentieth century. More empirical sociological research is needed to prove whether these myths are true or false, and there still remains the difficult question as to whether the false myths can be made true.

34. Frederick Jackson Turner, *The Frontier in American History* (New York: Henry Holt and Company, 1950), p. 284.

35. Harvard Committee, *General Education in a Free Society* (Cambridge, Mass.: Harvard University Press, 1945), p. 7.

could the schools for long offer a limited curriculum consisting of knowledge more ornamental than useful. There brewed in the nation a revolution in higher education which sought to educate all the people to the best of their abilities, create new knowledge through research, and seriously adopt a role of service to almost all sectors of the public life. As a vital part of the educational frontier, American institutions of higher learning underwent more significant change in the period 1870 to 1940 than in the entire period from the founding of Harvard College to 1870.

HIGHER EDUCATION

Many of the major renovations in American higher education were the result of three factors: the decline of the classical curriculum in the college with the introduction of the elective system; the utilitarian temper of the American people expressed through the rise of the state universities; and the impact of the German university on American higher education. All of these major trends in higher education were also the common consequences of the rapid development of technology and a vast expansion in knowledge.

Decline of the classics in the liberal arts college

Despite the limited effect of the Enlightenment on the college curriculum during the first half of the nineteenth century, the central core of a college education remained the classical course.[36] Such a course blended easily with the religious spirit of the period, as testified by the large number of denominational colleges founded during this era. Classicism, in alliance with Christianity, meant more than just the teaching of Greek and Latin. With the classics went a well-defined system of values and concepts with reference to man, society, and learning.

The decline of the classical curriculum in American higher education resulted not only from the utilitarian demands of American culture, the proliferation of useful knowledge, and the changing aims of American educational institutions, but also from a fundamental change in the way many viewed the nature of man and the nature of the "good" society toward which education must strive. Just as the demands of a technological society had undercut the practical values of the classics, so, too, the impact of Darwin on American social, philosophic, and psychological thought undermined the theoretical value of the classics. As one humanist, Phillip S. Richards, put it: "It is the theory of evolution, and nothing else, which has turned the tide of opinion decisively in favour of Naturalism. . . . Unless this assertion [of the continuity of nature] can be discredited, the cause of Humanism is already lost."[37] Although

---

36. For the effect of the Enlightenment on the college curriculum, see R. Freeman Butts, *The College Charts Its Course* (New York: McGraw-Hill Book Company, 1939), Chapter 4. Also, see Richard Hofstadter and Wilson Smith, eds., *A Documentary History of American Higher Education* (Chicago: University of Chicago Press, 1961).
37. Quoted in Butts, *College Charts Its Course*, p. 271.

Richards may have overstated his case by asserting that it was evolutionary theory alone which turned the tide, evolutionary theory did play a significant role in supporting alternative formulations of the nature of man, the good society, and learning which seriously challenged the classical reason for being.[38]

Ancients versus moderns

By the third decade of the nineteenth century, the security of classicists in the college was threatened by those who persisted in proposing that the teaching of a modern foreign language be included as part of the college course. Reacting negatively to this proposal and other pressures for college reform, Yale College, under the leadership of Jeremiah Day, responded by issuing what has become the definitive statement in defense of the classical curriculum. To the Yale faculty of 1828, the aim of a college course was to "lay the foundation of a superior education" and this superior education was a mastery of "intellectual culture." The two great points to be gained in intellectual culture were "the discipline of the mind; expanding its powers, and storing it with knowledge."[39] Espousing a faculty psychology which could be supported on either an Aristotelian or a Lockean base, the report sketched the characteristics of a disciplined mind and the curriculum most suited for its development. The Renaissance concept of a well-rounded man was transposed in the American college to mean a well-disciplined mind. The curriculum necessary for developing that mind was, of course, Greek and Latin. Essentially, the arguments presented to establish the superiority of Greek and Latin in developing "intellectual culture" were:

1. Only the Greek and Latin languages are suitable for mental discipline.

2. Modern languages require mere memorization and are not essentially disciplinarian.

3. Only Greek and Latin facilitate the development of esthetic taste.

4. Greek and Latin are essential in understanding divine truths of revealed religion.

5. Classical languages are useful in understanding history and modern literature.

6. Greek and Latin familiarize a student with languages and culture essentially different from his own.

Thus the battle between the ancients and moderns was engaged with full force; in college after college, bitter personal conflicts raged.[40] The

---

38. The impact of Darwinian evolution on American social thought will be examined more extensively in the next chapter. While in this chapter we are discussing the more practical forces which vied against the tradition, it is important to remember that classicism came under simultaneous attacks from both the theoretical and the practical side.

39. Silliman, *American Journal of Science and Arts*, p. 300.

40. The scars of such bitter conflict lasted well into the twentieth century. Paul Elmer More reported that when Irving Babbitt, a staunch defender of classical humanism, was under severe attack at Harvard, the classics department ignored him because he was in the department of French literature. See Frederick Manchester and Odell Shepard, eds., *Irving Babbitt: Man and Teacher* (New York: G. P. Putnam's Sons, 1941), p. 330.

first major break in the supremacy of the classics came with the entrance of modern foreign languages into the college curriculum as legitimate studies.[41]

Yale had set the standard for the defense of the classical tradition. Over and over throughout the nineteenth century such leading college figures as Noah Porter, James McCosh, Andrew F. West, and Paul Shorey could be heard restating the Yale faculty arguments. The classical curriculum changed very little with the onrush of time; neither did the opinions of its defenders. Almost a century after the Yale Report of 1828, J. W. Scudder of the Albany Academy, Albany, New York, penned his "Latinist's Creed" which reflected the same arguments:

> I believe in Latin, because it develops the memory, the reason, the judgment, the imagination;
> I believe in Latin, because it develops observation, accuracy and concentration of mind and thusly lays the foundation for success in business or professional life;
> I believe in Latin, because, through translation, it trains one to express himself in English with clearness and force—an indispensable requisite for civic influence;
> I believe in Latin, because it familiarizes one with the history and the thought of the greatest nation of antiquity, the nation that furnished us with the basis of our own laws and government, language, and literature;
> I believe in Latin, because there is no other school study in which one can find so *strong a combination* as this of thorough mental discipline, acquaintance with the language and the civilization at the basis of our own, and the ability to express one's views convincingly.[42]

Early attempts at college reform

Classicists in control of the American college curriculum during the first half of the nineteenth century fought a bitter delaying action against college reforms. Such reformers as Francis Wayland at Brown and George Ticknor at Harvard usually met with determined resistance and only limited success. Students, unable to tolerate the limited, fixed, classical curriculum, created an extra curriculum around which more significant educative experience occurred. By mid-nineteenth century, literary societies, debating societies, and Greek fraternities occupied a considerable amount of the time, energy, and interests of the college youth.[43] Other youth, however, turned away from college entirely so that the American college, far from being a viable institution, was actually faced with a crisis in rapidly declining enrollments. President Wayland at Brown put it succinctly when he said:

---

41. Once the modern foreign languages gained intellectual respectability on college campuses, many modern foreign language professors turned the same arguments, once used against them, against the entrance of the newer subjects of study, such as sociology, anthropology, economics, and education.

42. J. W. Scudder, "Latinist's Creed" in *The Practical Value of Latin* (New York: The Classical Association of the Atlantic States, 1915), p. 40.

43. See Rudolph, *American College and University*.

... colleges are not filled because we do not furnish the education desired by the people. . . . Is it not time to inquire whether we can not furnish an article for which the demand will be, at least, somewhat more remunerative?[44]

Wayland proposed and instituted an elective system at Brown; by 1856, however, it was curtailed. The elective system had previously been proposed but never successfully implemented by Jefferson at the University of Virginia and by Ticknor at Harvard College. The repeated failures of college reformers to institute an elective system in the antebellum period is patent evidence of the strength of the classical fixed-course tradition. The strength of this tradition is further evidenced by the fact that when college faculties were forced to respond to public demands for more scientific study and were threatened by the establishment of such practically oriented technical institutes as Rensselaer Polytechnic Institute (1824), they established separate scientific schools on college campuses.[45] In this way, faculties could protect themselves, temporarily at least, from pressure to change their course offerings.

The elective system

The classicists' hold on the American college was finally broken in the post-Civil War period. This was accomplished mainly through the introduction of an elective system. Harvard College, the oldest and one of the most revered colleges, led the way. Just as it was Harvard at the beginning of the nineteenth century which directed the course of liberalizing Protestant theology,[46] so it was Harvard which initiated one of the most revolutionary curricular changes in nineteenth-century higher education. While neither the Board of Overseers nor the faculty of Harvard were in unanimous agreement about the wisdom of such a revolution, a young professor of mathematics and chemistry at the Massachusetts Institute of Technology called to the Presidency of Harvard in 1869 was convinced of it. With unrelenting vigor, Charles W. Eliot moved Harvard from a small provincial college to a nationally renowned university. In the forty years of his administration (1869-1909), Harvard College grew from a faculty of sixty to six hundred with an increase in endowment from two million to twenty million dollars. This phenomenal growth is attributable in some measure to Eliot's leadership as well as to the increasing wealth of the country at large. In part, at least, this rapid growth was also made possible by the introduction of the elective system which allowed the newer physical and social sciences to develop and flourish as a legitimate part of a college course. "All requirements for particular subjects were abolished for seniors in 1872, for juniors in 1879, and for sophomores in 1884; then requirements for freshmen were reduced in 1885, and only English and a modern language were required after 1894."[47]

---

44. Quoted in Butts, *College Charts Its Course*, pp. 146-147.
45. Examples are the Sheffield Scientific School at Yale, the Lawrence Scientific School at Harvard, and the Chandler School of Science at Dartmouth. See Butts, *College Charts Its Course*, p. 130.
46. By 1805, the Hollis Professorship of Divinity was in the control of the Unitarians.
47. Butts, *College Charts Its Course*, p. 176.

In a series of articles and speeches, Eliot defended the elective system on the grounds that if all disciplines were pursued equally well, they would be of equal value. It was evident, he asserted, that a student could not possibly pursue in depth all disciplines and would therefore have to select fields of inquiry based on his own interests. The mature American student, Eliot argued, was equipped to make intelligent choices among options planned by the faculty. The liberating experience which is the aim of a liberal education was not confined only to those students pursuing the eternal verities of the noble dead in a classical course but was equally valid for those students plumbing the depth of knowledge in other fields, such as the physical and social sciences. The disappearance of required courses, he believed, would not only unleash the creative spirit of professors and students but would allow a university to be true to its name by seriously pursuing the truth in all areas of inquiry.[48]

As the leading spokesman for the elective system, Eliot became one of the outstanding leaders of collegiate reform of the century. Daring to be different, Eliot brought down upon himself the wrath of classicists for the next half century. Since what Eliot did at Harvard had its inevitable effect on other colleges, these institutions attempted to use their influence to curb what they considered Eliot's excesses. "His job was in jeopardy in 1885-6; the overseers were seeking his removal; eight New England college presidents were all but down on their knees, imploring, begging the corporation not to allow Eliot to drop Greek as an entrance requirement."[49] Eliot not only won this battle but went on to win others as well. As an accomplished speaker and debater, Eliot was more than equal to his task, proving his skills again and again in NEA meetings and university gatherings. In February 1885, at the meeting of New York City's Nineteenth Century Club, President Eliot of Harvard met his equal in President James McCosh of Princeton. Point for point, McCosh opposed Eliot's liberalism with arguments drawn from Christianity, Scottish philosophy, faculty psychology, and mental discipline. The issues were sharply drawn and the focal points around which liberals and conservatives rallied were clearly established. Colleges lined up on one side or the other.

. . . Yale and Princeton may serve as the archetypes of the conservative position held by such colleges as Wesleyan, Williams, Hamilton, Colgate, Rochester, Rutgers, Syracuse, Amherst, Bowdoin and Dartmouth. . . . On the other hand, colleges that more quickly tried to adopt 'university' methods were represented by such institutions as Harvard, Cornell, Columbia, Michigan, Northwestern, and Stanford.[50]

The 1880's and 1890's were fraught with intense debate over the elective issue. When the twentieth century dawned, it was apparent that

---

48. For a thorough elaboration of Eliot's ideas, see Edward A. Krug, ed., *Charles W. Eliot and Popular Education,* Classics in Education, No. 8 (New York: Bureau of Publications, Teachers College, Columbia University, 1961).
49. Rudolph, *American College and University,* p. 295.
50. Butts, *College Charts Its Course,* p. 231.

Eliot had been successful in renovating American academia. Even Yale and Princeton had, by this time, instituted a half-prescribed and half-elective curriculum, while other institutions, such as Indiana, Wisconsin, and California, were using a major-minor system. When Eliot retired in 1909 and President A. Lawrence Lowell took charge, Harvard itself backed away from a complete elective system and went to a partially prescribed curriculum. The effect of all this controversy was the evolution of a viable college, offering many different courses and programs within a complex university setting. A college education was no longer synonymous with a classical curriculum. As the college became adapted to the needs of the American people, the classicists' hold on the college was effectively destroyed. Eliot had, indeed, earned the wrath of the classicists and the praise of the American people. He was, in fact, hated and honored by both. A modern Harvard historian, Samuel Eliot Morison, in sympathy with the older tradition, concluded that "Mr. Eliot, more than any other man, is responsible for the greatest educational crime of the century against American youth—depriving him of his classical heritage."[51]

Of course, it was not Eliot's personal ideas alone which led to the decline of classicism in higher education. The proliferation of new knowledge gave realistic substance to most of his proposals. As early as 1873, Charles Francis Adams had noted the increasing difficulty of maintaining the classical ideal of the well-rounded orator when he said, "But Cicero did not have to learn in his day a thousandth part of what must be known now to complete the substance of an accomplished speaker."[52] The classical ideal of well-roundedness, even as an ideal, became increasingly difficult to maintain. Once the elective system was introduced and the classical core broken, the American college was deluged with new courses and new programs. College catalogs grew from the size of a select restaurant menu to that of a burgeoning mail-order catalog. The problem of general education versus specialized education in the face of a truly massive explosion in knowledge became the central issue for education in the twentieth century.[53] In response to these complex problems, Robert M. Hutchins, in *Higher Learning in America* (1936), suggested a return to the orderly structure of the medieval university, while another Harvard president, James B. Conant, reacting to the same problem at the Harvard Tercentenary, suggested:

The older educational discipline, whether we like it or not, was disrupted before any of us were born. It was based on the study of the classics and mathematics; it provided a common background which steadied the thinking of all educated men. We can not bring back this system if we would, but we must find its modern equivalent.[54]

---

51. Samuel Eliot Morison, *Three Centuries of Harvard* (Cambridge, Mass.: Harvard University Press, 1936), pp. 389-390.

52. Charles Francis Adams, *An Address Delivered at Cambridge Before the Society of Phi Beta Kappa* (Boston: John Wilson Press, 1873), p. 23.

53. See Harvard Committee, *General Education in a Free Society.*

54. David T. W. McCord, *Notes on the Harvard Tercentenary* (Cambridge, Mass.: Harvard University Press, 1936), p. 213.

The struggle in twentieth-century higher education has been a search for its modern equivalent.[55]

The state university and the ideal of service

Although the elective system was helpful in breaking the classical fixed-course tradition, and thus broadening the curriculum toward a greater university ideal, it was the growth and development of the state universities which pushed this ideal further to meet the practical needs of a rapidly expanding technological society. Even though some twenty states had established state universities before the Civil War,[56] the most significant growth and development of these institutions occurred after the Civil War. Under the impetus of war, Congress passed the Morrill Act (1862), which granted land to the states for the establishment of state colleges instituting programs in military training, mechanics, and agriculture. Although in most states the sale of land was poorly administered,[57] the act itself did stimulate states to establish colleges directed toward practical service to the people.

The early history of many of these frontier land-grant colleges was one of bare existence, privation, and a very real struggle for survival. Nevertheless, by the time Charles W. Eliot retired from the presidency of America's oldest college in 1909, the newer land-grant universities, such as Cornell, Minnesota, Wisconsin, and Illinois, had achieved national eminence and distinction in their own right. Eminence was achieved not by mimicking the older privately endowed universities but rather by developing their own unique functions of service to the community. While virtually all American institutions of higher learning expressed as a secondary aim the concept of service to a larger community, few seriously entertained such a goal as a primary function. The state universities and the land-grant colleges, holding service as a primary goal, put theory into practice by establishing massive extension programs and creating technical and professional schools. As "community service centers," these institutions, almost at will, called into existence courses, programs, and schools in the fields of commerce, journalism, agriculture, electrical, mechanical, civil and aeronautical engineering, mining, forestry, and education, all in the interest of serving the needs and demands of an advancing technological society.

However, if these institutions were to be more than trade schools, they needed to develop in basic research as well as applied technology and to translate this into practice through an emphasis on teaching. All state university presidents and boards struggled with the problem of

---

55. It is interesting to note that Charles W. Eliot, a professor of science and president of Harvard, had such a profound effect on higher and secondary education (Committee of Ten) at the end of the nineteenth century, just as another professor of science and president of Harvard, James B. Conant, by mid-twentieth century was exerting a significant influence on American secondary and higher education. Harvard, through its presidents alone, has had a profound effect in shaping the course of American education.

56. See Tewksbury, *Founding of American Colleges and Universities,* p. 170.

57. See Allan Nevins, *The State Universities and Democracy* (Urbana: University of Illinois Press, 1962), pp. 27-37.

maintaining some sense of balance between research, teaching, and service. The ideal of service to the people which came to permeate the state university placed the student of animal husbandry in the same classroom with the student of Hegelian philosophy, thereby producing the effect Edward D. Eddy suggested: "to make the liberal arts generally less formal and other-worldly, and consequently more related to the immediate needs of the students and of modern life."[58] At the beginning of the twentieth century, some of the more successful land-grant colleges and state universities came close to realizing Jefferson's dream of a university serving all the people and pursuing the truth in all realms of inquiry. The land-grant university of Cornell and the state University of Wisconsin are good representatives of the more successful land-grant institutions developed during this period.

The Cornell idea

New York State was extremely fortunate in enlisting the efforts of two very capable leaders in the establishment of its land-grant institution, Ezra Cornell and Andrew Dickson White. Cornell, a man of many occupations and interests, was anxious to endow a new college to serve the needs of the mechanic and farmer; he combined his own private donation with the federal land granted under the Morrill Act to New York State to found Cornell as a publicly supported land-grant college and a privately endowed university. It was, indeed, Cornell's honesty and shrewd financial abilities employed in the sale of the New York land scrip[59] that reaped for New York State's land-grant college more return per acre than any other state with the possible exception of California New York, which "had been given one-tenth of the Morrill Act bounty, was able finally to pocket more than one-third of all the money it yielded."[60]

Cornell's financial abilities seemed equaled only by his abilities to popularize his ideas. So well had Ezra Cornell made known the idea of the new university that when the institution opened its doors in 1868, the entering class was the largest in the history of American education to date—412 students.[61]

Called in 1865 to help organize and develop the new university, Andrew Dickson White, working closely with Ezra Cornell, ably guided the evolution of the Cornell idea.[62] At the inauguration ceremonies in Ithaca in 1868, President White charged that:

The university should foster the close union of liberal and practical studies, should forever be under nonsectarian control, and should develop a close relationship with the school system of the state. . . . Furthermore, there should be perfect equality among the different courses of study with no special privi-

---

58. Quoted in Nevins, *State Universities and Democracy,* pp. 88-89.
59. Much of which represented Wisconsin white pine timberland.
60. Nevins, *State Universities and Democracy,* p. 34.
61. Nevins, *State Universities and Democracy,* p. 41.
62. See Andrew Dickson White, *Autobiography of Andrew Dickson White,* 2 vols. (New York: The Century Company, 1905).

leges for particular subjects . . . also, an opportunity for the student to select the courses in which he desired to specialize. The ultimate aim of the university was the development of the individual in all of his intellectual, moral, and religious powers and the bringing of these powers thus developed to bear upon society and its welfare—'the adaptation of the university to the American people, to American needs, and to our own times.'[63]

Ezra Cornell followed:

I hope we have laid the foundation of an institution which shall combine practical with liberal education, which shall fit the youth of our country for the professions, the farms, the mines, the manufactories, for the investigations of science, and for mastering all the practical questions of life with success and honor.
I believe we have made the beginning of an institution which will prove highly beneficial to the poor young men and the poor young women of our country . . . as will enable any one by honest efforts and earnest labor, to secure a thorough, practical, scientific or classical education.[64]

Cornell himself best summarized his idea when he said, "I would found an institution where any person can find instruction in any study."[65] The Cornell idea took higher education a great distance from the time in 1828 when Jeremiah Day's Yale faculty defined the only true function of a college course in classical terms. Cornell University not only introduced the elective system and substantially departed from the traditional, classical curriculum, but as an institution, it took on humanitarian goals, emphasizing service to a community in progress.[66] In a state that long since had lost its frontiers, Cornell University, until well into the twentieth century, pioneered the new educational frontier for a democratic society.

The Wisconsin idea
The Wisconsin idea that "the borders of the campus are the boundaries of the state" was perhaps best expressed by Lincoln Steffens when he wrote in 1909:

In Wisconsin the university is as close to the intelligent farmer as his pigpen or his toolhouse; the university laboratories are part of the alert manufacturer's plant; to the worker, the university is drawing nearer than the school around the corner, and is as much his as his union, or his favorite saloon. Creeping into the minds of the children with pure seed, into the debates of youth with pure facts, into the opinions of voters with impersonal, expert knowledge, the state university is becoming a part of the citizen's own mind, just as the state is becoming a part of his will. And that's what the whole story means: the University

---

63. Paraphrased by Butts, *College Charts Its Course*, p. 186.
64. Quoted in Butts, *College Charts Its Course*, pp. 186-187.
65. Quoted in Butts, *College Charts Its Course*, p. 187.
66. For the character of Cornell as an institution, see Carl Becker, ed., *Cornell University: Founders and the Founding* (Ithaca: Cornell University Press, 1943).

of Wisconsin is a highly conscious lobe of the common community mind of the people of Wisconsin.[67]

During the first two decades of the twentieth century, the Wisconsin ideal of service to the community materialized under the able guidance of President Van Hise, 1904-1918.[68] The university became a national leader in extension programs which touched the lives of the people in almost everything from agriculture to fine arts. Professors in the arts and sciences, as well as in the professional schools, pooled their talents with farmers, workmen, businessmen, and politicians to solve pressing practical problems. Skillfully implementing the expert advice of sociologists, economists, and political scientists, Governor Robert La Follette instituted political, social, and economic reforms which placed Wisconsin state government in the vanguard of progressive reform. Wisconsin pioneered in "the effective regulation of public utilities, conservation, scientific agriculture, income and inheritance taxes, workmen's compensation, social security, and a dozen other measures that were later to emerge as part of the New Freedom or the New Deal."[69] University faculty played significant roles in virtually all these measures. Those university scholars who participated in the weekly informal Saturday afternoon luncheons with state legislators and public officials, and who served on state commissions under the encouraging eyes of La Follette and Van Hise, must have sensed that while they were profoundly shaping the American way of life, they were also pioneering the Jeffersonian ideal of a university into reality.[70]

The unique function of a state university was probably nowhere better enunciated than in Van Hise's inaugural address in 1909:

I, therefore, hold that the state university, a university which is to serve the state, must see to it that scholarship and research of all kinds, whether or not a possible practical value can be pointed out, must be sustained. A privately endowed institution may select some part of knowledge and confine itself to it, but not a state university. A university supported by the state for all its people, for all its sons and daughters, with their tastes and aptitudes as varied as mankind, can place no bounds upon the lines of its endeavor, else the state is the irreparable loser.

Be the choice of the sons and daughters of the state, language, literature, history, political economy, pure science, agriculture, engineering, architecture, sculpture, painting, or music, they should find at the state university ample opportunity for the pursuit of the chosen subject, even until they become creators in it. Nothing short of such opportunity is just, for each has an equal right to find at the state university the advanced intellectual life adapted to his

67. Quoted in Nevins, *State Universities and Democracy,* pp. 98-99.

68. See Merle Curti and Vernon Carstensen, *The University of Wisconsin* (Madison: University of Wisconsin Press, 1949), Vol. II.

69. Henry Steele Commager, *The American Mind* (New Haven: Yale University Press, 1959), p. 352.

70. As Commager put it, La Follette "was the first statesman since Jefferson to see the possibilities of the state university as a powerhouse to generate social and economic programs." *The American Mind,* p. 352.

need. Any narrower view is indefensible. The university should extend its scope until the field is covered from agriculture to the fine arts.[71]

In some states, the people came so to identify their interests with the state university that they not only supported the institution financially but also championed the teacher's right freely to teach and to inquire and the student's right to learn. Because of public support, the Board of Regents of the University of Wisconsin concluded their investigation in the now famous Ely Academic Freedom Case[72] by asserting that "Whatever may be the limitations which trammel inquiry elsewhere, we believe the great state University of Wisconsin should ever encourage that continual and fearless sifting and winnowing by which alone the truth can be found."[73] The state university not only had broadened the scope of higher learning in America but had also presented an ideal of academic freedom within a context which an enlightened public could support.

The state university in the twentieth century, so inexorably linked with the society, inevitably reflected in some measure the vices and virtues, the successes and failures, of that society. A society under internal and external threat and running scared is a society with a low tolerance for freedom of thought.[74] Thus by mid-twentieth century it was obvious that if academic freedom were to survive on state university campuses, it would have to depend on an enlightened public opinion, willing to tolerate that "continual and fearless sifting and winnowing by which alone the truth can be found."

Whether it was Wisconsin or Cornell or other state universities such as Michigan, Minnesota, California, or Illinois, the common thread which ran throughout all these institutions was the ideal of service to the people. This ideal translated into action meant joining the theoretical with the practical, the scholar with the practitioner to meet and solve the many-sided interests and needs of the people. The resulting curricula were as varied as mankind itself. In these respects, the state universities represented a major force in the transformation of American higher education.

Impact of the German universities

American higher learning radically changed as a result of the elective system, the development of the state universities and land-grant colleges, and the impact of the German universities on American education in general. If, indeed, one historical root of the elective system can be traced back to Jefferson's view of a state university, another root goes back to the German universities' effective use of the elective principle.

---

71. Quoted in Butts, *College Charts Its Course*, pp. 229-230.
72. For a detailed discussion of the case, see Curti and Carstensen, *University of Wisconsin*, I, 508-527.
73. Curti and Carstensen, *University of Wisconsin*, I, 525.
74. See James W. Silver, *Mississippi: The Closed Society* (New York: Harcourt, Brace & World, Inc., 1964).

For most of the nineteenth century, these institutions led the world in basic research. The German states had created a revolution in higher learning, which in turn directly or indirectly influenced all the educational institutions of the West. Taking as its single most important objective the creation of new knowledge and the development of students who could create knowledge, rather than the classical ideal to know "all the best that was said and thought in the past," the German university shook loose from tradition and created a new kind of higher education. Such a university was a place where professors were free to search for the truth, delving deeper and deeper into specialized areas, and where students were able to associate with professors who were doing research in areas of interest to them. In the informality of the seminar or the laboratory, students and faculty explored the depth of knowledge together, freely challenging one another.

As the focus of attention was taken off the institutionalized authority of the professor and placed on the problem of the serious, exciting quest for new knowledge, the creative talents of some of the most brilliant minds in the West were unleashed.[75] From Kant and Hegel to Marx and Engels, the German university produced social thinkers who profoundly influenced the course of Western civilization.[76] This same institution played a major role in developing the minds of those who ushered in the atomic age, the most significant revolution in the physical sciences since Newton. Max Planck, Werner Heisenberg, Albert Einstein, Enrico Fermi, and Robert Oppenheimer were all, at one time or another, students at a German university. Throughout most of the nineteenth century and part of the twentieth, German universities set the standard for scholarship in most fields of inquiry.

By leading the field in theoretical and experimental science, creating new knowledge through seminars and laboratory research, the German university played a crucial role in the massive proliferation of knowledge which affected all American educational institutions. The German ideal of *Lehrfreiheit und Lernfreiheit* (freedom to teach and freedom to learn), when effectively employed, resulted in creative, fruitful research. As a student at Göttingen in 1817, George Ticknor of Harvard commented that "a more perfect freedom, and in most cases a more perfect use of it can not be imagined than is now to be found in Germany. . . ."[77] In the same mood, at the end of the century, G. Stanley Hall referred to these institutions as the freest spot on earth.[78]

This freedom, however, was backed by a *Gymnasium* which prepared youth for university work by emphasizing not freedom but rigid discipline, not creativity but strict rote memorization. When Ticknor left

---

75. See Friedrich Paulsen, *German Universities and University Study* (New York: Charles Scribner's Sons, 1906).

76. One must qualify this point. The German university did not directly produce social critics. Kant and Hegel were philosophers of "the establishment," while Marx and Engels as real social critics were ostracized from the German university. Freedom of inquiry in the "German Republic" was, when it involved social criticism, primarily confined to those "philosopher kings" who knew the "truth."

77. Quoted in Butts, *College Charts Its Course*, p. 101.

78. Butts, *College Charts Its Course*, p. 79.

Göttingen and accepted an appointment to teach at Harvard in 1819, he returned to an institution more in line with the German *Gymnasium* than the German university. This was so much the case that it became customary for nineteenth-century graduates of Harvard, Yale, Princeton, or Columbia to feel their education incomplete until they took some work at the German university. The nineteenth-century mass migration of American students testified to the inadequacy of American higher learning and the superior offerings of the German university.[79] By mid-nineteenth century, such universities as Leipzig, Dresden, Berlin, Weimar, Jena, Halle, Wittenberg, and Göttingen literally served as graduate schools for the American college.

Touched by the German spirit of scholarship, American college leaders such as George Ticknor and Charles W. Eliot of Harvard, Henry Tappan of Michigan, Daniel C. Gilman of Johns Hopkins, Andrew D. White of Cornell, David Starr Jordan of Stanford, William R. Harper of the University of Chicago, and G. Stanley Hall of Clark University struggled to create in America a graduate education equal to their perception of the German model.

Although Ticknor, by 1835, had largely given up in his attempts to reform Harvard College, and Tappan, by 1863, had failed to Prussianize the University of Michigan, Tappan's colleague, Andrew D. White, succeeded in introducing the elective system and the seminar method and in generally raising the standards of scholarship at the new institution of Cornell. As a product of this new university, which seemed to glean the best from both the state university and German university ideal, David Starr Jordan, upon the strong recommendation of White, went on to become the first president of Leland Stanford University.[80] Jordan persevered in guiding Stanford toward the goal of a modified *Lehrfreiheit und Lernfreiheit*.[81]

The major development in graduate education, however, occurred when Daniel Coit Gilman was given the opportunity to form a new university in Baltimore. The German university idea, in a modified form, was obviously part of his earlier thinking; at his inauguration as president of the University of California in 1872, he had said:

We distinguish the requirements of young scholars, like those who have just left the high school and the academy, from those of advanced students, whose tastes, talents, and wants are specialized. Give the former prescription; give the latter freedom; but let the prescription vary with the varying peculiarities of individuals, and let the freedom allowed be the freedom which is governed and protected by law. College work for college boys implies daily guidance under prescribed rules; professional work implies voluntary, self-impelled enthusiasm in the acquisition of knowledge.[82]

---

79. For the impact of German thought on American culture see Henry A. Pochmann et al., *German Culture in America, Philosophical and Literary Influences, 1600-1900* (Madison: University of Wisconsin Press, 1957).

80. See *The Autobiography of Andrew Dickson White*, pp. 447-448.

81. See George T. Clark, *Leland Stanford* (California: Stanford University Press, 1931).

82. Quoted in Butts, *College Charts Its Course*, p. 195.

The German distinction between the *Gymnasium* as an institution emphasizing discipline and the university as an institution emphasizing freedom to inquire functioned significantly to shape Gilman's view of higher education. After spending a year touring various universities in Europe and America under the authorization of the Johns Hopkins Board of Trustees, Gilman returned to Baltimore to found the first graduate university in America. Although Johns Hopkins developed an undergraduate program, the central aim of this institution was to provide an environment where scholars could learn to create new knowledge by, in fact, creating new knowledge. The aim of Johns Hopkins as Gilman saw it was to encourage research and further "the advancement of individual scholars, who by their excellence will advance the sciences they pursue and the society where they dwell."[83]

Patterned after the German university, Johns Hopkins University stressed the use of seminar and laboratory methods, visiting lecturers, field work, individualized instruction, and intensive library research, all in the interest of developing scholars who could produce new knowledge. Thus, the classical ideal of the well-rounded gentleman gave way to the concept of the Ph.D. specialist. Extremely successful, Johns Hopkins quickly led the nation in the cultivation of the experimental sciences, as well as in many other areas of inquiry. By the end of the nineteenth century, this university became an important model for graduate study. With various modifications, other major institutions such as Chicago, Columbia, Harvard, Princeton, and Yale tended to emulate the Hopkins model in the development of their own graduate schools and programs.

By the dawn of the twentieth century, most major institutions of higher learning had grafted on to the American college graduate schools emphasizing the goals of research and professional schools emphasizing research and service in varying degrees. With Hopkins leading the way in graduate study, the state universities giving direction by establishing professional schools with emphasis on service to the community, and Harvard broadening the college curriculum through the use of the elective system, American institutions of higher learning underwent radical transformation.

While some institutions resisted the onrush of change and tried to ignore the utilitarian demands of a rapidly evolving technological society, none could ignore the startling proliferation of knowledge. In general, America entered the nineteenth century with the college as a single-purpose, classical seminary, often viewed as an alternate to a "people's college" or academy. A very different America entered the twentieth century with a public and private system of truly secondary schools, public and private universities, with a vastly expanded undergraduate college curriculum, often related to many different types of professional schools and capped by a graduate school.

The triple function of twentieth-century American higher education —teaching, research, and service—was clearly apparent at the dawn of

---

83. Quoted in Butts, *College Charts Its Course*, p. 195.

the century. To a considerable extent, A. F. Nightingale was correct when he asserted that:

> . . . before the twentieth century dawns in its glory there will be a broad highway thru which a pupil may walk unfettered, amid attractive associations, from the kindergarten to a degree at the end of the postgraduate course of the university and still will the people of the future be able to say, 'There were giants in those days.'

SUGGESTED READINGS

Barnard, Henry. *American Journal of Education,* I (1855).

Becker, Carl, ed. *Cornell University: Founders and the Founding.* Ithaca, Cornell University Press, 1943.

Brown, Elmer. *The Making of Our Middle Schools,* 3rd ed. New York, Longmans, Green & Company, 1907.

Butts, R. Freeman. *The College Charts Its Course.* New York, McGraw-Hill Book Company, 1939.

Childers, J. Wesley. *Foreign Language Teaching.* New York, The Center for Applied Research in Education, Inc., 1964.

Clark, George T. *Leland Stanford.* Stanford, Calif., Stanford University Press, 1931.

Commager, Henry Steele. *The American Mind.* New Haven, Yale University Press, 1959.

Curti, Merle, and Vernon Carstensen. *The University of Wisconsin,* Vol. II. Madison, University of Wisconsin Press, 1949.

Harvard Committee. *General Education in a Free Society.* Cambridge, Mass., Harvard University Press, 1945.

Henry, Jules. *Culture Against Man.* New York, Random House, Inc., 1963.

Hofstadter, Richard, and Wilson Smith, eds. *A Documentary History of American Higher Education.* Chicago, University of Chicago Press, 1961.

Krug, Edward A., ed. *Charles W. Eliot and Popular Education,* Classics in Education, No. 8. New York, Bureau of Publications, Teachers College, Columbia University, 1961.

———. *The Shaping of the American High School.* New York, Harper & Row, 1964.

Morison, Samuel Eliot. *Three Centuries of Harvard.* Cambridge, Mass., Harvard University Press, 1936.

Nevins, Allan. *The State Universities and Democracy.* Urbana, University of Illinois Press, 1962.

Paulsen, Friedrich. *German Universities and University Study.* New York, Charles Scribner's Sons, 1906.

Pochmann, Henry A., et al. *German Culture in America: Philosophical and Literary Influences, 1600-1900.* Madison, University of Wisconsin Press, 1957.

Rudolph, Frederick. *The American College and University.* New York, Alfred A. Knopf, Inc., 1962.

Sizer, Theodore R., ed. *The Age of the Academies,* Classics in Education, No. 22. New York, Bureau of Publications, Teachers College, Columbia University, 1964.

————. *Secondary Schools at the Turn of the Century.* New Haven, Yale University Press, 1964.

Tewksbury, Donald G. *The Founding of American Colleges and Universities Before the Civil War.* New York, Bureau of Publications, Teachers College, Columbia University, 1932.

Turner, Frederick Jackson. *The Frontier in American History.* New York, Henry Holt and Company, 1950.

West, Andrew F., ed. *Value of the Classics.* Princeton, N.J., Princeton University Press, 1917.

White, Andrew D. *The Autobiography of Andrew Dickson White,* 2 vols. New York, The Century Company, 1905.

Youmans, E. L. *The Culture Demanded by Modern Life.* New York, D. Appleton and Company, 1867.

CHAPTER 5

Nineteenth-century neo-Enlightenment views of the good society

. . . the Golden Age lies before us and not behind us, and is not far away. Our children will surely see it, and we, too, who are already men and women, if we deserve it by our faith and by our works.[1] EDWARD BELLAMY (1887)

Most nineteenth-century Americans held a faith that tomorrow would be better than today. To be sure, there were those who dwelled in the darker shadows of tragedy, but the American spirit generally moved toward a Golden Age in the future rather than from one in the past. Nineteenth-century views of the good society, whether derived from theological, metaphysical, or scientific formulations, usually reflected an explicit faith in the continuing progress of mankind. Such "rationalizations," as Max Weber put it, were concretely reinforced by the practical changes in Western life. Western society was indeed going somewhere; just where, for what purpose, and under whose control, however, were all debatable questions. Could men through conscious thought and collective action direct the course of human progress, as Condorcet and Saint-Simon had earlier suggested, or were there inexorable laws of nature which had predetermined their destiny? Were the social laws governing human society directly analogous to the physical laws of the universe; and if so, did they function mechanistically and dogmatically in the affairs of men, or were they susceptible to human purposes?

---

1. Edward Bellamy, *Looking Backward* (New York: The New American Library, 1963), p. 222.

COSMIC VIEWS OF THE GOOD SOCIETY

Some of the implicit paradoxes of the eighteenth-century thinkers—which suggested indefinite progress within a very definite Newtonian universe, stressed individual freedom and at the same time conformity to natural law, and honored human reason amidst a host of self-evident truths—became explicit problems for the nineteenth-century thinker. Regardless of how these apparent contradictions were resolved, most nineteenth-century thinkers assumed that the universe was governed by orderly law, that both the universe and man's place in it were ultimately comprehensible, and finally, that if man did discover the key to the universe, mankind would thereby benefit.

What took place in nineteenth-century thought was essentially a grandiose search for the meaning and purpose of life. Since individual men occupied but a small speck of time in the larger stream of humanity, and the present was in human experience but a fleeting moment of the future in the process of becoming the past, the search for the law or laws governing the human condition could proceed through the study of history and historic formulations. Cosmic histories, or those histories which explained past, present, and future, were more often the rule than the exception. To be sure, the ideas of Hegel, Marx, Comte, and Spencer were decidedly different, but they all held in common the belief that through the study of history one could decipher the law or laws of progress and from these extrapolate the nature of the future "good society." In this sense, all were users of cosmic history.

Although Enlightenment ideology tended to be modified by the romantic movement in Europe and transcendentalism in America, eighteenth-century thinkers had set the stage upon which nineteenth-century men acted out the logical consequences of certain Enlightenment assumptions. What took place on that stage was a dramatic contest between grandiose systems of thought for the loyalty of men. Among some of the varied contenders were those who evolved their thought either from Hegelian idealism, Comtean positivism, or Spencerian evolution.

Hegelian idealism

In searching for the law or laws which govern human experience, nineteenth-century thinkers evolved cosmic views of history which transcended the present and projected a future "good society." The German idealists led the field in this development; pre-eminent among them was Hegel. Hegel's view of history grew out of Kant's idealism, which affirmed the central importance of mind in dealing with reality. While Kant maintained a logically rationalized view of reason and history, Hegel went on to combine the rational and the intuitive to give reason and history a cosmic sweep.

In this process of attempting to combine the main elements of rationalism and romanticism into an organic unity, Hegel did considerable violence to Kant's view of reason as well as of history. Kant's view of history is well summarized by Lewis Beck as follows:

History has brought us to the present; there are indications, Kant thinks, that the progress will continue; but that it will continue is predicated upon our own faith in the autarchy of will and free acts, not on settled empirical knowledge of the past extended inductively to the future. The movement of history or the trend of the times does not, therefore, exempt men from their moral responsibility for seeking the reign of law over the whole world. The future will be the work of men, not a conclusion waiting to be drawn from premises already discovered by historians. Each moral act at the time it is done is, as it were, an absolutely new beginning, not determined by history or by Nature. History brings us to each present; but in each future we are on our own.[2]

In direct opposition, Hegel saw history not just as a series of events leading to the present where moral decisions are made but rather as the panoramic vision of a cosmic deterministic reason working its way in and through historical events. What happens had to happen. For the historian to render value judgments on past events is to render judgment on God Himself. "The Idea is the nature of God's will, and since this Idea becomes truly itself only in and through History, History is, as a modern writer has well characterized it, 'the autobiography of God.'"[3] The aged and dusty historical documents, if correctly read, would reveal the purpose of life and the reason for human progress. "Hegel and Marx believed in common that though history is the reality and the embodiment of reason, yet its grasp depends upon an understanding of the way history works and the goals toward which history strives."[4] Understanding of the way history works was found in the dialectical process of reason itself. Although many philosophers in the history of the West had reasoned dialectically, few, except perhaps the neo-Platonists, had so thoroughly fused the structure of thought with the content of historic evolution. The cement which bound the two was a romantic idealized spirit creating an organic whole. Through the conflict of thesis and antithesis and the resulting synthesis, the world spirit had been working its way through individuals, groups, and nations to arrive one day at the transcendental state in which rests the absolute Idea. Within this process, the greater reality exists in the universal abstraction of a state rather than in the specific, such as an individual. The individual becomes a pawn of the greater cosmic forces which require discipline to conform to a cultural destiny. In the hands of a conservative like Hegel, this system could justify the growing nationalistic spirit of a German state which required discipline to God, country, and emperor. In the hands of a revolutionary like Marx, this system could also subjugate the individual to a discipline in the name of a future classless society.

---

2. Lewis White Beck, ed., *Kant on History* (Indianapolis: The Bobbs-Merrill Company, Inc., 1963), p. xxvi.

3. Robert S. Hartman, trans., *Hegel's Reason in History* (New York: Liberal Arts Press, 1953), p. xxi. Also see Sidney Hook, *From Hegel to Marx* (New York: Humanities Press, Inc., 1950).

4. George L. Mosse, *The Culture of Western Europe* (Chicago: Rand McNally & Company, 1961), p. 142.

German idealism in America

As Perry Miller suggested, America of the nineteenth century absorbed two "Germanic invasions"—the first romantic and literary, the second rationalistic and philosophical.[5] The first came by way of England's Coleridge and Carlyle and culminated in the American transcendental movement; the second came by way of Kant and Hegel and culminated in the occupation of significant academic posts by men of German idealist persuasion. While transcendentalism in the first half of the century had only slight success in influencing the course of American academic philosophy, German idealism in the last half of the century was more successful.

The main philosophy taught in the American college during the first half of the nineteenth century was a Scottish realism, largely based on the middle-of-the-road philosophy of John Locke. In general:

> . . . Scottish Realism was a philosophy of 'common sense'—forthright, down-to-earth, rational and yet pious. It supported orthodoxy in the theology, raised no dangerous questions, invited no intellectual adventures. It was enlightened, and yet conservative. It was a restatement of Locke against David Hume, and contradicted Hume's scepticism by a blanket assertion that idea and object correspond so faithfully that Americans, intent upon their business, need never give a second thought to so unprofitable a worry.[6]

However, with the publication of Auguste Comte's *Cours de Philosophie Positive* (1830-1842), Herbert Spencer's *Social Statics* (1850), and Charles Darwin's *The Origin of Species by Means of Natural Selection* (1859), the pious and secure world of the Lockean "common sense" realists was threatened. By the closing decades of the century, Scottish realism, under constant attack by varied exponents of evolution, had been replaced by German idealism as the dominant "American" academic philosophy. German idealism, with its toughly reasoned dialectic method, its cosmic history, and its sweeping answers to the ultimate questions, was far better prepared to fight the battle for orthodoxy. By the end of the century, the triumph of idealism was symbolized by:

> . . . the capture of the major academic posts by philosophers trained—many of them in Germany—in the dialectic. George Trumbull Ladd at Yale, Borden Parker Bowne at Boston University, George Sylvester Morris at Michigan, James Edwin Creighton at Cornell, George Holmes Howison at California were only the best known of a regiment.[7]

Perhaps the best known of all the idealists in this period was Josiah Royce, who in *The Philosophy of Loyalty* confronted the issue of individual liberty versus conformity to law. In the end, Royce reconciled the contradictions and paradoxes of life in a transcendental ideal.

---

5. Perry Miller, ed., *American Thought: Civil War to World War I* (New York: Rinehart and Company, Inc., 1954).

6. Miller, *American Thought*, p. x.

7. Miller, *American Thought*, p. xii.

Apart from the academic community, the extent to which German idealism permeated American life was limited. The exception was the St. Louis Hegelian movement. Within the German settlement of St. Louis, the Hegelianism of Henry Conrad Brokmeyer and William Torrey Harris found congenial surroundings. There, in "Old Philosopher's Row," Harris and other members of the Philosophical Society learned their Hegelianism from Brokmeyer. In the shimmering lamplight of these Hegelian drawing rooms, Brokmeyer in his brusque but clear-headed way could be seen and heard using the sparks from the dialectic to light the path to the absolute. Out of these brilliant and sometimes abstruse discussions evolved the *Journal of Speculative Philosophy* (1867-1888), the first periodical in the English-speaking world devoted exclusively to speculative philosophy. Among the illustrious contributors to this organ of German idealism were G. Stanley Hall, Josiah Royce, Charles S. Peirce, John Dewey, and William James. As editor of this journal, William T. Harris kept one foot in speculative theory, and, as superintendent of the St. Louis schools (1869-1888), he kept his other foot in practice. Joining Hegelian theory with practice, Harris effectively shaped and molded the St. Louis system to be an educational showplace for the nation. Under his leadership, St. Louis developed an efficient graded public school system which included the first public kindergarten system in the nation. At a time when Boston was yet to support a public kindergarten, St. Louis had established fifty-five kindergartens as part of their public schools.[8]

No doubt the Hegelian philosophy that Harris internalized, emphasizing orderly systematic change in a rationally ordered universe, was reflected in the rationally ordered and structured model school system of St. Louis that he administered. It was that same Hegelianism which Harris carried to the Concord Summer School of Philosophy (1879-1888). There, in the cool, clear New England summers, the transcendentalism of Bronson Alcott engaged the Hegelianism of Harris in open debate. Although the perfect thesis and antithesis seemed to have been created, the grand synthesis was never effected.[9] With the death of Alcott and the end of the Concord School, Harris went on to become U.S. Commissioner of Education (1889-1906). Through his influence in that office and his leadership in the National Education Association councils, he aided and abetted the standardization of American education.

Using a Hegelian structure which framed his perceptions of the world, Harris built into that structure a conservative content which justified nationalism, industrial capitalism, social stratification, imperialism, and Christianity. To be sure, Harris was an educational innovator, but one

---

8. Kurt F. Leidecker, *Yankee Teacher* (New York: The Philosophical Library, 1946), p. 270. To what extent these kindergartens remained true to the Froebelian model is highly questionable. Harris had been critical of the Froebelians for being too child-centered. Leidecker asserted that Harris and Susan Blow saw the effect of the kindergarten as the "subtle conversion of play into work." If this is true, Harris' notion as to the function of play in education is more in accord with Plato's *Republic* than with Froebel's *Kindergarten*.

9. For an interesting discussion of this school, see Henry A. Pochmann, *New England Transcendentalism and St. Louis Hegelianism* (Philadelphia: Carl Schurz Memorial Foundation, 1948).

who advocated innovations that would make the school more efficient in achieving conservative goals. Just as it was a conservative Whig politician who led the struggle for the common school in the first half of the century, so it was a conservative Hegelian who systematized American education from the kindergarten through the high school at the close of the century. To Harris, the school was not to be used as a vehicle of social reconstruction. "As an Hegelian, he believed that improvement would take place in any case and by necessity; that the school was an agent not for guiding the change but for preserving the values of the past and adjusting the individual to society."[10] While Harris' conservatism was not too far removed from that of the "Royal Prussian Court Philosopher," other Americans, such as Walt Whitman and John Dewey, fused a more liberal content to a Hegelian structure and ended with a philosophy for democracy. Indeed, Hegel's cosmic dialectical sweep of history, when given the right content, could be used for almost any cause. Paradoxically, "The philosopher who equated what is with what ought to be, he released the greatest dissatisfaction with what is; and thus, as the greatest conservative, unchained the greatest revolution."[11]

Marxian idealism

Karl Marx (1818-1883), a brilliant son of that rather strange marriage of Enlightenment values and Hegelian history, also propounded a cosmic history which had profound revolutionary consequences. Using essentially the same historical methodology as Hegel and Leopold von Ranke, Marx also told the story of mankind as it actually occurred. As all idealists have done in the past, Marx searched for the one idea that could explain the many. Unlike Hegel who found God in history or Ranke who found history to be the objective handiwork of God, Marx found at the root of all historical change the one catalytic agent which shaped the content of the dialectic. That agent was the means of production, which in turn influenced all social institutions.[12] The school as a social derivative of the dominant economic system would inevitably follow the elite of that system. One then looked to the economic class struggle and not to the educational system as a lever of social change. History, cast in terms of the dialectic of economically rooted social class conflict, made man's past comprehensible, his present meaningful, and his future determined. As a believer in progress, Marx had built his view of history out of the idealist superstructure and fused it with a materialistic realism. This system, however, was never a raw materialism. Marx always viewed it as a complex series of interrelationships of man with his economic and cultural environment. Marx's theory of progress offered hope not only for an oppressed proletariat but also for those humani-

---

10. Merle Curti, *The Social Ideas of American Educators,* rev. ed. (Paterson, N.J.: Littlefield, Adams and Company, 1960), p. 345.

11. Hartman, *Hegel's Reason in History,* p. xi.

12. With respect to American educational institutions, it is far easier to make a case for Marx than it is to refute him. American educational institutions, from the colonial period to the present, have been heavily influenced by the economic system and the means of production which determined it.

tarians who saw in the classless society relief from the crass materialism of capitalism and the release of the creative energies of mankind for humane purposes. Thus "socialistic humanism" had its appeal.

Marx was, indeed, one of the last of the great system builders in the history of the West. Within a Newtonian universe, he evolved a dialectical, deterministic,[13] revolutionary, materialistic, utopian view of history. His system explained past, present, and future. Just as all the leaders of the Protestant revolution found God on their side, so Marx found the forces of the universe on the side of impending revolution. Just as Hegel read his past in such a way as to justify the status quo, Marx read his past so as to justify revolutionary change. Both men had found deterministic laws in history. When carried into practice, both grandiose systems were destructive of individual liberty. If Hegel lost the individual within the deterministic dialectic of reason which eventually culminated in an abstract "state," Marx lost the individual within the deterministic dialectic of economic and social forces which also culminated in an abstract "classless society."[14] Marx believed he had discovered the true story of mankind by way of scientific history. Truth, in this context, is dogmatic. Marx's inevitable legacy was a deterministic, revolutionary view of mankind.

On the surface, America—in the throes of industrial conflict, facing a growing proletariat and an increasingly depressing slum condition—might have been considered fertile ground for Marxian socialism. This, however, was not the case. America had its own social and economic critics—such as Henry George, Lester Frank Ward, Edward Bellamy, and Thorstein Veblen—and its own social action groups which made up the larger Progressive Reform era.[15] A vital part of the thought of these and other social critics of the American scene was a weeding out of deterministic thinking, whether that determinism originated in the conservative, classical economic theories of Herbert Spencer or the radical socialistic system of Karl Marx.[16] Most of these men "insisted that man can be master of his fate, that his own reliance is reason, that the State is his instrument, and that the planned society is the solution for social ills."[17] American social thinkers were more interested in adjusting the older system to humanitarian ends than in accepting a new deterministic system. The Marxian view of history fared rather poorly

---

13. For Marx both the end, the Communist state, and the means, violent class revolution, are predetermined by the force of history. Men are part of the force of history. While the dialectic of class struggle is inevitable and the victory of the proletariat is ultimately assured, the proletariat still have to develop class consciousness and battle to fulfill the apocalyptic vision. The inherent contradiction in Marx's thought with respect to determinism and revolution plagued the Communist left well into the twentieth century. See Chapter Ten.

14. A central problem for Marx was the issue of free will versus determinism which appears in his doctoral thesis. In the end, Marx transformed the liberal concept of freedom into a social determinism. See Mosse, *Culture of Western Europe*, pp. 173-174.

15. See Richard Hofstadter, *The Age of Reform* (New York: Alfred A. Knopf, Inc., 1955).

16. See Ralph Henry Gabriel, *The Course of American Democratic Thought,* 2nd ed. (New York: The Ronald Press Company, 1956), p. 226.

17. Gabriel, *Course of American Democratic Thought,* p. 225.

in both nineteenth- and twentieth-century America.[18] For the most part, the Communist party of America, which evolved in the twentieth century, remained true to Marx and looked not to the schools but to the economic institutions as means of social revolution. The role of the party with respect to American education, therefore, has tended to be minor with the exception of the 1930's, when the party increased not only its membership but also its involvement in public education. We shall return to these activities in Chapter Ten.

Comtean Positivism

While the cosmic histories, which evolved from German idealism, often minimized the importance of the individual in the name of dialectical reason, French positivism, which assumed the existence of natural law, minimized the importance of the individual in the name of positive law. The leading figure in the development of positive philosophy and the founder of sociology was Auguste Comte (1798-1857). As a student of Saint-Simon and a son of the Enlightenment, he believed in progress, natural law, and the efficacy of science to discover man's place in a Newtonian universe. What he lacked, however, was the Enlightenment faith in human reason. Comte found certainty in natural social laws which he was sure existed. The founder of sociology firmly believed that just as Newton had proved that there were universal physical laws, the science of society, or sociology, would discover those social laws which govern the human condition. These laws, empirically validated, would represent positive knowledge. To Comte, progress did not mean humanity charting its own future freely but rather the submission of humanity to those natural social laws, positively confirmed by the new science of society Thus, once the moral and social laws were validated, they could not be seriously challenged any more than could the law of gravity. The next step then would be:

> . . . the submission of all classes to the moral requirements of their position, under the instigation of a spiritual authority strong enough to enforce discipline. Thus might disturbing popular dispositions, now the constant source of political illusion and quackery, be reformed; and the vague and stormy discussion of *rights* would be replaced by the calm and precise determination of duties.[19]

The enforcer of the new moral discipline derived from a science of society would be education. "Thus the great characteristic office and privilege of the modern spiritual power will be the organization and working of a universal system of positive education, not only intellectual, but also, and more emphatically, moral."[20] The positive science of society

---

18. So much has this been the case that it is highly questionable if Marx's analysis of society has ever really had a fair hearing in American culture. See William Appleman Williams, *The Great Evasion* (Chicago: Quadrangle Books, Inc., 1964).

19. Auguste Comte, *The Positive Philosophy of Auguste Comte* (London: John Edward Taylor, Little Queen Street, Lincoln's Inn Fields, n.d.), II, 472.

20. Comte, *Positive Philosophy*, II, 473. In many ways, Comte suggested, as Helvétius had earlier, that "To guide the motion of the human puppet it is necessary to know the wires by which he is moved. . . ."

and education, Comte assumed, would one day bring order out of the chaotic social conditions which were so much a part of his post-revolutionary society. He was confident that this day was coming.

History, read through positivistic eyes, confirmed that mankind had evolved culturally. Mankind began its long trek upward from the state of being a "fetich-worshiper."[21] The first phase of cultural evolution proceeded as men rationalized their superstitions into codified theologies. Gradually, however, as religions failed to give satisfactory answers for the resolution of human problems, men turned increasingly to philosophy. Thus mankind advanced to the second stage of cultural evolution, the metaphysical stage. In time, philosophy too had failed to quench man's thirst for knowledge of himself and the universe. As men increasingly relied not on religion or philosophy but on science for the resolution of their more pressing problems, the third stage in man's cultural history dawned. This new stage, Comte asserted in the mid-nineteenth century, would be an age of science, an age in which neither the hand of God nor the mind of the philosopher would be a welcome visitor in the scientific laboratory. The scientific method would usher in the golden age in which men could create a scientific society based on positive knowledge. Of course, what Comte could not have known was that the very science in which he placed so much faith would, in the twentieth century, cast serious doubt on the certainty of ever gaining such positive knowledge. Nevertheless, his great stress on science and the scientific method marks him as a precursor of Lester Frank Ward and John Dewey, who also placed great faith in the scientific method as the "Great Panacea." However, neither Dewey nor Ward allowed their faith to dogmatize the method or its social applications as Comte had done.

In searching for the law of progress, Comte thought he had discovered the true course of history.

It certainly appears to me that the whole course of human history affords so decisive a verification of my theory of evolution, that no essential law of natural philosophy is more fully demonstrated. . . . A law which fulfills such conditions must be regarded as no philosophical pastime, but as the abstract expression of the general reality.[22]

Comte's age of positive science was to be ushered in not by the reason, will, and judgment of men but by deterministic force of evolutionary law. His faith in science was only equaled by his distrust of men's rational will. "Natural laws moved through natural, not human necessities; man could discover these laws, he could not change them."[23] Again the individual was viewed as a pawn swept along by the force of cosmic history.

Sociology was born in the search for the law of progress, in the framework of cosmic histories. In the process, both cofounders of sociology, Auguste Comte and Herbert Spencer, discovered cultural evolution. By the 1870's and 1880's, virtually every American social philosopher

---

21. Comte, *Positive Philosophy*, II, 186.
22. Comte, *Positive Philosophy*, II, 465.
23. Mosse, *Culture of Western Europe*, p. 199.

who thought seriously about the good society had to face not only the positivism of Comte but also the scientism of Spencer.

Spencerian evolution

While Marx found in history a record of progress which justified class conflict in the interest of a classless utopia, Herbert Spencer found in history a record of evolutionary progress which justified cutthroat individualism in the interest of an altruistic utopia. Both men found their golden age in the future. Spencer's philosophy, however, justified capitalism, while Marx's socialism condemned it. It was, then, no historical accident that Spencer and not Marx captured the imagination of capitalistic America in the post-Civil War era.[24] Popularizing the spirit of laissez-faire capitalism within a framework of evolutionary theory, Spencer seemed to reach his zenith of popularity in America during the 1880's.[25]

Spencer's philosophy was an ambitious attempt to organize and integrate all knowledge; the organizing theme used throughout most of his work was social evolution. Six years before Darwin published *The Origin of Species,* Spencer had coined the phrase "survival of the fittest." This seminal idea helped transform the law of progress into the law of evolution.

Both Darwin and Spencer walked in the shadow of another Enlightenment student of progress, Thomas Robert Malthus (1766-1834). Concerned with the problem of the perfectibility of human society, Malthus was struck by the great gap between the ideal world of human aspirations and the real world of human suffering. In typical Enlightenment fashion, Malthus, in his *Essay on the Principle of Population as It Affects the Future Improvement of Society* (1798), found rational natural laws at work in the world of human suffering. By raising war, famine, and disease to the level of natural law, Malthus explained, and others justified, human misery as checks on overpopulation.[26] The world of men was still rational, even if it lacked humanitarian virtues.

In the England of Charles Dickens, Karl Marx, Charles Darwin, and Herbert Spencer, the struggle to survive could not go unnoticed. While Malthus discovered the reason for the struggle, Spencer, Darwin, and Alfred Russel Wallace found the reason that some survived and others did not. The "elect" who did survive did so not because they were chosen by God but, as Spencer saw it, because they were chosen by nature.[27]

---

24. In the last forty years of the nineteenth century, more than 350,000 copies of Spencer's books were sold in the United States. See Nelson Manfred Blake, *A History of American Life and Thought* (New York: McGraw-Hill Book Company, 1963), p. 399.

25. See Richard Hofstadter, *Social Darwinism in American Thought,* rev. ed. (New York: George Braziller, Inc., 1959).

26. Although Malthus refused to make value judgments, others were not so restrained. The dignifying of poverty as "natural," however, has proved in the past two centuries of Western experience to be a curse for the poor and an opium for the social conscience of the rich. By placing a social problem in the realm of "nature," men escape responsibility.

27. There is a strong parallel between the older Calvinistic doctrine of predestination and Spencer's evolutionary determinism. The one invested absolute authority in God, the other in evolution.

Both Spencer and Darwin built their ideas on a Malthusian view of reality. As Darwin suggested, "It is the doctrine of Malthus applied with manifold force to the whole animal and vegetable kingdoms; for in this case there can be no artificial increase of food, and no prudential restraint from marriage."[28] Darwin expressed his indebtedness to Malthus[29] for the seminal insight which helped him formulate what he called "Natural Selection; or the survival of the fittest."[30] Although it is virtually impossible to discover with any great degree of certainty the exact origin of a particular idea, there is strong evidence to indicate that the idea of survival of the fittest which Darwin applied to vegetable and animal life originated in part, at least, in the minds of social theorists who observed the impoverished human conditions.[31] To a certain extent, Nietzsche was correct when he observed that "Over the whole of English Darwinism, there hovers something of the odor of humble people in need and in straits."[32]

The universe that Spencer observed could not be judged senseless; it had to have a purpose. The death of the weak would have a beneficial effect on the progress of the human race. Using Lamarck's theory of acquired characteristics being inherited, Spencer was completely convinced that progress was not only possible but inevitable.

The ultimate development of the ideal man is logically certain—as certain as any conclusion in which we place the most implicit faith; for instance that all men will die. . . . Progress, therefore, is not an accident, but a necessity. Instead of civilization being artificial, it is part of nature; all of a piece with the development of the embryo or the unfolding of a flower.[33]

This natural unfolding of the human flower would be seriously impaired if men tinkered with the natural law of survival of the fittest and allowed the weak to survive. The poor, the weak, the downtrodden, the stupid, and the lazy must be allowed to die off.[34] If medieval Christianity made poverty a virtue and Calvin made it a vice, Herbert Spencer made it a symptom of racial degeneracy. In the interest of progress, Spencer justified a system that would allow the strong to take from the weak and the smart to take from both. Government should not interfere with the struggle. Spencer therefore opposed tariffs, poor laws, state banking, public education, and all forms of government regulation of industry. The good society for Spencer was a highly competitive social system

---

28. Charles Darwin, *The Origin of Species and the Descent of Man* (New York: The Modern Library, 1936), p. 53.

29. See Hofstadter, *Social Darwinism in American Thought*, p. 25.

30. Darwin, *Origin of Species*, p. 63.

31. See Hofstadter, *Social Darwinism in American Thought*, p. 25; also Mosse, *Culture of Western Europe*, pp. 197-209; and Raymond P. Stearns, *Pageant of Europe* (New York: Harcourt, Brace and Company, Inc., 1947), pp. 497 and 518.

32. Quoted in Hofstadter, *Social Darwinism in American Thought*, p. 25. One is inclined to wonder what sort of evolutionary laws might have been discovered if Malthus, Spencer, and Darwin had lived in a world which emphasized cooperation instead of competition. Selective perceptions, no doubt, play a large role in what is "discovered."

33. Quoted in Hofstadter, *Social Darwinism in American Thought*, p. 27.

34. See Herbert Spencer, *Social Statics* (New York: D. Appleton and Co., 1892).

which maximized individualism and minimized collective social action. He believed that out of such a social system would evolve the superman who would be strong, intelligent, and altruistic.

Unlike Jefferson and his followers who embraced a theory of progress based on social meliorism, Herbert Spencer and his followers, in the name of scientific sociology and evolutionary progress, denied a collective approach to reform and instead espoused a rugged individualism. Inherent in the thought of both European cofounders of sociology was the idea that once the law of progress was delineated, men had no other recourse than to learn to use that law in pursuit of self-interest. To Spencer, the wise and the strong must use their reason in the pursuit of their own ends. Hence, wise men study science, which shows them how to achieve their goals. Properly educated individual reason is thus of tremendous importance in the struggle for survival and the progress of the individual. Alleged "social reason" and "social planning" are rejected on the grounds that such activity depends on mass support and will in the end be directed at aiding the weak and the unfit and hence retard progress.

Spencer's rapid rise to fame in America in the 1880's was equaled only by his rapid decline in popularity in the 1890's. Although it is highly questionable whether America ever had a truly laissez-faire economic system, the social gospel encouraging individualism which Spencer preached was far more appropriate for the society of the eighties than it was for the early decades of the twentieth century. As the muckrakers in the twentieth century depicted the corruption and vice that the competitive society had wrought, and the progressives proposed practical solutions which utilized government to ameliorate conditions, Spencer's social views became increasingly anachronistic.

In a society that was rapidly building a system of public education, Spencer's hostility toward public education generally fell on deaf ears. However, many of his other educational views found a receptive audience. His four essays on education published between 1854 and 1859 embodied much of the educational wisdom of the eighteenth and early nineteenth centuries. In a way, he translated and collected bits and pieces of various educational recipes into a coherent set of views around an intellectual core of utilitarian, evolutionary naturalism. As Charles W. Eliot put it:

Through him, the thoughts on education of Comenius, Montaigne, Locke, Milton, Rousseau, Pestalozzi, and other noted writers on this neglected subject are at last winning their way into practice, with the modifications or adaptations which the immense gains of the human race in knowledge and power since the nineteenth century opened have shown to be wise.[35]

Central to Spencer's view of education was his conception of the child as a product of evolution. Since the same general laws of evolution have functioned in the life of the race and continue to function in the life of

---

35. Herbert Spencer, *Essays on Education* (London: J. M. Dent and Sons, Ltd., 1949), p. viii.

the child in an unbroken fashion, and since we know how men have evolved through various historic epochs, each of which has assumedly left its mark on mankind, it was only reasonable to conclude that the child in his natural development will recapitulate, in an abbreviated form, that racial experience.

The education of the child must accord both in mode and arrangement with the education of mankind, considered historically. In other words, the genesis of knowledge in the individual must follow the same course as the genesis of knowledge in the race. In strictness, this principle may be considered as already expressed by implication; since both, being processes of evolution, must conform to those same general laws of evolution above insisted on, and must therefore agree with each other. Nevertheless this particular parallelism is of value for the specific guidance it affords. To M. Comte we believe society owes the enunciation of it; and we may accept this item of his philosophy without at all committing ourselves to the rest.[36]

While Spencer may have arrived at this parallelism of the child and the race by way of Comte's cultural epochs, others such as G. Stanley Hall and Sigmund Freud arrived at similar conclusions by way of German romanticism and German physiological science.[37]

The recapitulation idea was a logical consequence of cosmic history. As long as men read their past as functionally linked to their present and future, it was eminently reasonable to find that linkage in the life of the child. One could arrive at the recapitulation idea by way of English evolution, French positivism, or German idealism.[38] It is, then, not difficult to understand why the idea of recapitulation was so much a part of the intellectual atmosphere of the latter half of the nineteenth century in both Europe and America. It is also significant that, when cosmic views of history were rejected in the twentieth century, recapitulation ideas tended to be discarded with them.

Spencer found the parallelism of child and race "of value for the specific guidance it affords." The specific guidance, however, is dependent on how one reads his past. In the eyes of a practical engineer such as Spencer, history confirmed the need for the curriculum and the methods of the school to be practical and to proceed from the simple to the complex, the concrete to the abstract, and the empirical to the rational. In his classic essay—"What Knowledge Is of Most Worth?"— Spencer made science king and thus relegated the classics to a lesser role in the education of the young. In this respect, most of Spencer's educational views found a more receptive audience in America than in England. The general movement of American secondary and higher education—with the introduction of the elective system, the growth of

36. Spencer, *Essays on Education,* p. 60.

37. For an analysis of the avenues which Hall and Herbartianism followed, see unpublished dissertation (University of Wisconsin, 1963) by Charles Strickland, "The Child and the Race."

38. The classic example, here, is the Herbartians and their use of history in American education at the turn of the century. We shall turn to this movement in Chapter Nine.

the state universities, the rise of the sciences, and the decline of the classics—was in the direction to which Spencer pointed. Throughout the closing decades of the nineteenth century, Spencer was used as an authority by those who advocated a more practical, scientific, useful curriculum in the American schools. While it is difficult to assess the exact influence of Spencer on American educational practice, perhaps Charles W. Eliot was correct when he said:

On the whole, Herbert Spencer has been fortunate among educational philosophers. He has not had to wait so long for the acceptance of his teachings as Comenius, Montaigne, or Rousseau waited. His ideas have been floated on a prodigious tide of industrial and social change, which necessarily involved widespread and profound educational reform.[39]

CONSERVATIVE VERSUS LIBERAL SOCIOLOGY

While Spencer advocated educational reform, his overall social views derived from his conception of the history of mankind were basically individualistic. Using various cosmic views of history and searching for the law of progress, nineteenth-century thinkers justified evolution as well as revolution, rugged individualism as well as collectivism, radicalism as well as conservatism. Those who espoused the Spencerian social views at the end of the century in America represented one side of a great debate which has persisted in American social thought throughout the twentieth century. On the one side, William Graham Sumner (1840-1910) represented the Spencerian view, and on the other, Lester Frank Ward (1841-1913) ably enunciated the social melioristic position. Both men believed in evolution, and both were leading figures in the development of American sociology. Aside from these few similarities, the social views they professed were radically different.

William Graham Sumner

At the height of his American popularity, Spencer visited the United States. Climaxing this triumphant visit was a dinner held in his honor at Delmonico's (November 9, 1882). The guest register for this festive occasion read something like a "Who's Who" of American life. After dinner, one leading spokesman after another of American arts and sciences, business, and politics gave glowing testimonials. Among those who paid tribute was William Graham Sumner, professor of political economy at Yale. With reference to the science of sociology he said, "We still need the master to show us how to handle and apply its most fundamental doctrines. . . . Mr. Spencer is breaking a path for us into this domain. We stand eager to follow him into it."[40]

Although Sumner did follow in the footsteps of the master, his general

---

39. Spencer, *Essays on Education*, p. xvi.
40. Quoted in Henry Steele Commager, *The American Mind* (New Haven: Yale University Press, 1959), p. 204.

thought reflected far more than a carbon copy of Spencer's "synthetic philosophy."[41] In broad perspective, his ideas represent an amalgamation of at least three streams of thought: secularized Protestant ethical values, evolutionary naturalism, and the classical economics of Smith, Malthus, and Ricardo. In the hands of Sumner, the virtues of work, thrift, sobriety, and diligence meshed neatly with the idea of survival of the fittest and the idea of independent automatic economic law into a tight, coherent philosophy of social conservatism. From this intellectual position, Sumner rigorously attacked social meliorist efforts in the closing decades of the nineteenth century as "the absurd effort to make the world over."

William Graham Sumner was the son of a hard-working, frugal immigrant who managed to find employment as a railroad worker and save enough to send his son to Yale. After Sumner completed his work at Yale in 1863, a wealthy friend assisted him in buying a substitute for Civil War service and financed his continued education in Europe. In Geneva in 1863 and 1864, he studied French and Hebrew; at Göttingen in 1864, ancient languages and history; and at Oxford in 1866, Anglican theology. In 1866 he returned to Yale as a tutor, and in the following year, on December 27, he was ordained deacon in the Protestant Episcopal Church at Trinity Church, New Haven. In June 1872, he was called from a position as rector of the Church of the Redeemer at Morristown, New Jersey, to become professor of political and social science at Yale, where he remained the rest of his life.

At Yale, he quickly became one of the more popular but controversial professors. Daring to use Spencer's works in his course, Sumner brought down the scorn of the religiously orthodox, including President Noah Porter. Because he also opposed imperialism and the Spanish-American War, he was attacked by nationalistic groups; and when he further voiced opposition to protectionism as a form of plutocracy, he was held suspect in the eyes of certain members of the business community. Nevertheless, his advocacy of laissez-faire capitalism, his justification of poverty, and his relentless attacks on social reformers endeared him to the representatives of the more conservative side of the Yale establishment.

Sumner's social philosophy centered on the belief that cultures evolve and develop without the direction of human purpose and will. Ideas of honor, justice, truth, and nature are all rationalized as products of social conditions.[42] Ideologies are illusions generally used to dupe people for selfish purposes. Self-seeking is the key universal human instinct which propels the struggle, just as survival of the fittest is the law which governs it. Reflecting on this idea, Sumner suggested to his students that life is very much a case of "root, hog, or die."[43]

---

41. Sumner did not confuse evolution with progress, nor did he express any utopian faith in a Spencerian golden age. For an analysis of the differences between Sumner and Spencer, see Harris E. Starr, *William Graham Sumner* (New York: Henry Holt and Company, 1925).

42. This theme is clear in his last major work, *Folkways,* 1906, but it is also evident in his earlier essays. See Albert G. Keller and Maurice R. Davie, eds., *Essays of William Graham Sumner,* 2 vols. (New Haven: Yale University Press, 1934).

43. Hofstadter, *Social Darwinism in American Thought,* p. 39.

While man is a product of social evolution, he cannot direct the course of that evolution.

He is in the stream and is swept along with it. . . . . Therefore the tide will not be changed by us. It will swallow up both us and our experiments. The things which will change it are the great discoveries and inventions, the new reactions inside the social organism, and the changes in the earth itself on account of changes in the cosmical forces. These causes will make of it just what, in fidelity to them, it ought to be. The men will be carried away with it and be made by it. The utmost they can do by their cleverness will be to note and record their course as they are carried along, which is what we do now, and is that which leads us to the vain fancy that we can make or guide the movement. That is why it is the greatest folly of which a man can be capable, to sit down with a slate and pencil to plan out a new social world.[44]

Sumner flatly rejected the humanitarian position that through reason, education, and collective action men could create, if not the good society, at least a better society.

Sumner clearly came up on the darker, more pessimistic side of American thought. In this respect, he was a part of that tragically oriented tradition represented in American thought by Jonathan Edwards, Herman Melville, Henry Adams, and T. S. Eliot. Whether rooted in supernaturalism or naturalism, this tradition persisted in focusing its attention on the tragic aspects of the human condition. While some men could be optimistic because of their faith in a loving God, an enlightened man, or a beneficent nature, Sumner could not accept any of these illusions. That strange mixture of Calvin, Malthus, and Darwin which shaped Sumner's view of reality, combined with a relentlessly logical mind, led straight to his conclusion at the end of his life: "I have lived through the best period of this country's history. The next generations are going to see war and social calamities. I am glad I don't have to live on into them."[45]

Unlike Emerson, who faced the tragic elements of the human condition but then optimistically found a beneficent deity in a transcendental oversoul, Sumner found that his deity vanished with the years. " 'I have never discarded beliefs deliberately,' he said later in life. 'I left them in a drawer, and, after a while, when I opened it, there was nothing there at all.' "[46] Although Sumner may have lost his God in that drawer, he did not lose his Protestant ethical values. Sumner's attitude toward work, poverty, frugality, and prudence appear as starkly secularized Puritan values without the tempering of a just God or a humanitarian sentiment. Most of his social essays sound as if they were written by a latter-day Benjamin Franklin—but devoid of Franklin's humor and humanity.

As the century came to a close, Sumner thundered against almost every form of social meliorism, from poor laws to government regulation of sanitation systems. In a series of publications—*What Social Classes Owe to Each Other* (1883), "The Forgotten Man" (1883), "The Abolition of

---

44. *Essays of William Graham Sumner*, 1, 105-106.
45. Miller, *American Thought*, p. xxviii.
46. Gabriel, *Course of American Democratic Thought*, p. 230.

Poverty" (1887), and "The Absurd Effort to Make the World Over" (1894)—Sumner made his case for rugged individualism. Poverty could not be abolished, for it was a part of that necessary struggle to survive. Those who remain poor, outside of paupers and the physically incapacitated, are the moral or biological degenerates of the race and must be allowed to suffer the natural consequences. Those who reach the top of the economic ladder are the fittest and usually receive their just rewards. The forgotten man, however, is not the poor man but that honest, hardworking, middle-class individual who usually ends up paying his taxes to support the degenerate poor.

The paupers and the physically incapacitated are an inevitable charge on society. About them no more need be said. But the weak who constantly arouse the pity of humanitarians and philanthropists are the shiftless, the imprudent, the negligent, the impractical, and the inefficient, or they are the idle, the intemperate, the extravagant, and the vicious.[47]

These are the people who must be allowed to die off.

Vice is its own curse. If we let nature alone, she cures vice by the most frightful penalties. It may shock you to hear me say it, but when you get over the shock, it will do you good to think of it: a drunkard in the gutter is just where he ought to be. Nature is working away at him to get him out of the way, just as she sets up her processes of dissolution to remove whatever is a failure in its line.[48]

Like Comte and Spencer before him, Sumner was sure "that the social order is fixed by laws of nature precisely analogous to those of the physical order."[49] Under these circumstances, the best that a science of society might do is to describe these natural laws so that men might more readily comply with nature's dictates. Progress had, indeed, occurred, but it did not occur as a result of human purpose and will. It occurred because of the law of evolution. This process, however, might be assisted if education developed in the young a "critical faculty" to perceive reality as it really exists and inculcated in them the virtues of industry, self-denial, and temperance.

The sound student of sociology can hold out to mankind, as individuals or as a race, only one hope of better and happier living. That hope lies in an enhancement of the industrial virtues and of the moral forces which thence arise. Industry, self-denial, and temperance are the laws of prosperity for men and states; without them advances in the arts and in wealth mean only corruption and decay through luxury and vice.[50]

Education, Sumner thought, played a limited but significant role in human welfare. The school would best serve the cause of society by

---

47. *Essays of William Graham Sumner*, I, 476.
48. *Essays of William Graham Sumner*, I, 481.
49. *Essays of William Graham Sumner*, II, 107.
50. Quoted in Starr, *William Graham Sumner*, pp. 492-493.

Schools

inculcating the right mores and developing the critical intelligence of individuals. Such individuals would face up to the competitive, harsh realities of life and make the best of their circumstances, free of humanitarian illusions which were the cause of reformism. Although certain schools might become centers of new ideas which remold the mores, the chief function of the school is to transmit the social mores refreshed. It was not to reconstruct and reform society.

In the organization of modern society the schools are the institutional apparatus by which the inheritance of experience and knowledge—the whole mental outfit of the race—is transmitted to the young. Through these institutions, therefore, the mores and morality which men have accepted and approved are handed down. The transmission ought to be faithful, but not without criticism.[51]

Unlike Spencer, Sumner, who was educated in the public schools of Hartford, Connecticut, and served for twenty-five years on a state board of education, did not oppose public education.[52] He justified it as an expensive but necessary way of identifying and educating the gifted child. As he said, "The one thing which justifies popular education for all children is the immense value of men of genius to the society."[53] It is notable that others in the past, such as Horace Mann and Thomas Jefferson, had justified public education on decidedly different grounds. Although Jefferson was going to "rake from the rubbish annually," neither his proposed system nor Mann's was justified on the grounds of procuring genius but rather on the grounds of developing an enlightened electorate. Jefferson suggested that if he had to choose between the education of the genius and that of the people, he would choose the latter. The critical difference, here, is that William Graham Sumner would choose the education of the genius. Sumner's evolutionary sociology was distinctly devoid of either Mann's or Jefferson's humanitarian considerations.

While Sumner's thought integrated the past Protestant ethic with current nineteenth-century evolutionary theory, his last work was distinctively twentieth century. The thesis he developed in *Folkways* (1906), which described ideologies as intellectual by-products of the slowly evolving mores which, in turn, resulted from the practical immediate conditions of a culture, seemed to cut a furrow that many sociologists followed in the twentieth century. In Sumner's *Folkways,* there was no cosmic history, no utopian world view, no law of progress, but only cultural evolution. By 1906, Sumner had shifted from writing polemical essays about social systems and had begun to employ an inductive approach to gain more positive knowledge of society. This shift reflected a general trend in the field of sociology. The inductive approach, which rejected ideology, satisfied the conservative conscience of Sumner only because basically he believed men rational enough to understand the facts of scientific knowledge and live accordingly.

---

51. William Graham Sumner, *Folkways* (Boston: Ginn and Company, 1940), p. 635.
52. Starr, *William Graham Sumner,* p. 393.
53. Sumner, *Folkways,* p. 628.

In 1916, only ten years after Sumner published his classic *Folkways,* an Italian sociologist, who also rejected ideology in search of a positive science of sociology, published *Trattato di Sociologia generale.*[54] Vilfredo Pareto, however, read the mores as derivations or myths behind which existed the irrational residues or the real mainsprings of human action. At base, Pareto saw human nature as irrational and thus went on to construct a fascist sociological view of man and the good society. Although Sumner, too, rejected humanitarianism as illusory and called for a scientific, inductive approach to society, his rational image of the individual inhibited any fascist view. While many conservatives in the twentieth century took the fascist leap, Sumner never took that leap but maintained the position of the conservative until the end.

Sumner had effectively stated some of the major ideas espoused by social and educational conservatives in twentieth-century America. Whether they realized it or not, whenever twentieth-century social critics argued against government regulation of industry, social welfare, the planned society and for rugged individualism, laissez-faire capitalism, and the virtues of a competitive economic system, they inevitably echoed and re-echoed Sumner's social position. Again, whether they realized it or not, whenever twentieth-century educational critics argued that the schools could not and should not be used to reconstruct the society, that the main function of the school was to transmit the cultural past, that public education was justified only if it identified and educated the gifted, and that the school must be a miniature competitive society which prepares the young for entrance into the larger competitive society,[55] they were expressing a Sumnerian view of the social function of education.

Lester Frank Ward

At that same dinner at Delmonico's during which Sumner gave his tribute to Herbert Spencer, there sat a six-foot, broad-shouldered, full-chested Midwesterner who, before the close of the century, would be heralded by many in sociology as the "dean of American sociologists." One year after that dinner meeting, Lester Frank Ward published his *Dynamic Sociology* (1883), which refuted both Spencer and Sumner. It took Ward 14 years and 1400 laborious pages in two volumes to state his case. No doubt partly because of the forbidding style, as well as the conditions of the times, *Dynamic Sociology* got off to a slow start.[56] Nevertheless, by the end of the nineteenth century, no reputable American sociologist was unfamiliar with Ward's thesis. In this work, Ward

---

54. We will return to Pareto's analysis in Chapter Ten.

55. It is interesting that Sumner, like John Dewey, suggested that "A school is a miniature society." See *Essays of William Graham Sumner,* I, 40. The critical question which separates the educational ideas of these two men is, then: What is the nature of the good society of which the school must be a miniature?

56. Ward paid a substantial subsidy to D. Appleton and Company in order to get *Dynamic Sociology* published. In the ten years after its publication the book sold barely five hundred copies. See John C. Burnham, *Lester Frank Ward in American Thought* (Washington, D.C.: Annals of American Sociology Public Affairs Press, 1956), pp. 18-19.

launched a major attack on the Spencer-Sumner view of the good society. As Ward painstakingly dismantled the temple of social Darwinism, he constructed in its place the planned society. So carefully reasoned was this work that whenever liberals in politics or education in the twentieth century thought and acted in terms of social reform, they usually did so, consciously or not, along lines laid down by Ward in *Dynamic Sociology*.

Ward was born in 1841 of poor pioneer parents who moved westward from New York to Illinois. As a frontier youth, he was mainly self-educated, receiving little formal schooling. However, by 1860 or 1861 he was teaching school in Pennsylvania, and shortly thereafter he answered President Lincoln's call for 300,000 men. After being wounded twice at Chancellorsville, he was discharged from the service in 1864. From 1865 to 1906, he held various civil service posts in Washington, D.C., gaining some international recognition for his scientific research in paleobotany. During his years in Washington, he became the perennial night school student. Working by day and studying by night and attending Columbian (now George Washington) University, he earned several degrees and developed strong competency in many diverse fields of knowledge. Proficient in twelve languages, Ward was eminently qualified to teach one of the last university courses titled "A Survey of All Knowledge." At Brown University from 1906 to 1913, he also taught "The Sociological Aspects of Education." This was most fitting, for Ward had intellectually pioneered a path toward the educational frontier. *Dynamic Sociology,* sometimes called by Ward "The Great Panacea," concluded with education as the capstone of the planned society.

Ward built his thesis on a critical analysis of both Comte's positive philosophy and Spencer's synthetic philosophy.[57] He found both positions inadequate. Although he could accept much of what Comte had said, he could not accept Comte's narrow view of man, which left little freedom for thought or action and, if followed literally, "would so far cripple every department of science as to throw it back into medieval stagnation."[58] On the other hand, he saw that Comte's criterion of science "as its ability to foretell future unknown results from the coordination of present known phenomena,"[59] when applied to sociology, leads straight to the conclusion

. . . that the future of human society is in its own hands, and that a great and rapid progress can be artificially attained through clear and accurate scientific foresight of the necessary effects of present human modifications. . . . This is the department of active social dynamics, or 'sociocracy' (Vol. i P. 60), which Comte dimly saw but which his successors have thus far failed to recognize.[60]

While Comte's lack of faith in human reason obscured what he "dimly saw," Ward's strong humanitarian convictions facilitated the develop-

---

57. Lester Frank Ward, *Dynamic Sociology* (New York: D. Appleton and Company, 1883), I, 83-218.
58. *Dynamic Sociology,* I, 90.
59. *Dynamic Sociology,* I, 137.
60. *Dynamic Sociology,* I, 137.

ment of this key idea to its logical conclusions. That man was a product of natural evolution was accepted; that the laws of evolution must be allowed to continue to shape his destiny was rejected. Ward argued that man, using his intelligence, had "artificially" tampered with the laws of nature to improve their effects. Civilization itself is an artificial attempt at control and direction of nature. "We know that by precisely these means man has artificially modified the results of the operation of law in all other sciences, even down to biology, and there can be no longer a doubt of the same power over sociological phenomena."[61]

Although Ward was fundamentally a monist who believed that human intelligence was a product of evolution, he made a clear distinction between what he called "telic phenomena," or those phenomena controlled by human purpose and will, and "genetic phenomena," those phenomena governed by the blind and wasteful forces of nature. Unlike Emerson, who could love "nature" from the secure position of the Concord community, or William Graham Sumner, who could accept the harsher realities of nature from the security of the Yale campus, Ward, from his experience as a youth on the frontier and later his work in paleobotany, learned that nature, far from being beneficent or purposeful, was actually harsh, wasteful, and inefficient. When men applied their intelligence to agriculture, for instance, and thereby interfered with the natural law, both the land and animals became more productive. It was not natural selection at work here but intelligent selection.

In a series of publications—*Dynamic Sociology* (1883), *The Psychic Factors of Civilization* (1893), *Pure Sociology* (1903), and *Applied Sociology* (1906)—Ward carried out a sustained attack on the Malthus-Spencer-Sumner evolutionary equation. With critically pointed arguments, Ward slashed the laissez-faire school of economic and social thought and others who worshiped at the shrine of "nature." Neither the slums, crime, nor poverty could be blamed on nature but were produced by man's failure to apply intelligence to social phenomena.

Progress depends not on the romantic who views nature as good and beneficent, nor on the social Darwinist who justifies human suffering on grounds of its being natural, but rather on an enlightened society which coldly calculates the melioration of its problems. In looking toward the future, Ward said:

I insist that the time must soon come when the control of blind natural forces in society must give way to that of human foresight, or the highest civilizations of the earth must reach their culminating point and commence their decline. . . . And a time must certainly come when the maintenance of the healthy and progressive tone of society will be far more difficult than at present, or at any period of the past. Thus far, social progress has in a certain awkward manner taken care of itself, but in the near future it will have to be cared for. To do this and maintain the dynamic condition against all the hostile forces which thicken with every new advance, is the real problem of sociology considered as an applied science.[62]

---

61. *Dynamic Sociology*, I, 137.
62. Ward, *Dynamic Sociology*, I, 706.

Although Ward was not romantic, he was a neo-Enlightenment environmentalist who believed that progress was possible and that through science and universal public education an enlightened humanity could collectively chart its own future destiny. He saw his own position as a logical step forward from humanitarianism.

But from humanitarianism it is but one more step in the same direction to *meliorism*, which may be defined as humanitarianism *minus* all sentiment. Now, meliorism instead of an ethical, is a dynamic principle. It implies the improvement of the social condition through cold calculation, through the adoption of indirect means. It is not content merely to alleviate present suffering, it aims to create conditions under which no suffering can exist.[63]

To create these conditions, government would have to increase its positive, indirect, progressive legislation. Much of this indirect legislation would be educative as the planned scientific society emerged. As scientific psychology and sociology made available to government and public education more accurate knowledge upon which human behavior could be predicted, nineteenth-century individualism would be gradually surrendered for a greater collective freedom. Government, in this context, would be "transformed into a central academy of social science." Legislators as social scientists would then pass legislation not on the merits of rhetorical debate or pressure group interests but on the basis of anticipated social consequences, determined through carefully planned social experimentation. Thus men could collectively progress toward their true goal of "happiness."[64]

What safeguard did Ward suggest against the possibility that government would become just a more effective scientific tyranny? Unlike Comte, who advocated a scientific "priesthood," Ward, like Jefferson, advocated a greater universal diffusion of knowledge. Indeed, Ward assumed that an enlightened humanity would make government its servant rather than its master. Throughout Ward's thesis is a solid conviction that the common man can be educated not only to recognize tyranny but to prevent it.

Holding social views very similar to Sumner's, Edward L. Thorndike attacked Ward's sociocracy as a form of "intellectual communism."[65] Ward's sociocracy was not communism or socialism, however, but rather a democratic, scientifically planned society progressing teleologically. Indeed, Ward "criticized the socialists as excessively doctrinaire, seeking to solve all problems through government ownership. Sociocracy

---

63. Ward, *Dynamic Sociology*, II, 468.

64. Ward, *Dynamic Sociology*, II, 307.

65. See Edward L. Thorndike, "A Sociologist's Theory of Education," *Bookman*, V, 24 (1906-1907), 290-294. See also *Science* N.S. 24:299-301, September 1906. It is interesting that John Dewey criticized Ward mainly because of the faculty psychology he used; see *Psychological Review*, I (1894), 400-411. While Thorndike attacked his environmentalism, Thorndike's social views were very similar to Sumner's ideas; see Curti, *Social Ideas of American Educators*, Chapter 14.

would study each social problem with scientific objectivity and adopt whatever policies proved appropriate."[66]

Fundamental to Ward's social reconstruction views was a faith in the power of education to make a difference. Although Ward recognized the importance of the emotions and believed that intellect had evolved from the emotional, he believed that the intellect made it possible for man to achieve his desires. Mankind was governed by ideas. "Instill progressive principles, no matter how, into the mind, and progressive action will result."[67] However influenced by the ideas of Claude Adrien Helvétius, Ward's environmentalism did not extend to complete equality. Men's talents and intellect would differ; but the differences, he suspected, would not be so great as the inequities of society have led one to believe. Human nature was a physiological product of evolution. The child is born neither good nor bad but receptive to educative change. Unlike Sumner, who would consign the drunkard to the gutter to suffer the natural consequences of his vice, Ward was chiefly concerned with the kind of education and social conditions which made him a drunkard in the first place. Crime, Ward surmised, was a product of a corrupt education. "The inmates of our prisons are but the victims of untoward circumstances. The murderer has but acted out his education. Would you change his conduct, change his education."[68] The primary function of education is not so much to pass on the intellectual heritage of the past as to improve society.

The object of education is social improvement. Education is really needed for the purpose of making better citizens. This is practically the same thing as the higher end, social progress, which we saw to be the condition to increase human happiness. If education can not accomplish this end, it is worth nothing.[69]

Ward might have gone on to say that if education could not accomplish this end, his entire thesis was also worth nothing. His "great panacea" was based on the assumption that a free, universal, public system of education is the key instrument through which society can reform itself and progress teleologically.

In comparison to Sumner's, Ward's work has remained relatively obscure. The tragedy of Ward is that while he was ahead of his general culture, he was also out of step with the direction sociology was taking at the turn of the century. When George E. Vincent reviewed Ward's *Outlines of Sociology* in 1898 and called him the "dean of American sociologists," he qualified this praise: "His work must have a permanent value, in spite of the trend away from the interpretation of society as a whole. . . ."[70] By 1906, when Ward was elected the first president of the American Sociological Society, he was viewed by the younger gener-

66. Blake, *History of American Life and Thought,* p. 402.
67. Ward, *Dynamic Sociology,* II, 547.
68. Ward, *Dynamic Sociology,* II, 241.
69. Ward, *Dynamic Sociology,* II, 589.
70. Quoted in Burnham, *Lester Frank Ward in American Thought,* p. 9.

ation of sociologists as the grand old man of sociology, to whom one might pay his respects, but not as a person to turn to for guidance in the newer inductive approach to the field.[71] While many younger sociologists were taking a narrower, more inductive approach to their field, Ward continued to expound his grandiose theses, which changed very little between 1883 and 1913.

Ward was a part of that nineteenth-century search for the law of progress, using a cosmic view of history to integrate all knowledge within a rational whole. Ward reconstructed much of the American Enlightenment values which stressed rationality, science, progress, and education; he did this by intellectually making a place for man as the controller of social evolution rather than its victim. His cosmic view of history described the past, explained the present, and made man's future subject to human determination. Unlike those who saw man as a pawn of cosmic forces, such as Hegel and Harris with their conservative transcendental ideal, Marx with his radical materialistic ideal, Comte with the positive law, and Spencer with his evolutionary determinism, Ward saw man as potentially the master of his own cultural destiny. Although out of step with many sociologists, he lived to see the general culture catch up with many of his major ideas. As one reviewer of *Applied Sociology* put it in 1906: "Scientific legislation along the lines proposed by Ward . . . was not as unrealistic as in the America of 1883."[72] The Progressive era of social and educational reform had dawned. Indeed, most of the reform eras of the twentieth century—Progressive, New Deal, New Frontier, and Great Society—echoed in one form or another Ward's assumptions about the good society.[73]

The recognition that Ward did receive from the field of sociology was largely due to the efforts of Albion W. Small, founder of the first department of sociology on a university campus (University of Chicago, 1893). It was Small who popularized Ward's *Dynamic Sociology* among leading sociologists.[74] Although Small in his later years was highly critical of Ward's grandiose, unscientific assertions, he was deeply indebted to Ward for his social reconstructionist views.[75] Lester Frank Ward was the intellectual precursor of social reconstructionism in twentieth-century American education. When Small addressed the National Education Association in Buffalo in 1896 and challenged the teachers to use their leverage to reform society,[76] he reflected the War-

---

71. See Burnham, *Lester Frank Ward in American Thought.*

72. Quoted in Burnham, *Lester Frank Ward in American Thought,* p. 19.

73. For example, a familiar Wardian theme is clearly evident in the following excerpt: "The education of our people is the most basic resource of our society. Education equips man to think rationally and creatively in his quest for knowledge, for beauty, and for the full life; it provides the basis for effective political democracy; and it is the most important force behind economic growth, by advancing technology and raising the productivity of workers." *The Annual Report of the Council of Economic Advisors, Economic Report of the President,* transmitted to Congress in January 1965, p. 156.

74. See Burnham, *Lester Frank Ward in American Thought.*

75. In 1913, Small said, "I have often said, and it remains my estimate, that everything considered, I would rather have written *Dynamic Sociology* than any other book that has ever appeared in America." *American Journal of Sociology,* XIX (1913-1914), 77.

76. See *N.E.A. Addresses and Proceedings, 1896,* p. 77.

dian thesis. When George S. Counts, a student of Albion Small, shook the complacency of the Progressive Education Association in 1932 with his address "Dare Progressive Education Be Progressive?," and in the same year published *Dare the Schools Build a New Social Order?*, American society once again was confronted with a Wardian challenge. Social reconstructionism in American education has remained a viable, consistent tradition represented by Small at the beginning of the twentieth century, Counts in the thirties, and Theodore Brameld at mid-century, all reflecting Ward's view of the function of education.[77]

American society, however, has tended to be somewhat ambivalent to both Ward's and Sumner's views of the good society. In facing its major social problems in the twentieth century, American society has more often practiced a Wardian meliorism and verbalized a Sumnerian individualism, whereas American education has more often practiced a Sumnerian individualism and verbalized a Wardian social meliorism. Perhaps Perry Miller was correct when he said: "The nation has yet to decide for one against the other, a fact which may cause us to suspect that the debate will continue. Consequently, there is good reason why students should give careful scrutiny to these two opposing interpreters of the American spirit."[78]

By the end of the nineteenth century, most intellectuals in Europe pointed to the end of the Enlightenment as well as the end of ideology, and with it the fruitless search for the law of progress. While some could find solace in a return to the old Greek cyclical theories of history expounded by Spengler and Toynbee, others found that a nihilistic or an existentialist rejection of the past made more sense. In striking contrast to the European intellectuals' profound sense of despair at the turn of the century, many American intellectuals were in the midst of a neo-Enlightenment reconstruction of social philosophy which emphasized not pessimism but guarded optimism; not contemplation of irrational wellsprings but means of social action. In many respects, Ward reflected that reconstruction of enlightened values in American culture, while Edward Bellamy projected the enlightened aspirations of that culture.

At the beginning of the century it was Saint-Simon who spoke for the sons of the European Enlightenment when he said, "The golden age is not behind us, but in front of us. It is the perfection of social order. Our fathers have not seen it; our children will arrive there one day, and it is for us to clear the way for them." At the end of that century it was Edward Bellamy who spoke for the sons of the American Enlightenment when he said, "The Golden Age lies before us and not behind us, and is not far away. Our children will surely see it, and we, too, who are already men and women, if we deserve it by our faith and by our works."

---

77. We will return to a more critical analysis of social reconstructionism in Chapter Nine.

78. Miller, *American Thought*, p. xxx.

SUGGESTED READINGS

Beck, Lewis White, ed. *Kant on History.* Indianapolis: The Bobbs-Merrill Company, Inc., 1963.

Burnham, John C. *Lester Frank Ward in American Thought.* Washington, D.C., Annals of American Sociology Public Affairs Press, 1956.

Cargill, Oscar. *Intellectual America: Ideas on the March.* New York, The Macmillan Company, 1947.

Cohen, Morris R. *The Meaning of Human History,* 2nd ed. La Salle, Ill., The Open Court Publishing Company, 1961.

Comte, Auguste. *The Positive Philosophy of Auguste Comte,* Vol. II. London, John Edward Taylor, Little Queen Street, Lincoln's Inn Fields (undated).

Curti, Merle. *The Social Ideas of American Educators,* rev. ed. Paterson, N.J., Littlefield, Adams and Company, 1960.

Darwin, Charles. *The Origin of Species and The Descent of Man.* New York, The Modern Library, 1936.

Gabriel, Ralph Henry. *The Course of American Democratic Thought,* 2nd ed. New York, The Ronald Press Company, 1956.

Hartman, Robert S. *Hegel's Reason in History.* New York, Liberal Arts Press, 1953.

Hofstadter, Richard. *The Age of Reform.* New York, Alfred A. Knopf, Inc., 1955.

———. *Social Darwinism in American Thought,* rev. ed. New York, George Braziller, Inc., 1959.

Hook, Sidney. *From Hegel to Marx.* New York, Humanities Press, Inc., 1950.

Keller, Albert G., and Maurice R. Davie, eds. *Essays of William Graham Sumner,* 2 vols. New Haven, Yale University Press, 1934.

Leidecker, Kurt F. *Yankee Teacher: The Life of William Torrey Harris.* New York, The Philosophical Library, 1946.

Miller, Perry, ed. *American Thought: Civil War to World War I.* New York, Rinehart and Company, Inc., 1954.

Mosse, George L. *The Culture of Western Europe.* Chicago, Rand McNally & Company, 1961.

Pochmann, Henry A. *New England Transcendentalism and St. Louis Hegelianism.* Philadelphia, Carl Schurz Memorial Foundation, 1948.

Spencer, Herbert. *Essays on Education.* London, J. M. Dent and Sons, Ltd., 1949.

Starr, Harris E. *William Graham Sumner.* New York, Henry Holt and Company, 1925.

Stearns, Raymond Phineas, ed. *Pageant of Europe.* New York, Harcourt, Brace & Company, 1947.

Sumner, William Graham. *Folkways.* Boston, Ginn and Company, 1940.

Ward, Lester Frank. *Dynamic Sociology,* 2 vols. New York, D. Appleton and Company, 1883.

White, Morton, ed. *Age of Analysis: Twentieth-Century Philosophers.* New York, Mentor Books, 1959.

———. *Social Thought in America.* Boston, The Beacon Press, 1964.

Williams, William Appleman. *The Great Evasion.* Chicago, Quadrangle Books, Inc., 1964.

CHAPTER 6
Pragmatic conceptions
of man and society

*There remains the final reflection, how shallow, puny, and
imperfect are efforts to sound the depths in the nature of things.
In philosophical discussion, the merest hint of dogmatic certainty as to finality of statement is an exhibition of folly.[1]*
ALFRED NORTH WHITEHEAD

What began in the closing decades of eighteenth-century European
thought as an optimistic search for the law of progress culminated, at
the end of the nineteenth century, in a debilitating sense of despair.
After a century of intense intellectual conflict, few Enlightenment "self-
evident truths" remained self-evident. When Friedrich Nietzsche, in
the name of sincerity, rejected appearances and issued his anguished
cry—"God is dead. God remains dead. And we have killed him"—he
was reflecting not only on the supernaturalist's God but also on the
many gods implicit in Enlightenment ideology. The gods of reason,
nature, science, and progress could not be relied on to offer a way out
of the human predicament. Going beyond good and evil, and therefore
beyond tragedy, Nietzsche called for a transvaluation of values, stripped
clean of Enlightenment presuppositions. His work reflected the disillusionment and alienation of many European intellectuals at the end
of the century and, for many, Nietzsche symbolized a profound turning
point in Western thought.

Within this *Zeitgeist* of despair stood an alienated intellectual elite,
a frustrated proletariat interested in revolution, and an unauthentic
bourgeoisie, unsure of its own existence. Through these classes may have

1. Alfred North Whitehead, *Process and Reality* (New York: The Macmillan Company,
1929), p. x.

surged an *élan vital,* but it was an impulse which only confirmed a deeper disillusionment with reason, science, and spiritual values. In search of a rationally demonstrated certainty, the European became conscious of the uncertain and the irrational. Indeed, the rational was increasingly used to confirm the irrational as men searched behind the facade of bourgeois values for the meaning of existence. Nietzsche breathed life into a Machiavellian superman as he found only the lust for power at the center of his universe; ideology was rejected in the name of sincerity as Ernst Jünger placed his faith in a charismatic leader; and Vilfredo Pareto, in the name of scientific sociology, found the real mainspring for action in the "residues" of irrational behavior. Freud was not alone in his concern for the irrational. Probing the depth of their own ids, men like André Gide and Marcel Proust discovered no more than a lust for life in the murky waters of the irrational. What remained of the Enlightenment faith in reason, whether expressed in a Comtean positivism or a Spencerian science, was declared bankrupt by Ferdinand Brunetière; and what was left of Condorcet's faith in progress was declared dead by Georges Sorel in his *Reflections on Violence* (1908). Paul Valéry expressed the temper of the times when he said:

We do not know what will be born, and we fear the future, not without reason, we hope vaguely, we dread precisely; our fears are infinitely more precise than our hopes; we confess that the charm of life is behind us, but doubt and disorder are in us and with us.[2]

Within this tempest of fear, uncertainty, and insecurity, nihilism and existentialism evolved as two formidable literary-philosophic views on life. The difference between nihilism and existentialism is more in degree than in kind of rationality. The nihilist's world is so much in flux that it is basically inscrutable, while the existentialist's world, although absurd, is still comprehensible.[3] Both views, however, put great stress on the existence of man as part of the flux; the impotence of reason; the alienation of man from God, nature, society, and self; the fear and trembling in the face of nothingness; the death of ideology; and the assertion of man's subjective freedom to act in the face of the absurd. To a great extent, these movements represent a protest against the mechanization of man in a bureaucratic and technological society and at the same time reflect a keen sensitivity to the ethical malaise implicit in the process of a cultural transvaluation. Those who could not tolerate the ambiguity of such transvaluations often returned to past cultural traditions and attempted to resurrect older values. Thus men searched their ancient, medieval, and Renaissance past to develop such philosophies of certainty as neoclassicism, neo-Thomism, and neohumanism.

---

2. Hans Kohn, *Making of the Modern French Mind* (New York: D. Van Nostrand Co., 1955), p. 79.

3. A comparison of Kafka's *The Trial* and Camus' *The Stranger* reflects the difference between a nihilist and an existentialist view of reality. In *The Trial,* the protagonist never knows why he is being tried and ultimately punished; in *The Stranger,* the protagonist knows, in fact, the nature of the crime but then is convicted for the wrong reasons. The difference, here, is in the degree of rational comprehension of one's world.

While Darwin, Freud, Nietzsche, and others had given men good reason to question their Enlightenment conception of man and society, mathematicians and physicists proceeded to further destroy that block-type Newtonian view of the universe from which so many social ideas had evolved through analogous thinking. From the late Renaissance to the present, physical scientists have had a profound effect in subtly shaping Western social philosophies. The effective end of the Enlightenment came not with the tortured mind of Nietzsche but with the thought of Albert Einstein who suggested in 1916 that "neither time nor space had any determinable reality"; of Max Planck whose "quantum theory (1910) went far toward destroying Newton's world machine"; or of Werner Heisenberg who "proved by 1927 that small particles did not conform to the cause and effect sequence."[4] As Mosse put it:

The Newtonian universe of the seventeenth century had led to ideologies based upon it in the eighteenth and nineteenth centuries. It was difficult, if not impossible, to build a consistent ideology upon the new scientific developments. . . . For Newton, science had been a philosophy of life, a consistent world view; modern scientists not only destroyed his concept of the universe but also his linkage of ideology and science.[5]

The block-type universe with all its absolutes, within which so many nineteenth-century cosmic histories ended against a wall of determinism, was in the twentieth century effectively destroyed for most intellectuals. Comte's age of science had indeed dawned, but with it came not the certainty of positivism but the uncertainty of chance. Twentieth-century man, whether European or American, found himself in the midst of the most fundamental reconstruction in philosophy since the seventeenth century. The course America took in this reconstruction was unique.

PRAGMATISM: A NATIVE AMERICAN PHILOSOPHY

In striking contrast to the European profound sense of despair at the turn of the century, Americans generally looked to the future with a high degree of optimism, unshaken in their humanitarian faith in the possibility of progress and its principal corollary, social meliorism. American culture, in fact, was giving birth to a neo-Enlightenment world view. In the vanguard of this movement, attempting to pick up the shattered ideology of pre-Darwinian Enlightenment thinkers and to reconstruct their ideas in an open-ended universe, were such men as Charles Sanders Peirce, William James, and John Dewey. Such a reconstruction of philosophy emphasized not pessimism but guarded optimism; not contemplation of irrational wellsprings but means of intelligent social action.

Under the leadership of Peirce, James, and Dewey, pragmatism evolved as an explicitly native American philosophy. This philosophy,

---

4. George L. Mosse, *The Culture of Western Europe* (Chicago: Rand McNally & Company, 1961), pp. 285-286.
5. Mosse, *Culture of Western Europe,* pp. 286-287.

while rooted in those values which were implicit in the functioning behavior of American society, incorporated that society's reaction to European cosmic histories emerging from German idealism, French positivism, and English evolutionary thought. What evolved, however, was neither German, French, nor English, but a native American philosophy. As Mortimer Adler put it, "Dewey's philosophy, along with that of James, can be regarded as the most indigenous to this soil, the most original and originally American of all the philosophies we have produced."[6] Such a philosophy inevitably reflected the practical temper of American society. No doubt it was that temper which inclined Americans more toward hope than despair. A society which generally placed little faith in abstract metaphysical realities[7] could be expected to suffer little anguish over an increasing awareness that metaphysics might be only an intellectual rationalization for one's own peace of mind. Whatever the case, however, pragmatism in America—with its rejection of metaphysical absolutes, utopias, and ultimate truths, its stress on the possible in an evolving pluralistic society, and its application of rational intelligence to the process of social amelioration—tended to be the intellectual bridge across which many Americans passed from a closed Newtonian universe to a twentieth-century open-ended world view. In this sense, pragmatism was a transitional philosophy which reflected both the practical temper of American culture and a reaction to some of the main currents of both European and American thought.

While it is customary to consider Peirce, James, and Dewey as the founders of pragmatism and to treat pragmatism as a unified school of thought, close scrutiny of the personalities, life experience, and thought of each man reveals enough differences to dispel that idea. Peirce introduced the term *pragmatism* into American philosophic thought, and James popularized it; they disagreed vigorously, however, as to the meaning of the term. There is, indeed, serious doubt as to whether or not James ever really fully understood what his lifelong friend meant by "pragmatism." Ralph Barton Perry put it well when he said, "Perhaps it would be correct, and just to all parties, to say that the modern movement known as pragmatism is largely the result of James's misunderstanding of Peirce."[8]

This misunderstanding became most obvious when James introduced the term *pragmatism* to popular audiences in a series of lectures at the University of California in 1898 and ascribed its authorship to Charles Sanders Peirce.[9] James had so distorted the meaning of his idea that Peirce gave up the word and from then on called his philosophy *pragmaticism,* which he said "is ugly enough to be safe from kidnappers." This, however, was no minor play on words; behind it lies a very basic difference between James and Peirce. Peirce said, "Although James calls

6. Mortimer Adler, "S. F.'s Mortimer Adler Traces Our Philosophical Heritage," *Oakland Tribune,* Oakland, Calif., Jan. 27, 1957, p. 8B.

7. See Alexis de Tocqueville, *Democracy in America* (New York: Mentor Books, 1946).

8. Ralph Barton Perry, *The Thought and Character of William James* (Cambridge, Mass.: Harvard University Press, 1948), p. 281.

9. These lectures were later published with refinements; see William James, *Pragmatism* (New York: Longmans, Green and Company, 1907).

himself a pragmatist, and no doubt he derived his ideas on the subject from me, yet there is a most essential difference between his pragmatism and mine."[10] What, then, was the difference?

James asserted that pragmatism meant that

... the effective meaning of any philosophic proposition can always be brought down to some particular consequence, in our future practical experience, whether active or passive; the point lying rather in the fact that the experience must be particular, than in the fact that it must be active.[11]

In further popularizing the idea, James referred to the pragmatic method as a means of determining the "cash value in terms of particular experience." James seemed to merge pragmatism with that conventional wisdom of the average American, who when approaching abstract problems usually asks, "What difference does it make?" If no conceivable difference results in the acting out of the idea in dispute, then there is no point in further debate. The problem, however, is not that easily settled. There remains the question as to what kinds of differences one accepts as valid. To James, the difference would be found in "what sensations we are to expect from it, and what reactions we must prepare."[12] Because these sensations would, for James, always be particular, he further asserted that pragmatism "agrees with nominalism, for instance, in always appealing to particulars."[13] On these subtle but crucial points, James and Peirce were in serious disagreement. To Peirce,

In the first place, the meaning of a concept is construed in terms of conduct, and not in terms of sensation; and, in the second place, it is construed in terms of generality and not in terms of particularity. . . . For Peirce the good lies in coherence, order, coalescence, unity; for James in the individuality, variety, and satisfaction of concrete interests.[14]

There is, here, more than just the usual difference between the mind of a logician and that of a psychologist. To Peirce, the pragmatic method was a way of clarifying the meaning of ideas in the process of discovering general truths. To James, however, the pragmatic method was directed toward the immediate sensations of a particular experience and the discovery of personal truths. Peirce was more a realist[15] seeking general principles, whereas James was more a nominalist, resting his case ultimately on individual perceptions. James' radical empiricism had at its base a subjective character which neither Peirce nor Dewey would allow in his own thought. Both Peirce and Dewey were more concerned with public knowledge than James. Dewey said:

10. Quoted in Perry, *Thought and Character of William James,* p. 281.
11. Quoted in Perry, *Thought and Character of William James,* p. 280.
12. Gail Kennedy, ed., *Pragmatism and American Culture* (Boston: D. C. Heath and Company, 1950), p. 13.
13. Kennedy, *Pragmatism and American Culture,* p. 15.
14. Perry, *Thought and Character of William James,* pp. 281-282.
15. For the realism of Peirce, see James Feibleman, *An Introduction to Peirce's Philosophy Interpreted as a System* (London: George Allen & Unwin, 1960). See also John F. Boler, *Charles Peirce and Scholastic Realism* (Seattle: University of Washington Press, 1963).

In the literal sense of the word pragmatist, therefore, Peirce is more of a pragmatist than James. He is also less of a nominalist. That is to say, he emphasizes much less the *particular* sensible consequences, and much more the habit, the generic attitude of response, set up in consequence of experience with a thing.[16]

The *pragmaticism* of Peirce, the *radical empiricism* of James, and the *instrumentalism* of Dewey reflected considerable differences, some of which, no doubt, are attributable to the fact that one man was a logician, another a psychologist, and the other a social philosopher. Peirce's thought tended to be rationalistic, while James tended to combine the intuitive with the empirical, and Dewey's thought tended to be empirical within a modified Hegelianism. Their life experiences, their personal temperaments, their ideas, and their impacts on American educational thought, are different enough to warrant separate consideration. But these men had major areas of agreement. As pragmatists, all would agree that the meaning of an idea is to be found in both the passive and the active conceivable consequences of that idea put to the test through action. Beyond the pragmatic method, all agreed that the universe was open-ended, involving a large area of chance and novelty, that absolutes were dead, and that life was a process of evolutionary change. They further agreed that the application of science to this evolutionary process was vital, that human nature was largely plastic, and that the good society was the open, pluralistic society which maximized human freedom. Keeping these broad areas of consensus in mind, we will stress the unique characteristics of each and their respective contributions to twentieth-century American thought.

THE PRAGMATICISM OF CHARLES S. PEIRCE

A decade before Spencer made his triumphant visit to America, a group of young men, mutually concerned with the vital philosophic issues of the day, gathered at "Old Cambridge" and formed a discussion group which they "half-ironically" and "half-defiantly" called "The Metaphysical Club."[17] Sometimes, meeting in the study of Charles S. Peirce and at other times in the study of William James, such young men as Chauncey Wright, Oliver Wendell Holmes, John Fiske, and others gathered to discuss the burning issues implicit in the idealism of Kant and Hegel, the utilitarianism of Bentham and Mill, the positivism of Comte, and the evolutionary theories of Darwin and Spencer. All the leaders of this discussion group achieved distinction within their lifetime except one, Charles S. Peirce, who died in relative obscurity. It took another generation to resurrect and publish his works[18] and

---

16. John Dewey, "The Pragmatism of Peirce," supplementary essay in Charles S. Peirce, *Chance, Love and Logic,* ed. Morris R. Cohen (New York: George Braziller, Inc., 1956), p. 307.

17. For Peirce's description of this group, see *The Collected Papers of C. S. Peirce,* ed. C. Hartshorne and P. Weiss (Cambridge, Mass.: Harvard University Press, 1931-1935).

18. The beginning of this major effort was *The Collected Papers of C. S. Peirce.* Although, between 1935 and the present, there has been considerable work done on various aspects of his thought, a definitive biography of Peirce remains undone.

recognize that the recluse who died in 1914 in abject poverty on his farm at Milford, Pennsylvania, was perhaps the most brilliant philosopher America had produced.

Charles S. Peirce was the son of Benjamin Peirce, a leading Harvard mathematician who devoted much time and effort to giving his son an excellent education. Although Charles Peirce was reared and educated by and for an academic life, graduating *summa cum laude* from the Lawrence Scientific School, he was refused a place in the academic community except for a five-year instructorship at Johns Hopkins (1879-1884). Peirce's inability to conform to the established social conventions of the academic world militated against his ever gaining a position at an American university. Concerned about his friend's future, James said in 1869:

The poor cuss sees no chance of getting a professorship anywhere, and is likely to go into the Observatory for good. It seems a great pity that as original a man as he is, who is willing and able to devote the powers of his life to logic and metaphysics, should be starved out of a career, when there are lots of professorships of the sort to be given in the country to 'safe' orthodox men.[19]

James' concern for Peirce's welfare continued throughout his life. Twenty-six years later, James all but begged President Eliot to hire Peirce, but again to no avail.[20] Rejected by Eliot, James organized a series of lectures that Peirce eventually gave as a visiting lecturer. Toward the end of his life, James collected a sum of money from old friends to help Peirce keep the creditors from his door.

For the most part, Peirce found that the only employment opportunities open to him were those which were basically extraneous to his major talents and interests. He worked for the United States Coast Survey for much of his life and in later years did hack work for the *Century Dictionary, Nation,* and the *North American Review.* Nevertheless, Peirce persevered in his work in logic, metaphysics, and mathematics, increasingly at the expense of earning a living.

From 1900 to his death in 1914 from a cancer that afflicted him for two years Peirce lived with his French wife in extreme poverty; there was no money even for a decent burial. His widow sold all his manuscripts to Harvard University for $500.[21]

James never seemed to lose faith in the genius of his lifelong friend, and with prophetic accuracy he wrote to Peirce in 1903: "As things stand, it is only highly skilled technicians and professionals who will sniff the rare perfume of your thought, and *after you are dead,* trace

---

19. Quoted in Feibleman, *Introduction to Peirce's Philosophy*, p. 16.
20. See William James' letter to President Eliot, March 3, 1895, in Perry, *Thought and Character of William James*, p. 283.
21. Philip P. Wiener, ed., *Values in a Universe of Chance: Selected Writings of Charles S. Peirce* (Stanford: Stanford University Press, 1958), p. xvii.

things back to your genius."[22] Cut off from the academic community, financially embarrassed, and growing increasingly cantankerous with age, Peirce found himself with fewer and fewer friends. His inability to get along with others eventually forced him into a life of isolation. That this was not what he desired was evident:

. . . when, in 1887, he inherited some money it was used to buy a large plot of ground and to build a house, with an attic that was to be spacious enough to contain his many disciples. The house itself, of ambitious size, was never completed because of shortage of funds, and the attic designed to accommodate the many disciples was, symbolically enough, never finished. The Peirces occupied the house, but the attic only became a place in which to hide from creditors.[23]

Without many friends or disciples, feeling acutely the loneliness of alienation, Peirce would comment in his letters to James, "I have nobody to talk to."

Increasingly, James became Peirce's chief, if not sole, interlocutor as well as benefactor. In spite of Peirce's cryptic attacks on James' nominalistic leanings, the relationship between the two men remained warm and friendly. The two were, however, temperamentally and intellectually poles apart. James excelled in human relations, emphasized individualism, and would not allow his freedom to be fettered by logic, mathematics, or science; Peirce, on the other hand, often failed in his social relationships, opposed individualism, argued for means of developing universal scientific consensus, and excelled in the development of an impersonal symbolic logic. In a way, it is ironic that in real life Peirce, so much the individualist, should argue for the grounds of social consensus, and James, the greater conformist, should argue for such a strong individualism. No doubt each man saw in the other something he himself lacked. James was personally warm and intuitive, while Peirce was impersonal, cold, and analytic. Peirce probably put it best when he said, "Your mind and mine are as little adapted to understanding one another as two minds could be, and therefore I always feel that I have more to learn from you than from anybody."[24]

Although each learned something from the other, they expressed decidedly different views of pragmatism and the nature of truth. In a universe of "chance," Peirce was trying to synthesize the rationalism inherent in logic and mathematics with an objective empiricism, whereas James struggled to combine the subjectivism inherent in his own individualism with objective empiricism. In the end, they espoused vastly different grounds for truth. When James, with typical rhetorical flourishes, said "Truth is what works" and "The true is the expedient," he opened pragmatism to the charge of being a philosophy of expediency. By further emphasizing changing truths without placing equal emphasis on a method of inquiry which could allow rational public verification,

---

22. Quoted in Perry, *Thought and Character of William James*, p. 287.
23. Feibleman, *Introduction to Peirce's Philosophy*, p. 22.
24. Perry, *Thought and Character of William James*, p. 288.

he also exposed pragmatism to a charge of being anti-intellectual. In spite of these problems, James not only defined pragmatism in terms of *particular* consequences but ultimately verified truth on the basis of the individual's will to believe. James said, "A new opinion counts as 'true' just in proportion as it gratifies the individual's desire to assimilate the novel in his experience to his beliefs in stock."[25] Clearly, James' radical empiricism has at its center a subjectivism rooted in the phenomenological experience of the individual.

Peirce, in contrast, dedicated himself to the development of a method of inquiry which could be used to publicly verify general truths. "The opinion which is fated to be ultimately agreed to by all *who investigate,* is what we mean by the truth, and the object represented in this opinion is the real."[26] Peirce firmly believed that

There are real things, whose characters are entirely independent of our opinions about them; whose realities affect our senses according to regular laws, and, though our sensations are as different as our relations to the objects, yet, by taking advantage of the laws of perception, we can ascertain by reasoning how things really are, and any man, if he have sufficient experience and reason enough about it, will be led to the *one true conclusion.*[27]

To be sure, James also believed that "there are real things, whose characters are entirely independent of our opinions about them," but James' phenomenalism, which emphasized the individual's unique perceptions, led not to *one* but to *many* true conclusions. Peirce, as a logician, "sought the meaning of a proposition in its logical and experimentally testable consequences." James, as a psychologist, "looked for more immediately felt sensations or personal reactions."[28] In direct response to James' phenomenalism, Peirce said:

Pragmaticism does not intend to define the phenomenal equivalents of words and general ideas, but, on the contrary, eliminates their sential element, and endeavors to define the rational purport, and this it finds in the purposive bearing of the word or proposition in question.[29]

In response to those who argued that pragmaticism was an anti-intellectual philosophy which emphasized action at the expense of thought, Peirce said:

. . . if pragmaticism really made Doing to be the Be-all and the End-all of life, that would be its death. For to say that we live for the mere sake of action, as action, regardless of the thought it carries out, would be to say that there is no such thing as rational purport.[30]

---

25. Kennedy, *Pragmatism and American Culture,* p. 18.
26. Peirce, *Chance, Love and Logic,* p. 306.
27. Peirce, *Chance, Love and Logic,* p. 26. Italics mine.
28. Wiener, *Values in a Universe of Chance,* p. 181.
29. Wiener, *Values in a Universe of Chance,* p. 196.
30. Wiener, *Values in a Universe of Chance,* p. 196.

Although Peirce believed in a universe of chance, for him all was not flux; he also believed in universals and such a thing as rational purport. His lifework was an intensive attempt to join the laws of logic and mathematics with objective empiricism in a changing universe. Though it was still incomplete at his death, Peirce had been attempting to develop a functional metaphysics of change applicable to philosophical and empirical science. Well versed in the thought of most major Western philosophic thinkers of the eighteenth and nineteenth centuries, Peirce reached back to Duns Scotus to reopen the scholastic question of realism versus nominalism and to evolve his own unique form of realism.[31] To Peirce, science was at home with realism and fundamentally at odds with nominalism. The scientist seeks universal laws and cannot be satisfied by the unique character of particulars. Peirce's realism was in direct opposition to James' nominalistic leanings. From the vantage point of his own realism, Peirce attacked the nominalism of Mill and then went on to attack Spencer's notions of science and his mechanized conception of the universe, Darwin's law of survival of the fittest,[32] and Hegel's absolute,[33] long before it was popular to do so. Part of Peirce's misfortune was that many of his ideas were so far ahead of his time that he inevitably attacked many idols of nineteenth-century thought while they were still being worshiped.

Peirce did basic work on the validity of probability theory and laid the groundwork for the beginning of symbolic or mathematical logic, a contribution for which Bertrand Russell expressed his indebtedness.[34] "As early as 1867, in a paper 'Upon the Logic of Mathematics', he [Peirce] had clearly anticipated some of the notions that were embodied later in Whitehead's and Russell's *Principia Mathematica*."[35] There is, indeed, greater similarity between the thought of Peirce and that of Whitehead than there is between either Peirce and James or Peirce and Dewey. Although there is some doubt to what extent Whitehead was familiar with Peirce's work, since he makes no reference to Peirce in his major books,[36] it seems probable that Whitehead arrived at Peirce's philosophic position independently. Both men were mathematicians, both were acutely conscious of the same currents of nineteenth- and twentieth-century thought, and both were concerned with similar problems. Nevertheless, even given these common conditions, the similarity in ideas between the two men is astonishing. Many of the ideas that Alfred North Whitehead expressed in *Process and Reality* can be successfully matched point for point with various writings of Peirce.[37] Indeed, Peirce had cut a path which Whitehead later duplicated.

---

31. See Boler, *Charles Peirce and Scholastic Realism.*
32. Peirce, *Chance, Love and Logic,* p. 275.
33. Feibleman, *Introduction to Peirce's Philosophy,* p. 27.
34. See Feibleman, *Introduction to Peirce's Philosophy,* pp. xv-xvi, Foreword by Bertrand Russell.
35. Feibleman, *Introduction to Peirce's Philosophy,* p. 19.
36. See Feibleman, *Introduction to Peirce's Philosophy,* p. 459.
37. For a detailed comparison, see Feibleman, *Introduction to Peirce's Philosophy,* pp. 459-463.

In seeking to develop a fully articulated philosophic system based upon a rigorous logical and mathematical foundation, Peirce chose a road which only Whitehead has since followed. For both men understood that in an age of science, the right to believe cannot be won by ignoring science, still less by combatting science, but only by a path which 'lies through the thorniest mazes of a science as dry as mathematics.'[38]

Such was the path that Peirce took.

While the direct effect of Peirce's work on American educational practice was negligible, the indirect effect through Dewey and the symbolic logicians was more extensive. Dewey obtained his "Ph.D. in philosophy at Johns Hopkins while Peirce was teaching logic. Dewey tells us that he did not appreciate Peirce's work in logic until twenty years later."[39] By the time Dewey had discarded much of his Hegelian idealism and was developing his own instrumentalism, he was better able to appreciate Peirce's work. In later years, Dewey increasingly turned to Peirce's work rather than to James' as a source of support for his own instrumentalism. Even though Peirce's work was more in the direction of the theorizing of Whitehead and Dewey's instrumentalism was more directed toward social philosophy and social action, Peirce's emphasis of publicly testable knowledge and his de-emphasis of subjective choice made his thought far more compatible with Dewey's instrumentalism than with James' radical empiricism.

THE RADICAL EMPIRICISM OF WILLIAM JAMES

In Peirce's later correspondence with James, Peirce repeatedly admonished James that "truth is public" and that the greatest sin a man of science could commit was to use his terms "without anxious care to use them with strict accuracy."[40] Peirce's unhappiness with James' "loose talk" reflects his lifelong desire to bring some sense of universal order out of the chaos of personal experience. This same source of contention between the two men also reflects James' unwillingness to fetter his soul with any form of determinism, whether that determinism originated at the hand of God, nature, or the man of science.

While Peirce's life struggle was with other men, James' struggle was with himself. As a young man of twenty-eight, in revolt against his father's Swedenborgian religion and in quest of a moral philosophy with which to live, James drank dry the cup of despair. Brooding over the nature of good and evil and man's destiny in a universe of apparent illusions, he touched bottom, almost losing his will to live. As he recorded in his diary, he reached a turning point on April 30, 1870.

---

38. Murray G. Murphey, *The Development of Peirce's Philosophy* (Cambridge, Mass.: Harvard University Press, 1961), p. 295.
39. Wiener, *Values in a Universe of Chance*, p. xvii.
40. Perry, *Thought and Character of William James*, p. 291.

I think that yesterday was a crisis in my life. I finished the first part of Renouvier's second *Essais* and see no reason why his definition of free will—'the sustaining of a thought *because* I *choose to* when I might have other thoughts'—need be the definition of an illusion. At any rate, I will assume for the present—until next year—that it is no illusion. My first act of free will shall be to believe in free will.[41]

The long, dark, lonely road back to mental health was lighted for James by the "will to believe." Although he experienced no religious conversion, he was, indeed, twice born. He was one of those nonreligious individuals in whom "the new man may also be born either gradually or suddenly."[42] James' rebirth was gradual; he struggled throughout his lifetime, with some success, to overcome his neurasthenia. However, James knew full well that the road back led not to the once-born, healthy-minded innocence of an Emerson but to a deeper understanding of the human condition. Having tasted the forbidden fruit, there is, in fact, no return to original innocence.

Reminiscent of Søren Kierkegaard's *Fear and Trembling* (1841), James in describing the twice-born perceived that:

When disillusionment has gone as far as this, there is seldom a *restitutio ad integrum.* One has tasted of the fruit of the tree and the happiness of Eden never comes again. The happiness that comes, when any does come—and often enough it fails to return in an acute form, though its form is sometimes very acute—is not the simple ignorance of ill, but something vastly more complex including natural evil as one of its elements, but finding natural evil no such stumbling block and terror because it now sees it swallowed up in supernatural good. The process is one of redemption, not of mere reversion to natural health, and the sufferer, when saved, is saved by what seems to him a second birth, a deeper kind of conscious being than he could enjoy before.[43]

Unlike Kierkegaard, who in facing the absurd found an all-powerful God, James found in the darkness a "More" from which one's subconscious could draw strength. However, James' "More" or God was finite, plural, as well as a source of man's power.[44] Neither the universe, man, nor God had a predetermined end. Central to all of James' thinking is the idea that there is in each individual a residuum of pure freedom to become that which at present he is not. Because of this, he revolted against Hegelianism, Spencerian evolution, Comtean positivism, and any other system, whether scientific or not, that presumed to predetermine men's future and eliminate their freedom.

Of the three leading pragmatists, James was perhaps the best trained in the sciences; yet he recognized better than the others the inherent

41. Quoted in Perry, *Thought and Character of William James*, p. 121.
42. William James, *The Varieties of Religious Experience: A Study in Human Nature* (New York: Collier Books, 1961), p. 150.
43. James, *Varieties of Religious Experience*, p. 135.
44. See Ralph Henry Gabriel, *The Course of American Democratic Thought*, 2nd ed. (New York: The Ronald Press Company, 1956), pp. 340-343.

limitations of science in resolving the problems of mankind. To James, the pragmatic method was a way of viewing the consequences of ideas in terms of the *individual's* experience. In this context, he could say, "If theological ideas prove to have value for concrete life, they will be true, for pragmatism, in the sense of being good for so much."[45] While others were slamming doors by way of the scientific test, James was bent on keeping them open. He insisted "that conjunctive and disjunctive relations are, when experienced, equally real."[46] In a letter to François Pillon, James defined his philosophy as follows:

My philosophy is what I call radical empiricism, a pluralism, a 'tychism,' which represents order as being gradually won and always in the making. It is theistic, but not *essentially* so. It rejects all doctrines of the Absolute. It is finitist; but it does not attribute to the question of the infinite the great methodological importance which you and Renouvier attribute to it. I fear that you may find my system too *bottomless* and romantic. I am sure that, be it in the end judged true or false, it is essential to the evolution of clearness in philosophic thought that someone should defend a pluralistic empiricism radically.[47]

The virtue of James' system was that it was unsystematic enough to accept many different experiences as real. His classic work, *Principles of Psychology* (1890), although behavioristic in orientation and centrally concerned with habit formation, also included a place for the stream of consciousness to which John B. Watson and other "scientific" psychologists reacted negatively. James literally accepted "disjunctive concepts" as real. Of the three pragmatists, only James, with a clear conscience, could say to Freud when he visited America in 1909, "The future of psychology belongs to your work."[48] Dewey and others noticed repeatedly that in James' psychological views of human nature there is as much room for a phenomenological approach to psychology as for a behaviorist one.

In his varied published works,[49] as well as his personal correspondence, James more than either Peirce or Dewey reflected existential themes. His own encounter with despair, his turning away from despair to act, his assertion of freedom, his own estrangement from nature, God, and unauthentic metaphysical systems, his appreciation of the limitations of reason in dealing with the depth of human experience, and his persistent view of man as "becoming" and therefore incapable of being objectively defined—all are personal factors which help account for the existential themes implicit in James' radical empiricism. His quest

---

45. Kennedy, ed., *Pragmatism and American Culture*, p. 21. John Dewey could not accept this use of pragmatism. For Dewey's view on religion, see *A Common Faith*. Interestingly, one would suspect that James could accept *A Common Faith* while Dewey could not accept James' conclusions in *Varieties of Religious Experience*.

46. Perry, *Thought and Character of William James*, p. 277.

47. Quoted in Perry, *Thought and Character of William James*, p. 275.

48. Ernest Jones, *The Life and Work of Sigmund Freud* (New York: Basic Books, Inc., 1953-1957), II, 57.

49. Such as "On a Certain Blindness in Human Beings," *The Will to Believe*, and *The Varieties of Religious Experience*.

for existential moral values was taken by Mussolini to justify a nihilistic view of power. It was one of those existential themes in James' thought, emphasizing action in the face of the impotence of reason, which Mussolini confused with his nihilism of value when he said:

The pragmatism of William James was of great use to me in my political career. James taught me that an action should be judged rather by its results than by its doctrinary basis. I learnt of James that faith in action, that ardent will to live and fight, to which Fascism owes a great part of its success. . . . For me the essential was to act.[50]

James and existentialism

In broad perspective, James was the link between two major nineteenth- and twentieth-century traditions that stood for individual freedom against the demands of organized society. By mid-nineteenth century, the transcendentalism of Emerson and Thoreau had turned men away from social meliorism and taught them that the most important knowledge was that of self-knowledge and "being"; in mid-twentieth century, such existential-self theorists as Rollo May, Gordon Allport, Abraham Maslow, and Carl Rogers turned away from social meliorism and centered their attention on the process of individual self-actualization. Both nineteenth- and twentieth-century traditions placed heavy emphasis on feeling, emotions, intuition, individual perception, on being true to one's self, and both implied a faith in human nature to overcome the damaging effects of organized society on human personality and freedom. Although both traditions had their European counterparts, both were drastically Americanized. In this Americanization process is a stream of optimism which lies close to the vital nerve of American culture. American transcendentalists, in the process of Americanizing German and English romanticism, never approached the melancholy spirit of a Goethe or a Carlyle, and modern American existentialists, in Americanizing German and French existentialism, have not approached the *Fear and Trembling* of Kierkegaard or the *Nausea* of Sartre. There is in this phenomenon the persistent tendency of the American to dwell more on the bright side and less on the dark side of the human condition.

Transcendentalism can be viewed theoretically as a reaction against the rationalism of the Enlightenment and practically as a reaction against the beginnings of the Industrial Revolution. Similarly, twentieth-century existentialism may be seen as a reaction against nineteenth- and twentieth-century scientific views of man as well as a protest against the depersonalization of man in an industrial mass culture. In spite of these similarities, which demonstrate the continuity of individualism in American thinking, there are some differences which cannot be ignored. Although American existential psychology and philosophy rejects a classical Freudian view of man, it does accept a depth-psychological perspective of man in a present-reality context along with an empirical

---

50. Quoted in Perry, *Thought and Character of William James*, p. 317.

methodology for verification of its principles. In contrast, transcendental-ism endorsed neither a depth-psychological view of man nor an empirical methodology for verification. William James, in this context, is logically the connecting link between the two traditions. Personally acquainted with Emerson, James could not accept either his monistic Oversoul or his "religion of healthy-mindedness,"[51] for these seemed to ignore the problem of evil, lacked a sense of the tragic, and failed to appreciate the depth of the phenomenological experience of the individual. James advocated both a phenomenological and an empirical approach to psychology, and in so doing, he was a precursor of the existential-self theorists' thought.[52]

At the dawn of modern psychology, James realized, perhaps more than most, that of the many diverse routes psychology could and prob-ably would take, each psychology would begin with certain implicit assumptions concerning human nature, and that these assumptions would in turn affect the outcome of the study.

James warns psychologists that by their own theories of human nature they have the power of elevating or degrading this same nature. Debasing assumptions debase the mind; generous assumptions exalt the mind. His own assumptions were always the most generous possible.[53]

Although James appreciated the depths of existential despair, there was for him a way out, there was an *Exit,* and therefore an optimistic view of human nature was possible. Gordon Allport has aptly suggested that:

His view of the human predicament is as stark as that of a Kafka or a Camus, and his own countless acts of kindness reflect his effort to improve the lot of his fellow mortals. While many modern existentialists see no escape from the anguish in life, James, though acknowledging its gravity, would certainly point to the hopeful and redemptive capacities resident in most men, to their reservoir of courage, and to their freedom to find sustaining, and therefore true, beliefs.[54]

Influence on psychology and education

James the psychologist, rather than James the philosopher, influ-enced education. "It has been estimated that nine tenths of the teachers who studied any psychology at all in the years between 1890 and 1910 read James."[55] By 1890, James had published *Principles of Psychology,* which was a landmark in the history of American psychology. This work

---

51. James, *Varieties of Religious Experience,* p. 80.

52. For further analysis of the existential characteristics of James, see Rollo May, ed., *Existential Psychology* (New York: Random House, Inc., 1961). Also Adrian van Kaam, "The Impact of Existential Phenomenology on the Psychological Literature of Western Europe," *Review of Existential Psychology and Psychiatry,* I, 1 (1961), 62-91.

53. Gordon Allport, ed., *William James' Psychology: The Briefer Course* (New York: Harper Torchbooks, 1961), p. xxii.

54. Allport, *William James' Psychology,* p. xxii.

55. Merle Curti, *The Social Ideas of American Educators,* rev. ed. (Paterson, N.J.: Little-field, Adams and Company, 1960), p. 443.

was soon followed by *Psychology: The Briefer Course* and *Talks to Teachers,* which were attempts to make the detailed and involved concept of the earlier work more relevant to students and teachers. James' psychological pedagogy was permeated with his own individualism. Unlike Lester Frank Ward and John Dewey, and more in line with the transcendentalism of Emerson and the existentialism of Rollo May,[56] James did not deal with the social function of education. As Merle Curti has pointed out:

> . . . nowhere in *Talks to Teachers* does he speak of education as a social function. Maintaining that the basis of all education is the fund of native reactions with which the child is endowed, emphasizing interest as the motive power of all educational progress, and instinct as the beginning of interest, James conceived of education as the organization of acquired habits on the part of the individual in such a way as to promote his personal well-being.[57]

James' *Principles of Psychology,* as applied to educational practice, were decidedly individualistic. Ignoring the social melioristic function of education, James thought of the process of education as fitting the child to his environment. Without even a hint of social meliorism, James, in "Great Men and Their Environments," extolled the genius as the natural elite. Born into wealth and well insulated from the real conditions of poverty, James at various times fell into the practice of romanticizing the virtues of poverty. Convinced that social stratification was a part of the natural order, he also repeatedly justified private property as part of man's instinctive endowment. Education in this context should develop the right habits. Habit alone, as the "fly-wheel of society," "saves the children of fortune from the envious uprisings of the poor."[58]

In many respects, James' social ideas were more in keeping with the laissez-faire philosophy of William Graham Sumner than with the social consciousness of Dewey's instrumentalism. In spite of James' brilliant insights into the human condition, his ideas on social action were peculiarly naïve. Perhaps the difference between James and Dewey, in this respect, is due to the fact that James loved humanity from the perspective of Harvard Yard and Dewey from the perspective of Jane Addams' Hull House. James' radical empiricism was a philosophy of individualism, not of social action. Herein lies a distinctive strength as well as a weakness in the philosophies of individualism expressed at various times in American thought. While at times they might be used to justify social liberalism and at other times to justify the status quo, they often served to remind men that they could not escape individual responsibility by way of mass social reform. James' doctrine of habit and instinct was used by

---

56. See Rollo May, *Man's Search for Himself* (New York: W. W. Norton & Company, 1953).

57. Curti, *Social Ideas of American Educators,* p. 448.

58. William James, *The Principles of Psychology,* Vol. I (New York: Henry Holt and Company, 1890), p. 121. For the social conservatism of William James, see Curti, *Social Ideas of American Educators.*

American psychologists and teachers to justify the established social system.[59] That this was James' intent is highly questionable.

James' work in psychology, as well as in philosophy, is marked by both overstatement and contradiction. James would have been the first to admit that this contradiction was inevitable; man was too complex to be readily encompassed in one systematic view of psychology. If, in one chapter of *Principles of Psychology,* one finds man a poor creature of habit, unable to break the chains of habit he himself has forged, one has only to continue on to the next chapter to find man a free agent, undetermined by his past.[60] What is important, here, is not so much the contradiction but the fact that implicit in James' psychology are at least two different approaches to psychology—phenomenology and biological behaviorism. It was the latter which Dewey found significant for instrumentalism[61] and which G. Stanley Hall and Edward L. Thorndike, as students of James, nurtured in their own unique psychologies. James played a part in the early developments of an experimental psychology.[62] His psychology also put great stress on "the biological basis of mental development, the motor consequences of ideas and the emphasis on training not this or that faculty but the *whole* child, by forming habits on the basis of instincts. . . ."[63] By insisting that consciousness should be viewed as a functional kind of behavior in which the total organism is striving to adjust to its environment, and by further asserting that this process could be studied by employing scientific methods, James was directing attention toward a more empirical view of human behavior. This side of the many-faceted William James—emphasizing heredity, empirical psychology, and social conservatism—had a profound impact on American education in the first half of the twentieth century through the influence of his most famous pupil, Edward L. Thorndike.

The fact that one can find in James the basis of Thorndike's connectionism and also of May's existential-self theories may seem strange, but it is not unreasonable. James' empiricism was truly radical, emphasizing a pluralism of truth, method, and psychologies. Reminiscent of Emerson, James suggested that "a terrible flavor of 'humbug' marks the work of any psychologist who claims perfect consistency and exactitude for all his statements."[64] James' work in philosophy and psychology suffered from neither perfect consistency nor exactitude for all statements. In retrospect, James' radical empiricism seems strikingly different from the pragmaticism of Peirce, and it was also different from the instrumentalism of Dewey, which developed independently of both Peirce and James.

---

59. This is most clearly apparent in the social and educational views of Edward L. Thorndike, which are discussed in the following chapter.

60. See Allport, *William James' Psychology,* p. xv.

61. See John Dewey, *Philosophy and Civilization* (New York: Capricorn Books, 1931), pp. 27-29.

62. See Edwin G. Boring, *A History of Experimental Psychology* (New York: Appleton-Century-Crofts, Inc., 1950), pp. 508-517.

63. Curti, *Social Ideas of American Educators,* p. 450.

64. Allport, *William James' Psychology,* p. xv.

THE INSTRUMENTALISM OF JOHN DEWEY

The year in which *The Origin of Species* was published (1859) also witnessed the death of one of America's most famous educators and the birth of another. If for mid-nineteenth-century Americans the name Horace Mann symbolized the common school movement, the name John Dewey was associated in the minds of mid-twentieth-century Americans with the progressive education movement. Both men were New Englanders, reared in families of moderate means, both were acutely concerned with the social problems of their respective eras, and both came to appreciate the important role education could play in the resolution of those problems. The intellectual and social worlds of these men were vastly different, however. After Hegel, Comte, Darwin, and Spencer, it was difficult for some, and impossible for many, to conceive of human nature and the learning process as the Scottish realists had. It was just as difficult for those faced with the problems of immigration, industrialization, and urbanization to conceive of the good society in terms of Horace Mann's conservative view. The life of John Dewey (1859-1952) spanned critical years of American intellectual, social, and educational history. In each area profound transformation occurred, and in each area John Dewey was deeply involved.

Personally quiet, shy, and retiring, Dewey, upon graduation from Johns Hopkins, was taken aside by President Daniel C. Gilman and warned of his "seclusive and bookish habits."[65] Tempted by his natural bent toward the ivory tower with its rationalized systems, and yet painfully aware that thinking about ideas was not the same as acting them out, Dewey took conscious steps to overcome his natural "bookish habits." The major thrust of Dewey's philosophy was toward integrating his own personal world of thought with action. While all three pragmatists looked out upon the same changing, evolving universe, their personal quests, which marked the direction of their thought, were decidedly different. If Peirce's quest was for order and James' for freedom, Dewey's lifelong quest was for unity. Some forty-six years after Gilman's warning, Dewey, reflecting back on his life, said:

Probably there is in the consciously articulated ideas of every thinker an over-weighting of just those things that are contrary to his natural tendencies, an emphasis upon those things that are contrary to his intrinsic bent, and which, therefore, he has to struggle to bring to expression, while the native bent, on the other hand, can take care of itself. Anyway, a case might be made out for the proposition that the emphasis upon the concrete, empirical, and 'practical' in my later writings is partly due to consideration of this nature. It was a reaction against what was more natural, and it served as a protest and protection against something in myself which, in the pressure of the weight of actual experiences, I knew to be a weakness.[66]

---

65. Paul Arthur Schilpp, ed., *The Philosophy of John Dewey* (Evanston: Northwestern University Press, 1939), p. 16.

66. John Dewey, "From Absolutism to Experimentalism" in *Contemporary American Philosophy,* ed. G. P. Adams and W. P. Montague (New York: The Macmillan Company, 1930), p. 16.

In compensating for this "weakness," Dewey purposefully became involved in various action-oriented groups from the Settlement House Movement in Chicago to the Teachers' Union in New York City. As he evolved the main elements of his philosophy of instrumentalism, he drew heavily on his experiences both in abstract philosophy and in practically oriented action groups. As he put it:

Upon the whole, the forces that have influenced me have come from persons and from situations more than from books—not that I have not, I hope, learned a great deal from philosophical writings, but that what I have learned from them has been technical in comparison with what I have been forced to think upon and about because of some experience in which I found myself entangled.[67]

Dewey's early education at Burlington, Vermont, was distinguished by the separation of the formal, rather sterile schooling and the rich, face-to-face, informal education he received in his father's grocery business. To the young John Dewey, the gap between the school and life itself seemed excessive. Ultimately, Dewey dedicated much of his lifework to closing this gap. Although in the earlier years he showed little unusual ability, in his last year at the University of Vermont, stimulated by H. A. P. Torrey, Dewey's interest in philosophy quickened, and he began to demonstrate exceptional talents in that field. Even though Torrey was a Scottish realist, he introduced Dewey to some of the German philosophers and other evolutionary thinkers. Dewey's feelings that things seemed out of joint were reinforced by his reading of Harriet Martineau's exposition of Comte. Comte not only described the problem which he personally felt but also proposed a resolution for the difficulty. Dewey said:

I cannot remember that his law of 'the three stages' affected me particularly; but his idea of the disorganized character of Western modern culture, due to a disintegrative 'individualism,' and his idea of a synthesis of science that should be a regulative method of an organized social life impressed me deeply.[68]

The idea that science could and should be a "regulative method" for organized social life became a central axiom in Dewey's later philosophy.

After Dewey taught a few years in Vermont and Pennsylvania, his original interest in philosophy, once quickened by Torrey, was reinforced by W. T. Harris' favorable reaction to a philosophic article he had written. Upon deciding to make a career in philosophy, Dewey at the age of twenty-three borrowed five hundred dollars and traveled to Baltimore to attend the new university of Johns Hopkins. That same fall that Spencer was celebrated at Delmonico's (1882), Dewey was starting his work in philosophy at one of the most exciting educational institutions for advanced study in the nation. While the Scottish philosophers were receiving deadly blows at the hand of Spencer's social Darwinism,

---

67. Dewey, "From Absolutism to Experimentalism," p. 22.
68. Dewey, "From Absolutism to Experimentalism," p. 20.

John Dewey, educated in the Scottish tradition, came under the influence of the Hegelian, George S. Morris at Johns Hopkins. At Hopkins, he was also introduced to the experimental psychology of G. Stanley Hall, the logic of Charles S. Peirce, the history of Herbert Adams, as well as Edward Caird's attempts to reconcile the differences between science and religion.[69] In this richly charged intellectual atmosphere, with his own certainties rapidly dissolving, Dewey replaced his Scottish philosophy with Hegelian idealism.

At a time when philosophy and psychology were intimately joined, Dewey, as a student, found himself in the midst of a major contest at Johns Hopkins between the historical approach to the field represented by his mentor, Morris, and the experimental approach represented by Hall. Morris lost that struggle and in 1885 left for the University of Michigan, where Dewey had received an appointment in philosophy the preceding summer. "First as a teacher and then as a colleague at Michigan, he [Morris] helped shape the first fifteen years of Dewey's philosophical thought."[70] One of the major differences between Dewey and both James and Peirce is that, although James and Peirce studied German idealism,[71] neither became Hegelian. Although Hegelianism could not satisfy James' search for freedom nor Peirce's quest for precision and order, it did satisfy Dewey's personal need for organic unity. In spite of the changes which occurred as he evolved his own form of pragmatism, which he first called experimentalism and later instrumentalism, certain characteristics of his Hegelian experience remain central throughout Dewey's work.

Dewey's idealism

German idealism had essentially been founded on the work of Immanuel Kant, who struggled to resolve one of the more critical epistemological problems of the eighteenth century. Attempting to heal the breach between the empiricism of Hume and the rationalism of Leibnitz, Kant reasoned a place for empiricism by suggesting that the content of knowledge comes from the external world through experience. He also found a place for rationalism by arguing that the forms these raw experiences take are dependent on "transcendental categories," existing in "the minds of all rational beings prior to and above the external world of experience. Kant believed that there is an external world that causes our experience, but he insisted that we cannot *prove* it and therefore cannot *know* it. We know only our impressions and perceptions as ordered by the mind."[72] That which is known is a function of the operation of the transcendental categories. Kant had given Plato a significant

---

69. See Morton G. White, *The Origin of Dewey's Instrumentalism* (New York: Columbia University Press, 1943).

70. White, *Origin of Dewey's Instrumentalism*, p. 7.

71. Indeed, Peirce noted that his father had him study Kant two hours each day for three years.

72. R. Freeman Butts, *A Cultural History of Western Education*, 2nd ed. (New York: McGraw-Hill Book Company, 1955), p. 285.

twist. The universals exist not in the ideas, as Plato believed, but in "categories." Under these circumstances, ideas themselves lose their platonic metaphysical reality and become unrealized goals toward which human experience may be ordered.

Kant takes the word "Idea" from Plato, though he does not ascribe metaphysical reality and power to ideas, as Plato often did. An Idea for Kant is like Plato's Idea, however, in being a conception for which no experience can give us an exemplar, yet a conception which is not arbitrarily constructed by the imagination. But whereas Plato thought the Ideas were objects of pure reason in a noumenal world in which the world of sense participates by imitating the Ideas, Kant thought of them as necessary creations of the human mind with no known metaphysical existence. Necessary, though, for what? Kant believed that they were necessary for the guidance of our theoretical knowledge and practical or moral experience, holding before us an unrealized systematic goal for our piece-meal dealings with particular problems.[73]

Kant's concept of Idea is remarkably similar to the function of ideas that Dewey later developed. Dewey, however, came to Kant by way of Hegel; and to Dewey, it is Hegel that completes Kant.[74] In an article entitled "Kant and Philosophic Method,"[75] Dewey rigorously attacked Kant for separating reason and the material acted upon. Dewey interpreted Kant as saying that reason "acts only upon a material foreign to it."[76] The solution to the problem of a Kantian dualism was a Hegelian organism in which reason is seen as the living unity in all things. As Dewey put it, "The material which was supposed to confront reason as foreign to it, is but the manifestation of reason itself."[77] Dewey's quest for unity was fulfilled not by the formal logic of Peirce or the analytical reasoning of Kant but by the romanticized reasoning of Hegel, which seemed to dissolve all boundaries and resolve all opposites.

Although Dewey, at the University of Chicago from 1894 to 1904 and at Columbia from 1904 to 1930, evolved a realistic instrumentalism which he first applied to education and then to the broader social and political problems of the nation, he never lost certain characteristics of his Kantian-Hegelian experience. His use of ideas as unrealized goals, his war on dualism (the first shot fired at Kant), his quest for unity in all experience, his sense of an evolving community, his dialectical reasoning, his need for conflict, tension, or problematic situations in order to have

---

73. Lewis White Beck, *Kant on History* (Indianapolis: The Bobbs-Merrill Company, Inc., 1963), pp. xix-xx.

74. He did his doctoral dissertation (since lost) on Kant, and in the following years proceeded to write articles criticizing Kant from the perspective of Hegelianism. Dewey essentially followed in the footsteps of his mentor, Professor Morris. For an insight into the thought of Morris, see Robert Mark Wenley, *The Life and Work of G. S. Morris* (London: The Macmillan Company, 1917).

75. William T. Harris, ed., *Journal of Speculative Philosophy* (New York: D. Appleton and Company, 1889), XVIII, 162-174.

76. Harris, *Journal of Speculative Philosophy*, p. 168. For a discussion of the crucial point, see White, *Origin of Dewey's Instrumentalism*, p. 37.

77. Harris, *Journal of Speculative Philosophy*, p. 168.

any thought, and his heavy dependence on the past in order to explain the present—all are elements of his personal needs intertwined with his Hegelian experience, which became a basic part of his philosophy. Even though he rejected Hegel's absolute for an open-ended universe and rejected a future determined by history for a future determined by conscious choice, Dewey, as late as 1930, still said, "Were it possible for me to be a devotee of any system, I still should believe that there is greater richness and greater variety of insight in Hegel than in any other single systematic philosopher."[78] Dewey's encounter with Hegelian philosophy was no mere intellectual excursion but rather a very personal part of his development.

There were, however, also 'subjective' reasons for the appeal that Hegel's thought made to me; it supplied a demand for unification that was doubtless an intense emotional craving, and yet was a hunger that only an intellectualized subject matter could satisfy. . . . But the sense of divisions and separations that were, I suppose, borne in upon me as a consequence of a heritage of New England culture, divisions by way of isolation of self from the world, of soul from body, of nature from God, brought a painful oppression—or, rather, they were an inward laceration. . . . Hegel's synthesis of subject and object, matter and spirit, the divine and the human, was, however, no mere intellectual formula; it operated as an immense release, a liberation. Hegel's treatment of human culture, of institutions and the arts, involved the same dissolution of hard-and-fast dividing walls, and had special attraction for me.[79]

In Dewey's later works, the theme of unity still remained. To what extent this was merely a reflection of his personal need and to what extent it was the result of his Hegelian past remains a moot question. Perhaps it was both.

Still under the influence of his colleague, George S. Morris, Dewey published *Psychology* (1887), in which he attempted to reconcile the historical approach to psychology implicit in his own Hegelianism with the new experimental psychology of G. Stanley Hall and others. The result was forced and strained, hardly satisfactory to either Hall or Dewey. It was not until George Herbert Mead, Dewey's friend and colleague at Michigan and Chicago, began his development of social psychology that Dewey found a psychology compatible with the essential elements of his emerging instrumentalism. It is significant, however, that although Dewey came to accept and advocate experimentalism in psychology as well as in education, his own approach to treating problems remained anthropological if not historical. As much as Dewey stressed the present and the future, the past was not to be ignored. Whatever problem Dewey faced, he usually used the past to explain the present situation.[80] Indeed, if one were to delete all the historical interpretations from his major work, much of his analysis would be missing.

78. Dewey, "From Absolutism to Experimentalism," p. 21.
79. Dewey, "From Absolutism to Experimentalism," p. 19.
80. This was the same approach used by Sylvester Morris.

Nurtured and steadied by Hegelian cosmic history, which saw the past, present, and future as a continuous stream, Dewey as late as 1938 reflected this idea when he suggested: "The past is of logical necessity the past-of-the-present, and the present is the past-of-a-future-living-present."[81] Dewey, however, rejected Ranke's search for the true history and Hegel's determinism of history. He saw men reconstructing their past in light of new evidence and shaping their future in part by using the past as "a lever for moving the present into a certain kind of future."[82] The past, however, was viewed as a basis for more than just a convenient rhetorical device for winning current debate. To Dewey, the past was fundamentally a part of the larger dialectic—i.e., the past was the thesis, the newer forces of the present were the antithesis, and with the "future-living-present" rests the synthesis. With each new synthesis, the past will by necessity be reconstructed and the dynamic process of change continued indefinitely.[83]

Sensitive to the approach that Dewey and the Chicago school were using, Peirce reacted negatively to what Dewey called the "first declaration of the instrumentalists."[84] In his review of *Studies in Logical Theory* (1903), Peirce said that Dewey "seems to regard what he calls 'logic' as a natural history of thought." Peirce felt that such a history was commendable but that the confusion of logic with history was, indeed, a "suspicious beginning."[85] Peirce went on to say, "The Chicago school or group are manifestly in radical opposition to the exact logicians, and are not making any studies which anybody in his senses can expect, directly or indirectly, in any considerable degree, to influence twentieth-century science."[86] In personal correspondence, Peirce went on to point out to Dewey that his method was not only "loose" but "wretched." Peirce, however, acknowledged Dewey's pragmatic views and said, "I am simply *projecting upon the horizon,* where distance gets magnified indefinitely, the *direction* of your standpoint as viewed from mine."[87] It is interesting that James, more open to diversity than either Peirce or Dewey, enthusiastically reviewed the Chicago School's *Logical Studies.*[88]

81. John Dewey, *Logic: The Theory of Inquiry* (New York: Henry Holt and Company, 1938), p. 238. It is interesting that Dewey's definitive statement on historiography is to be found in his work on *Logic.* See p. 220. For an analysis of Dewey's view of history and its relationship to teaching see Sally G. Farrell, *Dewey's Philosophy of History: Its Implication For Teaching* (Inter-University Project One Publication Series, Cornell University, 1965).

82. Farrell, *Dewey's Philosophy of History,* p. 239.

83. Although no comprehensive critical review of Dewey's thought and influence on education exists at present, one suspects that when the definitive work is done, it will have to consider seriously not only Dewey's historical methodology but also his precise interpretation of the past.

84. Dewey, *Philosophy and Civilization,* p. 27.

85. *The Nation,* LXXIX, 2046 (Sept. 15, 1904), 220. For the confirmation of the authorship of this review, see Walter Burks, ed., *Collected Papers of Charles Sanders Peirce,* VIII (Cambridge, Mass.: Harvard University Press, 1958), p. 145. For further discussion of Peirce's disagreement with Dewey, see Burks, *Collected Papers of C. S. Peirce,* p. 180.

86. *The Nation,* LXXIX, 2046 (Sept. 15, 1904), 220.

87. Burks, *Collected Papers of C. S. Peirce,* VIII, p. 182.

88. Perry, *Thought and Character of William James,* p. 308.

Dewey's Chicago School was developing a philosophy of instrumentalism destined to have its major impact more in areas of social action than on the work of theoretical science. Dewey's instrumentalism, which conceived of ideas as instruments of social action, evolved gradually. As his Hegelianism began to fade and certain aspects of Darwinian naturalism became more pronounced, Dewey reacted, modified, and reconstructed his ideas as a result of his attempts to put these ideas into action. As Dewey put it:

I seem to be unstable, chameleon-like, yielding one after another to many diverse and even incompatible influences; struggling to assimilate something from each and yet striving to carry it forward in a way that is logically consistent with what has been learned from its predecessors.[89]

Instrumentalism

As head of the Department of Philosophy, Psychology, and Pedagogy at the University of Chicago (1894-1904), Dewey developed the philosophy of instrumentalism. If Hegel tended to dissolve the Scottish realistic certainties in the mind of the younger Dewey, it was the impact of Darwin on philosophy, psychology, and education that helped to dissolve the Hegelian certainties in the mind of the older Dewey.[90]

Human nature was conceived as neither bad nor good but as largely a product of cultural evolution. The child born with undifferentiated tendencies to act evolves his human characteristics in a transactional relationship with his social environment. The stress, then, was not on inherited characteristics, or the cultural epoch theory,[91] or even the survival of the fittest, but rather on the social environment which could develop and enhance the most valued human traits.

In cooperation with George Herbert Mead at Michigan and later at Chicago, Dewey worked out a functional social psychology compatible with instrumentalism.[92] While Dewey's and Mead's psychology of social behaviorism placed great stress on environment, their position was not a complete environmental determinism. The individual always stood in

89. Dewey, "From Absolutism to Experimentalism," p. 22.
90. See John Dewey, *The Influence of Darwin on Philosophy* (New York: Henry Holt and Company, 1910). Also see John S. Brubacker, "Darwinian Evolution and Deweyan Education," *Rhode Island College Journal*, I, 3 (December 1960).
91. In rejecting the determinism of Hegel's cosmic history, Dewey radically modified the recapitulation theory of the Herbartians and others who applied that theory to the curriculum of the school. It was not the past but the present which should determine the curriculum. As Dewey said, "Hence no past period should be selected except as it serves to increase the child's insight and appreciation of significant and valuable features of present civilization." See John Dewey, "Culture Epoch Theory," in *Paul Monroe Cyclopedia of Education*, II (1911), 240-242. It is significant that Dewey practiced what he preached. The curriculum of the Chicago Laboratory School was largely organized on the basis of an anthropological use of the past which could be considered most relevant at that time. See Katherine Mayhew and Anna Edwards, *The Dewey School* (New York: D. Appleton-Century Company, 1936).
92. For Mead's assessment of Dewey's instrumentalism, see G. H. Mead, "The Philosophies of Royce, James, and Dewey in Their American Setting," *International Journal of Ethics*, XL, 2 (January 1930), 211-231.

a *transactional relationship* with his environment—i.e., he changed his environment as his environment changed him. The ultimate outcome could not be completely determined. On the other hand, all was not flux or change; through the application of science to social inquiry and the use of reflective thought, man could, in large measure, deliberately shape his future and create a better social order. Dewey's good society was a pluralistic society, encompassing a maximum amount of freedom, where reasonable men were deeply involved in using intelligence to create a more humane society. Reminiscent of Lester F. Ward's sociocracy, Dewey suggested that the great scientific revolution would come when

. . . men collectively and co-operatively organize their knowledge for application to achieve and make secure social values; when they systematically use scientific procedures for the control of human relationships and the direction of the social effects of our vast technological machinery.[93]

Although progress was not inevitable, it was possible. Twentieth-century man need not be a victim of the Frankenstein of mass culture but could control his own destiny. Of all the American philosophers in the first half of the twentieth century, John Dewey came closer than any other to developing a neo-Enlightenment philosophy. As Dewey discussed the historical roots of pragmatism, he said, "If I were asked to give an historical parallel to this movement in American thought I would remind my reader of the French philosophy of the Enlightenment."[94] Placing great faith in the reasonableness of mankind, Dewey's instrumental philosophy carries with it strong echoes of the Jeffersonian ideal. For example, Jefferson could just as well have said:

It is the formation of a faith in intelligence, as the one and indispensable belief necessary to moral and social life. The more one appreciates the intrinsic esthetic, immediate value of thought and of science, the more one takes into account what intelligence itself adds to the joy and dignity of life, the more one should feel grieved at a situation in which the exercise and joy of reason are limited to a narrow, closed and technical social group and the more one should ask how it is possible to make all men participators in this inestimable wealth.[95]

While Dewey reconstructed the Enlightenment rational image of man along Darwinian lines, he failed to take into serious account a radically different but equally significant movement of his own time—the psychoanalytic movement. Whatever explanation is given for this oversight, it remains a striking fact that John Dewey, usually sensitive to the major trends of his age, missed or avoided one of the most original and influential of his contemporaries. If, however, Dewey had seriously attended

93. Quoted in Nelson Manfred Blake, *A History of American Life and Thought* (New York: McGraw-Hill Book Company, 1963), p. 408.

94. Dewey, *Philosophy and Civilization*, p. 34. Yet it must be noted that Dewey had abandoned one basic tendency of Enlightenment thought, i.e., that particular brand of faith in natural reason with its concomitant devotion to self-evident truths.

95. Dewey, *Philosophy and Civilization*, p. 35.

to Freud's dualistic view of man and stoic view of culture, he would either have had to reject much of Freud's basic ideology or modify his own ideas.[96]

Much of Dewey's philosophy emerged as a consequence of his Chicago Laboratory School experience. Under the influence of Francis W. Parker, principal of the Cook County Normal School in Chicago; Ella Flagg Young, District Superintendent of the Chicago Public Schools; Jane Addams of Hull House; and Mrs. Alice Chipman Dewey, Principal of the Laboratory School, Dewey joined theoretical pragmatism with educational practice.[97] Thus, philosophy came to mean for Dewey a general theory of education. Although in his later work at Columbia he tended more toward broader political and social interests, he did so by evaluating political and social institutions in terms of their educative functions, i.e., their influence in shaping human ability to react intelligently to novel situations. Some twelve years after he left Chicago, he continued to argue that "if we are willing to conceive education as the process of forming fundamental dispositions, intellectual and emotional, toward nature and fellow men, philosophy may even be defined *as the general theory of education.*"[98]

In Dewey's theory of education means and ends, freedom and responsibility, the child and the curriculum, and the school and society are viewed as fundamentally integrated. To separate one from the other results in all sorts of perversity and is destructive of the unity so necessary for the growth of the individual and society. To Dewey, the only single aim of education which could encompass all the diverse purposes of education was the idea of *growth*. In this context, the function of the teacher is to work himself out of a job. By using his psychological understanding of the child and his understanding of the way knowledge is created, the teacher would guide the child through a continuous, reflective learning experience which would culminate in an independent, creative, socially responsible thinker. Far from relieving the teacher from responsibility for what transpired in the classroom, Dewey challenged teachers with the Herculean task of not only understanding the child but also of understanding how knowledge was created in many diverse fields and then using those insights to enhance the intellectual, emotional, and social growth of the individual.

Unlike Robert Owen in the nineteenth century or G. S. Counts in the twentieth century, who saw the school as a vehicle for reforming society by blueprinting a new social order and then indoctrinating the young toward that end, Dewey saw the function of the school as a vehicle for reforming society by producing critical thinkers who as adults would make their own decisions. Dewey consistently refused to blue-

---

96. For some of the differences between Freud and Dewey, see Clarence J. Karier, "The Rebel and the Revolutionary: Sigmund Freud and John Dewey," *Teachers College Record,* LXIV, 7 (April 1963).

97. For an analysis of Dewey at Chicago, see the unpublished dissertation (University of Wisconsin, 1960) by Robert E. Tostberg, "Educational Ferment in Chicago, 1883-1904."

98. John Dewey, *Democracy and Education* (New York: The Macmillan Company, 1961), p. 328.

print the new social order, not only because he knew any long-range blueprint in a society of rapid change would be fallacious but also because such a blueprint implied a control and direction of learning in conflict with his conception of free and continuous growth. Dewey's social reconstructionist ideas were, therefore, at odds with such reconstructionists as G. S. Counts and Theodore Brameld, who advocated more direct action on the part of the school.

Although Dewey's name is often associated with the Progressive Education Association and especially the child-centered wing of the movement, which advocated an extremely permissive approach to education, throughout his lifetime Dewey remained a severe critic of these excesses. Repeatedly he warned against a hit-or-miss impressionistic curriculum and suggested that unless progressive educators evolved an intellectually coherent curriculum, they would fail.[99] In general, failing to heed his warning, progressive educators like William H. Kilpatrick and others used Dewey's criticism of the traditional school as a basis for advocating their own child-centered views.[100] Dewey conceived human nature as plastic and learning as a rationally organized experience. Neither conception is compatible with the romantic, child-centered educator who generally assumed the child's nature to be innately good and thought of the learning process as unrestrained, real-life experience.

Although Dewey cast a long and distinct shadow over much educational philosophy in the twentieth century, the extent of his influence on actual educational practice remains difficult to assess. It is, indeed, a moot question whether John Dewey was correctly interpreted as often as he was misinterpreted. If Emerson was right when he suggested that "to be misunderstood is to be great," Dewey had achieved greatness. Perhaps Peirce was correct when he warned the young Dewey that his use of old terms to mean new things could only lead to misunderstanding. Or perhaps Dewey's style of writing, which James described as "damnable, you might even say God-damnable,"[101] was the source of the difficulty. In spite of style, however, it was not difficult to misinterpret one who saw himself changing in chameleon-like fashion, and who at the same time was attempting to synthesize and reconstruct some of the major intellectual traditions of the nineteenth and twentieth centuries for modern educational practice. While elements of Comtean science, Hegelian organismic history, Darwinian evolution, and Wardian sociocracy can be found in Dewey's thought, all were reconstructed and wedded to a Yankee practicality in a fashion uniquely his own. His personal quest for unity destined him to become the great synthesizer of the American experience. As such, he, more than either Peirce or James, became at once both the hero and the villain of the twentieth-century educational frontier. Perhaps George Herbert Mead was correct

---

99. See John Dewey, "How Much Freedom in the New School?" *The New Republic* (July 9, 1930). See also John Dewey, "Progressive Education and the Science of Education," *Progressive Education,* V (1928).

100. See Lawrence Cremin, *The Transformation of the School* (New York: Alfred A. Knopf, Inc., 1961), Chapter 6.

101. Quoted in Cremin, *Transformation of the School,* p. 237.

when he said, "In the profoundest sense, John Dewey is the philosopher of America."[102]

THE PRAGMATIC CONSENSUS

The personal temperament, life experience, and intellectual bent of each of the leading pragmatists were different enough to explain why Peirce's pragmaticism, James' radical empiricism, and Dewey's instrumentalism were all so very different on many crucial points. Peirce found the dignity of man to rest in his ability to understand precisely the orderly laws of the universe, whereas James found man's dignity in his subjective ability to be free and Dewey seemed to find it in the creative ability of man to posit and realize his ideas socially. Peirce took the path toward the physical scientist's conception of science, James toward the American existential psychologist's conception of science, and Dewey toward the educational and social reformer's view of science. Taken alone, each has serious shortcomings; but taken together, they present a fairly broad picture of that mainstream of twentieth-century American intellectual life denoted by the term *pragmatism.*

Amidst diversity, there were certain unifying elements. All three men were evolutionary naturalists who conceived man and his universe as being in a state of evolutionary change. All were concerned with the application of science to control and order change for human purposes, and all three seemed to conceive of human nature as plastic and the good society as pluralistic. In rejecting the absolute, they gave up absolute certainty and in unison agreed on the tentative nature of truth. Unlike the European nihilist who, upon discovering the death of "God," and therefore of absolute truth, had swung to the opposite extreme and denied any possibility for truth, the pragmatists accepted the tentative nature of truth and assumed enough faith in the reasoned intelligence of men to shape their destiny, if not completely at least significantly. The pragmatist's belief—that the meaning of an idea is to be found in both the active and the passive consequences of that idea when tested in action—reflects in a very real sense the practical temper of American culture. The pragmatism of Peirce, James, and Dewey was a reconstruction of Enlightenment values, taking into account and influenced by both the intellectual trends and practical conditions of American life. Unlike their Enlightenment predecessors who assumed inevitable progress, the pragmatists could believe progress possible only if men applied their intelligence to the vexing problems of today in order to shape their tomorrows. That pragmatism was not a system, that it leaves many loose ends, that it was expressed in different ways in vastly different areas, and that it leaves one with a feeling of unfinished business all attest to the general belief of Peirce, James, and Dewey as to the unfinished universe of man and his culture. One can be quite certain all would have agreed with Alfred North Whitehead's observation that "In philosophical discussion, the merest hint of dogmatic certainty as to finality of statement is an exhibition of folly."

---

102. Mead, "Philosophies of Royce, James, and Dewey," p. 231.

SUGGESTED READINGS

Allport, Gordon, ed. *William James' Psychology: The Briefer Course*. New York, Harper Torchbooks, 1961.

Boler, John F. *Charles Peirce and Scholastic Realism*. Seattle, University of Washington Press, 1963.

Burks, Walter, ed. *Collected Papers of Charles Sanders Peirce*, Vols. VII and VIII. Cambridge, Mass., Harvard University Press, 1958.

Cremin, Lawrence. *The Transformation of the School*. New York, Alfred A. Knopf, Inc., 1961.

Dewey, John. "Culture Epoch Theory," *Paul Monroe Cyclopedia of Education*, II (1911), 240-242.

———. *Democracy and Education*. New York, The Macmillan Company, 1961.

———. *The Influence of Darwin on Philosophy*. New York, Henry Holt and Company, 1910.

———. *Logic: The Theory of Inquiry*. New York, Henry Holt and Company, 1938.

———. *Philosophy and Civilization*. New York, Capricorn Books, 1963.

Feibleman, James. *An Introduction to Peirce's Philosophy Interpreted as a System*. London, George Allen & Unwin, 1960.

Harris, William T., ed. *Journal of Speculative Philosophy*, XVIII, New York, D. Appleton and Company, 1889.

James, William. *Pragmatism*. New York, Longmans, Green & Company, 1907.

———. *The Principles of Psychology*, Vol. I. New York, Henry Holt and Company, 1923.

———. *The Varieties of Religious Experience: A Study in Human Nature*. New York, Collier Books, 1961.

Kennedy, Gail, ed. *Pragmatism and American Culture*. Boston, D. C. Heath and Company, 1950.

May, Rollo, ed. *Existential Psychology*. New York, Random House, Inc., 1961.

———. *Man's Search for Himself*. New York, W. W. Norton & Company, 1953.

Mayhew, Katherine, and Anna Edwards. *The Dewey School*. New York, D. Appleton-Century Company, 1936.

Mead, G. H. "The Philosophies of Royce, James, and Dewey in Their American Setting," *International Journal of Ethics*, XL, 2 (January 1930).

Murphey, Murray G. *The Development of Peirce's Philosophy*. Cambridge, Mass., Harvard University Press, 1961.

Peirce, Charles S. *Chance, Love, and Logic*, ed. Morris R. Cohen. New York, George Braziller, Inc., 1956.

Perry, Ralph Barton. *The Thought and Character of William James*. Cambridge, Mass., Harvard University Press, 1948.

Schilpp, Paul Arthur, ed. *The Philosophy of John Dewey*. Evanston, Ill., Northwestern University Press, 1939.

White, Morton G. *The Origin of Dewey's Instrumentalism*. New York, Columbia University Press, 1943.

Wiener, Philip P., ed. *Values in a Universe of Chance: Selected Writings of Charles S. Peirce*. Stanford, Calif., Stanford University Press, 1958.

CHAPTER 7

Psychological conceptions of man and society

When, then, we talk of 'psychology as a natural science,' we must not assume that that means a sort of psychology that stands at last on solid ground. It means just the reverse; it means a psychology particularly fragile, and into which the waters of metaphysical criticism leak at every joint, a psychology all of whose elementary assumptions and data must be reconsidered in wider connections and translated into other terms. . . . The Galileo and the Lavoisier of psychology will be famous men indeed when they come, as come they someday surely will, or past successes are no index to the future. When they do come, however, the necessities of the case will make them 'metaphysical.'[1] WILLIAM JAMES

When, in 1892, James suggested that the future Galileo of psychology would by necessity be a metaphysician, the fields of philosophy and psychology were still intimately joined. The history of American psychology in the twentieth century, however, has been largely distinguished by the separation of the two fields. In quest of solid ground under the banner of "science," many psychologists turned in despair from philosophy as just so much metaphysical speculation and proceeded to direct their attention toward a more objective model of behavior. In spite of this trend, no psychologist completely escaped dealing with philosophic problems. Whether it was G. Stanley Hall attempting to determine the content of children's minds, Sigmund Freud attempting to cure mental illness by way of psychoanalysis, Edward L. Thorndike attempting to

1. Gordon Allport, ed., *William James' Psychology: The Briefer Course* (New York: Harper Torchbooks, 1961), pp. 334-335.

classify and objectify human achievement by way of mathematical scales, or B. F. Skinner attempting to understand learning by observing the behavior of rats in a box, all were fundamentally concerned with defining human nature and the kind of society most fitting for that nature.[2]

Psychologists, freed from some of the confining strictures of academic philosophy and riding the *Zeitgeist* of "science," profoundly shaped man's image of himself in the twentieth century—more so than sociologists or philosophers. By way of the popular press, literature, drama, and the arts, as well as academic instruction, psychologists played the role of "high priests of culture," to borrow the terminology of G. Stanley Hall. Although few psychologists today would welcome such a title, all would readily admit that psychology as a field of inquiry has been extremely influential in shaping man's view of himself and society. In many ways, psychologists in the twentieth century were playing the role that philosophers and theologians had played in previous years. Whether it was the nineteenth-century philosopher philosophizing about psychological questions or the twentieth-century psychologist psychologizing about philosophical questions, both were products of their respective historical eras, and none seemed to fully escape the necessity of dealing with the metaphysical issues.

In spite of the vast professionalization and specialization which occurred in both philosophy and psychology, the two fields remained functionally related at a number of critical points. In the areas of defining man, truth, and social ideals, philosophy and psychology converge. Since psychology's central concern is with man and since different psychological conceptions of man usually lead to some very different social and educational implications, we shall focus primarily on psychological conceptions of human nature and secondarily on their social and educational implications. At the risk of omitting some significant material, we shall discuss only five conceptions of human nature: the primitivistic conception of G. Stanley Hall, the neoclassical conception of Sigmund Freud, the social behaviorist view of George H. Mead, the connectionist view of Edward L. Thorndike, and the behaviorist conceptions of John B. Watson and B. F. Skinner.

THE PRIMITIVISTIC CONCEPTION

It has been reported that when Granville Stanley Hall (1844-1924), a bright young student with unconventional ideas, gave his trial sermon at Union Theological Seminary, "the member of the faculty whose custom it was to criticize, despairing of mere criticism, knelt and prayed for his soul."[3] Indeed, well he might have, for neither the mind nor the

---

2. The social interests are reflected in such works as Edward L. Thorndike, *Human Nature and the Social Order;* G. Stanley Hall, "Fall of Atlantis"; Sigmund Freud, *Civilization and Its Discontents;* and B. F. Skinner, *Walden Two.*

3. Edwin G. Boring, *A History of Experimental Psychology* (New York: Appleton-Century-Crofts, Inc., 1950), p. 505.

soul of G. Stanley Hall would ever flirt with orthodoxy. Hall was unquestionably a trailblazer of American psychology. He was the first man in the United States to receive a Ph.D. in psychology (under William James), the first president of Clark University, the founder of the psychological laboratory at Johns Hopkins, the founder of the American Psychological Association, and the originator of such journals as the *American Journal of Psychology, Pedagogical Seminary, Journal of Religious Psychology,* and the *Journal of Applied Psychology.* Perhaps more important from the standpoint of education, he can be broadly considered one of the founders of educational psychology and, more specifically, of the child-study movement which by the twentieth century evolved into the field of child psychology. From the standpoint of his many accomplishments, it would be easy to get the impression that Hall was chiefly an administrator, spending his life in organizational activities. However, such was not the case; Hall was just as much a purveyor of unconventional social and educational ideas as he was a founder of organizations.

Edwin Boring has suggested that Hall's early intellectual interest was in philosophy, but when Hall discovered psychology, he "turned the tables by saying that psychology furnished the true approach to philosophy."[4] As Hall psychologized about philosophy, he evolved what may appear on the surface as erratic, if not unconventional, views of the nature of man and the good society. Recent studies of Hall's work, however, seem to indicate that his "synthetic psychology" was far less erratic than was earlier suspected.[5] Explicit in his works are some very definite views on the nature of man and the good society which seem to add up to what Josiah Royce referred to as a rather "strange ideal system."[6] Hall's idealism was strange indeed, for it carried the romantic faith of Fichte, the voluntarism of Schopenhauer, and the nihilism of Nietzsche, all steadied and anchored in a set of primitivistic beliefs based on the German concept of *Volk.*[7] Hall's study in Germany (1868-1871 and 1878 and 1880) was more than the usual nineteenth-century academic procession to the mecca of learning. While he studied philosphy, physiology, and experimental psychology,[8] he became deeply attached to German

---

4. Boring, *History of Experimental Psychology,* p. 508.

5. For two excellent but divergent analyses of Hall's ideas, see the unpublished dissertation (University of Wisconsin, 1963) by Charles Strickland, "The Child and the Race," and the unpublished dissertation (University of Wisconsin, 1962) by Charles Burgess, "The Educational State in America." See also Charles Strickland and Charles Burgess, *Health, Growth, and Heredity: G. Stanley Hall on Natural Education,* Classics in Education, No. 23 (New York: Bureau of Publications, Teachers College, Columbia University, 1965).

6. Quoted in Burgess, "Educational State in America," p. 158.

7. *Volk* is used here as George L. Mosse defined it in *The Crisis of German Ideology* (New York: Grosset and Dunlap, 1964), p. 4: "*Volk* is one of those perplexing German terms which connotes far more than its specific meaning. '*Volk*' is a much more comprehensive term than 'people,' for to German thinkers ever since the birth of German romanticism in the late eighteenth century '*Volk*' signified the union of a group of people with a transcendental 'essence.' This 'essence' might be called 'nature' or 'cosmos' or 'mythos,' but in each instance it was fused to man's innermost nature, and represented the source of his creativity, his depth of feeling, his individuality, and his unity with other members of the *Volk.*"

8. Hall was one of the first American students to study with Wilhelm Wundt at his Leipzig laboratory.

Kultur. Hall's need for what he called "delicious mysticism" was satisfied not by the rationalism of Kant or the rationalized romanticism of Hegel, but by the German concept of *Volk* which mystically dissolved individualism into a collectivized transcendental nature. In Germany, Hall found the "ultra-phenomenal identity" which James suggested his former pupil sought. Henceforth, Hall worshiped at the shrine of evolutionary nature, buttressed on the one side by a primitivistic romanticism and on the other by scientific biology cemented and fused together with a recapitulation theory.

The recapitulation theory that Hall evolved from his study of Darwin in combination with his German experience was quite different from the recapitulation theory of Herbert Spencer. While both men were users of cosmic history—i.e., they both used the past to explain the present and determine the future—Spencer, in typically English utilitarian fashion, rationalized the past so that the history of the race might give clues to help in organizing a curriculum to make men more knowledgeable. Spencer evinced little respect for man's primitive past; Hall, on the other hand, relished man's primitive past as part of the living present. As Hall put it:

Often even germs of sins and errors of all the past must be made to glow up for a moment, for the vestiges of evil are thus burned out, while at the same time their conflagration alone can arouse the next higher powers which control, or, it may be, repress them.[9]

Hall was deeply impressed by German primitivistic thought, the roots of which go back to Rousseau by way of Johann Gottfried von Herder.[10] Hall's romantic primitivism was reinforced by findings in biology, physiology, and especially embryology. If the student of embryology could see in the development of the fetus the evolution of the life stages which led to the first man, G. Stanley Hall could see in the anthropological history of the race and the stages of a child's growth and development the prehistoric evolution of the race. The preadolescent child was, for Hall, at the savage stage. At such a stage, reasoning with a child is useless. *Dressur* is the proper key to child rearing.[11] The child must be led to fear God, love country, and develop a strong body. As the child burns out the vestige of evil inherent in his nature, he needs a good share of authoritarian discipline, including corporal punishment, in order to develop his will. The child at this stage also needs and craves myths and superstitions to help him relive and thus burn out some of his primitivistic past. Church and state, fully integrated, could be used to furnish the appropriate myths.

---

9. Quoted in Strickland, "Child and the Race," p. 319.

10. For a history of the development of the recapitulation idea in German education, see Strickland, "Child and the Race."

11. *Dressur* is a term Hall frequently used to describe the desired approach to child rearing. In German, the term stands for a method of animal training developing unflinching obedience. See Burgess, "Educational State in America."

Central to Hall's conception of human nature was a strong emphasis on body culture at every stage of a human being's development. Nothing was more important than a strong, robust body. Since children and men both think with their wills, emotions, and bodies more than with their minds, physical health is crucial. Hall literally raised health to the stature of a religious cult. In a speech at Cooper Union in 1905, he said, "I almost believe that the boy or girl who has not enough vigor to play a good deal is hardly worth educating at all."[12] There were those degenerates of the race who should be sterilized as well as those who were so low on the evolutionary scale that any attempt at formal education would only pervert their true nature. Hall suggested there "are many who ought not to be educated, and who would be better in mind, body, and morals if they knew no school."[13] Of those who were selected for schooling, the weak would again be separated, at age six or seven, into a dullard school to meet their individual needs.

With the approach of adolescence, the child's nature changes and his education must change accordingly.[14] As the child passes from the primitive discipline of the Old Testament to the altruism of the New Testament, "we can no longer coerce and break but must lead and inspire."[15] At adolescence, where the primitive meets the civilized, the appeal in the school must be not to the child's reason but to his emotion; teachers, "with almost religious if not pentecostal fervor,"[16] should indoctrinate their pupils with a selfless dedication to the ideal of service. "The one word now written across the very zenith of the educational skies, high above all others, is the word service. This is coming to be, as it should be, the supreme goal of all pedagogic endeavor, the standard by which all other values are measured."[17] With charismatic teachers in control, the high school would take as its chief goals patriotism, body culture, military discipline, love of authority, awe of nature, and devotion to the state.

Interestingly, Hall rather consistently not only ignored but argued against intellectual attainment at all levels of public education. Open discussion of critical issues should not be tolerated in the high school, for such discussions would only "flatter the pupils by the subtle suggestion that they can form opinions that merit the name."[18] The student at this level thinks not with substantial thought but only in "thoughtlets." What he needs is not reasoned discussion but courses indoctrinating him in what Hall termed *heroölogy*. In this way, the individualism so damaging to the evolutionary progress of American culture could be overcome. The young could identify emotionally with heroes as they

---

12. Quoted in Burgess, "Educational State in America," p. 183.

13. Quoted in Burgess, "Educational State in America," p. 185.

14. Probably most recognized of all of Hall's work was his massive study of adolescence entitled, *Adolescence: Its Psychology and Its Relations to Physiology, Anthropology, Sociology, Sex, Crime, Religion, and Education.*

15. Quoted in Burgess, "Educational State in America," p. 196.

16. Quoted in Burgess, "Educational State in America," p 197

17. G. Stanley Hall, *Educational Problems* (New York: D. Appleton & Company, 1914), II, 667.

18. Quoted in Burgess, "Educational State in America," p. 200.

merged their "self" with what was basically a totalitarian collective ideal. In higher education, scientific research would proceed at a rapid pace, emphasizing the new science of psychology. Even here, however, Hall could not tolerate diversity; his ideal faculty was characterized by unanimity, always anxious and willing to teach only that which bettered the state.[19]

Convinced that individualism was contrary to nature, Hall believed that men not only need to but are anxious and willing to escape from freedom.

For most of us the best education is that which makes us the best and most obedient servants. This is the way of peace and the way of nature, for even if we seriously try to keep up a private conscience at all, . . . the difficulties are so great that most hasten, more or less consciously and voluntarily, to put themselves under authority again, reserving only the smallest margin of independence in material interests, choice of masters, etc.[20]

Unlike the evolutionary ideas of Spencer and Sumner, which led straight to rugged individualism, Hall's evolutionary ideas led straight to collectivism. Reminiscent of Sumner, Hall suggested that pity should not be reserved for the poor, sick, and defective, "because by aiding them to survive it interferes with the process of wholesome natural selection by which all that is best has hitherto been developed."[21] He went on to say, "Pity has its highest office . . . in removing the handicaps from those most able to help man to higher levels—the leaders on more exalted planes who can be of most aid in ushering in the kingdom of the superman."[22] In unison with Nietzsche, Hall believed "that man today is only a link, which ought soon to be a missing one, between the primitive cave dwellers and the superman."[23] Hall's "overman," however, was no rugged individualist but rather a charismatic leader, a picture of health, strength, and verve who lost himself in the total collective interests of a transcendent state.

Before World War I, Nietzsche's view of the *Übermensch* served as Hall's model man. During the disillusioning experience of World War I, however, Hall's superman looked increasingly less like Nietzsche's *Übermensch* of power and more like a Christ-like colossus, a product of the transcendent "mansoul."[24] At this time, Hall wrote of a new religion called "morale," which would embody all the virtues of the *Übermensch,* less his demonic egotism, which he assumed had been the cause of Germany's recent failings. As Charles Burgess summed up Hall's work:

19. See Burgess, "Educational State in America," p. 206.
20. G. Stanley Hall, *The Pedagogical Seminary* (Massachusetts: J. H. Orpha, 1914), II, 86.
21. Quoted in Burgess, "Educational State in America," pp. 215-216.
22. Quoted in Burgess, "Educational State in America," p. 216.
23. Quoted in Burgess, "Educational State in America," p. 214.
24. See G. Stanley Hall, *Jesus, the Christ, in the Light of Psychology* (New York: D. Appleton & Company, 1917).

With morale as the new religion of coercion for virtue's sake, with the colossus of a Christ-like superman standing on Liberty's vacated pedestal, with sublimation of self to the State therefore permeating every hierarchical layer from the slave to the *uebermensch,* Hall would at last be able to say that his battle had ended. The dawn of the new day would be upon the world.[25]

Through selective breeding, genetic psychology, and a well-planned educational system geared to the real nature of man and not the demands of vested social interests, the kingdom of the superman would be at hand.

Nevertheless, Hall recognized that America was not taking the path to this idyllic kingdom. Four years before he died, he published "The Fall of Atlantis,"[26] in which he projected the ideal kingdom where men practiced religion in all ways from fetishism to nature worship, according to their development on the evolutionary scale. Everyone in this society dedicated his total self to the interests of the society under the enlightened guidance of what Hall called "heart-formers" (psychologists). This idyllic society eventually ended in chaotic destruction. What caused the decline and fall of Atlantis was creeping individualism, which slowly but surely destroyed the collective self. This was Hall's warning to America. If she persisted in emphasizing the rights and dignity of the individual, she too would meet the ignominious end of Atlantis.

Beginning with a primitivistic conception of the nature of man, which assumed that "the child is vastly more ancient than the man, and that adulthood is comparatively a novel structure built upon very antique foundations,"[27] Hall went on to suggest the kind of education that would be compatible with his conception of man as well as the kind of society he thought most fitting. It is interesting that Hall—using a cosmic sweep of history in the name of human progress, as had Hegel, Comte, Marx, and others before him—would also destroy the individual. Hall's social vision was a socialistic state; this was socialism not of the left, however, but of the right.[28] Hall, with almost uncanny prophetic vision, blueprinted National Socialism at least a decade before it was realized in Germany. Very likely, Hall would have been repelled if he had lived to see the consequences of his ideas in action. Nevertheless, his primitivistic conception of human nature, the use of racial myths in education, the emphasis on nonintellectual purposes of education, the reliance on instinct as right, the vision of health as a religious cult, the submergence of the individual to the interest of the whole, and the faith in the coming superman and superrace all added up to what Josiah Royce described in 1919 as "a strange ideal system."

It was no accident, however, that Hall's sensitive, unconventional mind should anticipate many of the functional constructs of National

---

25. Burgess, "Educational State in America," p. 222.

26. G. Stanley Hall, *Recreations of a Psychologist* (New York: D. Appleton & Company, 1920), pp. 1-116.

27. Quoted in Strickland, "Child and the Race," p. 216.

28. He abhorred the development of Bolshevism, suggesting that Bolshevism was ". . . democratization gone mad." Burgess, "Educational State in America," p. 224.

Socialism, for he had integrated into his personal life numerous primitive beliefs of the *Völkische Kultur,*[29] many of which were antecedents to the later rise of National Socialism in Germany.[30] In 1923, the year before he died, Hall saw himself as a true prophet of the twentieth century. "I love but perhaps still more pity mankind, groping and stumbling, often slipping backward along the upward path, which I believe I see just as clearly as Jesus or Buddha did."[31] It is highly questionable whether Hall had the vision attributed to Jesus or Buddha, but he was a true prophet of a new twentieth-century extreme conservative idealism, an idealism which rejected the Enlightenment concept of rational man collectively resolving his problems and which assumed the irrational nature of man and turned to charismatic leadership to manipulate the instincts of the herd.

The difference between the mind of the conservative and the mind of the extreme conservative or fascist lies to a considerable extent in the conservative view of man as a reasoning being and the fascist view of man as a nonreasoning, instinct-driven animal. The difference between the two conceptions was reflected in the extended arguments between William T. Harris and G. Stanley Hall that rocked the National Education Association halls for decades. The difference, here, is a basic ideological conflict between two kinds of conservative minds, the one holding a rational conception of human nature and arguing that schools must act accordingly, the other holding a primitivistic conception of man and arguing that the schools must educate differently. Although neither man could have realized it at the time, Hall's ideas represented the wave of the future for at least one country.

While neither the conservatives nor the liberals in American education were willing to accept and adopt all of Hall's unconventional ideas, most accepted some of his work. Through more than 400 books and articles and 2500 lectures in over forty states and through his influence on his thousands of students,[32] Hall made an impact on American educational thought. As the founder of the child-study movement, which became a Department of Child Study of the National Education Association in 1893, Hall directed the attention of educators toward child growth and development. When this movement began to decline after the first decade of the century, many of Hall's students became leaders of the new field of child psychology. Among the most important of these leaders was Arnold Gesell, who agreed with his mentor's recapitulation theory.

It was Gesell who coined the word 'maturation,' a term which reflected Hall's emphasis on inner growth as opposed to learning. In 1912, together with his

---

29. See Hall, *Recreations of a Psychologist,* pp. 323-327.
30. For the functional relationship between German *Volk* beliefs and the rise of National Socialism, see Mosse, *Crisis of German Ideology.*
31. G. Stanley Hall, *Life and Confessions of a Psychologist* (New York: D. Appleton & Company, 1923), p. 596.
32. See Merle Curti, *The Social Ideas of American Educators,* rev. ed. (Paterson, N.J.: Littlefield, Adams and Company, 1960), p. 426.

wife, Gesell published *The Normal Child and Primary Education.* The book praised Hall as the 'Darwin of psychology,' and declared that recapitulation was 'one of the most wonderful of all scientific generalizations.' Gesell maintained that the present can be understood only in terms of the past.[33]

The recapitulation idea was nurtured in the field of child psychology well into the twentieth century. In spite of the accumulating evidence to the contrary in both biology and anthropology,[34] Hall and other educators persisted in arguing for a school based on the nature of the child viewed as a primitive.

The influence of Dewey's work at Chicago[35] and the general reluctance of sociologists, anthropologists, and historians to use the past as a cosmic determiner of the future contributed to the rapid decline of Hall's ideas and influence. Increasingly, American psychologists and educators looked to the cultural environment for clues in understanding child behavior rather than to the anthropological past. As an organizer and popularizer, Hall was successful, but as a purveyor of the superman and superrace idea, he failed. Nevertheless, William H. Kilpatrick was perhaps correct when he suggested, "America believes, as does no other country, that education must be based on a study of psychology. That this is so is due to no small degree to the influence of President Hall."[36]

THE NEOCLASSICAL CONCEPTION

In addition to popularizing psychology for American education, Hall also was responsible for introducing Sigmund Freud (1856-1939) and Carl Jung (1875-1961) to American audiences. Through Hall's efforts, such men as William James, James M. Cattell, and Edward B. Titchener met and heard Freud and Jung expound their views at Clark University's vigentennial celebration in 1909. At that time, the ideas of Jung and Freud were still compatible. Not until Jung published *The Psychology of the Unconscious* in 1912 did a major break with Freud appear imminent.

From 1913 to 1961, Jung shifted markedly from Freud's classical conception of man to a mystical view of the soul embodying the collective experiences of the race. In more than one respect, the ideas Jung propounded in *The Reality of the Soul* in 1932 were closer to the later ideas of G. Stanley Hall than to Freud's. In their views on religious mysticism, a collective unconscious, the primitivistic nature of man, and the necessity for charismatic leadership, Hall and Jung seemed to parallel each other. Although neither man was a native of Germany, neither were they foreigners to German *Völkische Kultur*. The general ideology

---

33. Strickland, "Child and the Race," pp. 317-318.
34. Franz Boas clearly repudiated the basis of the theory in 1911 by asserting that the difference between the mind of the savage and civilized man is attributable to environment. See Franz Boas, *The Mind of Primitive Man* (New York: The Macmillan Company, 1911).
35. For an intriguing analysis of Dewey's Laboratory School and the recapitulation idea, see Strickland, "Child and the Race."
36. Quoted in Curti, *Social Ideas of American Educators,* p. 396.

of both, however, came very close to elaborating a psychology compatible with the belief system of National Socialism. Perhaps George Mosse best identified Jung's position in relation to National Socialism when he said:

It is significant that Jung cited Mussolini as an example of such [charismatic] leadership. But Jung came ideologically closer to national socialism than to Italian fascism. As he elaborated his theories, the collective subconscious became transformed into a racial unconscious. The collective experiences of mankind which included his ancestors and his peoples were now unified as racial experiences. Not only did Jung's psychoanalysis and racial thought fuse, he himself took over an 'Aryanized' psychological journal in national socialist Germany.[37]

If Hall's and Jung's conceptions of man are indeed similar, both are markedly different from Freud's. Although Freud, too, was a product of that nineteenth-century cosmic use of the past, he did not romanticize the past but rather rationalized it to explain the cause and effect of current psychic phenomena. To be sure, Freud held an evolutionary conception of man—implicitly involving a recapitulation of man's instinctual past through the unconscious—which cast heavy emphasis on the nonrational origins of reason, but his psychology nonetheless remained an ego-oriented psychology. Freud's conception of man involved an explicit, classical dualism. Very much as some of the ancient Greeks pictured themselves, Freud saw the dual nature of man's passion and reason as inexorably linked through the unconscious. In Freud's psychoanalysis, as in much ancient literature, the black steed of passion had to be controlled and directed by reason. The ego (reason), however, was not alone, but received reinforcement from the superego (internalized social conscience) which helped maintain the dynamic tension so necessary for mental health. Too much or too little tension on the reins would result in destruction. Freud's conception involved not only a classical dualism but also a classical notion of the golden mean.

At various times, Freud has been accused of contributing to the irrationality of the Western mind. This charge, it seems, is more appropriately directed at the users and implementers of Freud (especially in the arts) than at Freud himself. Freud's own quest to make the irrational rational was the ultimate in rationality. The ancient maxim of "Know thyself" and Freud's psychoanalytic theory are, indeed, one. In assuming that reason could dispel the darkness in the human soul and light the path toward mental health, Freud firmly placed his faith in rationality. Yet Freud was a thoroughgoing materialist, always insisting that all that is true of man—his motives, behavior, self-image—is ultimately reducible to biochemistry. In this respect he is in diametric opposition to many classical theories. He explicitly rejected philosophic idealism and the Platonic dualism of spirit and matter. Freud, then, used the classical dual-

---

37. George L. Mosse, *The Culture of Western Europe* (Chicago: Rand McNally & Company, 1961), p. 271.

ism but gave it a biophysical content which resulted in a radically different image of man.

To Freud, the nature of man was neither good, as Emerson had thought, nor socially plastic, as George Herbert Mead and John Dewey had held. Rather, it consisted of the primordial "beast" against which mankind has been struggling through the course of evolution. The evolution of the beast to man was recapitulated in an abbreviated form in the life of the child. The idea that ontogeny recapitulates phylogeny provided the conceptual framework through which Freud could read into the clinical situation both the real and the imagined history of the racial experience.[38] Freud was using the past, putting great emphasis not only on the personal history of his patient but also on the racial history of man. Important, here, was Freud's development of the concept of the *Oedipus complex.* This complex first appeared at that point in historic time when the assumed protohominoid passed from a primitive, physiologically acting animal to a civilized, symbolically thinking animal. Freud believed that the Oedipus complex was recapitulated in an abbreviated form in the life experience of every child. Erich Fromm described the *Oedipus complex* thus:

. . . the decisive step from primitive to civilized history lies in the rebellion of the sons against the father, and the murder of the hated father. The sons then create a system of society based on a covenant which excludes further murder among the rivals and provides for the establishment of morality. The evolution of the child, according to Freud, follows a similar path. The little boy at the age of five or six is intensely jealous of his father and represses murderous wishes against him only under the pressure of the castration threat. In order to liberate himself from continuous fear, he internalizes the incest taboo and thus builds the nucleus around which his 'conscience' is to grow (superego). Later on, the prohibitions and commands voiced by other authorities and by society are added to the original taboos voiced by father.[39]

The Oedipus complex has been the center of much dispute among Freudians and non-Freudians alike. Some have interpreted it as an allegorical event to be viewed in a broad context as a developmental phase through which the human species passes;[40] others, especially in clinical practice, have reified it as a complex problem that a specific patient had to resolve under the guidance of a psychoanalyst. However much in dispute this concept remains, it is clear that Freud developed a functionally useful naturalistic doctrine of original sin. The problems resulting from the original murder of the father are reproduced in the life of each gener-

---

38. For his use of man's racial past to interpret the meaning of dream symbols, see Sigmund Freud, *A General Introduction to Psychoanalysis* (New York: Perma Book, 1957), pp. 209-210.

39. Erich Fromm, *Beyond the Chains of Illusion* (New York: Simon and Schuster, Inc., 1962), p. 34.

40. For an interesting modification of Freud's Oedipus concept as a universal developmental phase, see Ernest Becker, "The Significance of Freudian Psychology," *Main Currents,* XIX, 2 (December 1962), pp. 45-50. Also see Ernest Becker, *The Birth and Death of Meaning* (New York: The Free Press of Glencoe, Inc., 1962).

ation. Each generation, then, has to learn to repress its instincts in order to become human. Human nature, in this context, does not fundamentally change. There are always new actors, but the play remains the same. There is very little of the Enlightenment faith in social meliorism, utopian optimism, or any great hope of progress in Freud's psychoanalytic theories. Happiness is not attainable, for ultimately the fault lies not with society nor with the individual but is inherent in the very unchanging nature of man himself. The tragic tendency implicit in Freud's psychoanalysis was made explicit when, for example, he suggested that in therapy "a great deal will be gained if we succeed in 'transforming your hysterical misery into everyday unhappiness,' which is the usual lot of mankind."[41] Like Marx, Freud discovered what he thought was the one key that unlocked the door to understanding human history, but unlike Marx, who cast his economic determinism in the framework of a Hegelian theory of progress culminating in a utopia, Freud cast his sexual determinism in the framework of a classical dualism which could only end in tragic resignation. While Freud's image of man involved a classical dualism and a classical sense of tragedy, neither the dualism nor the tragedy was truly classical. Unlike the Stoics, who made their soul a desert, Freud insisted that one must pay careful attention to the affective state in order to enhance the domain of reason. Unlike Plato, who viewed the passions as something from which to escape in flight toward a transcendental reason, Freud was convinced that "Where id was, there shall ego be."[42] Although Freud's image of man involved many classical characteristics, his great contribution to the modern world was a fundamental reconstruction of the classical conception of man, which resulted in a very different image of man for the modern world.

To Freud, life was a struggle for existence, and human life was a struggle to achieve rational supremacy over the beast which is a part of man's instinctual endowment, a part of man's primordial past—a past which, try as he may, man cannot escape. He cannot escape from the beast, for it is in him and with him.

The element of truth behind all this, which people are so ready to disavow, is that men are not gentle creatures who want to be loved, and who at the most can defend themselves if they are attacked; they are, on the contrary, creatures among whose instinctual endowments is to be reckoned a powerful share of aggressiveness. . . . As a rule this cruel aggressiveness waits for some provocation or puts itself at the service of some other purpose, whose goal might also have been reached by milder measures. In circumstances that are favourable to it, when the mental counter-forces which ordinarily inhibit it are out of action, it also manifests itself spontaneously and reveals man as a savage beast to whom consideration towards his own kind is something alien.[43]

41. Quoted in Herbert Marcuse, *Eros and Civilization* (Boston: The Beacon Press, 1955), pp. 246-247.
42. Sigmund Freud, *New Introductory Lectures on Psychoanalysis,* trans. W. J. H. Sprott (New York: W. W. Norton & Company, 1933), p. 112.
43. Sigmund Freud, *Civilization and Its Discontents,* trans. and ed. James Strachey (New York: W. W. Norton & Company, 1962), pp. 58-59.

This concept of man was, then, logically extended in implication to society. Civilized society, Freud insisted, is always menaced with the problem of self-destruction. Man's basic hostility to man is so great, his instinctive passions so strong, that culture must call up every possible reinforcement in order to check these destructive instincts. The sanctions for censorship, repression, authoritarian leadership, etc., are not found in the existential world of common work or the necessity for group action but are embedded in the very nature of man. To Freud, the non-repressive culture is a psychological impossibility. The release of the pleasure principle at the expense of the reality principle could only end in nonculture. If culture is to survive, it can do so only if a newer, more restraining reality principle evolves from the conflict. In this context, every revolution which begins in the name of freedom inevitably ends in the name of restraint.[44] Freud saw this paradoxical nature of man working itself out over the broad scope of cultural evolution. Cultural evolution was, then, conceived as a struggle between *eros* and *thanto*, between the instinct for life and the instinct for death.[45] Freud transposed into a cultural world view the powerful insights about human nature that he derived from literature, anthropology, history, biology, medicine, his own personal psychology, and his own social milieu. In a true Platonic sense, he saw the individual writ large in culture, and the culture, in turn, reinforced his perception of the individual.

Psychoanalysis was culturally derived. Freud's bourgeois background not only influenced how he came to perceive man and culture, but it also provided the source of some of the basic ideas which he built into the very superstructure of psychoanalytic theory itself. While Freud, like Gide and others, attacked the bourgeois Victorian ethic, Freud himself, being of the bourgeoisie, reflected its values in his own personal life and built into his thinking a central concept of nineteenth-century economics, the static concept of wealth which assumes that one must rob from the rich to help the poor.[46] He adopted this view of wealth at an early age, then later applied it to sex energy, and concluded that sex energy, upon which all culture is based, is also limited. Man exists in the perpetual state of sacrificing some measure of his sexual life for his cultural life.

Civilization, then, originates not by the conscious extension of an individual's power, thereby achieving for each individual a greater freedom, but by the repression of sexual energy so that sublimation occurs. "Here as we already know, civilization is obeying the laws of economic necessity, since a large amount of the psychical energy which it uses for its own purposes has to be withdrawn from sexuality."[47] Civilization may progress as knowledge gives control over the environment, but

44. See Marcuse, *Eros and Civilization.*

45. See Freud, *Civilization and Its Discontents,* pp. 65-69.

46. For an analysis of this idea as implicit in the thought of Freud, see Erich Fromm, *Sigmund Freud's Mission* (New York: Harper & Brothers, 1959). Also, for a biography of Freud, see Ernest Jones, *The Life and Work of Sigmund Freud,* 3 vols. (New York: Basic Books, Inc., 1953-1957).

47. Freud, *Civilization and Its Discontents,* p. 51.

man must pay a price for this control. For Freud, civilized man must always exchange some part of his chance of happiness for the measure of security implicit in control. As Freud said, "It is impossible to overlook the extent to which civilization is built upon a renunciation of instinct, how much it presupposes precisely the non-satisfaction (by suppression, repression, or some other means?) of powerful instincts."[48] And, "The commandment [to love thy neighbor as thyself] is impossible to fulfil; such an enormous inflation of love can only lower its value, not get rid of the difficulty."[49]

Throughout Freud's work, there remained implicit assumptions as to the nature of man which shaped his perceptions of man in society. These assumptions reflected considerable faith in the rationality of man. However, it was not the rationality of the eighteenth-century Enlightenment but the rationality of classical antiquity. Unlike Hall, who closed his dualism in a monistic "mansoul," or Jung, who reconciled all opposites in a "collective unconscious" and then looked to the future for the "kingdom of the superman," Freud maintained to the very end that there was no hope of transcending the dualism to achieve the superrace.

The authoritarian personality of Freud cannot be concealed. Even the most devoted disciple of Freud, Ernest Jones, had difficulty in accounting for the dramatic personal trauma that Freud's colleagues repeatedly experienced as they challenged his ideas.[50] The pattern was repetitious. Breuer, Stekel, Fliess, Jung, Adler, Rank, Ferenczi, and Reich all found that an intellectual disagreement with the Master of Psychoanalysis meant a violent personal conflict as well. The "passionless science" of psychoanalysis was fraught with passion. Freud had a mission. He had founded a movement based on the "universal truths" of psychoanalysis as he developed them; and his mission was to spread the gospel. To carry out this mission, he needed, psychologically as well as practically, a coterie of dedicated apostles who would not question the word but would expand it, confirm it, and communicate it to a hostile world. Freud intended to cast a shadow on the minds of posterity that was sharp, clear, and distinct. In this endeavor, his best friends were his worst enemies. In spite of all his attempts to hold them in check, his shadow, after his death, became increasingly diffused. One recent writer has accounted for no less than thirty-six varieties of psychoanalysis.[51]

Even though the shadow of Freud's ideology became diffused, Freud, more than any other psychologist in the past century, was successful in profoundly changing Western man's image of himself, his childhood, and his sex. Through his many and varied interpreters, Freudian and neo-Freudian terminology became commonplace in the language of Western culture. Neither the home, church, school, factory, theater, nor the mass media remained unaffected by Freudian or neo-Freudian views of man and culture. Although Freudian psychology was used by some to justify

---

48. Freud, *Civilization and Its Discontents*, p. 44.
49. Freud, *Civilization and Its Discontents*, p. 90.
50. See Jones, *Life and Work of Sigmund Freud*.
51. See Mosse, *Culture of Western Europe*, p. 273.

sexual license, neither Freud nor his psychology sanctioned such a view. If he had to face this interpretation of his work, one would suspect that he would claim not to be a Freudian, much as Marx once claimed not to be a Marxian.[52] Both men had a profound effect on Western thought, the consequences of which they could neither foretell nor control.

The Americanization of Freud was led by such revisionists as Erich Fromm, Erik Erikson, Karen Horney, Harry Stack Sullivan,[53] Karl Menninger, Gardner Murphy, and others. Although these revisionists represented many divergent views, there were certain underlying areas of agreement. All seemed to reject Freud's emphasis on the importance of the race history of the patient as they directed their attention to the current life situation. In general, they were more interested in therapy than in doctrinaire ideology, for their work reflected a greater concern for the function of the social environment in developing healthy personalities. In his later work, Freud came close to developing a metaphysics of the mind by ignoring environmental influences and suggesting that "reality will forever be unknowable."[54] Freud's profound sense of tragedy was usually rejected by the revisionists, who, in turning to the present instead of the past, became vitally concerned with social meliorism.[55] At this point, many of the social ideas of Erik Erikson, Erich Fromm, Karl Menninger, and Gardner Murphy tended to merge with the social ideas of John Dewey and George Herbert Mead. In this way the revisionists, while rejecting Freud's tragic classicism, used many of his profound insights into the human condition for humanitarian purposes.

If John Dewey had explicitly dealt with Freud's conception of man, he would have had to either reject much of Freud or seriously modify his own views. Even though Dewey did not deal with this question directly,[56] he did criticize psychoanalysts for their "transformation of social results into psychic causes" and for treating "phenomena which are peculiarly symptoms of the civilization of the West at the present time as if they were the necessary effects of fixed native impulses of

---

52. See Philip Rieff, *Freud: The Mind of the Moralist* (Garden City, N.Y.: Doubleday & Company, 1961), p. 343.

53. Although Sullivan radically modified Freud's tripartite psyche into a "self system," he "opinioned that the meticulously fractionated Freudian system was a worthwhile preoccupation if one wanted to induce headaches. Sullivan traced his own thinking to the social psychology of George Herbert Mead, which stresses the social genesis of mind." See Becker, *Birth and Death of Meaning*, p. 48.

54. Quoted in Mosse, *Culture of Western Europe*, p. 268.

55. Freud's emphasis on the importance of early childhood, cast in terms of Erik Erikson's thesis that "basic trust" achieved very early in life tends to shape not only personality but also intelligence, has been given strong empirical validation by the extensive work of Benjamin S. Bloom in *Stability and Change in Human Characteristics* (New York: John Wiley & Sons, Inc., 1964). See also Bruno Bettelheim's review of Bloom's work, "How Much Can Man Change?" *New York Times Review of Books,* III, 2 (Sept. 10, 1964). For Erikson's basic work, see Erik H. Erikson, *Childhood and Society,* rev. ed. (New York: W. W. Norton & Company, 1964). The implications of Erikson's, Bloom's, and Bettelheim's work are of extreme importance for those interested in the education of culturally deprived children.

56. The present historical evidence seems to indicate this. Perhaps when the personal papers of John Dewey are released to the historian, they will prove otherwise.

human nature."[57] Dewey's view of the child, which employed the influence of the social environment in shaping human nature, was incompatible with Freud's dualistic conception of the child, which assigned history a much larger function.

While Freud's view of human nature was incompatible with that of John Dewey, it was equally unacceptable to the romantic humanitarians who, from Rousseau to A. S. Neill, proclaimed the nature of man as "good." Most romantic, child-centered educators ignored the fact that Freud saw in man a beast which would have to be repressed for cultural purposes. When these educators came in contact with psychoanalysis, as in the case of Margaret Naumburg in her Walden School in Greenwich Village and A. S. Neill at Summerhill, they maintained their original concept of man as basically good and proceeded to use, wherever possible, psychoanalytic ideas, not to repress for the sake of sublimation, but to free a child from the guilt and anxiety of what they viewed as a repressive culture. At the center of the extreme child-centered wing of the progressive education movement was a romantic educator applying key Freudian ideas to educational practice.[58] Thus Freud's influence on education has come to mean, to many educators and laymen, a highly permissive form of socialization. Other authors, however, point toward the more restrictive nature of psychoanalysis as applied to education.

The historical impact of Freud on American education remains an unanswered question. Even though the American teacher has learned to use the language of Freud, Adler, and sometimes Jung, it is difficult to determine the extent to which this has actually influenced pupil-teacher relationships. Indeed, how the American teacher has learned the language of psychoanalysis is open to question. An examination of many of the educational psychology textbooks used in training teachers during the twenties and even the thirties reveals little attention paid to psychoanalysis; by the forties and fifties, most texts had a separate chapter dealing with the subject, but with little consideration of its application in educational practice. One suspects that the average American teacher in the twentieth century learned more of psychoanalysis by way of the popular press than by formal instruction.

THE SOCIAL BEHAVIORIST VIEW

William James once cautioned philosopher-psychologists: "By their fruits ye shall know them, not by their roots." If the psychologies of Hall and Freud placed great stress on the "roots" of mankind, the social behaviorism of George H. Mead, the connectionism of Edward L. Thorndike, and the behaviorism of John B. Watson and B. F. Skinner placed far greater stress on the "fruits" of the human condition. In this respect,

---

57. Joseph Ratner, ed., *Intelligence in the Modern World: John Dewey's Philosophy* (New York: The Modern Library, 1939), p. 745.
58. See Lawrence A. Cremin, *The Transformation of the School* (New York: Alfred A. Knopf, Inc., 1961).

the former were characteristic of nineteenth-century thought and the latter of twentieth-century thought. Although all the behaviorists were evolutionary naturalists, agreeing as to the importance of the present by de-emphasizing the role of instincts and emphasizing the role of environment in shaping human behavior, they seriously disagreed as to the extent to which environment controls human behavior.

Implicit in such a dispute were competing conceptions of human nature. In the tradition of Helvétius and Owen, Watson and Skinner saw human nature as determined by the environment; whereas George H. Mead, in the manner of William Maclure and John Dewey, conceived of human nature as involving an emerging self which consciously and purposely shapes the environment. Even though Mead agreed with Watson's attack on introspective psychology and with his emphasis on behavior, he objected to Watson's casting the individual in terms of a physiologically behaving animal without the intervening variable of reflective thought. Reacting specifically to Watson's behaviorism, George H. Mead declared that his own psychology was a "social behaviorism." Mead's social behaviorism involved a conception of human nature very different from that held by other behaviorists.

The year John Dewey published *Psychology* (1887), George H. Mead (1863-1931) was studying psychology with William James and philosophy with Josiah Royce. Under their influence, he decided upon a career in psychology and philosophy. The following year he went abroad to study and remained there until 1891, when he accepted an appointment as an instructor in the Department of Philosophy and Psychology at the University of Michigan in Ann Arbor. The department chairman at the time was John Dewey. Four years later, Mead accompanied John Dewey to the new University of Chicago, where he remained until his death.

Even though Dewey left Chicago in 1904, the close intellectual alliance between Mead and Dewey continued unabated throughout their lives. Dewey's instrumentalism and Mead's social psychology evolved out of the searching dialog that took place between the two. Mead provided the psychology which was a base for Dewey's instrumentalism, while Dewey provided the philosophy which steadied Mead's psychology. Dewey repeatedly expressed his indebtedness to Mead. As Dewey said, "His mind was deeply original—in my contacts and my judgment the most original mind in the America of the last generation."[59] Dewey saw Mead's contribution to philosophy as the development of an evolutionary conception of nature and man which made man neither a pawn of the universal forces of nature nor a victim of individual subjectivism but which gave a rational explanation for social authority and yet preserved the free integrity of the individual. In relation to this problem, Dewey said:

His identification of the process of evolution with that of continuous reconstruction by which nature and man (as a part of nature that has become con-

---

59. Quoted in Alfred Stafford Clayton, *Emergent Mind and Education* (New York: Bureau of Publications, Teachers College, Columbia University, 1943), p. xii.

scious) solve the problem of the relations of the universal and the individual, the regular and the novel—this identification is his own outstanding contribution to philosophy.[60]

In rejecting Watson's determinism, Mead insisted that man is a social, reflective being that evolves his human characteristics from a social setting. At the base of his psychology rests the idea that

... any psychological or philosophical treatment of human nature involves the assumption that the human individual belongs to an organized social community, and derives his human nature from his social interactions and relations with that community as a whole and with the other individual members of it.[61]

As an avid student of Aristotle, Mead was saying that man is a social animal, but unlike Aristotle, who viewed human nature as fixed, Mead viewed human nature as emerging within a social context. Man, in the course of evolution, became human when he began to think reflectively. He began to think when, in a social context, he advanced from gestures to language which could be symbolically internalized. In contrast to Freud, who saw the original development of culture as the loss of some portion of one's happiness in order to attain security, Mead saw the development of culture as the origin of intelligence which increased man's chance for happiness. Indeed, while there was continuity between the mind of man and that of the animal, there remained a qualitative difference in the ability of man to symbolize his past, present, and future reflectively and to direct his actions accordingly. To Mead, stimulus-response psychology could explain how animals and humans learned certain habitual kinds of behavior, but it failed to explain adequately purposive behavior which was symbolically generated. In his view, mind, self, and society were functionally related in a transactional, continuous, and emerging process.

The child is born a physiological organism with undifferentiated tendencies to act. Through verbal gestures in a social context the child learns the meaning of the symbols held in common by the group. Once he learns language, the child can internalize conversation, and he becomes a thinking being. Through various kinds of social activities, the child learns to symbolically take the role of the other, and there gradually emerges a conception of self in which he sees himself as others see him. As the individual takes the role of the other and sees himself as others see him, there develops the "generalized other," which includes society's values, attitudes, and beliefs which are then internalized in the individual in the form of the "me." Thus far, one has substantially a picture of the "organization man." This, however, is not all. There is another side to the self—the "I"—which, unlike the "generalized other" or the "me," represents the novel, creative, impulsive side of the self which repeatedly

60. Quoted in Clayton, *Emergent Mind and Education,* p. xiii.
61. Quoted in Clayton, *Emergent Mind and Education,* p. 49.

surprises the "me." the "I's" behavior is never completely predictable.[62] In keeping with his mentor's (William James) opposition to determinism, Mead's social behaviorism also rejected the notion of complete determinism. Mead suggested that the ability of the self to introduce novel behavior in the social group forever confounds attempts at prediction of individual behavior as well as at complete standardization of group control. The group undergoes continuous change as individuals change within the group. To Mead, social institutions are basically made up of neither "I's" nor "me's" but of whole individuals with emerging selves behaving cooperatively to achieve greater freedom. This socialized individualism assumes that freedom is gained through society and not from society. Alienation of man from society can, in this context, only dehumanize man. Consistently, Mead rejected the classical dualism and refused to pit the individual against society. Man achieves his humanity and his freedom through society. While assuming that the individual internalizes the controlling limits of society, Mead defined freedom in terms of the ability of the whole self to act.

But in freedom the personality as a whole passes into the act. Compulsion disintegrates the individual into his different elements; hence there are degrees of freedom in proportion to the extent to which the individual becomes organized as a whole. It is not often that the whole of us goes into any act so that we face the situation as an entire personality. Moreover, this does not necessarily spell creation, spontaneity; it spells the identification of the individual with the act. Freedom, then, is the expression of the whole self which has become entire through the reconstruction which has taken place.[63]

This definition of freedom is a long way from the Jeffersonian idea of freedom based on the natural rights theory, but there are similarities. Mead's ideas were based on a concept of enlightened self-interest, in which the individual sees his own interests as intimately tied with the interests of others. Both definitions assumed that "no man is an island, entire of it self," and both assumed the individual's responsibility to society as well as society's responsibility to the individual.[64] Fundamentally, both assumed man to be rational enough to consciously examine alternatives and act on the basis of reasoned choice.

To Mead, the good society was a society which maximized freedom and allowed individuals to reconstruct their social institutions as they reconstruct themselves. Such continuous reconstruction was to be thought through consciously and reflectively. Crucial, here, was the use

---

62. In direct contrast to John B. Watson and B. F. Skinner, Mead assumed that an important part of human behavior would remain unpredictable. See Anselm Strauss, ed., "The Process of Mind in Nature" in *George Herbert Mead on Social Psychology* (Chicago: Phoenix Books, 1964), p. 105.

63. George H. Mead, *The Philosophy of the Act,* ed. Charles W. Morris (Chicago: University of Chicago Press, 1938), p. 663.

64. Once again, in direct contrast to Mead, B. F. Skinner argued that such ideas as freedom and responsibility have no place in a scientific analysis of human behavior. See B. F. Skinner, *Science and Human Behavior* (New York: The Macmillan Company, 1953), pp. 446-449.

of the scientific method in its broadest sense, reflective intelligence employed in resolving problems. Reminiscent of Lester Frank Ward's attitude toward crime, Mead argued, "What are the conditions out of which crime springs? How, on the one hand, can you protect society against the criminal and yet, on the other hand, recognize those conditions which are responsible for the criminal himself?"[65] Mead, like others before him, was sure that society could progress in this field. He said, "Progress has become essential to intelligent life. Now, how are we to get ahead and change those situations that need changing?"[66] The solution rests in the application of social-science knowledge to the social melioration process of a planned society.

In his essay on Auguste Comte, Mead paid tribute to the founder of sociology for "his emphasis on the dependence of the individual on society, his sense of the organic character of society as responsible for the nature of individuals."[67] On the other hand, Mead disagreed with Comte for worshiping the "Supreme Being in the form of society."[68] Mead held far more respect for the rational intelligence of the average man than did Auguste Comte or, for that matter, G. Stanley Hall or Carl Jung. Mead's optimism was based on a faith in man's ability to change himself and his environment, whereas the optimism of Comte was based on the ability of a scientific elite to shape human nature, and that of Hall rested on a faith in charismatic leadership and the future kingdom of the supermen.

Unlike Comte, Hall, Jung, or Freud, who used man's past to understand man's present, Mead argued that we must learn to understand the past through the present.[69] In *The Philosophy of the Present*,[70] Mead thoroughly rejected the nineteenth-century cosmic use of history to explain the present and project a future. There is only one reality, and that is the present. Similar to Dewey's later view of history was Mead's view of the past as "that conditioning phase of the passing present which enables us to determine conduct with reference to the future which is also arising in the present."[71] To Mead, the past is dead and has meaning only as we ascribe meaning to it from the present context. In this sense, we actually read history backward but create the illusion that we read it forward. For instance, the historical perspectives of Hegel, Marx, Comte, Freud, and Hall were all interpretations of the past derived from the present perspective of their individual lives. As Mead put it, "Every great social movement has flashed back its light to discover a new past."[72] There are, in this sense, as many pasts as there are futures demanding a new past. Mead said, "The novelty of every future demands a novel past."[73] He summarized his conception of history when he said:

65. Strauss, *George Herbert Mead on Social Psychology*, p. 23.
66. Strauss, *George Herbert Mead on Social Psychology*, p. 22.
67. Strauss, *George Herbert Mead on Social Psychology*, p. 292.
68. Strauss, *George Herbert Mead on Social Psychology*, p. 291.
69. See Strauss, *George Herbert Mead on Social Psychology*, pp. 319-327.
70. George H. Mead, *The Philosophy of the Present*, ed. Arthur E. Murphy (Chicago: The Open Court Publishing Company, 1932).
71. Quoted in Strauss, *George Herbert Mead on Social Psychology*, p. xxv.
72. Strauss, *George Herbert Mead on Social Psychology*, p. 321.
73. Quoted in Strauss, *George Herbert Mead on Social Psychology*, p. xxv.

The long and short of it is that the only reality of the past open to our reflective research is the implication of the present, that the only reason for research into the past is the present problem of understanding a problematic world, and the only test of the truth of what we have discovered is our ability to so state the past that we can continue the conduct whose inhibition has set the problem to us.[74]

Mead's pragmatic rejection of cosmic history, his rational conception of man and society, and his belief in social progress by way of social meliorism mark his views as part of the neo-Enlightenment pragmatic conception of man and culture. Within recent decades, Mead has received increasing recognition for his creative work in sociology and social psychology. He has been hailed, with C. H. Cooley, as the cofounder of social psychology. Mead's ideas on human nature were carried into educational thought by John Dewey,[75] into psychology by Harry Stack Sullivan,[76] and into social science theory by Talcott Parsons, Kingsley Davis, Robert K. Merton, and many others. Most social science theorists today would agree with Dewey that Mead was "deeply original."

Interestingly, however, in a world of publish or perish, George Herbert Mead would have perished. In the forty years of his academic work, Mead published not a single book. He was first and foremost a teacher, creating and re-creating ideas with students, which left little time for publication. In comparison with the massive publication lists of Hall, Thorndike, or Dewey, Mead's few articles look sparse indeed. Consequently, his influence on American thought cannot be gauged by his publication list but rather by the many influential people who were either formally or informally his students. The fact that Mead was at the University of Chicago, one of the leading institutions in the field of sociology during the first half of the twentieth century, no doubt contributed to his influence. As students from the new fields of sociology and social psychology flocked to his philosophy course, it was clear that Mead had something significant to offer. After his death in 1931, dedicated students compiled his notes and articles into three volumes: *Mind, Self and Society; The Philosophy of the Present;* and *The Philosophy of the Act.* These volumes continue to be a rich source of insight for students of human nature and culture.

THE CONNECTIONIST VIEW

In 1898, when James introduced the term *pragmatism* to popular audiences at the University of California, a former student of his, Edward

74. Strauss, *George Herbert Mead on Social Psychology*, p. 324.

75. For a perceptive analysis of Mead's thought and the implications of his ideas for educational practice, see Clayton, *Emergent Mind and Education*. It should also be recognized that the following cited work of Dewey's is subtitled "Social Psychology." There are many indications that Dewey's ideas here are a product of his extended dialog with Mead. John Dewey, *Human Nature and Conduct* (New York: Henry Holt and Company, 1922).

76. Sullivan traced his own thinking from the social psychology of Mead; see Becker, *Birth and Death of Meaning*, p. 48.

L. Thorndike (1874-1949), was completing an epoch-making dissertation: "Animal Intelligence: An Experimental Study of Associative
Processes in Animals." This work was quickly recognized as a landmark
in experimental psychology and, as a result, Thorndike's career skyrocketed. Within a few years he was a full professor at Columbia University, with major interests in human learning and educational psychology. For almost half a century, Thorndike held sway at Columbia, during
which time he taught thousands of teachers and administrators, published 50 books and 450 monographs and articles. His massive three-
volume work entitled *Educational Psychology* (1913) set the tone of
educational psychology for almost the next two decades. From his pen
flowed a prodigious number of educational maxims; psychological laws;
textbooks and scales of achievement for elementary, secondary, and
college courses in varied fields; dictionaries for elementary and secondary schools; and teacher manuals. Because he wrote so many of the texts
and the tests used in elementary and secondary schools, his impact on
American educational practice was both immediate and extended.

In 1901, in collaboration with Robert Woodworth, Thorndike published his now-famous paper on the transfer of training, which attempted
to refute empirically the claims made by the exponents of the traditional
doctrine of formal discipline. At a time when the attacks on the classical
languages were increasing at a feverish pitch, the findings of Thorndike
and Woodworth were received with great enthusiasm. The classicists,
down through the years, had argued that Greek and Latin were to be
valued not so much for their specific content as for their power to develop the faculty of reasoning. The experiment of Woodworth and
Thorndike seemed to demonstrate that ability developed in one line
of work was specific and did not transfer except in cases where it could
be utilized in a concrete way.[77] Thorndike concluded that school subjects are to be valued for their specific content and not for any generalized disciplinary powers.[78] For the next thirty years, the battle raged
with relentless fury until Greek was eliminated from the public school
and Latin was reduced to an elective course. Although many factors
contributed to the decline of the classics in American education,[79]
Thorndike's timely arguments were of major importance.[80]

---

77. See Edward L. Thorndike and Robert S. Woodworth, "The Influence of Improvement in One Mental Function upon the Efficiency of Other Functions," *Psychological
Review*, 8, (1901), 247-261, 384-395, 558-564.

78. Charles H. Judd, at the University of Chicago, found a different alternative to
Thorndike's explanation. Judd argued that when a subject is taught for "generalizations,"
these generalizations transfer. Various experiments have since confirmed Judd's hypothesis. See Charles H. Judd et al., *Education as Cultivation of Higher Mental Processes* (New
York: The Macmillan Company, 1936). If one pushes Thorndike's thesis to its logical
extreme, the formal school might best return to an apprenticeship system. For a critical
appraisal of Thorndike's theory that only identical elements transfer, see Pedro T. Orata,
The Theory of Identical Elements (Columbus: Ohio State University Press, 1928).

79. See Chapter Four.

80. Whether the ready acceptance of Thorndike's work on this subject was due to the
impressive evidence he presented or because Thorndike found what the culture wanted
is indeed a moot question. See Walter B. Kolesnik, *Mental Discipline in Modern Education*
(Madison: University of Wisconsin Press, 1958).

In more ways than one, Thorndike was a man of the hour who rode the *Zeitgeist* of his time. Such a *Zeitgeist* saw science as an instrument to organize the public school on the model of a business establishment.[81] As George P. Strayer, a leading light in the efficiency movement in education, put it: "All our investigations with respect to the classification and progress of children in the elementary schools, in high schools, and in higher education are based upon Professor Thorndike's contribution to the psychology of individual differences."[82]

In 1904, when Dewey went to Columbia, Thorndike published *Introduction to the Theory of Mental and Social Measurements.* From this point on, Thorndike became one of the leading figures in the test and measurement movement. In 1917 and 1918, Thorndike chaired the Committee on Classification of Personnel of the United States Army, and for the first time group intelligence tests were introduced to American culture on a massive scale. In the postwar era, Thorndike's influence led to the use of various tests in business and industry as well as in education. By serving on the National Research Council, he helped develop the popular National Intelligence Test used in the elementary schools. By 1926, he published *The Measurement of Intelligence,* which deals with the well-known C A V D test. Throughout the 1920's and 1930's, Thorndike stood in the middle of the storm which raged over the nature of intelligence as well as the nature-nurture argument. His response to both these problems was consistent with his psychological conception of man.

As an evolutionist, Thorndike believed that "amongst the minds of animals that of man leads, not as a demigod from another planet, but as a king from the same race."[83] Because men's minds were continuous with the minds of animals, the study of animal learning could give a simplified key to understanding human intelligence. From his study of animal intelligence, he derived his theory of *connectionism.*

Connectionism as conceived by Thorndike can be defined in rather simple terms. In all species of animals, including man, certain neurobiological connections of such a nature that the application of a given stimulus tends to elicit a particular type of response (S-R bonds) are found to exist. Some of these connections have already been established in the normal animal at the time of birth; others, which he is potentially capable of forming, are acquired as a result of post-natal experiences.[84]

Connections are "stamped in" by way of the law of *exercise* and the law of *effect.* The law of exercise implied that repetitions strengthen connections, and the law of effect suggested that rewards also strengthen con-

81. For one aspect of this development, see Raymond E. Callahan, *Education and the Cult of Efficiency* (Chicago: University of Chicago Press, 1962).

82. Quoted in Curti, *Social Ideas of American Educators,* p. 483.

83. Edward L. Thorndike, "The Evolution of Human Intellect," *Popular Science Monthly,* LX (November 1901), 65.

84. Florence L. Goodenough, "Edward Lee Thorndike, 1874-1949," *American Journal of Psychology,* LXIII (1950), 292.

nections while punishment weakens them. Later research by T
and others seemed to indicate that punishment did not weake
tions.[85]

With the law of effect stripped of punishment, Thorndike
theory of reinforcement which Watson and Skinner later ᴜᴄ..⸺
more fully. However, Thorndike radically disagreed with Watson as to
the origin of differences among individuals. While Watson attributed
the differences to environment, Thorndike attributed them to heredity.
"Thorndike early concluded that heredity is the major reason for human
variation in intellect and character, that no other factor is more significant than innate and inherited inequalities in the capacity to learn."[86]
The differences between Watson and Thorndike on this key aspect of
human nature led the one psychologist to advocate social radicalism and
the other to advocate social conservatism more compatible with the
values of an emerging middle-class America. Thorndike's emphasis on
heredity did not lead to the primitivism of Hall[87] or the tragic sense of
Freud but rather to the social conservatism of W. T. Harris. Like Harris,
he was no laissez-faire advocate but insisted that the "original nature has
achieved what goodness the world knows as a state achieves order, by
killing, confining or reforming some of its elements."[88] Even though
there were innate differences in learning capacity, the function of the
school was to take each child as he was and train each to the limits of
his capacity.

The major thrust of Thorndike's thought and influence was along
quantitative lines. "Whatever exists at all exists in some amount,"[89] he
asserted early in his career, and then he spent the rest of his life trying
to measure what exists.

His influence in establishing and popularizing the fact-finding, statistical, and
experimental technique in education has been immeasurable. Taking over the
methods of the physical and natural sciences, and using the more quantitative
devices of such pioneers as Pearson, Galton, Cattell, Rice, and Boas, Thorndike,
together with Judd, revolutionized American educational technique.[90]

Advising teachers to think in terms of measurable behavioral objectives[91]
and to conceive of learning as a stamping-in process, Thorndike went

---

85. Thorndike's connectionist view of human learning accounts for his persistent attitude that intelligence must not be viewed as general but as specific kinds of behavior. The
quantitative speed of making these connections he attributed to heredity.

86. Geraldine M. Joncich, ed., *Psychology and the Science of Education: Selected Writings
of Edward L. Thorndike,* Classics in Education, No. 8 (New York: Bureau of Publications,
Teachers College, Columbia University, 1962), p. 21.

87. Thorndike had explicitly rejected the recapitulation theory. See Joncich, *Psychology
and the Science of Education.*

88. Edward L. Thorndike, *Educational Psychology* (New York: Bureau of Publications,
Teachers College, Columbia University, 1921), Vol. I, *The Original Nature of Man,* p. 281.

89. National Society for the Study of Education, *Seventeenth Yearbook* (Bloomington,
Ill., 1918), part II, p. 16.

90. Curti, *Social Ideas of American Educators,* p. 460.

91. See Edward L. Thorndike, "The Contributions of Psychology to Education," *The
Journal of Educational Psychology,* I (January 1910), 5-6.

on to suggest that the new science of psychology might quantitatively determine not only the best methods to be used but the best objectives of education as well.[92] Thorndike's unbounded faith in a quantitative science of education led him into areas of defining not only what is but what ought to be.[93] The fact that what he thought ought to be was predetermined by his own personal values did not seem to restrain him.

In many respects, Thorndike's personal values were akin to the rugged individualism of William Graham Sumner, harnessed to the educational activism of W. T. Harris. Progress depended not on the extension of culture to the masses but rather on the education of the gifted elite. Repeatedly, he argued against the upward extension of the compulsory education law on the grounds that such attempts at further education of the mentally unfit were doomed to failure. Thorndike's emphasis on individual differences and objective classification of students led to the logical conclusion of segregating, for educational purposes, the superior intellects, whom he believed to be of superior moral character and good will as well. As Thorndike put it:

> But, in the long run, it has paid the 'masses' to be ruled by intelligence. Furthermore, the natural processes which give power to men of ability to gain it and keep it are not, in their results, unmoral. Such men are, by and large, of superior intelligence, and consequently of somewhat superior justice and goodwill. They act, in the long run, not against the interests of the world, but for it. What is true in science and government seems to hold good in general for manufacturing, trade, art, law, education, and religion. It seems entirely safe to predict that the world will get better treatment by trusting its fortunes to its 95- or 99-percentile intelligences than it would get by itself. The argument for democracy is not that it gives power to all men without distinction, but that it gives greater freedom for ability and character to attain power.[94]

Thorndike was quite sure that "to him that hath a superior intellect is given also on the average a superior character."[95] His own white middle-class values seemed obvious when he suggested that his scientific observations of men indicated that "the abler persons in the world in the long run are the more clean, decent, just and kind."[96] Between money-making, intelligence, and moral character, he asserted, there exists a positive correlation. In many ways, Thorndike was a twentieth-century sample of that long tradition of the spirit of capitalism which, from Benjamin Franklin to William Graham Sumner, equated virtue with wealth. The difference, however, is that Thorndike equated it "scientifically."

---

92. In 1903 he admitted that the aim and goal of education was determined "not by facts but by ideals." It was not long, however, before he asserted ideals and values were proper subjects of scientific investigation and control. See Robert Woodworth, "Edward Lee Thorndike (1874-1949)," *National Academy of Science*, XXVII (1952), 217.

93. In this way, Thorndike was well along the route that Watson and Skinner took to behavioral engineering.

94. Edward L. Thorndike, "Intelligence and Its Uses," *Harpers*, CXL (December 1919-May 1920), 235.

95. Thorndike, "Intelligence and Its Uses," p. 233.

96. Thorndike, "Intelligence and Its Uses," p. 235.

Man is not solely a product of his environment; there are moral and intellectual differences which are due to one's ancestry. Because "mental and moral inheritance from near ancestry is a fact,"[97] Thorndike was also sure that "racial differences in original nature are not mere myths."[98] He objectively tested Negro and white children and found that even though there was considerable overlap between the two races, the white pupils were demonstrably superior in scholarship, and this, he concluded, was attributable to original nature since "the differences in the environment do not seem at all adequate to account for the superiority of the whites."[99] Thorndike's emphasis on heredity led him to de-emphasize the importance of environment. In a later work, he concluded that:

By selective breeding supported by a suitable environment we can have a world in which all men will equal the top ten percent of present men. One sure service of the able and good is to beget and rear offspring. One sure service (about the only one) which the inferior and vicious can perform is to prevent their genes from survival.[100]

Thorndike included in his twenty-point program for social progress such advice as: Society should practice scientific "eugenics"; "the able and good should acquire power"; and "quality is better than equality."[101] To Thorndike, quality and equality were diametrically opposed concepts. Interestingly, this is exactly what he had found wrong, some thirty-three years earlier, with Ward's *Applied Sociology*. Thorndike had attacked Ward for ignoring the Galton thesis which made ancestry so significant. Ward's equalitarianism, Thorndike surmised, was nothing more than a "defense of intellectual communism."[102] Throughout his life, Thorndike held fast to a conception of human nature which saw man as a product of biologic evolution with some men higher and others lower on the genetic scale. His massive studies of individual differences confirmed, for Thorndike and others, that social and economic classes were largely caused by differences in inherited intelligence. Thorndike's original view of human nature was confirmed by the statistical charts of a lifetime of work. Men could progress if they recognized the pernicious nature of Ward's "equalitarianism" and proceeded to practice eugenics to bring forth the mental and moral best.

Thorndike had objectified, standardized, and typed both the individual and society. In this respect, he played a significant role, indirectly at least, in the "scientific management" movement in business and directly

---

97. Edward L. Thorndike, *Individuality* (Boston: Houghton Mifflin Company, 1911), p. 40.
98. Thorndike, *Individuality*, p. 36.
99. Thorndike, *Individuality*, pp. 37-38.
100. Edward L. Thorndike, *Human Nature and the Social Order* (New York: The Macmillan Company, 1940), p. 957.
101. Thorndike, *Human Nature and the Social Order*, pp. 957-962.
102. Edward L. Thorndike, "A Sociologist's Theory of Education," *Bookman*, XXIV (1906-7), 294. See also Edward L. Thorndike, "Scientific Books," *Science*, XXIV (September 1906), 299-301.

in the efficiency movement in education.[103] Through his many disciples in education, his textbooks, tests, achievement scales, and teachers' manuals, he had a profound impact on American education. Thorndike, perhaps more than any other single individual, helped standardize and structure American education in the twentieth century.[104] Through the efforts of Thorndike and others, American school administrators, teachers, and curriculum experts learned to regard their students objectively and quantitatively. The question of whether this standardization of the educational frontier enhanced social mobility or decreased it, and questions concerning the value system on which the standards were based, proved to be embarrassing for most American educators by mid-twentieth century.

Thorndike's vast influence on American education may be accounted for in part by the fact that his own values were those of a white, middle-class America, but more important was the fact that his empirical findings were essentially what a business-minded America wanted to hear. His positive correlations of wealth, morality, intelligence, and social power could ruffle no one on the upper end of the power structure. Nor, indeed, would a well-washed, growing, middle-class America be upset to find that science had substantiated the fact that "the abler persons in the world in the long run are the more clean, decent, just and kind." The conservative social values of Thorndike were fundamentally compatible with a business-minded, conservative, middle-class America. It is interesting that it took Horace Mann, a conservative Whig politician, to establish the common school in the first half of the nineteenth century; William T. Harris, a conservative Hegelian philosopher, to organize American secondary education in the second half of the century; and Edward L. Thorndike, a conservative psychologist, to standardize education in the twentieth century.

BEHAVIORAL ENGINEERING

Thorndike's law of effect, his study of animal learning, and his quantitative research all contributed to the rise of behaviorism. Nevertheless, his emphasis on inherited characteristics, as well as his reliance on physiological explanation to fill in where empirical observation failed, marked his psychology as still mentalistic. It remained for another student of animal learning, John B. Watson (1878-1958), to lead psychology out of the wilderness of introspection.

---

103. In certain respects, some of Thorndike's ideas on individual differences and their educational implications found limited acceptance by progressive education reformers. For the role Thorndike and educational science played in progressive education movements, see Cremin, *Transformation of the School*, and Joncich, *Psychology and the Science of Education*.

104. For a comprehensive biography of Thorndike, see Geraldine Joncich, *The Sane Positivist: A Biography of Edward L. Thorndike* (Middletown, Conn.: Wesleyan University Press, 1968). For a more critical view, see Curti, *Social Ideas of American Educators;* also see Clarence J. Karier, *Scientists of the Mind: Intellectual Founders of Modern Psychology* (Urbana: University of Illinois Press, 1986).

Watson was attracted to the University of Chicago by the fame of John Dewey, of whom he later confided, "I never knew what he was talking about and, unfortunately, still don't."[105] Under the influence of Angell, Donaldson, and Loeb, Watson's interests veered away from the social behaviorism of Mead to the experimental study of animal behavior, the field in which he completed his Ph.D. dissertation in 1903. After five years as an instructor in experimental psychology, Watson left Chicago for a full professorship at Johns Hopkins, where from 1908 to 1920 he developed and popularized his ideas on behaviorism. In 1920, due to a sensationally publicized divorce suit, he was asked to resign from Johns Hopkins. From 1921 to 1946 he was vice-president of a number of prominent Madison Avenue advertising agencies and thus influenced the course of commercial advertising.

Even though Watson's academic career was cut short and much of his work reflects exaggerated enthusiasms, his significance lies not in what he discovered but in the direction he moved a generation of research psychologists. This influence was emphasized by the American Psychological Association when it cited him in the paperback edition of *Behaviorism:*

To Dr. John B. Watson, whose work has been one of the vital determinants of the form and substance of modern psychology. He initiated a revolution in psychological thought, and his writings have been the point of departure for continuing lines of fruitful research.[106]

What Watson wrought was indeed a revolution. The beginnings of this revolt first appeared in his 1913 *Psychological Review* article, "Psychology as a Behaviorist Views It," quickly followed by *Behavior* in 1914, and his most important book, *Psychology from the Standpoint of a Behaviorist,* in 1919. By 1925, when he published *Behaviorism,* based on a series of lectures he had given at the New School for Social Research and at Cooper Union, his major thesis was well known by both psychologists and the lay public.

Persuasively, Watson asserted that the proper study of human psychology was not human consciousness but human behavior. Explicitly attacking Freud and James for their introspective psychologies, he argued that if psychology was ever to become a science, psychologists must quit making up introspective explanations for behavior and concentrate on observed behavior. He further asserted that much of what has been attributed to consciousness could now be explained through Pavlovian conditioning in conjunction with a functional physiological view of the human being. "Behavior, from Watson's point of view, consists of motor and glandular responses to sensory stimuli; it is always sensorimotor."[107]

---

105. Quoted in B. F. Skinner, "John Broadus Watson, Behaviorist," *Science,* N.S. 129 (1959), 197-198.
106. John B. Watson, *Behaviorism,* rev. ed. (Chicago: University of Chicago Press, 1958), p. iii.
107. Robert S. Woodworth, "John Broadus Watson: 1878-1958," *American Journal of Psychology,* LXXII (June 1959), 304.

Man thinking, to Watson, was man talking to himself, subvocally exercising his vocal cords. Reacting strongly to conscious-oriented psychologists, Watson developed his own muscular theory of thinking which tended to place the process of thought in the muscles rather than the brain. It was the total physiological organism that was thinking, and therefore the total organism should be the concern of the psychologist.[108]

For a man who advocated an empirical approach to behavior, Watson was peculiarly gifted in speculating beyond his data. This was due as much to his crusading spirit as his reaction to opponents. Watson had both a cause and a vision to promote; his cause was a call for psychologists to concern themselves with the prediction and control of human behavior, and his vision was the creation of a better man and a better society through behavioral engineering. In the thick of the storm which raged about him, Watson came to the conclusion "that there is no such thing as an inheritance of capacity, talent, temperament, mental constitution and characteristics. These things depend on training that goes on mainly in the cradle."[109] As some social reformers in the past had done, Watson went to a position of extreme environmental determinism.

Give me a dozen healthy infants, well-formed, and my own specified world to bring them up in and I'll guarantee to take any one at random and train him to become any type of specialist I might select—doctor, lawyer, artist, merchant-chief and, yes, even beggar-man and thief, regardless of his talents, penchants, tendencies, abilities, vocations, and race of his ancestors. I am going beyond my facts and I admit it, but so have the advocates of the contrary and they have been doing it for many thousands of years.[110]

Watson conceived of human nature as a physiological product of evolution which was shaped and molded by environment. His conception of man was opposed to Hall's primitivism, Freud's classical dualism, Thorndike's connectionism, as well as Mead's social behaviorism. Although Mead's behaviorism came closest to Watson's conception, Mead's social self included a reflectively thinking being which was never totally predictable. Watson well understood the revolutionary social implications of his science of behavior. If the individual is a product of his environment, he could not be held responsible for his actions but needed "unconditioning."[111] Watson further indicated that a science of human behavior concerned with control and prediction could not assume freedom but must, on the contrary, seek to determine and control the significant variables of human behavior. Indeed, if thought and action are determinably linked, then the freedom of thought allowed can be no more than that freedom of action tolerated by the community. As Watson put it, "All true speech does stand substitutive for bodily acts,

---

108. Watson's speculations set off a series of sensorimotor studies in both psychology and educational psychology in the 1920's and 1930's.
109. Quoted in Woodworth, "John Broadus Watson: 1878-1958," p. 305.
110. Watson, *Behaviorism*, p. 104.
111. Watson, *Behaviorism*, pp. 184-186.

hence organized society has just as little right to allow free speech as it has to allow free action, which nobody advocates."[112] Very much in the tradition of Helvétius, Watson would have agreed with the dictum that "To guide the motions of the human puppet it is necessary to know the wires by which he is moved." Although Watson had not discovered the right wires, other behaviorists took up the search. Among those who by mid-century thought they had found the right wires was B. F. Skinner (1904-   ).

In 1926, Skinner graduated from Hamilton College as an English major. Shortly thereafter, his interest in behaviorism and psychology was quickened by a series of articles by Bertrand Russell in *Dial* magazine on the epistemology of John B. Watson's behaviorism. As Skinner put it:

Many years later when I told Lord Russell that his articles were responsible for my interest in behavior, he could only exclaim, 'Good Heavens! I had always supposed that those articles had demolished Behaviorism!' But at any rate he had taken Watson seriously and so did I.[113]

So seriously did Skinner take Watson that a few years later he ranked Watson alongside Darwin and Lloyd Morgan as representing the "three critical changes in our conception of behavior."[114] Skinner, as a behaviorist, had caught what he termed Watson's "brilliant glimpse of the need for, and the nature and implications of, a science of behavior.[115] He was determined, however, not to follow Watson into the realm of physiological speculation. In his doctoral thesis at Harvard, Skinner

... defended the proposition that the psychologist should regard the reflex as a correlation between stimulus and response. He ignored the possibility of intervening physiological links, which for the psychologist, are often a queer make believe physiology, a dummy physiology doing duty for truth when facts are missing.[116]

So consistently has he refused to postulate explanatory internal variables that some, in jest, have suggested that Skinner deals with an "empty organism."[117]

The reinforcement theory Skinner developed, which includes both respondent and operant conditioning, has proven extremely useful in

---

112. Watson, *Behaviorism*, pp. 303-304. This question of degree and nature of freedom has become a serious problem for man in a totalitarian century. Assuming the linkage between thought and action, the focus of attention is on thought control. For example, in the current scene *treason* is defined by many not as an "overt act against the United States government" but as compliance or noncompliance with an ideology of "Americanism."

113. B. F. Skinner, "A Case History in Scientific Method," *The American Psychologist*, XI, 5 (May 1956), 222.

114. B. F. Skinner, "John Broadus Watson, Behaviorist," *Science*, N.S. 129 (1959), 197.

115. Skinner, "John Broadus Watson, Behaviorist," p. 198.

116. Boring, *History of Experimental Psychology*, p. 650.

117. Boring, *History of Experimental Psychology*, p. 650.

the training of both animals and humans. In this respect, Skinner was one of the key leaders in the application of reinforcement theory to education by way of programed instruction.[118]

Persistently, Skinner argued that his reinforcement ideas were not the product of predetermined theories of behavior but the result of practical laboratory attempts simply to control and predict behavior. Under such circumstances, theories of behavior lose their significance. "When behavior shows order and consistency, we are much less likely to be concerned with physiological or mentalistic causes. A datum emerges which takes the place of theoretical fantasy."[119] In the discovery that reinforcement is, indeed, the "wire" which controls the human puppet, a datum emerges about human nature and the good society. Man is a product of evolution whose inheritance plays a minimal role in behavior.[120] His nature, from the height of his rationality to the depths of his emotions, is shaped by forces which lie outside the individual.

Determined by a complex series of reinforcements, men are neither free nor responsible. They do not have "consciousness" or "mind" and exhibit no capacity for spontaneous action. Skinner, like Watson before him, knew that a scientific behaviorism was incompatible with a philosophy of personal freedom. As Skinner said:

The hypothesis that man is not free is essential to the application of scientific method to the study of human behavior. The free inner man who is held responsible for the behavior of the external biological organism is only a prescientific substitute for the kinds of causes which are discovered in the course of a scientific analysis.[121]

While the conception of the individual "which emerges from a scientific analysis is distasteful to most of those who have been strongly affected by democratic philosophies,"[122] much of our difficulty arises because

We have not wholly abandoned the traditional philosophy of human nature; at the same time we are far from adapting a scientific point of view without reservation. We have accepted the assumption of determinism in part; yet we allow our sympathies, our first allegiances, and our personal aspirations to rise to the defense of the traditional view.[123]

The way out of the problem of social value transition was, for Skinner, to follow increasingly the way of science. Science, he believed, might eventually develop the moral standards upon which mankind can agree.

---

118. Interestingly, behaviorism has also entered the area of psychotherapy. See the chapter on "Psychotherapy" in B. F. Skinner, *Science and Human Behavior* (New York: The Macmillan Company, 1953). See also William Glasser, *Reality Therapy* (New York: Harper & Row, 1965), and Joseph Wolpe, Andrew Salter, and L. J. Reyne, eds., *The Conditioning Therapies* (New York: Holt, Rinehart & Winston, Inc., 1964).

119. Skinner, "Case History in Scientific Method," p. 231.

120. Skinner, *Science and Human Behavior*, p. 26.

121. Skinner, *Science and Human Behavior*, p. 447.

122. Skinner, *Science and Human Behavior*, p. 449.

123. Skinner, *Science and Human Behavior*, p. 9.

If a science of behavior can discover those conditions of life which make for the ultimate strength of men, it may provide a set of 'moral values' which, because they are independent of the history and culture of any one group, may be generally accepted.[124]

Skinner knew that a science of behavioral engineering was in the making and the dream of the Enlightenment—that man could control his future destiny by controlling his environment—was near at hand. Yet, for many, the dream had turned into a nightmare. The question of who controls, and for what purpose, was, as Skinner put it, "a frightening one." A year after Skinner projected, in *Walden Two,* what a good society would look like, Orwell projected another view in *1984.* In Skinner's good society men had lost their freedom, responsibility, and capacity for spontaneity but had in turn learned to love without hate and to live without fear. They had, indeed, exchanged their illusions of personal freedom for the reality of a collective happiness. The people of Oceania, on the other hand, fell victim to a most effective behaviorally engineered tyranny. While much of the utopian literature by mid-century was direly pessimistic, projecting many present fears onto future horizons, Skinner's utopia, in comparison, was optimistic. Men could, he believed, engineer a better man and a better society.

Skinner was part of the Enlightenment tradition which, in the spirit of science, lost faith in human reason, freedom, and initiative as it found the key to progress. In mid-nineteenth century, Marx looked to cosmic history and found the key to progress in economic determinism; by mid-twentieth century, B. F. Skinner looked to animal learning and found the key to human progress in a theory of reinforcement. Both utopian sons of the Enlightenment had lost confidence in human freedom. Even though their methods and approach were radically different, the quest of each was the same—the perfectibility of man and society. While behaviorism has become a popular stream of educational psychology, many humanist critics have raised the delicate question of whether or not Watson's and Skinner's concerns correctly lead to the perfectibility of man or the perfectibility of rats. Joseph Wood Krutch made this point clear when he said:

There remains, nevertheless, the cheerful possibility that we actually know less about the Science of Man than we do of the less difficult sciences of matter and that we may, just in time, learn more. Perhaps Hamlet was nearer right than Pavlov. Perhaps the exclamation 'How like a god!' is actually more appropriate than 'How like a dog! How like a rat! How like a machine!' Perhaps we have been deluded by the fact that the methods employed for the study of man have been for the most part those originally devised for the study of machines or the study of rats, and are capable, therefore, of detecting and measuring only those characteristics which the three do have in common.[125]

---

124. Skinner, *Science and Human Behavior,* p. 445.
125. Joseph Wood Krutch, *The Measure of Man* (Indianapolis: The Bobbs-Merrill Company, Inc., 1954), pp. 32-33.

By mid-twentieth century, it was clear to most that at the base of many of the varied psychologies rested some very difficult philosophical questions. Whether it was Hall's primitivistic view of man, Freud's classical stoicism, Mead's social behaviorism, Thorndike's connectionism, Watson's and Skinner's behaviorism, or numerous others,[126] all seemed to project very different views of human nature and society. If Hall's view of "Atlantis" appeared as socialism of the right, Skinner's view in *Walden Two* appeared as socialism of the left, and Mead's *Mind, Self and Society* reflected social liberalism, Thorndike's conservatism seemed most compatible with the growing temper of a middle-class America. Each had an influence in shaping the twentieth-century American's image of himself both in and out of the schoolroom. In a very real sense, psychologists were playing the role that philosophers and theologians had played for other generations.

It is interesting that psychologists were just as divided on the important issues as philosophers and theologians had been in the past. While some students of psychology joined the ranks of a well-developed psychological school, others, faced with as many different psychologies as there are philosophies of man, took the eclectic way out. Such a position was easier to take than to defend. Sooner or later, the eclectic had to face the tough questions and, in so doing, develop his own unique philosophy and psychology of man. When he did this, however, the eclectic position often looked more like the Hydra of Hercules than a coherent philosophy or psychology of man. Perhaps the problem with a science of man is that "the Galileo and the Lavoisier of psychology" have not yet arrived on the scene. While many would have some doubts about their ever coming, most would agree with William James that if such men did arrive, "the necessities of the case will make them 'metaphysical.'"

SUGGESTED READINGS

Becker, Ernest. *The Birth and Death of Meaning.* New York, The Free Press of Glencoe, Inc., 1962.
Bloom, Benjamin S. *Stability and Change in Human Characteristics.* New York, John Wiley & Sons, Inc., 1964.
Boas, Franz. *The Mind of Primitive Man.* New York, The Macmillan Company, 1911.
Boring, Edwin G. *A History of Experimental Psychology.* New York, Appleton-Century-Crofts, Inc., 1950.
Erikson, Erik H. *Childhood and Society,* rev. ed. New York, W. W. Norton & Company, 1964.

126. Unfortunately the scope of this book does not permit adequate treatment of many other significant schools of psychology. An examination of these schools of thought would demonstrate a greater philosophical pluralism underlying psychological thought. For example, a study of Carl Rogers' conception of human nature contrasted with that of B. F. Skinner would reveal some remarkable differences.

Freud, Sigmund. *Civilization and Its Discontents,* trans. and ed. James Strachey. New York, W. W. Norton & Company, 1962.

———. *A General Introduction to Psychoanalysis.* New York, Permabook, 1957.

Fromm, Erich. *Beyond the Chains of Illusion.* New York, Simon and Schuster, Inc., 1962.

———. *Sigmund Freud's Mission.* New York, Harper & Brothers, 1959.

Glasser, William. *Reality Therapy.* New York, Harper & Row, 1965.

Hall, G. Stanley. *Life and Confessions of a Psychologist.* New York, D. Appleton & Company, 1923.

———. *Recreations of a Psychologist.* New York, D. Appleton & Company, 1920.

Joncich, Geraldine M., ed. *Psychology and the Science of Education: Selected Writings of Edward L. Thorndike,* Classics in Education, No. 8. New York, Bureau of Publications, Teachers College, Columbia University, 1962.

Jones, Ernest. *The Life and Work of Sigmund Freud,* 3 vols. New York, Basic Books, Inc., 1953-1957.

Marcuse, Herbert. *Eros and Civilization.* Boston, The Beacon Press, 1955.

Mead, George H. *The Philosophy of the Act,* ed. Charles W. Morris. Chicago, University of Chicago Press, 1938.

———. *The Philosophy of the Present,* ed. Arthur E. Murphy. Chicago, The Open Court Publishing Company, 1932.

Rieff, Philip. *Freud: The Mind of the Moralist.* Garden City, N.Y., Doubleday & Company, 1961.

Skinner, B. F. *Science and Human Behavior.* New York, The Macmillan Company, 1953.

Strauss, Anselm, ed. "The Process of Mind in Nature," *George Herbert Mead on Social Psychology.* Chicago, Phoenix Books, 1964.

Strickland, Charles, and Charles Burgess. *Health, Growth, and Heredity: G. Stanley Hall on Natural Education,* Classics in Education, No. 23. New York, Bureau of Publications, Teachers College, Columbia University, 1965.

Thorndike, Edward L. *Educational Psychology,* Vol. I. New York, Bureau of Publications, Teachers College, Columbia University, 1921.

———. *Human Nature and the Social Order.* New York, The Macmillan Company, 1940.

Watson, John B. *Behaviorism,* rev. ed. Chicago, University of Chicago Press, 1958.

Wolpe, Joseph et al., eds. *The Conditioning Therapies.* New York, Holt, Rinehart & Winston, Inc., 1964.

CHAPTER 8

Humanist conceptions of man and society

There are two laws discrete,
Not reconciled—
Law for man, and law for thing;
The last builds town and fleet,
But it runs wild,
And doth the man unking.[1]
RALPH WALDO EMERSON

At the center of much of the social and educational conflict in twentieth-century America lie some basically conflicting positions with respect to the nature of man and the good society. From the standpoint of those who believe in a pluralistic society, this condition is as it should be. A society that is truly pluralistic should reflect differences at a fundamental as well as a superficial level. There are, however, inherent dangers in such a social system. If, for instance, basic differences are allowed to immobilize a society and prevent action, then such a society is committed to its own self-destruction. A pluralistic social ideal assumes free, open debate on fundamental issues, but it also assumes that man will strive for consensus in terms of action even though they may never reach consensus on basic questions.

In this respect, it was the pragmatist, James B. Conant, in the midst of the stormy educational debate at mid-century, who sought consensus for educational action, not by analyzing the virtues and defects of fundamentally conflicting positions with respect to educational thought, but rather by purposely focusing attention on those educational practices

---

1. Edward Waldo Emerson, ed., *The Complete Works of Ralph Waldo Emerson* (Cambridge, Mass.: Riverside Press, 1904), IX, 78.

on which he could obtain the greater consensus. Conant, as the great compromiser of mid-twentieth century, was a pragmatist who believed in a pluralistic society. While Conant sought consensus in practice, he knew full well that many of the fundamental values over which men are divided are not reconcilable. Indeed, even though one might get John Dewey, Robert Maynard Hutchins, and Jacques Maritain to agree on a specific educational practice, one could not expect them to agree on the nature of man or the nature of the good society. These, then, are not very useful questions, as Conant recognized, in achieving a consensus for action. On the other hand, they are extremely useful for understanding the pluralism underlying American thought. In fact, it is this pluralism which causes much of the educational conflict and which creates the need for consensus in the first place.

Contrary to considerable popular opinion, which holds that educational criticism began with Russia's successful launch of Sputnik, American education had been persistently criticized throughout the twentieth century. To be sure, many in education seemed to ignore the criticism until after Sputnik; nevertheless, many of the more effective arguments heard in the fifties were also heard in the twenties and thirties. Among those who consistently registered pointed and effective criticism from the vantage point of a well-defined philosophic position were the humanists.

From Isocrates on, the humanists have functioned as the schoolmasters as well as the social critics of Western culture. In American education, they held their own—especially in the colleges—until the latter half of the nineteenth century. With the rise of Darwinian naturalism, which suggested the continuity of man and animal, the humanist's assumption as to the dualistic nature of man was challenged; with the rise of science, specialization, research, and the explosion in human knowledge, the humanist educational ideal of the well-rounded man was laid waste; and with the increasing democratization of American culture, the humanist ideal of an ordered aristocratic society was devastated. The humanists, then, were struggling against some of the main currents of twentieth-century educational and social thought. As they continued the struggle, they were true to their tradition and soon became leading critics of American society and education.

Even though there were broad general areas of agreement within the humanist position, there still remained considerable differences. While all found eternal verities in tradition, not all found the same truths. Although all would agree that man's nature is divided, not all could agree as to a precise definition of his dualistic nature. In general, the humanists believed in a well-ordered, stable society, but again, not all found refuge in the classical ideal of an aristocratic social order. Indeed, some became exponents of a democratic society. One reason for these differences is that some humanists seemed more sensitive to the realities of the twentieth century and thereby moderated their traditional position, while others seemed quite content to rest their case on eternal truths. The marked differences among various humanists might further be accounted for by the fact that even though all relied on the unchanging aspects of tradition to define man's nature and his education, each group's center of interest was on a different aspect of the Western tradition. In one way or another, at least three major currents of Western thought—the rhetorical, the philosophical, and the religious—were reflected in twentieth-century American humanism. Although Irving Babbitt and Paul Elmer More reflected a narrow, classical, literary humanism, and Jacques Barzun and Gilbert Highet held a more modern, urbane, literary humanist's perspective, both groups were essentially part of the rhetorical humanist tradition. Rooted in the thought of Isocrates, Cicero, and Erasmus, this was a formidable educational tradition. Although Robert M. Hutchins and Jacques Maritain both went back to Thomas Aquinas and Aristotle for their philosophic bases, Maritain's religious humanism relied more on the revealed truths of Christianity, while Hutchins' rational humanism was based more on an Aristotelian conception of man. In spite of these differences, the common grounds of agreement among all humanists should not be overlooked. All humanists found eternal verities in tradition, spoke of the unchanging elements of human nature, emphasized the unchangeable in a rapidly changing society, and were intimately concerned with education and the growth of scientific naturalism.

RHETORICAL HUMANISM

Neohumanism

In the first two decades of the twentieth century, Paul Elmer More (1864-1937) as the stylist and Irving Babbitt (1865-1933) as the inquiring scholar joined forces to present neohumanism to the world as an alternative to the scientific naturalist perspective of man, education, and society. From the serenity of Harvard Yard, Babbitt poured forth the *Weltanschauung* of neohumanism in *Literature and the American College* (1908), *New Laokoön* (1910), *The Masters of Modern French Criticism* (1912), *Rousseau and Romanticism* (1919), and *Democracy and Leadership* (1924). From the marketplace, Paul Elmer More, as literary editor of *The Independent* (1901-1903) and *The Evening Post* (1903-1909) and as editor-in-chief of *The Nation* (1909-1914), took up the cudgel against the romantic and naturalist writers. Together, they presented a united front against the humanitarian values of the pragmatists in philosophy as well as against the Darwinian naturalism implicit in the thought of most psychologists, sociologists, and educators in the twentieth century.

From Babbitt's point of view, America was rapidly becoming hopelessly caught in the grip of a relativistic naturalism. The cause was to be found in the growth of humanitarianism, which consisted of romantic naturalism on the one side and scientific naturalism on the other. The romantic tradition as epitomized by Rousseau and the scientific tradition as epitomized by Bacon were viewed as corrupting the civilized standards of the West. Science and romanticism together fed the Frankenstein of mass culture, the myth of progress, and the idea of the perfectibility of man.

Babbitt asserted that men have a choice of living on one of three levels. At one extreme, they may accept the discipline of supernatural religion and thereby become subject to restraints that are "exterior and anterior" to man himself; or they may go to the other extreme and live as naturalists in a confused state without standards, taste, or restraint, becoming puppets of their naturalistic passions. If there were only these two choices, Babbitt insisted, he would take the supernaturalist way of life.

There was another position, however, which he defined as humanistic. The humanists would develop an internal discipline that would free man from his naturalistic instability and yet not subject him to the external discipline of the religious life. The history of the West, Babbitt surmised, had been largely a history of humanism providing ethical standards of taste and judgment for the leadership class and supernatural religion providing the necessary restraints for the great masses of people. From the Enlightenment on, however, man had espoused the new religion of humanitarianism, which ran roughshod over orthodox religious restraints as well as humanistic discipline. Modern Western man, as he intellectually rejected Christianity, still lived unconsciously off the moral capital of the past, a moral capital that was rapidly being eroded by the growth of humanitarianism. In this sense, Western man was heading straight for the abyss of naturalistic destruction. The religious as well as the humanistic sanctions for restraint were simply disappearing from Western culture.

During the eighteenth and nineteenth centuries, in an attempt to find standards in the natural world as the myths of Christianity lost their credibility, the pseudo-classicists, empiricists, and rationalists placed their faith in reason to the exclusion of feeling and imagination. As a consequence of this intellectual debacle, the doctrine of knowledge as power earlier promulgated by Francis Bacon was given realistic expression in the form of scientific naturalism. However, unable to hold feeling in check for very long, reason implicit in scientific naturalism gave way to a surge of romantic naturalism, and the imagination was released to wander freely under the guise of native genius. Jean-Jacques Rousseau epitomized (for Babbitt) the romantic sentimentalism which, when worshiping the "noble savage," could as readily turn to the primitivism of G. Stanley Hall as it could to the permissive child-centered education of Margaret Naumburg.[2]

Man could only oscillate between the extremes of unbridled reason and undisciplined imagination. What eventually followed, Babbitt surmised, was a complete disillusionment with both reason and imagination, to the extent that all civilized standards were lost in a world of nihilism. Neither the romantic who viewed his fleeting imagination as genius nor the utilitarian scientist who specialized to know more and more about less and less could be relied upon to preserve standards so necessary for a humane culture. Baconian science and Rousseauian romanticism were the two pillars which supported the humanitarian lintel under

---

2. Lawrence A. Cremin, *The Transformation of the School* (New York: Alfred A. Knopf, Inc., 1961).

which modern man walked to his own self-destruction. Although at times these two strains of naturalism seemed antagonistic, the utilitarian idea of knowledge as power nicely complemented the romantic's cry for service to a highly sentimentalized notion of the brotherhood of humanity. Science, in the service of unrestrained sentiment, was corrupting the house of intellect.

The solution to all this rested not in a return to supernaturalism but in a revival of the standards and taste of classical humanism. The humanist, as Babbitt defined him, was one who "moved between an extreme of sympathy and an extreme of discipline and selection, and became humane in proportion as he mediated between these extremes."[3] Reason, imagination, emotions, and sense experience must all be subservient to a higher ethical "will to refrain." "A person who has sympathy for mankind in the lump, faith in its future progress, and desire to serve the great cause of this progress,"[4] and is committed to either the utilitarian ideal of knowledge for power or the romantic goal of service to humanity should be called a humanitarian, not a humanist.[5]

At the center of Babbitt's and More's conception of human nature was the ethical "will to refrain." This will "eludes all attempts at analysis" and exists as a "residuum of pure and abstract liberty, not to be expressed in terms of time and space."[6] The neohumanist's quest for certainty ended with the universal, superrational will of man, based not on *a priori* assumptions but rather on what they termed the experience of man. As Babbitt said:

... the opposite of the subrational is not merely the rational but the superrational, and ... this superrational and transcendent element in man is a certain quality of will. This quality of will may prove to be alone capable of supplying a sufficient counterpoise to the various 'lusts,' including the lust of feeling, that result from the free unfolding of man's natural will.[7]

Unlike Henri Bergson's concern with the *élan vital,* Babbitt's interest was in a *frein vital.* The truly educated man was one who had developed and disciplined his ethical will not to act but to refrain from action. Such a discipline could be developed only through a serious study of the ancient classics in the original languages. Translations would not suffice. While the logic of the ancients may survive translations, the finer esthetic shades of meaning so necessary for the disciplining of the ethical will do not survive. Since Hutchins and Adler assumed a universal logic to be at the center of man's nature, they could accept translations in their Great Books curriculum, but Babbitt and More could not. The

3. Irving Babbitt, *Literature and the American College* (Boston: Houghton Mifflin Company, 1908), p. 22.

4. Babbitt, *Literature and the American College,* p. 7.

5. For a similar conception of humanism, see Paul Elmer More, *Shelburne Essays* (Boston: Houghton Mifflin Company, 1913), Vol. I.

6. Irving Babbitt, *The Masters of Modern French Criticism* (Boston: Houghton Mifflin Company, 1912), p. 247.

7. Irving Babbitt, *On Being Creative* (Boston: Houghton Mifflin Company, 1932), p. 199.

difference in their educational recommendations is largely due to a difference in the way they defined human nature.

Since the kind of knowledge best designed to develop and strengthen one's "will to refrain" is known, then the question remains: Can the great mass of men rise to the heights of self-discipline necessary to taste the fruits of classical virtue? In a resounding chorus, almost as an echo out of the dead ruins of classical antiquity, the neohumanists answered "No!" The great masses were trainable in the humanitarian sense but uneducable in the humanist sense. As Babbitt put it:

Some persons will remain spiritually anarchical in spite of educational opportunity, others will acquire at least the rudiments of ethical discipline, whereas still others, a small minority, if we are to judge by past experience, will show themselves capable of more difficult stages of self-conquest that will fit them for leadership.[8]

Babbitt's and More's classical view of human nature and knowledge culminated in a classical aristocratic view of the good society. Both were fully convinced that the great mass of men were incapable of rising to the heights of excellence necessary for self-rule. Since most men will remain intemperate, it follows that most men neither deserve nor are capable of freedom. "It is ordained in the eternal constitution of things, that men of intemperate minds cannot be free. Their passions forge their fetters."[9]

Interest in mankind must begin at the top and progress downward. The gifted must not only be the exemplars of culture worthy of emulation but must be allowed to exercise economic, political, and social power if civilization is to survive.[10] These leaders must learn that the main purpose of the machinery of government is not to raise the material welfare of the masses but to create advantages for the upward striving of the exceptional.[11] Harking back to Aristotle's *Politics,* which intellectually justified slavery on the basis of a dualistic conception of human nature, More found equality only among equals. Majority rule, he concluded, is nothing more than a conceit on the part of the mass man. In every social institution there are leaders and followers, and it behooves the American people to realize that what really rules is not a nebulous will of the people nor a popular majority but a small leadership minority.[12] It is the education of that small leadership minority which will determine the standards of a just society. As Babbitt suggested, "Our real hope of safety lies in our being able to induce our future Harrimans

8. Irving Babbitt, *Democracy and Leadership* (Boston: Houghton Mifflin Company, 1924), p. 310.

9. More, *Shelburne Essays,* IX, 26. This is a quotation from Burke which More used to express his own sentiment.

10. For More's concept of aristocracy see "Natural Aristocracy," *Shelburne Essays,* IX, 3-38.

11. See More, *Shelburne Essays,* IX, 31.

12. See Babbitt, *Democracy and Leadership,* p. 16. Babbitt's and More's distrust of the people is much like that of Emile Faguet who expressed his ideas in *The Cult of Incompetence.*

and Rockefellers to liberalize their own souls, in other words to get themselves rightly educated."[13]

American education had been so thoroughly corrupted by romantic naturalism at the elementary school level and by scientific utilitarianism at the graduate level, said Babbitt, that there was serious danger that the liberal arts college, so necessary to train the elite, would itself be overrun by the spirit of humanitarian naturalism. The humanitarianism of Charles W. Eliot, John Dewey, George Herbert Mead, Edward L. Thorndike, and many others had thoroughly corrupted American education. The only hope for the survival of civilized standards rested in the recall of the liberal arts college to the discipline and content of the classics.

Not only the education of the young but the entire society, Babbitt and More asserted, showed signs of being afflicted by cancerous humanitarianism. From Jefferson on, America had been led down the primrose path of naturalism. Under the false ideal of progress, Americans had come to believe in mass social meliorism. As More said, "The works of Miss Jane Addams and a host of other modern writers [are] in fact only one aspect of the slow drift from medieval religion to humanitarianism."[14] Such a drift was from personal integrity to communal charity and collective socialism. In a similar vein Babbitt argued that

We may be sure that stalwart believers like St. Paul or St. Augustine or Pascal would look upon our modern humanitarians with their talk of social problems and their tendency to reduce religion to a phase of the tenement-house question as weaklings and degenerates.[15]

The just society was a hierarchical society which distributed its rewards of power, privilege, and property according to the superiority of persons. The humanitarians, however, had encouraged the inferior to utilize the power of government to dip their hands into the pockets of the superior in the name of mass philanthropy and social justice. Under such conditions, Babbitt believed that:

It is not yet clear that it is going to be possible to combine universal suffrage with the degree of safety for the institution of property that genuine justice and genuine civilization both require.[16]

The rights of property must be ensured not only for the sake of social justice but also because inequalities of wealth based on the superiority of persons is essential in maintenance of the hierarchical nature of the good society. Indeed, "to the civilized man *the rights of property are more important than the right to life.*"[17] Since, to More, the main purpose

---

13. Babbitt, *Literature and the American College,* p. 71.
14. More, *Shelburne Essays,* IX, 197.
15. Babbitt, *Literature and the American College,* pp. 10-11.
16. Babbitt, *Democracy and Leadership,* p. 207.
17. More, *Shelburne Essays,* IX, 136. The attitude of Babbitt and More toward property and social meliorism is very much akin to that of another decided opponent of social meliorism, William Graham Sumner.

of government was to create advantages for the exceptional, and since property was more important than life, the humanitarians with their gospel of social reform via social and educational meliorism were viewed as the deadly foe of civilization. The critical error of humanitarianism was faith in progress and humanity. Science had reinforced this myth as the mass of men confused material progress with moral progress. Because men collectively could create better automobiles, they were deluded into thinking they could collectively create a better man and a better society.

The ancients, together with the Christian theologians, knew that moral striving was always an individual affair. Salvation could not be made a collective affair. The humanitarians not only offered salvation in this world, but they proposed to save men collectively through urban renewal projects, settlement houses, and mass philanthropy. All the advocates of these efforts ignored the ancient wisdom that virtue begins and ends with the individual and has relatively little to do with the workings of a bureaucratic agency. This delusion of progress was a part of the modern mind not found in the classical world. The ancients, Babbitt argued, appreciated the tragic nature of man too well to be caught up in such mass delusions.

Men have always dreamed of the Golden Age, but it is only with the triumphs of modern science that they have begun to put the Golden Age in the future instead of the past. The great line that separates the new era from the old is, as Renan remarks, the idea of humanity and the cult of its collective achievements.[18]

This naïve faith in progress and the perfectibility of man, supported by science, served to break down the old Ciceronian idea of beneficence. Cicero had clearly warned against the dangerous effects of indiscriminate giving. Beneficence, he cautioned, must always be judged in terms of its possible consequence for individual virtue.[19]

The old philanthropy, as we have said, has been profoundly modified and converted into humanitarianism by being more closely connected with this idea of progress; and the idea of progress in turn rests mainly on a belief in the benefits that are to come to mankind in the mass as the results of a closer cooperation with nature.[20]

The neohumanists' disdain for mass philanthropy turned on the classical ideal of social justice and social order. Mass philanthropy, they believed, tended to destroy personal integrity and responsibility as it emphasized the nebulous needs of humanity in mass. Since true charity begins at home, the personal touch—the real character-building attributes of giving and receiving—are lost in the impersonal characteristics of a bureaucratic agency.

18. Babbitt, *Literature and the American College,* p. 34.
19. See Moses Hadas, ed., *The Basic Works of Cicero* (New York: The Modern Library, 1951).
20. Babbitt, *Literature and the American College,* p. 34.

"Am I my brother's keeper?" The whole American people had replied in an 'ecstatic affirmative.' One should note in passing the intolerable dilution of the principle of obligation that is implied in extending to men indiscriminately what one owes to one's own brother. At all events, no small issues are involved in the question whether one should start with an expansive eagerness to do something for humanity or with loyalty to one's self. There may be something after all in the Confucian idea that if a man only sets himself right, the rightness will extend to his family first of all, and finally in widening circles to the whole community.[21]

The classical virtue of beneficence had been perverted not by science alone but also by the "religion of humanity" missionaries who insisted on carrying the Christian gospel of brotherhood into the realm of social reform. These reformers had repeatedly failed to make a correct distinction between religious and secular virtues.[22] This error was further compounded when, under the guise of the good Samaritan, these missionaries substituted the second commandment for the first[23] and replaced the Bible with the tenement house as a center of religious interest.[24] This kind of perversion of the religious sentiment to humanitarian ends would eventually lead to nothing more than communal socialism in which individual integrity would be but a meaningless term.

Consistently, the literary humanists in the twentieth century, from Irving Babbitt in *Literature and the American College* (1908) to Jacques Barzun in *The House of Intellect* (1959), have warned of the corrupting influence of mass philanthropy on society and education. In 1908, Babbitt's protest was a lonely protest, but by mid-century the more moderately liberal voice of Jacques Barzun, arguing essentially the same point with respect to philanthropy, reached a much larger receptive audience. As masses of people appeared as second- and third-generation recipients of welfare, it was clear to most that something was wrong. While urban renewal projects and public housing failed in many cases to produce a more responsible humanity, Russell Kirk and other conservatives were quick to point out not only that philanthropy can corrupt but that you cannot really change human nature. Increasingly, men of more conservative temper were saying that the thorny bush—which Edward Bellamy in *Looking Backward* suggested might bloom as a beautiful rose bush if transplanted from the bog to a more healthy environment—was, after all, nothing more than just another thorny bush. The humanitarians, on the other hand, insisted that we have not controlled the environment and handled the transplant with enough scientific care

21. Babbitt, *Democracy and Leadership*, p. 201.
22. See More, *Shelburne Essays*, I, 251.
23. More, *Shelburne Essays*, IX, 288.
24. More, *Shelburne Essays*, I, 250-251. One would suspect that both Babbitt and More, if alive today, would view the current activities of various churches in the civil rights movement as a continuation of the same humanitarian sentiment. The recent "War on Poverty" would probably also be viewed as another humanitarian venture which fattens the budgets of the bureaucracy and collectively alleviates the guilt and anxiety of people escaping their individual responsibility.

to warrant such conclusions.[25] By the sixties, amidst racial conflict and considerable economic, social, and educational deterioration in America's major urban centers, many voices reflecting a Sumner-Babbitt point of view could be heard; but when action was taken, it usually followed the humanitarian tradition of Bellamy and Ward.

The neohumanist attack on social reform was only one side of the attack on humanitarianism. The other side of the attack focused on educators who were corrupted by the same ideas. The progressive educators who believed in the progress of humanity by way of education and who assumed, like Rousseau, that the child's nature was good, were "impressionistic" educationists. Those who viewed human nature as neither good nor bad but subject to learning experience and who proposed a science of education were viewed as Baconian specialists or "intellectual fractions," interested in the dissemination, not of knowledge, but of bits and pieces of information. In 1924, Babbitt warned: "We have been permitting Professor Dewey and his kind to have an influence on our education that amounts in the aggregate to a national calamity."[26]

Because Babbitt and More were chiefly concerned with the education of the elite and were willing to write off the masses as only capable of being humanitarianly trained, their educational interests were primarily at the college level. At that level they reserved their bitterest invectives for the social sciences or, as they termed them, the "pseudo-sciences," which presumed to be developing a science of man and society. Departments of anthropology, sociology, psychology, and education came under fire not only because they were the most recent departments to gain. university status but because these fields presumed to be seeking answers for questions already answered by the humanists. In this respect, the social sciences were poaching on humanist preserves. Referring to the social sciences, More suggested, "Better the frank unreason of mythology than this labyrinth of intellectual deception."[27] Indeed, dragging the student

. . . through the slums of sociology, instead of making him at home in the society of the noble dead, debauches his mind with a flabby, or inflames it with a fanatic, humanitarianism. . . . He is narrow and unbalanced, a prey to the prevailing passion of the hour, with no feeling for the majestic claims of that within us which is unchanged from the beginning.[28]

The pseudo-sciences, from sociology to education, were permeated with Darwinian naturalism. While a student trained solely in science is likely to be left in "a state of relative imbecility,"[29] the student trained solely in the social sciences is likely to be left with a more dangerous, in-

25. Some even suggested that the solution to the educational problems of the urban centers lay in the creation of public boarding schools, much as Robert Dale Owen had proposed earlier in the nineteenth century.
26. Babbitt, *Democracy and Leadership,* p. 313.
27. More, *Shelburne Essays,* I, 300.
28. More, *Shelburne Essays,* IX, 37.
29. More, *Shelburne Essays,* IX, 47.

flamed, flabby conceit. The psychologists, whether they were connectionist, behaviorist, or Freudian, were equally rebuked for their rejection of dualism and for their naturalistic assumptions.[30] Responding to the psychologists who had undercut the humanistic tradition, Babbitt argued that "the behaviorists and other naturalist psychologists . . . are to be accounted at present among the chief enemies of human nature."[31] So, also, More suggested: "Certainly the afterclap of that orgy of illicit science, the thing called behaviorism in this country, is no better than a lifeless bogey dressed up to frighten college boys and to delight illiterate psychologists."[32]

The neohumanists attacked modern psychologies not only because they as humanists placed their faith in a competing faculty psychology, but because modern psychologies had undercut the humanist's dualistic view of human nature which, in turn, undermined their learning theory. This theory was based on the assumption that a liberal education was concerned with the discipline of the mind while a vocational education was concerned with training in physical skills. The one education dealt with ideas and the other with things. Although discipline was held to be a vital part of a liberal education, the neohumanist passed beyond this point to emphasize the process of "imitation." "The very essence of education is . . . to set before [youth] the stirring examples of those who have found their joy and consolation in higher things."[33] As one comes to imitate the excellence of the great minds of the past, a catharsis occurs which unifies his being and frees him for truly creative work.

The neohumanist was careful to distinguish between rote Ciceronianism, the curse of the classical tradition, and true imitation. True imitation involved an element of creativity. "The imitation of models, it is well to remember, is not necessarily barren. Many of the neo-classics showed that this type of imitation is compatible with genuine creation."[34] By imitating the excellence of the classical authors, one transcends the limits of self to the higher universal life and at the same time gains in self-knowledge, which is the only virtue achievable by man. In rejecting the Baconian doctrine of knowledge as power, Babbitt and More revived the ancient doctrine of knowledge as virtue. Obviously, not everyone could reach this stage of purification. "Those who can receive the higher initiation into the Hellenic spirit will doubtless remain few in number, but those few will yield a potent influence for good, each in his own circle."[35]

---

30. It is interesting that neither Babbitt nor More recognized the classical dualism of Freud and consistently typed him as a Rousseauian romantic. It seems clear that Babbitt did not get the same insights into human nature as Freud from Sophocles' *Antigone* and *Oedipus Rex*. See Edmund Wilson, "Sophocles, Babbitt, and Freud," *New Republic*, LXV (Dec. 3, 1930), 68-71.

31. Irving Babbitt, "What I Believe," *The Forum* (Feb. 1930), 83.

32. Paul Elmer More, *The Skeptical Approach to Religion*, 5th ed. (Princeton, N.J.: Princeton University Press, 1958), p. 100.

33. Paul Elmer More, *The Demon of the Absolute* (Princeton, N.J.: Princeton University Press, 1928), p. 26.

34. Irving Babbitt, *On Being Creative* (Boston: Houghton Mifflin Company, 1932), p. 14.

35. Babbitt, *Literature and the American College*, p. 180.

While in a Thorndikean view of education, one might "stamp in" all kinds of information, and in the Skinnerian sense train men in a scientific way, to the humanists the real education of man was fundamentally an art. The art of educating man takes as its chief goal the shaping and creating of the amateur, the man of taste and self-discipline—in short, the man who thinks for himself. Babbitt's and More's man of taste, capable of judging eloquence, was very much akin to Cicero's orator whose "power will never be able to effect its object by eloquence, unless in him who has obtained a thorough insight into the nature of mankind, and all the passions of humanity, and those causes by which our minds are either impelled or restrained."[36] To Cicero it was the *orator* and to Babbitt it was the *man of taste* who needed vigorous training in many fields of knowledge and who must guard himself against sheer specialization. Their educational ideal was a universal man, a man whose knowledge was not encyclopedic but selective and eminently useful for a well-rounded amateur. In the course of his education, he must have developed a disciplined, intuitive sensitivity for the beautiful, the good, and the true.

In many ways the educational ideal of Babbitt and More was very similar to that held for the orator by both Cicero and Quintilian. The difference in educational ideals, however, lies mainly in the fact that Cicero's orator would be a speaker, and Babbitt's man of taste would be a writer. The sacred ground of the rhetorical tradition has always been the art of communication, both written and spoken. Whether one emphasizes the one or the other, the educational rationale for both remains very similar. In this respect, the neohumanists attempted to reconstruct the classical rhetorical ideal in twentieth-century American education.[37]

In an age which was becoming increasingly uncertain, the neohumanists presented an educational rationale that featured as its chief virtues stability, order, and certainty. Their educational views maintained such internal and external consistency that their attitude toward various educational problems was predictable with almost scientific accuracy. With respect to internal consistency, their aristocratic views of the good society were supported by an aristocratic view of education. The belief in a universal, unchanging essence of man, complemented by insistence upon the unchanging essence of education and the concept of knowledge as virtue, was realized in their learning theory of imitation. With respect to external consistency, it can readily be seen that when facing educational problems, they were extremely consistent with the "noble dead." As Babbitt and More spun their classical rationale into social and educational ideas, it became apparent that neohumanism was mainly a rigorous, classical protest against modern thought.

During the first two decades of the century, Babbitt and More presented a stern, united front against the humanitarian currents of American society. After 1915, when More retired as editor of *The Nation* to

---

36. J. S. Watson, trans., *Cicero on Oratory and Orators* (New York: Harper & Brothers, 1860), p. 19.

37. One might, however, recognize that Cicero's orator was more a man of action, whereas the neohumanist man of taste tended more toward the contemplative life.

live the life of a scholar on the Princeton campus, his views began to drift away from those of Irving Babbitt. Unable to find satisfaction in Babbitt's humanism, which cut between naturalism and supernaturalism, More moved to a Christian humanism just as another student of Irving Babbitt, T. S. Eliot, had done.[38] The dilemma for More was that Babbitt's humanism did not seem to lead to any secure haven.

And so I ask myself, reluctantly, almost wishing my answer were mistaken, whether those who advocate humanism, as an isolated movement, are not doomed to disappointment. It is not that the direction in itself is wrong; every step in the program is right, and only by this path can we escape from the waste land of naturalism. But can we stop here in security? For purpose that will not end in bitter defeat; for values that will not mock us like empty masks, must we not look for happiness based on something beyond the swaying tides of mortal success and failure? Will not the humanist, unless he adds to his creed the faith and the hope of religion, find himself at the last, despite his protest, dragged back into the camp of the naturalist?[39]

Unlike T. S. Eliot, who joined the Anglican Church, More, though he moved to a religious humanism,[40] remained outside the church. More's religious experience led him to conclude that good and evil have real existence. The orthodox Christian explanation for evil—i.e., the absence of good—left More unsatisfied. Therefore, he was unwilling to close the dualism of good and evil in an all-perfect, all-powerful God. Like the traditional Christian, More was convinced that God existed, but unlike the traditional Christian, he was sure that evil existed as an active force which limits the power of God. Too unorthodox to enter and too orthodox to leave, More ended his quest of certainty on the very steps of the Anglican Church.

Neohumanism recast

During the 1930's, there appeared in the neohumanist constellation, alongside the bright shining stars of Babbitt and More, such lesser stars as John Jay Chapman, W. C. Brownell, G. R. Elliott, Stuart P. Sherman, George E. Woodberry, and Norman Foerster.[41] Of these lesser stars,

---

38. See Robert M. Davies, *The Humanism of Paul Elmer More* (New York: Bookman Associates, Inc., 1958).

39. Paul Elmer More, *On Being Human* (Princeton N.J.: Princeton University Press, 1936), p. 20.

40. The direction of More's thought is clearly portrayed in the titles of his books: *Platonism* (1917), *The Religion of Plato* (1921), *The Christ of the New Testament* (1924), *Christ the Word* (1927), *The Catholic Faith* (1931), *Anglicanism* (1935).

41. See Norman Foerster, *Toward Standards* (New York: Farrar & Rinehart, Inc., 1930), p. 157. See also Norman Foerster, ed., *Humanism and America* (New York: Farrar & Rinehart, Inc., 1930), p. ix. To be sure, all these men did not exactly duplicate the thought of Babbitt and More. There were minor differences, and some defected from the neohumanists' ranks early. Thus, Stuart P. Sherman was viewed by other neohumanists as a renegade. As Foerster put it, "He drifted from his humanistic position into an ever vaguer faith in the common man, and at length as a literary journalist in New York, into a rather indulgent impressionism."

it was Norman Foerster who carried the neohumanist ideology to mid-century.[42]

As a student and close disciple of Irving Babbitt, as a teacher of American literature in the state universities of Wisconsin and North Carolina, and as director of the School of Letters at the State University of Iowa, Norman Foerster was in a unique position to carry the neohumanist gospel to foreign parts, the state university. To Foerster, the state universities "were the expression in terms of higher education, of Jacksonian democracy and the humanitarian movement."[43]

How close was Norman Foerster's conception of neohumanism to that held by Irving Babbitt and Paul Elmer More? In most respects, Foerster's formulation appears to be an exact replica of Babbitt's and More's rationale. Nevertheless, Foerster introduced certain critical changes. Unlike his mentor, who understood Jefferson's humanitarianism, Foerster, at the price of considerable distortion of historical evidence, changed Jefferson to qualify as a precursor of the neohumanist tradition. Implicit in Foerster's work is a great eagerness to sell the neohumanist rationale even at the expense of some contradictions, which neither Babbitt nor More tolerated in their own thinking. Babbitt and More found the modern foreign languages unsuitable either as an instrument of discipline or as a medium of communing with the great ideas of the "noble dead," whereas Norman Foerster allowed French or German as a substitute for Greek and Latin in his new liberal education.[44] What prompted Foerster to make this shift remains unknown. Undoubtedly, one factor of considerable importance was the apparent decline in the percentage of students taking classical languages in the American public secondary schools.[45] Greek had virtually disappeared from the curriculum, and Latin was diminishing as a major study.

When Foerster abandoned classicism for modern literary humanism, it became apparent that his humanism would be more acceptable to the rational humanism of Hutchins and Adler. If the neohumanists and the rational humanists disagreed in theory, at least in practice a major obstruction had been removed. Given Babbitt's and More's conception of human nature and education, their insistence on the ancient languages was eminently logical. Foerster broke the neohumanist's logic by allowing modern foreign languages to substitute for the ancient languages. There was something approaching contradiction when, on the one hand, he insisted, "While it may suffice to read works of science and philosophy in translations, it does not suffice so to read works of imaginative

---

42. As Louis J. A. Mercier put it, "But Foerster alone developed a systematic and prolonged exploitation of Babbitt's humanism." Louis J. A. Mercier, *American Humanism and the New Age* (Milwaukee: Bruce Publishing Company, 1948), p. 166.

43. Norman Foerster, *The American State University* (Chapel Hill: University of North Carolina Press, 1937), p. 59.

44. See Foerster, *American State University*, pp. 261-263.

45. By 1934 the number of students in public high school taking Greek was so small that Greek was no longer listed as a subject of study in the public secondary school. See *The Biennial Survey of Education in the United States, 1934-1936* (Bulletin 1937, No. 2, U. S. Printing Office, 1939), Chapter 1, Vol. II, "Statistical Summary of Education, 1935-1936," p. 20.

literature";[46] and on the other hand, he proceeded to accept French and German as substitutes for the classical languages. Foerster was aware of this discrepancy and admitted, "Eventually the logic of the situation might well send us back to the despised classical languages, for Greek especially."[47] Nevertheless, the rational humanists and the neohumanists could now talk about the Great Books curriculum as if they meant the same thing.

The rational humanism of Hutchins and Adler, which emphasized the logical syllogism, a metaphysics, and the universal reason of man, was theoretically closer to the neo-Thomism of Maritain than to the classical-literary humanism of Babbitt and More. In contrast with the rational humanists, Babbitt, More, and Foerster rejected any absolute metaphysics and placed their faith not in "reason" but in the "will to refrain," the higher intuitive imagination. As Foerster put it, "Unlike the conceptions of life that grow out of science, humanism seeks to press beyond reason by the *use of intuition or imagination.*"[48] The difference might be further demonstrated by recalling the frequent contests in the late medieval and Renaissance periods between those who emphasized rhetoric at the expense of logic and those who emphasized logic at the expense of rhetoric. The one was part of a literary tradition and the other was part of a philosophic tradition. Although Foerster could not bring himself to accept a reasoned metaphysics, he flirted with the rational humanists when he said:

Our Occidental love of reason might drive us to the last step, the formulation of the metaphysics or the theology latent in this humanistic philosophy. Admittedly, this would give us more order than we easygoing Americans are ready for today. On the other hand we do yearn, in our bewilderment, in our empty aimlessness, for order. We are weary of the chaos within our minds.[49]

It is clear that Foerster was more interested in closing ranks with the rational humanists than in refuting them. Once humanitarianism was laid low, there would be time enough to resume the age-old conflict between the logical and the rhetorical traditions.

Foerster also sought an alliance with orthodox religion as he insisted that humanism and religion could work together in stemming the tide of naturalism. On the one hand, Foerster had to admit that "pure humanism is incompatible with a dogmatic, revealed religion"[50] and that "old religious solutions are inadequate"[51] for the neohumanist; but on the other hand, he was quick to point out that "humanism may be regarded as auxiliary to religion. It attracts, not only those seeking order as critical

---

46. Foerster, *American State University,* p. 261.
47. Foerster, *American State University,* p. 262.
48. Foerster, *Toward Standards,* p. 167.
49. Norman Foerster, *The Future of the Liberal College* (New York: D. Appleton-Century Company, 1938), p. 77.
50. Foerster, *Toward Standards,* p. 205.
51. Foerster, *Toward Standards,* p. 202.

individualists, but also those who feel the need of order as members of a visible Church."[52]

One might go further, Foerster surmised, and emphasize the common grounds of humanism and Christianity by recognizing that both conceive of reality in dualistic terms.

Of the trend of past experience there can be no doubt; both of the old guiding traditions, the Greek and the Christian, however different outwardly, were absolutely at one in their sharp contrast between the human and the natural.[53]

Although it is difficult to view the worldly temper of the Christian as a mere outward difference, it becomes clear that Foerster, for the sake of harmony, was emphasizing the very point that made it possible for the early Church fathers to blend classical dualism into Christian dualism, even though the Christian dualism was fundamentally very different from the classical. While Foerster recognized that "pure humanism was incompatible with a dogmatic revealed religion," he sought the support of orthodox religion as an ally against the common enemy, naturalism.

Neohumanism, as recast by Norman Foerster, took on many of the characteristics of an opposition party willing to minimize basic differences between itself and possible supporters in order to dislodge a common foe. Behind this façade of rapprochement, which evoked a limited degree of flexibility, remained the rigid dualistic humanism of Irving Babbitt. Babbitt's and More's conception of human nature, the good society, the purpose of knowledge, and the nature of a liberal education are all aptly paraphrased in most of the work of Norman Foerster. As Foerster himself said, "I know of nothing better than the dualistic humanism which Irving Babbitt set forth with great learning and critical power."[54] Foerster, like his mentor before him, squared off against Darwinian naturalism, which assumed a continuity of man and animal, by asserting that man is forever separate from nature, not in degree, but in kind. The world of man is a world of moral values, the world of nature "amoral, blind, and pitiless." One must recognize that "human nature is in all times and places of recorded history fundamentally the same and that it will not be changed tomorrow."[55] Just as Babbitt and More had earlier argued, Foerster thundered against Baconian science and Rous-

---

52. Foerster, *Toward Standards*, p. 204. One might also consider the practical support the churches gave to neohumanism through their emphasis on the classical languages. It was the private schools which persistently held Latin and Greek in the curriculum of the secondary schools. In 1934, the percentage of students taking Latin in public secondary schools had dropped to 16.04 per cent and Greek to almost nothing. In 1933, the private high schools reported 56.0 per cent in Latin and 1.6 per cent in Greek. In spite of the fact that the enrollment of the private schools more than doubled between 1900 and 1933, one can note a rise in the percentage of students taking Latin from 46.9 per cent in 1900 to 56.0 per cent in 1933. The great bulk of these private high schools were church-affiliated schools; 2113 were reported sectarian and 522 nonsectarian. See *The Biennial Survey of Education in the United States, 1934-1936*, "Statistical Summary of Education," pp. 23-24.

53. Foerster, *Toward Standards*, p. 161.

54. Foerster, *Future of the Liberal College*, p. 17.

55. Foerster, *Future of the Liberal College*, p. 75.

seauian naturalism. The true humanist function of knowledge is virtue, and virtue, in the end, is being true to oneself, true to what one ought to be in the higher sense.

The philosophy of humanism finds its master truth, not in men as they are (realism) or in men as worse than they are (naturalism) or in men as they 'wish' to be (romanticism), but in men as they 'ought' to be—'ought,' of course, not in the usual restrictedly moral sense, but with reference to the perfection of the human type.[56]

Foerster's educational ideal was the same as Babbitt's, and so was his belief in the ideal society as a stable aristocratic society. Just as Irving Babbitt had found that "in substituting the love of man for the love of God the humanitarian is working in a vicious circle,"[57] so Foerster argued that "humanitarianism found no meaning in the primary law, *Love the Lord thy God,* and therefore perverted the meaning of the secondary, *love thy neighbor as thyself."*[58] "Christian love," Foerster insisted, "was metamorphosed into natural sympathy, and the old faith in personal immortality yielded to the new faith in social progress."[59]

Once again a neohumanist attacked the social meliorists largely, one would suspect, because a society predicated on a "slave class,"[60] as Aristotle viewed it, or an "indoctrinated class,"[61] as Foerster saw it, or a class "compelled by fear or blind obedience,"[62] as Paul Elmer More saw it, was not possible so long as men persisted in viewing mankind as perfectible and insisted on being their brother's keepers. Most of organized philanthropy was, Foerster insisted, "nothing but a form of communal materialism,"[63] which administered to the needs of the body but rigorously failed to minister to the needs of the soul. "Freedom from physical suffering is a good thing, but it is not the best. Relatively [sic] to ethical and spiritual values it is not important."[64] Physical suffering has not increased but actually decreased; humanitarianism has increased man's sensitivity to physical pain to the extent that the very moral fibers of civilization are threatened with deterioration. In the Middle Ages, when charity was under proper controls, Foerster concluded,

. . . there was none of the instinctive repugnance to *bodily* suffering that is so marked in the eighteenth century and later. On the contrary, the mortification of the flesh was held to be praiseworthy, torture was allowed by common consent, and burning at the stake was regarded with positive satisfaction. Not that such things are desirable. But it is clear that when humane and enlightened men

---

56. Foerster, *Toward Standards,* p. 188.
57. Babbitt, *Democracy and Leadership,* p. 283.
58. Foerster, *American State University,* p. 32.
59. Foerster, *American State University,* p. 32.
60. See Benjamin Jowett, trans. and ed., *The Politics of Aristotle* (Oxford: The Clarendon Press, 1885).
61. Foerster, *American State University,* p. 179.
62. More, *On Being Human,* pp. 154-155.
63. Foerster, *Future of the Liberal College,* p. 19.
64. Foerster, *Future of the Liberal College,* p. 9.

could endure and approve such sights the valuation of physical pain in the Middle Ages, the great age of Christianity, was quite different from our own.[65]

The fact that humane and enlightened men could view human sacrifice on the altar of religious unity with "positive satisfaction" seemed, to Foerster, *prima facie* evidence that theirs was an age which at least had its values straight. This age had not confused the second commandment with the first. Foerster believed that humanitarianism had made us a soft, flabby people.

We are a coddled people. . . . Certainly people used to make little of bodily suffering which they could not stand at all today, such as floggings of five hundred lashes, or operations without anaesthetics. I do not recommend such suffering, for myself or others; I am simply affirming that a civilization based upon the avoidance of suffering is an empty and hollow affair.[66]

Although at times Foerster may seem extreme, he was only making more explicit the neohumanist social ideology. The classical concept of charity invariably carried with it the corollary virtue of stoic fortitude. Fortitude, the ability to withstand pain and suffering, was viewed as a positive good. The humanitarian attempt to reduce pain to a minimum deprived people of the opportunity to develop virtue.

At this point, many of the conservative social ideas of William Graham Sumner and Edward L. Thorndike seemed to merge with those of the neohumanists. Although each arrived at his conclusions from a radically different set of conceptions of human nature, they all saw the ideal society as inevitably hierarchical and therefore rested their hopes for the future in the education of the gifted child. All argued against the social meliorists, who assumed that human nature as well as society was capable of intelligent collective change, and all viewed the masses as trainable but not educable. While Sumner arrived at his conclusions by way of social Darwinism, and Thorndike by way of testing and measuring society as it exists, Babbitt and More arrived at what they thought society ought to be by way of ancient models. However, neither Foerster nor Babbitt was content to amass the classical evidence to support his case but each used humanitarian evidence whenever it seemed useful. It should be recalled that Paul Shorey, Irving Babbitt, and Paul Elmer More had attacked Edward L. Thorndike on the grounds that he was a pseudo-scientist who failed to recognize the duality of human nature and therefore his research amounted to nothing more than a compendium of errors. Although Foerster rejected the connectionist school of psychology, he looked with great favor on Thorndike's social views. Since Foerster insisted that the growth of the state universities, as well as our secondary schools, had been a waste of taxpayers' money in a foolish philanthropic venture to educate the uneducables, he was delighted to find Thorndike saying the same thing.

---

65. Foerster, *Future of the Liberal College*, p. 8.
66. Norman Foerster, "The College, the Individual, and Society," *The American Review,* IV, 2 (December 1934), 139.

Unimpressed by pseudo-idealism, Professor Thorndike boldly opposes the growing tendency to keep youth in school and college as long as possible. 'Indiscriminate advances in the compulsory school age beyond sixteen seem, in view of the facts, a weak and wasteful procedure. . . . We need laws to prevent greedy or perverse parents from depriving gifted children of schooling, not laws to force them to keep in school children who have neither the ability nor the interest to profit thereby.'[67]

Obviously, Thorndike and Foerster were both interested in education of the gifted child. They were both interested in developing and maintaining a conservative social order, and they arrived at their common conclusion from opposing traditions. Both Babbitt and Foerster frequently pointed with satisfaction to the fact that the intelligence testers in World War I had confirmed what the humanists had been saying all the time; namely, that our society cannot afford to be governed by the average since "the average mental age of our male voter is about fourteen."[68] While Babbitt was quick to point out the social implications of the tests and measurement movement, Foerster was even more apt at seeing the implications for educational practice.

If we are prepared to take the psychologists' word for it most pupils may at that age [12] be divided into three groups. The first is composed of pupils who have reached, or already passed, their natural limits of educability. They are so low in endowment that further instruction would involve definite waste. The second group is composed of pupils who can be trained in preparation for some activities of citizenship and some types of vocation. Receptive of authoritative instruction, they can be indoctrinated. . . . The third group is composed of pupils who can do more than passively learn items of fact, thought, and habit, who are capable of active assimilation and expression of mind and personality.[69]

The American school might best be concerned with "indoctrination" for the masses and "education" for the gifted children. A concept of a democracy of the people, by the people, and for the people, and an education compatible with this conception were untenable. Interestingly enough, they were made untenable by the humanitarian social scientists themselves. "Even the intellectual turned against democracy, Old Style, partly because it had not worked, and partly because its dogmas could not endure the facts being amassed against them by political scientists, psychologists, and biologists."[70] Indeed,

. . . if psychology proved anything, it seemed to prove not only that people differed in intelligence but that in the aggregate they had very little of it—that,

---

67. Foerster, *American State University*, p. 176.

68. Babbitt, *Democracy and Leadership*, p. 264. Also see Foerster, *American State University*, p. 171.

69. Foerster, quoting a *New York Times* excerpt (March 20, 1932) of an address by Thorndike; *American State University*, p. 179.

70. Foerster, *American State University*, p. 137.

if not a great beast, as Hamilton had opined, the people were certainly a great fool.[71]

The neohumanism of Norman Foerster had reached some kind of ultimate in sophistry when he denied the validity of certain knowledge and then used that same knowledge to support his own position. While Irving Babbitt, in the first two decades of the twentieth century, had written about the deterioration of the ideas of equalitarian democracy, social progress, and optimistic faith in the moral improvement of humanity as if this was something to be expected in the near future, Norman Foerster, writing in the next two decades, marshaled with considerable satisfaction evidence to show that this deterioration had already come to pass. John Dewey[72] and Norman Foerster both recognized the disillusionment of the American intellectual, and both saw it as an opportunity to introduce their own ideas. The disillusionment, to Dewey, was caused by a rejection of traditional values, whereas, to Foerster, the disillusionment was caused by a rejection of naturalistic values and the eroding of Enlightenment concepts. To Dewey, the opportunity lay in the development of a science of man based on the reconstruction of Enlightenment values; to Foerster, the opportunity lay in the renaissance of humanism. Both men, however, sensed certain features in this crisis in American values which Daniel Bell aptly described some decades later as a profound distrust on the part of the younger generation for any neat, systematic philosophy of human nature or the good society.[73]

As Foerster carried the neohumanist ideology to mid-century, certain subtle changes in his attitude may be noted. He himself did not report any major changes in his thought, nor did his last important educational work, *The Humanities and the Common Man* (1946), indicate any fundamental change in his concept of the nature of man, the function of knowledge, the nature of the good curriculum, or the nature of the teaching-learning process. Nevertheless, there was an explicit shift from a more aristocratic to a more equalitarian view of the function of the humanities. Less emphasis was given to the evils of mass education and "indoctrination" for the masses, and more emphasis was given to the ideal of a liberal education for all men. The humanities, he commented, "are not exclusive, not for any class, not for an artificial aristocracy of birth or wealth, not for a natural aristocracy of intelligence, but for all men and women."[74] He further suggested that:

To say that what is great is for the few is to insult the common man, to deny the element of greatness in his nature. He has a stake in spiritual as well as material

---

71. Foerster, *American State University*, p. 138.
72. See John Dewey, "What I Believe," *Forum*, LXXXIII, 3 (March 1930), 176-182.
73. See Daniel Bell, *The End of Ideology* (New York: The Free Press of Glencoe, Inc., 1960).
74. Norman Foerster, *The Humanities and the Common Man* (Chapel Hill: University of North Carolina Press, 1946), p. vii.

wealth. The century of the common man calls for a better distribution of material wealth; it needs, no less, a better distribution of spiritual wealth.[75]

This, indeed, was not neohumanism as Babbitt or More developed it, nor was it the same as Foerster's own ideas as expressed in his earlier works. One can only speculate as to why this shift occurred. Perhaps Foerster was pragmatically sensitive to the postwar atmosphere which had little tolerance for elitist systems and felt it necessary to redirect neohumanism toward a more democratic view of the good society. One thing was clear, however. As Norman Foerster began to write about the humanities for all men, without making distinctions between the freemen (the liberally educable) and the slave class (the uneducable), he brought neohumanism more closely in line with the more liberal ideas of such literary humanists as Mark Van Doren and Jacques Barzun and the rational humanism of Hutchins and Adler, who insisted that liberal education in a democratic society must be for all.

By mid-century, neohumanism had been redefined by Norman Foerster to mean something very different from what Babbitt and More had envisioned at the beginning of the century. Foerster, sensitive to the trends of the times, displayed a greater willingness to modify his position than had any of his predecessors. In his attempt to make Jefferson the precursor of neohumanism, and in his later, more explicit concern for the "greatness" of the common man's nature, he demonstrated a sensitivity to the major trend of the twentieth century, the democratization of American culture. It is important to recognize, however, that at no time did Foerster explicitly recognize a conflict between the American concept of democracy and the classical conception. Nor did he change his conception of human nature. Whether Foerster's change from aristocratic to democratic emphasis was sophistical, superficial, or sincere remains an unanswered question.

In his willingness to substitute the modern for the classical languages, Foerster represented a sharp break with the educational tradition in which both Babbitt and More placed their faith. While neohumanism, under Foerster, continued to bear the marks of the classical tradition, the classical languages no longer were held to be an absolute requirement for a liberal education. The terms *classical humanism* and *neohumanism* ceased to be interchangeable. Although Foerster in his earlier works carried the neohumanist's conception of charity to its logical conclusions, there is a distinct absence of the suffering wisdom of Parzival in his later works. Here again, Foerster may have been sensitive to the social thought of the American citizenry, as the American public increasingly came to look at poverty and physical suffering as an evil breeding vice and delinquency, and less as a human condition which would enable the moral athlete to vault to spiritual virtue.

Although Babbitt's and More's neohumanism ceased with Norman Foerster, much of the classical rationale of Babbitt and More resounded in the great debate in American education at mid-century. Voices calling for discipline, community of values, narrow and prescribed curriculum,

---

75. Foerster, *Humanities and the Common Man*, p. viii.

elimination of electives, elimination of educational frills, separation of utilitarian from liberal studies, education for the leadership class, and education as transmission of our cultural heritage could be heard with increasing vigor. Though the exact formulation of neohumanism changed with Norman Foerster, the educational values inherent in this tradition remained very much alive.

New conservatism

No sooner had Norman Foerster begun to find a place for the humanities in the education of the common man than others took up the cudgel against humanitarianism in the interest of the conservative society as Babbitt and More defined that society. Peter Viereck in *Conservatism: From John Adams to Churchill* (1956), Russell Kirk in *A Program for Conservatives* (1954), and Gordon Keith Chalmers in *The Republic and the Person* (1952) clearly resurrected Irving Babbitt's view of the good society. As an editor of *Modern Age* and a frequent contributor to the *National Review*, Russell Kirk led the attack on social and educational humanitarianism. Although there are differences between the neohumanists and the neoconservatives, their conception of the good society as aristocratic, their scathing denunciation of democratic values, their abhorrence of mass culture, their retreat into tradition, and their attack on education are all common characteristics. Thus, Russell Kirk said:

A truly conservative system of learning, aimed at some restoration of the ideal of the unbought grace of life, cannot breathe until the stifling empire of the doctrinaire Deweyites is overthrown. For no one in our time is more old-fashioned than a hard-and-fast pupil of John Dewey; the weight of this being upon our schools and colleges and universities is the weight of an intellectual corpse.[76]

Very much in line with Norman Foerster's view, Kirk went on to attack the naïve democratic notion of majority rule. The masses are not going to save civilized culture from destruction, Kirk pointed out, for "no mysterious wisdom abides in the bosom of the people." Only through the education of the gifted will humanity find stability enough to survive in the twentieth century. The steps required were clearly pointed out by Kirk:

The *public* is not going to save us from the decay of reason; we must save ourselves, and thereby society. The first step is to confess that any society, no matter how democratic politically, requires leaders of opinion and taste and serious thought, and that the primary purpose of any system of education is to encourage and instruct those leaders, the guardians of the World and unbought grace of

---

76. Russell Kirk, *A Program for Conservatives* (Chicago: Henry Regnery Company, 1954), p. 63.

life. The second step is to resuscitate that liberal learning which teaches men the meaning of time and duty, and which nurtures the idea of a gentleman.[77]

The liberal learning that Kirk proposed to resuscitate bore the familiar marks of neohumanism. When it came to education, however, the new conservatives proposed a greater militancy against the doctrinaire Deweyites. As Kirk put it, "the modern thinking conservative [when dealing with education] must employ some of the methods of revolutionaries, and echo the Jacobin cry of Danton, 'audacity, and again audacity and always audacity.'"[78] Repeatedly, the neohumanists provided the ammunition with which the neoconservatives attacked education with audacity. Since the neohumanists were the disfranchised educationists of the twentieth century, their arsenal was well stocked with educational criticism. By mid-century, such neoconservatives as Russell Kirk, Gordon Keith Chalmers, and such leaders in the Council for Basic Education as James D. Koerner, Harold Clapp, and Douglas Bush seemed to find the neohumanists' ammunition extremely useful for attacking humanitarians in education. In Koerner's *The Case for Basic Education,*[79] and Clapp's and Bush's frequent essays in the Council for Basic Education *Bulletin,* the educational views of Babbitt and More reached a wider audience.[80] In general, most neoconservatives not only sympathized with the educational views of Babbitt but also found considerable grounds for agreement with his conception of human nature and the good society. By 1956, in the twilight of the McCarthy era, amid growing attacks on the schools, Russell Kirk felt that things were looking up for the neohumanists:

. . . nowadays their number is increasing rapidly. University and college presidents like Dr. Nathan Pusey and Dr. Gordon Keith Chalmers have been his disciples; some of the best-known Catholic writers and some of the most able Protestant clergymen acknowledge their debt to him and the rising generation is rallying round the memory of Irving Babbitt who died in 1933.[81]

Kirk went on to say: "The Marxist, Freudian, instrumentalist, and naturalist schools of opinion against which Babbitt and Paul Elmer More

---

77. Kirk, *Program for Conservatives,* p. 76.
78. Kirk, *Program for Conservative,* p. 63.
79. See also James D. Koerner, *The Miseducation of American Teachers* (Boston: Houghton Mifflin Company, 1963). For a more detailed study of neohumanism, see unpublished dissertation (University of Wisconsin, 1960) by Clarence J. Karier, "The Neo-Humanist Protest in American Education, 1890-1933." For the relationship between the neohumanists and the Council for Basic Education, see Robert H. Beck, "The New Conservatism and the New Humanism," *Teachers College Record,* LXIII (May 1962), 435-444.
80. To be sure, not all who sympathized with the Council's position were neohumanists or neoconservatives. For example, when the Council sponsored Admiral H. G. Rickover's book, *Swiss Schools and Ours: Why Theirs Are Better* (Boston: Little, Brown and Company, 1962), they were supporting not a humanist who looked to the past for the eternal verities but a scientist whose main concern was with the present development of academic talent for a scientific technological age. Both Rickover and the Council called for a radical reconstruction of American education, but for very different reasons.
81. Russell Kirk's introduction to Babbitt's *Literature and the American College* (Los Angeles: Gateway Editions, Inc., 1956), p. vii.

and their friends contended so stoutly are now in their marked decline."[82] Babbitt, according to Kirk, had won the battle after all. One is inclined to wonder if, again, Kirk might have mistaken the end of the Marxist, Freudian, instrumentalist, and naturalist schools for what was really the end of ideology, and the end of systematic schools, including humanism, in which the younger generation could no longer place their faith.

Literary humanism

While neoconservatism was, in a very real sense, the authentic heir of neohumanism as Babbitt defined it, there were other humanists who rejected Babbitt's narrow, aristocratic social and educational views and yet were a significant part of the literary humanist tradition. This group, represented by such men as Mark Van Doren, Gilbert Highet, and Jacques Barzun, reflected far more liberal humanitarian social views. In many ways, this group was more akin to the sweetness and light of Matthew Arnold than to the narrowed stoicism of Irving Babbitt.

These literary humanists kept alive the role of the well-rounded amateur whose function it was to act as an influential social and educational critic. Just as it was the orator's function to use the spoken word artistically to persuade, so it was the function of the man of literature, the man of taste, to use the written word to persuade. One might well ask: Persuade humanity to what? The answer was clear: To persuade humanity toward those truths which the disciplined, well-rounded amateur senses are true. As word artists, these men exerted a powerful influence on the literate population.[83] They could, in a sense, paint a picture of American education and society as bright or as dark as they felt it warranted.

As heirs of the rhetorical tradition, the literary humanists were the modern-day orators who employed their talents not on the public platform of oral debate but on that of written debate. Thus, when Jacques Barzun in *Teacher in America* (1945) painted with verve and humor the picture of the "Ph.D. octopus," one could not help but sense the ideal of the well-rounded gentleman lurking in the shadows. One could also recall that it was that same Ph.D. specialist who advanced the cause of technological and theoretical science at the expense of the humanist's well-rounded man. The ideal of the Ph.D. was not to know all the best that was thought and said in the past, but rather to create new knowledge. As the Ph.D. replaced the amateur at the head place of the table of culture, many humanists such as Barzun were seriously concerned about the humanist's loss. When Barzun further suggested that the "three great forces of mind and will—Art, Science, and Philanthropy—

---

82. Kirk, Introduction to *Literature and the American College*, p. viii.

83. Perhaps the best example of this occurred when William H. Whyte, trained in literature, attacked the social scientist's methodology and then went on to verbally paint a picture of what the Organization Man really looked like: *The Organization Man* (New York: Simon and Schuster, Inc., 1956). As an amateur, disciplined in literature, Whyte carried on the great dialog with many people as he intuitively sensed what was taking place. He, then, verbally painted the picture of the "new suburbia." It is interesting that some social scientists mistook a literary approach to social criticism for social science research!

have, it is clear, become enemies of Intellect,"[84] one could detect strong overtones of Babbitt's concern with Rousseauian art, Baconian science, and humanitarian philanthropy. In Barzun's attack on philanthropy, one could not help but sense a reflection of Cicero's attitude toward benevolence as dangerously corrupting, if not discriminately controlled. As Barzun pictured "education without instruction" and "instruction without authority"[85] as characteristic of the American school, he portrayed the failings and excesses of mass education in a humanitarian society as a modern humanist sees them.

The humanists, as schoolmasters, represented the oldest educational tradition in the history of the West. As such, their central focus was on the education of the well-rounded man. Aside from the educational ideal of the orator-courtier-gentleman, there remained the consistent recognition that the teaching process is fundamentally an art. Whether it was Quintilian, concerned with the education of the orator, Erasmus with the Christian prince, Matthew Arnold with the English gentleman, or Gilbert Highet with the liberally educated man, all viewed teaching as an art which involved discipline, discrimination, emotion, and imitation. While the teaching process involved orderly planning and some degree of precision, it could not be made scientific.[86] As Gilbert Highet aptly put it:

Teaching is not like inducing a chemical reaction: it is much more like painting a picture or making a piece of music, or on a lower level like planting a garden or writing a friendly letter. You must throw your heart into it, you must realize that it cannot all be done by formulas, or you spoil your work, and your pupils, and yourself.[87]

In a narrower, more conservative, polemical fashion, A. Whitney Griswold lamented the decline of liberal education in America. The cause of this decline he attributed not only to the elective system espoused by Charles W. Eliot, the instrumentalism of John Dewey, and the rise of departments of education on university campuses, but, more important, to the influence on American education of the immigrant, whose children filled the classrooms of the twentieth-century educational frontier. The parents of such children did not "comprehend" the meaning of a liberal education, and consequently they failed to support it.[88] However, what Griswold failed to realize was that much of the classical conception of a liberal education was premised on the assumption that only the few were educable and that many of the staunchest defenders of the tradition, such as Paul Shorey, Irving Babbitt, Paul Elmer More,

---

84. Jacques Barzun, *The House of Intellect* (New York: Harper & Brothers, 1959), p. 27.
85. Barzun, *House of Intellect*, pp. 88-144.
86. It is interesting that on this point John Dewey could agree with the humanists. While much scientific work could be done with respect to education, Dewey believed the teaching process itself was an art. See John Dewey, *The Sources of a Science of Education* (New York: Liveright Publishing Corporation, 1929).
87. Gilbert Highet, *The Art of Teaching* (New York: Vintage Books, 1954), p. viii.
88. A. Whitney Griswold, *Liberal Education and the Democratic Ideal*, rev. ed. (New Haven: Yale University Press, 1962), p. 25.

Norman Foerster, and Albert Jay Nock,[89] had failed to heed Matthew Arnold's warning that the age of the common man was about to dawn. Considerably more sensitive to this advent, Mark Van Doren insisted: "The notion of Nock is that only a few are educable, whereas the thesis of this book is that many are and indeed all men."[90] In the fifties, many literary humanists took a similar position and attempted to define a liberal education for all men in terms of a democratic society. Few, however, were optimistic that a future American culture would be any more receptive to their educational ideas than had been the case in the immediate past. The flood of new knowledge had inundated virtually all the humanist's hallowed ground. It was symptomatic of the times that, more often than not, the literary humanist spoke of re-creating the educational ideal rather than preserving it. If Joseph Wood Krutch was correct when he said, "The modern novels most discussed in advanced circles during the fifties are nihilistic. . . . They preach despair rather than, as Lewis did, the benefits of a culture accessible to all who want it,"[91] then the literary humanists, in re-creating their educational ideal, would have to contend not only with the naturalistic pragmatism of James or Dewey but, more important, with the nihilism of a Nietzschean view of reality. Such a view had become increasingly popular with the *avant-garde* of the younger generation.

PHILOSOPHIC HUMANISM

The rational humanism of Hutchins and Adler relied heavily on St. Thomas Aquinas and Aristotle for its definition of man. Rational humanism was to the Middle Ages what literary humanism was to the Renaissance; i.e., where the Renaissance emphasized rhetoric and esthetic taste, the Middle Ages emphasized logic and scholastic reasoning. Hutchins and Adler defined man's nature as divided between his reason and his passions in basically Aristotelian terms. The essence of man's nature that distinguishes him from the animal world was his ability to reason. This was viewed as a universal characteristic of man in every time and place. It followed, then, that a truly liberal education was that education which liberates man's mind from his passions, an education which teaches men to think rationally; a vocational education, on the other hand, teaches men to use their hands. As a result of American pragmatism and many other materialistic and naturalistic influences, this innate dualism has been ignored, and American education has become permeated from the early grades through the university with a confused vocationalism. Very much in the rationalistic tradition, Hutchins assumed universal truths, a universal metaphysics as well as a universal nature of man. Just as Aristotle was concerned with the

---

89. See Albert Jay Nock, *The Theory of Education in the United States* (New York: Harcourt, Brace and Company, 1932).

90. Mark Van Doren, *Liberal Education* (Boston: The Beacon Press, 1959), p. 70.

91. Joseph Wood Krutch, "Reflections on the Fifties," *Saturday Review* (January 2, 1960), 9.

essence of man but not his accidents and Aquinas was concerned with the unity of truth, so Hutchins argued that the essence of man, truth, and education were everywhere the same. As he put it:

One purpose of education is to draw out the elements of our common nature. These elements are the same in any time or place. The notion of educating a man to live in any particular time or place, to adjust him to any particular environment is therefore foreign to a true conception of education.[92]

What follows, then, is an oft-quoted but questionable syllogism. "Education implies teaching. Teaching implies knowledge. Knowledge is truth. The truth is everywhere the same. Hence education should be everywhere the same."[93] If education is rightly understood, it will inevitably be "the same at any time, in any place, under any political, social, or economic conditions."[94]

Starting with a universal conception of human nature and a universal conception of education, Hutchins went on to sketch a blueprint of higher education in terms of the trivium and quadrivium as he understood them. Ultimately, the aim of higher education was wisdom. "Wisdom is knowledge of principles and causes. Metaphysics deals with the highest principles and causes. Therefore metaphysics is the highest wisdom."[95] Metaphysics became for Hutchins and Adler the highest science. Herein lies one of the major differences between the religious humanism of Jacques Maritain and the rational humanism of Hutchins and Adler. While Hutchins and Adler stopped at metaphysics, Maritain completed the Thomist system with theology as the "queen of science" and the ultimate source of wisdom.

From Hutchins' and Adler's point of view, the disintegration of American education was of such a nature that this was no time to quibble about theology. What was needed was a clear definition of man as a rational animal and a clear set of educational aims that proceed from first principles. The education which follows must be that kind of education which develops men's intellectual virtues.

I suggest that the cultivation of the intellectual virtues can be accomplished through the communication of our intellectual tradition and through training in the intellectual disciplines. This means understanding the great thinkers of the past and present, scientific, historical, and philosophical. It means a grasp of the disciplines of grammar, rhetoric, logic, and mathematics; reading, writing, and figuring. It does not, of course, mean the exclusion of contemporary ma-

---

92. Robert Maynard Hutchins, *The Higher Learning in America* (New Haven: Yale University Press, 1962), p. 66.

93. Hutchins, *Higher Learning in America,* p. 66.

94. Hutchins, *Higher Learning in America,* p. 66. Adler said essentially the same thing: "The *ultimate* ends of education are the same for all men at all times and everywhere." Mortimer J. Adler, "In Defense of the Philosophy of Education," *The Forty-First Yearbook of the National Society for the Study of Education* (Chicago: University of Chicago Press, 1942).

95. Hutchins, *Higher Learning in America,* p. 98.

terials. They should be brought in daily to illustrate, confirm, or deny the ideas held by the writers under discussion.[96]

At St. John's College in Annapolis, Maryland, under the presidency of Stringfellow Barr, Hutchins had his chance to test his ideas in action. With the trivium and quadrivium as loose guidelines, the four-year college curriculum was designed around the one hundred "great books" of Western civilization.[97] Such a reconstruction of the liberal arts curriculum was designed to develop those intellectual powers necessary for a rational man. Neither Hutchins nor Barr nor Adler was concerned with vocational, technical, or professional education, but rather that education which is necessary for developing those characteristics common to all men's nature. Once one was liberally educated, he could then proceed to apply himself to whatever specialty he selected. Thorndike had not convinced everyone that mental discipline did not work. This was most clearly illustrated when Stringfellow Barr argued:

The man who has learned to practice these arts successfully, can 'concentrate' on anything, can 'apply himself' to anything, can quickly learn any specialty, any profession, any business. That man can deliberate, can make practical decisions by other means than tossing a coin, can understand his failures, can recognize his obligations as well as his opportunities. He is in short what an earlier generation eloquently termed 'an educated man.'[98]

Although few institutions at the college level followed the direction of St. John's, Hutchins and Adler went on to argue that a similar curriculum should be organized at the high school level. They both believed that if all men have a common nature and there is a common content best designed to develop this common nature, then a democratic society which has equalized the right to vote must be primarily concerned with the development of the intellectual arts in *all* children, and not just the gifted few.[99] What is needed is not, as Thorndike would have it, one kind of content for the slow learner and another kind of content for the gifted, nor, as Babbitt would have it, a humanistic education for the few and humanitarian education for the many, but rather the same content for all children. "I insist, however, that the education I shall outline is the kind that everybody should have, that the answer to it is not that some people should not have it, but that we should find out how to give it to those whom we do not know how to teach at present."[100] Hutchins

---

96. Robert M. Hutchins, *Education for Freedom* (Baton Rouge: Louisiana State University Press, 1943), p. 60.

97. See "A Report on a Project of Self-study," *Bulletin of St. John's College in Annapolis,* VII, 2 (April 1955). Also see Russell Thomas, *The Search for a Common Learning: General Education, 1800-1960* (New York: McGraw-Hill Book Company, 1962), pp. 230-243.

98. Quoted in V. T. Thayer, *Formative Ideas in American Education* (New York: Dodd, Mead & Company, 1965), p. 341.

99. It is interesting that although many high schools do seem to follow a modified Great Books approach in their special education of the gifted, few seem to entertain the idea that such courses should be open to the so-called average learner.

100. Hutchins, *Higher Learning in America*, p. 61.

and Adler consistently pressed their point that any educational system which presumes to take as its goal critical thinking for the gifted and something less than this for the average or less-than-average student is an educational system designed for something less than a free democratic society. Under the guise of meeting individual needs, Hutchins charged, American educators avoided the tougher problem of how to liberally educate the common man.[101]

Hutchins' and Adler's good society was the democratic society where all men were equipped to carry on the "great conversation." Such a society was predicated not on a slave class as in ancient Greece, nor on a serf class as in the Middle Ages, but on the idea that all men can be free. The rational humanists were selective with respect to what aspects of the historic tradition they chose to espouse. Aristotle, for instance, had made a mistake when he concluded that some men are by nature slaves. As Hutchins said, "Aristotle's views on the natural slave are refuted by a simple reference to his basic proposition that man is a political animal. If all men are men, none of them can by nature be a slave."[102]

Aristotle had come to his conclusions from a study of man within Greek society, which depended on slavery; and Robert Hutchins derived his view of human nature within a society that rejected slavery. If, in one social context, one can conclude natural slavery, and in another, rational freedom for all, either human nature or our perspective of that nature has changed. There was something in the rational humanist's position approaching contradiction. If neither human nature nor education had changed, then the social system had changed our conception of that nature. As much as Hutchins and Adler universalized education and human nature outside of society, many of their views on human nature, as well as on education, were conditioned by their own conception of the good society—which was neither ancient nor medieval, but very modern indeed.

While Hutchins and Adler proved to be formidable educational critics who prepared the way for other critics by mid-twentieth century, the direction they attempted to push American education was not followed. The multiplicity of purposes of education in a pluralistic society were not easily rationalized into a single purpose, nor in actual practice was it as easy to distinguish the liberal from the technical as both Hutchins and Adler had argued. To a considerable extent, both men were voices crying in the wilderness of a technocracy. A technological society which valued change and relied on specialists in many fields of human knowledge for its very survival was neither able nor, indeed, willing to trust its educational fortunes to the idea of Stringfellow Barr that a St. John's type of education adequately educates one for "any specialty, any profession, any business." The age when John Milton

---

101. By mid-century the question of what is the appropriate education of a free man in a free society was a critical question for many both in and out of the humanist fold. See, for example, the report of the Harvard Committee, *General Education in a Free Society* (Cambridge, Mass.: Harvard University Press, 1945).

102. Robert M. Hutchins, *The Democratic Dilemma* (Uppsala, Sweden: Almquist and Wirsells Boktryceri AB, 1952), p. 36.

could define a liberal education as that education "which fits a man to perform justly, skillfully, and magnanimously all the offices, both private and public, of peace and war" had passed.

RELIGIOUS HUMANISM

Throughout the history of the West, there has existed a dynamic tension between supernaturalism and naturalism. From Darwin on, however, the major thrust of Western culture has been toward a naturalistic definition of man and culture. So much has this been true that men have frequently described the modern era as the "post-Christian era." Paralleling this trend in Europe at the beginning of the century and in America by mid-twentieth century has been the decline of certain key Enlightenment ideas which seem to undermine man's confidence not only in God but also in himself. Not only the gods of the supernaturalists had come under question but also the gods of reason, nature, and science. In the midst of this transvaluation emerged both a nihilistic and an existential view of reality.

In the context of this *Zeitgeist* of disillusionment, there also emerged various reassertions of older traditional religious values in terms of Protestant neo-orthodoxy and neo-Thomism. While the neo-orthodoxy of Karl Barth, Reinhold Niebuhr, and Paul Tillich evolved from an existential base, the Thomism of Jacques Maritain was clearly a reconstruction of St. Thomas Aquinas' thirteenth-century synthesis of faith and reason, naturalism and supernaturalism, cast in terms of the twentieth century. Although Thomism cannot be judged an influential philosophy outside of Roman Catholic education in America, within that faith it is a vitally significant philosophy. In American education, however, it not only nicely illustrates a tightly reasoned position with respect to the problem of defining human nature and its implications for educational practice but also clearly illuminates those areas where beliefs in supernatural revelation do make a difference in practice.

For American educators, Jacques Maritain (b. 1882) was among the more influential leaders in the revival of the philosophy of St. Thomas Aquinas in the twentieth century. For almost fifty years as a teacher and writer at the Collège Stanislas and the Institut Catholique in Paris, at the Institute of Mediaeval Studies in Toronto, and at Princeton University, Maritain reworked and reconstructed Thomistic philosophy. As had Aquinas, Maritain insisted that there was no conflict between the natural and the supernatural if they were rightly understood. There was a place for philosophy and a place for theology within a unified cosmology. While man's nature is divided between a spiritual soul and a natural body, the two are integrally a part of the unified man. Although neither Maritain nor Aquinas could accept a strict Cartesian dualism, on close analysis there always remained a functional dualism of body and soul, matter and spirit.

Just as Aquinas conceived of universal Christendom with one body politic and one church, Maritain conceived of the good society as a democratic Christian world society. If there was a universal natural law, which Aquinas thought he had arrived at through Aristotelian reasoning, and a universal divine law revealed in Christian scripture and tradition, then the ideal society was not to be found in the national state but in a universal world state. In the post-World War II period, both Hutchins and Maritain argued for an international world order based on a Thomistic model.[103] Such a society would be permeated by the "Christian spirit." As Maritain put it:

Well, those Christians who are turned toward the future and who hope—be it a long range hope—for a new Christendom, a new Christianly inspired civilization, know that 'the world has done with neutrality. Willingly or unwillingly, states will be obliged to make a choice for or against the Gospel. They will be shaped either by the totalitarian spirit or by the Christian spirit.' They know that a new Christianly inspired civilization, if and when it evolves in history, will by no means be a return to the Middle Ages, but a typically different attempt to make the leaven of the Gospel quicken the depths of temporal existence.[104]

The possibility of the development of the world state as a purely Christian civilization was recognized by Maritain as remote. But he retained the possibility that men could arrive at the idea of natural law through the use of their natural reason, as Aquinas had suggested. Perhaps Hutchins and Adler were more realistic on this point. Humanity with its many faiths might be expected to use its natural reason to arrive at a universal metaphysics more readily than it could come to accept a universal theology. Nevertheless, Maritain stayed with the synthesis of Aquinas and insisted that theology was functionally related to a correct definition of man, society, and education.

Jacques Maritain shared Paul Elmer More's concern, late in life, that an educational humanism without a theology seems to lead back to the humanitarian camp in the end, and if not there, nowhere. Fundamentally, Maritain argued that the education of man today suffers from a false definition of man and, as a consequence, a false definition of the ends of education. The sociologist who conceives of man in terms of his social needs, the psychologist who conceives of man in terms of psychological needs, and the pragmatist who insists on reconstructing ends as well as means give, at best, a partial view of man's nature and the appropriate education, and at worst, a very false conception. The true education of man must be based on the Christian idea of man if it is to be well grounded. Such an idea incorporates and assumes the divine destiny of man. Man is defined

. . . as an animal endowed with reason, whose supreme dignity is in the intellect; and man as a free individual in personal relation with God, whose supreme righteousness consists in voluntarily obeying the law of God; and man as a sin-

103. See Robert M. Hutchins, *St. Thomas and the World State* (Milwaukee: Marquette University Press, 1949). Also see Jacques Maritain, *Man and the State* (Chicago: University of Chicago Press, 1951).
104. Maritain, *Man and the State*, p. 159.

ful and wounded creature called to divine life and to the freedom of grace, whose supreme perfection consists of love.[105]

Maritain never lost sight of this end. Education is an art, an artistic endeavor in the creation of the Christian man who uses all his faculties for the ultimate glory of God.[106]

While Hutchins separated the vocational from the liberal in a very rigorous fashion, Maritain viewed the technical as an integral part of a liberally educated man. Maritain had far more confidence that the technical could be humanized as part of a unified educational experience. On this point, interestingly, there is a greater consensus between John Dewey and Maritain than there is between Maritain and Hutchins. In fact, when Maritain left the "aims of education" and discussed the "dynamics of education," there were numerous points upon which pragmatic and naturalistic educators were in hearty agreement with him.[107] Nevertheless, the fundamentally supernaturalist view of man held by Maritain remained irreconcilable with the fundamentally naturalistic philosophy of John Dewey. If, however, those on the naturalistic side found it difficult to reach consensus as to the nature of man or the good society, those on the supernaturalist side were just as divided. Once one got beyond the definition of the Christian man and Christian civilization to its meaning in action, the pluralistic religious character of American society came into play. American society reflected a fundamental secular as well as religious pluralism by mid-twentieth century. In view of this pluralism, perhaps Conant was correct in not asking the ultimate questions but rather directing attention to those educational practices upon which a greater consensus could be reached.

Humanism itself could not be characterized as an educational philosophy which defined man's nature, the good society, and educational practice with complete unanimity. While the narrow classicism of Babbitt and More might be favorably compared with the neoconservatism of Russell Kirk, neither position would fit well with the urbane literary humanism of Jacques Barzun or Gilbert Highet, nor would Hutchins' and Adler's emphasis on a universal reason and universal metaphysics set well within the literary humanist tradition. More important was the fact that the rational and literary humanists were divided in their conception of the good society all the way from a very elitist position on the one hand to a great concern for a democratic society on the other.

There were, however, broad areas of agreement. All found eternal verities in tradition and, more often than not, conceived of human nature as unchanged by time and place and of education as a changeless art. If pragmatists were concerned with a scientific view of man in a universe

---

105. Jacques Maritain, *Education at the Crossroads* (New Haven: Yale University Press, 1943), p. 7.

106. As Maritain put it, "May I confess at this point that, although I believe in natural morality, I feel little trust in the educational efficacy of any merely rational moral teaching abstractly detached from its religious environment." Maritain, *Education at the Crossroads*, p. 68.

107. Maritain, *Education at the Crossroads*, pp. 29-57.

of change, the humanists were concerned with the literature and philosophy of man in a universe of stability and eternal truths. On the surface, most humanists would agree with Dewey's suggestion that educators must learn "to make acquaintance with the past a *means* for understanding the present" and with Whitehead's assertion that "the only use of a knowledge of the past is to equip us for the present."[108] Most humanists found in their past more certitude to explain their present than either Dewey or Whitehead had found. The humanist quest for present certainty was satisfied by their study of the past. The eternal truths were not only revealed in the past, but the past explained how humanity had gone astray. Repeatedly, it was scientific naturalism, the idea of progress, social meliorism, mass philanthropy, and romantic art which had corrupted American society, which in turn had corrupted American education. The humanists, then, provided some of the main social and educational criticism in twentieth-century American education. As such, they disagreed at times with each other as to the nature of the good society and at various points as to the meaning of a liberal education, as well as the nature of man. Nevertheless, all would firmly agree with Emerson when he said:

> There are two laws discrete,
> Not reconciled—
> Law for man, and law for thing;
> The last builds town and fleet,
> But it runs wild,
> And doth the man unking.

SUGGESTED READINGS

Adler, Mortimer J., and Milton Mayer. *The Revolution in Education.* Chicago, University of Chicago Press, 1958.

Babbitt, Irving. *Democracy and Leadership.* Boston, Houghton Mifflin Company, 1924.

———. *Literature and the American College.* Boston, Houghton Mifflin Company, 1908.

———. *On Being Creative.* Boston, Houghton Mifflin Company, 1932.

Barzun, Jacques. *The House of Intellect.* New York, Harper & Brothers, 1959.

Beck, Robert H. "The New Conservatism and the New Humanism," *Teachers College Record,* LXIII (May 1962), 435.

Davies, Robert M. *The Humanism of Paul Elmer More.* New York, Bookman Associates, Inc., 1958.

Foerster, Norman. *The American State University.* Chapel Hill, University of North Carolina Press, 1937.

———. *The Future of the Liberal College.* New York, D. Appleton-Century Company, 1938.

---

108. Quoted in Mortimer J. Adler and Milton Mayer, *The Revolution in Education* (Chicago: University of Chicago Press, 1958), p. 155-156.

————. *The Humanities and the Common Man*. Chapel Hill, University of North Carolina Press, 1946

————. *Toward Standards*. New York, Farrar & Rinehart, 1930.

Griswold, A. Whitney. *Liberal Education and the Democratic Ideal,* rev. ed. New Haven, Yale University Press, 1962.

Highet, Gilbert. *The Art of Teaching*. New York, Vintage Books, 1954.

Hutchins, Robert M. *The Democratic Dilemma*. Uppsala, Sweden, Almquist and Wirsells Boktryceri AB, 1952.

————. *The Higher Learning in America*. New Haven, Yale University Press, 1962.

————. *St. Thomas and the World State*. Milwaukee, Marquette University Press, 1949.

Kirk, Russell. *A Program for Conservatives*. Chicago, Henry Regnery Company, 1954.

Krutch, Joseph Wood. "Reflections on the Fifties," *Saturday Review* (January 2, 1960), 9.

Maritain, Jacques. *Education at the Crossroads*. New Haven, Yale University Press, 1943.

Mercier, Louis J. A. *American Humanism and the New Age*. Milwaukee, Bruce Publishing Company, 1948.

More, Paul Elmer. *The Demon of the Absolute*. Princeton, N.J., Princeton University Press, 1928.

————. *On Being Human*. Princeton, N.J., Princeton University Press, 1936.

————. *The Skeptical Approach to Religion,* 5th ed. Princeton, N.J., Princeton University Press, 1958.

Nock, Albert Jay. *The Theory of Education in the United States*. New York, Harcourt, Brace and Company, 1932.

Van Doren, Mark. *Liberal Education*. Boston, The Beacon Press, 1959.

CHAPTER 9

The nature of the child versus the interests of society

God makes all things good; man meddles with them and they become evil. He forces one soil to yield the products of another, one tree to bear another's fruit. He confuses and confounds time, place, and natural conditions. He mutilates his dog, his horse, and his slave. He destroys and defaces all things; he loves all that is deformed and monstrous; he will have nothing as nature made it, not even man himself, who must learn his paces like a saddle horse, and be shaped to his master's taste like the trees in his garden.

. . . but what can be done . . . when instead of training man for himself you try to train him for others? Harmony becomes impossible. Forced to combat either nature or society, you must make your choice between the man and the citizen, you cannot train both.[1] JEAN-JACQUES ROUSSEAU

With these words, Rousseau initiated a revolution in Western educational thought, a revolution of the "heart" which reappeared in the thought of numerous nineteenth- and twentieth-century educational theorists and practitioners. In the mysticism of Froebel, the loving paternalism of Pestalozzi, the "new education" of Francis W. Parker, and the transcendentalism of Emerson and Thoreau, one can sense the spirit of the rebellion of the heart at work in the nineteenth century. In the twentieth century, one can perceive some of the same spirit, with, however, a different psychological basis, in the Jungian mysticism of Margaret Naumburg, the romantic Freudianism of A. S. Neill, and the romantic existentialism of Carl Rogers.

These people conceived of human nature differently, but they had in common a strong interest and respect for the subjective claims of

---

1. Jean-Jacques Rousseau, *Émile*, trans. Barbara Foxley (London: J. M. Dent and Sons, Ltd., 1955), pp. 5-7.

the individual against the demands of an organized society. This tradition looked to the heart, feelings, emotions, and the unconscious for sources of truth and generally asserted the rights of the child against the demands of society which "destroys and defaces all things." The true education of man must follow the natural unfolding of human potentialities. This tradition usually looked to the child for clues on how to organize the school. The clues that each individual found most significant were determined by his mental set toward either nature or the unconscious. As a result, curriculum and methodology varied from person to person as well as time and place. While none completely ignored the interests of society, all tended to place greater emphasis on the needs of the individual than on the needs of organized society, and thus they usually represented a revolt against the formal institutions and traditions of the established social system.

Contending against the child-centered educators were many diverse groups. From decidedly different perspectives, humanists, Hegelians, Herbartians, and social reconstructionists repeatedly took positions against the rebels of the heart. While the humanism of Irving Babbitt centered on the development of a stable, classical, aristocratic society, and the Hegelianism of W. T. Harris reflected a strong concern for maintaining the conservative social order, the Herbartians, representing one of the last major waves of German idealism to break on the educational shores of America in the nineteenth century, asserted the importance of history, tradition, and the transcendental nature of ideas in understanding the evolving society. While each group used a different kind of history, a different model of the good society, and a different conception of human nature, the weight of their educational efforts seemed to fall on the side of the interests of society. Just as these groups looked to the traditional wisdom of Western culture for clues to organize the school, the social reconstructionists—such as Lester Frank Ward, Albion Small, George S. Counts, and Theodore Brameld—looked at the present problems of society to determine future needs and thereby to discover the clues for organizing the schools of today. If the former groups looked to the past and the latter group looked to the present and a projected future for their rationale for organizing the school, both emphasized the education necessary for the "citizen."

Repeatedly, Dewey and others in the twentieth century argued against extreme positions either on the child-centered or on the society-centered side of the educational dialog. In the midst of the heated debate between the culture-centered Herbartians and the child-centered Pestalozzian and Froebelian educators, Dewey insisted in *The Child and the Curriculum* (1902) that these points of view represent two ends of the same continuum. He further argued that it is as much a mistake to ignore the interests of society as it is to ignore the needs of the child. Dewey consistently held that the education of "man" and the education of the "citizen" were two aspects of the same education. Within the next few decades, William Heard Kilpatrick, a student of Dewey, attempted to take a similar position while applying Dewey's philosophy to educational practice. In so doing, however, Kilpatrick seemed to shift the center of gravity toward a more child-centered approach. By mid-century,

Kilpatrick's synthesis, as well as other more extreme child-centered approaches, came under attack. As James B. Conant searched for educational consensus amidst considerable conflict, it became evident to most that the educational dialog had shifted more toward the needs of society. Whether it was Dewey, Kilpatrick, or Conant attempting to find the workable synthesis, each was vitally concerned with the kind of education he thought necessary for the development and maintenance of free men in a pluralistic society.

Although there were many educational reformers in the nineteenth and twentieth centuries, the focus of this chapter is on those individuals and groups who best represent either a child-centered or a society-centered point of view and on those who attempted to steer a middle course. As will be seen, each individual lived within a different society and was influenced by a different set of social circumstances. In spite of these differences, one may still detect some continuity within these opposing traditions. While it is necessary to extract extreme positions to sharpen our analysis and demonstrate something of the issues at stake, there are no clear black and white positions in much of the following educational dialog and often these positions tend to blend into the grays, which become the operational basis for educational practice. With these limitations in mind, we shall consider both the Pestalozzians and Froebelians in contrast to the Herbartians in the last half of the nineteenth century. We shall also consider the child-centered education advocated by Margaret Naumburg in the first half of the twentieth century in juxtaposition with the educational views of the social reconstructionists, G. S. Counts and Theodore Brameld. The views of William H. Kilpatrick and James B. Conant will then be considered in terms of their respective attempts to synthesize the education of man and of the citizen.[2]

NINETEENTH-CENTURY CHILD-CENTERED PERSPECTIVE

Pestalozzian movement

Although Johann Heinrich Pestalozzi (1746-1827) boasted that he had not read a book in thirty years, he had, it seems, read Rousseau's *Émile* carefully. Pestalozzi had, in fact, socialized the education of Émile. If Rousseau would educate Émile in the country away from the corrupting influences of the town, Pestalozzi would educate Émile as a member of a socialized group in the town. Pestalozzi's school was modeled after what he considered the loving atmosphere of the ideal home. Such a school, Pestalozzi believed, could radiate intellectual and moral reform which would eventually have a salutary effect on an entire community.[3] The education that Pestalozzi sought to develop would create, he believed, a moral man exhibiting those natural instincts which governed

---

2. No attempt is made here to cover the development of progressive education in the twentieth century. For an excellent treatment of that subject see Lawrence Cremin, *The Transformation of the School* (New York: Alfred A. Knopf, Inc., 1961).

3. See Pestalozzi's *Leonard and Gertrude*, 1781.

man in his original state of innocence and which still exist as traces in the early life of the child. As he said:

In this condition, before his deterioration has begun, man is a simple child of his instincts. He gives himself up absolutely to their innocent enjoyment. He loves the gazelle and the marmot, his wife and his child, his dog and his horse. He knows not God, he knows not sin.[4]

When he stumbled out of this garden of Eden, "primitive man knew not what he was losing when he took the step. He was seeking primitive pleasures, and he lost infinitely in this regard."[5] Primitive man, in becoming civilized, was deformed, and so we find him as Rousseau saw him, mutilating "his dog, his horse and his slave." This miseducation of man occurred at an early stage in the development of the race and was repeated over and over again in the education of the children of each new generation. Children are taught to bear the yoke of the citizen before they have had a chance to feel and trust the free play of instincts, before they have tasted that original spirit of innocence. "Only by such mutilation can man become a citizen. It is not easy . . . and it is often done at the cost of introducing a poison into his nature which destroys his humanity. . . . The man enters the citizen yoke without having known the charm of his primitive condition."[6] A natural education must maintain and develop the natural instincts as being trustworthy in a state of civilized culture.

The rights of childhood, whether asserted by Rousseau, Pestalozzi, Froebel, or Emerson, were usually based on the belief that the child is a product of nature and nature's God and is, therefore, born good, and that it is this natural goodness which must be preserved and developed. Most of these men tended toward a pantheistic view; i.e., they viewed God and nature as one. As long as men believed that this God was beneficent, and men like Pestalozzi, Froebel, and Emerson could read into the child's nature many of the more humane virtues of traditional Christianity, the respect for, if not the worship of, the child's nature seemed innocent enough. When, however, this notion of God had died and G. Stanley Hall's "mansoul" replaced Emerson's "oversoul," the age of innocence had ended. While Pestalozzi could find in the child's nature a strong susceptibility to love, tenderness, and kindness, Hall found a savage susceptible to myth, superstition, and discipline.[7]

---

4. J. A. Green, ed., *Pestalozzi's Educational Writings* (New York: Longmans, Green & Company, 1912), p. 61.

5. *Pestalozzi's Educational Writings,* p. 66.

6. *Pestalozzi's Educational Writings,* p. 71.

7. Charles Strickland and Charles Burgess have both aptly pointed out the relationship between Rousseau's primitivism and the primitivism of G. Stanley Hall. The road from Rousseau to Hall, however, is by no means straight. Rousseau tended to have more faith in the efficiency of reason than Hall, just as Rousseau and his interpreters tended, unconsciously at least, to read into the child's nature more of the benevolent Christian virtues. The intellectual climate in which each man lived made a difference; nevertheless, the historical link is there. See Charles Strickland and Charles Burgess, eds., *Health, Growth, and Heredity: G. Stanley Hall on Natural Education,* Classics in Education, No. 23 (New York: Bureau of Publications, Teachers College, Columbia University, 1965), p. viii.

If men have been miseducated along the road from the primitive to the civilized state, the new education must concentrate on the natural education of the child so as to rejuvenate "man" first, and then slowly this education would rejuvenate society. There are certain key Platonic assumptions implicit in much of the child-centered position which should be noted. First, there is assumed a "nature," which, though it may be hidden and distorted, exists as a transcendental entity. Second, it is further assumed that if each individual were educated according to that which nature has ordained him to be as a man, each would function in the ideal society as a worthy citizen. The educational reform of the individual would indirectly but inevitably result in bringing the society closer to an ideal social system. For these reasons, Rousseau declared Plato's *Republic* "the finest treatise on education ever written."[8]

As Pestalozzi proceeded to reform the education of man, he found that it was not only the harsh discipline of a stern teacher in a poorly lit and ventilated classroom, so typical of the schools of his day, which perverted a child's nature, but equally devastating was the effect of a curriculum that was remote from childhood experience, abstract, and taught by rote. Not as a theoretician but as a practical educational reformer, Pestalozzi exerted a profound influence on educational practice in both Europe and America. At Newhof, Stanz, Burgdorf, and Yverdon, Pestalozzi turned his reformer's zeal into educational practice. Although many of his schools were closed for economic, political, or social reasons, his actual teaching was markedly successful. In 1799, after visiting his school at Burgdorf, The Society of Friends of Education said of his work, "Pestalozzi's pupils learn to spell, read, write and calculate quickly and well, achieving in six months results which an ordinary village schoolmaster's pupils would hardly attain in three years."[9] What, then, was the secret of his success? Pestalozzi's answer to this question was as follows:

Here is the principle upon which I acted: Seek first to open the heart of the children, and, by satisfying their daily needs, mingle love and benevolence with all their impressions, experience, and activity, so as to develop these sentiments in their hearts; then to accustom them to knowledge in order that they may know how to employ their benevolence usefully and surely in the circle around them.[10]

To Pestalozzi, a sound education must involve the hand, the head, and the heart. The education of the whole child must include manual training, not only because it had vocational value but because it was part of a natural education which liberates the mind. Learning to work with one's hands was as much a part of a sound education as learning to work with one's mind. This idea was often used in late nineteenth- and early twentieth-century American education to support the notion that all students should take some manual training in the comprehensive high

---

8. Rousseau, *Émile*, p. 8.

9. Quoted in S. J. Curtis and M. E. A. Boultwood, *A Short History of Educational Ideas* (London: University Tutorial Press, Ltd., 1961), p. 329.

10. Quoted in Paul Monroe, *A Text-Book in the History of Education* (London: The Macmillan Company, 1916), p. 606.

school. Although in his personal life Pestalozzi lacked the practical ability to be successful,[11] the education he advocated was practical and highly successful.

Just as Emerson suggested that "the secret of education lies in respecting the pupil," Pestalozzi suggested the key was to be found in love and respect for the child. Since it is always more difficult to teach teachers to love and respect children than it is to teach them a set of rules to use when teaching, for many teachers in the nineteenth century Pestalozzian education came to mean a set of rules for classroom instruction. One must follow nature. The child's natural growth was always from the simple to the complex, from the concrete to the abstract. Therefore, as a teacher, one must move with nature and order the experiences of the child from the thing to the word, from the immediate experience to the distant. Direct experience was to be preferred over any vicarious experience, and therefore nature study and geography were to take place in the fields and woods near the schools. The child could best learn the meaning of a word by first touching the thing for which the word stood and then learning the word. Much of what the child needed to learn could be taught by way of object lessons. Almost any object, from a sea shell to a flower, could become the center around which the child's world of experience could be daily broadened to include the skills, knowledge, and moral lessons so necessary for civilized life. Thus, the hallmark of the Pestalozzian movement both in Europe and America became the object method.

In many ways, this method was to the Pestalozzian movement of the nineteenth century what Kilpatrick's "project method" was to "progressive education" in the twentieth century.[12] Both methods emphasized direct-experience learning following Rousseau's dictum of "teach by doing"; both cut across traditional fields of knowledge and assumed a reorganization of knowledge on the basis of the natural growth and development of the child; and both became rallying points for major educational reform movements.[13] Within the child-centered educational tradition, there is a distinct preference for direct-experience learning, which gives rise to an antibook attitude.[14] Thus, Pestalozzi argued:

It is indisputable that the mania for words and books, which has absorbed everything in our popular instruction, has been carried so far that we cannot possibly remain long as we are. Everything convinces me that the only means of preserving us from remaining at a civil, moral, and religious dead level is to abandon the superficiality, the piecemeal, and infatuation of our popular instruction and to recognize intuition as the true fountain of knowledge.[15]

---

11. He did not start teaching until he was fifty years old, before which time he failed at numerous occupations.

12. Kilpatrick's project method, however, tended to rely somewhat more on the spontaneous interest of the child, and therefore tended to be somewhat more child-centered.

13. See William Heard Kilpatrick, *The Project Method* (New York: Bureau of Publications, Teachers College, Columbia University, 1919).

14. This is reflected in Rousseau's *Émile,* Pestalozzi's *How Gertrude Teaches Her Children,* and Emerson's *The American Scholar,* as well as in Kilpatrick's *Foundations of Method.*

15. Quoted in Monroe, *Text-Book in the History of Education,* p. 610.

If one follows one's intuition, education can become pleasant, simple, practical, realistic, and within the reach of all.

The widespread influence of Pestalozzi was largely due to the fact that he proposed a practical way of educating the masses to love God and country and to become more effective workers, without threatening the elite class of wealth and power. While virtually all of Pestalozzi's work was with culturally deprived children, his social ideas were far from revolutionary. Even though the education of the poor would improve their lot, at no point could one expect education to change fundamentally their divinely allotted station in life. Booker T. Washington, in facing the power elite in America, argued for a practical education for the newly freed slaves and won great applause from the governing class for concluding that "in all things that are purely social we can be as separate as the fingers, yet one as the hand in all things essential to mutual progress."[16] So, too, Pestalozzi argued for a practical education for the new proletariat and was looked upon with favor by the power elite for suggesting that "'the poor must be educated for poverty' for in order 'to enjoy the best possible state, both of soul and body . . . it is necessary to *desire little and be content with still less.'*"[17] Under the circumstances, it is little wonder that Fichte's call for the rejuvenation of the Prussian nation along Pestalozzian lines[18] could be met with such electrifying and positive support by the aristocratic classes of Prussia. Here was an education which could meet the needs of the masses and the nation without threatening the class structure.

By the time Pestalozzi died, his educational principles had become the standard operating procedure for the German *Volkschules* and the normal schools which trained the teachers. In 1843, it was these Pestalozzian practices which so impressed Horace Mann on his visit to the Prussian schools.[19] However, neither Horace Mann, who advocated Pestalozzian methods for American schools, nor Joseph Neef, who introduced them to the United States at Philadelphia in 1809, nor Robert Owen and William Maclure, who made extensive use of Pestalozzian ideas at New Harmony, accepted Pestalozzi's social ideas with respect to education for poverty. On the contrary, Maclure and Owen used Pestalozzian methods to reconstruct the society at New Harmony.

Pestalozzian practices had a peculiar attraction in America during the nineteenth century. While transcendentalism called for greater respect for childhood, as well as more humane treatment of children, transcendentalism as a movement never developed a coherent educational reform program. The Pestalozzian movement tended to fill much of this need. The method also had an appeal to the practical temper of American culture. Pestalozzi, after all, was a practicing schoolmaster who demonstrated that his ideas worked.

---

16. Quoted in Merle Curti, *The Social Ideas of American Educators*, rev. ed. (Paterson, N.J.: Littlefield, Adams and Company, 1960), p. 297.

17. Quoted in the unpublished dissertation (University of Wisconsin, 1962) by Charles Burgess, "The Educational State in America," p. 18.

18. See Johann Gottlieb Fichte, *Addresses to the German Nation, 1807-1808* (Chicago: The Open Court Publishing Company, 1922).

19. See Horace Mann, *Seventh Annual Report*, 1843.

By 1862, Edward Sheldon, Superintendent of Schools at Oswego, New York, was well on his way toward making Oswego the center of Pestalozzian education in America. The Oswego movement provided teachers trained in the object method for normal schools from Maine to Mississippi and as far west as California. As the apostles of Pestalozzi fanned out across the country, carrying the object lesson into the educational wilderness, both the Oswego Normal School and its students seem to have lost rather quickly the spirit of Pestalozzi. The staff at Oswego itself became highly specialized in various aspects of the method. Within a short time, Oswego had an expert teacher of object lessons on "Animals and Moral Instruction," another on "Color and Geography," and another of "Advanced Lessons on Plants and Objects." Pestalozzi's dislike of specialized fields of knowledge as well as methodologies seems to have been ignored at Oswego. Under the influence of experts, the method became a set of rules and recipes to be memorized and often, by the less imaginative teacher, employed purely by rote.[20]

Not all teachers, however, slavishly followed the object method. Francis W. Parker, the man whom Dewey once called the "father of progressive education,"[21] could not be rightly accused of slavishly following any theory or method. From 1873 to 1880, as superintendent of the Quincy, Massachusetts, schools, Parker initiated exciting educational reforms throughout the school system. More in the spirit of men like Pestalozzi and Froebel than in the letter, Parker became one of the leading educational reformers at the end of the century. Just as Emerson, Pestalozzi, and Froebel could see the divine in the child's evolving nature, Parker believed that "the spontaneous tendencies of the child are the records of inborn divinity."[22] To Parker, the child must be the center of the educational experience, and everything he is taught must have meaning for him.

After 1880, Parker became the director of the Chicago Cook County Normal School. Freely borrowing from what he considered the best of Froebel, Pestalozzi, Herbart, and many others, Parker developed the Cook County Normal School as a showplace for the new education of the nineteenth century. So well developed was this image that G. Stanley Hall once said he visited Cook County annually "to set my educational watch."[23] By 1896, Dewey and his laboratory school at Chicago together with Parker and his Cook County Normal School represented a large part of the educational ferment in the nation at the turn of the century.[24]

---

20. For an example of a typical object lesson, see Ellwood P. Cubberly, *Public Education in the United States,* rev. ed. (Boston: Houghton Mifflin Company, 1934), pp. 347-349. See also the paper given at the National Teachers Association convention in August 1873 by E. A. Sheldon, "Object Teaching," *NEA Proceedings,* I and II (1857-1873), compiled by H. Barnard, Syracuse, New York, 1909.

21. John Dewey, "How Much Freedom in the New Schools?" *The New Republic,* LXIII (July 9, 1930), 204.

22. Quoted in Cremin, *Transformation of the School,* pp. 134-135.

23. Quoted in Cremin, *Transformation of the School,* p. 135.

24. See the unpublished dissertation (University of Wisconsin, 1960) of Robert E. Tostberg, "Educational Ferment in Chicago, 1888-1904." See also Robert E. Tostberg, "Colonel Parker's Quest for 'A School in Which All Good Things Come Together,'" *History of Education Quarterly,* VI, 2 (Summer 1966), 22-42.

While Dewey attempted to test in school practice some of the hypotheses he had evolved from his philosophy and his psychology, Parker started from practices others had employed which he intuitively thought would work. In this way, Parker exemplified a romantic approach to educational reform, whereas Dewey exemplified a pragmatic, experimental approach. Interestingly, both approaches became part of the progressive education movement in the twentieth century. Parker's role as an educational reformer was aptly reflected in the following response to criticism of the methods he used at Quincy.

There are some criticisms that are made on a certain experiment in education at Quincy that I want to notice, mainly to endorse. It is said, first, that there is nothing new in the Quincy method. No one has claimed that there is; at least, I put forward as the best argument that it is old. This experiment is the outcome of the experience of the last 100 years. It is indebted to all the great teachers and theorists of the past.

It is claimed I stole all my ideas. The thing I commend in that charge is that it is solid truth. I did steal—stole it all. I stole from Cleveland, Cincinnati, Aristotle, Pestalozzi, Spencer, and everybody else I could find in possession of anything worth stealing. I am going to keep at it, and I advise all of you who are earnest teachers to steal—steal all you can; and then you will not get half enough for the famished minds of children.[25]

Parker did steal and all in the interest of what his intuition told him the famished minds of children needed.

From Pestalozzi, Parker borrowed the object lesson, which he fused with Froebel's concern for "self-activity." However, when he borrowed the Herbartian idea of "concentration" in curriculum planning, he dropped the emphasis on history and replaced it with the child as the center of concentration.[26] In general, Parker was more at home with such child-centered reformers as Pestalozzi and Froebel than with the tradition-oriented Herbartians.

Froebelian movement

By the time Friedrich Froebel (1782-1852) had established his school (1837) at Blankenburg, Germany, and two years later named it the *Kindergarten,* he had fairly well completed the development of his major ideas. Critically important to all his work was the idea of unity in all things. All existence—physical, mental, moral, organic and inorganic— was unified in a pantheistic God.

In all things there lives and reigns an eternal law. . . . This all-controlling law is necessarily based on an all-pervading, energetic, living, self-conscious, and hence eternal Unity. . . . This Unity is God. All things have come from the Divine

---

25. Francis W. Parker, "On New Ideas in Education. A Response to Criticism of Quincy Experiment." Report in the *NEA Addresses* (1880), 49.

26. See Francis W. Parker, *Talks on Pedagogics* (New York: John Day Company, 1937.)

Unity, from God, and have their origin in the Divine Unity in God alone. . . . The divine effluence that lives in each thing is the essence of each thing.[27]

Froebel's quest of certainty was part of that nineteenth-century search for the one idea which would unlock all the secrets to both physical and mental existence. Froebel found it in God, unfolding His meaning in all things. "There is no other power but that of the idea; the identity of the cosmic laws with the laws of our mind must be recognized, all things must be seen as the embodiment of *one* idea."[28] In the life experience of every man, "there is repeated the history of the creation and development of all things, as the holy books relate it. . . . Every human being who is attentive to his own development may thus recognize and study in himself the history of the development of the race to the point it may have reached, or any fixed point."[29] Froebel, like many others in the nineteenth century, saw the history of the race writ small in the life of the child, but unlike those who gave this recapitulation idea an anthropological content, Froebel saw it "as the holy books relate it."

Plato, in his theory of remembrances, accounted for both good and evil implicit in man's nature by way of an obscure racial past but was not interested in bringing forth the evils of that past; similarly Froebel was most concerned with that education of man which would bring forth his nobler virtues. These virtues, to Froebel, were reflected in the unity of experience. Reading Froebel from a strictly Hegelian point of view, William T. Harris asserted that "Froebel, accordingly, attempts to organize a system of education that will unfold the rational self and chain down the irrational."[30] Harris missed the point. The irrational and the volitional, from Froebel's standpoint, are to be used as an integral creative part of the rational self. The end of education is not reason per se, but rather the happy, unified man who need not keep his instincts and impulses chained down, for they are functionally a part of the integrated man at peace with himself, his universe, and his God.

This, indeed, was the potentially explosive and highly significant contribution of Froebel to Western educational thought. Like Rousseau before him, Froebel insisted: *"The child, the boy, man, indeed, should know no other endeavor but to be at every stage of development wholly what this stage calls for.'*[31] While the man can be expected to put away the things of the child, he must nonetheless maintain those "child-like" qualities, to use Pestalozzi's word, or those "God-like" qualities, to use Froebel's word, derived from his childhood play experiences. The spirit of play must be maintained in the man if he is to be truly creative and express his humanity. This concept of play was well expressed by Schiller in his *Letters on Aesthetic Education,* when he said, "The plays of children often have deep meaning, for, to speak plainly and concisely, man plays

27. Friedrich Froebel, *The Education of Man,* trans. W. N. Hailmann (New York: D. Appleton and Company, 1892), pp. 1-2.
28. Froebel, *Education of Man,* p. 3.
29. Froebel, *Education of Man,* pp. 40-41.
30. Froebel, *Education of Man,* p. vii.
31. Froebel, *Education of Man,* p. 30.

only where he is a human being in the fullest sense of the word, and he has reached full humanity only where he plays."[32] In the same mood, Froebel insisted that:

Play is the purest, most spiritual activity of man at this stage, and at the same time, typical of human life as a whole—of the inner hidden natural life in man and all things. It gives, therefore, joy, freedom, contentment, inner and outer rest, peace with the world. It holds the source of all that is good.[33]

The age-old dichotomy between play and work is a false dichotomy. The man who has not learned to work with "joy, freedom, contentment" is a sadly miseducated man. A true vocational aim in life is to find that occupation where one can play at his work.[34] Froebel insisted that work should be a creative endeavor which, to be truly creative and bring forth the best God-like character in man, must embody the play spirit. It should be recognized that:

The debasing illusion that man works, produces, creates only in order to pre-serve his body, in order to secure food, clothing, and shelter, may have to be endured, but should not be diffused and propagated. Primarily and in truth man works only that his spiritual, divine essence may assume outward form, and that thus he may be enabled to recognize his own spiritual divine nature and the innermost being of God.[35]

True education, therefore, is not a prescriptive, interfering education but one which keeps alive the spirit of play and allows for considerable self-activity and social participation in meaningful, worthwhile experi-ence. Educators once again were reminded that they must be concerned with the whole child, his personality and moral character as well as his intellectual development. This, then, was the purpose of the children's garden—to provide a place where children might grow naturally.

Permeating all of Froebel's educational ideas was his mysticism. The objects with which the children played were "gifts" of God, each having a different symbolic meaning; and the activities in which the children were engaged were called "divine occupations." The circle the youngsters formed represented the mystical unity in all things. While these ideas seemed necessary as a rationale for many nineteenth-century Froebel-ians, most twentieth-century kindergarten advocates turned to psy-chology for their rationale. More important than the rationale employed was the fact that Froebel had instituted a radical child-centered reform movement which, if not contained at the kindergarten level, could have serious implications for the elementary school.

---

32. Quoted in Froebel, *Education of Man*, p. 58.
33. Froebel, *Education of Man*, p. 55.
34. For an interesting analysis of competing attitudes toward play and work in edu-cational thought, see Merle Borrowman, "Traditional Values in Shaping of American Education," *The Sixtieth Yearbook of the National Society for the Study of Education* (Chicago: University of Chicago Press, 1961).
35. Froebel, *Education of Man*, p. 32.

In 1856, Mrs. Carl Schurz organized one of the first German-speaking kindergartens in America at Watertown, Wisconsin; in 1860, Elizabeth Peabody established her English kindergarten in Boston; and in 1873, under the leadership of William T. Harris, the kindergarten became part of the St. Louis public school system on a large scale. Harris, the Hegelian, did not, however, rest easy with the mystical Froebelians. Froebel, after all, had really argued for more than just the kindergarten. His education called for reform based on the life stages of the child's development and for an educational program of self-activity that would keep alive the spirit of play at all levels of instruction. Froebel's belief that education must be such that the young would experience "joy, freedom, contentment" at all levels was a revolutionary idea for his day or, for that matter, any day. Harris consistently warned of the dangers in "excessive cultivation of self activity through a sentimental theory which apotheosizes childhood and infancy."[36] Although Harris was basically opposed to the sentimental Froebelians, he supported the development of the kindergarten in St. Louis for its work in rescuing the poor child from the slums. To Harris the purpose of the kindergarten was to "chain down the irrational" and prepare the youngster for the life of reason that would presumedly follow in further schooling. Because Harris viewed the kindergarten as only a preparatory school for the rational work of the first grade, its radical character could be effectively isolated from the rest of the school system in terms of its own unique function. Thus, the explosive nature of Froebel's ideas would be quietly and effectively curbed. The educational time bomb which Froebel so neatly planted at the base of the educational system, set to go off whenever men realized that the true aim of education was to follow the nature of the child and not the rationalized interests of society, was effectively disarmed at that point when the kindergarten became incorporated into American education as a play school which prepared the young for schoolwork.

Not only Harris but many other Americans came to view the function of kindergarten in just such a light. It is easier, then, to understand why many frustrated Froebelians overlooked Hall's primitivism and rallied to support his efforts to establish a department of child study in the NEA. In 1893, at a meeting of the NEA, Hall proudly proclaimed a victory for the child when he exclaimed, "that unto you is born this day a new Department of Child Study."[37] Amidst that gathering of dedicated child-centered educators stood not only disciples of Hall but also many disciples of Froebel. Radical ideas are not easily quarantined. By way of the child study movement, child psychology, and the teaching of Francis W. Parker and many other progressive educators in the twentieth century, Froebel's ideas were modified, reconstructed, shorn of their mysticism, given the sanction of a "scientific" psychology, and carried into the educational battle against a tradition-oriented society. Through the haze and smoke of battle, one could still detect, however, somewhat of

36. Quoted in unpublished dissertation (University of Wisconsin, 1963) by Charles Strickland, "The Child and the Race," p. 128.
37. Strickland and Burgess, *Health, Growth, and Heredity*, p. 16.

the same outline, the figure of the child. In 1928, Harold Rugg and Ann Shumaker, echoing the reform temper of many twentieth-century child-centered progressive educators, aptly expressed something of this ongoing child-centered tradition when they said:

For the progressive schools of today, for the first time in history, are actually working out in practice something which Rousseau perceived and only vaguely described to his contemporaries; which Pestalozzi apprehended only in the personal love and goodness of his heart; toward which Froebel strove through an obscure mysticism; which Dewey partially phrased and could not entirely exemplify. In spite of the errors and gropings and mistakes of an imperfect methodology one fact stands supreme: The new education has reoriented educational thinking about its true center—the child. And all those other things are slowly being added unto it.[38]

NINETEENTH-CENTURY SOCIETY-CENTERED PERSPECTIVE

Unlike Pestalozzi and Froebel, who placed great emphasis on the child as an unfolding flower, Johann Friedrich Herbart (1776-1841) shifted the center of importance to the teacher, as representing the interests of society. While Pestalozzi and Froebel tended, éach in his own way, to be revolutionaries of the heart, Herbart was more a conservator of the mind. Even though Herbart was in basic agreement with Hegel's dictum—"whatever is rational is real and whatever is real is rational"—Herbart set out to create a philosophy, a psychology, and an ethical system distinct from those of Hegel. His lifework might best be characterized as an attempt to replace Hegel as the philosopher of Germany. That he came out second best in this endeavor is evident. Perhaps his bitterest disappointment in life came in 1833, when he failed to succeed Hegel at the University of Berlin.

Many have suggested that Herbart's great misfortune was that he lived in the shadow of Hegel, but in a sense this cannot be viewed as a misfortune, for Hegel provided a solid intellectual position against which Herbart developed his ideas. Herbart attempted to cut an intellectual swath between the rational philosophy of Kant and the romantic rationalism of Hegel. Like Kant, Herbart started with a fundamental dualism between what is and what ought to be—a metaphysics and an ethical system—and like Kant, he turned to the question of how we come to know (epistemology) in order to resolve the issue. Kant, on the one hand, concluded that we can never know reality, and Hegel, on the other hand, found reality in the unfolding of the absolute spirit. Herbart insisted that it was not possible to reduce everything to a single principle and therefore posited a pluralistic metaphysics based on many unchanging "reals." As Herbart intellectually moved from his metaphysics to his associationist psychology and then to his ethical system, the metaphysical "reals" became "ideas" in his psychology and "ideals"

---

38. Harold Rugg and Ann Shumaker, *The Child-Centered School* (Chicago: The World Book Company, 1928), pp. 324-325.

in his ethical system.[39] Although Herbart liked to describe himself as the "Kantian of the year 1828," he went beyond Kant in establishing more of an organic system than Kant, and yet he stopped short of Hegel's absolute system.

Herbart's thinking was very much a product of that nineteenth-century neoclassical revival implicit in German idealism. This revival employed Platonic assumptions, developed transcendental notions of *Kultur,* and put them in motion in the form of a cosmic, moving history. Within certain limitations, the philosophy of Herbart can best be compared with that of Plato in *The Republic.* To Plato, as to Herbart, the critical problems of philosophy were eventually to be resolved in the education of man and the citizen. To Plato, and Herbart, the end of education was virtue. Both philosophers thought virtue was achieved by an education which used ideas as instruments to achieve the good life. Both believed that behind appearances, there were unchanging reals, reals ultimately existing as knowable transcendental ideas. Herbart, as well as Plato, understood that in order to educate for virtue, the process must be delicately controlled to bring the young intellectually and emotionally into closer and clearer union with these ideas. Just as Plato had warned of confusing the young mind with complex ideas and advocated using only those models which brought forth the "good," Herbart was very concerned with clear ideas which would eventuate in "good" character.

In spite of these striking similarities, Herbart, nonetheless, was working in a post-Lockean age where Platonic notions of innate ideas had been generally discredited. During the nineteenth century, the shift was made, however, from innate ideas in the child to innate processes and stages of growth and development. Herbart, like so many others in the nineteenth century, had found the corresponding link between *Kultur* and the growth stages of the child.[40] To Herbart, "History ought to be the teacher of humanity."[41] The crucial question then becomes: what kind of history? As a good classicist, Herbart began his history with the Greeks. Education should begin with Homeric poems because the interests of the youth of the race were naturally the same as the interests of present-day youths. For Herbart and his followers both in Europe and America, the "concentration," or core, of the curriculum around which all other areas of study were to be correlated was a combination of history and literature. Where factual history began and literary fiction ended, however, was not quite clear.

---

39. In certain aspects of Herbart's psychology, one can find elements of Hegel's dialectic cast in different terminology, and in Herbart's ethics, one can find elements of Kant's categorical imperatives, again cast in different terms. There were some very basic contradictions implicit in Herbart's system which remained unsolved. For a carefully reasoned analysis of some of these contradictions, see John Angus MacVannel, *The Education Theories of Herbart and Froebel* (New York: Bureau of Publications, Teachers College, Columbia University, 1905), pp. 66-80.

40. For instance, when Dr. W. Rein pointed out in his *Outline of Pedagogics* in 1893 that this had been the consensus of the best informed observers, he cited the following to support the idea: Lessing, Herder, Goethe, Schiller, Kant, Fichte, Shilling, Hegel, Comte, Huxley, Spencer, Rousseau, Pestalozzi, Froebel, Herbart, Ziller, etc.; pp. 96-98.

41. Johann Friedrich Herbart, *Letters and Lectures on Education* (Syracuse, N. Y.: Bardeen School Supplies, Inc., 1898), p. 237.

As a follower of Herbart, Tuiskon Ziller, at the University of Leipzig, developed the culture-epoch idea more explicitly in terms of a practical curriculum and, together with Dr. W. Rein at Jena, applied these ideas to the *Volkschule.* The curriculum Ziller set forth started with Grimms' *Fairy Tales* for the first grade, *Robinson Crusoe* for the second grade, and at the third grade the core was divided between Jewish and German history. On the one side, the child worked his way from the Bible stories of the Old Testament to the New Testament, and on the other side, he worked his way from the legends of *Thuringia* through the *Niebelungen* and on to the restoration of the German Empire. With Ziller, the rational emphasis of Herbart was lessened for an apparently increasing emphasis on *Volk* myths.[42]

The American disciples of Ziller and Rein, Charles and Frank Mc-Murry and Charles De Garmo, led the Herbartian movement in American education with considerable success. The curriculum they advocated was also based on the culture-epoch theory, but the content of history was modified to fit the American scene. The core of the curriculum that Frank McMurry recommended proceeded with the following sequence:

First grade—"The Fir Tree" by Hans Christian Andersen
Second grade—"Louise, the Child of the Western Forest"
Third grade—"Robinson Crusoe"
Fourth grade—Fremont's Expedition
Fifth grade—Story of John Smith
Sixth grade—Causes of the French and Indian War.[43]

Here, then, was a curriculum which could take the youngster from "The Fir Tree" to the "Causes of the French and Indian War," all based on the assumed correspondence of the natural growth of the child and the history of the race.

However, there was a problem which reappeared throughout Herbart's, Ziller's, and McMurry's use of history. If the aim of education was virtue, as Plato and Herbart suggested, and history was the teacher of humanity, as Herbart believed, then historical data should be selected with less care for historical accuracy and more concern for the moral effect that such knowledge would have on the student. Herbart's use of history was very compatible with those chauvinistic groups in both Europe and America who persistently advocated a patriotic history. As Herbart put it, "Patriotic history is not the same for each country," but whichever country and whatever patriotic history is to be taught, one must always remember that "great care should be exercised in selecting only that which can be understood by boys, and will increase their patriotic feelings."[44] Although few of the American Herbartians would care to admit it, at the center of their core curriculum was the use of history as a mythical vehicle for teaching moral and patriotic lessons.

---

42. See Charles De Garmo, *Herbart and the Herbartians* (New York: Charles Scribner's Sons, 1896), p. 119.
43. De Garmo, *Herbart and the Herbartians,* pp. 123-129.
44. Herbart, *Letters and Lectures on Education,* pp. 237-238.

The impact of the Herbartians on American education was greatest at the secondary school level. By the turn of the century, Herbartians occupied many of the key posts in the newly formed departments of education on university campuses which prepared secondary school teachers. Most of Herbart's ideas were more compatible with the academic orientation of the high school than with that of the elementary school. Herbart, more than Pestalozzi or Froebel, had developed a rational psychology of learning and a related methodology of teaching which, if one ignored the culture-epoch idea, could be effectively used to sustain the traditional disciplines.

The psychology Herbart developed was essentially an associationist psychology. The child's mind, at birth, is a blank slate which can only enter into ideational relationship with its environment by way of the nervous system. The mind has neither innate ideas nor innate faculties but builds up a content on the basis of "presentations" of sense perceptions. Through assimilation of these presentations, or ideas, the mind develops clearer, more complex, and higher mental processes. This process of *apperception*, if properly controlled, eventually produces a self, a will, and, in the end, character. All this seems reminiscent of Locke, except that the ideas Herbart dealt with are basically transcendental, Platonic entities, all of which have logical relationships. Knowledge becomes transcendental presentations which the teacher must order in a logical sequence so that the child learns. Significant learning occurs not only when the child incorporates ideas into his own mental repertoire but, more important, when he becomes interested and seeks out other related ideas. Interest, then, is not only a means but also an end. As Herbart said:

The ultimate purpose of instruction is contained in the notion, virtue. But in order to realize the final aim another and nearer one must be set up. We may term it *many-sidedness of interest*. The word *interest* stands in general for that kind of mental activity which it is the business of instruction to incite. Mere information does not suffice; for this we think of as a supply or store of facts, which a person might possess or lack and still remain the same being. But he who lays hold of this information and reaches out for more takes an interest in it. Since, however, this mental activity is varied, we need to add the further determination supplied by the term *many-sided.*[45]

Learning, then, involves more than the mere passive reception of information; it includes an active, intellectually alive mind. Somewhat like a magnet, the ideas already constituting the "mind" are attracted by some ideas and repelled by other ideas. That which determines whether a particular idea will be attractive is largely determined by the content of ideas already existing in both the conscious and the subconscious mind. The teacher, therefore, must study what ideas the child already commands and determine what logical steps can be used to present new ideas, so that further learning can take place. Herbart, then, developed a general method of instruction that had universal application.

---

45. Monroe, *Text-Book in the History of Education*, p. 633.

The method was based not on the nature of the content, nor on the nature of individual differences, but on the way *all* minds learned.

Based on the associationist psychology of Herbart, Ziller went on to standardize the method in terms of the five formal steps of teaching: preparation, presentation, association, generalization, and application. The knowledge to be imparted was organized in logical units of study. The teacher would skillfully prepare the student for the new ideas by drawing his conscious attention to older ideas which were logically related to those new ideas about to be presented. The new ideas, then, are presented and quickly associated with other ideas the student already commands. Next, the youngster is helped to make generalizations on the basis of what he has learned, and finally he is expected to make a practical application of the new idea. Lesson plans and unit plans are, thus, logically and sequentially ordered and become the building blocks of the larger curriculum with its concentration on history and literature.

Much of Herbart's logically organized philosophy, psychology, methodology, and curriculum design was attractive to the secondary school teachers in both Europe and America. The Herbartian movement placed great stress on the role of the teacher in the dissemination of ideas and the shaping of moral character. Thus, the traditional interests of society were reasserted. By 1892, the Herbartians occupied the center of the educational stage with the formation of the National Herbart Society.[46] Advocating a science of education along Herbartian lines, such men as Frank M. McMurry, Charles De Garmo, Charles A. McMurry, and C. C. Van Liew wrote books, gave speeches, and argued their case at annual meetings of the National Education Association. By 1900, when the movement had already been discredited, it was evident that the influence Herbart had exerted in American education was not so much through his philosophy or his psychology as through his methodology. For the next two decades, many Herbartian teachers continued to teach future teachers Herbart's five formal steps, lesson plans, and unit plans, along with scattered bits of his philosophy and psychology. Dewey's philosophy and Thorndike's psychology, however, intellectually eclipsed the Herbartian movement in the twentieth century. By 1918, William Heard Kilpatrick took the next logical step and attempted to create a method based on the new philosophy and the new psychology which he named "the project method."

The last decade of the nineteenth century was, in many ways, a watershed for twentieth-century educational thought. At almost any annual meeting of the National Education Association, one might hear spirited, serious debate on a variety of issues as Herbartians, Pestalozzians, Froebelians, Hegelians, pragmatists, social reconstructionists, and classical humanists confronted each other in open debate. Outside these halls of active debate existed a society in fundamental transition from an agrarian to an industrial economy and from a rural to an urban society. Whether it was the McMurry brothers, Francis W. Parker, John Dewey, Albion Small, Lester Frank Ward, William T. Harris, or Paul Shorey

---

46. The National Herbart Society later became the National Society for the Scientific Study of Education and later The National Society for the Study of Education.

who periodically occupied the center of the stage, all seemed to sense, in one way or another, that America was in the throes of fundamental social change.

The Western frontier had closed and the new educational frontier was about to open. That problems and dangers lay ahead, few would deny. But these were what Van Wyck Brooks aptly called "the confident years." Such massive problems as urbanization, industrialization, and immigration were only a challenge to the optimistic American self-confidence. Undismayed by the closing of the frontier, the confidence which broke the sod of the Dakotas and felled the timbers of the great Northwest was readily transferred to the educational frontier. If free land contributed to democratic values in an agrarian economy, free education could contribute to democratic values in an industrial economy. If rural society provided the place where diverse ethnic groups learned to respect one another on the basis of merit, perhaps education could perform that same function in an urban society. If, then, the schools were to perform all these functions adequately in the new society of the twentieth century, the schools would have to be reformed. But few could agree on a suitable procedure and the right purposes. The Progressive Education Association (1919) was born largely as a response to that strong vocal public demand for educational reform in the early decades of the century. The history of the association, which included both child-centered and society-centered educators, was marked by a lack of unanimity of purpose and method.[47] Both in and out of the Progressive Education Association were educators who looked to the child and others who looked to society for insights into organizing the curriculum of the schools. When Rugg and Shumaker in 1928 said that "one fact stands supreme: The new education has reoriented educational thinking about its true center—the child," and a few years later G. S. Counts dared the progressive educators to use the schools to build a new social order, the issue was again effectively restated in a twentieth-century context.

TWENTIETH-CENTURY CHILD-CENTERED PERSPECTIVE

Reminiscent of Froebel's insistence that play gives joy, freedom, and contentment, and that it holds the source of all that is good in education, Margaret Naumburg, founder and director of Walden School, also insisted that:

. . . for young children, work and play are one and the same thing—work and play, or whatever you may choose to call that all-absorbing activity, in which children lose themselves, for either long or short periods of time. That state of being is to my mind the starting-point of real education.[48]

---

47. See Cremin, *Transformation of the School.*
48. Margaret Naumburg, *The Child and the World* (New York: Harcourt, Brace and Company, 1928), p. 10.

The one great contribution of Froebel, Margaret Naumburg found, was his recognition of the importance of self-activity. Both these child-centered educators believed that if the child is given freedom and cultural opportunity, he will grow and develop into a constructive, creative, purposeful human being. If society would just stop inhibiting the child, the good that is latent in his natural soul could be released.

However, in defining human nature, they differed. While Froebel defined the child's nature from the perspective of a mystical pantheist who could see the hand of God at work in the creative spontaneity of the child, Miss Naumburg, from the perspective of the mystical primitivism of Jungian psychology, could see in this same spontaneity the release of the creative good latent in both the personal and the collective unconscious of the race. Finding the rationalism of Freud somewhat wanting, Miss Naumburg concluded that:

The Jungian approach acknowledges the existence and importance of the personal unconscious, but regards such an approach as incomplete; to Jung the universal or collective unconscious contains images which deal not only with past experiences that have been repressed, but also with future experiences that have not yet been related to consciousness but may be in the process of such development.[49]

Primitivism in American educational thought did not end with Hall. Indeed, it was carried to the present on the mystical collective soul of Jungian psychology. As late as 1950, Margaret Naumburg said that:

The young child and the primitive wait for no rules of art before expressing themselves in forms so vivid that we all respond. A sense of rhythm, a feeling for color, and an image-making capacity belong to the human race and were never imposed from without. As man draws upon the limitless resources of the unconscious he evokes again ancient images which preceded words as a direct form of communication. Ability to create is inherent in humanity and may at any moment win further release in such fulfillment and integration.[50]

Miss Naumburg felt that education should provide the inner and outer freedom that allows an individual to express his true human nature, rather than thwart the child in order to create a citizen.

The life of Margaret Naumburg was dominated by one great passion —to reform society. After graduation in 1910 from Columbia, where she had completed her major work with John Dewey and had been president of the Socialist Club, Miss Naumburg came to believe that social reform by way of collective social action was not only possible but necessary.[51] Continuing her studies at the London School of Economics under the direction of Sidney and Beatrice Webb, however, Miss

49. Margaret Naumburg, *Schizophrenic Art: Its Meaning in Psychotherapy* (New York: Grune & Stratton, Inc., 1950), p. 20.

50. Naumburg, *Schizophrenic Art*, p. 37.

51. For much of the biographical material on Miss Naumburg, I am indebted to Robert H. Beck, "Progressive Education and American Progressivism: Margaret Naumburg," *Teachers College Record*, V. 60 (May 1959), 198-208.

Naumburg became increasingly disillusioned with the possibilities of any real reform by way of collective action. Any real, lasting reform, she surmised, must begin with individual renewal, not with urban renewal. Thus, any reform, to be truly effective, must get back to the very basis of the problem: the education of the child. She then traveled to Italy and studied with Dr. Montessori at her *Casa dei Bambini.* Upon her return to the United States, she attempted to put into practice the Montessori method at the kindergarten of the Henry Street Settlement House in New York City. As Naumburg used Montessori's method, she increasingly came to believe that while Montessori's method worked on a principle similar to Froebel's idea of self-activity, it tended, through the use of objects, so to structure and channel the emotional energies of the child that those energies were not released in a truly creative way. Dissatisfied with the Montessori method, Miss Naumburg set out to establish her own school and her own approach. In 1914, she founded the Children's School which later was renamed the "Walden School."[52]

As Margaret Naumburg proceeded to release the creative energies of children, she attempted to release her own creative energies by way of psychoanalysis with the Jungian analyst, Dr. Beatrice Hinkle. One could not understand, she surmised, the emotional life of children unless one first understood one's own emotions. At her urging, it is estimated that at least half the staff at Walden School undertook analysis.[53] The teachers, freed from their own inhibitions, could then allow the students the same freedom to release their creative energy. Walden School became a highly permissive school, free of teacher-imposed lessons. As Agnes De Lima put it, "Walden School has dared to create a child's world and then for the most part to stand aside and watch the children grow in it under conditions of real freedom."[54]

The "child's world," however, did turn out to have a focus. Under the able guidance of Mrs. Florence Cane,[55] Margaret Naumburg's sister, the creative arts became the center of the school activities.[56] Music, dramatics, writing, drawing, and painting all became highly important vehicles of expression. In the area of creative drawing and painting, the Walden School children excelled. By studying the child's free expression in painting, Miss Naumburg and Mrs. Cane came to understand the inner struggles of the child to free himself.[57] The social free-

---

52. Aptly named in honor of the man who, in attempting to escape the demands of society, reminded his countrymen "that they are to be men first, and Americans only at a late and convenient hour." Walden School began as a nursery school, and expanded year by year. By 1928, the school had two hundred boys and girls, ranging in age from two to eighteen.

53. See Cremin, *Transformation of the School,* p. 213.

54. Agnes De Lima, *Our Enemy the Child,* 2nd ed. (New York: New Republic, 1926), p. 203.

55. Mrs. Cane also had undergone analysis under the direction of Dr. Beatrice Hinkle.

56. See Beck, "Progressive Education and American Progressivism," p. 201.

57. Later in life, Margaret Naumburg made significant contributions to art therapy at the New York State Psychiatric Institute. See *Schizophrenic Art: Its Meaning in Psychotherapy* and *Studies of the "Free" Art Expression of Behavior Problem Children,* 1947. Margaret Naumburg's educational views represented in no small way the fusion of expressionism in art and the growing popular interest in psychoanalysis.

dom of the school was, then, only a means to achieving that more important inner freedom to express oneself creatively. The school, as described by Agnes De Lima, became a virtual beehive of meaningful activity where children created not only at drawing boards and painting easels but in workshops and laboratories. At Walden School Lewis Mumford taught English, Hendrik Willem Van Loon taught history, Ernest Bloch instructed music, and Dr. A. A. Goldenweiser of the New School for Social Research freely discussed with inquisitive minds such topics as primitive culture, taboos, superstition, religion, morality, and inheritance of acquired characteristics.[58]

Encouraged by her success with Walden School, Margaret Naumburg, in *The Child and the World* (1928), launched her attack on what she considered to be the society-centered school of John Dewey and others. Much as Jung had warned of the herd instinct, and therefore the need for leaders, Miss Naumburg saw Dewey's social behaviorism as one which sacrificed individual leadership for the good of the group and therefore "is nothing but instinctive herd psychology, translated into modern terms."[59] Just as Jung insisted that man must learn to trust the inherent goodness of his unified unconscious, Margaret Naumburg asserted that "we trust the innate social instincts of children so profoundly that we find it unnecessary to force socialization from above."[60]

Miss Naumburg had clearly understood the critical difference between her position and Dewey's. The child, Dewey believed, was born with undifferentiated tendencies to act; there were, however, no innate social instincts to be trusted. He also believed that the social learning experience of the young must be carefully planned by adults if it was to be intelligent and progressive. Miss Naumburg insisted that Dewey's laboratory school was just that: a school planned and structured by adults to socialize youngsters for little more than a herd existence. Dewey, Miss Naumburg charged, had ignored subjective experience and downgraded the emotions by calling them "reflexes of action." Such a philosophy, Naumburg concluded, leads to the deadening condition of "group-mindedness."

Two years before Margaret Naumburg published her attacks on Dewey's psychology, philosophy, and educational views, Dewey, in *Art and Education* (1926), had already branded the permissive child-centered school as "really stupid." Cremin summarized Dewey's ideas thusly:

Freedom . . . is not something given at birth, nor is it bred of planlessness. It is something to be achieved, to be systematically wrought out in cooperation with

---

58. See Beck, "Progressive Education and American Progressivism," p. 202, and De Lima, *Our Enemy the Child*, p. 205.

59. Naumburg, *Child and the World*, p. 59.

60. *Child and the World*, p. 121. The parallel with Jung is even closer. For example, one is strongly reminded of Jung's notion of the collective unconscious as mystically rooted in the native soil when Naumburg suggested that what is wrong with America is "that we lack the spiritual equilibrium of those who grow from their native soil. This very want is, I think, what makes us Americans subject to tides of slavish imitation." *Child and the World*, p. 26.

experienced teachers, knowledgeable in their own traditions. Baby, Dewey insisted, does not know best![61]

This heated argument continued. In *The New Republic*,[62] Naumburg repeated her charge that Dewey's philosophy was typically American with its emphasis on mass action, group-mindedness, and group psychology. All this she saw as leading to "a dull and gloomy picture, this technological utopia."[63] In the following issue, Dewey responded by arguing that the progressive revolt of Francis W. Parker was essentially a sound revolt against the formalized traditional school which needed reconstruction. What was needed now, however, was the creation of a new, intellectually meaningful subject matter, based on the many varied fields of human knowledge. There were some child-centered educators, he noted, who look to the immature minds of children to create their own subject matter. As a consequence of this approach, the fear of adult imposition had become of supreme importance, and as a result, some of these schools allowed pupils unrestricted freedom in all things. They had, indeed, carried the idea of freedom to the point of anarchy. "Ultimately it is the absence of intellectual control through significant subject matter which stimulates the deplorable egotism, cockiness, impertinence and disregard for the rights of others apparently considered by some persons to be the inevitable accompaniment, if not the essence, of freedom."[64]

While he recognized some of the successes of the child-centered school, Dewey went on to argue firmly that neither the individual nor society can afford to depend on subjective license for its sustenance or its survival in the twentieth century. A truly progressive school must extend rational freedom and rational intelligence which is itself the "fruit of objective knowledge and understanding." Such schools cannot be secured through the study of children alone but must also consider the moving forces of society. Once again, Dewey reflected the neo-Enlightenment faith in the rational man and the rational purposes of education, and once again, he asserted that education cannot afford to neglect the claims of the child's nature or the interest of society.

While there were fundamental differences between Dewey and Naumburg, Dewey's philosophy, psychology, and approach to education were not as society-oriented as Margaret Naumburg claimed. Dewey had rather consistently attempted to chart a middle course. Margaret Naumburg had clearly developed an extreme child-centered approach, and although she could not be considered representative of the mainstream of American educational thought, Miss Naumburg, and many others like her, did represent one significant side of the twentieth-century

---

61. Quoted in Cremin, *Transformation of the School*, p. 234.
62. See Margaret Naumburg, "The Crux of Progressive Education," *The New Republic*, LXIII (June 25, 1930), 145. See also John Dewey, "How Much Freedom in the New Schools?"
63. Quoted in Beck, "Progressive Education and American Progressivism," p. 207.
64. Dewey, "How Much Freedom in the New Schools?" p. 206.

educational dialog.[65] It was evident that Miss Naumburg's position had historical antecedent in the thought of men like Rousseau and Froebel. The influence of the newer psychoanalytic movement on the child-centered tradition was also unmistakable. Margaret Naumburg, then, was not so much a nineteenth-century rebel of the heart as a twentieth-century rebel of the unconscious.

TWENTIETH-CENTURY SOCIETY-CENTERED PERSPECTIVE

Although Margaret Naumburg had, rather early in life, lost faith in the possibility of American society's being reformed by way of collective action, G. S. Counts, as a son of the American frontier, never lost that optimistic faith. The one element which appeared consistently in his lifelong work was a passion to translate and reconstruct what he considered the virtues of the Western frontier in the new educational frontier. Born in 1889 on a small farm near Baldwin, Kansas, Counts as a youth witnessed the closing of one frontier and, with it, a way of life he intensely valued. As an adult he witnessed the opening of a new educational frontier. From the first, he derived his basic values, and from the second, the challenge of his life.

While Margaret Naumburg was establishing her Children's School in New York City (1914), Counts was at the University of Chicago, working on his Ph.D. under Charles H. Judd and Albion W. Small. At Chicago, he became thoroughly engrossed in the theories of Hegel, Comte, Spencer, Ward, Sumner, Veblen, and Dewey. Much of what he studied tended to confirm his growing faith that man is both a product and a creator of his own culture. It is through social institutions that men profoundly shape their future destinies as well as their present realities. In the spirit of Lester Frank Ward, Counts came to believe that the school was one of the more important social institutions that shape

---

65. There were others early in the twentieth century such as Caroline Pratt and Marietta P. Johnson, just as there were some later in the century such as A. S. Neill, Carl Rogers, Rollo May, Herbert Maslow, and Ashley Montagu, who tended to represent a child-centered point of view. All these people held very different conceptions of human nature and generally espoused different psychologies. Whether it was the romantic Freudianism of A. S. Neill, the Emersonian optimism of Carl Rogers, or the existentialism of Rollo May, all seemed to emphasize the needs of the individual against the demands of an unauthentic society. Perhaps of all the current child-centered educators, A. S. Neill, as he described his school in Summerhill, 1960, came closest to the Naumburg position. Yet Naumburg appears to have had a far better grasp of the psychology she and her staff were using than did A. S. Neill. By most accounts, Walden School was also more culturally productive. By 1961, Harold H. Hart and Benjamin Fine had organized a Summerhill School Society which received a charter to operate a private school in New York State. Another offshoot of A. S. Neill's influence in the United States was the attempt of George Von Hilsheimer to develop a Summerlane School and camp in the Blue Ridge Mountains of North Carolina. On July 12, 1963, the school was burned to the ground by 400 mountaineers, aroused by reports of nudism, immorality, and integration. As the sheriff of Transylvania County put it, there were reports of sexual promiscuity at the camp, but "when they brought in Negroes and told it over town before they did it, they were inviting trouble." *Rochester Democrat and Chronicle,* July 13, 1963. Obviously, the child-centered school could not completely ignore the demands of the larger society!

the course of cultural evolution. The child could no more grow independently of cultural imposition than he could live without breathing. The very life-giving element which nourishes the child, Counts insisted, is socially derived from the larger culture.

Counts' early work reflected his concern for keeping open the new educational frontier. In *The Selective Character of American Secondary Education* (1922), Counts pointed out that the poor drop out of school while the wealthy manage to finish. Furthermore, the secondary schools were biased against the interests of the common people. In *The Social Composition of Boards of Education* (1927), he pointed out the social and economic class bias of American school board members, and in *School and Society in Chicago* (1927), he discussed the vulnerability of educators who failed to organize and deal realistically with politics.[66] By 1928, when Margaret Naumburg published *The Child and the World,* reflecting an extreme child-centered position, and Rugg and Shumaker published *The Child-Centered School,* a somewhat less extreme position, Counts was clearly building his case for a society-oriented school.[67]

In 1932, Counts' speech before the Progressive Education Association —"Dare Progressive Education Be Progressive?"—shook the Association to its very roots. Observers on the scene recalled the reaction of stunned silence when he had finished. In this electrified atmosphere, the Association forgot its planned program and went on to discuss Counts' challenge.[68] As Counts stripped away the educational jargon, he laid bare one of the most pressing issues facing educators in the twentieth century. Few times, indeed, have educators been so clearly and forcibly brought face to face with their social responsibilities as educators.

Progressive education, Counts asserted, had accomplished some good by focusing its attention on the child, but its concept of education was too narrow.

The weakness of Progressive Education thus lies in the fact that it has elaborated no theory of social welfare, unless it be that of anarchy or extreme individualism. In this of course, it is but reflecting the viewpoint of the members of the liberal-minded upper middle class who send their children to the Progressive schools. . . .[69]

---

66. For an interesting historical confirmation of what Counts was saying, see Raymond E. Callahan, *Education and the Cult of Efficiency* (Chicago: University of Chicago Press, 1962).

67. The year 1929 marked the beginning of the depression. Harold Rugg moved during the next decade from a child-centered to a more society-centered social reconstructionist's position. Rugg's series of social science texts were the clearest and most concrete attempt on the part of any social reconstructionist in the twentieth century to change the curriculum of the schools directly along social reconstructionist lines.

68. Before the Department of Superintendence and the National Council of Education in Washington, Counts continued the attack with such addresses as "Education Through Indoctrination" and "Freedom, Culture, Social Planning, and Leadership." All three speeches are published under the title, *Dare the Schools Build a New Social Order?* Our discussion here is drawn from all three speeches to get the whole of the argument.

69. G. S. Counts, *Dare the Schools Build a New Social Order?* (New York: John Day Company, Inc., 1932), p. 6.

Such people pride themselves on their open-mindedness and tolerance, support mild social reform, and are full of noble sentiments for humanity; on the other hand, these same people, with ample material comforts, live within their own class, shun conflict, have very little courage of their convictions, and consistently view the harsher realities of life only from the distance of their soft-carpeted living rooms. These, then, are the people who can value an education which dotes on a child's interest, and it is this class which has captured progressive education. If progressive education is ever to be progressive, it must develop a sense of direction, free itself from this class, squarely face all social issues, establish a relationship with the power structure of the community, develop realistic social aims, and "become less frightened than it is today at the bogies of *imposition* and *indoctrination*. In a word, Progressive Education cannot place its trust in a child-centered school."[70] While Counts insisted that there must be "no deliberate distortion or suppression of facts to support any theory or point of view,"[71] he did insist that:

. . . all education contains a large element of imposition, that in the very nature of the case this is inevitable, that the existence and evolution of society depend upon it, that it is consequently eminently desirable, and that the frank acceptance of this fact by the educator is a major professional obligation.[72]

The romantic child-centered educator cannot dodge this obligation by hiding behind a presumed notion that the nature of the child is good. Clearly and concisely, point after point, Counts ticked off the fallacies at work in the child-centered schools.[73] First of all, "There is the fallacy that man is born free. As a matter of fact, he is born helpless." The most fundamental decisions on such matters as language, religion, economic and social tradition are made not by the child but by the group to which he belongs by accident of birth. Furthermore, he insisted:

My thesis is that such imposition, provided the tradition is vital and suited to the times, releases the energies of the young, sets up standards of excellence, and makes possible really great achievement. The individual who fails to come under the influence of such a tradition may enjoy a certain kind of freedom, but it is . . . the freedom of mediocrity, incompetence, and aimlessness.

The second major fallacy is the assumption that the child is by nature good. The child is neither good nor bad, he is merely a "bundle of potentialities." Direction for such potentialities is to be found not in nature but in culture. Very much as Small and Ward had previously argued, Counts insisted, "There can be no good individual apart from some conception of the character of the *good* society; and the good society is not something that is given by nature; it must be fashioned by the hand and brain of man." The third fallacy is that "the child lives in

---

70. Counts, *Dare the Schools Build a New Social Order?* p. 10.
71. Counts, p. 10.
72. Counts, p. 12.
73. Counts, pp. 13-26.

a separate world of his own." If this were true, Counts argued, the child would have no incentive to mature as an adult. The fourth fallacy is "that education is some pure and mystical essence that remains unchanged from everlasting to everlasting." The people who hold this idea believe that as education somehow unfolds out of the nature of the child, it exists as a pure experience, freed of the political and social context. Such a view is hardly realistic, Counts surmised.

The fifth great fallacy is "that the school should be impartial in its emphases, that no bias should be given instruction." This is an untenable position; every teacher and every school must select some things and reject others, and by this very selection, they impose a bias. The sixth fallacy is that "the great object of education is to produce the college professor," that kind of individual who keeps on balancing pros and cons, always waiting for more facts, who never makes up his mind, and therefore never takes a stand on any significant social issue. If this were true, and it could be achieved with all students, society would be seriously impaired, if not completely immobilized.

The seventh fallacy is the belief on the part of some educators that "education is primarily intellectualistic, free of passion and great faiths." American society and American education "are touched by no great passions. We can view a world order rushing rapidly toward collapse with no more concern than the outcome of a horse race. . . ." Such a generation is destined "to a life of absorption in self, inferiority complexes, and frustration. The genuinely free man is not the person who spends the day contemplating his own navel, but rather the one who loses himself in a great cause or glorious adventure." The eighth fallacy is "that the school is an all-powerful educational agency." This is typical of the overzealous romantic idealism of many progressive educators who have confused what is with what they think ought to be. The ninth fallacy is reflected by those child-centered educators who think ignorance rather than knowledge is the way to wisdom. "Here is the doctrine of *Laissez faire,* driven from the field of social and political theory, seeking refuge in the domain of pedagogy. Progressive Education wishes to build a new world but refuses to be held accountable for the kind of world it builds."

Last, but not least, is the fallacy espoused by many educators "that in a dynamic society like ours the major responsibility of education is to prepare the individual to adjust himself to change." Therefore, the individual "must possess an agile mind, be bound by no deep loyalties, hold all conclusions and values tentatively and be ready on a moment's notice to make even fundamental shifts in outlook and philosophy." Such value-change artists cannot be relied upon for the stable, rational judgment necessary for bringing industrialism in line with human purposes.

Counts, with his ten fallacies, had fairly well destroyed the pedestal upon which the child-centered educators had placed the child. What, then, must be done to make progressive schools truly progressive? First, the teachers must realistically learn to assert what little social and political power they do have. Second, they must not be satisfied with merely studying contemporary society; they must "give to our children a vision of the possibilities which lie ahead and endeavor to enlist their loyalties and enthusiasms in the realization of the vision."[74] The school, then, not only must pass on the traditions of society as the Herbartians and the humanists would have it, but it must also become an instrument in the reconstruction of that society. The schools should "become centers for the building, and not merely for the contemplation, of our civilization."[75] Counts would ask of his students not only understanding but commitment to the new social order. What was the vision, the blueprint, toward which the young must be committed? To Counts, it must be our democratic heritage which was largely a product of the Western frontier, free land, a simple agrarian society. It was part of the American dream which sought to enrich and ennoble the life of the common man. He was not talking about political institutions but rather about the spirit of democracy, which he saw thus:

. . . it is a sentiment with respect to the moral equality of men: it is an aspiration towards a society in which this sentiment will find complete fulfillment. A society fashioned in harmony with the American democratic tradition would combat all forces tending to produce social distinctions and classes; repress every form of privilege and economic parasitism; manifest a tender regard for the weak, the ignorant, and the unfortunate; place the heavier and more onerous social burdens on the backs of the strong; glory in every triumph of man in his timeless urge to express himself and to make the world more habitable; exalt human labor of hand and brain as the creator of all wealth and culture; provide adequate material and spiritual rewards for every kind of socially useful work; strive for genuine equality of opportunity among all races, sects, and occupations; regard as paramount the abiding interests of the great masses of the people; direct the powers of government to the elevation and the refinement of the life of the common man; transform or destroy all conventions, institutions, and special groups inimical to the underlying principles of democracy; and finally be prepared as a last resort, in either the defense or the realization of this purpose, to follow the method of revolution.[76]

These values, Counts surmised, have their roots in the past, as part of the American dream. If they are to survive, they must become the central ingredients in the blueprint of the new social order.[77] The choice, Counts argued, is not "between individualism and collectivism. It is rather between two forms of collectivism: the one essentially democratic, the other feudal in spirit; the one devoted to the interests of the people, the other to the interests of a privileged class."[78]

74. Counts, p. 37.
75. Counts, p. 37. This position was very close to that of Albion Small and Lester Frank Ward.
76. Counts, pp. 41-42.
77. The right of revolution which Counts asserted was, indeed, an authentic root of the American heritage. This blueprint, however, clearly reflected the economic crisis of the depression and was somewhat left of center. Nevertheless, the Communists vigorously disagreed both with Counts' assumption that the school could help reconstruct the social order and with his blueprint. For an extended criticism of Counts' social reconstructionism from a Marxian standpoint, see Zalmen Slesinger, *Education and the Class Struggle* (New York: Covici Friede, 1937).
78. Counts, p. 49. What Counts could have mentioned, but did not, was the fact that one form of corporate feudalism was already developing in Fascist Italy.

The Progressive Education Association's response to Counts' challenge was typical of any organization facing such a controversial question. The matter was referred to a committee, and the troublemaker was appointed chairman.[79] The following year, the committee reported back essentially along the lines Counts had laid out the previous year. After some debate and charges of socialism and radicalism, the report of the committee was not approved by either the Board of Directors or the Association itself. The report of the committee was then published as a separate document entitled "A Call to the Teachers of the Nation." Neither the Progressive Education Association nor the American teacher responded to the call. While the initial shock of Counts' speech soon wore off, Counts had, indeed, touched the main weakness of the Progressive Education Association. For two more decades, the Association sought its social purpose, but to no avail.[80] In 1941, less than a decade after Counts delivered his address, the United States went on a wartime economy which has kept the American economy functioning ever since. Under the circumstances of a cold war existence, Counts' concern for depression conditions appears dated and out of phase with the main trends of the post-World War II era.[81]

By the end of the war, Theodore Brameld had developed his philosophy of social reconstruction much in the tradition of Ward, Small, and Counts. To be sure, the world had radically changed and so had social reconstructionism—in content, but not in basic perspective. While Counts found progressivism wanting a sense of direction, Brameld said progressivism overemphasized means at the expense of ends and failed to delineate goals.[82] Just as Counts had called for not only understanding but commitment on the part of students, so too Brameld argued that teachers must strive by way of the "method of defensible partiality" to help students achieve group consensus and commitment toward a new social vision. The social vision, however, had changed markedly. While Counts' blueprint was for a greater economic and social democracy in America, Brameld's social vision was for a world democracy. Brameld believed that the many varied schools of psychology, from behaviorism to psychoanalysis, were increasingly coming to a consensus on the question of the nature of man. This, coupled with his study of anthropology, which reveals the common elements in all men's nature, led him to the rather happy conclusion that self-government is not only possible for all mankind but is a basic drive of all men.

---

79. Such men as Merle Curti, Sidney Hook, and Jesse H. Newlon were also appointed to the committee.

80. See Cremin, *Transformation of the School,* pp. 264-271.

81. There is, however, the exception of those very serious centers of very serious poverty which are coupled with racial segregation in our large urban areas. The schools today are being asked by society to reconstruct the social order with respect to racial conflict and the culturally underprivileged. The "bogey of imposition" is again raised as neither teachers nor their organizations seem to have any clearer notion as to their social obligations in this reconstruction than did the PEA in the thirties. In this area, Counts' questions are still relevant and still begging for answers. See "Dare the Schools Build the Great Society?" *Phi Delta Kappan,* XLVII, 1 (September 1965), 27.

82. See Theodore Brameld, *Education for the Emerging Age* (New York: Harper & Row, 1965), p. 26.

Or, still more relevantly, the capacities of human beings for appreciating the requisites of complete self-government are now proving to be, not merely a pleasant sentiment, but a demonstrable expectation—an expectation supported even by scientific recognition that the desire for self-government, as one form of participation, is itself a basic drive of man.[83]

The mandate, then, is clear: Teachers, without suppression of evidence, must teach so as to encourage students' commitment to the ideals and purposes of the new world democracy.[84]

Consistently, the social reconstructionists have placed the school on the cutting edge of social reform. As they have developed their position, they have pressed educators with some difficult questions. Can the schools reconstruct the social order? To what extent, in a pluralistic society, is a single blueprint realistically possible even if desirable? If, indeed, it can be done and should be done, then upon whose shoulders must fall the task of designing the blueprint? To what extent do teachers who judge their success or failure by the degree to which they have successfully committed their students to a new social vision become mere propagandists for a particular point of view?[85] Is there a difference between teaching for understanding and teaching for commitment?

It is significant that John Dewey never drew up the blueprint. To Dewey, it was enough to get students to think, for "if we once start thinking no one can guarantee where we shall come out, except that many objects, ends and institutions are doomed. Every thinker puts some portion of an apparently stable world in peril and no one can wholly predict what will emerge in its place."[86] To Dewey, the school could not become the *main* determiner of social change, but it could become a significant *participant* in change. While Dewey was in disagreement with the child-centered educators, he also disagreed with an extreme social reconstructionist position.[87] The function of the school, at best, was to produce social reformers and not to presume to reform society directly. Indeed, if the schools succeeded in turning out critically alert, socially sensitive adults, capable of making sound decisions, this would be revolution enough.

To the more conservative humanist and Herbartian educators, Dewey appeared as a radical social reconstructionist because he called for a new curriculum based on present-day experience. His philosophy went against the use of the past as a cosmic determiner of the present and the future. To the social reconstructionist, like Brameld, Dewey lacked a

---

83. Brameld, *Education for the Emerging Age,* p. 83.

84. See Theodore Brameld, *Education as Power* (New York: Holt, Rinehart & Winston, Inc., 1965). See also Theodore Brameld, *Philosophies of Education in Cultural Perspective* (New York: Henry Holt and Company, 1955).

85. One is reminded of our earlier discussion of William Maclure and Robert Owen at New Harmony.

86. Quoted in Joseph Ratner, ed., *Intelligence in the Modern World: John Dewey's Philosophy* (New York: The Modern Library, 1939), p. v.

87. See John Dewey, "Can Education Share in Social Reconstruction?" *The Social Frontier,* I (1934-5), 11-12. See also John Dewey, "Education and Social Change," *The Social Frontier,* III (1937-8), 237.

sense of direction. Dewey did refuse to blueprint a new social order. On the other hand, to many child-centered educators, Dewey was far too academically and socially oriented. Here again, Dewey emphasized the importance of society, and he called for more defensible intellectual content in the schools. These groups had not misinterpreted Dewey; quite to the contrary, from their perspective they understood him only too well and disagreed with him on real issues.[88] When he broke radically with nineteenth-century thought, Dewey was attempting to find a middle course between the two ends of what he thought of as the continuum between the individual and the society. Such a position is as difficult to develop as it is to defend and maintain. Many other educators attempted to find a middle course, and they, too, became subject to legitimate attack from many sides as well as being the object of considerable misunderstanding.

TWO VIEWS OF THE MIDDLE WAY

William Heard Kilpatrick

Dewey once said, "In the best sense of the words, progressive education and the work of Dr. Kilpatrick are virtually synonymous."[89] Dewey chose to emphasize "best sense of the words" because some child-centered educators had taken *progressive education* to mean essentially a planless curriculum which operated on "flashy, spur-of-the-moment improvisation," and such was not the case with Dr. Kilpatrick. Those who follow "the immediate and spontaneous activities of children in the schoolroom" are hardly progressive, for progressive implies "that there must be a point of view from which to select materials and arrange them in some kind of order."[90] If one critically and carefully reads Kilpatrick's major works, he finds Dewey was correct in saying that Kilpatrick was no extreme child-centered educator who followed the "spontaneous activities of children in the schoolroom." However, uncritically read and loosely interpreted by the thousands of teachers he taught, Kilpatrick could be taken as one who stood for a planless curriculum, because he tended to emphasize the needs of the child more than the needs of society.

Considered by Dewey as one of his best students, Kilpatrick taught about 35,000 teachers and administrators at Teachers College, Columbia, from 1909 to 1937.[91] In the minds of many educators, Kilpatrick was Mr. Progressive Education. His fame as a teacher and his ability to per-

88. Dewey's position lent itself not only to attacks from many sides, but taken out of context, it could easily be misinterpreted. For example, see Arthur Bestor's treatment of Dewey in *Restoration of Learning* (New York: Alfred A. Knopf, Inc., 1955) and *Educational Wastelands* (Urbana, Ill.: University of Illinois Press, 1953).

89. Quoted in Samuel Tenenbaum, *William Heard Kilpatrick* (New York: Harper & Brothers, 1951), p. vii.

90. Tenenbaum, *William Heard Kilpatrick*, p. vii.

91. See Robert J. Schaefer, "William Heard Kilpatrick: An Appreciation," *Teachers College Record*, LXVI, 4 (January 1965).

sonalize large-group instruction are almost legendary and may well out-live his educational ideas. His educational ideas, some have argued, involved the direct application of Dewey's philosophy to educational practice. Kilpatrick's *The Project Method* (1918) is often thought of as the application of Dewey's *How We Think* (1910). A critical problem arose, however, because Dewey emphasized teacher planning and or-ganized subject matter more than Kilpatrick. Indeed, while Dewey in-sisted that "baby does not know what is best," Kilpatrick subtly but distinctly tended to place more responsibility on baby. Kilpatrick, then, seemed to cut a path between Dewey and Naumburg.[92]

The educational philosophy of Kilpatrick owed as much to Pestalozzi and Parker as it did to Dewey. If one disregards the spiritual temper of Pestalozzi and the transcendentalism of Parker, their ideas—with a Deweyan cast—would be the educational ideas of William Heard Kil-patrick. After hearing Francis W. Parker speak in Albany, Georgia, in 1892, and then reading *The Quincy Method,* Kilpatrick recalled, "It went into all that I did. It helped me to see a new vision in education."[93] Kil-patrick never seemed to forget that vision. Such a vision oriented edu-cation toward its true center—the child. He went on to say:

Francis Parker was the greatest man we had to introduce better practices into the country's schools. I would say now that he took Pestalozzi's ideas and im-proved and enriched them and carried them forward. He preceded Dewey, but Dewey came along with a much finer theory, a much better worked-out theory.[94]

Here was a mission befitting a minister's son. If Parker implemented and improved upon Pestalozzi's ideas, Kilpatrick thought he would do the same for John Dewey. Kilpatrick seemed to take Parker as a model for his educational career and Dewey, Pestalozzi, and Parker as sources of his educational ideas.

After completing his study of such child-centered educators as Montessori and Froebel,[95] Kilpatrick was prepared to take the methodo-logical leap. In 1918, he published *The Project Method,* which propelled him into the educational limelight overnight.[96] The "purposeful act," set in the project method, should, he argued, become the center of the educational experience. The child purposing, planning, and executing a project could learn in a meaningful, real-life way. Like Pestalozzi's object method, Kilpatrick's project method cut across all formal sub-

---

92. Lawrence Cremin reasonably argued that Boyd H. Bode of Ohio State University came closer to a Deweyan position. See Cremin, *Transformation of the School,* pp. 220-224. One might, however, go further and recognize that the more current "discovery method" as espoused by Jerome S. Bruner in *The Process of Education* and others is probably closed to Dewey's concern for intellectual growth.

93. Tenenbaum, *William Heard Kilpatrick,* p. 26.

94. Tenenbaum, *William Heard Kilpatrick,* p. 26.

95. See Kilpatrick's *The Montessori System Examined* (1914) and *Froebel's Kindergarten Principles Critically Examined* (1916).

96. It is interesting that when Kilpatrick wrote *The Project Method,* he attempted to reconcile and combine the psychologies of both Thorndike and Dewey. By the time he wrote *Remaking the Curriculum* in 1936, he had clearly given up any reconciliation attempt and he went on to base his psychology on social behaviorism.

jects, freed the child from the tyranny of empty, formalistic instruction, capitalized on his natural interests, took the child back to the concrete, and made him the center around which learning would take place. Unlike Pestalozzi's object lesson, Kilpatrick's project method placed far more emphasis on the purposing and planning of the child. By 1925, in *Foundations of Method,* Kilpatrick standardized the steps of his method to purposing, planning, executing, and judging. Each of these steps must be effectively performed in the course of the project by the student himself. The teacher's role should be that of a guide, with one eye on the child's growth and the other on the project, always ready to say "no" when the project does not lend itself to growth, but also ready to contribute advice when it does. It is clear that such a procedure could easily drift from the child's purposes and be standardized as routine in the curriculum. It is also possible that trivia might become standard educational experience, in the name of children actively purposing. Both of these factors seriously plagued the implementation of the project method.

Reminiscent of both Parker and Pestalozzi, Kilpatrick also warned teachers against teaching physics, arithmetic, and geography as separate disciplines and as intellectualistic tools in isolation from one another. He advocated that the child must learn all these things through whole-hearted, purposeful activity and that such activity must deal mainly with the concrete, real-life experience of making and doing. Much of Kilpatrick's *Foundations of Method* was against fixing subjects in advance. A civilization under rapid change, he surmised, needs more "changing-civilization teachers" and fewer "fixed-civilization teachers." The kind of teacher most needed was the one who would teach *how* to think and not *what* to think.[97] While Kilpatrick popularized this slogan, other educators revised the older corollary cliché: that they teach children and not subjects. With such easy-going slogans, some educators projected, if not an anti-intellectual bias, at least an anti-academic bias, which tended to bring down massive criticism of education upon the heads of all educators in the fifties. Indeed, while much of the failure of progressive education cannot fairly be attributed to the work of Kilpatrick, the net effect of his war on fixed subject matter was to discredit the functional role of the disciplines in educating the younger generation, and thus the weight of his influence was toward a more child-centered perspective. Kilpatrick insisted from the very beginning that:

We contemplate no scheme of subordination of teacher or school to childish whim; but we do mean that any plan of educational procedure which does not aim consciously and insistently at securing and utilizing vigorous purposing on the part of the pupils is founded essentially on an ineffective and unfruitful basis.[98]

---

97. See William Heard Kilpatrick, *Foundations of Method* (New York: The Macmillan Company, 1925), p. 266.
98. William H. Kilpatrick, *The Project Method* (New York: Bureau of Publications, Teachers College, Columbia University, 1919), p. 12.

From Kilpatrick's position it was only reasonable that any scheme to reconstruct the social order by way of indoctrinating the younger generation must be rejected.[99] Consistently, he argued for the freedom of the student to learn and to test his ideas freely. In *Education For a Changing Civilization* (1926), for example, he pointed out that the older moral sanctions were vanishing and that we must now prepare to accept criticism and put our most cherished values to the test.

Our duty is so to prepare the rising generation to think that they will think for themselves, even ultimately, if they so decide, to the point of revising or rejecting what we now think. Our chosen beliefs will have to stand this ordeal.[100]

Kilpatrick could take this stand, for he believed that all our social institutions had grown out of human purposing and that "there is no necessary conflict in kind between the social demands and the child's interests."[101]

In the real world of existence, however, there are some very basic conflicts of interest. To extricate himself logically from this most fundamental educational problem, Kilpatrick did as other theorists from Plato to Dewey had done: He idealized society. While to most Platonists this ideal society has a transcendental reality behind the curtain of appearances, to most pragmatists this ideal society was a functional goal cast in terms of an evolving culture, always in the process of becoming. Kilpatrick most often spoke of this idea as the "worthy life" or the "good life." Richard Hofstadter once suggested, "If the new educators really wanted to reproduce life, they must have had an extraordinarily benign conception of what life is."[102] Kilpatrick did not want to reproduce real life in the classroom, but rather "the good life," which he understood to be personal, humane, cooperative, and authentic. The other characteristics of society, such as competition, impersonal structure, institutional authority, and unauthentic social relationships, he proposed to leave outside the classroom whenever possible.

That such a view was humanely idealistic was certain; that such a view could easily be misinterpreted was understandable; but that such a view was possible to realize in the contemporary world was extremely doubtful. Even while thousands flocked to hear Kilpatrick at Teachers College, Columbia University, speak in benign terms about the good life, the books were burning in front of the University of Berlin. Many signs indicated that the twentieth-century contribution to the social life of mankind was to be in the direction of developing not more humane democratic societies but rather totalitarian societies. Counts hit the critical point when he said:

---

99. See William H. Kilpatrick, *Philosophy of Education* (New York: The Macmillan Company, 1951), p. 124.

100. Quoted in V. T. Thayer, *Formative Ideas in American Education* (New York: Dodd, Mead & Company, 1965), p. 288.

101. Kilpatrick, *Project Method*, p. 12. One should note, here, the similarity between Dewey and Kilpatrick on many of these questions.

102. Quoted in Charles Frankel, "Appearance and Reality in Kilpatrick's Philosophy," *Teachers College Record,* LXVI, 4 (January 1965), 360.

If life were peaceful and quiet and undisturbed by great issues, we might with some show of wisdom center our attention on the nature of the child. But with the world as it is, we cannot afford for a single instant to remove our eyes from the social scene or shift our attention from the peculiar needs of the age.[103]

James B. Conant

By mid-century, it was the "peculiar needs of the age" which had shifted the educational dialog from a child-centered to a society-centered discussion. The man who emerged as the most influential participant in that discussion, critically sensitive to the needs of the age, was James B. Conant. Steadied by a pragmatic realism, yet driven by a Puritan sense of duty, Conant was both intellectually and temperamentally suited to fill the role that Lester Frank Ward had earlier sensed was needed in the new "sociocracy" of the twentieth century. Ward had pointed out that the time was rapidly approaching when American society would have to coldly calculate its social and educational legislation with scientific realism if that society could be expected to survive. It was with something of that coldly calculating sense that Conant devoted his lifework to the survival of a free, democratic society.

On October 9, 1933, the same day that students were preparing to burn their books at the University of Berlin, James B. Conant became president of Harvard University.[104] During his twenty-year presidency, 1933 to 1953, Conant was actively and deeply involved in public service. In the days of "America Firsters" before World War II, Conant tirelessly and relentlessly argued that the American nation must mobilize to stop Fascism. In June 1940, even before the U. S. entered the war, Conant was appointed by Franklin D. Roosevelt to the National Defense Research Committee which was eventually to oversee the development of the atomic bomb. Later, as advisor to the Atomic Energy Commission, first chairman of the National Science Foundation, board member of the Office of Defense Mobilization, and actively involved in the creation of the G. I. Bill, Conant distinguished himself as a public servant. In 1953, he became High Commissioner for Germany, and in 1957, he retired as United States Ambassador to the German Federal Republic.

After a decade of destructive criticism of the American public school system by many different forces, Conant decided to enter the conflict-laden arena of public education. The world of Kilpatrick and the world of Conant were very different. These two men were alike in their concern for the preservation and development of a free society, but as to be expected, they differed as to what that society needed most. If Kilpatrick seemed to reflect the spirit of Parker and Pestalozzi in his concern for the child, Conant reflected more of the spirit of Jefferson and Mann in his concern for the needs of society.[105] To Conant, the good society

---

103. Counts, *Dare the Schools Build a New Social Order?* p. 32.
104. For much of the biographical information used here, I am indebted to Paul F. Douglass, *Six Upon the World* (Boston: Little, Brown and Company, 1954), pp. 329-409.
105. See James B. Conant, *Thomas Jefferson and the Development of American Public Education* (Berkeley: University of California Press, 1962).

was free, pluralistic, socially mobile, open, and classless. Such a society was one where men freely competed and were duly rewarded not on the basis of social station, race, or creed, but on the basis of virtue and talent. This Jeffersonian ideal which Conant incorporated in his philosophy is both democratic and aristocratic—democratic in its emphasis on equality of opportunity, aristocratic in its emphasis on excellence. As he put it, "The American tradition requires an elite of excellence and of character, an elite chosen anew with each succeeding generation with neither the accidents of birth nor of education sufficing to give a man a high place among his fellowmen."[106] Modern scientific and industrial society requires the development of all talents to the fullest and highest degree of human excellence. This can be done only if men and ideas are free to compete and the best of men and ideas are duly rewarded. This assumes that all men have free and equal access to educational opportunity, and it further assumes free competitive use of ideas within education itself. As Conant said, "A free market of ideas assumes an educational system which believes in a free market and impresses this belief in a free market on children."[107] However, it is not enough to develop the natural talents; the development of virtue is also necessary. To be sure, this was an ideal, but for Conant it was the guiding principle by which he approached problems in American public education.

It is interesting that the key word which describes Kilpatrick's view of the good society is *cooperation,* while the key word for Conant's view is *competition.* One man seemed to walk on the child's side of the educational street and the other on society's side. Neither man, however, went to the extreme. From Conant's standpoint, competition is to be valued but must not be overemphasized to the point of becoming destructive. Under the demands of the times, men must periodically reach consensus and decide on the best course of cooperative action. At this point, Conant brought together his pragmatic realism and his Jeffersonian idealism. What then emerges is a sense of community not too far removed intellectually from that of Jefferson and Mann.[108] Like Jefferson and Mann, Conant believed that the public schools were a vital instrument in maintaining and developing this community.

By the 1950's, the American public schools, especially the comprehensive high school, came under severe searching criticism from many sources, both conservative and liberal.[109] With the launching of Sputnik,

---

106. Douglass, *Six Upon the World,* p. 385.

107. Douglass, *Six Upon the World,* p. 385.

108. This same view of the public schools as crucial in the development of a democratic community, interestingly enough, led Jefferson, Mann, and Conant into conflict with various religious interests. In 1952, Conant attacked the parochial schools as being a divisive influence in the American community. See Douglass, *Six Upon the World,* pp. 392-393.

109. For instance, see Arthur E. Bestor's *Educational Wastelands,* 1953, and his *Restoration of Learning,* 1955; Albert Lynd's *Quackery in the Public Schools,* 1956; Admiral Rickover's *Education and Freedom,* 1959; Fred M. Hechinger's *Big Red Schoolhouse,* 1959; and C. Winfield Scott's and Clyde M. Hill's *Public Education Under Criticism,* 1954. For a representative reply to some of this criticism, see R. W. Burnett and Harold Hand, "Two Critiques of *Educational Wastelands,*" *Progressive Education,* XXXI, 3 (January 1954); and *Educational Theory,* IV (January 1954).

extremist groups fanned the educational flames to such a heat that it appeared to many that the comprehensive high school might be lost in the blaze.[110] In this context, Conant undertook his study of the American high school. He had already partly developed the procedure for such a study with his *General Education in a Free Society* (1945). In January of 1943 he had appointed a committee of experts to study the problem and to strive to reach some consensus. The result was one of the best works on the subject at mid-century. Freed from the demands of government service in 1957, Conant became more directly involved in the investigation. By selecting a committee of experts to visit and study the schools with him and then reach some kind of agreement as to appropriate recommendations, Conant employed an approach that was sadly lacking in the work of many educational critics of the fifties. Few critics of American education had bothered to study what the schools were actually doing. The results of Conant's studies drastically weakened the arguments of those who were attacking public education from a purely ideological position. What followed, then, was a series of studies based on Conant's judgment, enlightened by direct experience in the schools and by the advice of a panel of selected experts. Financially supported by the Carnegie Foundation from 1957 to 1963, Conant, with his staff, produced *The American High School Today, The Junior High School, Slums and Suburbs,* and *The Education of American Teachers.*

In *The American High School Today,* he argued that the comprehensive high school was basically a sound institution serving the needs of a democratic society.[111] Basing his report on what he and his committee considered the best practices in the schools, Conant went on to list thirty-one recommendations for the high school. Many of those recommendations clearly reflected Conant's social concerns; for example, his strong support for guidance and counseling reflected his concern for society's need of appropriate manpower,[112] just as his emphasis on ability grouping, programs of the academically talented, and the highly gifted pupils reflected his concern for society's need of highly trained talent. He assumed that the academic honors list he recommended would help stimulate the competition necessary for producing that talent. Lastly, his insistence that the twelfth-grade social studies class be made up of a cross section of all youngsters in the school, learning together the basis of the American form of government and the economic basis of our free society, reflected his sense of community.

Just as Jefferson and Mann had to temper their ideal with the possible, so Conant often had to modify his recommendations, which usually reflected his notion of an ideal society, to the possible. The electrifying response of the public to his study of the American high school seemed to indicate that Conant had hit the possible. As thousands of citizen

---

110. See Thayer, *Formative Ideas in American Education,* pp. 342-348.

111. James B. Conant, *The American High School Today* (New York: McGraw-Hill Book Company, 1959), p. 8.

112. Conant, in this work, unquestionably gave a powerful lift to the new and struggling field of guidance. However, while Conant conceived of guidance as primarily vocational, the trend of the field since has been more in the direction of psychological therapy.

groups, teachers, administrators, and boards measured their schools by
Conant's standards, it became clear to most observers that Conant had
a more profound influence on actual educational practice than any other
single critic of American education in the fifties. The salutary effect was
almost immediate in at least two ways. First, the destructive criticism
that threatened to destroy the comprehensive high school waned; and
second, as it did wane, public attention was more clearly drawn toward
the practical problem of improving instruction.

Realizing that one does not get agreement for action by asking ultimate questions, Conant consistently concentrated on the best practices
now employed in the schools. "Best," however, was determined by his
own model of the good society and what he judged to be possible. Since
his model was a classless society where all men were free to compete
on the basis of merit, it was not surprising that Conant, in *Slums and
Suburbs* (1961), became one of the leading figures to draw public attention to the inequities in public education. As Conant discussed the
"social dynamite" that was building up in the cities—which only a few
years later exploded[113]—he directed attention to the need for greater
expenditure of funds in slum schools, vocational guidance until age
twenty-one, employment opportunities for youth, on-the-job training,
and practical vocational training. As he emphasized a practical education
for a practical job, his ideal of a classless, open, competitive society gave
way to what he judged was possible. Always working between his ideal
social model on the one hand and the pragmatically possible on the
other, he faced the problem of de facto segregation in the urban centers,
and once again, his sense of ideal community gave way to what he judged
was practically possible.

Much as I admire the comprehensive high school in the town with one high
school and see it as an instrument of democracy, it seems impossible for school
authorities in a large city to create artificially a series of such schools. If a policy
were to be adopted that, as an ideal, every neighborhood school should have a
widely heterogeneous school population represented by all socio-economic
backgrounds, school administrators would be forced to move children about as
though they were pawns on a chessboard.[114]

Conant at this point clearly sacrificed his ideal of a common school
serving a classless open society for a ghetto school which has served the
interests of a class society and has to a considerable extent negated the
possibility of equal educational opportunity, all in the name of the
pragmatically possible. Conant, however, did not rest easy with this
apparent negation of his common school ideal, and by 1963 he published a retraction of his earlier attitude toward this issue.

If Conant's ideal gave way on this point to the pragmatically possible,
his later work seemed to come up stronger on the ideal side than on the

113. Such as the riots which occurred in the summer of 1964 in Rochester, New York,
and New York City.
114. James B. Conant, *Slums and Suburbs* (New York: McGraw-Hill Book Company,
1961), p. 31.

pragmatically possible side.[115] In *The Education of American Teachers,* he dared the liberal arts and education professors to put away the hatchet which had long been used to cripple teacher education in America; he challenged liberal arts professors to become seriously and responsibly involved in the problem of effectively preparing teachers for the public schools, and he challenged professors of education to put an end to education courses which lacked any meaningful substance.

Assuming that the professors in the colleges of education and the arts would take collective responsibility for teacher education, Conant went on to propose that teachers should be certified by the educational institution rather than by the state.[116] Again, Conant's basic faith in the efficacy of free competition was reflected in his proposal to reduce the power of the state, regional, and national accrediting agencies so that teacher-training institutions might freely compete in the development of excellent training programs. Indeed, while Conant's suggestions on teacher education were already in practice in some institutions, his proposals amounted to a radical reconstruction for the great bulk of teacher education institutions. Although it was too early, perhaps, to judge the impact of Conant's work on teacher education, his idealistic proposals seemed to have outreached his sense of the possible.[117]

Since the publication of *The American High School Today,* Conant has been attacked by the social reconstructionists as being too conservative, by conservatives as being too liberal, and by child-centered educators as being too academic. If Conant was conservative, he was conservative in the Jefferson-Horace Mann sense of conservatism. Most of Conant's educational commitments evolved from his sense of the needs of a democratic society. In this way, he was reflecting the demands of the present society. Such a technological society, internally threatened by racial conflict and externally threatened by the cold war, attempting to preserve and develop democratic values in a mass culture, repeatedly demonstrated a greater concern for the education of the citizen than for the education of the man. In an age in which totalitarian societies cast a darkening shadow over the optimistic spirit of a democratic society, the Harvard men who gathered in the Memorial Church no doubt appreciated hearing that Yankee of Puritan extraction assert that a republic of free men still had a contribution to make,

... not in abstract thought nor in art or poetry, but rather in a demonstration that a certain type of society long dreamed of by idealists can be closely approached in reality—a free society in which the hopes and aspirations of a large part of the members find enduring satisfaction through outlets once reserved for only a small minority of mankind.[118]

---

115. Judging from the response of much of the educational establishment to Conant's report. For example, see Harry S. Broudy, "Conant on the Education of Teachers," *The Educational Forum* (January 1964).

116. James B. Conant, *The Education of American Teachers* (New York: McGraw-Hill Book Company, 1963), p. 210.

117. It is difficult to make an assessment of Conant's influence on American education largely because his influence is still in the process of development.

118. Douglass, *Six Upon the World,* p. 376.

None of the child-centered educators like Froebel, Pestalozzi, Parker, Naumburg, or Kilpatrick completely ignored the interest of society; and none of the society-oriented educators like Herbart, Counts, Brameld, or Conant completely ignored the claims of the child. The one tradition took for its chief concern the education of man, and the other the education of the citizen.

In both traditions, one can clearly sense both continuity and change. In Froebel's self-activity method, Pestalozzi's object lesson, Parker's spontaneous tendencies of the child, Naumburg's expressionism, and Kilpatrick's project method, one can see a consistent call for the active involvement of the child in the growth process. Change is also apparent. These nineteenth-century rebels found their basis for action in either mysticism or romanticism, while the twentieth-century rebels relied more heavily on a naturalist psychology or philosophy.

Throughout the thought of Herbart, Counts, Brameld, and Conant is the critical need for society to prepare the child for citizenship. Change, again, is equally apparent, from the Herbartians who emphasized the past tradition and used history in a cosmic sense, to Counts and Brameld who thought the past should be used as a relief against which the future should be projected and controlled, to Conant who sought to conserve and nourish what he saw to be the wisdom of the American heritage. Each man and each movement was a product of, and participant in, the economic, political, social, and intellectual milieu of the times. These two traditions represent two ends of a dynamic dialog which has repeatedly recurred as part of the American educational experience.

It is not unreasonable to expect that such a dialog may continue. Indeed, as men in literature increasingly write of alienation, sociologists talk of anomie, psychologists discuss the problem of depersonalization, and the younger generation flirts with existentialism if not nihilism, one senses the demands of the individual against the needs of society. What society may be buying in education under cold war pressure may not in fact be what the individual in that society needs. While many disagree with Rousseau's conception of man or society, few deny the fact that he touched one of the critical perennial issues in Western educational thought when he said, "Forced to combat either nature or society, you must make your choice between the man and the citizen, you cannot train both."

SUGGESTED READINGS

Borrowman, Merle. "Traditional Values in the Shaping of American Education," *The Sixtieth Yearbook of the National Society for the Study of Education.* Chicago, University of Chicago Press, 1961.

Brameld, Theodore. *Education for the Emerging Age.* New York, Harper & Row, 1965.

———. *Philosophies of Education in Cultural Perspective.* New York, Henry Holt and Company, 1955.

Broudy, Harry S. "Conant on the Education of Teachers," *The Educational Forum,* January 1964.

Callahan, Raymond E. *Education and the Cult of Efficiency.* Chicago, University of Chicago Press, 1962.

Childs, John L. *American Pragmatism and Education.* New York, Henry Holt and Company, 1956.

Conant, James B. *Thomas Jefferson and the Development of American Public Education.* Berkeley, University of California Press, 1962.

Counts, C. S. *Dare the Schools Build a New Social Order?* New York, John Day Company, 1932.

Cremin, Lawrence A. *The Transformation of the School.* New York, Alfred A. Knopf, Inc., 1961.

De Garmo, Charles. *Herbart and the Herbartians.* New York, Charles Scribner's Sons, 1896.

De Lima, Agnes. *Our Enemy the Child,* 2nd ed. New York, The New Republic, 1926.

Douglass, Paul F. *Six Upon the World.* Boston, Little, Brown and Company, 1954.

Frankel, Charles. "Appearance and Reality in Kilpatrick's Philosophy," *Teachers College Record,* LXVI, 4 (January 1965).

Froebel, Friedrich. *The Education of Man,* trans. and ed. W. N. Hailmann. New York, D. Appleton and Company, 1892.

Hand, Harold. "Two Critiques of Educational Wastelands," *Progressive Education,* XXXI, 3 (January 1954); and *Educational Theory,* IV (January 1954).

Herbart, Johann Friedrich. *Letters and Lectures on Education.* Syracuse, N.Y., Bardeen School Supplies, Inc., 1898.

Kilpatrick, William Heard. *Foundations of Method.* New York, The Macmillan Company, 1925.

———. *Philosophy of Education.* New York, The Macmillan Company, 1951.

———. *The Project Method.* New York, Bureau of Publications, Teachers College, Columbia University, 1918.

MacVannel, John Angus. *The Education Theories of Herbart and Froebel.* New York, Bureau of Publications, Teachers College, Columbia University, 1905.

Naumburg, Margaret. *The Child and the World.* New York, Harcourt, Brace and Company, 1928.

Parker, Francis W. *Talks on Pedagogics.* New York, John Day Company, 1937.

Rugg, Harold, and Ann Shumaker. *The Child-Centered School.* Chicago, The World Book Company, 1928.

Slesinger, Zalmen. *Education and the Class Struggle,* New York, Covici Friede, 1937.

Thayer, V. T. *Formative Ideas in American Education.* New York, Dodd, Mead & Company, 1965.

CHAPTER 10

A Fascist and a Communist view of the function of the American school

The school must be one of the instruments of government of the group culture. The group culture should be the expression of the will of the dominant element of the elite, whose values are validated by the power to enforce them.[1] LAWRENCE DENNIS

A revolutionary proletarian system of education necessarily involves indoctrination as an essential feature. . . . The school system must itself be revolutionized, before it can become an instrument of revolution—or of any serious social change.[2] EARL BROWDER

Many historians characterize the nineteenth century as an age of democratic republics; with equal justification the twentieth century might be characterized as an age of totalitarian societies. Both the Communist and the Fascist held totalitarian conceptions of man and society, and both sought to organize and control the total man—i.e., his deepest thoughts and convictions as well as his actions. Although many religious, political, and social systems in the past had solicited the unwavering loyalty of masses of people, and in the process had developed some very effective techniques of control, few could match the control of the totalitarian society in the twentieth century. This increased effectiveness was made possible, though not inevitable, by advances in the social sciences and in communications.

As social scientists found surer ways of predicting and controlling

1. Lawrence Dennis, "Education—The Tool of the Dominant Elite," *The Social Frontier,* I, 4 (January 1935), 14.
2. Earl Browder, "Education—An Ally in the Workers' Struggle," *The Social Frontier,* I, 4 (January 1935), 22-23.

human behavior, and the mass media provided a vehicle for reaching a larger audience, a major moral crisis evolved. At the very heart of that crisis was the question of how to use the new knowledge. Because of the greater ability to achieve selected ends, the ends and the means demanded greater care and scrutiny. With the increasing possibility that men could collectively achieve whatever goal they chose, the burden of choice was increased, not lessened. The crucial decisions, previously left to fate, nature, or the gods, were now in the hands of man. Man in the twentieth century was fulfilling most of the wildest dreams of the eighteenth-century philosopher Condorcet. Progress in human knowledge had occurred very much as Condorcet had anticipated, but his easygoing corollary idea of moral progress seemed to have fallen by the wayside. There was, after all, a nonrational component to man which most of the religious traditions had recognized and utilized and which many of the Enlightenment thinkers tended to ignore. The importance of the nonrational factors in human behavior was reasserted by Freud, Jung, and others, and the Enlightenment conception of a rational man, freely reasoning his way to a better society, was devastated.

Indeed, as twentieth-century man pursued the Enlightenment idea of social meliorism and gained objective freedom through the creation of bureaucratic structure, he lost his subjective freedom at the hands of the very institutions giving him the greater objective freedom.[3] As a consequence of such twentieth-century alienation, philosophies of existentialism and nihilism, which emphasized man's subjective freedom, were born. The Enlightenment formula for the progress of humanity carried with it the unexpected depersonalization of the individual. It is a curious phenomenon that at the point when Western society had begun to achieve its greatest progress in human knowledge, it had become profoundly disillusioned with the Enlightenment respect for the dignity of man.

In the interest of a science of society and the progress of that society, the ideologues of both the left and the right, such as Karl Marx and Vilfredo Pareto, subverted the Enlightenment concept of the free individual. While Marx found the solution for the evils of society in the dictatorship of the proletariat, Pareto, as the philosopher of the right, found the solution in the ordered society controlled by the elites of power. Ideologically, Marx incorporated in his socialistic humanism more of the Enlightenment values than did Pareto. But, when the Marxist dictatorship of the proletariat was put to the test of action in the Russian Revolution (1917) and Benito Mussolini fulfilled Pareto's conception of the elite in Italy (1923), it was apparent that there was little practical

---

3. *Objective freedom* is defined as having practical alternative choices, and *subjective freedom* is the feeling of being free. In this sense, man in the twentieth century has increased his objective freedom and at the same time decreased his subjective freedom. This distinction is essentially the same as that made by Herbert J. Muller in *Issues of Freedom* (New York: Harper & Brothers, 1960). For an interesting analysis of the role of the communications media in the increasing alienation of man in the twentieth century, see Marshall McLuhan, *Understanding Media: The Extensions of Man* (New York: McGraw-Hill Book Company, 1964); see also Richard Schickel, "Marshall McLuhan: Canada's Intellectual Comet," *Harper's Magazine* (November 1963), 62-68.

difference between the systems. Both totalitarian systems submerged the individual in the cause of the state, and both used the same media of mass persuasion and control.

Although there are many similarities between the two systems, Communism has tended to grow in those underdeveloped nations that have a minimum capital base, while Fascism has developed in those countries where the industrial capital was threatened by social and economic disorder.[4] Fascism was ultimately a totalitarian defense of established industrial capitalism, and Communism was an alternative to the established order. Both placed less value on the dignity of the individual than on the greater good of society.

While, in a very real sense, Fascism and Communism were a response to the economic conditions of life in the twentieth century, they were also influenced by the nineteenth-century European revolution against Enlightenment values. What began as a romantic reaction to the Enlightenment at the beginning of the nineteenth century culminated in a storm of intellectual nihilism at the end of that century. Western society, in its search for certainty in an uncertain world, had in its weary disillusionment rediscovered irrationalism—an irrationalism more profound and despairing than anything the West had experienced since the decline of the ancient world. Literate intelligence would henceforth focus not on the joys of life and the future millennium, but rather on the crisis of death and the absurd existence of man alienated from culture, nature, or God.

By the time Nietzsche had passed beyond tragedy, beyond good and evil, Kierkegaard had discovered the value of fear and trembling, Melville had emphasized the indestructible nature of evil, and Dostoevski had written, "There are three powers, three powers alone, able to conquer and to hold captive forever the conscience of these impotent rebels for their happiness—those forces are miracle, mystery, and authority."[5] In the twentieth century both Fascists and Communists made ample use of "miracle, mystery, and authority" to control the conscience of those "impotent rebels for their happiness."

Georges Sorel in *Reflections on Violence* (1915) carefully and explicitly considered the functional utility of miracle, mystery, and authority for the syndicalist cause of class war and violence.[6] Sorel found these chains of humanity to be vital instruments for controlling and directing the masses for the coming class war.[7] On the other side, Pareto in his brilliant

---

4. While America in the nineteenth century had achieved its capital base through a philosophy of individualism within a distorted Protestant ethic which sacrificed the weak for the financially strong, the Communist party in the twentieth century used the collective power of the state to amass its capital base through a totalitarian system within a distorted Marxian ethic which destroyed the individual in the interest of the collective.

5. Fyodor Dostoevski, *The Brothers Karamazov* (New York: The Macmillan Company, 1912), p. 269.

6. See Georges Sorel, *Reflections on Violence,* trans. T. E. Hulme (New York: Peter Smith, 1935).

7. It is interesting that the same year Sorel published his famous work on violence, a young man from Wichita, Kansas, joined the Syndicalist League of North America. That young man was Earl Browder, who would shortly lead the Communist party in America through its more prosperous years, 1930-1945.

but laborious *Trattato di sociologia generale*[8] (1916) realistically examined these same characteristics under the classification of the "non-logico-experimental" and found them to be the vital tools of the elite in controlling the herd in mass formations and mass actions. While Sorel advocated nonrational manipulation of the masses in the interest of class warfare and Pareto found similar nonrational factors the key to successful leadership by the elite, both reflected the general European rejection of the Enlightenment conception of a rational man. As many European social thinkers at the turn of the century declared the Enlightenment notions of man and the good society either dead or bankrupt, it was clear to most that a transvaluation was taking place not only in literature, art, drama, and philosophy, but also in social thought.

This shift of values focused increasingly on the absurdity of life and the irrationality of human motivations and actions. Individual existence was to be secured not by fulfilling one's duties to the mass or herd, which lived by illusions, not by placing one's faith in the humanitarian future or in the rationalistic past, but rather by the sheer assertion of one's self in a nihilistic world. In the name of "sincerity," all ideology had to be rejected. Youth without a banner, youth without a cause, became the rallying cry of many in the twentieth century. From such a view, representative democracy was nothing more than a bourgeois facade behind which petty, selfish, vested interests developed. Democracy appeared a sham when one passed beyond appearances to the reality of nihilism. Even science, the goddess of the Enlightenment, which once offered so much hope for a suffering humanity, increasingly came to be viewed as Frankenstein's monster, ushering in an age of mass organization and mass culture that alienated the individual and destroyed his identity.

While many were experiencing a clear loss of faith in science and the rationality of man, science continued to give man greater power. Advances in natural science increased man's control over physical phenomena, and, similarly, advances in the social sciences increased man's control over human behavior. Under these conditions, freedom became psychologically unbearable for many. This, then, was the phenomenon to which Erich Fromm addressed himself in *Escape from Freedom* (1941), and at which Adolf Hitler aimed when he said, "Providence has ordained that I should be the greatest liberator of humanity. I am freeing man from the demands of a freedom and personal independence that only a few can sustain."[9] The paradox of modern existence was that while the options had clearly increased, the depersonalization of the individual had also increased. The problem of maintaining individual identity and dignity in the face of mass organization became a critical problem for most societies in the twentieth century.

By the beginning of the twentieth century, when America was still reflecting its optimism through the neo-Enlightenment views of Peirce, James, and Dewey, the European intellectual had already been caught in

---

8. Vilfredo Pareto, *The Mind and Society*, ed. Arthur Livingston, trans. Andrew Bongiorno and Arthur Livingston, 4 vols. (New York: Harcourt, Brace and Company, 1935).

9. Quoted in Muller, *Issues of Freedom*, p. 36.

the undertow of nihilistic pessimism. To the European, the wave of the future could readily be seen as some form of elitism,[10] while to the American, the wave of the future seemed to be some form of democracy. This was not the case, however, fifty years later. By mid-century, many Americans came to understand what the European literati of a generation earlier were talking about when they described man as being in a state of alienation. Increasingly, such phrases as "the feeling of not belonging," "being a member of the lonely crowd," or "a victim of the organization man's system" became part of the conventional wisdom of the American mind. By mid-century, America had developed its own Fascist and Communist organizations, its own nihilism in the literary and performing arts, its own existential pessimism, and its own awareness of alienation, all stimulated by problems of bureaucracy, cold war tensions, racial conflicts, and economic privation in some sectors of American life.

Repeatedly in the twentieth century America was threatened internally, as well as externally, by the rise of Fascism and Communism. While neither group, ideologically or practically, ever came close to dominating American educational thought, both were significant pressure groups in American education in the twentieth century. Both extremes of the totalitarian spectrum reflect some realistic ideas with respect to the function of the school in modern society which cannot be ignored. Since it is impossible to discuss here the total influence of both groups on American education, the focus of this chapter is limited to a single Fascist and a single Communist ideological model of man and society, and the educational views of one leading Fascist and one leading Communist. We will consider the ideas of Lawrence Dennis as an avowed American Fascist and Earl Browder as an avowed American Communist, and their respective views concerning the function of the American school in the modern world.

A FASCIST MODEL

In the minds of many, the term *Fascism* represents all that is evil, eliciting painful memories of such infamous centers of human degradation as Auschwitz, Buchenwald, Dachau, and Belsen; others view Fascism as a mere accident of history, to be quietly and quickly tucked away in the pages of the schoolboy's history book. It seems as much a mistake to use the term *Fascism* as a label for all generalized evil as it is to view it as germane only to German and Italian social history. In the one case the term becomes meaningless, and in the other case the issue is treated with considerable detachment and is viewed as insignificant with respect to our own thinking. Those holding either view ignore the possibility that Fascism is a unique twentieth-century ideological response of Western man to the conditions of life in an industrial, bureaucratic society. The significant fact is that both the ideology of Fascism and the conditions that perpetuated it persist in American and European centers of culture.

---

10. See George L. Mosse, *The Culture of Western Europe* (Chicago: Rand McNally & Company, 1961), pp. 296-297.

Just as Communism can be viewed as an ideology which has evolved from nineteenth-century thought and conditions, so Fascism can be viewed as an ideology conceived in the late nineteenth century and born in the twentieth. Interestingly, the same year that marked the publication of *The Communist Manifesto* also marked the birth of the man who was to be acclaimed the Karl Marx of Fascism, Vilfredo Pareto (1848-1923). The direct influence of Pareto's thought on the course of Fascism was limited in comparison with Marx's influence on Communism; nevertheless, Pareto did for Fascism essentially what Marx did for Communism—that is, he developed a comprehensible and systematic ideological basis for the forthcoming movement. As Pareto developed the intellectual basis for the coming of Fascism, he predicted the wave of the future. He lived to see his prediction come true and, in the end, joined the Fascist ranks as a senator in Benito Mussolini's government.[11]

As an engineer who turned first to economics and then to sociology, Vilfredo Pareto was a sensitive, perceptive student of his time. Propounding a science of human behavior, he reflected the positivist's concern for certainty. In going beyond what most positivists considered positive knowledge by dealing with the nonrational aspects of human behavior, Pareto was unquestionably trying to correct what he considered a major weakness in the positivist's rationale. Pareto's thought, however, reflected his historic period; it was more than merely an attempt to improve and develop positivism. While he purported to develop a scientific analysis,[12] unencumbered with bias or personal values, his own bitter disillusionment with humanitarianism, liberalism, and representative democracy turned his analysis into a series of biting polemics. The overall model which Pareto used is itself premised on philosophic assumptions, assumptions which Pareto failed to make explicit. The most basic of these assumptions is that by nature man is fundamentally controlled and moved to action by nonrational forces. While Pareto began his analysis with a discussion of the scientific approach, and while he saw all human thought and action as logico-experimental (rational behavior) or non-logico-experimental (nonrational behavior), his three-volume *Trattato di sociologia generale* is for the most part a dissertation on the latter dimension of human behavior. The inadequate development of the logico-experimental can hardly be viewed as an oversight. Investigation of Pareto's model reveals that

11. In spite of the fact that Pareto joined the Fascist ranks the year he died (1923), it is extremely doubtful whether, had he lived, he would have remained a Fascist. Certain characteristics of Pareto, his own love of freedom to inquire as well as his positivistic approach, would have run counter to the populism so characteristic of the later Fascist development. Nevertheless, his basic analysis of power for the sake of power is a fundamental concept of Fascist thought. For Pareto's role in the historic development of Italian Fascism, see Mosse, *Culture of Western Europe*, pp. 296-297. For Pareto's prediction of the rise of a Fascist dictator for Italy and his conclusion that such a victory would be "beneficial to the nation as a whole," see Pareto, *Mind and Society*, IV, 1789-1790.

12. It is interesting that Pareto also believed that Georges Sorel in his *Reflexions sur la Violence* also ascended "to the altitudes of science." See Pareto, *Mind and Society*, IV, 1535.

for Pareto the nonrational aspects of human nature constitute the critical factor in controlling human behavior. Closer examination demonstrates that the aspect of nonrational behavior which is most significant to Pareto is the *instinctive residues.* Thus, we are face to face with Pareto's basic assumption: The nature of man is fundamentally moved by nonrational determinants.

This assumption made, Pareto's analysis turned out to be a massive compendium of arguments supporting his major assumptions. Pareto, thinking in dualistic terms, proceeded to divide the non-logico-experimental into *derivations* (myths), which are comprehensible expressions of *residues* (sentiments). The residues were first listed in six classes, but gradually, as Pareto continued his analysis, he returned to a dualism by emphasizing Class I, instinct for combinations (need for change), and Class II, group persistence (need for certainty and security). Here, in the nonrational residues, Pareto found stability and continuity in human behavior. While the derivations (myths)—which included all ideologies, religions, philosophies, rationalistic histories, and humanitarian values— changed at a rapid pace, the residues that gave rise to the derivations or that existed behind the facade of appearances remained relatively stable. Thus, for Pareto, the nonrational residues basically determined human behavior.

The problem of predestination has repeatedly recurred in Western thought, usually in different forms, but it almost always reflects the intellectual climate of the period. While some Puritans believed that God had predestined men, and many late-nineteenth-century social Darwinists found human behavior predetermined by the law of evolution, the Fascist in the twentieth century, who had rediscovered the irrational, concluded that human behavior in a mass bureaucratic society was basically predetermined by nonrational urges. Pareto surmised that modern man, as a result of industrialization and individual alienation, was experiencing a slow but perceptible increase in the residue of group persistence (need for certainty and security). Thus, there developed a need for new and better myths to integrate man with the herd. As derivations or myths were created to satisfy the residues, they could be validly tested only by their effectiveness in satisfying the nonrational need for security. Outside of this kind of utility, the "true" leader would not take the derivations seriously. To study the differences in ideologies, religions, or reasoned thought as if these differences were significant in human behavior—in any sense other than satisfying irrational needs—is to be deluded by the chimerical world of myth.

Because all ideologies are mere myths, Pareto, and the Fascists who followed his analysis, did not consider distinctions between competing social-political ideologies as important. One myth or ideology is as good as another as long as it works, and it works as long as it satisfies the nonrational needs of mass man for security. This aspect of Pareto's thought attacks the very foundations of freedom. When reasonable ideological differences are no longer viewed as significant and the way people think does not make a difference, it is then relatively easy to label all groups either Communist or Fascist. The day when men cease to make distinctions between socialist and Communist, or democrat and socialist, is the day when the freedom to exist, at least for the middle groups, has already been lost. The Fascist belief that man is fundamentally a non-rational creature who can be manipulated by techniques which appeal to and satisfy man's irrational sentiments attacks the academic community's very reason for being—that is, the rational understanding of man and his environment.

It can reasonably be argued that the German university flowered in the Platonic authoritarian culture of nineteenth-century Germany, and that such noble ideals as *Lehrfreiheit* and *Lernfreiheit* functioned as living ideals, because both professor and student were members of the guardian class. This institution, which was nourished and sustained by a Platonic authoritarian culture, collapsed under the Paretoan authoritarianism of Fascism. Fascism destroyed not only the freedom to inquire but, far more significant, the reason for inquiry in the first place. To Pareto, mass man was motivated by sentiments and satisfied by myths, representative democracy was but a humanitarian facade, and the Enlightenment idea of man rationally participating in social progress was but an ineffective myth; it followed, therefore, that mass man needed leadership. The Fascist mind of the twentieth century called for charismatic leadership which recognized the sentiments and manipulated the myths, unrestrained by ethical responsibilities. To Pareto, the true elite would eventually break through the trappings of the humanitarian edifice and assert that leadership.

Using a concept of leadership not too far afield from Pareto, both Benito Mussolini and Adolf Hitler asserted that their leadership was more democratic than any other existing in the Western democracies, since they represented the people in their most significant needs. The need of the herd was not for more food, clothing, and shelter, but rather for the psychological security of belonging. Man's nonrational need for security necessitated myths that would help make man feel a part of something greater than his existential self and thereby help destroy that alienation so characteristic of the individual in modern industrial society. In union with Dostoevski's Grand Inquisitor, the Fascists agreed that what these "impotent rebels need for their happiness" is not the enlightenment of reason, but the miracle of charismatic authority and the mystery of a meaningful mythology.

Statism, racism, or personality cults could serve as myths to fulfill the needs of the nonrational sentiments. All means of education—whether it be the mass media through which members of the adult world continue their education or the school through which the young are formally indoctrinated—came to be recognized as arteries through which flow the lifeblood of the nation's cultural derivations.

Although Pareto had worked out his "scientific sociology" unencumbered with humanitarian values, his sociology embodied many of the central features of a fascist social philosophy. His attack on Enlightenment values and representative democracy, his conviction regarding the vulnerability of man to manipulation resulting from man's nonrational nature, and his theory of elites all provided the intellectual groundwork for a nonintellectual system. The questions Pareto asked and answered, the assumptions he made, and the social and intellectual trends he represented can all be recognized as significant characteristics of the Fascist mind, whether that mind is colored by the cultural myths of Germany, Italy, Spain, Portugal, or the United States. If we turn, for example, to American thought to examine the ideology and educational views of Lawrence Dennis, an American Fascist in the thirties and forties, the similarity of thought is striking.

LAWRENCE DENNIS AND THE AMERICAN SCHOOL

Not until Lawrence Dennis retired from the diplomatic service and a later career in international banking did he become a significant figure in American social thought. By 1930, in semiretirement on his farm near Becket, Massachusetts, Dennis began writing and publishing materials on pressing social problems. His first book, *Is Capitalism Doomed?* (1932), set the direction for his later works, *The Coming American Fascism* (1936) and *Dynamics of War and Revolution* (1940), which made Lawrence Dennis the leading American intellectual exponent of Fascism in the thirties and forties.

Dennis' rejection of humanitarian democracy, his awareness of the irrationality and alienation of the masses, his view of education as a means of manipulation, and his solution to the mounting crisis through charismatic leadership are all essentially Paretoan. Lawrence Dennis clearly summarized his point of view when he said:

The role of education in our present crisis is to make the masses susceptible as they never were before to propaganda and demagogic manipulation. The greater the number of people who can vote and read, the greater the irrationality, the greater the conflict of minority interests, and the greater the anarchy in the political and economic processes under a system of parliamentary democracy. The people can rule with rationality and success only through a single leader, party and governing agency. Public order and welfare require administration, not conflict; the imposition and performance of duties, not the playing of a competitive game.[13]

As Dennis turned to education in the broader culture, he pointed to the necessity of controlling the mass media in the national interest of good citizenship.

The church, the press, the theatre, the moving pictures, and the radio undoubtedly do more educating than the school, if for no other reason than that they educate people throughout their entire lifetimes. These institutions also educate with definite social purposes. Sometimes these purposes harmonize with the larger purposes of the social plan, and sometimes they certainly do not. In the fascist view of things, all institutional formation of character, mind, social attitudes, and opinions with a social purpose, must harmonize with, and not be antagonistic to, the larger purposes of the national plan. This means that fascism

---

13. Lawrence Dennis, *The Dynamics of War and Revolution* (New York: The Weekly Foreign Letter, 1940), p. 125.

holds that no institution forming people's minds, characters, and attitudes should have among its purposes or effects the unfitting of people for good citizenship as the state defines good citizenship.[14]

To Dennis, democracy had died not from the crisis of youth but from the crisis of old age. As democracy reached maturity with universal suffrage and mass public education, the chief fallacy of the liberal ideal lay exposed for all to see. The common man simply did not make intelligent decisions based on reasoned evidence; moreover, through the advancing techniques of psychological control, not only could he be induced to let his decisions be made for him, but he could also be made to enjoy the process. The question, then, was not whether the masses should be manipulated, but, rather, who should do the manipulating?

To Dennis, the problem of American society in the thirties was the condition of anarchy that resulted from the failure of the natural elite to shed outworn nineteenth-century ideas of liberal freedom for a tighter discipline of national purpose. While the twentieth-century elite exercised freedom in manipulating the masses for their own vested interests, only anarchy and conflict resulted, to the detriment of all. The effort of the elite must be integrated through a national government concerned with national purpose. Only in this way could the myths be manipulated so as to truly satisfy the sentiments of the masses.

As a tool of the dominant elite, the school was to indoctrinate the young with the right myths clearly defined by the elite.

The group culture should be the expression of the will of the dominant element of the elite, whose values are validated by the power to enforce them. This method of validating values is the only one by which an argument can ever be ended and cooperative activity made possible.[15]

The function of mass education, then, is not to produce free men, freedom being an illusion, nor is it, as Jefferson had maintained, "to help one recognize tyranny and revolt against it"; on the contrary, its major function is to educate men to accept the tyranny of the dominant elite. While the formal school must be concerned with the production of efficient and effective workers, it must also be concerned with the effective integration of the individual into the social order. As Pareto had pointed out earlier, Dennis concluded that:

To be successfully adjusted, an individual does not have to have two cars or even a full stomach. He merely needs to have a place, or, to belong. . . . People don't mind suffering. On the contrary, some of them love to suffer all of the time. What people cannot endure is not belonging. The tragedy of capitalism —unemployment—does not inhere in the phenomena of want and privation, but in the spiritual disintegration of large numbers of people from the group culture. Hitler can feed millions of his people acorns, and, yet, if he integrates

---

14. Lawrence Dennis, *The Coming American Fascism* (New York: Harper & Brothers, 1936), pp. 211-212.
15. Dennis, *Coming American Fascism*, p. 224.

them in a spiritual union with their community, they will be happier than they were while receiving generous doles from a regime which gave them no such spiritual integration with the herd.[16]

Once again, one is reminded that men do not live by reason alone, but by miracle, mystery, and authority. Implicit in Lawrence Dennis' work is the basic assumption of the irrationality of the mass man, the alienation of this man from his culture, and the need to integrate him into the social order through the manipulation of the cultural myths.

Out of the chaos and confusion of a dying parliamentary government must come a new charismatic elite, for it alone could save the culture from total disintegration. Dennis argued that the most rational and realistic approach to modern life was to feed the masses the irrational myths they needed. Hitler was not only

. . . the greatest political genius since Napoleon, but also the most rational. . . . Even Hitler's much caricatured emotionalism is one of the most rational things about him. He knows that the masses can be united and led only by their emotions, and he knows how to unify and lead them through their emotions. Anyone who thinks that the masses can be unified and led otherwise may be a rationalist, but he is no more rational than a man who pours water instead of gasoline into the tank of his automobile.[17]

Dennis said that the American power elite must and would learn to use the appropriate Madison Avenue techniques to manipulate the masses. In this process, Dennis argued, the school—in comparison with the home, the workplace, the marketplace, the press and radio—is only one of the lesser agencies of education.[18] Those who look to the school to dispense social facts and ideas neutrally, as if these ideas "can be dispensed like cigarettes wrapped in cellophane,[19] are as ridiculously naïve as those who look to the schools to reconstruct the social order. The school can do neither. Teachers are, in fact, only a tool of the dominant elite. The elite will not tolerate any effective revolutionary-minded teacher. They will fire him. Under the circumstances, the teaching ranks are largely filled by the personality types which follow rather than lead.

Furthermore, there is a self-selection process among those who go into teaching which militates against any real revolutionary becoming a teacher, according to Dennis. The person who goes into teaching gets satisfaction from leading children, not men. Such a person lacks the personality traits of the leader. Afraid of conflict, lacking in courage, unable to suffer and enjoy the travail of leadership, the American teacher escapes the hard knocks of society by retiring to the security of the classroom. The true rebels like Socrates and Jesus had what it takes to know how to die for a cause, but the teacher does not. Indeed,

---

16. Dennis, *Coming American Fascism*, pp. 225-226.

17. Maximilian John St. George and Lawrence Dennis, *A Trial on Trial* (Chicago: M. J. St. George, 1946), p. 442.

18. Dennis, "Education—The Tool of the Dominant Elite," p. 12. See also McLuhan, *Understanding Media*.

19. Dennis, "Education—The Tool of the Dominant Elite," p. 11.

Because we admire Socrates and Jesus is no reason why we should suppose that the purpose of the school, necessarily conducted by a host of salaried mediocrities, is to create social rebels. The social rebels will happen . . . in spite of the school, not because of it.[20]

The schools and the teachers as instruments of the power elite can only follow those who either have or seize power. Once in power, the new elite will inevitably force the schools to use any and all means to indoctrinate the younger generation with the new "right" values. The teacher, then, is one of the propagandizing agents through which the elite in power effectively organize and secure their control of the social system.

As the war clouds in Europe thickened, and many Americans argued for the entrance of the United States in the war against Fascism, Dennis vigorously asserted that since most signs indicated that America was rapidly developing its own brand of Fascism, it would be absurd to become involved in a war against Fascism. If such a war ended in victory, the war itself would only accelerate the development of American Fascism, and in the end American Fascism would inevitably have to contend against the Communism of the Soviet Union. On April 17, 1944, Lawrence Dennis was formally charged with sedition. The government case against Dennis was based on the charge that Dennis' later books, *The Coming American Fascism* and *The Dynamics of War and Revolution,* were written and distributed to further a conspiracy of insubordination in the United States Armed Forces. Interestingly, some officers in the armed forces did find Dennis' ideas "stimulating." One army reviewer for the U.S. Army Information Service, reviewing *The Dynamics of War and Revolution* in Dennis' "The Weekly Foreign Letter," regretted the fact that:

'Elite' readers lacking such equipment [an understanding of such authors as Adam Smith, Malthus, Veblen, and Marx] are more likely to damn Mr. Dennis as anti-British, pro-Hitler, pro-communist or just plain 'subversive' than to gain any thought stimulation from his observations, and it is the sad truth that starry-eyed dreamers in the ivory towers of endowed educational institutions, and parlor pinks of the literary teas, are more likely to be familiar with the literature mentioned than are the dynamic types capable of influencing the trend of political action.[21]

The reviewer went on to suggest that while he disagreed with some of the premises set forth by Dennis, he found the book stimulating and therefore:

The book is recommended to army officers for reading because it gives in lucid, smoothly moving English the viewpoint of a thinker who has become disgusted with the easy-going habits of the democracies and favors radical change to put an end to such habits.[22]

---

20. Dennis, "Education—The Tool of the Dominant Elite," p. 14.
21. St. George and Dennis, *Trial on Trial,* pp. 451-452.
22. St. George and Dennis, *Trial on Trial,* p. 449.

On December 7, 1944, before Dennis could defend himself against the charges that apparently amounted to no more than that some members of the armed forces found his ideas "stimulating," a mistrial was declared due to the death of the judge. After the war, the government failed to prosecute and eventually dropped the case for lack of substantial evidence. As the sedition trials of 1944 disappeared from the front page, Dennis himself retired from public life.

During the thirties and early forties, Dennis, more than any other American, had carefully delineated the Fascist view of man and society and the function of the school in that society. In developing his rationale, Dennis repeatedly touched on a series of basic questions which American teachers, their professional organizations, and the American public have consistently failed to answer. For example, to what extent does American society need charismatic leadership to make decisions and to weld diverse groups together for efficient, effective action? Can the values of freedom and rationality, which were born in a rather simple agrarian culture, survive in a threatened, complex, bureaucratic society? Can or should the psychological alienation of modern man be alleviated by manipulating the myths to satisfy the "residues"? To what extent is the teacher in America a tool of the power elite, indoctrinating the young with the "right" values? How free is the American teacher? On precisely what grounds should teachers in a pluralistic society assert their freedom and responsibility?

Although many have insisted on academic freedom for the college teacher on the grounds that such freedom is basic and necessary for the creation of new knowledge, far fewer have agreed that such freedom is also basic and necessary for the elementary and secondary school teacher in order to create free men in a free society. The failure of the public to reach consensus as to the function of the school in the American social order has in turn contributed to the inability of teachers, their organizations, and the public to come to grips with the problem of delineating the rights and responsibilities of teachers on the basis of their functions. Lacking such consensus, the American teacher has remained vulnerable and susceptible to the pressures of many different kinds of well-organized groups. During the "red scare" of the twenties and the depression of the thirties, the American Legion and the Daughters of the American Revolution, along with many other "patriotic" groups, clearly demonstrated the vulnerability of American teachers to organized pressure-group activity.[23] Since the McCarthy era attempts to censor textbooks, school activities, and teachers have been common occurrences in the American educational experience.

---

23. See Howard K. Beale, *Are American Teachers Free?* (New York: Charles Scribner's Sons, 1936). See also William Gellerman, *The American Legion as Educator* (New York: Bureau of Publications, Teachers College, Columbia University, 1938); and Richard Seelye Jones, *A History of the American Legion* (Indianapolis: The Bobbs-Merrill Company, Inc., 1946). For an analysis of the similarity of thought between Lawrence Dennis and the current right-wing pressure groups in American education, see Clarence J. Karier, "Totalitarianism of the Right," *Educational Theory,* XIV, 1 (January 1964), 40-49.

A COMMUNIST MODEL

It has often been suggested that the two major intellectual streams of German idealism represented by Hegel and Marx in the nineteenth century met each other in the twentieth century at the Battle of Stalingrad. The road from Hegel to Hitler, however, is as rugged and twisted as the road from Marx to Stalin. To be sure, Hegel was the great conservator who lost the individual in the concept of the state, and Marx was the great radical who lost the individual in the interest of class warfare; nevertheless, the utopian state of Hegel and the utopian socialistic humanism of Marx remained far short of the totalitarian tyranny of either Hitler or Stalin.

Although one may go back to Marx, Pareto, Hegel, or others to find the ideological roots of totalitarianism and, indeed, to find certain key ideas which pointed to the direction and function these ideas might play in shaping modern Communism or Fascism, the end results were by no means predestined. The additions and corrections that men such as Friedrich Nietzsche, Giovanni Gentile, and Ernst Jünger made to the development of totalitarianism of the right were matched by the work of Georges Sorel, V. I. Lenin, Leon Trotsky, and others who contributed to the development of totalitarianism of the left. Furthermore, it was neither ideologies nor revolutionaries which gave rise to totalitarianism, but rather the combination of these factors in the social, economic, and political milieu of a pre- and post-World War I environment. Given all these contributing factors, Marx still remains the chief ideologue of the left.

As discussed earlier, Marx had found the means of production to be the governing law of history, which shaped the course of all social institutions. Few would care to deny that Marx had hit upon one of the most important catalysts of social change in both the nineteenth and twentieth centuries, and most would agree that changes in means of production have been one of the most significant causes of social change throughout history. Marx, however, went beyond this thesis to argue that each major change in production resulted in a reorganization of the class system which in turn resulted in class struggle. This struggle was inevitable. The outcome of such a struggle would result in a greater synthesis and, in the end, the utopian communist society. Marx was materialistic and realistic when he examined the forces of change, and he was highly idealistic when he viewed the end toward which that change was ultimately directed.

Marx's system was deterministic and revolutionary at the same time. Although class war was inevitable and the victory of the proletariat ultimately assured, the proletariat still had to develop class consciousness and battle to fulfill the apocalyptic vision. Just as the Puritan struggled to prove to himself as well as to others that he was one of the elect, predestined by God, the Communist in the twentieth century struggled to prove to himself and to others that Marx's cosmic use of history to explain the present and predict the future was valid.

Just exactly how and when the class conflict would begin and end remained open to question. Should the dedicated Marxist work toward an immediate political revolution to overthrow the capitalists, or should he work to develop the proletariat class consciousness, and then organize the worker through unions to destroy the capitalist means of production? Should a revolutionary look upon the coming revolution as an immediate event and work toward it, or should the good Communist be content to compromise and take milder measures along the way to capitalistic destruction? To what extent should the revolutionary fraternize with the enemy? If, for example, a Communist controlled a labor union, should he work against the immediate interest of the worker and thus increase the worker's hatred of the capitalist and hasten his downfall; or should he work for immediate reforms for the worker and thus risk the chance of aiding and abetting the survival of capitalism? Such questions of tactics were implicit problems of Marx's analysis of class warfare which persisted in plaguing the left-wing movement in both Europe and America in the nineteenth and twentieth centuries.

Although Marx recognized the importance of the means of production as a determiner of social change, his idealistic dialectic structure of class warfare led him to neglect the possibility that a new managerial class and an increasingly larger and larger middle class might evolve from the new industrial means of production. The illusion that a highly self-conscious proletariat would yet prove Marx correct persisted in Communist leadership long into the twentieth century. The fact that the Communists have been most successful in the feudal agrarian cultures of Russia and China and not the highly industrial societies of the West bears out the fatal flaw in Marx's prophecy. Living in a world of Dickens, Marx could easily mistake the workers' struggle for better living conditions for a struggle to control the means of production. In spite of their willingness to strike, riot, and destroy the machinery of production, neither the English nor the American worker was as much interested in class wafare as he was in gaining his share of the fruits of his labor.

The use of violence to redress grievances was not a concept foreign to the American worker. The Irish immigrant riots of the 1830's, the Molly Maguires in the anthracite regions in the 1860's, the Haymarket Square Riot in Chicago in 1886, the battle between hundreds of Pinkerton men and steel workers in Homestead, Pennsylvania, in 1892, and the many strikes in which federal troops fought the workers on the streets in the 1890's, all attest to the continuing use of violence in American history.[24] Out of the violent traditions of the Western states evolved the Industrial Workers of the World (I.W.W.) and other syndicalists who met the social forces aligned against them with a well-placed stick of dynamite. The various action-oriented groups of the American left wing, such as the Syndicalist, the Socialist Labor Party, the Socialist Party, and others—which by 1905 made up the united front of the I.W.W.—were distinctive for their lack of ideology. What ideological commitments they did possess were more Bellamyite utopian than Marxian.[25]

---

24. See Theodore Draper, *The Roots of American Communism* (New York: The Viking Press, 1957), pp. 21-22.

25. See Draper, *Roots of American Communism*, pp. 15-16.

The popularity and strength of the American left wing throughout the closing decades of the nineteenth century stemmed, for the most part, from the conditions and frustrations of the worker rather than from an ideological basis. The central battle within labor unions and the socialist left itself was largely between the majority, who were willing to take the position that one had to work for immediate reforms, and the minority on the extreme left, who insisted that organized effort must be directed not toward reforming but toward destroying the system. From the latter standpoint, there was, after all, a real danger that the worker as a revolutionary could be bought off by bourgeois reforms.

Marx and Engels viewed the American working-class struggle as well advanced but woefully deficient in ideological basis. After Engels visited America in 1888, he concluded that American workers were "ahead of everyone else in practice and still in swaddling clothes in theory."[26] The native American radical from the Western states who was concerned with violent immediate action did not need the theory of Marx or Engels to help make up his mind whether or not to dynamite the company store. The immigrant socialists, on the other hand, who knew the theory and prided themselves on their superior knowledge thereof, tended to form separate groups and isolate themselves from the mainstream of American labor. The doctrinaire socialist ideology, furthermore, did not fit the conditions of a budding capitalist system in a society which lacked a feudal class tradition. In the midst of severe labor conflict, Samuel Gompers, as head of the American Federation of Labor, tapped into the real mainstream of American laborers' motivations by advocating higher wages, shorter hours, and better working conditions. On the political side, Robert La Follette organized the Progressive Party to agitate for practical political institutional reform. Between the political work of La Follette and the union activities of Gompers and many other socialists of milder persuasion, the radical left began to lose its major reason for existence.

Although socialists did well at the polls before World War I, the entrance of America into the war marked for many the end of their political influence. As many socialists took an unpopular stand against the war, they lost the support of their constituency. During the war years, the extreme left was further weakened by government mass trials which sent hundreds of I.W.W. and Syndicalist League leaders to prison. As membership, power, and influence of the radical left in America began to decrease, the revolutionaries had good cause to be pessimistic. Then, in October 1917, came the electrifying news that the Bolsheviks had seized power in Russia. Almost overnight the radical left was revived.

The impact of the Bolshevik revolution on the American Left Wing was stunning. It was as if some Left Wing Socialists had gone to sleep and had awakened as communists. The Bolshevik revolution had a dazzling, dreamlike quality, all the more glamorous because it was far away, undefiled by any contact with the more recalcitrant American reality.[27]

---

26. Quoted in Draper, *Roots of American Communism,* p. 26.
27. Draper, *Roots of American Communism,* p. 101.

If the Bolshevik Party of eleven thousand members could take control of Russia, then a small, tightly organized party of zealous revolutionaries might, under the right conditions, meet with equal success in the United States. The only question was who would be the American Lenin. One did not have to wait for the proletariat to develop class consciousness to carry out the revolution. Oddly enough, Lenin and Trotsky were proving Marx wrong, at the same time that they had achieved their greatest success for the Communist cause. The Russian Revolution was not a proletarian revolution, but a Bolshevik revolution. The Marxian vision of a proletarian revolution had yet to occur. Still a Marxian believer six months after the October Revolution, Lenin continued to look to industrialized Germany for the real proletarian revolution and insisted that "it was an 'absolute truth' that they were 'doomed' without a German revolution."[28] Neither was the Russian Revolution doomed nor did the German proletarian revolution materialize. However, little more than a decade later, German industrialists, fearing a Communist revolution, supported the National Socialist solution of Adolf Hitler.

The Communist Party of America was born largely as a consequence of the Russian Revolution. As the Bolsheviks successfully completed their October Revolution in Russia, the Russian revolutionaries in Boston, New York, and Chicago gained status, influence, and power over the American left wing. In the fall of 1919, the left wing converged on Chicago to organize the Communist Party of America. In amalgamation with the old-line radical socialists and syndicalists were foreign-language federations led by the Russians. It was the latter who controlled the convention and who, throughout the twentieth century, controlled the Communist Party of America.

The old question of tactics still came to the fore: Should a good Communist work for immediate reforms for the worker or against these reforms in order to hasten the eventual collapse of the capitalistic system? This question, however, was now resolved by the discipline of the party itself. The good Communist working in any organization would always be working for the interest of the party, and the interest of the party was ultimately defined in Moscow. Whether in a labor union or a teachers' union, the needs of the party came before the needs of the worker or the teacher. The Communist, like the Fascist, demanded a disciplined, dedicated membership who knew where their first loyalties rested. Here, then, was an organization which could fraternize with the enemy, burrow from within, establish united fronts and popular fronts, and still not be bought off by bourgeois reform.

The party was no sooner organized then it was driven underground by the red scare that followed World War I. In 1920, Earl Browder was released from Leavenworth Prison after having served sixteen months of a three-year sentence for attempting to block the draft during World War I. He immediately joined the underground party and was given charter membership. Browder was recognized by the party as a solid revolutionary. As a Kansas youth, he had followed his father from Unitarianism to Populism to Socialism, and in his mid-teens, he was a tire-

---

28. Quoted in Draper, *Roots of American Communism,* p. 104.

less worker for the Syndicalist League of North America, which was then led by William Z. Foster. As a lifelong friend and compatriot, Foster followed Browder into the Communist party, and within a decade they became the key leaders of the party.

When America entered World War I, Browder refused to register for the draft and organized the League for Democratic Control, which attempted to get a court order to restrain the Governor of Missouri from executing the draft laws. For this he received his three-year prison sentence. At Leavenworth, he studied economics, sociology, read Marx and Engels, and became acquainted with "Big Bill" Haywood, the leading Syndicalist labor leader who was also imprisoned at Leavenworth.

Browder's background equipped him well for a rapid rise within the party. In 1921, he was a delegate to the Congress of the Red International of Labor Unions at Moscow, and in 1926, he was back in Moscow as a member of the Executive Committee of the same organization. That same year he traveled to China with a labor delegation and reached Hankow just when Chiang Kai-shek had decided to massacre the Communists that Chiang and Sun Yat-sen had invited from Moscow to help in organizing China. Browder stayed on as an underground editor of the *Pan-Pacific Worker* in Hankow. Upon returning to the United States in 1929, he found his old friend Foster in a struggle with Jay Lovestone and others for control of the party. The Foster-Browder forces won. In 1930, Foster, because of ill health, stepped aside, and Earl Browder became the head of the Communist party until 1945.[29] Browder directed the fortunes of the party during the strongest, most powerful period of its existence in American culture. It was also during this period that the party became more directly involved in education.

EARL BROWDER AND THE AMERICAN SCHOOL

From Karl Marx to Joseph Stalin, the Communists maintained a consistent attitude toward the function of the school in any society. The school, it was repeatedly asserted, will inevitably indoctrinate the young for whatever social system happens to exist. The school, therefore, cannot be expected to lead a revolution; it can only follow the revolution. The mainspring of social change is the means of production. When the proletariat develop enough class consciousness to take command of the political and economic institutions of society, they will then proceed to revolutionize the bourgeois family, school, and all means of education. Both the Communist and the Fascist conceived of education as an instrument for shaping and molding children to meet the needs of society. The argument between the two views was not how much social indoctrination but rather what kind of indoctrination. Bourgeois individualism had been repudiated by both the Communist and the Fascist. The concept of educating free men for a free society was viewed as the edu-

---

29. See Nathan Glazer, *The Social Basis of American Communism* (New York: Harcourt, Brace & World, Inc., 1961).

cational by-product of the Enlightenment and the French Revolution, and as such it was part of the dying bourgeois past.

The educational policy for the radical left was set in *The Communist Manifesto:*

And your education! Is not that also social, and determined by the social conditions under which you educate; by the intervention, direct or indirect, of society by means of schools, etc.? The Communists have not invented the intervention of society in education; they do but seek to alter the character of that intervention, and to rescue education from the influence of the ruling class.[30]

The communist position was further crystallized when Lenin announced, after the successful Russian Revolution, that the party

. . . sets itself the aim of concluding the task begun by the October Revolution of 1917 of converting the school from a weapon for the class domination of the bourgeoisie into a weapon for the destruction of this domination, as well as for the complete destruction of the division of society into classes. The school must become a weapon of the dictatorship of the proletariat.[31]

By 1934, Stalin further simplified the Communist position by suggesting that "education is a weapon the effect of which is determined by the hands which wield it, and by who is to be struck down."[32] This was the position that the American Communist party held under the leadership of Earl Browder, except for some slight modifications when expediency warranted.

As Lawrence Dennis and Earl Browder expressed their ideas in *The Social Frontier* (1935) on the question of "Indoctrination: The Task Before the American School," it was evident that both believed the school to be an instrument of the power elite. They further agreed that the classroom teacher was not only vulnerable to external power control, but that through a kind of self-selection process, the individual who selected teaching as an occupation clearly lacked the necessary personal characteristics of leadership. A timid, bourgeois teacher, afraid of real conflict, could hardly be expected to incite anyone to revolt or to offer any serious leadership toward the coming revolution. Browder made it plain when he said:

Those of us whose analysis of the crisis of capitalism leads us to the revolutionary solution, and who see the institutions of learning as inextricably involved in this crisis, must therefore be pardoned for our scepticism toward any program of social change which relies upon the school system as an important instrument in bringing that change about. The school system must itself be revolutionized, before it can become an instrument of revolution—or of any serious social change.

---

30. Karl Marx, *Capital, The Communist Manifesto, and Other Writings,* ed. Max Eastman (New York: The Modern Library, 1932), p. 339.

31. Quoted in Robert W. Iversen, *The Communists and the Schools* (New York: Harcourt, Brace and Company, 1959), p. 62.

32. Quoted in Iversen, *Communists and the Schools,* p. 63.

A revolutionary proletarian system of education necessarily involves indoctrination as an essential feature (indoctrination being defined, not as the preaching of a body of doctrine, but as the inculcation of a positive attitude in favor of a specific type of social activity). In the present educational system of the United States, however, the general trend of indoctrination is, because of the capitalist control, necessarily reactionary in character.[33]

Browder concluded that the problem of indoctrination and its function "cannot be answered by the educational field; the answer must be given to our educators by all the progressive forces of society, as our common directive to them on the conduct of their special sector of a common battle-front."[34] All was not lost, however. The Communists in education might best align themselves with the progressive educators who rejected the Communist analysis of the society but who were bent on stopping the rise of Fascism.

By 1935, Browder was broadening the Stalinist attitude toward education by asserting that something could be done in spite of capitalist control of the schools. The following series of events led to a change in party tactics: By 1935 Adolf Hitler had stopped the Communists in Germany; capitalism was in a state of economic collapse the world over; the membership of the Communist party in America was increasing as a result of the depression; the Communist party had made some successful inroads into the American Federation of Teachers; and the social reconstructionists were making a persuasive case that the schools could be used to reconstruct the social order. When all these factors were put together, it was clear to the party leadership that a broader, more flexible line toward the schools was necessary.

In 1935, Browder attended the Seventh Congress of the Communist International in Moscow, where it was decided that a new line of united fronts must be established to stop Fascism. Since the capitalist system was crumbling, there was serious danger that Fascism, as a totalitarian extension of capitalism, would pluck victory from the hands of the Communists. What was needed was an alliance with radical and liberal bourgeois forces to halt the Fascist development throughout the world. After returning to America, Browder called for a popular front against Fascism in an attempt to enlist the progressives of American society to the cause. In education, the Communists would support and aid liberal educators, especially those liberals who would dare the schools to build a new social order. As Browder said:

We who are revolutionaries understand that the majority of progressive educators, while rejecting fascism with abhorrence, do not embrace the communist program. We do not draw the conclusion that he who is not entirely with us is against us; on the contrary, we say that all those who are sincerely against fascism, who will fight against fascism, should be united in a single anti-fascist front, ranging from mild progressive to communist.[35]

---

33. Browder, "Education—An Ally in the Workers' Struggle," pp. 22-24.
34. Browder, "Education—An Ally in the Workers' Struggle," p. 24.
35. Browder, "Education—An Ally in the Workers' Struggle," p. 24.

Although the Communist teacher could not militantly indoctrinate the Marxist-Lenin doctrine, he could work to organize the class consciousness of the teachers, move the teachers' organizations to take anti-Fascist stands, and perhaps teach children some of the major tenets of the class struggle. While in the latter area Browder still remained highly skeptical, he and other party members increasingly came to believe that they had a larger role to play in the field of education. The Fascist threat and increased party membership as a result of the depression led the party to this conclusion; perhaps even more persuasive was the gaining of control over New York's Local No. 5, the largest local of the American Federation of Teachers (A.F.T.).

By 1933, John Dewey was battling against the Communists who were pressing to take control of the union. On April 29, 1933, at Commerce High School in New York City, about eight hundred members of the A.F.T. heard Dewey call for the suspension of a former pupil of his, not on the grounds that he was a Communist, but on the grounds that he was attempting to use the organization for other than union purposes.[36] Dewey had hit the key difference between a left-wing socialist and a Communist—the latter's loyalties were to the party and eventually to Moscow and not to the teachers' union. Dewey, however, lost this first engagement with the Communists. Repeatedly during the next decade, Dewey fought to break the Communist control of the teachers' union. In 1939, he organized the Committee for Cultural Freedom, consisting of such men as G. S. Counts, William H. Kilpatrick, Horace Kallen, Sidney Hook, Carl Becker, and Harry Gideonse. It was this committee which eventually wrested control of the teachers' union from the Communists.

In 1939, G. S. Counts spearheaded the counterattack. Counts charged that the

... Communists were, in fact, 'the midwives of fascism.' Communists preach democracy, ... but they 'violate the most elementary virtues of fairness and integrity, and by their methods bring inevitable discord into the ranks of the popular cause ... ends and means cannot be separated.'[37]

Counts called for the expulsion of Communist-controlled locals, but with little success. Failing in this, he ran for the presidency of the American Federation of Teachers against the Communist candidate. Counts had an uphill fight on his hands. When he went to the Buffalo convention in the summer of 1939, the odds were good that the party would maintain control and Counts would be defeated. However, the news of the Nazi-Soviet Pact, which came before the vote was taken, so shook the liberals supporting the Communists in the united front against Fascism in the convention that Counts won by a vote of 344 to 320.[38] By 1941, through the efforts of Counts and others, the Communist-controlled locals had been expelled from the A.F.T.

---

36. See Iversen, *Communists and the Schools*, pp. 42-43.
37. Iversen, *Communists and the Schools*, pp. 200-201.
38. See Iversen, *Communists and the Schools*, p. 115.

What limited success the party had achieved in the late thirties was due largely to the support of liberals who were concerned with the rise of Fascism. The beginning of the decline of the Communist party in America came with the Nazi-Soviet Pact.[39] The pact itself not only shook the popular front, but the overnight shift in party policy from a militant anti-Fascist position to one of peaceful coexistence made it clear to most liberal supporters who still had any doubts that the party was, in fact, controlled by Moscow.[40] Under these circumstances, the campaign that Counts, Dewey, Kilpatrick, Hook, and others mounted to wrest control of the A.F.T. was successful. By 1941, a decade before the McCarthy era, some of the major leaders in American education had effectively checked and turned back the Communist influence in the American Federation of Teachers.[41]

Strangely enough, it was Counts, a leading social reconstructionist, who effectively fought the Communists within the teachers' union, and it was also the social reconstructionists who seemed to have influenced the party into a more active role within the schools. The party was always reluctant to believe that any serious indoctrination toward a new social order could take place within the halls of a bourgeois school, but when it became allied with the social reconstructionists and other liberals in the united front, there was a noticeable shift of party policy toward use of the schools for Communist purposes. As Iversen put it:

In examining the crystallization of the Communist Party line on the schools, one is struck by the fact that the party seemed almost to have been forced into assigning a greater role to the schools by the Frontier Thinkers, with whom they were allied in the united front.[42]

Theodore Brameld, as a social reconstructionist, led the way. Far ahead of Browder or the party at the time, Brameld spelled out what a Marxist teacher could do in the present crisis in an article entitled "Karl Marx and the American Teacher."[43] As Brameld saw it, there were many who believed that Marx had erred in certain respects but that he had nonetheless correctly diagnosed the disease of capitalism. While it is true that Marx predicted the inevitable decline of capitalism, he also advocated the violent overthrow of capitalist tyranny.

Marx, however, was not merely a philosopher intent upon demonstrating the inevitable course of history: he was also a methodologist interested in the con-

---

39. See David A. Shannon, *The Decline of American Communism* (New York: Harcourt, Brace and Company, 1959).

40. Granville Hicks was a typical example of a liberal socialist who joined the Communist party in 1934 and left it in 1939 because of the pact. Sidney Hook, on the other hand, joined the party, tried to reinterpret Marx, and was publicly denounced by Browder for crossing the party line. Both men found that they were not free to think and inquire within the party. See Iversen, *Communists and the Schools,* pp. 194-200.

41. At present, the NEA and the A.F.T. both take the stand that the party member is essentially a committed agent of a foreign power and cannot teach freely and therefore should not be allowed to teach in the schools.

42. Iversen, *Communists and the Schools,* p. 73.

43. *The Social Frontier,* II (November 1935), 53-56.

scious transformation of society, and as such he advocated violence because he believed that workers as intelligent, willful beings are justified in advocating and practicing varying degrees of militancy against the employing class.[44]

It was the tough-mindedness of Marx and his willingness to face the class struggle, with its necessity of violence, which made Marx a revolutionary instead of a dreamy idealist.

Brameld went on to address himself to the implication of the Marxist method for teachers. From Marx's standpoint:

The teacher who wishes to conduct his activity—within the school and without—in behalf of the collectivist ideal must free himself from the fallacy that the choice before him is naught or all. The question is not whether he as citizen and as worker *can* or *cannot* direct his energies along lines indicated by Marxian tactics. The question is rather *in what degree can he.*[45]

What, then, can the Marxist teacher do?

Teachers, first, should recognize that unless they choose to follow the older educational philosophy of neutrality they must accept a point of view consonant with the requirements of the new America. They must then influence their students, subtly if necessary, frankly if possible, toward acceptance of the same position. This does not mean that fair and intelligent analysis of 'the other side' should be avoided; on the contrary it becomes an indispensable means in the teacher's hands.[46]

The Marxist teacher, however, must emphasize the limits on freedom of speech in a capitalist society and the conditions of the Negroes, miners, and other oppressed workers under the present system.

The Marxist teacher must further recognize that disobedience of law is, under certain conditions, not only necessary but highly ethical.

Marx almost admits that successful insurrection against the capitalist class is the highest moral act possible in our society. . . . Let us avoid violence when at all feasible, Marx would assert. Let us never resort to it indiscriminately. Meanwhile, let us achieve by the vote all the rights we can. But let us not characterize violence categorically as immoral under all circumstances.[47]

Finally, the teacher must organize and develop class consciousness and realize that economically he is closer to the ditch-digger than to the college trustee. Brameld was careful to point out that he was not arguing for or against collectivism but was simply arguing that those "who do advocate this goal" must face the necessity of "a frank, thorough consideration of the Marxian means to their common end."

---

44. Brameld, "Karl Marx and the American Teacher," p. 56.
45. Brameld, "Karl Marx and the American Teacher," p. 55.
46. Brameld, "Karl Marx and the American Teacher," p. 56.
47. Brameld, "Karl Marx and the American Teacher," p. 56.

Brameld had pushed the function of the Communist teacher in the American classroom considerably beyond anything either the party or Browder had dared to advocate openly. In the following spring, Dewey, in an article in *The Social Frontier,* criticized such a Marxian position because it substituted class struggle and conflict for "our democratic traditions and its methods."[48] In the following issue, William H. Kilpatrick, in "High Marxism Defined and Rejected," addressed himself to the Marxian position as developed by Brameld, analyzed it, and point for point rejected it. Kilpatrick took care to point out that, as he understood it, "Dr. Brameld did not so much state his own position as portray the essential logic of high-Marxism."[49] Kilpatrick insisted that American education should openly and definitely reject high-Marxism and "so much the more reject communism." He stated:

And this I say (in part) because high-Marxism, as I see it, rejects democracy, rejects education as a process of social change, and rejects (at least during its revolutionary program) the ethical regard for the personality of others. It may, of course, turn out that the democratic process might under certain circumstances involve violence, a recalcitrant minority might force it. But as things now appear I cannot in advance and on principle accept violence as essential to a social program. For these and many other reasons I conclude that American education should not hesitate to make its position clear as to the rejection of high-Marxism and communism.[50]

Kilpatrick went on to point out that there were very few Communists or high-Marxians within the ranks of American professors, and although he would not deny their right to be Communists, he would firmly and emphatically deny their position in the academic world.

Communist writers on education increasingly took up positions in line with Brameld. After attacking the bourgeois position of Dewey and Kilpatrick, Howard Langford, in *Education and the Social Conflict* (1936), went on to explain how the teacher might use history, geography, literature, and even the project method in the elementary school to increase class consciousness and facilitate the interests of the party. Richard Frank, in "The Schools and the People's Front,"[51] attacked the pragmatism of Dewey and others for its lack of clear direction and sense of purpose. Frank went on to describe what the party thought the Communist teacher could do in the bourgeois school. "The task of the Communist Party must be first and foremost to arouse the teachers to class-consciousness and to organize them into the American Federation of Teachers, which is in the main current of the American Labor Movement."[52] The teachers must rally to the slogan, "out of the morass of

---

48. John Dewey, "The Class Struggle and the Democratic Way," *The Social Frontier,* II (May 1936), 242.

49. William H. Kilpatrick, "High Marxism Defined and Rejected," *The Social Frontier,* II (June 1936), 272.

50. Kilpatrick, "High Marxism Defined and Rejected," p. 274.

51. *Communist* (published by the Communist Party of the United States of America in Chicago and New York), XVI (May 1937), 432-445.

52. Frank, "Schools and the People's Front," p. 439.

pragmatism, away from medievalism, forward Marxian-Leninism." As class-conscious members of the proletariat, teachers must be thoroughly instructed in Marxian-Leninism so that "they will be able skillfully to inject it into their teaching at the least risk of exposure and at the same time to conduct struggles around the schools in a truly Bolshevik manner."[53]

At no time were either Browder or other Communist party leaders naïve enough to believe that the revolution could be wrought from skillful teachers indoctrinating the youngsters. School boards were still dominated by business and professional representatives; the teachers almost en masse were bourgeois individualists attracted to a Dewey-Kilpatrick "morass of pragmatism"; and the entire system was legally controlled by a capitalistic state government. Under these circumstances, Zalmen Slesinger concluded that educators in the broader sense—such as journalists, lecturers, artists, writers, and labor leaders—could be considered far more free to influence the masses than any public school teacher.

[These] molders of the minds of the masses must assume the role of the propagandist, the political strategist, using whatever techniques may be effective in convincing and in converting the minds of the masses as speedily and as effectively as possible. Failure to do so is to expose the masses to the destructive demagogy of the ruling class.[54]

Turning then to the public schools, Slesinger reverted to Browder's realistic appraisal of the conditions when he concluded that:

The public school, apparently, can render little if any direct service to the revolutionary cause. Under present conditions the public schools must be considered mainly a closed area for significant education in the direction of revolutionary social reconstruction.[55]

All of this, Slesinger concluded, meant that Dewey, Kilpatrick, Counts, Childs, and others were dead wrong and Browder was correct when he said, "The school system must itself be revolutionized before it can become an instrument of revolution—or of any serious social change."[56]

Repeatedly, Communist ideologues came back to Browder's position. As political realists, the Communists had to admit that in spite of the fertile depression years, they were singularly unsuccessful with the schools. Although they had gained control over Local No. 5 of the New York teachers' union, they were able to do this primarily because the party itself drew from one third to one half of its membership from New York City. With respect to total numbers of teachers, their success, even here, was minimal. When the Communists gained control of Local

---

53. Frank, "Schools and the People's Front," p. 440.
54. Zalmen Slesinger, *Education and the Class Struggle* (New York: Covici Friede, 1937), p. 293.
55. Slesinger, *Education and the Class Struggle,* p. 294.
56. Slesinger, *Education and the Class Struggle,* p. 294.

No. 5, representing approximately 1,200 teachers, there were some 30,000 teachers employed in New York City and more than 850,000 teachers in the nation at large. Even in the teachers' union, the Communists found that they had to fight Dewey, Kilpatrick, Childs, Counts, and others along the way. By 1941, the Committee for Cultural Freedom had taken control of the American Federation of Teachers. Nevertheless, the Communist party did have a limited influence in American education during the thirties and early forties.[57] Earl Browder's "united front," "people's front," and "popular front" were successful in enlisting the support of many American liberals both in and out of education. The strength of the party rested not only on a small, hard-core following but on the support the party could muster from the liberal wing of American political and social life.

In spite of the Nazi-Soviet Pact of 1939, Browder managed to keep enough liberal support so that when the war in Europe closed, the party itself was at peak strength with from 75,000 to 85,000 members.[58] Within the next decade, under cold war pressure, the party lost its liberal support and went into a rapid decline.[59] As the cold war developed, Browder's alliance with American liberalism collapsed. In 1945, Browder lost control of the party. He was charged with bourgeois "revisionism," and the following year, he was expelled from the party. A harder line was demanded by the new Soviet cold war policy. Once again, Moscow's control of the American Communist party was demonstrated.

During the more radical period of the depression and the heyday of American liberalism, the Communists in America reached their greatest influence on the social scene, as well as in the schools. In the more conservative era of the fifties and sixties, extreme right-wing groups demonstrated a greater influence. Just as Dewey, a moderate liberal, found himself being attacked, his ideas distorted, and his character maligned by Communists in an era of liberalism, so Dwight D. Eisenhower, a moderate conservative, found himself being attacked, his ideas distorted, and his character maligned by right-wing groups[60] in an era of conservatism.

The end result of the Communist influence was to confuse, distort, and discredit much of American liberalism. It remains to be seen to what extent the contemporary extreme rightists will confuse, distort, and discredit the conservative tradition. While the Fascists evolved their ideas and support out of the conservative side of the social-political-educational spectrum and the Communists out of the liberal side, both grew in influence, depending on the conditions of the time, and both were equally destructive of what may be very humanitarian causes. Both were radical in the sense that they advocated front organizations and any method which could achieve their particular purpose. The end clearly justifies the means for each group. If myth satisfies the irrational

---

57. For an objective and more extensive account of the Communist influence in the schools, see Iversen, *Communists and the Schools.*
58. See Shannon, *Decline of American Communism,* p. 3.
59. See Shannon, *Decline of American Communism.*
60. See Robert Welch's *The Politician* (Belmont, Mass.: Robert Welch, 1963).

need of the masses in a mass society and if it serves as an efficient vehicle of manipulating the people, then both would use it for their own purposes.

Both totalitarian views conceive of education as a weapon of indoctrination to be wielded by the power elite. In both cases the freedom of students and teachers is lost. Both the Communist and the Fascist were extremely realistic when they recognized the teachers' vulnerability to the vested power interests of society, and when they realized that any effective indoctrination of their values in the school would depend on who controlled the groups controlling the schools.

Both the Communists and the Fascists have raised some fundamental questions with respect to the function of the school and the teacher in modern American society. If education involves nothing more than indoctrination, it logically follows that neither the teacher nor the student can, or even should, be free. As more and more voices in the twentieth-century American pluralistic society have called for indoctrination of the right values in the schools, the battles on the educational frontier have been most often fought over whose values should control. Much less concern has been demonstrated for the need of the schools to maintain an intellectually free environment of inquiry so as to produce free men. The failure of the teachers, their organizations, and the public to face this issue realistically and squarely and reach some consensus as to the rights, freedoms, and responsibilities of the teacher based on the function of the school in developing free men in a free society, in effect, has made the schools and the teachers vulnerable to whatever pressure group happens to mount the strongest attack. American society, it seems, has yet to decide on this issue. If and when it does decide, one might expect to hear arguments such as Lawrence Dennis presented when he suggested that the schools will inevitably express the "will of the dominant element of the elite, whose values are validated by the power to enforce them," and such as those of Earl Browder who asserted that "The school system must itself be revolutionized, before it can become an instrument of revolution—or of any serious social change." One might, however, still hope to hear the argument of a Jefferson who could say: "I know of no safe depository of the ultimate powers of the society but the people themselves; and if we think them not enlightened enough to exercise their control with a wholesome discretion, the remedy is not to take it from them, but to inform their discretion by education."

SUGGESTED READINGS

Beale, Howard K. *Are American Teachers Free?* New York, Charles Scribner's Sons, 1936.

Brameld, Theodore. "Karl Marx and the American Teacher," *The Social Frontier,* II (November 1935).

Browder, Earl. "Education—An Ally in the Workers' Struggle," *The Social Frontier,* I, 4 (January 1935), 22.

Dennis, Lawrence. "Education—The Tool of the Dominant Elite," *The Social Frontier*, I, 4 (January 1935), 14.

———. *The Coming American Fascism.* New York, Harper & Brothers, 1936.

———. *The Dynamics of War and Revolution.* New York, The Weekly Foreign Letter, 1940.

Dewey, John. "The Practical Promise of a Social Point of View," *The Social Frontier*, II (May 1936).

Draper, Theodore. *The Roots of American Communism.* New York, The Viking Press, 1957.

Dunbar, Ernest. "The Plot to Take Over the P.T.A.," *Look*, XXIX, 18 (September 7, 1965).

Frank, Richard. "The Schools and the People's Front," *Communist*, XVI (May 1937), 432.

Gellerman, William. *The American Legion as Educator.* New York, Bureau of Publications, Teachers College, Columbia University, 1938.

Iversen, Robert W. *The Communists and the Schools.* New York, Harcourt, Brace and Company, 1959.

Jones, Richard Seelye. *A History of the American Legion.* Indianapolis, The Bobbs-Merrill Company, Inc., 1946.

Kilpatrick, William H. "High Marxism Defined and Rejected," *The Social Frontier*, II (June 1936), 272.

Marx, Karl. *Capital, The Communist Manifesto, and Other Writings,* ed. Max Eastman. New York, The Modern Library, 1932.

Mosse, George L. *The Culture of Western Europe.* Chicago, Rand McNally & Company, 1961.

Muller, Herbert J. *Issues of Freedom.* New York, Harper & Brothers, 1960.

National Education Association. "The John Birch Society," *Defense Bulletin*, No. 88 (April 1961).

Pareto, Vilfredo. *The Mind and Society,* ed. Arthur Livingston, trans. Andrew Bongiorno and Arthur Livingston. 4 vols. New York, Harcourt, Brace and Company, 1935.

Schickel, Richard. "Marshall McLuhan: Canada's Intellectual Comet," *Harper's Magazine*, November 1963, p. 62.

Shannon, David A. *The Decline of American Communism.* New York, Harcourt, Brace and Company, 1959.

Sherwin, Mark. *The Extremists.* New York, St. Martin's Press, 1963.

Slesinger, Zalmen. *Education and the Class Struggle.* New York, Covici Friede, 1937.

Sorel, Georges. *Reflections on Violence,* trans. T. E. Hulme. New York, Peter Smith, 1935.

St. George, Maximilian John, and Lawrence Dennis. *A Trial on Trial.* Chicago, M. J. St. George, 1946.

CHAPTER 11

War by peaceful means

*If the radiance of a thousand suns
were to burst into the sky,
that would be
the splendor of the Mighty one—*[1]

BHAGAVAD-GITA

After a four-minute run over Hiroshima, the bomb dropped away from the Enola Gay at 0915, August 6, 1945, and the only words a shaken copilot recorded in his flight book were "My God!" In that instant of time, history seemed to stand still, take notice, and then proceed on a new, more treacherous course for all humanity. While some who were there felt themselves to have been present at the dawn of creation, others were equally sure that that same "radiance of a thousand suns" would be present at the end of human history. Was the time, then, 0001 or 2359? No one was certain. What was certain, however, was the fact that, for the first time in history, we held within our grasp the power to destroy the entire human race.

As ten million men and women mentally packed their duffle bags, they, no doubt, dreamed of home and hearth. However, they could never return to the homes they left behind. The world had changed, and most of all they, themselves, had changed with it. The America that marched off to war in 1941 was still, in large part, an immigrant nation, always distrustful and suspicious of its military and the power and mind that went with it. The America that marched home from the war in 1945 was not only more sympathetic toward the military, but it was much more respectful of its' thinking and leadership, and more willing to commit its fortunes and destiny to military direction. The changed attitude on the part of the veterans and their families toward military leadership was a significant ingredient in the complex of circumstances which helped pro-

---

1. Quoted in Robert Jungk, *Brighter than a Thousand Suns* (New York: Harcourt Brace Jovanovich, Inc., 1958).

pel America, in the next four decades, to becoming the leading arms producer and distributor, and the most powerful thermonuclear nation in the world.

The bombing of Hiroshima and Nagasaki not only signaled the birth of the atomic age and the end of World War II, but it also provided the situational context out of which emerged a strange new kind of war, a war carried on by peaceful means, called the *cold war*. More than any other single phenomenon, it was the cold war which profoundly shaped America's political, economic, and educational institutions for the next four decades.

Even as America, with its prewar, antimilitary reflexes still in place, moved to dismantle one of the largest military forces in history, the signs of the cold war began to appear, justifying and rationalizing the need for ever-larger military expenditures. While there were those in San Francisco at the founding of the United Nations who thought they felt the soothing breeze of a world at peace, there were others who stood at Ellis Island and felt the chilling effects of the cold war as they observed the United States Immigration Agency officials speed the entrance of suspected war criminals in exchange for their possible service against the Soviet Union.[2]

The war crimes trials at Nuremberg were prematurely brought to a close in the summer of 1948 under pressure to remobilize Germany for the cold war. The effect of the cold war on those trials was perhaps no better exemplified than when Carl Krauch, "Father of I. G. Auschwitz" Counsel, read into the court record his closing arguments for his client's defense, reminding the court of the fear that Adolf Hitler had of the "Bolshevist menace" and how "right" he was in his policy which was, as Krauch put it, "confirmed by the political situation which has developed in recent months in Europe."[3] Even though the Nuremberg trials came to a close, and many Nazi leaders in both the government and private industry returned to their previous positions of power and authority under the mantle of the cold war, it became increasingly clear that, given the nature and extent of the crime against the Jewish people, no trial, no set of new laws, no judgment at Nuremberg, could close the book on the Holocaust.

As the survivors began their exodus from Europe to form the new state of Israel, the story of what had taken place at Auschwitz, Buchenwald, Dachau, Belsen, and other infamous centers of human degradation began to unfold. The most advanced scientific and cultural nation in the West, a nation that had given the West such great scientists as Albert Einstein and Max Planck, as well as such great humanists as Goethe, Kant, Schelling, and Lessing, now gave the world Adolf Hitler, Heinrich Himmler, the S.S., and the death camps in which some ten million people, of whom more than six million were Jews, were systematically murdered.

Out of those haunting shadows of darkness came, for many, the realization that Western culture had undergone a fundamental break. As George

---

2. See Howard Blum, *Wanted* (New York: Quadrangle/N.Y. Times Book Co., 1977). Also see John Loftus, *The Belarus Secret*, ed. Nathan Miller (New York: Alfred A. Knopf, 1982).

3. Quoted in Joseph Borkin, *The Crime and Punishment of I. G. Farbin* (New York: The Free Press, 1978), p. 149.

Steiner put it, we have lived through "a season in Hell" and passed into a *"post culture"* where we have literally learned to create a Hell on earth for ourselves and our posterity. He said, "In locating Hell above ground, we have passed out of the major order and symmetries of Western civilization."[4] To Steiner and to other thoughtful observers, this was a turning point, a breaking away from the progressive humanizing character of Western culture, toward an ominous new form of barbarism.

The fact that this new barbarism should emerge in one of the major scientific and spiritual leading nations of the West would be seen by some as a clear indicator of deep problems embedded in the very heart of Western culture itself. Some wished to wipe away the stain, and immediately reacted by suggesting that those who ran the camps must have been insane. They were, however, repeatedly proven wrong, as more and more camp commanders turned out to be typical middle-class people who seemed to love their families, who tended their gardens, and who usually appeared as the mainstay of the general culture.[5] There were others who attempted to prove that within the personality structure of most modern individuals is the potential to inflict pain on others readily, especially if requested to do so in the interest of a new cause such as "science."[6] As the guilt seemed to slip from individual to society, and present to past, other observers pointed to the fact that Hitler's S.S. was largely made up of Germany's so-called best, its professional classes trained at the university. It was that class which brought intelligence to the process of exterminating people. What had occurred, then, was not just a fluke of history or the work of an unruly mob, but rather was a planned, legalized program of mass murder carried out by some of the best-educated people in the culture.

The future of Western civilization was indeed open to question. Richard Rubenstein perceptively analyzed the holocaust phenomenon in terms of the larger process of depersonalization of human relationships which had been occurring within modern bureaucratized society. He went on to analyze it in conjunction with the increasing secularization of the culture and the declining respect for human life, all of which made it possible to treat human beings as surplus population, and thereby target them for extermination.[7] The process in Germany had, in fact, begun with the feeble-minded and aged being targeted as a surplus, nonproductive population. The social problem of surplus populations could be easily resolved in the interest of all through mercy killing. The cultural acceptance of legal euthanasia programs was an important step *Into That Darkness.*[8]

As Rubenstein and others analyzed it, the problem lay with the En-

4. George Steiner, *In Bluebeard's Castle: Some Notes Towards the Redefinition of Culture* (New Haven: Yale University Press, 1979), p. 56.

5. Perhaps the best character study along these lines is to be found in Gitta Sereny, *Into That Darkness: From Mercy Killing to Mass Murder* (New York: McGraw-Hill Book Company, 1974).

6. Hans and Michael Eysenck, *Mindwatching* (London: Michael Joseph, 1981), pp. 35-59.

7. Richard L. Rubenstein, *The Cunning of History: Mass Death and the American Future* (New York: Harper & Row, 1975).

8. See, for example, Sereny, *Into That Darkness.*

lightenment ideology which had sustained Western culture, especially American culture, since the eighteenth century. The idea of progress, grounded in science, reason, education, freedom, and the morality of enlightened self-interest, as reflected in the thought of Thomas Jefferson, Horace Mann, John Dewey, and others, became seriously open to question in 1945. Europeans had earlier questioned those values when Ferdinand Brunetière, George Sorel, and Paul Valéry looked into the bloody trenches of World War I and declared the Enlightenment notion of progress dead. Out of that inability to reconstruct the Enlightenment values came the development of an even deeper malaise, which resulted in the search for order through Fascism. In contrast, America maintained its Bellamy-like faith in progress and Enlightenment virtues well into the closing days of World War II. As Hitler assumed power in Germany in 1933, and America suffered from the grips of its worst depression, the American nation, with its Enlightenment faith undaunted, launched the Chicago World's Fair as "A Century of Progress," with its subtitle "Science Explores: Technology Executes: Mankind Conforms."[9]

Not until after World War II did Huxley's *Brave New World* seem to take on real relevance, as Americans became engulfed in reading George Orwell's *1984*. Even Golding's *Lord of the Flies*, based, as it was, on some of Freud's more pessimistic moments, as reflected in *Civilization and Its Discontents*, became a best-seller. Increasingly, America's literary and visual artists began to reflect the theme of a worried future. Tomorrow might not be better than today; it might, in fact, be far worse. Science and social meliorism did not necessarily lead to a better future, but they could lead to a Hiroshima or a death camp. Existential literature and psychology, born in the crucible of war and crisis, became more popular to American readers. Increasingly, Americans appeared less sure of the future and reflected growing signs of disenchantment with a basic Enlightenment philosophy of life which had sustained them since the eighteenth century.

Science was not proving to be the benign beneficiary of humanity that so many had assumed it would be. After the "scientific" experiments in the death camps, people began to doubt, and these doubts only deepened when it was revealed that the United States Public Health Service, from 1932 to 1972, in Macon County, Alabama, had carried on a study of the effects of syphilis on poor blacks locked in poverty. American doctors, employed by the United States government, coldly withheld available, effective treatment to hundreds of blacks for the sole purpose of recording the damage to the brain and vital organs that the disease would produce. As part of the experiment, in the interest of the advancement of "science," the government provided "free" autopsies. Thus, American men and women of science demonstrated that they, too, were just as interested in the pursuit of science as their German counterparts had been in the experiments on Jews in the death camps.[10]

Science and scientific knowledge were clearly not as benign as once be-

---

9. Lewis Mumford, *The Myth of the Machine* (New York: Harcourt Brace Jovanovich, Inc., 1970), p. 213.

10. See James H. Jones, *Bad Blood: The Tuskegee Syphilis Experiment* (New York: The Free Press [Macmillan], 1981).

lieved. Men and women did not appear as rational as once thought, the state as a vehicle of social meliorism was rapidly becoming much more problematic, and public education, as an arm of that state, was not proving to be the workable panacea it was once expected to be. The underlying ethic of enlightened self-interest seemed to work for some, but not for others. Evil, itself, seemed to be more than just ignorance which could be banished by enlightenment. As some Americans began to lose faith in these basic ideological constructs, they also lost faith in their future. Progress no longer seemed possible. The Bellamy-like future to which so many Americans had subscribed at the turn of the century seemed to fade by mid-century, as more and more literary artists saw their future in terms of Huxley's *Brave New World* or Orwell's *1984*.

America had always been an optimistic nation. That optimism was expressed in terms of the Enlightenment, and was sustained in the nineteenth century by the wealth of the frontier and the opportunities it afforded. So, too, was the neo-Enlightenment faith of John Dewey practically sustained by the newly developing educational frontier, as it emerged in the twentieth century. The educational frontier, itself, was realized as a consequence of a growing monopoly capitalism, which provided the surplus wealth necessary to sustain and develop the system. The progressive, liberal regulatory state which emerged by World War I was ideologically sustained by the neo-Enlightenment philosophy of John Dewey, George Herbert Mead, and others. This overall system survived the depression of the 1930's through greater social ameliorative activities on the part of the New Deal. Thus, the idea of progress managed to survive the breadlines and soup kitchens which marked the urban landscape of the 1930's. Although even John Dewey, late in life, began to have some doubts, for most Americans the Enlightenment ideology still remained a viable philosophy by which to live. Not until the post-World War II period did a reconstruction of American philosophy seem not only probable, but eminently desirable.

If the intellectual and social climate seemed to call for a thoroughgoing reconstruction in this nation's thinking, so, too, did the economic system. The monopoly capitalist system which had been nourished under the progressive regulatory state had far outgrown its national boundaries. Some Americans became conscious of this phenomenon as they learned that corporate conglomerates such as General Motors, Ford, and Standard Oil, prior to World War II, were all deeply involved in cartel arrangements which not only produced the motor vehicles, synthetic fuels, and rubber for the creation of the new German military, but had patent agreements which directly interfered with the American war effort.[11] By the end of World War II, the prewar cartel system emerged as the multinational

---

11. See Bradford C. Snell, *American Ground Transport,* presented to the Subcommittee on Antitrust and Monopoly of the Committees on the Judiciary of the U.S. Senate, 93rd Cong., 2nd Sess., Feb. 26, 1974 (Washington, D.C.: U.S. Government Printing Office, 1979). Also see Joseph Borkin, *Crime and Punishment of I. G. Farbin;* and Charles Higham, *Trading with the Enemy: An Exposé of the Nazi-American Money Plot 1933-1949* (New York: Delacorte Press, 1983).

system, a world-wide system of monopoly capitalism which functioned outside of any single national, politically controlling force. Free of such controls, the multinationals readily exploited the national resources of so-called underdeveloped nations, and with equal ease exploited the cheap labor supply of those countries for heavy industrial production, the latter often at the expense of the United States itself.

Economic structures which were first developed on a national level began to appear on an international level. Just as earlier in the century, when big business, labor, government, and banking interests voluntarily came together in the National Civic Federation to help institutionalize the regulatory state in the interests of eliminating "wasteful" competition, so, too, by 1973 the Trilateral Commission was formed, made up of big business, labor, government, and banking interests who voluntarily came together for the purposes of eliminating wasteful competition between three regions of the world: Japan, the United States, and Europe.[12] While the multinationals found the trilateral agreements useful in eliminating wasteful competition and facilitating both production and consumption, they also found the C.I.A. and American military aid equally useful in maintaining the political and social stability necessary to support and sustain their economic investments.[13]

As the cold war began, it was apparent that the economic system had far outgrown the national political system once used to regulate it.[14] It was equally apparent that not only did the neo-Enlightenment ideology of the new liberalism require reconstruction, but what was also needed was a thorough reconstruction of the political system so as to bring the economic system within responsible limits. Thus, as World War II closed and the cold war began, it became clear to most thoughtful observers that America required a thorough, critical reconstruction of its political, economic, and educational institutions if the Enlightenment values were to survive the very real threat of Fascism as a twentieth-century way of life.

As Albert Camus wisely warned, if men and women do not take care, the *Plague* will return. Perceptively, Camus advised his fellows, at the close of the war, that what the world needs is "dialog," really honest dialog. The great tragedy for America—and, indeed, the world—was that just when that dialog was needed most, it was rendered impossible by cold war conditions. A nation under constant threat, real or perceived, was not prepared to question its fundamental beliefs or carry on a sustained dialog long enough to reconstruct its ideology or its institutions. When the issue is portrayed as military survival, all questions quickly tend to be reduced to the simplicity of military solutions. Thus, the cold

---

12. See Michael J. Crozier, Samuel P. Huntington, and Joji Watanuki, *The Crisis of Democracy: Report on the Governability of Democracies to the Trilateral Commission* (New York: New York University Press, 1975).

13. See Noam Chomsky and Edward S. Herman, *The Washington Connection and Third World Fascism* (Boston: South End Press, 1979).

14. For data, see Jill Bullitt and Michael Locker, *CDE Stock Ownership Directory No. 4 Energy* (New York: Corporate Data Exchange, Inc., 1980). Also see Edward Herman, *Corporate Control, Corporate Power* (Cambridge: Cambridge University Press, 1981).

war fears in the four postwar decades seemed to dominate and stifle any possibility for effective reform. In place of reform, floundering institutions tended to be propped up, and only temporary, superficial remedies seemed possible in an increasingly complicated, uncertain world of threat and violence. The great tragedy remained that, under cold war conditions, the reconstruction of American institutions would not be achieved.

REFLECTIONS ON AN EDUCATIONAL PAST

As the war came to a close that September of 1945, Americans looked back over the last half century with a real measure of pride in their accomplishments. They had created the largest mass production, industrial system in the world, and with that system came a mass consumer-oriented society, with a highly sophisticated news and information media and an advertising and entertainment industry which cultivated the "desires," if not the "needs," of the American people. Complementing this vast social and economic system was the development of the largest and most complete public educational system in the world. The growth in this area alone was truly remarkable. In the seventy years between 1870 and 1940, the American population trebled, while the American high school population increased ninety-fold, and the college and university population increased thirty-fold.[15]

While it was in the predominantly rural America of the nineteenth century that the structure of American education, with its public ladder system from the kindergarten, elementary school, high school, and university, emerged, it was not until the development of urban America of the twentieth century that the system was fully populated. The enforcement of child labor laws, combined with the passage of compulsory education laws early in the century, resulted in a massive expansion of elementary and secondary schooling. While, in large measure, the common school was the accomplishment of the nineteenth century, it was the high school that became the dominant institution in the first half of the twentieth century, and the university the dominant educational institutional development in the second half of the century.

With the new wave of immigrants from southern and eastern Europe swelling American urban centers from 1890 to 1910, the pressure for educational reform intensified in the elementary schools. The early pressure on the high school for reform came from a different source. In 1892, the universities and colleges were most interested in the creation of a standard, uniform, academically acceptable college preparatory high school curriculum through which the few expected to attend college might pass. By 1900, still only 10 per cent of American youth, ages fourteen to seventeen, attended a secondary school, and an even smaller number could ever be expected to attend college. Thus, the Committee of Ten (1892), domi-

---

15. Harvard Committee, *General Education in a Free Society* (Cambridge, Mass.: Harvard University Press, 1945), p. 7.

nated by university personnel and chaired by Charles W. Eliot, the president of Harvard, concluded that, within limited options, everyone who attended high schools, whether they intended to go to college or not, should take a similar academic course.[16] The committee still viewed the high school as serving a relatively small population.

By 1913, however, a new NEA committee, the Commission on the Reorganization of Secondary Education, called for fundamental change in educational direction of the high school. This commission was not dominated, as the earlier committee had been, by university personnel, but rather by vocational and social efficiency enthusiasts who came from state educational agencies, colleges of education, and the public schools themselves. David Kingsley chaired the commission and worked under David Snedden in the State Department of Education of Massachusetts.[17] In a speech before the NEA, Kingsley called for an education devoted to more than a vocation. What was needed, he said, was "the adjustment of the individual to life."[18] The commission, under the leadership of this "adjustment to life" curricular enthusiast, worked from 1913 until 1918. The culminating product was the *Cardinal Principles of Secondary Education* (1918).[19] Teachers in training would be required for the next thirty years to commit to memory the following "cardinal principles": (1) health, (2) command of fundamental processes, (3) worthy home-membership, (4) vocation, (5) citizenship, (6) worthy use of leisure time, and (7) ethical character.

The social efficiency and life adjustment mentality of the leading members of the committee was so strong that, in the development of that report, the "command of fundamental processes" was added almost as an afterthought.[20] While the influence of academic, university-based disciplines was present in the 1892 report of the Committee of Ten, it was clearly absent from the 1918 report of the Commission on the Reorganization of Secondary Education. Professors of education and state education personnel, especially those who had extensive backgrounds in the rapidly expanding vocational education field, had assumed their place of influence.

With this commission report came the social efficiency standard against which traditional academic subjects were to be evaluated and dropped from the school. As a result, the subjects most frequently added were commercial studies, social studies, industrial arts, physical and biological sciences, and home economics. The subjects most frequently dropped

16. Edward A. Krug, *The Shaping of the American High School 1880-1920* (Madison: University of Wisconsin Press, 1969), p. 65. The recommended options were labeled *Classical, Latin Scientific, Modern Languages,* and *English* (pp. 61-62).

17. For a detailed discussion of the report, see Krug, *Shaping of the American High School*, pp. 378-406. For an analysis of David Snedden and the social efficiency movement in education, see Walter H. Drost, *David Snedden and Education for Social Efficiency* (Madison: University of Wisconsin Press, 1967).

18. Krug, *Shaping of the American High School*, p. 379.

19. CRSE, *Cardinal Principles of Secondary Education* (U.S. Bureau of Education, Bulletin No. 35, Washington, D.C., 1918).

20. See Krug, *Shaping of the American High School*, pp. 378-406.

were Latin, ancient history, French, and advanced mathematics.[21] From 1910 to 1930, America seemed to have espoused Herbert Spencer, as the efficiency craze swept through its educational institutions.[22] This same kind of practical, efficiency-minded thinking reappeared periodically in American education on the wings of vocational education. It appeared again under the guidance of Charles Prosser in the late 1940's and early 1950's as the "life adjustment" movement, and in the 1970's under the term *career education*.[23]

A common psychology which ran throughout these movements was a Thorndikean connectionist psychology which conceived of learning as a "stamping in" process and that which was to be learned as discrete quantifiable elements. Thorndike had led the attack on the classicist's argument for mental discipline and transfer of training. To the school administrators looking for excuses to drop Latin, Thorndike's arguments appeared "scientifically" persuasive. In retrospect, they appear particularly weak.[24] Nevertheless, the new, vastly expanded American educational system was being reorganized on a business model.[25] With the efficiency measure in hand, Greek disappeared from the public high school curriculum while Latin was greatly reduced.

Latin had been slipping from the high school as a major field of concentration for some time, but after the "cardinal principles" were applied, it went into a steep decline. The loss of Latin meant far more than the loss of a single subject. With it was lost a larger view of what a liberal conception of education meant, which was embodied in the classical tradition, the longest educational tradition in the West. As educators busily created new, more practical life adjustment kinds of courses to meet the presumed needs of immigrant children, Latin declined as a primary course of study, and with it went the classical authors who had been studied.[26] In meeting the needs of individuals and their presumed destinies, "differentiated" curriculums were devised, whereby not only life adjustment vocational courses would be taught, but whole programs were devised which could track youth into the vocational occupation that the newly professionalized guidance personnel would help select.

The tracking structure that emerged in the comprehensive high school served class interest and was determined by controlled vocational choice. In order to help educators to "differentiate" their students on something other than pure class lines, leaders of the testing movement promised a

---

21. Krug, *Shaping of the American High School*, p. 399.

22. See Raymond E. Callahan, *Education and the Cult of Efficiency* (Chicago: University of Chicago Press, 1962). Also see Samuel Haber, *Efficiency and Uplift* (Chicago: University of Chicago Press, 1964).

23. See Joel Spring, *The Sorting Machine* (New York: David McKay, 1976).

24. See Walter B. Kolesnik, *Mental Discipline in Modern Education* (Madison: University of Wisconsin Press, 1958).

25. See David Tyack, *The One Best System* (Cambridge, Mass.: Harvard University Press, 1975). Also see Paul Violas, *The Training of the Urban Working Class* (Chicago: Rand McNally & Co., 1978).

26. Latin as a subject of study because of religious reasons remained somewhat more of a significant course of study in Roman Catholic schools until mid-century. The elite Ivy League prep schools to which the wealthy classes sent their youngsters also maintained the classical curriculum well into the second half of the twentieth century.

"scientific" measurement of differences in terms of both I.Q. and achievement scores.[27] Embedded in those tests to help differentiate students were not only class bias but also ethnic and racial bias as well.[28] The schools would thus "scientifically" track the coal miner's son back to the coal mine and the steel worker's prodigy back to the steel mills. One cannot read the literature of the educational tracking enthusiasts of that period without entertaining the very real possibility that for many immigrant children who, in fact, did achieve a degree of social mobility, it must have been in spite of the schools rather than because of them.

The scientific testing movement that significantly helped structure American education was financed, for the most part, by the philanthropic foundations that had emerged at the turn of the century. Indeed, throughout the twentieth century, every significant reform movement in American public education was funded at some time in its life history by one or more of the private philanthropic foundations. The rise of the large foundations representing the interests of corporate wealth registered an increasingly significant influence over the course of political and educational reform in the twentieth century.[29] This influence was effected through the dissemination of large blocks of funds for research, development, and criticism of educational institutions and their practices. Foundation leaders saw themselves on the cutting edge of reform. As one spokesman for the foundation, Fred M. Hechinger, put it: "The ideal foundation-sponsored enterprise is one that blazes a new trail, thrives for a while on sponsored dollars, gathers momentum, and is quickly taken over as a permanent program by the local board, the state education authority, or a university's own budget."[30] To be sure, not all foundation programs achieved their goals. Some backfired and got out of control, as did the local control experiment at the Ocean Hill-Brownsville district in Brooklyn in the spring of 1968. However, funds were quickly cut off for those kinds of projects. In the first half of the century, the foundations were heavily involved in sponsoring and attempting to shape the direction of black education,[31] medical education,[32] the mental hygiene movement,[33] the testing

27. See Merle Curti, *The Social Ideas of American Educators* (Paterson, N.J.: Littlefield, Adams and Co., 1959), pp. 459-498. Also see Clarence J. Karier, Paul Violas, and Joel Spring, *Roots of Crisis: American Education in the Twentieth Century* (Chicago: Rand McNally & Co., 1973), pp. 108-137.

28. See Clarence J. Karier, *Shaping the American Educational State* (New York: The Free Press [Macmillan], 1975), pp. 127-244.

29. See David W. Eakins, "The Development of Corporate Liberal Policy Research in the United States, 1885-1965" (unpublished Ph.D. diss., University of Wisconsin, 1966). Also see James Weinstein, *The Corporate Ideal in the Liberal State, 1900-1918* (Boston: Beacon Press, 1968).

30. As quoted in Warren Weaver, *U.S. Philanthropic Foundations* (New York: Harper & Row, 1967), p. 245.

31. See James D. Anderson, "Philanthropic Control over Private Black Higher Education," in *Philanthropy and Cultural Imperialism,* Robert F. Arnove (Bloomington: Indiana University Press, 1982).

32. See C. Richard Brown, *Rockefeller Medicine Men: Medicine and Capitalism in America* (Los Angeles: University of California Press, 1979).

33. See Christine M. Shea, "The Ideology of Mental Health and the Emergence of the Therapeutic Liberal State: The American Mental Hygiene Movement 1900-1930," (unpublished Ph.D. diss., University of Illinois, 1980).

movement, the guidance and vocational education movement, as well as the progressive educational movement.[34]

In effect, the rise of foundations to key power positions in policy formation amounted to the development of a fourth branch of government, which effectively represented the interests of American corporate wealth.[35] In retrospect, the concerned voices of the majority of the Industrial Relations Commission investigating the role of foundations in 1914 seemed most prophetic as they warned the nation that "the domination of men in whose hands the final control of a large part of American industry rests is not limited to their employees, but is being rapidly extended to control the education and social service of the nation."[36] Those warnings seemed to fall on deaf ears, as foundations developed as active participants in shaping educational and social policy throughout the century.

The foundations heavily supported the progressive education movement which was led by the Progressive Education Association. While the Association was made up of people holding many different philosophies and psychologies and often could reach consensus only on the fact that the schools needed reforming, they leaned toward a romantic child-centered position.[37] Throughout its history, from 1918 to 1955, the Progressive Education Association reflected a strong middle-class bias, as George S. Counts had charged in his ringing criticism of the Association in his 1932 speech, "Dare Progressive Education Be Progressive?"[38] Although in its early years the Association was dominated by middle-class lay people, in its later years it tended to be dominated by middle-class professors of education. For much of the period from 1920 to 1950 the most influential and dominant center for teacher education in America was Teachers College, Columbia University. Stanwood Cobb, an early lay founder of the Progressive Education Association, once suggested that the professors at Teachers College, Columbia, took the Association "away from them."[39] This feeling was understandable. Teachers College, with its powerful cadre of educators such as John Dewey, William Heard Kilpatrick, John L. Childs, Harold Rugg, George S. Counts, Edward L. Thorndike, and a host of others, in no small measure set the parameters and dominated the education debate through the decades of the progressive years. After World War II, when the Progressive Education Association was caught in a withering cross fire of criticism, their leadership failed to respond adequately, in large part because they were retired or about to retire from Teachers College. Thus, as the Association collapsed in 1955, so, too, did Teachers College, Columbia, lose its grip as the singular, most significant institutional spokesperson for teacher education in America.[40]

---

34. While much of the progressive education movement was supported by foundations, they also paid for the research and writing of its history. For one such history, see Lawrence A. Cremin, *The Transformation of the School* (New York: Alfred A. Knopf, 1961).

35. See Karier et al., *Roots of Crisis,* p. 110.

36. As quoted in John Lankford, *Congress and the Foundations in the Twentieth Century* (River Falls: Wisconsin State University, 1964), p. 31.

37. See Cremin, *Transformation of the School.*

38. See p. 241.

39. See Cremin, *Transformation of the School,* p. 250.

40. Teachers College also had its satellites during the P.E.A.'s later days. One such in-

While the Progressive Education Association had a number of educational reform projects, most of which reflected interests in the experimental private elementary schools and only to a limited extent public elementary schools, perhaps the most significant project developed was that directed at the secondary schools, called the *Eight Year Study*.[41] This project was a massive experimental attempt to demonstrate the effect of progressive educational reform on the secondary schools, and the subsequent effect those reforms had on students as they proceeded through their college careers. The study was financed by the Carnegie Foundation and the General Education Board at costs running into the millions of dollars. The project, which ran from 1932 to 1940, was successful for the most part. In general, it demonstrated that students in the experimental schools did as well academically as those in the more traditional schools, while at the same time the students from the experimental schools had developed stronger leadership qualities. The report was published in the midst of the war (1942) and, therefore, failed to receive the attention it deserved. By the end of World War II the Association, though showing signs of age, was, in fact, still very much alive.

EDUCATION AT THE CROSSROADS

The *Eight Year Study* seemed to indicate that the traditional secondary school curriculum did not make much difference, at least in terms of college success. "Life adjustment" educators continued to press for a more trivialized course of study, while others called for the reconstruction of both secondary and higher educational curricula. The war in Europe was not quite over when James B. Conant, as president of Harvard University, penned the introduction to *General Education in a Free Society*. The report came to represent one of America's most serious attempts to find an adequate replacement for the classical curriculum.

Although the loss of the classical curriculum had important implications for the secondary schools, it had even more significance for the liberal arts college. Much as Irving Babbitt had predicted in *Literature and the American College* (1908), once the classical languages disappeared, the very existence of a liberal education would be in doubt. Liberal education was threatened not only by students heavily saturated in Rousseauistic romanticism, but, more importantly, by the Baconian "scientism" and its narrow-minded research orientation that increasingly pervaded the thinking of the younger liberal arts professors. Nevertheless, the loss of the classical curriculum went largely unnoticed for decades, because the teaching staff of both the colleges and the secondary schools still tended to be teachers who had come out of that tradition and who carried with them educational values and sympathies reflecting a substantial level of literary expectations.

---

stitution was the University of Illinois, which published the P.E.A.'s *Journal* in its declining years. Thus, Arthur Bestor appropriately targeted the College of Education at the University of Illinois, along with Teachers College, Columbia, for his criticism.

41. See Wilford M. Aikin, *The Story of the Eight Year Study* (New York: McGraw-Hill, 1942).

That educational matrix was gradually lost in the next generation of professors and teachers. America had been living on the educational capital of its past. The pragmatic Harvard president James B. Conant took note of this problem when, at the Harvard Tercentenary in 1936, he said:

The older educational discipline, whether we like it or not, was disrupted before any of us were born. It was based on the study of the classics and mathematics; it provided a common background which steadied the thinking of all educated men. We cannot bring back this system if we would, but we must find its modern equivalent.[42]

With these thoughts in mind, Conant appointed a committee of Harvard professors to find the "modern equivalent" for what was the older classical course. After lengthy deliberations, the committee outlined what they believed was the necessary goal of a general education, or "liberal education," at the college level in terms of the humanities, the social sciences, science, and mathematics, and how these areas might be utilized in secondary school education. The authors went on to note that, in the past, it had been necessary to "surrender" the training of teachers to new and "far less well-equipped institutions," because the colleges failed to introduce changes in their curriculum and thus assume leadership in teacher preparation. As a consequence, the colleges lost touch with the schools.[43] The cadre of teachers trained in teachers colleges and normal schools, they believed, were inadequately trained in subjects which they were required to teach. This, coupled with the low salaries which pushed the intellectually abler persons away from teaching, compounded the problem of teacher preparation for the schools. The committee misjudged the future as they looked for the resolution of this problem by hoping that the expansion in postwar industry would not be as competitive as it had been in the past and, therefore, abler persons could be expected to enter the teaching force. They could not have been further from the mark of what transpired than when they hoped that the "peculiar violence of expansion in commerce and industry which took able people from it during the last half-century will be less strong in the next."[44]

While the committee failed to sense the kind of economic growth the country was about to undergo in the coming decades, they also missed what would become a growing middle-class ground swell for a college education. In many ways, they continued to think, as did most college administrators, in terms of a college population limited to 20 to 25 per cent of the overall population. Most significant of all, however, was that while the committee attempted to define what it meant by a liberal education, and to make explicit its curricular significance for the secondary schools and for the training of secondary school teachers, it failed to meet the problem of the education of the college professor. Babbitt's point, with

---

42. David T. W. McCord, *Notes on the Harvard Tercentenary* (Cambridge, Mass.: Harvard University Press, 1936), p. 213.
43. Harvard Committee, *General Education in a Free Society*, p. 23.
44. Harvard Committee, *General Education in a Free Society*, p. 25.

respect to the training of a Ph.D. research specialist as fundamentally dysfunctional when it came to preparing college professors to teach in a liberal arts-oriented college, remained unanswered.[45] While the committee did an admirable job in analyzing the relationship of specialization versus generalization, and in determining that of which a liberal arts college program might consist, it did not resolve the critical problem of the training of professors for service in such a college. The problem still remained unsolved. As a consequence, the liberal arts college continued to be fractionalized by a scientism pervading the humanities and social sciences, which by 1980 made Irving Babbitt's analysis, in retrospect, appear prophetic.

While *General Education in a Free Society* was being written, another somewhat wider cross section of educators, including James B. Conant, met as members of the Educational Policies Commission of the National Education Association and issued their report on *Education for All American Youth*.[46] In this document, the commission repeatedly made the point that the great bulk of American youth will never go to college and, under such circumstances, will need an education which adjusts them to the world of work and community values. Furthermore, the commission seemed to adopt much of what had been expressed in the progressive education literature of the 1930's. The commission also embraced the social efficiency, life adjustment thrust of men like George D. Strayer and others on the commission, whose careers went back to the days when the "cardinal principles" were being implemented. James B. Conant endorsed both *General Education in a Free Society*, for the academically talented, and *Education for All American Youth*, for the less-than-talented masses of people. Taken together, these documents fit his vision of the ideal meritocratic society.[47]

The overall thrust of *Education for All American Youth* was in the direction of life adjustment education. One of the strongest, best-organized groups that nourished this thrust was the vocational education group. These educators were not only the key participants who helped reorganize secondary education along the lines of the "cardinal principles," but also the major lobbyists to ensure the passage of the Smith-Hughes Bill early in the century.

One of the leaders in that political action was Dr. Charles Prosser. As a lobbyist for the National Society for the Promotion of Industrial Education, Prosser, along with a large cadre of teachers, administrators, and professors, cultivated the idea that what the bulk of the American people needed was a simple, practical, "how to"-oriented curriculum which would presumably adjust one for life. For the most part, the "life adjustment" educators reduced education to a narrow process of training the masses in terms of specific, elementary behaviors which they believed were

---

45. This issue would remain the most important question regarding the survival of a liberal arts college, yet it was seldom confronted. Jacques Barzun discussed its elements in *Teacher in America* (Boston: Little, Brown and Co., 1945).

46. Educational Policies Commission, *Education for All American Youth* (Washington, D.C.: National Education Association, 1944).

47. See Charles Burgess and Merle L. Borrowman, *What Doctrines to Embrace* (Glenview, Ill.: Scott, Foresman and Co., 1969), pp. 128-130.

essential for a person to be adjusted to modern living.[48] On June 1, 1945, at a conference sponsored by the United States Office of Education, entitled "Vocational Education in the Years Ahead," Prosser summarized the work of the conference and laid out the vocational educators' agenda for the future. As he put it,

. . . the vocational school of a community will be able better to prepare 20 percent of the youth of secondary school age for entrance upon desirable skilled occupations; and that the high school will continue to prepare another 20 percent for entrance to college. We do not believe that the remaining 60 percent of our youth of secondary school age will receive the life adjustment training they need and to which they are entitled as American citizens—unless and until the administrators of public education with the assistance of the vocational education leaders formulate a similar program for this group.[49]

While vocational educators looked to the postwar future and thought about how they might prepare 60 per cent of American youth for life adjustment, few had bothered to look over their shoulders and note that Robert M. Hutchins, just a year earlier, had given a devastating critique of vocational education, the implications of which did not call for an expansion of vocational education but did call for a very severe restriction of it. Hutchins minced no words as he pointed out:

In an age in which industrial management has simplified most industrial operations to the point where they can be performed by twelve-year-olds, vocational training is a fraud. In a period of unemployment, it becomes a most vicious kind of fraud. In the depression year of 1934, 150,000 students finished their schooling in bookkeeping, and 36,000 new bookkeepers were hired. In the same year 100,000 students were trained as Diesel engineers and 5,000 new men were added to the 20,000 employed in the industry. The American Youth Commission found in 1940 that more than two thirds of all occupations required nothing beyond elementary education, and that workers without any vocational training reached normal production on 70 percent of all jobs in less than a week.[50]

While attacking vocational education as a fraud, Hutchins also challenged the larger educational myth that unemployment was somehow caused by the lack of training in a field. This myth reappeared throughout the postwar period whenever unemployment surfaced as a major social problem. Hutchins' voice, however, tended to fall on deaf ears as more and more

---

48. See Spring, *Sorting Machine*, p. 19. For an analysis of the life adjustment movement in the context of citizenship education, see Clarence J. Karier, *Education of the American Citizen: An Historical Critique* (Philadelphia: Research for Better Schools, Inc., 1978). For one example of a number of "how to" trivialized life adjustment citizenship textbooks used in the public schools at that time, see E. Crawford, E. G. Cooley, C. C. Trillingham, and E. Stoop, *Living Your Life* (Boston: Heath and Co., 1953).

49. As quoted in part by Cremin, *Transformation of the School*, p. 334.

50. Robert M. Hutchins, "The Threat to American Education," *Collier's* (Dec. 16, 1944), 20. Hutchins' criticism in 1944 is not far removed from Ivan E. Berg's later analysis in *Education and Jobs: The Great Training Robbery* (New York: Praeger, 1970).

school leaders began extolling the life adjustment slogans as well as the progressive cliches drawn from *Education for All American Youth*.

In many ways the educators who espoused the new social efficiency, progressive ideology, were at the opposite ends of the educational spectrum from those professors who authored *General Education in a Free Society*. They were similar, however, in two respects. First, they both clearly misjudged the intellectual capabilities of the greater mass of the American people; and second, they both clearly failed to appreciate the growth of the middle class and the growing desire of that class for a college education. Whether it was the authors of *Education for All American Youth*, those of *General Education in a Free Society*, or Charles Prosser leading the school people in their "life adjustment movement," all made the same mistake of assuming that in the postwar period, approximately the same number of people would attend college as had in the past. They made that mistake on the very eve of the most significant expansion of American higher education in the twentieth century.

THE G.I. BILL

Little more than two weeks after American troops swarmed ashore on the beaches of Normandy, President Roosevelt signed into law the Serviceman's Readjustment Act of 1944, known as the G.I. Bill. The bill was a product of a combination of efforts on the part of veterans' organizations, Franklin Delano Roosevelt and his National Resources Planning Board, and the Congress. In its initial form the bill contained provisions for preferential treatment for veterans in terms of job placement, mortgage guarantees, unemployment benefits, and educational benefits. The education package, though limited, still included provisions for a variety of vocational training programs, as well as for college. It provided government subsidies for tuition and fees, books, and cost-of-living allowances for all who were eligible. The original bill contained provisions which restricted it to only one year of educational benefits and made only veterans under age twenty-five eligible for such benefits. Through the efforts of the American Legion and other veterans' organizations, these restrictions were quickly removed, making virtually all veterans eligible for four years of educational benefits.

The bill was originally thought to be an anti-depression bill which would channel veterans back into suitable civilian occupations. Again, under pressure of the American Legion, it developed into something more. As early as the spring of 1942, President Roosevelt had charged the National Resources Planning Board with the task of postwar planning. At the time, the war was still in its early stages; therefore, the president advised the committee to assume a low public profile. Thus, the committee proceeded with its work with little publicity long before the outcome of the war was even assured.[51] From the outset, the National Resources Plan-

---

51. David R. B. Ross, *Preparing for Ulysses: Politics and Veterans During World War II* (New York: Columbia University Press, 1969), p. 53.

ning Board was concerned about what might happen if the veteran returned to a society in economic depression. The committee recalled the experience of the twenty-year-bonus battle and the unruly march on Washington. More importantly, they noted that most revolutions in the twentieth century, whether Bolshevist or Fascist, were led by unemployed, disgruntled veterans. There was a very distinct fear that a veteran who returned from the battlefront to the breadline might turn to street fighting in desperation, as his counterparts had done in Germany, Italy, and Russia after World War I.

The Great Depression was fresh on the committee's mind. The year before America entered the war in 1940, the unemployment rate was still 15 per cent.[52] Faced with as many as fifteen million returning veterans, economists were predicting a steep depression with as many as eight or nine million people unemployed.[53] As the law evolved, the committee determined that it was clearly going to be a manpower channeling bill in which educational benefits were to be restricted to just those occupations in need of manpower. As one committee put it: "The primary purpose of any educational arrangements which we may recommend should be to meet a national need. . . . We have regarded any benefits which may be extended to individuals in the process as incidental."[54] While the committee saw the bill as a manpower control bill, the American Legion saw it as a veterans' bonus bill. Under the circumstances, the Legion pressured for the elimination of the key provision which would restrict support to only those occupations in need of manpower. The Legion also pushed to make every veteran eligible for four years of college training if they could get themselves admitted to a college. Thus, under political pressure, the G.I. Bill emerged more as a bonus bill than as the manpower channeling bill which was originally intended.

While the National Resources Planning Board was reporting to the president, the War Department surveyed American troops to determine how many might attend college on return to civilian life. All surveys missed the mark by wide margins.[55] By the summer of 1945, colleges were alerted and the American Council on Education prepared special guidelines for college administrators. Leading private college presidents were skeptical and critical of the final legislation.

James B. Conant, president of Harvard University, found the original act 'distressing' because it failed 'to distinguish between those who can profit most by advanced education and those who cannot.' His ideal G.I. Bill would have financed the education 'of a carefully selected number of returned veterans.' Reflecting a distrust of colleges and universities to maintain academic standards, Conant feared that because of the G.I. Bill 'we may find the least capable among the war generation . . . flooding the facilities for advanced education.'[56]

---

52. Keith W. Olson, *The G.I. Bill, the Veterans and the Colleges* (Lexington: University Press of Kentucky, 1974), p. 3.

53. Olson, *G.I. Bill, the Veterans and the Colleges*, p. 8.

54. Report of the Armed Forces Committee on Post-War Educational Opportunities for Service Personnel, July 1943, in Olson, *G.I. Bill, the Veterans and the Colleges*, p. xi.

55. Olson, *G.I. Bill, the Veterans and the Colleges*, pp. 29-30.

56. Olson, *G.I. Bill, the Veterans and the Colleges*, p. 33.

In a similar vein, Robert M. Hutchins, president of the University of Chicago, in a *Collier's* magazine article, found the proposed bill to be a "threat to American education."[57] Hutchins reiterated his belief in the need to develop a liberal education for all men and women in a democratic society. His democratic paideia, however, had not yet arrived. As he put it, "If every citizen is to be free, every citizen must be educated for freedom. We must recognize, however, that the educational system has not yet worked out this education."[58] Hutchins' ideas about the relationship of a liberal education and a free society were correct. His logic was flawless. Nevertheless, at the crucial point of implementation, he, like so many other classical liberals, seemed to falter. The educational system was not yet ready to deliver an education appropriate for free men and women.

Hutchins correctly noted, however, that higher education had been reserved mostly for the rich: "As for the higher levels of education, they remained the preserve of the relatively rich. Before the war only 14 percent of young people of college-age were in college. Repeated studies have shown that these students were not the best; they were the richest."[59] While he liked the principle implicit in the proposed legislation, that "there must be no relation between the education of a citizen and the income of his parents,"[60] he feared that when the veterans applied for college admission, the colleges would perpetrate the same educational fraud on the veterans as the vocational educators had perpetrated on high school youth. Colleges and universities might further succumb to the lure of money and higher enrollments, and thereby would not keep out "unqualified veterans," nor would they be inclined to "expel those who fail." Under such circumstances, Hutchins believed colleges and universities would become "educational hobo jungles" for unemployed veterans unable to find work. On this point both Hutchins and Conant agreed. The two men felt the colleges would not be selective enough. In spite of all the empirical evidence, then, which indicated that college entrances had not been based on merit but rather on wealth, when push came to shove and veterans already were at the gates of Harvard and Chicago, both presidents returned to the principle of allowing admission to only those the universities and colleges were sure might "profit" from the experience.

Fortunately for many veterans, the Congress failed to follow the advice of such leaders and, while enthralled in the euphoric climate of victory, proceeded to liberalize educational benefits for returning veterans. The G.I. Bill made it possible for millions to attend college who under ordinary circumstances would not have had the financial wherewithal to do so. The longstanding financial barrier to a college education had been breached. Thus, one of the most significant educational experiments in American education began to unfold. Within the next four years, two major myths which had dominated the thinking of American leaders in higher education and in the area of general social policy were exposed. The first was the notion that only a few people were interested in attending college and

---

57. See Hutchins, "Threat to American Education," pp. 20-21.
58. Hutchins, "Threat to American Education," p. 21.
59. Hutchins, "Threat to American Education," p. 20.
60. Hutchins, "Threat to American Education," p. 20.

competing for the higher-level occupations; and the second was that only a few could be expected to profit from what the colleges had to offer. Higher education had been, as Hutchins remarked, the "preserve of the relatively rich." Most of the government planners, university and college presidents, public school people, and select citizens who served on educational policy committees clearly misjudged the desire of the growing middle class for a higher level of education. Of the sixteen million veterans eligible for the G.I. Bill, as many as eight million availed themselves of the scholastic advantages of Public Law 346 and inundated the colleges, universities, high schools, and trade schools.[61] Many colleges doubled their enrollments as the nation's institutions of higher education quickly accommodated a 75 per cent increase over their prewar enrollment.[62] Some fourteen billion dollars were spent on this most ambitious program.[63] The nation profited immeasurably from such a vastly expanded, well-trained manpower pool.

While the first myth that only a few were interested in higher education was effectively exposed, the second, and perhaps the more significant, myth—that only relatively few could "profit" from what the colleges had to offer—was also disproved. As veterans took up their academic pursuits, they outdistanced their younger classmates academically and quickly came to dominate the honor rolls at most colleges. Survey after survey revealed the same thing. Veterans were not only profiting from what the colleges had to offer, but they were generally pushing college standards upward. Within a few years, Conant and Hutchins reversed themselves and went along with the general conclusion that the class of 1949, made up of approximately 70 per cent veterans, was one of the "best." At least 20 per cent of those veterans would not have attended college without the help of the G.I. Bill.[64] Thus, the myth that what the colleges had to offer was appropriate for only the few was temporarily, at least, laid to rest.

The interesting thing about this experiment is that it took place so fast. Colleges did not have the time to adjust the curriculum to "meet the needs of the veterans," because within a year over a million veterans were enrolled. To be sure, the colleges met the problem with larger classes, flexible schedules, early morning and evening classes, as well as pressing into teaching positions less than fully trained instructors. There was not enough time, however, to reorganize the college curriculum in any fundamental way as, indeed, the high school had done earlier in the century when it, too, faced a new and different population. Veterans in this sense were lucky. They were not faced with a watered-down curriculum constructed out of someone's estimate of their presumed abilities and contrived needs, but rather, as a consequence, the colleges attempted to deliver that which existed as the traditional intellectual fare. Thus, veterans profited from—and, indeed, proved themselves against—the standard existing curriculum.

The greater maturity of the veterans had its effect on campus life, not only academically, but socially as well. As the hazing and "Animal House"

---

61. See "The G.I. Bill: In 10 Years, 8 Million," *Newsweek* (Oct. 4, 1954).
62. Olson, *G.I. Bill, the Veterans and the Colleges*, p. 103.
63. See "Beginning of the End," *Time* (July 30, 1951).
64. Olson, *G.I. Bill, the Veterans and the Colleges*, p. 47.

antics temporarily disappeared from campus, marriage and children became an accepted part of student life. The overall tone of the campus became more serious and academically competitive. As Dean Wilbur J. Bender of Harvard complained, "There is a kind of unhealthy determination to get ahead, a grim competitive spirit, an emphasis on individual careerism and success which is disturbing. . . . the lights are burning very late and there is not much leisurely talk or fellowship or group spirit."[65]

Fortune magazine, in its survey of the class of 1949, picked up on these characteristics and suggested that this veteran-dominated class was the "soberest, most trained graduating class in U.S. history."[66] It went on to suggest further that this was a group which looked to big business for security, and characterized the class as a cautious generation which turned its back on speculative ventures.[67] Most members of this class wanted to join big corporations and not risk themselves in small business enterprises. They would, the magazine insisted, become great "technicians— not owners." Perceptively, the survey found that "above everything else security has become the great goal."[68] Having served in a large military and having been educated in large universities, the veterans tended to seek out employment with the large corporations. They had learned to function well within large institutions, and that satisfied their need for security. This quest for security was ultimately reflected in the suburban life-style they adopted and the political and social events they tended to support in the postwar period.

Although the G.I. Bill started out as a manpower control bill to avoid a postwar depression, it quickly turned into a veterans' bonus bill. Even though the bulk of the government expenditures for the bill went for educational purposes, it also included mortgage guarantees by the Veterans Administration for new housing, which spurred the development of the suburbs at the expense of the cities. This bill had long-range social consequences as well. Just as the veterans carried new attitudes toward military life into the cold war period, and their search for security underwrote a growing conservative political future, so, too, did their experience in higher education have a much longer-reaching impact than simply achieving a higher standard of living through occupational mobility. Having been to college and settled into newly built suburbs, these veterans reared their families with the very real expectation that their children, too, would go to college. It was the veterans' children who would burst the seams of the colleges in the 1960's. The veterans' college careers were the beginning of a rapidly expanding role for the colleges and universities. It was also their children who would be threatened by service in Vietnam and their children who would lead the college protest against the Vietnam War.

If the G.I. Bill was so successful, one wonders why it was not permanently institutionalized, at least for those who served in peacetime military service. When Congress considered such proposals in the 1950's, the

---

65. "G.I. Bill: In 10 Years, 8 Million."
66. "The Class of '49," *Fortune* (June 1949), 84.
67. "The Class of '49," 84.
68. "The Class of '49," 85.

political circumstances that propelled the earlier bill no longer existed. The major veterans' organizations continued to see the G.I. Bill as a bonus bill for participation in war. They did not view it as a bonus for service in the peacetime armed forces. Under the circumstances, the veterans' associations did not support it. Pentagon officials testified to the effect that a peacetime G.I. Bill would detract from the efforts of the military to keep career personnel in service. Finally, the older elite values of college and university administrators reappeared as they, too, testified against the bill. Elite values, especially in higher education, do not die easily. When the Korean War Bill came up for consideration, it was higher education officials who testified against it.

Despite the almost unanimous conclusions of studies that documented the superiority of veterans over nonveteran academic achievement, the nation's 'college groups and college administrators' consistently felt that 'many veterans' had enrolled in college 'for the purpose of securing subsistence payments, rather than a primary interest in education,' and for this reason the academic community favored less generous benefits for the Korean veterans.[69]

In retrospect, it is clear that college administrators and government planners rather consistently misjudged the veterans' desire for an education, as they did their academic ability. In the same vein, the government military planners misjudged the lack of desire of Americans to maintain a large military establishment. Americans were still not ready to accept the idea of a large standing militia. The public outcry that overwhelmed Congress and the president to "bring the boys back home" reflected the fact that America, in spite of four years of war, was still not a militarized nation. It was not prepared to make the sacrifices that would be required of it to maintain a large military force around the world. As the demobilization moved with breakneck speed, Admiral Chester Nimitz publicly complained, "Less than five months after the defeat of Japan, your Navy has not the strength in ships and personnel to carry on a major military operation."[70] General Eisenhower testified before a Senate Committee, "I am frank to say that I had never anticipated this emotional wave [to get men out of the Army] would reach proportions of near-hysteria."[71]

While President Harry S. Truman blamed Congress and the press, others, such as Secretary of the Navy James V. Forrestal, saw the country's lack of militarism as a Communist conspiracy. The Russians must have been amazed as they watched the most powerful nation in the world dismantling its armed forces. Most commentators, however, had forgotten the strong overall prewar American antagonism toward a standing militia which was embodied in its large immigrant population, many of whom had left their native lands to escape military service. Peace to that population, by and large, meant a world in which the military was severely restricted.

---

69. Olson, *G.I. Bill, the Veterans and the Colleges,* p. 103. Quoted from 82nd Cong., 2nd Sess., H.R. 1375, p. 79.

70. Ross, *Preparing for Ulysses,* p. 187.

71. Ross, *Preparing for Ulysses,* pp. 186-187.

The war, however, had changed the attitude of that population's sons and daughters. While not yet willing to accept for themselves the notion that peace could be maintained through force, as all militarists in the past have maintained, they were highly respectful of military leadership and counsel. It was this attitude that helped underwrite the cold war, which began almost immediately after the close of World War II. Within a short period, the general population came to accept the idea of peace through military force. The basic principle of the cold war—arms for peace—was reflected by President Truman when, only two months after the peace treaty was signed, he warned, "At the rate we are demobilizing troops, in a very short time we will have no means with which to enforce our demands—a just and fair peace—and unless we have that means we are heading directly for a third world war."[72]

We were "heading" into a third world war, a war by other means called the cold war. For the next forty years, America's foreign policy and its internal, political, social, and educational developments were locked into that war. In this strange new war America turned to its military men, such as General George C. Marshall, General Douglas MacArthur, and General Dwight D. Eisenhower, for leadership. As the Russian armies remained in place in the Balkans, East Germany, and the Baltic states, and Winston Churchill gave his Fulton, Missouri, speech in which he talked about an "Iron Curtain" descending over Eastern Europe, the Chinese Communists were winning their revolution in China. American veterans went to college and settled into the suburbs as the country was prepared for a new red scare.

THE RED SCARE A SECOND TIME

The first red scare occurred when a Bolshevik party of 11,000 succeeded in taking control of Russia in 1918. The American nation reacted to that event by working itself into a state of hysterical fear. Not until 1920, when the attorney general ordered sweeping dragnet-type raids on innocent American citizens, did the hysteria seem to subside. The fear remained, however. Throughout the 1920's, 1930's, and 1940's, the fear of Communism was a consistent theme reflected in the hundreds of groups who worked to combat the Communist influence in education.[73] Throughout this period the Communist party remained small, reaching its peak membership of 80,000 in 1944.[74]

During the 1930's, under Earl Browder, the Party developed its "popular front" against Fascism, in which it aligned itself with liberal organizations and movements to strengthen the cause against Fascism. As noted in Chapter Ten, the Communists were never very strong in American educa-

---

72. Ross, *Preparing for Ulysses,* p. 187.

73. See Howard K. Beale, *Are American Teachers Free?* (New York: Scribner's and Sons, 1936). Also see Paul Violas, "Fear and the Constraints on Academic Freedom of Public School Teachers, 1930-1960," *Educational Theory,* XXI (Winter 1971), 70-80.

74. Fred J. Cook, *The Nightmare Decade: The Life and Times of Senator Joe McCarthy* (New York: Random House, 1971), p. 24.

tion. They did not view the schools as a vehicle of revolution; nevertheless, by the mid-1930's they had taken control of Local #5 of the American Federation of Teachers in New York City.[75] By 1939, John Dewey, George S. Counts, Sidney Hook, and others organized the Committee for Cultural Freedom to break the Communist influence. By 1940, after a prolonged, bitter battle, the committee had broken the Communist influence with the election of George S. Counts to the presidency of the Federation.[76] One of the younger leaders in this battle was the ex-Marxist-turned-liberal, Sidney Hook.

It was not the conservatives, as one might expect, but the liberals who stopped the Communist influence in the American Federation of Teachers. Long before Senator Joseph McCarthy appeared on the scene, Sidney Hook, in "Academic Freedom and 'The Trojan Horse' in American Education" (1939), sketched out themes which would become commonplace in the cold war decades ahead. We must, he insisted, expose the dangers of Communists and "fellow-travelers" within academia through a concentrated effort for "public investigations" which turn "the searchlights of pitiless publicity and analysis upon it, [so that] we can compel every dark figure lurking in its shadows to emerge into the light, and fight for his ideas in the open."[77] Hook made the case for guilt by association and trial by "pitiless publicity" through "public investigations" well before McCarthy launched his program. It was Hook who effectively led the anti-Communist campaign in American education throughout the development of the cold war. By mid-century, Hook, along with others, had persuaded the Educational Policies Commission, the National Education Association, the American Federation of Teachers, and the Association of American University Presidents that membership in the Communist party constituted *prima facie* evidence for dismissal from teaching. In contrast, the American Association of University Professors rejected the assumption of guilt by association. Not until 1967, in *Keyishian* v. *Board of Regents*, did the United States Supreme Court declare this practice unconstitutional.

By 1951, Sidney Hook helped reorganize the Committee for Cultural Freedom into the American Committee for Cultural Freedom. With Hook as its first president, the organization became a subsidiary of the Central Intelligence Agency-sponsored Congress for Cultural Freedom.[78] Deeply involved in the cold war, he attempted to mobilize the professional educators against the dangers which "lurked from within." As an outspoken anti-Communist, Hook complained about the "cultural vigilantism" that was sweeping the nation, and felt that Senator McCarthy was weakening the anti-Communist cause through his broad attacks. Hook specifically

75. See Chapter Ten.

76. Robert W. Iversen, *The Communists and the Schools* (New York: Harcourt, Brace and Co., 1959), p. 202.

77. Sidney Hook, "Academic Freedom and 'The Trojan Horse' in American Education," *American Association of University Professors Bulletin* (Dec. 1939), 555. Also see Karier, *Shaping the American Educational State*, p. 80.

78. See Christopher Lasch, "The Cultural Cold War," in *Toward a New Past*, Barton J. Bernstein (New York: Pantheon Books, 1968).

complained of such harm when McCarthy attacked the Voice of America.[79] He believed that it was up to the organized professional expert to take charge and eliminate the Communist threat from within. In numerous speeches and articles, Hook tirelessly argued that Communists were unfit to teach at any level in American schools, and he always insisted that it was the professionals' responsibility to clean their own house. However, when faculty were called to testify before congressional committees and exercised their right against self-incrimination, supposedly guaranteed them by the Fifth Amendment, he said:

> It is morally and professionally inadmissible to refuse to answer questions relevant to one's educational fitness and integrity on the ground that a truthful answer would be self-incriminating. Such a refusal should be construed as presumptive evidence of unfitness, final determination to be left to faculty committees elected for that purpose.[80]

Thus, Hook advocated the firing of a professor for the exercise of his constitutional rights. However, neither Hook nor McCarthy invented the idea of guilt by association or the terms *fellow travelers* or *Fifth Amendment Communist*. This practice and terminology was well in place when Representative Martin Dies headed the House Un-American Activities Committee in the 1930's.

Much of the character of the second red scare, which seemed to burst forth in what has been labeled the "nightmare decade," had been brewing in the closing years of the New Deal. Immediately after the war, the New Deal suffered its final blow with the 1946 election of the Eightieth Congress, celebrated as the most conservative Congress in twenty years. That Congress included Senator Joseph McCarthy. In the context of a dying New Deal administration, the House Un-American Activities Committee intensified its investigations of the possible Communist infiltration into the cultural areas of the theater, radio, and movie industries. The fear of possible investigations by the House Un-American Activities Committee set local and state authorities to adopt their own security laws and to develop their own lists of subversive organizations. At the national level, democrats such as Senators Hubert Humphrey and Paul H. Douglas got on the bandwagon and introduced a bill to outlaw the Communist party.[81] President Truman issued Executive Order 9835 (March 12, 1947) in order to, as he said, "take the ball away" from Parnell Thomas, then head of the House Un-American Activities Committee.[82] Truman's loyalty order provided

---

79. See Sidney Hook's letter to the *New York Times*, May 8, 1953. For the relationship between the C.I.A. and the very significant role the Voice of America played in the maintenance of the cold war, see Erik Barnouw, *The Image Empire*, vol. III (New York: Oxford University Press, 1970).

80. Sidney Hook, *Common Sense and the Fifth Amendment* (New York: Criterion, 1957), p. 90.

81. Cook, *Nightmare Decade*, p. 18.

82. Cook, *Nightmare Decade*, p. 64.

. . . as one standard for dismissal 'membership in, association with, or sympathetic affiliation with any . . . organization, movement, group or combination of persons, designated by the Attorney General as . . . subversive.' Even a 'sympathetic affiliation,' whatever that might be, with a 'combination of persons,' whatever that might be, was enough to make a man suspect.[83]

Thus, the full weight of the executive branch of government, while embracing the principle of guilt by association and disregarding the individual's Fifth and Sixth Amendment rights, was used to jeopardize the lives of its citizens in the interests of national security. Hundreds of thousands of people who participated in liberal left causes in which Communists had participated in the 1930's "popular front" now stood threatened. Their jobs in and out of government were jeopardized as informal black listing became commonplace. The liberal left was now clearly open to attack with impunity by the conservative Congress.

For a decade, the fears which gripped so many Americans were both real and imaginary. While the internal fear of subversion was no doubt inflated, the fear of having one's career destroyed at the hands of the House Un-American Activities Committee was real enough. While the committee swung into action in the radio and movie industries, there were those who resisted and ultimately paid the price with the loss of their jobs and careers. The black list was a lethal weapon in the silencing of a generation. Thus, the real loss in each major area of cultural development and transmission, whether in theater, radio, movies, art, music, literature, religion, or education, occurred not only to the few hundred who lost their careers and livelihoods and were socially banished, but included millions who learned the habit of looking over their shoulders out of fear, and thus were frozen into silence.

This, then, was the "silent generation" who followed the espionage trial of Ethel and Julius Rosenberg, who became familiar with such names as Whittaker Chambers and Alger Hiss, and who became accustomed to reading in their newspapers about Fifth Amendment Communists. While there were those who still doubted the validity of the conspiratorial notions that passed for interpretive news analysis, they were shortly overwhelmed by two events which rocked America's security. By January 1949, China had fallen to the Communists as Chiang Kai-Shek retreated to the island of Formosa; and by September of that year, the world was awakened to be informed that Russia had exploded its first atomic bomb. The effect of both events simply heightened the hysterical fears already rampant in the American body politic.

Most Americans had difficulty understanding that the knowledge that went into making the atomic bomb was not secret but, in fact, was known to atomic physicists the world over, and that it was but a matter of time before other nations would produce the bomb.[84] Nevertheless, American "military" experts promised a ten- to twenty-year period of grace. Given

83. Cook, *Nightmare Decade*, pp. 62-63.
84. See Jungk, *Brighter than a Thousand Suns*.

the general population's lack of knowledge with respect to Soviet scientific capabilities, it was not hard to conclude, as many Americans did, that the answer must lie in superior Soviet espionage.

By February 6, 1950, the Republican National Committee excoriated the Truman administration for ". . . the dangerous degree to which communists and their fellow travelers have been employed in Government posts," and for permitting vital secrets to fall into the hands of ". . . alien agents and persons of questionable loyalty."[85] Three days later, Senator Joseph McCarthy launched his anti-Communist campaign in earnest at Wheeling, West Virginia. Lifting into the air a handful of papers, he charged, "I have in my hand hard evidence of 205 communists in the State department." Repeating these tactics and charges in speech after speech, McCarthy skyrocketed to instant fame as he flayed the Democrats with charges of high treason. Throughout the Korean War, from 1950 to 1953, McCarthy was one of the most feared men in Washington. He rode the crest of the anti-Communist wave until 1954, when he began to attack the secretary of the army under the presidential leadership of Dwight D. Eisenhower. Through the process of televised hearings, he was publicly discredited and shortly thereafter censured by the Senate and effectively silenced. With his demise in 1954 came the effective end of the second red scare, often termed "the McCarthy era."

While the end of McCarthy signaled the end of his demagogic attacks on a variety of people, it did not mean the end of the fear of Communist subversion, nor in any sense the lessening of the cold war. The cold war race with the Soviet Union was a race not only in weaponry but also in industrial production, manpower training, education, and cultural ideology. It was a total war. Military production increased as the lucrative "costs-plus" contracts, so profitable to industry during World War II, were continued throughout the Korean War and the cold war. Together, industry and the military gradually grew to have a vital political stake in the cold war and its maintenance. By 1961, in his farewell address to the nation, President Eisenhower warned of this growing and powerful alliance. As he put it,

In the councils of Government, we must guard against the acquisition of unwarranted influence, whether sought or unsought, by the military-industrial complex. The potential for the disastrous rise of misplaced power exists and will persist. We must never let the weight of this combination endanger our liberties or democratic processes.[86]

As the military and industrial complex grew in power, so, too, did universities, as they profited from huge government contracts serving both of these sectors. University research institutions, as well as the professors who served them, all profited from these cold war developments. The universities' role was to provide highly skilled manpower, research personnel,

---

85. As quoted in Cook, *Nightmare Decade,* p. 147.
86. As quoted in Borkin, *Crime and Punishment of I. G. Farbin,* p. i.

and facilities. The linkage was made clear when in March of 1947 Conant testified before a House Committee that was considering the establishment of a National Science Foundation and said, "The bottleneck of our scientific advance is essentially a manpower shortage"; and to eliminate that bottleneck in engineering and science, we "need a Science Foundation both to forward our domestic economy and to strengthen our military establishment."[87] Spurred on by large government contracts, the universities prospered along with the domestic economy and the military. One particular industry which grew very fast was the electronics industry.

America in the "nightmare decade" had entered the television era, an era which radically changed the country's political and cultural way of life. The cold war was a total war, requiring the manipulation of people, events, news, and entertainment, as well as general ideology. The television media became a useful instrument in that war. As Americans settled back to watch panels of experts interpreting the news for them, they came to vicariously enjoy and fear the cold war through such entertaining television shows as "I Was a Communist for the F.B.I.," "Mission: Impossible," and "The Man from U.N.C.L.E." They also became accustomed to hearing that news reports had come from "a reliable source." That source was usually the government, which was supplying the media with information, attempting to shape people's attitudes through information control and release.[88] Throughout the forty-year postwar cold war period, the government and advertising agencies had become increasingly more sophisticated in shaping public opinion. For this purpose, prior to February 11, 1976, the Central Intelligence Agency alone employed "approximately 50 journalists or personnel of U.S. media organizations."[89]

The C.I.A. was formed by the National Security Act of July of 1947, in which the military was reorganized to meet the contingencies of the cold war. It was organized as a super-secret organization, growing out of the Central Intelligence Group, which had emerged from the Office of Strategic Service during World War. II. Organized for both intelligence gathering and counter-insurgency activities, with a secret, virtually unlimited budget, the Agency grew to extensive proportions and had a vital role in shaping cold war events and both public and private thinking about those events. The C.I.A. invested heavily in covert propaganda to sustain and facilitate the cold war. As part of that process, the Agency entered the publishing industry. Books were important weapons in the cold war. As the chief of the C.I.A. Covert Action Staff in this area testified before a congressional committee,

Books differ from all other propaganda media, primarily because one single book can significantly change the reader's attitude and action to an extent unmatched by the impact of any other single medium . . . this is, of course, not true of all books

---

87. As quoted in Karier et al., *Roots of Crisis*, p. 194.
88. See Barnouw, *Image Empire.*
89. Foreign and Military Intelligence, Book I, *Final Report of the Select Committee to Study Governmental Operations with Respect to Intelligence Activities,* U.S. Senate, 94th Cong., 2nd Sess., Report No. 94-755 (Washington, D.C.: U.S. Government Printing Office, 1976), p. 195. Henceforth this report will be footnoted as the *Church Report.*

at all times and with all readers—but it is true significantly often enough to make books the most important weapon of strategic (long-range) propaganda.[90]

Thus, the Agency played a major role in helping to shape American thought about the cold war via books. "Well over a thousand books were produced, subsidized or sponsored by the C.I.A. before the end of 1967."[91]

Among the many and varied C.I.A.-sponsored books and reports were a series of manpower studies which greatly influenced educational policy in the late 1950's. For a variety of demographic and economic factors, America suffered a relative shortage of highly trained manpower in the decade of the 1950's.[92] In the context of the cold war, these shortages appeared ominously dangerous. Long before Sputnik, the C.I.A. had issued reports in which it compared Soviet and American manpower and America's educational development. As Burgess and Borrowman put it:

By 1950 President Eisenhower, of Columbia University, had launched a major manpower study under the direction of Eli Ginsberg, and the C.I.A. had issued its first ominous report about the Soviet threat to overtake the United States in its supply of such human resources. The National Science Foundation had also begun to express grave concern about the growing shortage of scientific and engineering personnel.[93]

In the thinking of such influential education critics as James B. Conant, Admiral Hyman Rickover, and Jerold Zacharias, the C.I.A.-sponsored manpower studies provided a baseline against which American education would be evaluated and remedial action proposed. These men saw education as a major part of the cold war manpower development process, and by the late 1950s they became major participants in the education debate. Their criticism of education was thus very different from that of the more typical anti-Communist groups, such as the American Coalition of Patriotic Societies, the Anti-Communist League of America, the Christian Nationalist Crusade, the John Birch Society, the Defenders of American Education, and numerous other groups which were active in searching out and exposing Communist activities in the schools.

There were still other critics of American education whose concerns grew not so much out of cold war fears as they did out of their general dissatisfaction with Prosser's "life adjustment" progressive reform movement and the perceived anti-intellectual stance of American educators, who from the "cardinal principles" forward had been attempting to meet "individual needs" through a differentiated curriculum that appeared to be increasingly trivialized.[94]

---

90. *Church Report*, I, p. 193.
91. *Church Report*, I, p. 193.
92. The lower birthrate of the 1930's, combined with the expanding demands for more highly trained engineers in the electronic and defense industries, in part accounted for the problem. See Burgess and Borrowman, *What Doctrines to Embrace*, pp. 113-141.
93. Burgess and Borrowman, *What Doctrines to Embrace*, p. 124.
94. For an example of that "trivialized curriculum," see Karier, *Education of the American Citizen*, pp. 57-64.

PROGRESSIVE EDUCATION UNDER ATTACK

While progressive education always had its critics, it seems that those who appeared by mid-century were both more aggressive and more effective. When Mortimer Smith published *And Madly Teach: A Layman Looks at Public School Education* (1949), and Bernard Iddings Bell published *Crisis in Education* (1949), it was apparent that circumstances had changed and more people were now listening to the critics than had in the past. The new critics were not only more incisive, but they directed their criticism at specific people and groups. Albert Lynd, in *Quackery in the Public Schools* (1950), took on the "world of Professor Kilpatrick." In that world of "neo-pedagogues' palaver" about "real needs," Lynd insisted, "the pupils are learning less and less about the arts of word and number, the history and the literature, the science and the esthetics, and the rest of the painfully accumulated culture of this harassed civilization."[95] Both he and Arthur E. Bestor, in *Educational Wastelands* (1953), criticized the anti-intellectualism that they believed had come to pervade the thinking of many American educators.

Lynd and Bestor both pointed to the speech of A. H. Lauchner, principal of the junior high school in Champaign, Illinois, before the National Association of Secondary School Principals as illustrative of the state to which "educationists" had fallen.[96] Lauchner said:

Through the years we've built a sort of halo around reading, writing, and arithmetic. We've said they were for everybody . . . rich and poor, brilliant and not-so-mentally endowed, ones who liked them and those who failed to go for them. Teacher has said that these were something 'everyone should learn.' The principal remarked, 'all educated people know how to write, spell, and read.' When some child declared a dislike for a sacred subject, he was warned that, if he failed to master it, he would grow up to be a so and so.

The Three R's for All Children, and All Children for the Three R's! That was it.

We've made some progress in getting rid of that slogan. But every now and then some mother with a Phi Beta Kappa award or some employer who has hired a girl who can't spell stirs up a fuss about the schools . . . and ground is lost. . . .

When we come to the realization that not every child has to read, figure, write and spell . . . that many of them either cannot or will not master these chores . . . then we shall be on the road to improving the junior high curriculum.

Between this day and that a lot of selling must take place. But it's coming. We shall some day accept the thought that it is just as illogical to assume that every boy must be able to read as it is that each one must be able to perform on a violin,

---

95. Albert Lynd, *Quackery in the Public Schools* (Boston: Little Brown and Co., 1950), p. 14.

96. A. H. Lauchner, "How Can the Junior High School Curriculum Be Improved?" *Bulletin of the National Association of Secondary School Principals,* XXXV, 177 (1951), 299-300. I am using the word *educationist* as Bestor defined it, to include school administrators and principals, state education agency personnel, as well as professors of education.

that it is no more reasonable to require that each girl spell well than it is that each one shall bake a good cherry pie. . . .

When adults realize that fact, everyone will be happier . . . and schools will be nicer places in which to live. . . .

If and when we are able to convince a few folks that mastery of reading, writing, and arithmetic is not the one road leading to happy, successful living, the next step is to cut down the amount of time and attention devoted to these areas in general junior high-school courses. . . .

One junior high in the East has, after long and careful study, accepted the fact that some twenty percent of their students will not be up to standard in writing . . . and they are doing other things for these boys and girls. That's straight thinking.[97]

Lauchner had put into words what many progressive, child-centered educators of the 1950's and "life adjustment" vocational educators had been thinking all along. Under the guise of "life adjustment" and meeting the "needs" of "*all* American youth," many educationists worked to develop a "how to"-oriented curriculum which might free as many as 20 per cent of youth from the burdensome tasks of learning to read, write, and do arithmetic. At this point, exclusive of cold war influence, progressive educators who espoused such doctrines were clearly vulnerable to criticism.

Of all the criticisms of education in the early 1950's, none was as serious, perceptive, and on target as that of Arthur Bestor. In *Educational Wastelands* (1953) and his follow-up work, *Restoration of Learning* (1955), Bestor delivered a wide-ranging, in-depth critique of American education. He argued that the function of the school was not to help people adjust to life but to help people learn to think. This was done through the disciplines of science, mathematics, history, literature, English, and foreign languages. The great tragedy of American education, Bestor insisted, resulted from the separation of these disciplines from what went on in the public schools. He believed that what went on was an increasingly insignificant vocational curriculum which was getting more and more anti-intellectual. The public schools, he argued, had lost their natural moorings, the disciplines of knowledge.

As Bestor saw it, the problem had evolved for historical reasons. Teacher education had developed separately from the disciplines. As a consequence, teachers trained at Teachers College (Columbia), the University of Illinois, and elsewhere were not adequately trained in the disciplines, but rather heavily trained in education courses that were fundamentally lacking in substance. Along with that training there emerged an "interlocking directorate" made up of school administrators, state education department personnel, professional education association representatives, and professors of education, who collectively controlled the curricula of the schools and the training of teachers. Educational reform could come only when

---

97. As quoted in part by Arthur E. Bestor, *Educational Wastelands: The Retreat from Learning in Our Public Schools* (Urbana: University of Illinois Press, 1953), pp. 55-56. Also see Lynd, *Quackery in the Public Schools,* p. 46.

teacher education was limited to methods of teaching and the university disciplines assumed a larger responsibility for training teachers.

Bestor correctly sensed that the problem was not just a matter of weak teachers with slovenly teaching habits, but rather was a fundamental problem of goals and purpose. He proceeded to endorse John Dewey's analysis of curriculum construction while citing the glaring weaknesses in the curriculum reconstructionist position that, from William Heard Kilpatrick to Florence Stratameyer, advocated an "integrated," "core," and "common learning" curriculum.[98] These attempts at integration, he pointed out, were not integration at all, but rather were superficial attempts by educationists to put together fundamental disciplines of knowledge which they did not understand or appreciate. As a consequence, they often assumed the arrogant position that they could create a new "discipline" of knowledge at the drop of a pen. Unable to do so, they repeatedly confused inert bits of information, called "subject matter," with the principle of living knowledge which grows out of the discipline. Failing to appreciate how living knowledge is produced, they put together the artifacts of the disciplines' "subject matter" in new and strange combinations. As a result, the curricula usually advocated by these educationists often looked more like impromptu abstract collages rather than systematic, coherent bodies of knowledge.

In developing his historical critique, Bestor worked his way back to the problem of the aims of education as reflected in the "cardinal principles" and the failure of the liberal arts college to adjust to the needs of the times and assume leadership in teacher education. Continuing, he squarely faced the fundamental issue that has plagued American education throughout the twentieth century. That issue usually appears when one defines a liberal education as crucial in the development of a free people, and when one also sees education as vital in developing a democratic society. It then logically follows that such an education must be made available to *all*, and not just an elite few. Bestor defined a liberal education as "the communication of intellectual power." He also insisted that if a society was to be "democratic," everyone must have a chance to develop his or her intellectual powers. These powers are derived not from "subject-matter fields," which are a "mere aggregate of facts," but from the study of the disciplines as living knowledge, which become "ways of thinking."[99] These ways of thinking prepare one to meet new problems as they arise. As Bestor put it: "The ability to face unprecedented situations by using the accumulated intellectual power of the race is mankind's most precious possession. And to transmit this power of disciplined thinking is the primary and inescapable responsibility of an educational system."[100]

American educationists from the turn of the century, with their test-and-measurement movement under the guise of "meeting individual needs," had so differentiated the curriculum that they produced a tracking system which reinforced social, racial, and ethnic class lines.[101] Bestor

98. Bestor, *Educational Wastelands*, pp. 52-53.
99. Bestor, *Educational Wastelands*, pp. 18-19.
100. Bestor, *Educational Wastelands*, p. 19.
101. See Karier, et al. *Roots of Crisis*, pp. 108-137.

pointed out that while many educationists spoke of democracy in education, they were often the least democratic when it came to educating the
masses of people and developing their capabilities to their fullest. The true
elitists were those educators prepared to write off 20 per cent of the population as functionally illiterate.

According to Bestor, that part of progressive education which culminated in life adjustment education was "regressive." He was quick to
point out, however, that he was not opposed to progressive education
when it came to improvement of instruction, but only when it came to
curriculum construction. Progressive educators somehow had gotten off
the right track. As he nostalgically looked back to 1922–1926, at the
high school education he had received at one of America's most progressive
schools, Lincoln School of Teachers College, Columbia University, he said:

With uninfluential exceptions the faculty of that school did not think of defining
the aims of secondary education apart from the aims of liberal education generally.
They believed thoroughly in the intellectual purposes that had always been central in education as a whole. They knew that the work of the secondary school
must intermesh with the advanced work carried on by scientists and scholars.[102]

In many ways Bestor's critique was right on target, especially as he analyzed the work of educationists and the declining respect for intellectual
life that seemed to pervade much of their thinking. He often, it seemed,
put his finger on the right people and, more importantly, on the right
issues. However, his critique fell short in one critical area, and that was
the problem of higher education itself. Those teachers at Lincoln School
who offered him intellectual disciplines were, like John Dewey and others
of that generation, products of an intellectual culture that had been rooted
in the classical tradition. Bestor had been the beneficiary of the educational capital of an ancient tradition, which by mid-century had ceased to
be the steadying focus of American education that it once had been. His
blind side was not only in viewing the training of his former teachers, but
also in visualizing the problem of training professors for the liberal arts
college. As early as 1908, Irving Babbitt, in *Literature and the American
College*, had warned that intellectual culture was threatened not only by
Rousseauistic romanticism, which had come to dominate elementary educators' thinking, but was more vulnerable to Baconian scientism, which
had come to pervade the training of the Ph.D. expert. It was the "scientism" that pervaded the training of young scholars preparing to teach in
the liberal arts college which ultimately proved most damaging to the liberal arts college. Doctoral training, Babbitt claimed, was conducive to
producing new knowledge, but not conducive to producing liberally educated teachers for the liberal arts.

While many, including Bestor, had talked about specialization versus
generalization in the arts curricula, none adequately came to grips with
the problem Babbitt had so clearly analyzed. Thus, even as Bestor was
carrying on his crusade for intellectual culture, the very meaning of a lib-

---

102. Bestor, *Educational Wastelands,* p. 45.

eral education was lost in the liberal arts colleges themselves. As highly specialized, scientifically trained young scholars assumed the leadership of liberal arts departments and colleges, these units of higher education became indistinguishable from the graduate colleges in which their leaders were nourished. Babbitt had correctly warned that the very survival of a liberal education was at stake. The great tragedy for future generations was that they were about to lose something without ever having known it. Bestor's analysis of the crisis in education was sound as far as he took it. However, it ran far more deeply and pervasively than even he suspected.

Not only were the high schools and liberal arts colleges in crisis because of the decline in the classical education tradition, but there also was emerging a popular culture which was gradually pervading the popular media and school curricula. This was accompanied by a lessening of intellectual standards and lower levels of expected performance. Bestor had accurately sensed a serious decline in expected levels of performance since he had attended school in the 1920's and since he taught at the University of Illinois in the 1950's. The older school texts, especially the English anthologies used in the public schools of the 1920's, demanded a higher level of intellectual performance than those used in the 1950's. The latter texts contained a pronounced intrusion of popular culture with a built-in, lower standard of performance.[103] The textbooks, from civics and English to the sciences, were increasingly taking on a more popular cultural dimension, for gradually more and more of them were being written by authors who were not the significant leaders in these disciplines. As fewer and fewer leading scholars had the time or inclination to write, or even pass judgment on, the texts that were being developed in the public schools by both public school teachers and professors of education, the separation about which Bestor once complained continued to increase. It has progressively worsened to the point that, today, many school textbooks, though they may carry a university professor's name, are, in fact, often mainly written by the publishing house editor.

Hoping to create an organization that might work for the educational reform he had in mind, Bestor helped organize the Council for Basic Education, and became its first president in 1956. Men such as Harold Clapp, Harry Fuller, Mortimer Smith, and others of like mind quickly joined. As a group, they stood against the educationists' influence and their differentiated curriculum. By 1959, their platform was laid out and edited by James D. Koerner, executive secretary to the council, in *The Case for Basic Education*. Koerner further carried these ideas into the 1960's in *The Miseducation of American Teachers* (1965) and *Who Controls American Education?* (1968). By the time Bestor formed the Council for Basic Education, the popular press had begun picking up on his and others' criticisms. *U.S. News and World Report* published interviews with Bestor under such pro-

---

103. See Gail Armstrong Parks, "Adolescence in the Twenties as Represented in American Novels, Popular Magazines, and Literature Anthologies of the Decade" (unpublished Ph.D. diss., University of Illinois, 1977). Also see James Warren Olson, "The Nature of Literature Anthologies Used in the Teaching of High School English 1917-1957" (unpublished Ph.D. diss., University of Wisconsin, 1969).

vocative titles as, "We Are Less Educated than Fifty Years Ago," and "What Went Wrong with U.S. Schools?"[104] Popular magazines carried regular sections on the education critics.

Amid all of this criticism, the Russians launched Sputnik I in October 1957. Once again, for the second time in less than a decade, America was stunned by a significant Soviet scientific achievement. This time the Russians were not trying to catch up, as in the case of the atomic bomb, but were clearly ahead of the United States in space technology and development.

The Russians had started their space program in 1945, whereas the United States did not get its program underway until 1954. Professor Donald H. Menzel, director of the Harvard Observatory; T. Keith Glennan, head of the National Aeronautics and Space Administration; General James M. Gavin, former chief of research and development at the Pentagon; and Werner Von Braun, space scientist, all made clear in public interviews with the press and electronic media the reasons why America was so far behind the Russians in space. Uniformly, they pointed to the failure of high-level officials in the Pentagon to appreciate the importance of space research and their active resistance to missile and satellite development. Clearly, the problem was a case of bad judgment on the part of both political and military planners.[105] Such, however, was not where the fault was to be found.

Given the state of the cold war mentality, with Senator Joseph McCarthy barely having passed from the scene, and the tide of educational criticism mounting, it was all very tempting to put the blame on education. The connection quickly was made. Even Bestor succumbed when, in his interview with *U.S. News and World Report*, "What Went Wrong with U.S. Schools?" on January 24, 1958, he charged that the schools had failed to give the necessary training and "that's why the first satellite bears the label 'Made in Russia.'"[106] Bestor, along with others, fell into the easy trap of linking the cold war failures and problems with American schools. Clearly, the schools had nothing to do with the failure of Pentagon planners to push for a space program. However, they had a lot to do with providing the trained technical manpower that was necessary to catch up quickly and to surpass the Russians in that field.[107] Nevertheless, the schools became easy cold war scapegoats, as columnist after columnist picked up the cudgel. When *Life* published "It's Time to Close Our Carnival" on March 24, 1958, it was clear that much of the earlier serious

---

104. See *U.S. News and World Report,* Nov. 30, 1956; June 7, 1957; Jan. 24, 1958.

105. See James M. Gavin, *War and Peace in the Space Age* (New York: Harper, 1958). Also see Donald H. Mengel, "The Astronomer's Stake in Outer Space," *Atlantic Monthly,* Nov. 1958. For an extended treatment of this period, see Frederick M. Raubinger and Harold C. Hand, "Later than You Think," undated ms., Archibald Anderson Library, College of Education, University of Illinois at Urbana-Champaign.

106. As quoted in Raubinger and Hand, "Later than You Think," chap. 5, p. 18.

107. The engineers and space technologists who made up the manpower pool which put the United States ahead in space had been graduated from high school long before Bestor started criticizing schools; indeed, many of them had been trained in the very schools Bestor and others had been criticizing.

criticism of education which Bestor and others had leveled, and which had nothing to do with the cold war, was now about to be buried in cold war hysteria. Ironically, even Bestor himself contributed to the burial.

TOWARD COLD WAR MANPOWER SOLUTIONS

Although President Eisenhower and many groups were steadfast in their opposition to federal aid to education, they could not resist the pressure that mounted as a consequence of Sputnik. The National Defense Education Act (1958) was a direct result of the launching of the Soviet satellite. In that act, fellowships and loans were granted for studies in science, mathematics, and foreign languages, and payments were authorized for equipment and building construction. The act set the pattern for federal involvement in education, which would become massive over the next two decades. The schools were thus linked with the federal government and increasingly tied to our national defense posture. Admiral Hyman G. Rickover characterized the schools as "Our First Line of Defense."[108] The manpower studies which the Central Intelligence Agency had developed earlier now became a persuasive part of the educational dialog. As Rickover put it:

Mr. Allen Dulles, director of our Central Intelligence Agency, estimated that between 1950 and 1960 Soviet Russia will have graduated 1,200,000 scientists and engineers compared with 900,000 in the United States. And by 1960 it is estimated she will have more scientists and engineers than we. Thereafter the situation will steadily worsen unless we take steps to upgrade mathematics and science teaching in the high schools and increase enrollment in our engineering colleges. Russia has been catching up with us so fast because each year she now graduates about twice as many engineers as we do.[109]

Repeatedly, Rickover related to television audiences the problems he had in finding suitable engineers for building an atomic-powered submarine. In the military mind of Rickover, the cold war was a total war, in which the schools played a direct role in training the personnel who were crucial in determining what he called "lead time"—the length of time this society took to produce new and more devastating weapons. Superior schools would shorten the lead time and thus help beat the Russians in weapons production. Weaker schools, he argued, would lead to disastrous results in the arms race with the Soviet Union.[110] Thus, for Rickover, education was the key to survival.

Although Rickover often supported Bestor's Council for Basic Education and its criticism of the educationists, his chief solution to the problem was not to be found in Bestor's concern for a new, more vital liberal education for everyone, but rather in a more tightly differentiated curricu-

---

108. H. G. Rickover, *Education and Freedom* (New York: E. P. Dutton and Co., 1959), p. 15.
109. Rickover, *Education and Freedom*, p. 45.
110. Rickover, *Education and Freedom*, pp. 39-52.

lum, where the best and the brightest might be more quickly and efficiently trained. The most intelligent youth, Rickover urged, ought to be tracked into special secondary schools, where they could be given the best science curriculum the nation had to offer. While the educationists had maintained and developed the elite tracking program within the comprehensive high school, Rickover wanted to take it one step further and abandon the idea of the comprehensive high school entirely. In his proposal he stepped beyond what most Americans were willing to accept.

While Rickover was calling for the creation of special science high schools for the gifted, the comprehensive high schools' math and science programs were receiving special attention. In 1950, the National Science Foundation, with Conant as its first president, was organized to promote basic research and education in the sciences, primarily at the college level. By mid-decade the NSF began to shift its support to high school curricular projects; and by 1956, it had funded M.I.T. physicist Jerrold Zacharies' Physical Science Study Committee project. At the University of Illinois, in 1952, the Carnegie Foundation funded an education professor, Max Beberman, who headed a group of mathematicians from the engineering and mathematics departments to develop a new math curriculum based on the way mathematicians think. These projects, and others like them, attempted to bring the university scholars into closer, direct relationship with public school curricular development. Over the next two decades, both the federal government and various foundations invested heavily in developing curricular materials for the new physics, math, and foreign language programs in the schools. While many of these activities reflected Bestor's concern for getting university scholars active in high school curriculum reform, they did not reflect any of his concerns for the importance of a liberal education. The underlying generating force out of which these curricular changes grew was not concern for the need for an improved liberal education for all, but rather a concern for producing enough engineers for the cold war.

As the criticism of education worsened, and some critics, such as Rickover, talked of doing away with the comprehensive high school, the Carnegie Corporation, under the leadership of John W. Gardner, in late 1956 asked James B. Conant to make a study of public education. Conant was a highly respected national leader with a long record of involvement in weapons production, from mustard gas in World War I to the atomic bomb in World War II. When it came to national security, Conant was always a strong advocate of military preparedness. In 1940 he served on the Committee to Defend America by Aiding the Allies, which called for mobilization of America long before Pearl Harbor was attacked; and by 1950 he had served on the Committee on the Present Danger, which also called for the mobilization of America for the cold war battle against Communism at home and abroad. Conant was an active leader in structuring cold war policies, which went all the way from weapons research and production to the shaping of American educational thought and practice.

A year before Sputnik, and well before he retired as ambassador to the German Federal Republic in 1957, Conant accepted Gardner's offer to become more directly involved in the educational criticism of the 1950's. As high commissioner for Germany, and later as ambassador, he had helped reorganize German education.[111] He had been deeply involved in most cold war manpower policies and was well aware of the earlier C.I.A. studies of the Soviet Union. His interest in public education went back to the 1930's when, as president of Harvard, he had been concerned with public education as a training ground for the university's student population. Throughout his career, Conant saw educational policy-making largely in terms of manpower planning. This was as true when he served on the Educational Policies Commission in the 1940's as it was when he helped found and head the National Science Foundation in the 1950's. Conant's manpower perspective was reflected in his testimony before Congress on the military draft and the G.I. Bill, and in his active involvement in establishing the Educational Testing Service at Princeton, New Jersey. In each case he saw education as the vital mechanism for sorting and channeling manpower.

As earlier noted, Conant thought of himself as a Jeffersonian who conceived of the ideal society as the meritocratic society, where talent and virtue would be rewarded.[112] Within that framework, Conant's many and varied educational policy-making activities fell into place. Thus, he did not see any conflict between the more academic thrust of *General Education in a Free Society* and his endorsement of the more "life adjustment" focus of *Education for All American Youth*. He was not as opposed to progressive "life adjustment" education for the masses as was Bestor. Neither was he as opposed to the work of the educationists in developing the comprehensive high school, with all of its differentiated curriculum, as Bestor had been. At heart, Bestor was far more an egalitarian democrat than Conant.

Conant knew that if we were going to "rake from the rubbish annually," as Jefferson put it, then it was necessary to develop a rake that was legitimately acceptable by not only the elite who succeeded, but, more importantly, by those who failed. Therefore, Conant was always interested in the college entrance examinations and the necessity to standardize their development, thereby achieving a kind of social credibility that was necessary in order to make his meritocratic view of society work. It was not surprising, then, that on December 19, 1947, when five men and their associates, representing the Carnegie Foundation for the Advancement of Teaching, the Carnegie Corporation of New York, the College Entrance Examination Board, and the American Council on Education, were chartered under New York State law as the Educational Testing Service, the man to be chosen to head such an operation was Conant's former dean at Harvard in charge of entrance examinations, Henry Chauncey.[113]

The Educational Testing Service was an instant success:

111. See Chapter Nine. Also see Stephen Preskill, "Raking from the Rubbish: Charles W. Eliot, James B. Conant, and the Public Schools" (unpublished Ph.D. diss., University of Illinois, 1984).

112. See p. 252. For an extended treatment of Conant's cold war activities, see Preskill, "Raking from the Rubbish." Also see Spring, *Sorting Machine*.

113. E.T.S. was a key part of the growing interlocking directorate of American education in the cold war period. For example, according to the annual report for 1948-1949, E.T.S. had 111 employees, all of whom were previously employed by the founding organizations. See Allan Nairn, *The Reign of E.T.S.* (Ralph Nader Report on the Educational Testing Service, 1980), p. 400.

I.B.M. (International Business Machines), Pepsi Cola Corporation, the Association of American Medical Colleges, Harvard University, the U.S. Department of State, the U.S. Atomic Energy Commission, and more than fifty leading universities, foundations, government agencies and corporations greeted the new testing firm with advisory services and contracts.[114]

Reporting to the newly formed board of trustees, Chauncey spoke of the power of testing, which could be viewed as "frightening, if not downright objectionable." Yet he predicted that we would become "accustomed to it and will find ourselves better off for it." This knowledge, he insisted, had greater possibilities for constructive use than misuse. Through more objective scientific testing, he said, "Educational and vocational guidance, personal and social adjustment most certainly should be greatly benefited. Life may have less mystery but it will also have less disillusionment and disappointment. Hope will not be a lost source of strength, but it will be kept within reasonable bounds."[115]

Chauncey and Conant both were vitally concerned with keeping the American dream of social mobility within "reasonable bounds." Over the next thirty years, the Educational Testing Service, as a private corporation, became the gatekeeper for virtually all American institutions of higher education and business life. By 1974, it had in place the kind of sorting device that Conant had long sought, an "objective" test which was accepted as legitimate by both those who succeeded as well as those who failed. The Scholastic Aptitude Test was the key to a college education and economic opportunity. The meritocracy seemed to have arrived when John Gardner, a former E.T.S. trustee, proclaimed, "The tests couldn't see whether the youngster was in rags or in tweeds, and couldn't bear the accents of the slum."[116] In general, the American public came to accept the notion that tests such as the S.A.T. were legitimate discriminators. E.T.S. President William W. Turnbull summarized such beliefs when, in a speech before the American-Jewish Congress in 1974, he said, "The ability to perform well on tasks sampled by examinations, along with other common indices of accomplishment, has come largely to replace considerations of family or wealth or religion or ethnicity as a basis for acceptance into selective colleges and professional schools."[117]

While Chauncey, Gardner, Turnbull, Conant, the Educational Testing Service, the foundations, and a large cadre of professional testers managed to convince the public that the tests were not based on considerations of "family or wealth or religion or ethnicity," the troublesome fact remained that S.A.T. scores correlated very well with parents' mean income. In many ways, this test reflected the economic and social class order. For example, comparing S.A.T. average scores with parents' mean income for 1973–1974, one gets the following results:

---

114. Nairn, *Reign of E.T.S.*, p. 2. For a further treatment of the relationship of Chauncey to Conant, see Preskill, "Raking from the Rubbish." Also see Raubinger and Hand, "Later than you Think."

115. Nairn, *Reign of E.T.S.*, p. 4.

116. Nairn, *Reign of E.T.S.*, p. 199.

117. Nairn, *Reign of E.T.S.*, p. 199.

S.A.T. Average	Parents' Mean Income
750–800	$24,124
700–749	21,980
650–699	21,292
600–649	20,330
550–599	19,481
500–549	18,824
450–499	18,122
400–449	17,387
350–399	16,182
300–349	14,355
250–299	11,428
200–249	8,639

Source: College Bound Seniors, 1973–1974, table 21, p. 27.[118]

The development of the Educational Testing Service as the accepted gatekeeper for education and business occupations in America, representing corporate wealth and serviced by interlocking personnel drawn from government, university, and corporate life, was the single most important educational institutional development in the postwar period. That organization was instrumental in sorting the manpower required to fulfill Conant's Jeffersonian, meritocratic vision of the social order. When Conant launched his 1957 study of the American high school, he not only had the educational establishment, including many government agencies and leaders, behind him, but he was supported by an interlocking directorate of foundational leaders, as well as the Educational Testing Service itself. Bestor's Council for Basic Education seemed to pale into political insignificance in comparison to Conant's forces.

The real issue for Conant was not the "educationist"; it was the problem of the cold war and how America might best mobilize its manpower resources to meet the challenge that lay ahead, while still preserving the meritocratic system it had been developing. He rejected Rickover's suggestion to dismantle the comprehensive high school and came through with twenty-one recommendations of his own, which he believed would strengthen the comprehensive high school and improve its tracking function. Among those recommendations were many which educationists advocated, such as improved guidance systems and school consolidation. In those recommendations he outlined a school program for "all American youth." While he put considerable emphasis on improved courses for able students in science, math, and foreign languages, he also called for more ability grouping and a guidance program to career track youngsters through the schools. The almost immediate massive federal funding of

---

118. Nairn, *Reign of E.T.S.*, p. 201.

new guidance programs in the schools was a direct consequence of Conant's recommendations.[119]

While much of what he recommended was designed to improve the education of the gifted, the more democratic function of the school was to be served by extracurricular programs, a well-developed homeroom system, and a senior social problems course, where all students of different tracks would meet to discuss social problems of the day. The major function of the comprehensive high school was to sort students into their life occupations. Therefore, Conant put great stress on the guidance program. In short, he advocated no "radical changes in the basic pattern" of secondary education, but rather called for sharpening its sorting function and an improved curriculum for the academically talented.[120]

The Carnegie Corporation and the Educational Testing Service immediately put into action a massive publicity campaign to sell Conant's recommendations. Thousands of school boards and administrators were supplied with free copies of the report, as professional reviewers, newspapers, and television personnel participated in the media blitz which followed. The campaign worked. For the most part, school leaders breathed a sigh of relief as they found themselves in general agreement with the report. School boards around the country took out full-page ads in their local newspapers to show how their system favorably compared with Conant's recommendations. As *The American High School Today* (1959) was being distributed, Conant hit the campaign trail to make the details of his program more explicit. Repeatedly, he warned that there must be a closer relationship between our educational planning and the struggle against Communism. People must awaken to the dangers and take practical, educational action. As he put it, "One can only conclude that many people are quite unconscious of the relation between high school education and the welfare of the United States. They are still living in imagination in a world which knew neither nuclear weapons nor Soviet imperialism."[121] For Conant, the cold war was the dominant determining factor of the times.

Many harassed school people, threatened by a decade of criticism, found a face-saving way out of the "nightmare decade" in Conant's report. His reports, starting with *The American High School Today* (1959), and followed by *Slums and Suburbs* (1961) and *The Education of American Teachers* (1963), had the general effect of mollifying various factions and even closing off the educational debate. Amid all the furor of that decade, it was clear that American educational rhetoric had passed from that of the progressive "life adjustment" manpower planners of the late 1940's to the rhetoric of the cold war manpower planners of the late 1950's. Progressive education as a movement disappeared in the midst of all that criticism and redirection of government policy, as did much of the thoughtful criticism

---

119. Conant thought of high school guidance as primarily vocational. He was most disappointed when the field, using federal funds, moved more to psychological counseling rather than vocational channeling.

120. James Bryant Conant, *The American High School Today* (New York: McGraw-Hill Book Co., 1959), p. 96.

121. James Bryant Conant, *The Child, the Parent, and the State* (New York: McGraw-Hill Book Co., 1959), p. 39.

that Bestor had raised with respect to the role of a liberal education for a free people in a democratic society. The cold war manpower concerns had overtaken and swept aside much of the serious educational dialog that had begun to surface earlier in the decade.[122]

As teachers attended N.D.E.A.-sponsored summer workshops in the new math and science in the early 1960's, they also read Conant's *Slums and Suburbs* (1961), in which he warned of the "social dynamite" building up in the ghettos of the major cities. The segregated ghetto schools, themselves a product of racial and economic class bias, put Conant's ideas about a comprehensive high school, i.e., where all youngsters rich and poor, of all races and creeds, might fairly compete, to a severe reality test. Facing the segregated nature of the school, Conant opted for preserving the neighborhood school at the expense of providing equal educational opportunity for all. He was opposed to moving "children about as though they were pawns on a chessboard."[123] However, by 1963, unable to maintain even the illusion of equal opportunity and fairness, he changed his mind in favor of some kind of busing to achieve racial, ethnic, and class diversity in the comprehensive high school. Conant vacillated on this issue, just as the American public did, for the next twenty-five years. The issue of busing was really only an educational reflection of a much deeper malaise of racial and economic injustice which remained the nation's single most difficult unresolved problem.

A STRUGGLE FOR SOCIAL JUSTICE

Throughout its history, America has suffered from the cancer of racism. Although the Civil War put an end to slavery, it did not put an end to racism. After that war, America institutionalized its racism in the form of segregation. After centuries of slavery, American blacks were forced to live their lives under the yoke of segregation for the next century. This meant that blacks lived in the worst housing available, had the highest rate of unemployment, were employed at the most menial tasks, received the poorest medical attention, suffered the greatest instances of disease, had the highest infant mortality rates and the shortest life expectancy rates, sent their children to second-rate schools, suffered the highest crime rate, and could look forward only to a life of poverty.

Behind this American apartheid society functioned a pervasive, deep-seated racism, one that should not be confused with the kind of prejudice which existed and worked against each new wave of ethnic and religious group who emigrated to America. For the most part, the Irish, Greeks, Poles, Jews, and others who broke through the barriers of prejudice woven in place by former immigrants had alternative courses of action through which they could assimilate into the mainstream of American life. In a racially segregated society, blacks suffered both from de jure as well as de facto segregation. In those areas of the country where de jure segregation

---

122. See Spring, *Sorting Machine,* and Burgess and Borrowman, *What Doctrines to Embrace.*

123. See p. 254.

did not exist, de facto segregation was maintained through an unwritten and often unspoken quota system in which the number of blacks was controlled. More than Irish Catholics, Greeks, Poles, or Jews, blacks suffered from this unspoken quota system because, in a racist society, they were more quickly and easily identifiable. They were a marked people.

The battle against racism in America, which evolved in the 1940's, 1950's, and 1960's, focused heavily on the elimination of de jure segregation. This was but the first phase of a larger struggle for social justice which continues to the present and whose outcome is still very much in doubt. Once the legal barriers of segregation fell in the late 1950's and early 1960's, blacks were quick to learn that the social justice of which they dreamed was still not at hand. The pattern of discrimination embedded in American institutions continued to maintain a segregated society. As a consequence of the civil rights struggle of the 1960's, a greater proportion of blacks were going on to higher education and some were even moving into higher-level occupations. But between 1975 and 1980, the proportion of black and Hispanic high school graduates going on to higher education had already declined.[124] When blacks were employed, they were usually overeducated for the position held.[125] When black unemployment is compared to white unemployment over the entire period of the cold war, it becomes clear that the situation worsened. Black unemployment went from 1.6 times that of whites in 1948[126] to 2.4 times that of whites in 1978, which in fact was the widest gap between the two groups since the government began recording employment statistics by race.[127]

As a consequence of this progressively worsening employment picture, black families became more and more devastated. In 1982, 37.7 per cent of all black families were headed by single women and 70 to 80 per cent of the female-headed nonwhite families lived in poverty. By 1984, one of every two black children came from families who lived below the poverty level.[128] The result of such destructive economic and social conditions was that, even though blacks represented only 12.5 per cent of the population as of 1978, they outnumbered whites in state and federal correctional facilities and made up 47 per cent of the total prison population.[129] The racism deeply embedded in America's social institutions continues to function. While wreaking havoc on the black race, it remains a cancer on the conscience of the American nation. However, in spite of this rather dismal

124. American Council on Education, Office of Minority Concerns, "Minorities in Higher Education," 1983, p. 9.

125. Dorothy K. Newman, *Protest, Politics, and Prosperity: Black Americans and White Institutions, 1940-1975* (New York: Pantheon Books, 1978), p. 70.

126. See Newman, *Protest, Politics, and Prosperity*, p. 64.

127. U.S. Department of Commerce, Current Population Reports Special Studies Series P-23, No. 80, *The Social and Economic Status of the Black Population in the United States: 1790-1978*, p. 188.

128. American Council on Education, Office of Minority Concerns, "Minorities in Higher Education," p. iii. Also see House Select Committee on Children, Youth and Families, *Report* (Washington, D.C.: U.S. Government Printing Office, 1984).

129. Timothy J. Flanagan, David J. VanAlstyne, and Michael R. Gottfredson, *Source Book of Criminal Justice Statistics—1981* (Albany, N.Y.: Criminal Justice Research Center, U.S. Department of Justice, 1982), p. 482.

picture, progress was made in the civil rights movement of the 1950's and 1960's, at least in the areas of breaking down some of the legal and social segregation that had emerged since the Civil War.

THE CIVIL RIGHTS MOVEMENT

Early in 1941, when America was beginning to mobilize for war, A. Philip Randolph, a labor leader, called a meeting of black leaders to discuss the racial segregation that was emerging in the new war industries. They planned a march on Washington for July 1, 1941, to protest such developments. As a response to that threat, President Roosevelt issued Executive Order No. 8802, which required the inclusion in all government contracts of a nondiscrimination clause and the establishment of a federal Fair Employment Practices Committee. Although some progress was made during the war toward an integrated work force, there were over 14,000 complaints registered against employers for discriminating practices.[130] With peace came the return of the more segregated work force.

By 1944, the National Association for the Advancement of Colored People had won its United States Supreme Court case, *Smith* vs. *Allwright,* in which legal barriers to blacks' right to vote in the Democratic primaries in the deep South were declared unconstitutional. Blacks, however, still faced the threat of lynching by unruly mobs if they tried to vote. Senator Theodore Bilbo recognized the immediate threat to white supremacy when he "urged whites to employ any means to bar Negroes from voting."[131] In spite of such threats to life and limb, blacks continued to press for free exercise of the franchise. As they did so, they increasingly made a significant political difference.

In 1948, President Truman, threatened with black resistance to segregation practices in the armed forces, issued Executive Order No. 9981, which mandated the desegregation of the armed forces. Even though the military, with its clear and direct command structure, might be expected to move quickly, they, too, moved slowly. In the late spring of 1953, the military was still attempting to desegregate combat units on line during the Korean War. Truman went further by pushing for a stronger civil rights plank in the 1948 Democratic platform, ordering the creation of a Fair Employment Board and asking Congress to create a permanent Civil Rights Commission. As the Dixiecrats walked out of the Democratic Convention, it appeared that Truman was in political trouble. He completed his 1948 whistle-stop campaign through the industrial Northern states, ending up in Harlem. While the Chicago *Tribune* inauspiciously announced the election of Thomas Dewey, it was Harry Truman who won. "On election day, two-thirds of the blacks voting voted for Truman, giving him the victory."[132] Truman was the first, but not the last, president to be elected by the black swing vote. In the close election of 1960, John Kennedy's election was made possible by a large proportion of black votes.

---

130. Newman, *Protest, Politics, and Prosperity*, p. 12.
131. As quoted in Newman, *Protest, Politics, and Prosperity*, p. 14.
132. Newman, *Protest, Politics, and Prosperity*, p. 14.

While some progress was made through the executive branch of government, and only slight progress was made through Congress, a major breakthrough in the judicial branch came with the Brown decision of 1954. In that case, the Supreme Court declared the separate-but-equal principle, as applied to education, inherently unequal, and therefore a violation of the equal-protection clause of the Fourteenth Amendment. Thus, segregation in America's public schools was declared unconstitutional. The decision was the culmination of six previous decisions made by the Supreme Court in cases the N.A.A.C.P. had brought to them from 1938 to 1954.[133] The Brown Case itself was not one, but five cases; it represented the legal culmination of a long, tedious struggle. A unanimous court ruled against de jure segregated schools. In the follow-up decision, the justices ruled that desegregation should proceed with "all deliberate speed." President Eisenhower, however, was reluctant to take action to implement the decision. His policy was to stay clear of the issue as much as possible. When Emmett Till was killed in Mississippi on August 28, 1955, and civil rights leaders requested federal troops, Eisenhower refused, ominously suggesting that the Communist party was involved in the civil rights movement.[134]

When the courts proceeded with "all deliberate speed" to integrate Central High School at Little Rock, Arkansas, in the fall of 1957, and Governor Orval Faubus used the state-controlled National Guard to block the federal court order, it was only after he withdrew his troops and mob violence ensued that President Eisenhower sent federal troops to restore order. While the issue was clearly one of fundamental importance involving both federal versus state power, and the enforcement of the law and the civil rights of American citizens, the president found it necessary to justify his decision to send troops to Little Rock on September 24, 1957, in terms of the cold war and what America's enemies abroad would make of such events.[135] Deeply involved with the cold war, Eisenhower saw the civil rights movement as reflecting an image that was damaging to America's security interests around the world. It was during his administration that F.B.I. surveillance of the leadership and the organizations of the civil rights movements was increased. Included in that surveillance was a young civil rights leader named Martin Luther King, Jr., who had just organized the Southern Christian Leadership Conference, which had developed out of the 1955–1956 Montgomery, Alabama, bus boycott.

On December 1, 1955, when Rosa Parks, secretary of the Alabama chapter of the N.A.A.C.P., boarded a bus and refused to give up her seat to a white patron, a new, more powerful mechanism for social change was introduced into the civil rights movement. Nonviolent resistance was now applied as Martin Luther King, Jr., directed the Montgomery bus boycott. The practice of nonviolent resistance required discipline, courage, and a willingness to sacrifice oneself and one's children to the brutality of a punishing society, all for a higher cause. The idea of nonviolent direct action, or *Satyagraha,* was effectively used by Mahatma Gandhi to free India

---

133. See Newman, *Protest, Politics, and Prosperity,* p. 290.
134. See Spring, *Sorting Machine,* p. 158.
135. Spring, *Sorting Machine,* p. 160.

from the yoke of British rule. Gandhi, himself, pointed to Thoreau's *Essay on Civil Disobedience* as the most significant piece of American literature ever written in this regard. The practice of *Satyagraha* was endorsed in the 1930's by the Christian Student movement, under the leadership of the Fellowship for Reconciliation. It was further adopted by James Farmer and others, who helped organize the Congress of Racial Equality, in 1942, at the University of Chicago.[136] King first became acquainted with the method of nonviolent resistance when he read Thoreau at Morehouse College in Atlanta, sometime in the mid-1940's, and he became reacquainted with it when he heard A. J. Muste lecture on nonviolent resistance at Crozier Theological Seminary in Chester, Pennsylvania, in the late 1940's. At the seminary, he became familiar with Walter Rauschenbusch and the Social Gospel movement, which placed religion at the center of economic and social concerns of humanity. At Crozier, he also studied Marx and came to reject the materialism that undergirded Marxist philosophy.[137]

At Boston University, from 1951 to 1953, King completed his doctoral studies while working out his philosophy of nonviolent resistance and developing deep concerns for economic and social justice. In September 1954, he accepted a ministerial position at the Dexter Avenue Baptist Church in Montgomery, Alabama. From his church he directed the successful Montgomery bus boycott, using nonviolent resistance ideas. The following year, 1957, he organized the S.C.L.C. and pressured the Eisenhower-Nixon administration to take national action in the civil rights movement. Under such pressure, the president signed the Civil Rights Act of 1957, the first such act since 1885. Although it was a relatively weak piece of legislation, it was the first in a series of such acts which would grow in strength. By 1957, within months of the formation of the S.C.L.C., King and his new organization were placed under F.B.I. surveillance, and remained so until he was assassinated.[138]

Across the South, students and nonstudents alike began using King's nonviolent technique to breach the segregation laws which separated the races in lunchrooms, restrooms, buses, railroads, at drinking fountains, swimming pools, and even in churches. By April 1960, the Student Non-Violent Coordinating Committee was organized in Raleigh, North Carolina, to further the cause. S.C.L.C., S.N.C.C., C.O.R.E., as well as the N.A.A.C.P. now worked feverishly to dismantle the segregated society of the South. In 1960, over 50,000 people demonstrated, and over 3,600 people went to jail.[139]

As the segregated walls of the South began to crumble, it became clear that the de facto segregated conditions of the Northern cities were as bad, and in some respects worse, than they were in the South. While white veterans with V.A.-sponsored mortgages moved from the cities to develop the de facto segregated suburbs, and financially prospered from cold war industrial development, blacks migrated from the South to the urban North in search of employment. From 1940 to 1970, over four million

---

136. Spring, *Sorting Machine*, p. 162.
137. See Spring, *Sorting Machine*, pp. 162-165.
138. See *Church Report*, III, p. 87.
139. Newman, *Protest, Politics, and Prosperity*, p. 20.

black people migrated to the inner cities of the North.[140] The great bulk of those blacks were from Southern cities, reasonably well-educated, hoping to better themselves through new job opportunities.[141] What followed was a national disaster. Jobs were not forthcoming. Black unemployment rose to more than double that of whites. Blacks did not participate to any significant extent in the cold war affluence which blessed the white, growing, suburban middle class. Black families which had so long withstood the barbarism of slavery now broke under the devastating crush of urban poverty.[142] Thus, the Northern urban centers spontaneously burst in protest against the degraded, poverty-ridden conditions which millions of blacks, adults and children, were forced to accept as a way of life. In 1964, Harlem rioted, followed by Bedford-Stuyvesant and Rochester, New York; Jersey City, Paterson, and Elizabeth, New Jersey; Philadelphia and Chicago. In the following summer of 1965, Watts rioted, causing millions of dollars in damage, 34 dead, and 856 wounded. In 1967, between June and August, 67 cities experienced black rebellion; and that summer, as Detroit burned, 41 people were killed and over 1,000 were wounded.[143] In the spring of 1968, with the assassination of Martin Luther King, Jr., came extensive rioting and destruction throughout the black ghettos.

By the time of King's death, there were many blacks who had turned away from his nonviolent strategy. While Stokely Carmichael called for "Black Power" and Malcolm X argued for black nationalism and black liberation, others, such as the Black Panthers of Chicago and the Black Slaves of Los Angeles, spoke of revolutionary action. Through the use of counterinsurgency tactics, the F.B.I. and the local police managed to destroy most of the extreme black revolutionary movements. With the death of King, the civil rights movement effectively came to a close. In many ways it had been overtaken, as King believed it would be, by the growing problems of the Vietnam War.[144]

Despite the violence and the difficulties of the 1960's, great strides were made in breaking down de jure segregation in the South, and, to a lesser extent, de facto segregation in the North. Laws were passed which proved useful in the long struggle ahead for social justice. One such law was the Civil Rights Act of 1964. John F. Kennedy had called for a stronger civil rights act but had met stiff resistance in Congress. Just five days after Kennedy's assassination on November 22, 1963, in Dallas, Texas, President Johnson appeared before Congress and said, "No memorial oration or eulogy could more eloquently honor President Kennedy's memory than the earliest possible passage of the civil rights bill for which he fought so long."[145] By the spring of 1964, the act was signed into law and the fed-

---

140. Newman, *Protest, Politics, and Prosperity*, p. 45.
141. Newman, *Protest, Politics, and Prosperity*, p. 46.
142. See Herbert Gutman, *The Black Family in Slavery and Freedom, 1750-1925* (New York: Pantheon Books, 1976).
143. Newman, *Protest, Politics, and Prosperity*, p. 21.
144. See David Levering Lewis, *King: A Biography* (Urbana: University of Illinois Press, 1979), p. 360.
145. As quoted in Spring, *Sorting Machine*, p. 175.

eral government was now authorized under eleven different titles to become directly involved in voting rights, education, public accommodations, and employment. Title VI of the act empowered the federal
bureaucracy to withhold federal funds from any educational institution if
it discriminated against persons on the basis of race, creed, color, or national origin. Title VII prohibited sex discrimination. In light of the
widening scope of federal funding for education at all levels in the decades
ahead, the act proved to be a substantial bureaucratic vehicle for forcing
some institutional change.

BLAMING THE VICTIMS

While the "social dynamite" was building up in the central cities, as
James Conant had warned, many Americans settled back to read Michael
Harrington's best-seller, *The Other America*,[146] which informed them of the
poverty they had difficulty seeing from their suburban backyards. The
crush of urban poverty on Southern black families, newly migrated in
search of jobs, was devastating. The failure of the American economic system throughout the cold war period to provide jobs and economic opportunity for all Americans remains one of the most difficult unresolved problems this nation has faced. When this problem became entwined with
racism, the issue became a volatile, social mixture with a real potential for
destroying both white and black cultures. The destiny of white suburban
and black urban Americans was inevitably linked. The Kerner Commission on Civil Disorders aptly stated the case: "What white Americans have
never fully understood—but what the Negro can never forget—is that
white society is deeply implicated in the ghetto. White institutions created it, white institutions maintain it, and white society condones it."[147]
The problems of unemployment and racism hung heavy on the American social conscience of the 1960's. President Lyndon Johnson began his
"War on Poverty" with the Economic Opportunity Act of 1964, followed
by the Elementary and Secondary Education Act of 1965. It became clear
that his major emphasis was not directed at the cause of poverty, such as
lack of jobs, but rather at the victims of poverty, who presumably were
responsible for their economic predicament. The practice of blaming blacks
for their poverty through the process of analyzing their deteriorating family
and educational conditions became a commonplace, mainstream practice,
in which the white community avoided the tougher problems, such as the
elimination of unemployment, the elimination of racism, and the elimination of an apartheid society. President Johnson went before Congress to
urge passage of the Elementary and Secondary Education Act of 1965, as
part of his "War on Poverty," informing the nation's lawmakers: "Very
often, a lack of jobs and money is not the cause of poverty, but the symptom. The cause may lie deeper—in our failure to give our fellow citizens a

---

146. Michael Harrington, *The Other America: Poverty in the United States* (New York:
Macmillan Co., 1962).

147. Otto Kerner, *Report of the National Advisory Commission on Civil Disorder* (Washington, D.C.: U.S. Government Printing Office, 1968), p. 1.

fair chance to develop their own capacities in a lack of education and training."[148] Thus, the cause of poverty was once again portrayed not as a lack of jobs and money, but rather as a lack of education and training.

This was not the first time, nor the last, that education was used to avoid some difficult issue. Recall Robert Maynard Hutchins' earlier suggestion that without the available jobs, the vocational training programs of the 1930's and 1940's were a "pernicious fraud"; remember, too, the blame that education received for what was the actual failure of the Truman and Eisenhower administrations to allocate enough resources for the space program. This kind of displacement of blame has repeatedly occurred. On close analysis, one usually finds at the heart of the matter some difficult economic, social, or political problem the society is not prepared to face. For example, when the Kerner Commission on Civil Disorders clearly and explicitly stated that "white racism is essentially responsible for the explosive mixture which has been accumulating in our cities since the end of World War II,"[149] and then went on to recommend special education for black children rather than for white children, the displacement practice of blaming the victim was clearly evident.

Repeatedly, the difficult problems of unemployment and racism have been systematically avoided through the process of expanding federal programs which call for special education for black children. As "head start," "culturally disadvantaged," and "compensatory education" entered the educationist's lexicon, it became clear that for the professionals there was money to be made in poverty. Both the educationists and the social scientists profited from the millions of federal dollars that poured into the creation, development, and evaluation of these programs. While some black children made gains, these programs did little to solve the major problems of unemployment and racism.[150]

THE CASE OF MARTIN LUTHER KING, JR.

Throughout the cold war, the American intelligence agencies actively shaped American life. From 1956 until 1971, when it was exposed, the Federal Bureau of Investigation operated a counter-intelligence program which directly shaped the civil rights movement of the 1960's. This was only one of a number of such agencies, each with its own secret counter-intelligence program, active in the internal affairs of the nation. The F.B.I. program targeted individuals and groups and employed techniques

---

148. As quoted in Julie Roy Jeffrey, *Education for Children of the Poor: A Study of the Origins and Implementation of the Elementary and Secondary Education Act of 1965* (Columbus: Ohio State University Press, 1978), p. 3.

149. Otto Kerner, *Report of the National Advisory Commission on Civil Disorder*, p. 5.

150. While the evaluations of these programs were difficult, especially because of the hidden kinds of expectations many people entertained, the "scientific" credibility of many social scientists was open to question. In the 1960's, they produced "empirical" studies to indicate certain programs would work; and in the 1970's, when the political picture had changed, the same scientists produced studies to indicate that these programs did not work. Many social scientists thus often appeared to be more servants of power than servants of truth.

that were useful during World War II and against Soviet agents in the cold war. William Sullivan, the former assistant director of the Bureau, in testimony regarding the use of "female plants" to discredit Martin Luther King, Jr., said: "This is a common practice, rough, tough, dirty business. Whether we should be in it or not, that is for you folks to decide. We are in it . . . no holds barred. We have used that technique against Soviet agents. They have used it against us."

QUESTION. The same methods were brought home?

MR. SULLIVAN. Brought home against any organization against which we were targeted. We did not differentiate. This is a rough, tough, business.

SENATOR MONDALE. Would it be safe to say that the techniques we learned in fighting . . . true espionage in World War II came to be used against some of our own American citizens?

MR. SULLIVAN. That would be a correct deduction.[151]

Sullivan went on to testify that any technique, legal or not, was used against King, including "real character assassination." When further asked whether anyone in the Bureau objected to these tactics, he said:

Never once did I hear anybody, including myself, raise the question, is this course of action which we have agreed upon lawful, is it legal, is it ethical or moral? We never gave any thought to this realm of reasoning, because we were just naturally pragmatists. The one thing we were concerned about will this course of action work, will it get us what we want, will we reach the objective that we desire to reach?

As far as legality is concerned, morals or ethics, was never raised by myself or anybody else. . . . I think this suggests really in government we are amoral.[152]

Almost from its founding in 1957, the S.C.L.C., along with King and every other major civil rights leader and organization, came under F.B.I. surveillance. However, as King and his organization rose to prominence in the movement, the Bureau intensified its investigation. Within a short time, F.B.I. activities shifted from surveillance and normal intelligence gathering to counter-insurgency, in which King was targeted by the Bureau to be destroyed as an effective black leader. Just why this occurred remains an open question.

While some commentators have come to believe that the Bureau's attacks on King resulted from his public criticism of that agency in the early 1960's, to which J. Edgar Hoover and the Bureau took serious offense, others have laid it to the racism of Hoover and the F.B.I. itself. Still others point to the voyeuristic personal character of Hoover, who seemed to relish the process of exposing important people's private sexual lives, as well as blackmailing those people with the threat of exposure. Some, however, have noted that the agency saw itself as a guardian of the status quo, and as such, it was prepared to do battle with any individual or group that tried

---

151. *Church Report*, III, pp. 134-135.
152. *Church Report*, III, p. 135.

to significantly change that order. Lastly, there are those who point to the development of the anti-Communist mission of the Bureau, which had become one of its compulsive, overpowering objectives, to the extent that, in its own thinking, it was justified in violating any individual's legal and constitutional rights.[153] Perhaps the best explanation for the F.B.I.'s behavior can be found in some kind of composite picture which includes all of these reasons. Nevertheless, the most significant and self-justifying factor welding all the factors together is the anti-Communist role in which the Bureau cast itself, the guardian of America's political and social life.

Throughout the decade 1958–1968, when the F.B.I. set out to investigate King, discredit him, and then remove him from the civil rights leadership, there existed the constant refrain that he was being advised by Communists. The Bureau made these charges to attorneys general, presidents, the Congress, and numerous newspapers and media personnel. King, himself, investigated these charges and found them unwarranted. He took the position that if a person had been a Communist but later rejected such a philosophy, he or she was welcome in the S.C.L.C. The F.B.I. was not of the same mind and identified two of King's advisors as Communists. Throughout the 1960's, and even during the Church Committee hearings of 1976, the F.B.I. refused to state why they considered Advisor A and Advisor B to be Communists.[154] However, in the late 1970's, the Bureau released a number of its files to David J. Garrow, and the information contained therein helped explain why the Bureau thought King's advisors were Communists.[155]

Advisor A was Stanley Levison; Advisor B was Jack O'Dell, who had been appointed by King to the S.C.L.C. staff on Levison's recommendation. Both Robert Kennedy and John F. Kennedy advised King to sever his connections with the two men, but King was reluctant to do so. He could find no evidence that either man was a Communist or was connected with the Communist party in any way. The F.B.I. took the matter out of King's hands by planting a front-page story in the Birmingham *News*, on June 30, 1963, entitled "King's SCLC Pays O'Dell Despite Denial."[156] Just fifteen days later, Governor George C. Wallace of Alabama testified before a Senate Committee in opposition to the Civil Rights Bill, S. 1732, charging that King's friends and associates were Communists. As evidence, he introduced the Birmingham *News* article. Two days later, on July 17, at a news conference, President Kennedy said, "We have no evidence that any of the leaders of the civil rights movement in the United States are communists."[157] On July 23, Robert Kennedy sent the following response to the Commerce Committee to questions put to him as the attorney general as a result of Wallace's earlier testimony:

153. See *Church Report*, III. Also see Lewis, *King: A Biography;* and David J. Garrow, *The FBI and Martin Luther King, Jr., from Solo to Memphis* (New York: W. W. Norton and Co., 1981), p. 82.

154. This is the way the Church Committee labeled them.

155. See Garrow, *FBI and Martin Luther King, Jr.*

156. James Free, "King's SCLC Pays O'Dell Despite Denial," *Birmingham News,* June 30, 1963, p. 1. Also see Garrow, *FBI and Martin Luther King, Jr.*, pp. 61-62.

157. *Church Report*, III, p. 99.

Based on all available evidence from the F.B.I. and other sources, we have no evidence that any of the top bodies of the major civil rights groups are Communists, or Communist controlled. This is true as to Dr. Martin Luther King, Jr., about whom particular accusations were made, as well as other leaders.

It is natural and inevitable that Communists have made efforts to infiltrate the civil rights groups to exploit the current racial situation. In view of the real injustices that exist and the resentment against them, these efforts have been remarkably unsuccessful.[158]

These public statements were made to save the civil rights bill then pending before Congress. They were also made under the assumption that King would break all connections with Levison and O'Dell. Robert Kennedy had just received a carbon copy of King's letter to O'Dell requesting that he resign from the S.C.L.C., not because he was a Communist, but because of the bad publicity his continued presence might bring to the movement.[159] Under these circumstances Robert Kennedy turned down the first F.B.I. request for a wire tap on King's home phone, but he approved a tap on Stanley Levison's home phone. The latter approval was given because the F.B.I. informed Kennedy that Levison had been an active member of the Labor Youth League in 1953–1954.[160] Angered by Kennedy's refusal to authorize a wire tap on King's home phone, J. Edgar Hoover sent him a memo on July 29, entitled "Martin Luther King, Jr: Affiliation with the Communist Movement," which detailed all of the F.B.I. allegations. Thus, the same day King was giving his famous "I Have a Dream" speech before the Lincoln Memorial, the F.B.I. was informing the attorney general and the president that their public statements about Communists in the civil rights movement were wrong.

Throughout the following fall, the F.B.I. reported to Robert Kennedy that King continued to have contact with Levison through a third party. Under such circumstances, Kennedy believed that King had broken a trust, and thus he authorized a wire tap on King's home phone on November 8, 1963.[161] Unknown to the attorney general, the F.B.I. program just getting under way included breaking and entering, as well as bugging King's hotel rooms, all as part of a larger plan to "discredit," "neutralize," and "destroy" Martin Luther King's leadership of the civil rights movement,[162] and to replace him with a Bureau-approved leader.[163]

Much of the F.B.I. case against King hinged on the question of whether or not Levison was a Communist while he was involved with the civil rights leader from approximately 1957 until 1968. All of the very close surveillance of Levison and King during this period failed to reveal any evidence that Levison was a Communist or a secret agent of the Communist party. In spite of all this cumulating evidence to the contrary, then, why did the F.B.I. continue to insist that Levison was a Communist? Fur-

158. *Church Report*, III, p. 100.
159. *Church Report*, III, p. 98.
160. *Church Report*, III, p. 101.
161. *Church Report*, III, pp. 111-115.
162. *Church Report*, III, p. 112.
163. *Church Report*, III, pp. 136-137.

thermore, why did the Bureau, as late as 1976, still refuse to reveal to the Church Committee its reasons for thinking Levison was a Communist? Having had access to F.B.I. files, David J. Garrow suggests that the reason the Bureau refused was because they did not want to expose the extent to which they had penetrated the Communist party in the United States at its very top echelons. Garrow further suggests that through their double agents, the F.B.I. was deeply involved in laundering Soviet money for the American Communist party. The F.B.I.'s Solo Project was so successful that one American official remarked, "For years the F.B.I. practically had been paying Gus Hall's salary, and with Soviet money."[164] Garrow argues that Levison was involved in this process from 1952 until the late summer of 1956, when he moved out of the business entirely. While Garrow claims that the Childs brothers (F.B.I. double agents) were the ones who pointed the finger at Levison, Levison himself repeatedly blamed his troubles with the F.B.I. on a close business associate named Jay Richard Kennedy, the former Samuel Richard Solomonick.[165]

Jay Kennedy had an interesting career and appears to be the person for whom the Solo Project was named. Levison first met Kennedy when the latter was part-owner of Unique Specialties Corporation, a tool-and-die firm. Levison was hired by Kennedy as a legal counsel and troubleshooter for the company during the war years. Jay Kennedy, as Samuel Solomonick, had been circulation manager for the *Daily Worker* until his disillusionment with the Communist party in 1939, when Hitler signed a non-aggression pact with the Soviet Union. Breaking with the Communist party, Solomonick became jobless and fell into some financial difficulties. Subsequently, he was befriended by Andrew Loewi, of the Loewi family, who owned Park Management Corporation and various other holdings throughout New York City.[166] It was at this point that Solomonick changed his name, and soon thereafter he managed to put together $50,000 with a partner to buy the Unique Specialties Corporation. A short time later, Jay Kennedy extended his business ventures to the Kennedy Real-Estate Management Corporation. By December 1941, Levison had moved from Unique Specialties to Kennedy Management, and had become an active partner with Kennedy in the affairs of the corporation. A few years later, Kennedy married Levison's former wife and they moved to California, where he made propaganda films for the State Department, to be used in Central and South America.[167] The Kennedy firm, now managed by Levison, developed extensive business holdings all the way from a large Ford dealership in New York to a wholesale laundry business in Ecuador. Levison became a successful, respected businessman, involved in the work of the American Jewish Congress. By 1949, Kennedy and Levison had had a heated falling-out, resulting in the dissolution of their partnership, with Levison retaining control of the Kennedy Management Corporation.

While Garrow insists that there was no connection between the F.B.I.

164. Garrow, *FBI and Martin Luther King, Jr.*, p. 38.
165. Garrow, *FBI and Martin Luther King, Jr.*, p. 40.
166. Garrow, *FBI and Martin Luther King, Jr.*, pp. 31-32.
167. Garrow, *FBI and Martin Luther King, Jr.*, p. 31.

and Jay Kennedy, Elizabeth Gurley Flynn and other Communists were suspicious that Kennedy was an F.B.I. informer, and they believed that the government movie contracts were a payoff for that activity.[168] What seems more plausible, however, is that the F.B.I. Solo Project originated with Solomonick who, with financial assistance from the Bureau, helped set up the Kennedy business enterprises, which were used to launder Soviet money for the Communist party. The fact that Party members were becoming suspicious of Kennedy might account for his quick move to California, leaving the business to Levison. According to F.B.I. informers, Levison was still trusted by Gus Hall and other Party members right up to 1956, when he decided not to launder any more money for the Party. While some F.B.I. agents are reported to have suggested that Levison was a "secret financial benefactor" of the Communist party as early as 1945 or 1946, it seems clear that it was Kennedy, alias Solomonick, who created the original corporate structure used for the "Solo" laundering system.[169] By 1960, after Levison had cut his ties with the Communist party, the F.B.I. trusted him enough to try to hire him as an informer. He refused.[170] Some years later, before Senator James O. Eastland's Internal Security Subcommittee, Levison testified under oath: "I am a loyal American and I am not now and never have been a member of the Communist Party." In regard to all other questions involving his possible financial dealings with the Party, he took the Fifth Amendment.[171] Thus, not only Levison's financial dealings but the F.B.I.'s Solo Project escaped public detection. As late as 1964, the F.B.I. was offering the S.C.L.C. tainted money through its "Solo" apparatus, and on Levison's advice, King turned it down.[172]

What, then, happened to Jay Richard Kennedy? He continued working as an entertainers' agent and gradually became more involved in the civil rights movement. He cultivated his friendship with James Farmer, director of C.O.R.E., from 1960 to 1970, while he served as a key informant, not for the F.B.I., but for the C.I.A. In 1965, after the Selma confrontation, Jay Kennedy reported his concern to the C.I.A. of the necessity of finding a replacement for King, if and when he was "either exposed or assassinated."[173]

The question of Levison's and Kennedy's exact participation in the Solo Project, as well as the F.B.I. and C.I.A. roles in the project, may never be known. All seemed to have been deeply involved in one form or another, and all had a significant impact on the civil rights movement. It may well be that Kennedy set up the Solo Project and Levison continued to financially profit from the arrangement. Perhaps Levison was not a Communist party member and his problems with the F.B.I. resulted from his partnership with Kennedy, as he claimed. Whatever the case, it is clear that

168. Garrow, *FBI and Martin Luther King, Jr.*, p. 33.
169. Garrow, *FBI and Martin Luther King, Jr.*, p. 40.
170. Garrow, *FBI and Martin Luther King, Jr.*, p. 42.
171. Garrow, *FBI and Martin Luther King, Jr.*, p. 48.
172. Garrow, *FBI and Martin Luther King, Jr.*, p. 158.
173. Garrow, *FBI and Martin Luther King, Jr.*, p. 140.

King apparently accepted Levison's explanation, while the F.B.I. did not. Levison continued to be listed by the F.B.I. on their top-ranked "Security Index" until his death. Such listing clearly indicated their belief that he was a Communist party member. King's name was placed in the next category below Levison's, in "Section A" of the "Reserve Index."[174]

On December 29, 1963, *Time* magazine chose Dr. King as its "Man of the Year," describing him as the "unchallenged voice of the Negro people . . . [who] has infused the Negroes themselves with the fiber that gives their revolution its true stature."[175] King, however, had already been targeted for character assassination. Just six days earlier, on December 23, 1963, a nine-hour conference was held at F.B.I. headquarters in Washington, D.C., in which a list of twenty-one techniques to discredit King was discussed, including the use of "female plants" and the appropriate surveillance devices. Microphones were installed in more than fifteen motels and hotels in which King stayed during the period from January 5, 1964, to November 29, 1965.[176] Some tapes were reproduced, while others were transcribed and put on mimeograph for distribution. The material was sent to world figures and to American political, religious, educational, and social leaders. One tape was sent to King, with a note suggesting that he commit suicide.[177]

In addition, through its easy access to the news and publishing channels, the Bureau prevented King from getting his own material published, while its agents wrote critical news stories which were quickly printed. Using information gained through wire taps, they exploited rifts between King and other civil rights leaders by sending them false and misleading information. They initiated an Internal Revenue Service investigation of King, and sent materials to all S.C.L.C. contributors, insinuating that King had been misusing funds. Throughout this massive campaign, the Bureau injected false information and false charges designed to discredit and destroy King as a leader.

The agency left no stone unturned. When Marquette University considered giving King an honorary degree, they were persuaded by the F.B.I. not to do so. The campaign was also carried into all churches of every denomination. When King requested an audience with the Pope, the F.B.I. approached Cardinal Spellman of New York to advise the Pope not to grant King's request. In October of 1964, when King was named to receive the Nobel Peace Prize, the Bureau quickly contacted European leaders as to King's flawed character. They paid particular attention to discouraging any "welcome home" ceremonies that might be initiated in his honor after the award was presented. The civil rights leader was, indeed, a "marked" man, as the assistant director of the F.B.I. wrote the day after King's famous "I Have a Dream" speech in Washington:

---

174. This was the index the Agency kept of all persons they believed should be rounded up and detained in the event of a national emergency. They were not necessarily enemy agents or Communists, but were influential people who could be used by the Party and therefore were considered dangerous.

175. *Church Report,* III, p. 135.

176. *Church Report,* III, p. 120.

177. *Church Report,* III, pp. 158-161.

Personally, I believe, in the light of King's powerful demagogic speech yesterday, he stands head and shoulders over all other Negro leaders put together when it comes to influencing great masses of Negroes. We must mark him now, if we have not done so before, as the most dangerous Negro of the future in this Nation from the standpoint of communism, the Negro and national security.[178]

Thus, King was marked, not because he was a violent revolutionary, but because of his leadership potential as an effective nonviolent leader. As the blacks' strongest leader, he was repeatedly listed as potentially the most dangerous, and the one who had the highest "potential for violence."[179]

The F.B.I. had targeted for destruction the most effective black leader, the one who stood most opposed to violent action. With respect to Communist influence in the movement, it was ironic that with all the very close surveillance of Levison, King, and the S.C.L.C., no Communist connections could be found.[180] Nevertheless, the agency continued its campaign.

The nonviolent demonstrations that worked so well from Montgomery to Selma began to run into increasing difficulty. As early as 1965, King had taken a position against the increasing involvement of the United States in the Vietnam War. This resulted in an immediate falling-out with the Johnson administration. It was not until the Mississippi voter registration drive that King became aware of the full implication of that estrangement. With his demonstrators badly beaten up, he called President Lyndon Johnson from Canton, Mississippi, for help, but his call was never answered. Equally important was the effect the Johnson administration had in quietly supporting Mayor Daley against King in his Chicago campaign. Not only were the Northern urban ghetto problems different from those in the South, but in many ways they seemed even more intractable. In addition, King now had the F.B.I. and the weight of the federal government's executive branch against him. Increasingly, he found himself facing many political and economic issues which were not amenable to solution by way of demonstrations.

King supported the Mississippi Freedom Democratic party and its attempt to be seated at the 1964 Democratic Convention in Atlantic City. President Johnson ordered a special F.B.I. surveillance squad to work the rooms of the M.F.D.P. at the convention. Through White House aides Bill Moyers and Walter Jenkins, information was channeled to the president, and he was able to make effective use of the information by countering each move that was made and breaking the M.F.D.P.'s attempt to be seated.[181] The F.B.I. proved to be a valuable tool in the manipulation of American politics. Most of King's actions in the civil rights movement were known to the president long before they were carried out.

King's nonviolent approach to social change ran into problems from other quarters. As the S.N.C.C., C.O.R.E., and others called for "black power," many young people interpreted that to mean all-black demonstra-

---

178. *Church Report*, III, pp. 107-108.
179. *Church Report*, III, pp. 20-21.
180. Even the F.B.I., at times, had to admit it. See *Church Report*, III, p. 106.
181. See Garrow, *FBI and Martin Luther King, Jr.*, p. 119.

tions and more aggressive, if not violent, action against the controlling white community. King's nonviolent approach was now made to appear weak and conservative, as many black youth were attracted to the Black Panther party and other militant protest groups. These radical extremist organizations were even more heavily infiltrated by the F.B.I. than was the S.C.L.C. The Bureau exploited and nurtured the violent versus nonviolent rift in the civil rights movement. King repeatedly warned young people against following a course of violence, which he said would beget violence. He told them that a black minority can never succeed against a white majority through violence. On the eve of the Cicero march, surrounded by blacks chanting "get whitey" and "black power," King said: "Even if every Negro in the United States comes to think that Negroes ought to riot, I am going to stand as that lone voice and say, it's impractical, it's unsound, and we'll never get our own way that way."[182] The media, heavily saturated with F.B.I. materials against King, and in the context of the social turmoil of the country at large, now depicted King as a weak, indecisive, conservative figure whose day had passed.

If one defines a radical as a person who goes to the root of the problem and takes effective action to solve that problem, then Martin Luther King, Jr., was, indeed, one of the most radical black leaders of the decade. After his Chicago campaign, he reflected: "For years I labored with the idea of reforming the existing institutions of the society, a little change here, a little change there." He went on to say: "Now I feel quite differently. I think you've got to have a reconstruction of the entire society, a revolution of values."[183] The goal of social and economic justice, he came to realize, could never be achieved as long as racism continued to separate and, thereby, politically disarm poor blacks and poor whites. Together, free of the crippling effects of racism, blacks and whites could provide a most powerful political force for social and economic justice.

Having successfully broken down the legal barriers of segregation in the South through nonviolence, this champion of civil rights now planned to go to the root of the problem and break through the chains of racism that subjugated poor whites and poor blacks, organizing them to take political action to achieve social justice. From the standpoint of both the F.B.I. and the C.I.A., King was becoming even more dangerous, not because he advocated the violent overthrow of the federal government, as Communists did, but because he insisted on using effective nonviolent democratic means to solve the nation's problems. In attempting to organize the poor of all races in America, King was on a course that he and the F.B.I. knew was an extreme threat to the existing social order. On a national television program during the summer before his assassination, he reflected: "It didn't cost the nation anything to guarantee the right to vote, or to guarantee access to public accommodations, but we are dealing with issues now that will cost the nation something."[184]

King was clear in his own mind as to what had to be done. He saw the relationship of the Vietnam War to the problem of poverty at home. Not

---

182. As quoted in Lewis, *King: A Biography,* p. 337.
183. Lewis, *King: A Biography,* p. 354.
184. Lewis, *King: A Biography,* p. 403.

only did the war withdraw much-needed money from poverty programs, but, even more cruelly, the poor were forced to take on a disproportionate share of fighting and dying. As King said,

Perhaps a more tragic recognition of reality took place when it became clear to me that the war was doing far more than devastating the hopes of the poor at home. It was sending their sons and their brothers and their husbands to fight and die and in extraordinarily high proportions relative to the rest of the population. . . . I could not be silent in the face of such cruel manipulation of the poor.[185]

As the numbers increased, the Vietnam War became, as King called it, a poor peoples' war. Thus, for him, the issue of the war had clearly fused with his proposed poor peoples' march.

King was building a potentially powerful political coalition against very significant opposition. As plans for the march on Washington progressed, he became involved in the garbage strike in Memphis, Tennessee. After leading one demonstration that ended in violence, King confronted the Invaders, the youthful gang who caused the violence, and persuaded them to desist. He then proceeded to schedule a new march.[186] In the interim, news came that Lyndon Johnson would not run again for the presidency. Overnight the political scene had changed, and King postponed his poor peoples' march on Washington to reconsider his strategy. A very real potential for political, social, and economic change appeared just off the horizon, but it would disappear with the successive assassinations of Martin Luther King, Jr., on April 4, 1968, and presidential candidate Robert Kennedy, on June 5, 1968. With the deaths of these two men, the voice of the poor was effectively stilled.[187]

King arrived in Memphis on the morning of April 3, with Ralph Abernathy and Jim Harrison, comptroller for the S.C.L.C. and key F.B.I. informer, after a plane delay because of a bomb scare.[188] He had come to recognize that he was a marked man and that he very well could pay for his beliefs and activities with his life. His last sermon that evening in the Masonic Temple reflected this awareness, as he moved the congregation to tears by saying,

Like anybody, I would like to live a long life. Longevity has its place. But I'm not concerned about that now. I just want to do God's will. And He's allowed me to go up to the mountain. And I've looked over, and I've seen the promised land.

I may not get there with you, but I want you to know tonight that we as a people will get to the promised land. So I'm happy tonight. I'm not worried about anything. I'm not fearing any man. 'Mine eyes have seen the glory of the coming of the Lord.'[189]

---

185. Lewis, *King: A Biography*, p. 359.
186. The F.B.I. had informers as members of the Invaders at that meeting.
187. Although for most of Robert Kennedy's political career he was liberal, and at times even conservative, close analysis of his political behavior in the last year of his life reveals that he was becoming radicalized, much as Martin Luther King, Jr., was radical.
188. Garrow, *FBI and Martin Luther King, Jr.*, p. 198.
189. Lewis, *King: A Biography*, p. 387.

While the Bureau busied itself with a news release designed to get King to stay at the Lorraine Hotel,[190] Memphis police chief Frank Holloman, a former F.B.I. agent and administrative assistant to J. Edgar Hoover, recalled the police officers who were guarding King because he had heard that there was a murder plot against one of them.[191] Thus, the first person to reach the fallen leader was Merril McCullen, an undercover F.B.I. informant who had successfully infiltrated King's official family. Just two minutes after the fatal shots were fired, an unidentified voice came across the police radio frequency, repeating in five sequenced broadcasts: "Information, subject may be in late model Mustang going north on Main." The suspected killer, James Earl Ray, was, in fact, in a white Mustang going in the opposite direction.[192]

The death of Martin Luther King, Jr., did not end the F.B.I.'s attempt to discredit him. That project continued for the next fifteen years, and came to the fore whenever Congress considered making Martin Luther King's birthday a national holiday. In the fall of 1983, when Congress finally decided to so honor the slain civil rights leader, it was Senator Jesse Helms who stood up in Congress and requested that the F.B.I. material be made public so as to disgrace King once and for all. The Bureau's campaign to discredit the man continues unabated. David J. Garrow, having been granteed access to certain F.B.I. files, reports that the Bureau is reputed to have a "Top Secret" file in which they have a quotation from King saying "I am a Marxist."[193] This not only flies in the face of King's repeated disclaimer of any Marxist connections, but, more importantly, it flies in the face of the fact that King believed in God, explicitly rejected materialism as a philosophy of life, and all his life stood opposed to violent revolution. Martin Luther King, Jr., was not a Marxist, nor a Communist, nor does the evidence suggest he associated with Communists. He was a radical black leader who came to believe that a fundamental redistribution of wealth and power was essential to fulfill a dream of social justice for both black and white America. He was not a Communist, but a Christian minister who took the social gospel of his ministry seriously.

While it is often difficult to ascertain what the F.B.I.'s exact role was in determining events with respect to Martin Luther King, Jr., and the civil rights movement, it becomes even more difficult to analyze the F.B.I.'s involvement in the history of the Black Panther party and other extremist groups. The Bureau's covert program to destroy the Black Panthers and other such groups was most thorough.[194] It had so penetrated the leadership of the Black Panthers, the United Slaves of Los Angeles, and the Blackstone Rangers of Chicago, that any serious attempt to assess accurately what really took place is a virtual impossibility. The F.B.I. programs were deeply involved in creating conflict between groups and individuals, to such an extent that it is not possible to determine where the

---

190. *Church Report*, III, p. 182.
191. See James Coates, "Why Many See Ray as Conspirator," *Chicago Tribune*, Aug. 21, 1978, p. 7. Also see Lewis, *King: A Biography*, p. 401.
192. Lewis, *King: A Biography*, pp. 402-403.
193. Garrow, *FBI and Martin Luther King, Jr.*, p. 213.
194. See *Church Report*, III, pp. 187-220.

Bureau's involvement in bombings and assassinations either begins or ends. Most of the leadership of the violence-prone Black Panthers died either in gun battles with police or at the hands of other black street gang leaders. The exact circumstances surrounding all those deaths may never be determined without complete access to F.B.I. files, which cover their covert action within those organizations.[195]

THE ANTIWAR MOVEMENT

Martin Luther King, Jr.'s assessment of the developing Vietnam War was accurate. It was a war in which blacks were killed and wounded in disproportionate numbers: they made up 12.5 per cent of the general population but 25 per cent of those killed and wounded in Vietnam.[196] Blacks and lower-class whites were the groups least able to avoid serving in what became the most unpopular war in America's history. The major avenue for escape from that war was the deferment offered to college students. Some collegians were moved to an anti-Vietnam War position by the conscience-pricking arguments of Martin Luther King, Jr., Yale University's William Sloan Coffin, M.I.T.'s Noam Chomsky, the Berrigan brothers, Dr. Benjamin Spock, and many others. Most, however, remained committed to support the government policy until the spring of 1966.[197] At that point, the government changed its college deferment policy and decided to draft students who were ranked among the lower levels of their class. Thus, when the Selective Service System asked colleges and universities to submit class rankings, the antiwar movement, as well as pressure for grade inflation, became a major campus problem.[198] What developed was a firestorm of campus unrest and demonstrations. Peace would not return to college campuses until either the draft system was changed or the war in Vietnam ended. The former occurred first because it was easier to do. By late 1969, President Nixon began taking steps toward a volunteer, professional army, and the demonstrations on campus began to dwindle, well before the war in Vietnam actually came to an end. While the motives of those who took part in the antiwar demonstrations were often varied and complex, and many youths opposed the war for highly ethical, selfless moral reasons, a critical factor with regard to campus demonstrations appears to have been the self-interest factor of the draft.[199] Nevertheless, the

---

195. A survey of the *Church Report,* III, pp. 187-220, leads one to this conclusion.

196. As reported in "The Different Drummer: Blacks in the Military," Part II, P.B.S. documentary, Feb. 20, 1984. Also see Wallace Terry II, "Bringing the War Home," *The Black Scholar,* II, 3 (Nov. 1970), 6-16.

197. A variety of campus surveys indicate that student opposition to the war did not pass the majority mark until some time in 1968.

198. See Arthur M. Schlesinger, Jr., *The Imperial Presidency* (Boston: Houghton Mifflin Co., 1973), p. 199.

199. There were, of course, other factors at work as well. The Education Commission of the States and other organizations had developed a variety of plans and procedures to restore campus order. Most of these worked on the "self-interest" of both faculty and graduate students. As the government closed down its postdoctorate fellowships, as did the major foundations, the effect was an instant surplus of faculty who now had to compete for a limited number of positions. The same effect was produced as graduate student fellow-

antiwar movement swept together and fused a wide diversity of groups for a short period of time.

One such group was the Students for a Democratic Society, first formed at an inspirational conference held in Port Huron, Michigan, on June 11–15, 1962, long before the Vietnam War became an issue. The students who met at Port Huron and organized the S.D.S. were, for the most part, children born during World War II to leftist, liberal parents, who had been actively engaged in a variety of liberal reform movements in the 1930s, but had been frozen into silence during the McCarthy era, with all the black-listing threats that it entailed. The children of that generation's activists were now prepared to speak out. They had their own dream, born of cold war experiences, and they articulated it in the *Port Huron Statement*, an "Agenda for a Generation":

As we grew, however, our comfort was penetrated by events too troubling to dismiss. First, the permeating and victimizing fact of human degradation, symbolized by the Southern struggle against racial bigotry, compelled most of us from silence to activism. Second, the enclosing fact of the cold war, symbolized by the presence of the Bomb, brought awareness that we ourselves, and our friends, and millions of abstract "others" we knew more directly because of our common peril, might die at any time. We might deliberately ignore, or avoid, or fail to feel all other human problems, but not these two, for these were too immediate and crushing in their impact, too challenging in the demands that we as individuals take the responsibility for encounter and resolution.[200]

The *Port Huron Statement*, a liberal document, called for an end to racial bigotry, discrimination in all forms, poverty, violence, and exploitation of all peoples. It specifically demanded programs which would lead to an end to the policy of deterrence and toward a universally controlled disarmament program and a negotiated peace with the Soviet Union. The document spoke out for world peace, the demilitarization of America, and the cultivation of the promise of American democracy. Stimulated by the promise of the Kennedy administration for social change and the civil rights movement for social justice, the S.D.S. was born as a liberal leftist coalition of students opposed to the cold war. Its early growth was slow but steady on larger campuses. However, as the Vietnam War developed, it became, almost overnight, the leading student antiwar organization, joined by the liberal mainstream youth as well as the more radical students, such as those from the Progressive Labor party. It also became, at most, only a loose coalition of diverse groups, held together by a common antiwar cause. In spite of its original statement on the civil rights movement and the participation of many of its early leaders in that movement in the South, the S.D.S. was primarily an all-white organization which never did effectively overcome its racial identity. While blacks pressed for

---

ships were cut at all levels. In those states that had the most severe campus disruptions, state-wide budget freezes were instituted which had an immediate effect on hiring practices. These and other bureaucratic measures were taken to pacify the campuses.

200. Tom Hayden, *The Port Huron Statement* (Chicago: Students for a Democratic Society, 1962), p. 3.

their place on campus in terms of organizations, student aid, and curricula, the common ground between the black student organizations and the S.D.S. was never really established, except in terms of the antiwar cause which unified all such groups.

As the demonstrations increased in size, and opposition to the continuing war grew both on and off campus, frustrations intensified. Strikes and sit-ins brought police riot squads and then military units onto campuses, and the ensuing confrontations led to violence in which many were injured and some died. Long before the antiwar campus conflicts of 1968 and 1969 had occurred, the F.B.I., C.I.A., and D.I.A. agents[201] had infiltrated a number of student organizations on campus and were employing the same counter-intelligence tactics on antiwar groups and their leadership that they had employed on the civil rights movement. As the violence escalated and bombings increased, it once again became difficult to determine just where F.B.I., C.I.A., and D.I.A. involvement in such activity began and ended.

The antiwar movement grew in size because the sentiments of mainstream college youths shifted, along with their parents, against the war. Although much has been made of the alienation that surfaced in the 1960's between parent and child—the so-called generation gap—the great bulk of the children of the suburbs who entered college reflected the values and career aspirations and desires for mobility that had been instilled in them by their parents. That aspect of the mainstream did not appreciably change. What had changed, however, was the critical position that both parents and students found themselves in as the war expanded and college deferment slipped away. An antiwar or pacifist stand was repugnant to the self-image of many mainstream college students and their parents, many of whom were war veterans themselves; nevertheless, the Vietnam War cut deeply into the aspirations they held for their children as well as those their children held for themselves. Even though many middle-class suburban families suffered the agony of divisive generational conflict, the antiwar movement on campus did not markedly increase until the parents of that class shifted to an antiwar position.

Once the middle class shifted from a pro- to an antiwar stance, the so-called light at the end of the tunnel was in view. The security-minded class of 1949 was not about to have their dreams for their children—to have a larger share of the material and social rewards of the culture—jeopardized. The values of this class were clearly reflected in the ease with which the antiwar protestors' younger siblings so quickly and easily adapted to the careerism which came to dominate the universities in the 1970's.

Not all middle-class youth were satisfied with their parents' suburban way of living, however. Some sought a better life-style by experimenting with various means of escape, including communal living, employing ancient religious practices, modern psychic manipulation, and heavy use of mind-altering drugs. Others, while remaining in the mainstream of the system, followed in the footsteps of their parents and used marijuana and

---

201. D.I.A. stands for Defense Intelligence Agency. It is primarily a military intelligence agency, usually employed when military interests are involved.

alcohol to escape the contradictions of their lives. The dream which some held of ending the cold war and fulfilling the promise of American democracy was not to be realized.

EDUCATIONAL RHETORIC AND REFORM

Many of the university practices developed after World War II that were instituted to manage larger numbers of students came under severe criticism during the antiwar movement of the late 1960's. Most of the university reforms of that period, designed to counter those criticisms, tended to be only cosmetic and temporary in nature. After the Vietnam War, the university returned to its prewar course, emphasizing research by its professors and vocational career training for its students. The trend of vocationalism and research, against which Irving Babbitt, Paul Elmer More, and Robert M. Hutchins had earlier warned, had overtaken the liberal arts colleges in most institutions, so that what remained was liberal in name only. For most students and parents, career training became the dominant function of the university.

As quiet returned to the campuses during the 1970's, college students and parents read of a new criticism of education. While the educational rhetoric of the early 1960's was dominated by society's cold war needs, which were reflected in such federally sponsored programs as the "new" math, physics, and foreign language programs, new, more child-centered voices began to be heard in the late 1960's. A continuing child-centered theme that often reached back to Paul Goodman's earlier work, while expressing immediate dissatisfaction with the deteriorating conditions in the urban and suburban schools, was reflected in John Holt's *How Children Fail* (1964), Nat Hentoff's *Our Children Are Dying* (1966), Jonathan Kozol's *Death at an Early Age* (1967), James Herndon's *The Way It Spozed to Be* (1968) and *How to Survive in Your Native Land* (1971), and George Dennison's *The Lives of Children: The Story of the First Street School* (1969). Some found the bureaucratic structures so intractable that they advocated and developed alternative schools, which became small educationally innovative enclaves within the system. Others, such as Ivan Illich in *Deschooling Society* (1970), suggested that society ought to return to a preindustrial age and abandon its dependence on schools entirely.

As some educators talked and wrote, it seemed as though progressive education was about to be born again in the form of "open education." The movement, however, was stillborn, and fairly quickly passed into oblivion. Amid all these diverse voices of criticism, the Carnegie Corporation, as it had done with James B. Conant in the 1950's, now came to the fore by heavily financing and popularizing Charles Silberman's *Crisis in the Classroom* (1970). Silberman, as had his predecessor, attempted to chart a pragmatic middle-of-the-road course.

By 1969, Arthur Jensen, in "How Much Can We Boost I.Q. and Scholastic Achievement?"[202] had trucked out the older, badly flawed research

---

202. Arthur Jensen, "How Much Can We Boost I.Q. and Scholastic Achievement?" *Harvard Educational Review*, XXXIX (1969), 1-128.

to "prove" once again the genetic superiority of whites over blacks. His article, almost like a weather vane, pointed to a marked shift in educational rhetoric. The liberal winds of the 1960's gave way to the conservative winds of the 1970's. As the political climate changed, so, too, did the work of professional education and social science experts. Those who once had produced "objective scientific" studies to justify expanding federal government education programs, now, in the 1970's, produced equally "objective scientific" studies to suggest that such programs ought to be shut down. While educationists and social scientists followed the decreasing flow of dollars and rode the wave of conservatism in the 1970's, education, itself, entered a period of "benign neglect" at virtually all levels of instruction.

Having spent more than $1,000 billion on the cold war from 1945 to 1965, fewer and fewer new resources were to be found for urban renewal and education in general. These developments were exacerbated as the multinational corporations, in pursuit of larger profits and cheaper labor, began closing down America's heavy industry and relocating it in less-well-developed nations. These developments, in conjunction with increasing automation and trilateral economic arrangements, spelled extremely high rates of unemployment and a devastating increase in poverty. By 1984, one of every five children and one of every two black children lived in poverty.[203]

As infant mortality, malnutrition, crime, child abuse, and drug addiction rates climbed, along with unemployment rates and poverty indicators, the schools reflected not only the "benign neglect" of the 1970's, but also the devastating economic and social circumstances in which children lived. In many urban areas, the schools were in a state of virtual collapse, as more and more new funding was diverted to house a growing prison population. The "social dynamite" of urban America had built up to massive proportions.

In the context of these economic and social conditions, the federal government and leading foundations launched a series of studies which focused attention on education, rather than economics, as the source of the problem. The United States Department of Education's *A Nation at Risk* (1983) was quickly followed by a study of the Education Commission of the States' Task Force on Education for Economic Growth, entitled *Action for Excellence*. The Carnegie Corporation produced *Education and Economic Progress: Toward a National Educational Policy;* the Carnegie Foundation for the Advancement of Teaching, in cooperation with the Atlantic Richfield Foundation, produced *High School: A Report on American Secondary Education;* and numerous other foundations and organizations financed their own studies. All of these reports analyzed and documented the faltering educational system. Some reports, more than others, obliquely seemed to recognize the social and economic conditions which gave rise to the educational malaise. None, however, squarely faced the fact that the problem rested with the economic system which had consistently failed to produce enough jobs. Furthermore, as a consequence of America's institutional racism,

---

203. See House Select Committee on Children, Youth and Families, *Report.*

blacks, Hispanics, and other minorities were made to carry a disproportionate share of the burden of that failure. Once again, one could observe the cycle of unemployment, devastating poverty, and social dynamite, followed by educational critiques which in effect continued to blame the victims by treating the symptom rather than the cause of the malady. For millions trapped in the morass of institutional racism and the chaos of poverty, the dream of which Martin Luther King, Jr., had spoken had not just failed to come true; instead, it had turned into a nightmare in the face of the reality of urban life. Social justice, as King had come to recognize it, would "cost something." America was not yet willing to pay that price.

THE WOMEN'S MOVEMENT

Clearly, the American community was not ready to do what was required to resolve its economic and racial difficulties, just as it was not quite ready to grant the American female full equality. The struggles for social justice for women and blacks have been historically linked. The women's rights movement is often traced to the pre-Civil War era, when American women abolitionists, at the 1840 World's Anti-Slavery Convention in London, were not allowed on the convention floor, but were allowed only to observe from the galleries.[204] The women's struggle for social justice which began to unfold at the Seneca Falls, New York, conference in 1848, under the leadership of Elizabeth Cady Stanton, Lucretia Mott, and others, was in many respects largely overshadowed by the abolitionist movement and the events of the Civil War. The struggle for women's rights, with respect to the right to vote, was a difficult one, even as such women as Lucy Stone and Susan B. Anthony became legendary suffragettes. While blacks were given the constitutional right to vote with the passage of the Fifteenth Amendment in 1870, it was not until 1920 that women were given that right, with the passage of the Nineteenth Amendment. Free exercise of the franchise by blacks was not to be realized until a century later, just as exercise of the franchise by women would not be fully realized on an operational par with men until the 1980's.[205]

While the black movement and the women's movement are indeed very different, they are similar in that they both represent a repressed class struggling for equity. Racist and sexist stereotypes have similar psycho-social components. In periods of heightened consciousness, as regards social justice involving one group, it is reasonable to find that consciousness reverberating with regard to other groups as well. Thus, it is not surprising that the same decade of the 1960's which spawned the civil rights movement generated renewed life in the feminist movement as well.

---

204. See Aileen S. Kraditor, *The Ideas of the Woman's Suffrage Movement, 1890-1920* (New York: Columbia University Press, 1965). Also see Eleanor Flexner, *Century of Struggle: The Women's Rights Movement in the United States* (Cambridge, Mass.: Harvard University Press, 1975); and William Henry Chafe, *The American Woman, Her Changing Social, Economic, and Political Roles, 1920-1970* (New York: Oxford University Press, 1972).

205. See Sandra Baxter and Marjorie Lansing, *Women and Politics: The Visible Majority* (Ann Arbor: University of Michigan Press, 1983).

The first phase of the women's movement, which began in the nineteenth century, focused heavily on the right to vote. After seventy-two years of struggle, which included picketing, marching, and going to jail, women received the right to vote in 1920. By that time the movement seemed to have peaked. However, women still faced a male-dominated society which not only continued to discriminate politically and socially against them, but was also culturally and institutionally sexist in character. The new, male-dominated advertising and entertainment industries of the 1930's and 1940's exploited and cultivated a sexist image of women for commercial purposes.[206]

The place of women in society radically changed as a result of World War II. By 1940, the majority of women still saw their careers in terms of a lifetime commitment to rearing a family. Only 25 per cent of all women of working age were in the work force in 1940, the same as it had been in 1910.[207] By 1945, as a result of the war, that figure had jumped to 36 per cent, and it never again returned to the prewar figure. With the war over, veterans were given job preferences, and men squeezed women out of the work force, especially in traditional male-dominated areas of employment. By 1950, the number of all women of working age in the work force had dropped to 34 per cent; in the next decade, it rose to 38 per cent, and increased in every decade thereafter until it reached 53 per cent by 1980.[208] The escalating number of women in the work force was a major stimulus in creating the new women's movement.

In spite of the continuing male-inspired ideology that a "woman's place is in the home," women were now moving into the work force in larger numbers. This shift was cultivated, on the one hand, by the desires of a growing middle class for more consumer goods and services associated with suburban living, and, on the other hand, by a rapid expansion of the new consumer industry's need for cheap labor.[209] Many women entered the labor market and helped pay for the mortgages, the television sets, the second cars, and the children's college educations. The jobs they took were almost invariably the lower-paying ones.[210] As they sought mobility in the work force, women ran into sexist, discriminatory practices that were well-institutionalized. Along with blacks, women were largely overeducated for their occupational level of work. They were also guided into certain lower-paying occupational levels. Today, approximately 80 per cent of all women work in only 25 of the 420 occupations. Such occupations as secretaries are 99 per cent female; nurses are 97 per cent female; elementary school teachers are 84 per cent female; and clerks are 86 per cent fe-

206. See Stuart Ewen, *Captains of Consciousness* (New York: McGraw-Hill Book Co., 1976), pp. 113-177.

207. See Mary Leach, "Women's Lives and Women's Liberation: Opportunities and Imperatives" (unpublished Ph.D. diss., University of Illinois, 1986), p. 3.

208. Baxter and Lansing, *Women and Politics*, p. 28.

209. For the implication for women in the labor market, see Veronica F. Nina and Barbara A. Gutek, *Women and Work: A Psychological Perspective* (New York: Praeger, 1981). Also see the Cambridge Women's Studies Group, *Women in Society* (London: Virago Press, 1981).

210. Leach, "Women's Lives and Women's Liberation," p. 5.

male.[211] As a result of this process, even though women have now entered the work force in comparable numbers to men, they continue to earn approximately sixty cents of every dollar earned by their male counterparts.[212] While pressure has been brought to raise pay levels for jobs of "comparable worth," there is still a major unfinished struggle to pay women the same as men for the "exact same" work.

Black women have suffered doubly from racism and sexism. By 1966, their average income, which was often the sole family income, was only 71 per cent of what white women received.[213] Under such depressing economic conditions, in 1980 black and white women and their children together made up 95 per cent of all welfare recipients and 70 per cent of all those who received food stamps.[214] Thus, the increasing numbers of women in the 1960's entering the work force, directly experiencing the effects of discrimination, combined with an increase in social consciousness emerging from the civil rights movement, helped produce the social context out of which a new feminist movement emerged.

In 1961, President Kennedy appointed a Presidential Commission on Women, to be headed by Eleanor Roosevelt. The work of the commission resulted in the first major piece of federal legislation prohibiting sex discrimination in the work force: the Equal Pay Act of 1963.[215] While the commission was correctly given credit for producing this important piece of legislation, it had more importantly created a network of highly educated women who became the leaders for the new women's movement. By 1964, when the Civil Rights Act was passed, these same women were active in lobbying to include, in Title VII of that act, prohibition against sex discrimination. Although, at the time, this act had many exemptions and was not enforceable, it was a major first step.[216] The Civil Rights Act was amended in 1972, and many of the exemptions were removed. The same Congress passed the Higher Education Act, including Title IX, which authorized the federal government to withhold financial assistance from those institutions which discriminated on the basis of sex. Thus, by the middle 1970's, the power of the federal government was effectively mobilized to move against sex discrimination in higher education and the workplace.

Behind this legislation was the work of thousands of women in organized effort carrying through an effective congressional lobbying campaign. Although many books reflecting the women's position were published during that era, such as Germaine Greer's *The Female Eunuch* (1971) and Kate Millett's *Sexual Politics* (1971), perhaps none was as significant as Betty Friedan's *The Feminine Mystique* (1963). In this work, Friedan caught and developed some of the major themes which held the feminist move-

---

211. "Paying Women What They're Worth," Report from the Center of Philosophy and Public Policy (University of Maryland, College Park), III, 2 (Spring 1983), pp. 1-2.
212. "Paying Women What They're Worth," p. 1.
213. Leach, "Women's Lives and Women's Liberation," p. 14.
214. "Paying Women What They're Worth," p. 5.
215. For a discussion of this act, see Leach, "Women's Lives and Women's Liberation," p. 23.
216. See Leach, "Women's Lives and Women's Liberation," p. 23.

ment together. She also was one of the key founders of the National Organization of Women, in 1966, which became the mainstream organization for the feminist movement. Although there were radical groups, such as the New York Radical Feminists, which grew out of the later days of the S.D.S. movement and tended to espouse women's liberationists' causes and lesbian interests, N.O.W. became the chief voice for the feminist movement.[217] By 1970, Betty Friedan and N.O.W., with its 3,000 members, led a successful national women's strike, commemorating the fiftieth anniversary of the passage of the Nineteenth Amendment; by 1983, the organization consisted of some 200,000 members.[218]

While N.O.W. grew rapidly and the membership found themselves easily agreeing on antidiscrimination activities with respect to legal rights, as well as political action to achieve equal pay for equivalent work, they rather quickly found themselves embroiled in fundamental differences regarding lesbian issues and influences. Many of the extreme antimale positions taken by certain lesbian leaders were unacceptable to the rank and file within the organization. More important issues were those involving abortion and the right of women to control their own reproductive processes. By 1973, the United States Supreme Court had legalized abortion up to the first trimester of pregnancy. Although most studies seemed to indicate that more than a majority of women favor abortion under certain circumstances, since the ruling, both the feminist movement and the general society have been deeply, emotionally divided over this issue.

In spite of such deep divisions within society and the women's movement itself, progress in women's rights was being made in higher education and the work force. Through organized effort on the part of N.O.W. and other groups, the Equal Educational Opportunity Commission and the Office of Civil Rights brought pressure on universities and major corporate employers to curb their sex-discriminative practices. Higher education began to change. While not all the barriers were breached by the end of the 1970's, women outnumbered men in undergraduate work and were increasing their numbers significantly in medicine, law, science, and engineering. However, the ratio of females to males in those fields remained relatively low as discrimination in education, as well as in the workplace, continued.

The sexist problem was a deeply rooted cultural phenomenon, much like racism. A task force of N.O.W. carefully studied the sex stereotyping that was evident in children's literature and produced a pamphlet which clearly documented the problem.[219] N.O.W. called the problem to the attention of the Office of Civil Rights and brought federal pressure to bear on publishing companies to change their sexist orientations. On a broader scale, a campaign was successfully waged to raise the consciousness levels of authors to change the sexist character of their language, which made use of such terms as *man, mankind,* the *nature of man,* as well as numerous

---

217. See Leach, "Women's Lives and Women's Liberation," p. 23.
218. See Leach, "Women's Lives and Women's Liberation," p. 23.
219. See *Dick and Jane as Victims: Sex Stereotyping in Children's Readers* (Princeton, N.J.: Women on Words and Images, 1972). Reprinted in part from Karier, *Shaping the American Educational State,* pp. 244-253.

other sexist terms.[220] By the 1980's, offensive sexist language was beginning to disappear from practical usage.[221]

While the 1970's reflected a slowing down in the black struggle for social justice, other groups concerned with gay rights, American Indians, the handicapped, Hispanics, and the women's movement seemed to pick up momentum. But the women's movement, like the civil rights movement, ran into serious difficulty when it passed beyond the political and legal barriers and turned to bread-and-butter economic issues. Recall that the civil rights movement experienced difficulty when Martin Luther King, Jr., had pointed out that it was going to "cost something." In both cases, the signs clearly indicated that society was still not willing to pay the costs of eliminating racism and sexism from the culture.

In March of 1972, when Congress first passed the Equal Rights Amendment by an overwhelming margin, and state after state quickly rushed to ratify it, few suspected that it would eventually fail to pass. Resistance to the amendment grew in the middle 1970's, however, as Title VII of the Civil Rights Act and Title IX of the Higher Education Act began to be enforced in higher education and in the general work force. The price of equality, especially in the work force, was going to be costly. By the close of the decade, Phyllis Schlafly and her heavily financed Eagle Forum emerged to focus the opposition's arguments in three key states where defeat of the amendment was considered necessary. Abortion, lesbianism, the survival of the family, as well as military service, all served to cloud the equal rights issue. For the most part, this resulted in the diversion of public attention from the fact that the E.R.A. would have made a significant difference in eliminating discrimination against women in terms of inheritance and property ownership laws in many states, and far more significantly, would have provided a constitutional basis from which women might derive equal pay for equal work. Nevertheless, in spite of the fact that 63 per cent of the women and 60 per cent of the men in 1980 supported the E.R.A., the amendment went down to defeat on June 30, 1982.[222]

As the smoke of battle began to fade away, it was clear that Schlafly and her Eagle Forum had picked up strong support from a variety of conservative groups, and had managed to focus that support politically in key states. While a number of explanations have been given for the defeat of the amendment, perhaps the best is to be found in N.O.W. president Eleanor Smeal's suggestion in 1982 that business organizations had quietly become the chief, but most effective, force against the amendment.[223] They, of course, had at that point in time the most to gain by its defeat.

The failure of the E.R.A., as well as the failure of women to receive equal pay for equal work, was matched by the clear failure of women to enter the political arena in anywhere near equal numbers to their male counterparts. By 1980, women still occupied only 13 per cent of the seats

---

220. See the preface to this edition.

221. Nevertheless, an analysis of preservice teacher-education texts as late as 1980 found them to be characterized by omission and imbalance with respect to treatment of sexism. See Myra Pollack Sadker and David Miller Sadker, "Sexism in Teacher-Education Texts," *Harvard Educational Review*, L, 1 (Feb. 1980), 36-96.

222. Baxter and Lansing, *Women and Politics*, p. 208.

223. See Leach, "Women's Lives and Women's Liberation," p. 56.

in the state legislatures, 5 per cent in the United States House of Representatives, and 2 per cent in the United States Senate.[224] However, by 1980, for the first time women were entering the voting booths in larger numbers than men, and as they did so, the political circumstances which had tended to obstruct the women's movement started to change.[225]

TOWARD FEDERALLY MANDATED PROGRAMS IN THE PUBLIC SCHOOLS

The practical technique of organization, congressional lobbying, and the creation of federal legislation to mandate specific programs, which was developed in the civil rights and women's movements, began to be used by other groups as well. Under considerable organized pressure, the Bureau of Education for the Handicapped was established as part of the Office of Education, in the Department of Health, Education, and Welfare, and in 1970, Congress proceeded to pass legislation which expanded the meaning of "handicapped" to include "learning disabled," itself an ill-defined term. By 1973, Congress had passed the Rehabilitation Act, of which Section 504 prohibited discrimination against handicapped people in all federally funded programs. The cost of implementing this law was prohibitive, and presidents have repeatedly backed away from full compliance.

By 1975, the Education for All Handicapped Children Act (Public Law 94-142) had been passed. This act was written in specific behavioral terms to reflect the interests of professional special education experts, who themselves were heavily influenced by Skinnerian psychology. The language of the act creates, perhaps, the most specific piece of educational legislation ever written. Included in it is both a provision for mainstreaming mentally retarded children in "the least restrictive environment," and an expression of Congress to fund up to 40 per cent of the additional costs. Congress has not come close to meeting its obligation in this matter. Nevertheless, the attempt to mainstream handicapped children has proceeded at local district and state expense. This, in itself, has produced a negative public reaction. Costs aside, however, the question of what constitutes "a handicap," as well as what is a free, "appropriate" public education as specified in the law, are questions not easily answered. By 1980, the courts were increasingly being asked to address the meaning of the law.

While some of the mainstreamed children were borderline mentally retarded, the bulk of them tended to be suffering from learning disabilities. The term *learning disability* was a relatively new one; and in the hands of professional special educators, it had grown to include virtually all children who had a learning problem the cause of which might run the gamut from some kind of physical disability to some kind of teacher or parental failing.[226] Yet in spite of such confusion, by 1980, a variety of handi-

---

224. Leach, "Women's Lives and Women's Liberation," p. 56.
225. See Baxter and Lansing, *Women and Politics,* pp. 17-39.
226. For a discussion of this problem and the early history of special education as a field, see Judith Ann Mogilka, "A Day of Inquiry: The Rise of Special Education in America" (unpublished Ph.D. diss., University of Illinois, 1986). Also see H. Svi Shapiro, "So-

capped children had begun to appear in the nation's regular classrooms. In implementing the law, some professional educators spoke of equal educational rights for the handicapped, others questioned the educational wisdom of mainstreaming, and some of the more cynical minded suggested that in the long run, the act would turn out to be a cheaper means of educating the handicapped. Whatever the original intent of this mandated legislation, it was being implemented.

If the original intent and the practical educational implications of the legislation regarding the handicapped seemed unclear at times, the federal government's policy regarding languages taught and used in the public schools seemed even more uncertain.[227] As the Hispanic populations of Texas, California, New York, Florida, and many urban centers rapidly grew because of political and demographic reasons, the pressure for special language programs for Spanish-speaking children in the public schools mounted. A variety of groups turned to the federal government to mandate language programs, and the issue of what was to be the federal government's language policy became critical. Were English language programs to be devised, as they had been earlier in the century for immigrant children to learn English exclusively, so as to replace their native language as quickly as possible? Or, were English language programs to be developed as simply a second language? While the merits of both positions were debated, there were those who suggested that English ought to be taught alongside the native language, and it ought to be taught with the expressed intent of both maintaining the native language and maintaining the native culture of the people. This bilingual-bicultural position gained considerable support from Hispanic Americans. Thus, cultural homogeneity versus cultural pluralism once again became a fundamental issue.

While the Hispanic community saw bilingual education as an opportunity for their children to learn English while maintaining proficiency in their native language and preserving their cultural heritage, the legislators who voted for the Bilingual Education Act of 1968 saw it primarily as a way of teaching English to Spanish-speaking children. The wording of the act was so vague that virtually all groups could read their own interpretation into it. Thus, the question of what bilingual education meant became debatable, even as new language programs were being implemented in the schools.

With the 1974 and 1978 legislation, however, bilingual education was defined primarily in such terms as to "allow a child to achieve competence in the English language." The legislation was not designed to support the maintenance of other languages or linguistic separatism.[228] When the Office of Civil Rights looked at school districts and found them at fault, it

---

ciety, Ideology and the Reform of Special Education: A Study in the Limits of Educational Change," *Educational Theory,* XXX, 3 (Summer 1980), 211.

227. See Rudolph C. Troike, "The Influence of Public Policy on Language Assessment of Bilingual Students," in *Language Assessment and Curriculum Planning,* ed. Stanley S. Seidner (Springfield, Ill.: State Board of Education, 1983), pp. 179-181. Also see Timothy Gerald Reagan, "Language, Ideology, and Education: A Comparative Analysis of Bilingual Education Programs and the Question of Black English" (unpublished Ph.D. diss., University of Illinois, 1982).

228. Troike, "Influence of Public Policy on Language Assessment," p. 179.

was usually because the districts had failed to provide English-language instruction where needed, not that they had failed to maintain the native languages. The same was true in *Lau* v. *Nichols* (1974). Even though, in that case, the United States Supreme Court did not designate a remedy, they ruled that San Francisco schools had violated the Civil Rights Act by failing to provide special assistance to students of limited English abilities. The Office of Civil Rights' guidelines, sometimes referred to as the "Lau remedies," called for school districts to classify their students by their English ability and to develop programs for those with minimal competencies. In general, it was clear that the weight of the federal government was operationally for an assimilationist policy; nevertheless, the fear of linguistic separatism persisted, especially in regard to communities which were essentially non-English-speaking.

Those who conceived of bilingual programs in terms of some form of cultural integration were concerned with what they thought the programs accomplished. Gary Orfield, a social scientist from the University of Illinois, testified before a House committee in 1977 that "some programs pursue not successful integration in American society but deeper cultural and linguistic identity and separation."[229] Just seven years later, another University of Illinois bilingual education specialist, Rudolph C. Troike, concerned with the loss of America's linguistic and cultural pluralism, pointed out that "the goal of most of these bilingual education programs as they presently exist is *not*, contrary to widespread belief, the cultivation of the native language skills of non-English-speaking students, but rather the assimilation of these students into English-only instruction as rapidly as possible."[230]

The continuing differences which surround American education regarding its bilingual programs are but reflections of the federal government's failure to reach a suitable consensus with regard to a language policy which all Americans can support.

TOWARD THE IDOLS OF CONSUMPTION

Throughout the twentieth century, America has changed from primarily a producer nation to a consumer nation. For most of the first half of the century, the society lived and thought in terms of production values. During the second half of the century, however, Americans seem to have adopted a consumatory value system, which has derived many of its ideals and values not from the social fabric of production, but rather from the social fabric of consumption. In the early 1940's, Leo Lowenthal conducted a most perceptive study of American "idols," carefully analyzing

---

229. As quoted in part by Diane Ravitch, *The Troubled Crusade: American Education, 1945-1980* (New York: Basic Books, 1983), p. 277.

230. Rudolph C. Troike, "Developing America's Language Resources for the Twenty-First Century: Foreign Language Teaching and Bilingual Education" (ms., 1983, Urbana, Ill.), p. 4.

the popular magazine biographies that Americans tended to read.[231] What he found was that, unlike the earlier period of the century when Americans read in detail about the lives of major political and industrial leaders and took them for their idols, the country's popular reading had radically changed and was now dominated by figures from the sports and entertainment sectors of society. As he put it,

If a student in some very distant future should use popular magazines of 1941 as a source of information as to what figures the American public looked to in the first stages of the greatest crisis since the birth of the Union, he would come to a grotesque result. While the industrial and professional endeavors are geared to a maximum of speed and efficiency, the idols of the masses are not, as they were in the past, the leading names in the battle of production, but the headliners of the movies, the ballparks, and the nightclubs.[232]

Lowenthal went on to point out that,

We observe that today the hero-selection corresponds to needs quite different from those of genuine information. They seem to lead to a dream world of the masses who no longer are capable or willing to conceive of biographies primarily as a means of orientation and education. They receive information not about agents and methods of social production but about the agents and methods of social and individual consumption.[233]

Vilfredo Pareto may have been correct when he suggested, earlier in the century, that the driving need of humanity in modern society was for "security," which was attainable through manipulation of myths; and Leo Lowenthal may have been correct in his analysis of American "idols." If so, and if one really wants to examine the ideals by which most Americans live, it is perhaps not the schoolhouse or the church that needs to be considered, but rather the movie theater, the television, and the ballpark. A society which takes its ideals for living from its movies, television, and sports arenas is a society which is educated to live in a dream world, where truth and reality are lost to image construction. Image construction, itself, becomes the key determinant, not only in the selection of consumer goods and services to satisfy the need for both bread and circuses, but, more importantly, in shaping the political, social, and religious life of the nation.[234] In such a world, language becomes detached from reality as image making and information control become powerful vehicles in determining what is to be the "reality" that is acted upon.

America, in the latter half of the twentieth century, has become a con-

---

231. See Leo Lowenthal, "Biographies in Popular Magazines," in *Radio Research, 1942-1943,* ed. Paul Lagarsfield and Frank N. Stanton (New York: Essential Books, 1944), pp. 507-548.
232. Lowenthal, "Biographies in Popular Magazines," p. 517.
233. Lowenthal, "Biographies in Popular Magazines," pp. 517-518.
234. See Clarence J. Karier, *Scientists of the Mind: Intellectual Founders of Modern Psychology* (Urbana: University of Illinois Press, 1986), chap. 4.

sumatory society which takes its idols from the entertainment industry. By 1984, it was conceivable that the best training for the presidency was no longer that of the law but rather that received in motion pictures. A society which takes its "idols" from the movies, which relies on that industry for leadership, and which has difficulty separating image from reality, is surely ill-prepared to grapple with the difficult problems engendered by the cold war, with its external and internal threats.

THE COLD WAR IN RETROSPECT

In 1967, while writing the last chapter for *Man, Society and Education,* I said,

The fundamental question, then, is: Can a society remain free in the face of constant external threat? And the corollary question is: Can a system of education maintain freedom of inquiry in a society filled with fear? One may argue that the freedom to teach is dependent on the answer to the first question; however, the answer to the first question may very well depend on the second—whether this society can educate a citizenry that is alert enough and that values freedom enough to withstand the erosion of individual liberty in the name of crisis. The resolution of these questions will have serious implications not only for the future of education but for the future of American society.[235]

These questions now, in 1986, seem as fundamentally important—indeed, in some respects, even more important. The question of whether this society can educate a citizenry that is alert enough and that values freedom enough to withstand the erosion of individual liberty in the name of crisis remains the critical, and yet unanswered, question for this generation of teachers. The real challenge is to find and develop such an education in the face of increasingly more difficult circumstances. The cold war has obviously taken its toll.

The fear of the enemy from without and within has been the dominating factor shaping the structure of events from 1945 to the present. That fear was there when the Nuremberg trials were prematurely called off to make way for the cold war; it was there during the spy trials of Alger Hiss and Ethel and Julius Rosenberg; and it was also there when America began designing its military-industrial complex and its super-secret intelligence agencies. The cold war chill was there when the Russians exploded their first atomic bomb and were the first in space. Fear can be read in virtually every major educational reform from the National Defense Education Act, to the National Education Commission report on *A Nation at Risk.* Fear was as vital a part of the manpower studies of the 1950's and 1960's as it was in Admiral Hyman Rickover's criticism of education and James B. Conant's prescribed solutions. It was there in the inordinate number of assassinations of America's political and social leaders in the 1960's, and it forever stalked Martin Luther King, Jr., and the civil rights movement.

---

235. See pp. 395-396.

Fear of the enemy without and within fueled the fires of the Vietnam War and shaped America's foreign policy, as well as America's internal social and educational policies.

In virtually every step along the way in the cold war, Americans learned to fear both the enemy without as well as within. And as they did so, they developed the habit of looking over their shoulders, and managed to survive without freedoms they once guarded as sacrosanct. The price of forty years of cold war cannot be measured in terms of dollars and cents; it has had far greater dimensions. When the time came to reconstruct American political, economic, social, and educational institutions, it was clear that the cold war had engendered not only an unnoticed loss of freedoms, but had also cultivated a polity with a constricted imagination and limited horizons. Although the need for such reconstruction was clearly evident, the dialog that must necessarily precede any such reconstruction was not readily forthcoming. A society dominated by fear, ever-desirous of security, satiated with image rather than reality, and frantically willing to make any sacrifice to check the enemy without and within, was not a society in any condition to face up to its many problems in order to fulfill the promise of America as the last great hope of humanity. Herein lies the real American tragedy.

Of all the many government committee and commission reports on the state of American education and society which emerged during the cold war, none was as ominously disturbing as the six-volume report of the Senate Select Committee to Study Governmental Operations with Respect to Intelligence Activities (1976). That report clearly documented the fact that, throughout the cold war, America's intelligence agencies had permeated virtually the entire social fabric of our society, and as they did so, violated with impunity the First, Fourth, and Sixth Amendment rights of hundreds of thousands of American citizens. The Bill of Rights was regularly being truncated in the name of national security. While some were disturbed to find the president of the United States violating the oath of office by approving the Huston Plan, others were even more disturbed to learn that when the president changed his mind, such agencies as the F.B.I., C.I.A., N.S.A., and D.I.A. continued to carry on illegal and unconstitutional practices, even after having been ordered not to do so by the chief executive.[236]

The secret undercover agencies in which America had invested its fortunes for its own security were now, in fact, employed against its own citizens, as they had once been employed against its foreign enemies. The enemy within was viewed as even more dangerous than the enemy without. Perhaps the most disturbing aspect of the six-volume report was not so much the fact that the agencies were out of control, or that they opened mail, broke into homes and offices, tapped telephones and bugged hotel rooms, targeted significant leaders for destruction, and engaged in direct political action for their own purposes; but, more important, was the fact that each agency had direct and immediate access to the press and electronic news media, and with ease could readily shape the public "image"

---

236. See *Church Report*, III, pp. 923-982.

as to what was taking place. In the period from 1950 to 1976, Americans grew accustomed to hearing their news reported in terms of either a direct government report or an "informed source reported"—which often was simply another covert government report. The intelligence communities' direct involvement in press and media information manipulation remains, perhaps, the most dangerous threat to this society's free institutions since the founding of the republic.

Prior to America's entrance into World War II, Attorney General Robert Jackson strongly supported the F.B.I.'s domestic surveillance program, and repeatedly came to its defense in terms of the need to maintain national security. Only in retrospect, when he became a United States Supreme Court Justice, did he change his mind and seriously worry about the dangers that clearly had come to pass. Shortly before he died in 1954, Jackson said,

I cannot say that our country could have no central police without becoming totalitarian, but I can say with great conviction that it cannot become totalitarian without a centralized police. . . . all that is necessary is to have a national police competent to investigate all manner of offenses, and then, in the parlance of the streets, it will have enough on enough people, even if it does not elect to prosecute them, so that it will find no opposition to its policies. Even those who are supposed to supervise it are likely to fear it. I believe that the safeguard of our liberty lies in limiting any national policing or investigative organization, first of all to a small number of strictly federal offenses, and second to nonpolitical ones.[237]

Within the last three decades, America's intelligence agencies have become more and more deeply involved in covert political action in the interest of cold war fears and national defense. As they have done so, it has become increasingly difficult to determine what is news and what is an agency message. Under such circumstances, one cannot help but pause and reflect on the wisdom of Thomas Jefferson, who drew together the inherent relationship between a free press and a free educational system for a free society, when he said, "Where the press is free and every man able to read, all is safe."[238] After that "radiance of a thousand suns" which mushroomed into the sky over Hiroshima that late summer day in 1945, nothing would ever again seem quite so "safe." Nevertheless, that Jeffersonian dream of developing and maintaining a free education for a free people within a free society remains the critical challenge for this generation of teachers.

SUGGESTED READINGS

Bernstein, Barton J. *Toward A New Past*, New York, Pantheon Books, 1968.
Bestor, Arthur. *Educational Wastelands*, Urbana, University of Illinois Press, 1985.

---

237. *Church Report*, III, pp. 411-412.
238. Gordon C. Lee, *Crusade Against Ignorance* (New York: Teachers College Press, 1961), p. 81.

Blum, Howard. *Wanted,* New York, Quadrangle/N.Y. Times Book Co., 1977.

Borkin, Joseph. *The Crime and Punishment of I. G. Farbin,* New York, The Free Press, 1978.

Burgess, Charles, and Merle L. Borrowman. *What Doctrines to Embrace,* Glenview, Ill., Scott, Foresman and Company, 1969.

Cook, Fred J. *The Nightmare Decade: The Life and Times of Senator Joe McCarthy,* New York, Random House, 1971.

Crozier, Michael J., Samuel P. Huntington, and Joji Watanaki. *The Crisis of Democracy,* New York, New York University Press, 1975.

Drost, Walter H. *David Snedden and Education for Social Efficiency,* Madison, University of Wisconsin Press, 1967.

Educational Policies Commission. *Education for All American Youth,* Washington, D.C., National Education Association, 1944.

Eysenck, Michael, and Hans Eysenck. *Mindwatching,* London, Michael Joseph, 1981.

Flexner, Eleanor. *Century of Struggle: The Women's Rights Movement in the United States,* Cambridge, Mass., Harvard University Press, 1975.

Foreign and Military Intelligence. Book 1–6, *Final Report of the Select Committee to Study Governmental Operations with Respect to Intelligence Activities,* U.S. Senate, 94th Cong., 2nd Sess., Report No. 94-755, Washington, D.C., U.S. Government Printing Office, 1976.

Garrow, David J. *The F.B.I. and Martin Luther King, Jr., from Solo to Memphis,* New York, W. W. Norton Company, 1981.

Gutman, Herbert. *The Black Family in Slavery and Freedom, 1750–1925,* New York, Pantheon Books, 1976.

Harvard Committee. *General Education in a Free Society,* Cambridge, Mass., Harvard University Press, 1945.

Jones, James H. *Bad Blood: The Tuskegee Syphilis Experiment,* New York, The Free Press, 1981.

Karier, Clarence J. *Shaping the Educational State,* New York, The Free Press, 1975.

Karier, Clarence J., Paul Violas, and Joel Spring. *Roots of Crisis: American Education in the Twentieth Century,* Chicago, Rand McNally & Company, 1973.

Krug, Edward A. *The Shaping of the American High School 1880–1920,* Madison, University of Wisconsin Press, 1969.

Lewis, David Levering. *King: A Biography,* Urbana, University of Illinois Press, 1979.

Mumford, Lewis. *The Myth of the Machine,* New York, Harcourt Brace Jovanovich, Inc., 1970.

Newman, Dorothy K. *Protest, Politics, and Prosperity: Black Americans and White Institutions, 1940-75,* New York, Pantheon Books, 1970.

Olson, Keith W. *The G.I. Bill, the Veterans and the Colleges,* Lexington, University Press of Kentucky, 1974.

Ravitch, Diane. *The Troubled Crusade: American Education, 1945-1980,* New York, Basic Books, 1983.

Ross, David R. B. *Preparing for Ulysses: Politics and Veterans During World War II,* New York, Columbia University Press, 1969.

Rubenstein, Richard L. *The Cunning of History,* New York, Harper & Row, 1975.

Sereny, Gitta. *Into That Darkness,* New York, McGraw-Hill Book Company, 1974.

Snell, Bradford C. *American Ground Transport,* presented to the Subcommittee on Antitrust and Monopoly of the Committees on the Judiciary of the United

States Senate, 93rd Cong., 2nd Sess., Feb. 26, 1974, Washington, D.C., U.S. Government Printing Office, 1979.

Spring, Joel. *The Sorting Machine,* New York, David McKay, 1976.

Violas, Paul C. *The Training of the Urban Working Class,* Chicago, Rand McNally & Company, 1978.

CHAPTER 12

The United States
Supreme Court
and education, to 1967

The Constitution is an experiment, as all life is an experiment.[1]
OLIVER WENDELL HOLMES

In the nineteenth century, Jefferson conceived of the Constitution as a social contract subject to change with the changing needs of the people. In the twentieth century, such men as Oliver Wendell Holmes and Louis Brandeis led the Supreme Court toward a similar pragmatic view of the Constitution.[2] In the period separating Jefferson and Holmes, American society and government underwent fantastic change, while the written Constitution changed relatively little. Even though Jefferson believed in a strict interpretation of the Constitution and Holmes believed in a loose interpretation, they both felt that government and the law must change with society. Because Jefferson believed in a strict interpretation of the Constitution as well as a progressively changing society, he concluded that each new generation would have to hold a new constitutional convention. Society changed rapidly, and yet no constitutional convention was ever convened. Furthermore, from 1791, when the first ten amendments were enacted, until 1966, the Constitution was amended only twelve times. This created the illusion of an unchanging Constitution. The fact is, however, that the Constitution has changed radically over the past century, not in word but in meaning, through court interpretation.

---

1. Saul K. Padover, *The Genius of America* (New York: McGraw-Hill Book Company, 1960).
2. It should be recalled that Holmes, William James, and Charles S. Peirce were all members of the Metaphysical Club at Harvard. James was the pragmatist in psychology, Peirce the pragmatist in mathematics, and Holmes the pragmatist in the law. See Chapter Six.

One must then distinguish between the written Constitution as formally stated with all its amendments and the living Constitution which consists of the meaning of the document as interpreted by the court at any given time. So fundamental is this point that if the United States government today was forced to operate within a strict interpretation of the Constitution it would immediately collapse for lack of constitutional authority. The schoolboy who studies the written Constitution and its amendments alone studies only a small part of the Constitution of the United States. To fully understand what the Constitution is at any given point is to understand what is and what is not constitutional at that time as interpreted by court decisions.

Even while Jefferson held to a strict interpretation of the Constitution, the first Chief Justice of the Supreme Court, John Marshall, had already loosely interpreted the constitutional authority of the court to extend the right of the court to declare null and void acts of Congress and of state legislatures. In a series of decisions from *Marbury* v. *Madison* (1803) to the Dartmouth College Case (1819), Marshall effectively took the first steps toward making the United States Supreme Court one of the more powerful courts in the Western world. The authority of the court, then, is based both on precedent and on explicitly delegated constitutional power.

Even though the court, in its many and varied decisions, places considerable emphasis on precedent, it is never free from current considerations. Every decision involves a current problem and a current reinterpretation of the past. Both the Supreme Court jurist and the historian are, in this sense, users of the past. The past can be used, depending on the weighing and selecting of evidence, as a conservative or a liberal force in judging any current controversial issue. Furthermore, the court in the twentieth century has come to place more emphasis on the present and future consequences of its decisions than did the nineteenth-century court, which relied more heavily on precedent. It is difficult, however, to determine when the court has made its decision primarily on present and future consequences or on past traditions; for in either case, precedents are used to establish the case, and in those cases where precedents are clearly at odds with the current decision, the court can reverse its previous stand.

The net social effect of a court which places more weight on precedents than on present and future considerations is conservative. On the other hand, the net effect of a court which places greater weight on present and future consequences is liberal, facilitating, if not initiating, social change. Most students of the law agree that the Supreme Court of the twentieth century has tended to operate as a more liberal court than that of the nineteenth. In this respect, the court reflected the pragmatic temper of American culture which required a changing Constitution to fit the needs of a changing society. The pragmatic role of the court involved more, however, than merely following cultural change. In basing decisions on expected consequences, the court became an agent of social change.[3] To what extent the court can or should lead in the

---

3. This is very apparent in areas such as segregation and legislative reapportionment, where federal and state legislatures have been unable to act.

process of social change and to what extent society can afford to have a court which merely follows are highly controversial and disputable questions.

In this process of constitutional change, the law loses much of its illusion of certainty. Perhaps this idea was best stated by Oliver Wendell Holmes, a pioneer exponent of the pragmatic function of the law, when he suggested that while men longed for certainty in the law through "delusive exactness, . . . certainty generally is illusion, and repose is not the destiny of man."[4] Although the living Constitution of the United States offers no ultimate certainty, it does serve as a vital vehicle of intelligent stability in a fluid, changing, pluralistic society. The court, in this respect, serves as the final arbiter of some of the most fundamental issues which divide society. Public education, as a vital aspect of that society, is inevitably involved in many of those issues, and as a consequence, many of the significant decisions of the court in the twentieth century have dealt with education.[5]

Education is a function of the states by virtue of the fact that the word *education* does not appear in the Constitution and the Tenth Amendment explicitly states: "The powers not delegated to the United States by the Constitution, nor prohibited by it to the States, are reserved to the States respectively, or to the people." The reserved power of the states in the field of education does not, however, prohibit the federal government from aiding education. The federal government has aided education from the Land Ordinance of 1785 to the most recent Elementary and Secondary Education Act of 1966. Federal economic power in education has been increasingly asserted at all levels of instruction.

While federal power has always been exercised in the form of financial aid to education,[6] the use of federal judicial power in matters dealing with education is largely a twentieth-century development. The Supreme Court's involvement in education in the twentieth century has resulted from the court's interpretation of the Fourteenth Amendment in such a way that both the equal-protection[7] and the due-process[8] clauses of that amendment bind the states and make the First Amendment[9] applicable to the states—although at present not all the citizen's rights under the Bill of Rights are protected against state interference. Since the case of *Meyer* v. *Nebraska* in 1923, the court has been consistently extending the ban of the Fourteenth Amendment so as to protect more and more of the citizen's rights against state infringement. School boards and state

---

4. Quoted in Padover, *Genius of America,* p. 257.

5. For example, the Brown decision involving segregation in the public school was, perhaps, one of the most important decisions of the court in the twentieth century.

6. For example, the Land Ordinance of 1785, the Morrill Act of 1862, and the Smith-Lever Act of 1914.

7. "No State shall . . . deny to any person within its jurisdiction the equal protection of the laws."

8. "No State shall . . . deprive any person of life, liberty, or property, without due process of law."

9. "Congress shall make no law respecting an establishment of religion, or prohibiting the free exercise thereof; or abridging the freedom of speech, or of the press; or the right of the people peaceably to assemble, and to petition the government for a redress of grievances."

educational agencies are legal arms of the state and therefore come under this restriction. In *West Virginia State Board of Education* v. *Barnette* (1943), Justice Robert Jackson, in delivering the opinion of the court, aptly stated this principle when he said:

The Fourteenth Amendment, as now applied to the States, protects the citizen against the State itself and all of its creatures—Boards of Education are not excepted. These have, of course, important, delicate, and highly discretionary functions, but none that they may not perform within the limits of the Bill of Rights. That they are educating the young for citizenship is reason for scrupulous protection of Constitutional freedoms of the individual, if we are not to strangle the free mind at its source and teach youth to discount important principles of our Government as mere platitudes.[10]

In his initial draft of the First Amendment, Madison attempted to bind the states as well as the federal government,[11] but when he failed to gain enough support, he rewrote the amendment so that it applied to the federal government alone. For example, the last of the original thirteen colonies to give up multiple establishment of religion and prohibit the use of public funds for all religions was Massachusetts in 1833, some forty-two years after the First Amendment was ratified. In *Barron* v. *Baltimore* (1833), the court concluded that the Bill of Rights limited the federal government but not the states. The division of authority between the state and federal government in the first half of the nineteenth century rested on a precarious balance. By 1860, the slavery issue added fuel to the fiery question of the division of national and state authority. The ultimate supremacy of the federal power seemed assured with the victory of the federal forces in the Civil War and with the ratification of the Fourteenth Amendment in 1868. This amendment not only made the Negro a citizen but also placed severe limitations on state power.

No State shall make or enforce any law which shall abridge the privileges or immunities of citizens of the United States; nor shall any State deprive any person of life, liberty, or property, without due process of law; nor deny to any person within its jurisdiction the equal protection of the laws. . . .

In the Slaughterhouse Case (1873), however, the court refused to interpret the amendment so as to bind the states. Considering the clause which prohibits states from abridging "the privileges or immunities of citizens of the United States," the court made a distinction between state and federal "privileges or immunities," holding that the state did not come within the purview of the federal authority. Not until 1923 in *Meyer* v. *Nebraska* and 1925 in *Pierce* v. *Society of Sisters* did the court

---

10. *West Virginia State Board of Education* v. *Barnette,* 319 U.S. 624, 63 Sup. Ct. 1185 (1943). For an extremely helpful secondary source, see Clark Spurlock, *Education and the Supreme Court* (Urbana: University of Illinois Press, 1955).
11. See Chapter Two.

begin to extend the meaning of the due-process clause so as to limit the states. In *Gitlow* v. *New York* (1925), the court interpreted *liberty* in the Fourteenth Amendment as including liberty of speech (First Amendment). In 1940, in *Cantwell* v. *Connecticut,* the court extended the due-process clause of the Fourteenth Amendment to include religious liberties, and by 1943, in *West Virginia State Board of Education* v. *Barnette,* it was evident that the court had ruled virtually all of the First Amendment applicable to the states by way of the Fourteenth Amendment. The Supreme Court involvement in public education has come about either through interpreting the Fourteenth Amendment due-process clause so as to make the First Amendment applicable to the states, as in the religion and academic freedom cases, or through interpreting the equal-protection clause of the same amendment so as to nullify the judicial precedent of "separate but equal" as established in the *Plessy* v. *Ferguson* decision (1896). By mid-century, the court was deeply involved in public education issues, most of which fell under one of three headings: religion, race, or academic freedom.

As more and more people in the twentieth century came to look upon education as a frontier through which one achieved social mobility for himself and his children, public education took on heightened significance. The school dropout in 1900 still had many avenues open for gainful employment, most of which were closed for his counterpart fifty years later. As it became increasingly clear that many decisions made at the elementary and secondary school level had a vital influence on the future economic, social, political, and religious life of the individual, the school became the center of considerable social conflict. Various economic, political, religious, and social groups also came to believe that their own beliefs and values could best be maintained through the increased influence of the school. Under these conditions, conflict on the educational frontier took on some of the characteristics of the Western frontier. It was no longer a question of free land or water rights, but questions of equal educational opportunity, religious freedom, racial conflict, and patriotism which dogged the heels of school teachers, administrators, and school board members across the country.

Strangely enough, school men were suffering, in part at least, from the success of their own attempts to sell the importance of public education. From Horace Mann on, educators insisted that education might be used to cure virtually everything from juvenile delinquency, religious bigotry, and racial prejudice to economic depression and poverty. As the public came to believe this, they automatically turned to the schools to solve the most pressing issues of the times. School boards, administrators, and teachers were made to assume responsibility for the Herculean task of educating the young for a pluralistic society which itself was fundamentally in conflict. As the conflict increased, many more cases were taken to the judicial system for resolution. Under these circumstances, the Supreme Court was rapidly becoming a school board for the nation, at least in some of the more fundamental areas where state educational policy conflicted with individual rights under the Constitution. The court, however, was reluctant to assume this role. Justice Felix Frankfurter protested:

But the court-room is not the arena for debating issues of educational policy. It is not our province to choose among competing considerations in the subtle process of securing effective loyalty to the traditional ideals of democracy, while respecting at the same time individual idiosyncrasies among a people so diversified in racial origins and religious allegiances. So to hold would in effect make us the school board for the country. That authority has not been given to this Court, nor should we assume it.[12]

Even while Justice Frankfurter argued that the Supreme Court should not become the school board for the nation, numerous cases involving education were being placed on the federal court dockets. The cases which the court handled were a good index of some of the major areas of cleavage, such as race, religion, and freedom. The court might also be viewed as a barometer of social conflict in American education. As the importance of education increased and conflict heightened, the court was pressed to take on more and more cases.[13] The number of Supreme Court decisions on education from the adoption of the Constitution to the present is itself revealing.

Number of Supreme Court cases concerning education [14]

1789-1808 . . . 0	1849-1868 . . . 1	1909-1928 . . . 5
1809-1828 . . . 1	1869-1888 . . . 0	1929-1948 . . . 14
1829-1848 . . . 1	1889-1908 . . . 3	1949-1965 . . . 40

In the thirty-six years from 1928 to 1964, the court made five times as many decisions involving education as it had made in the previous 139 years of its existence. Most of these decisions dealt with problems involving religion, race, or loyalty. We shall consider some of the major decisions in each area which have had a significant impact on educational policy.

RELIGION AND EDUCATION

The right of the private school to exist

The Supreme Court's first decision regarding education involved the legal right of the private school to exist. In 1816, the state legislature of New Hampshire passed a law which undertook to turn Dartmouth College, a privately endowed institution, into a public institution. Daniel

---

12. *Minersville School District* v. *Gobitis,* 310 U.S. 586, 60 Sup. Ct. 1014 (1940).

13. For instance, from 1889 to 1948, the general work load of the court increased, but cases involving education increased at approximately twice that rate.

14. Ward W. Keesecker, "Supreme Court Decisions Affecting Education," *School Life* (February 1949), 4. Keesecker's chart covered only the period until 1948; this author added the data on the period 1949-1965.

Webster argued the case for the original Board of Trustees before the United States Supreme Court. Chief Justice Marshall, in delivering the opinion of the court, concluded that the New Hampshire Legislature had violated Article I, Section 10, of the United States Constitution which prohibits the states from "impairing the obligation of contracts." The charter granted to a private college by the state or, as in this case, by the English Crown must be viewed as a contract which cannot be broken except with the consent of those who made the contract. In declaring the New Hampshire law null and void, Marshall not only protected the citizens' right of contract against arbitrary state infringement but at the same time extended the authority of the court to declare acts passed by a state legislature unconstitutional.[15] The effect of this decision on education was to protect private schools from state confiscation and to establish the legal basis for their existence in the rights of private contract.

Just how free and independent could the private school be in the face of the state's growing authority over education? Could the state, for instance, regulate the private schools, control their curriculum, or determine what was taught? In the twentieth century the extent of state control over private schools varied from state to state, depending on statutory and constitutional requirements. However, even when the statutes clearly called for regulation of the private schools, public officials were usually reluctant to assert their authority. This authority usually was not asserted until an inflamed public opinion, crystallized around a single issue, spurred officials to take action. For example, this was the situation which brought the case of *Meyer* v. *Nebraska* (1923) to the United States Supreme Court.

Perhaps no other area of the school curriculum is more subject to fluctuating enrollments because of the international outlook of the nation than foreign languages.[16] As a result of the nationalistic fervor which swept the country during and after World War I, state after state outlawed the teaching of German in the public schools, and one community after another burned its German textbooks at public demonstrations. As a direct result, the enrollment in German dropped from 24.4 per cent of the total high school population in 1915 to 0.6 per cent in 1922.[17] This nationalistic fervor also created the suspicion that many of the private foreign-language schools which catered to the various immigrants were a threat to American unity. The children of the immigrant, it was believed, must be Americanized by way of the English language as rapidly as possible. It was, then, not enough to eliminate

---

15. This was not the first time the U.S. Supreme Court nullified a state act, but it was one of a series of cases which solidly established the court's right to declare state laws null and void.

16. For an interesting analysis of the fluctuating enrollments of Spanish, French, and German in the American high school as influenced by World Wars I and II, see J. Wesley Childers, *Foreign Language Teaching* (New York: The Center for Applied Research in Education, Inc., 1964), pp. 5-28.

17. The teaching of German never recovered its prestigious place in the curriculum. By 1934, the enrollment in German rose to 2.4 per cent, but with the entrance of America into World War II, it again dropped to 0.8 per cent. By 1960, it was back to 1.7 per cent.

the teaching of foreign languages in the public schools; the private schools must also be brought in line with the public temper. This was part of the historical context in which the Nebraska Legislature, on April 9, 1919, passed the following law:

Section 1. No person, individually or as a teacher, shall, in any private, denominational, parochial or public school, teach any subject to any person in any language other than the English language.

Section 2. Languages, other than the English language, may be taught as languages only after a pupil shall have attained and successfully passed the eighth grade as evidenced by a certificate of graduation issued by the county superintendent of the county in which the child resides.[18]

In *Meyer* v. *Nebraska*, the United States Supreme Court declared this act unconstitutional. In so doing, the court made it clear that it was not questioning the states' right to make reasonable regulations for all schools nor their right to regulate their own public schools. The question before the court was whether or not the state had unreasonably interfered with the liberty of the teacher to follow his chosen occupation and the liberty of the parent to educate his children. The court, in applying the due-process clause of the Fourteenth Amendment, was radically departing from its own precedent in the Slaughterhouse Case of 1873. In that case, the court refused to apply the Fourteenth Amendment so as to bind the states. From *Meyer* v. *Nebraska* (1923) to the present, the court has gradually come to use the due-process clause, and the equal-protection clause, to extend the meaning of *liberty*—in effect, to federalize the First Amendment and make it applicable in limiting the authority of the state.[19] The states' authority in education is not unlimited. The parent's right to educate his child is a right shared with the state. Exactly where the state's rights end and the parent's rights begin remains a clouded issue.

Even though this case dealt specifically with the narrow grounds of a state law which prohibited the teaching of foreign languages in a private school, the court made its decision on the broader, more fundamental grounds of the parent's liberty to educate his child and the teacher's liberty to practice his profession in a private school which meets all reasonable state regulations. What, then, constitutes reasonable regulation of the private school? The court, of course, does not lay down any blanket guidelines for such questions but instead considers each case on its own merits. In this respect, the court merely considers whether or not the state has violated a citizen's rights under the Constitution. Just how far a state may go depends on the desire of the state legislature to

---

18. *Meyer* v. *Nebraska*, 262 U.S. 390, 43 Sup. Ct. 626 (1923).

19. There is a logical problem here. If the freedoms of the First Amendment are unqualified, does not "without due process of law" qualify a state to abridge these freedoms with due process? The court has ignored this problem. Perhaps Leo Pfeffer was correct when he said, in discussing how the court tried to correct the Slaughterhouse decision, "It sometimes requires an illogical decision to undo the work of a previous illogical decision." See Leo Pfeffer, *Church, State and Freedom* (Boston: The Beacon Press, 1953), p. 130.

extend its authority and the ruling of the court, which may or may not limit it.

The question still remained—could the state reasonably regulate the private school out of existence? Even before the court laid down its ruling in the Nebraska Case, the people of Oregon, on November 7, 1922, had passed by initiative an act which required all children of school age to attend public school. There could be no mistake; both the intent and the effect of this act was to abolish the parochial schools in the state of Oregon. In *Pierce* v. *Society of the Sisters of the Holy Names of Jesus and Mary* and *Pierce* v. *Hill Military Academy* (1925), the court held that the Act of 1922 "unreasonably interferes with the liberty of parents and guardians to direct the upbringing and education of children under their control"[20] and, furthermore, deprives the appellees of their property without due process of law. The liberty of parents to educate their child was once again asserted as one of the legal bases upon which the rights of the private school exist.

The fundamental theory of liberty upon which all governments in this Union repose excludes any general power of the state to standardize its children by forcing them to accept instruction from public teachers only. The child is not the mere creature of the state; those who nurture him and direct his destiny have the right, coupled with the high duty, to recognize and prepare him for additional obligations.[21]

In *Meyer* v. *Nebraska* and *Pierce* v. *Society of Sisters,* the court extended the meaning of the Fourteenth Amendment and at the same time clearly established the legal grounds upon which the private schools exist at the elementary and secondary level. If, then, the state could not use its compulsory education laws to eliminate the private school, could it go to the other extreme and use public funds to support them? Don't these private schools, in meeting the "reasonable regulations" of the state's compulsory-education machinery, carry out a public service, and therefore shouldn't they be financially reimbursed for that service? Under what conditions may the state aid, directly or indirectly, the private school? Since most private schools are sectarian, with the avowed purpose of teaching a specific religious faith, doesn't public aid for these schools constitute public aid for religion and thus violate the First Amendment's prohibition against an "establishment of religion," made applicable to the states by the Fourteenth Amendment? These were a few of the more difficult questions the court has increasingly been called upon to face.

The use of public funds for parochial school children

Only three years after the Supreme Court had, in effect, protected the Roman Catholic parochial schools from state-wide abolition in

---

20. *Pierce* v. *Society of the Sisters of the Holy Names of Jesus and Mary,* 268 U.S. 510, 45 Sup. Ct. 573 (1925).

21. *Pierce* v. *Society of Sisters,* p. 573.

Oregon, the State of Louisiana, with a much larger Catholic population, passed an act which provided free textbooks for all the children of the state. The books provided were those used in the public schools and were made available to all children regardless of the school they attended. In the resulting case, *Cochran* v. *Louisiana State Board of Education* (1930), the state was charged with diverting public property for private purposes and thus violating the citizen's right under the Fourteenth Amendment. Did this legislation aid the private school, or was the state merely carrying out its public function in aiding all the children of the state? The court unanimously concluded, "The schools, however, are not the beneficiaries of these appropriations. They obtain nothing from them, nor are they relieved of a single obligation because of them. The school children and the state alone are the beneficiaries."[22]

In upholding the Louisiana statute, the court developed the "child benefit theory"; i.e., such aid as free textbooks benefits the child and not the private school. Such a theory had serious implication for the meaning of the principle of separation of Church and State, especially as Madison and Jefferson had viewed it.[23] Just how far could the state go in benefiting the child attending a parochial school and still not be aiding religion? Could the state provide such things as tuition grants to parents of children in private schools, bus transportation, teachers' salaries, libraries, scientific laboratory equipment, free lunches, medical and psychological services, or even funds for private school construction on the grounds that all of these things benefit the child? The Cochran decision cracked the traditional wall of separation of Church and State enough that within the next seventeen years the court found itself forced to define explicitly the principle of separation of Church and State.

In *Everson* v. *Board of Education* (1947), Everson brought charges that the New Jersey statute which provided funds to parents for transportation of their children to and from the parochial school was a violation of his right under the First Amendment to be free of an establishment of religion, made applicable to the states by the due-process clause of the Fourteenth Amendment. The court was unanimous in defining the principle of separation of Church and State as follows:

The 'establishment of religion' clause of the First Amendment means at least this: Neither a state nor the federal government can set up a church. Neither can pass laws which aid one religion, aid all religions, or prefer one religion over another. Neither can force nor influence a person to go to or to remain away from church against his will or force him to profess a belief or disbelief in any religion. No person can be punished for entertaining or professing religious beliefs or disbeliefs, for church attendance or non-attendance. No tax in any amount, large or small, can be levied to support any religious activities or institutions, whatever they may be called, or whatever form they may adopt to teach or practice religion. Neither a state nor the federal government can, openly or secretly, participate in the affairs of any religious organizations or groups and

---

22. *Cochran* v. *Louisiana State Board of Education*, 281 U.S. 370, 50 Sup. Ct. 335 (1930).
23. See Chapter Two.

vice versa. In the words of Jefferson, the clause against establishment of religion by law was intended to erect 'a wall of separation between Church and
State.' . . .[24]

Although the court was unanimous in principle, the justices were very
much in disagreement as to the practical application of that principle.
In a five-to-four decision, the court upheld the New Jersey statute. The
majority of the court insisted that when the state provided bus transportation to and from school, the state was merely exercising its police
powers to protect children. The child benefited from such action, not
the school. Justice Hugo L. Black, in writing the majority opinion, recognized that incidental benefits might accrue to the school, but he insisted that this was true for all governmental services.

And parents might refuse to expose their children to the serious danger of traffic
accidents going to and from parochial schools, the approaches to which were
not protected by policemen. Similarly, parents might be reluctant to permit their
children to attend schools which the state had cut off from such general government services as ordinary police and fire protection, connections for sewage
disposal, public highways and sidewalks. Of course, cutting off church schools
from these services, so separate and so indisputably marked off from the religious
function, would make it far more difficult for the schools to operate. But such
is obviously not the purpose of the First Amendment.[25]

In the application of the New Jersey statute, the township of Ewing
had reimbursed bus fares only for public school and Catholic school
children. The minority of the court objected to this practice on the
grounds of discrimination against other religious sects. Furthermore,
Justice Wiley B. Rutledge argued that where transportation is necessary,
it is just as vital as school buildings, library facilities, and teachers'
salaries for the functioning of the denominational school.[26] Under the
circumstances, public bus transportation for parochial school children
constituted a public subsidy of parochial education. Justice Robert
H. Jackson argued:

But we cannot have it both ways. Religious teaching cannot be a private affair
when the state seeks to impose regulations which infringe on it indirectly, and
a public affair when it comes to taxing a citizen of one faith to aid another, or
those of no faith to aid all. If these principles seem harsh in prohibiting aid to
Catholic education, it must not be forgotten that it is the same Constitution
that alone assures Catholics the right to maintain these schools at all when predominant local sentiment would forbid them. Pierce v. Society of Sisters, (268
U.S. 510). Nor should I think that those who have done so well without this aid
would want to see this separation between Church and State broken down. If
the state may aid these religious schools, it may also regulate them.[27]

---

24. *Everson* v. *Board of Education,* 330 U.S. 1, 67 Sup. Ct. 512 (1947).
25. *Everson* v. *Board of Education,* p. 512.
26. See Spurlock, *Education and the Supreme Court,* p. 88.
27. *Everson* v. *Board of Education,* p. 517.

From the standpoint of the dissenting justices, the child benefit theory was instrumental in providing precedents which eventually would cloud the difference between the private and the public sector and the Church and State. As Justice Rutledge saw it, America was in the midst of violating the principle of separation of Church and State.

Two great drives are constantly in motion to abridge, in the name of education, the complete division of religion and civil authority which our forefathers made. One is to introduce religious education and observance into the public schools. The other, to obtain public funds for the aid and support of various private religious schools. . . . In my opinion both avenues were closed by the Constitution. Neither should be opened by this Court. The matter is not one of quantity, to be measured by the amount of money expended. Now as in Madison's day it is one of principle, to keep separate the separate spheres as the First Amendment drew them; to prevent the first experiment upon our liberties; and to keep the question from becoming entangled in corrosive precedents.[28]

As bus transportation took its place alongside free textbooks for parochial school children on the list of child benefits, the question still remained how far the federal and state governments might go in granting aid to parochial school children without violating the First Amendment. Within the next decade, federally subsidized school lunch programs were in operation across the nation. This practice, as well as the extension of medical and psychological services to parochial school children, has never been tested before the court, primarily because of the strong possibility that these practices would come under the child benefit policy of the court.

In addition to these aids, there has been steadily mounting pressure for more aid for parochial schools. This pressure has resulted from the extremely rapid rate of expansion of the parochial schools in America during a time in which the cost of education has also skyrocketed. R. Freeman Butts pointed out the practical reasons for the increasing demands for public support of parochial schools:

In recent years, Catholic schools have grown at a much more rapid rate than the public schools. In 1900, Catholic schools represented about five per cent of the total elementary and secondary school enrollments. For forty years this proportion rose only gradually; in 1940 it was still around six or seven per cent. But during the past twenty years, the rise has been spectacular. While public school enrollments increased 36 per cent, nonpublic enrollments increased 118 per cent. Today, about 14 per cent of all school children are in Catholic schools, perhaps as much as 16 per cent in all nonpublic schools.[29]

As a result of this vast expansion and the rising costs of education, strong pressure for financial aid has been exerted at the local, state, and national levels.

---

28. *Everson* v. *Board of Education*, pp. 534-535.
29. R. Freeman Butts, "Public Funds for Parochial Schools?" *Teachers College Record*, LXII, 1 (1960), 10.

In response to this pressure, "shared-time" programs have been instituted in many urban centers.[30] Under such programs, the parochial school students take a selected number of courses in the public school and the remainder of their program in the parochial school.[31] The secular courses are selected by parochial school officials on the basis of parochial school deficiencies, especially those areas which require the more expensive facilities such as laboratories, gyms, machine shops, etc., and on the basis of those secular subjects least offensive to the Roman Catholic Church.

Supporters of the shared-time programs are quick to point out that the Roman Catholic Church in America, by joining in shared-time programs, has moderated its traditional position as enunciated by Pope Leo XIII: "It is necessary not only that religious instruction be given to the young at certain fixed times, but also that every other subject taught be permeated with Christian piety."[32] The courses taken in the public school under the shared-time program, such as physical education, machine shop, chemistry, physics, and mathematics, would no longer be "permeated with Christian piety."[33] Opponents of the program, however, are also quick to point out that the net effect of shared time is to facilitate the educational goal, as enunciated by Pope Pius XI, of "Catholic education in Catholic schools for all the Catholic youth."[34] By accepting secular public school instruction as an integral part of parochial school education, the Roman Catholic schools would proportionately increase their capability to educate more Catholic youth. At the present time, approximately 50 per cent of Roman Catholic children are in Catholic schools. Through an intensive use of public school facilities and instruction, that percentage could be expected to increase markedly.

Does shared time benefit the parochial schools or the child? If on the one hand 100 per cent of the student's compulsory school time can be released by the state for parochial school education and on the other hand a small portion of the time can be released for religious instruction,[35] then what could be unconstitutional about releasing the child so he takes half of his instruction in the parochial school and the other

---

30. See Research Division, National Education Association, *Shared Time Programs: An Exploratory Study,* Research Report (1964), p. 10.

31. For an analysis of the legal and educational implications of the shared-time practices, see Henry E. Butler, Jr., "Religion, Government and Education," *Wall or illusion* (report of the 1965 School Law Conference at Miami University, Oxford, Ohio, May 7, 1965).

32. Gerald C. Treacy, S. J., ed., *Five Great Encyclicals* (New York: The Paulist Press, 1939), p. 60.

33. For the way in which religion is wedded to what, on the surface, may appear secular subjects, see George R. La Noue, "Religious Schools and 'Secular' Subjects," *Harvard Educational Review,* XXXII, 3 (1962), 255-291.

34. Treacy, *Five Great Encyclicals,* p. 61. Pope Pius went on to say: "If such education is not aided from public funds, as distributive justice requires, certainly it may not be opposed by any civil authority ready to recognize the rights of the family, and the irreducible claims of legitimate liberty. Where this fundamental liberty is thwarted or interfered with, Catholics will never feel, whatever may have been the sacrifices already made, that they have done enough, for the support and defense of their schools and for the securing of laws that will do them justice."

35. This practice was held constitutional in *Zorach* v. *Clauson* (1952).

half in the public school? From the perspective of the Roman Catholic parent, who pays taxes to support public education, it is difficult to understand why his child should not be allowed to avail himself of some of the public school instruction. If and when a test case on the constitutionality of shared time is made, such questions will undoubtedly be raised. If, however, shared time is upheld as constitutional and develops as a major practice in the schools, it is likely to change radically the character of American public education. The Elementary and Secondary Education Act of 1965, which provided federal funds for the support and development of shared-time programs, encouraged this trend.[36]

Increasingly, the public school can be expected to diminish its role as a common school as conceived by Horace Mann and to increase its new role as a service agency which supplements the education of children in sectarian schools. Although at present Roman Catholic schools are the chief sectarian schools involved in shared-time programs, it seems highly probable that Henry Butler was correct when he suggested that "federal support of shared time plans will encourage the establishment of part-time church schools by many denominations which have been unable or unwilling to carry the financial burden of operating full-time schools."[37] If, then, the denominational and public schools continue to move toward larger shared-time commitments, not only the principle of separation of Church and State may change radically but also the nature and function of public education itself.

There have also been numerous proposals made which would give public funds to parents who send their children to private and parochial schools at the elementary and secondary level. Sometimes these proposals have been argued from the standpoint of "distributive justice,"[38] sometimes from the standpoint of the child benefit theory, and sometimes from the standpoint of the First Amendment. In this last case, the argument usually consists of making a distinction between the establishment clause and the free-exercise clause of the First Amendment. In this frame of reference, the establishment clause is narrowly conceived of as a single establishment. This, of course, ignores Jefferson's and Madison's battle against multiple establishment and, furthermore, ignores the establishment-of-religion definition of the court as developed in the Everson Case, which rules out aid to *all* religions. The second phase of the argument usually proceeds on the grounds that the free-exercise clause of the First Amendment is a guaranteed right, and in order to exercise that right, one must have the means to exercise it. If, then, the parent has the right to educate his child according to his own religious persuasion by sending his child to a denominational school,

---

36. For decades, the Roman Catholic Church, the National Association of Manufacturers, and the Chamber of Commerce were the major lobbyists against any general federal aid to education bill in Congress. With the assurance that a portion of the federal funds would, in effect, go to the support of parochial schools by way of shared time, the major opposition to federal aid to education disappeared and the first general federal-aid-to-education bill (Public Law 89-10) was passed on April 11, 1965.

37. Butler, "Religion, Government and Education," pp. 21-22.

38. As discussed by Pope Pius XI in his encyclical on the "Christian Education of Youth." See Treacy, *Five Great Encyclicals.*

he should be free to do so, but he is not, in fact, free to exercise this right unless he has the financial wherewithal to do so. Under the circumstances, parents of the parochial school child should be financially reimbursed through either tax rebates or direct grants for the financial sacrifice they are making in exercising their right to free exercise of religion. Although the court has not been faced with the question of state financial grants to parents of parochial school children, Justice William O. Douglas, in *Sherbert* v. *Verner* (1963), said:

. . . the fact that government cannot exact from me a surrender of one iota of my religious scruples does not, of course, mean that I can demand of government a sum of money, the better to exercise them. For the Free Exercise Clause is written in terms of what the government cannot do to the individual, not in terms of what the individual can exact from government.[39]

Justice Douglas reflected a rather consistent view of the court here —namely, that government does not have to finance freedom to act in order to guarantee such freedom. By 1965, the court had ruled that textbooks and bus transportation for parochial school children were not in violation of the First Amendment. How far the court would go in extending the child benefit theory remained unknown. As the pressure for public aid to parochial schools mounted in recent decades, the words of Justice Rutledge sounded most prophetic when he said, in the Everson Case (1947), "Two great drives are constantly in motion to abridge, in the name of education, the complete division of religion and civil authority which our forefathers made." He saw the one as a struggle to obtain public funds for private religious schools and the other as an attempt to use the public schools for religious purposes. Both approaches, he believed, were prohibited by the First Amendment.

The use of public schools for religious purposes

No sooner had the court made its decision in the Everson Case than it was faced with the question of the use of the public schools for religious instruction in *McCollum* v. *Board of Education* (1948). Since 1940, the Champaign, Illinois, School Board had allowed the Council on Religious Education, composed of representatives from the Catholic, Jewish, and Protestant faiths, to hold religious instruction for forty-five minutes a week, during school time and in the school classrooms. Religious instruction was given to those children whose parents signed request cards and designated the kind of instruction desired. Those children whose parents refused to sign were taken to another room to continue their secular study during the religious instruction period. Vashti McCollum charged that this released-time program was, in effect, an establishment of religion by the State of Illinois. The State Supreme Court of Illinois upheld the board's action. The case was then appealed to the United States Supreme Court, and in an eight-to-one decision,

---

39. Quoted in Butler, "Religion, Government and Education," p. 24.

the court upheld the claim of McCollum that this was an establishment of religion prohibited by the First Amendment.

In handing down the decision, Justice Black pointed out that the establishment clause of the First Amendment, as defined in the Everson Case, prohibited the state and federal governments from rendering assistance not only to one religion but to *all* religions.

Pupils compelled by law to go to school for secular education are released in part from their legal duty upon the condition that they attend the religious classes. This is beyond all question a utilization of the tax-established and tax-supported public school system to aid religious groups to spread their faith. And it falls squarely under the ban of the First Amendment (made applicable to the States by the Fourteenth) as we interpreted it in Everson v. Board of Education, 330 U.S. 1.[40]

The decision of the court on this issue was clear. The state had been rendering assistance for religious instruction in two ways: by allowing the use of school property for religious instruction and by allowing the use of the compulsory public school machinery to get the child to attend religious instruction.

Here not only are the state's tax-supported public school buildings used for the dissemination of religious doctrines. The state also affords sectarian groups an invaluable aid in that it helps provide pupils for their religious classes through use of the state's compulsory public school machinery. This is not separation of Church and State.[41]

This decision stirred up question and debate over the constitutionality of many different types of released-time programs in use across the country.

Further refinement came with *Zorach* v. *Clauson* in 1952. New York State allowed the release of youngsters during school time to attend religious instruction off school grounds. In a six-to-three decision, the Supreme Court reasoned that since school property was not being used, the state was not using its power to coerce youngsters to attend religious instruction, and therefore the New York statute was not in violation of the First Amendment. The majority of the court, in this decision, seemed to ignore the coercive aspects of the compulsory public school machinery which it had emphasized four years earlier in the McCollum Case. It was precisely on this point that the minority sharply disagreed with the majority opinion. Justice Douglas, in rendering the opinion of the majority, said:

We are a religious people whose institutions presuppose a Supreme Being. We guarantee the freedom to worship as one chooses. We make room for as wide a variety of beliefs and creeds as the spiritual needs of man deem necessary.

---

40. Illinois Ex. Rel. *McCollum* v. *Board of Education,* 333 U.S. 203, 68 Sup. Ct. 464 (1948).

41. Illinois Ex. Rel. *McCollum* v. *Board of Education,* pp. 465-466.

We sponsor an attitude on the part of government that shows no partiality to any one group and that lets each flourish according to the zeal of its adherents and the appeal of its dogma. When the state encourages religious instruction or cooperates with religious authorities by adjusting the schedule of public events to sectarian needs, it follows the best of our traditions. For it then respects the religious nature of our people and accommodates the public service to their spiritual needs. To hold that it may not would be to find in the Constitution a requirement that the government show a callous indifference to religious groups. That would be preferring those who believe in no religion over those who do believe. Government may not finance religious groups nor undertake religious instruction nor blend secular and sectarian education nor use secular institutions to force one or some religion on any person. But we find no constitutional requirement which makes it necessary for government to be hostile to religion and to throw its weight against efforts to widen the effective scope of religious influence. The government must be neutral when it comes to competition between sects. It may not thrust any sect on any person. It may not make a religious observance compulsory. It may not coerce anyone to attend church, to observe a religious holiday, or to take religious instruction. But it can close its doors or suspend its operations as to those who want to repair to their religious sanctuary for worship or instruction. No more than that is undertaken here.[42]

In dissent, Justice Frankfurter responded: "The essence of this case is that the school system did not 'close its doors' and did not 'suspend its operations.' There is all the difference in the world between letting the children out of school and letting some of them out of school into religious classes."[43] The question, then, was whether or not New York State was using its compulsory education law to support religion. Justice Jackson argued:

The greater effectiveness of this system over voluntary attendance after school hours is due to the truant officer who, if the youngster fails to go to the Church school, dogs him back to the public schoolroom. Here schooling is more or less suspended during the 'released time' so the nonreligious attendants will not forge ahead of the church-going absentees. But it serves as a temporary jail for a pupil who will not go to Church. It takes more subtlety of mind than I possess to deny that this is governmental constraint in support of religion. It is as unconstitutional, in my view, when exerted by indirection as when exercised forthrightly.[44]

Reminiscent of Madison's argument in his *Memorial and Remonstrance Against Religious Assessment* in 1785—"Who does not see that the same authority which can establish Christianity, in exclusion of all other Religions, may establish with the same ease any particular sect of Christians, in exclusion of all other Sects?"[45]—Justice Jackson further argued in dissent:

---

42. *Zorach* v. *Clauson,* 343 U.S. 306, 72 Sup. Ct. 684 (1952).
43. *Zorach* v. *Clauson,* p. 687.
44. *Zorach* v. *Clauson,* p. 689.
45. Quoted in R. Freeman Butts, *The American Tradition in Religion and Education* (Boston: The Beacon Press, 1950), p. 62.

And, after all, if we concede to the State power and wisdom to single out 'duly constituted religious' bodies as exclusive alternates for compulsory secular instruction, it would be logical to also uphold the power and wisdom to choose the true faith among those 'duly constituted'. We start down a rough road when we begin to mix compulsory public education with compulsory godliness.[46]

Compulsory godliness or not, the Zorach decision upheld the New York State program, and as a result other states quickly moved to pattern their own programs after the New York State released-time program.[47]

The problems involved in maintaining a public school system in a religiously pluralistic society which adheres to a principle of separation of Church and State continued to plague school men and the court. Just how neutral can or should the public schools be with respect to the teaching of moral values? Is sectarian religion a necessary basis for the teaching of moral values? Should the public school teach the common elements of all religions as Horace Mann suggested? If so, to what extent is the state merely creating a new kind of common-elements religion? Can it be assumed that the Bible represents the common elements of all religions, and if read as Horace Mann suggested, without comment, whose Bible is to be read: Roman Catholic, Protestant, Old Testament, or New Testament? What, then, is the purpose of prayer, Bible reading, and religious exercises in the public schools? If the school is viewed as the major vehicle of indoctrinating political, social, and economic values, why shouldn't society be vitally concerned with the use of these schools for indoctrinating moral and spiritual values? On most of these questions, American society remained fundamentally divided.

The failure of the American public to reach any solid consensus on the function of the public schools served to complicate further the issue of the place of religion in American public education. By 1953, for example, twelve states required daily reading from the Bible in the public schools and eleven states explicitly prohibited such a practice.[48] Throughout the 1950's, the Supreme Court consistently refused to deal with the issue of prayer and Bible reading in the public schools. In *Doremus* v. *Board of Education* (1952), a New Jersey statute which required Bible reading was challenged. After some delay, the court refused to hear the case on the grounds that the appellants did not show enough serious injury to warrant a case, and, furthermore, the court said that since the child had already graduated, "obviously no decision we could render now would protect any rights she may once have had, and this Court does not sit to decide arguments after events have put them to rest."[49]

---

46. *Zorach* v. *Clauson*, p. 689.

47. New York State, however, unlike other states, allows school boards to grant released-time credit toward graduation. Since this practice originated not in the law but in a decision of the state Education Department and was never a part of the Zorach Case, the constitutionality of this practice was never tested. In light of what the majority said in the Zorach Case about the very limited role the state may play in released-time programs, the constitutionality of this New York State practice is extremely doubtful.

48. See Gordon C. Lee, *An Introduction to Education in Modern America* (New York: Henry Holt and Company, 1953).

49. *Doremus* v. *Board of Education*, 342 U.S. 429, 72 Supt. Ct. 396 (1952).

Two years later, in *Gideons International* v. *Tudor,* the court once again refused to become involved in the Bible-reading issue by denying certiorari, and thereby leaving the case in the state courts.[50]

By 1962, however, the court was ready to become involved in the highly controversial area of prayer and Bible reading in the public school. The New York State Board of Regents, under considerable public pressure for more religious exercises in the public schools, responded to such pressure by developing the following prayer to be used in the schools: "Almighty God, we acknowledge our dependence upon Thee, and we beg Thy blessings upon us, our parents, our teachers, and our country." In *Engel* v. *Vitale* (1962), the court concluded that New York State violated the establishment clause of the First Amendment by creating and using a prayer in the public schools to further religious beliefs. The following year, in a combined case involving a Pennsylvania statute and a Maryland school board regulation requiring daily Bible reading and recitations of the Lord's Prayer,[51] the court declared in an eight-to-one decision that such practices were also a violation of the First Amendment. Public education, as an arm of the state, cannot advance or inhibit the cause of religion but must remain neutral. With respect to this point, the court said:

The test may be stated as follows: What are the purpose and the primary effect of the enactment? If either is the advancement or inhibition of religion, then the enactment exceeds the scope of legislative power as circumscribed by the Constitution. That is to say that to withstand the strictures of the Establishment Clause there must be a secular legislative purpose and a primary effect that neither advances nor inhibits religion. . . .[52]

When the state uses prayers and Bible reading as a devotional exercise in the public schools, the state has exceeded the bounds of the Constitution. The court was careful to point out that nothing in this decision should be construed as prohibiting teaching about religion or reading the Bible for its historical and literary effects.[53]

The public reaction to this series of decisions was immediate and explosive. "In Congress a total of 111 members of the House of Representatives introduced 150 proposed amendments to the United States Constitution intended to permit prayers and Bible reading in the public schools."[54] As the hearings on these amendments proceeded, it became evident to most congressmen that the bulk of church leadership was

---

50. It should be noted that by 1954 the court was preparing its epoch-making Brown decision on segregation in the public schools.

51. *School District of Abington Township, Pennsylvania* v. *Edward Lewis Schempp* (1963) and *William J. Murray* v. *John N. Curlett* (1963).

52. Quoted in Butler, "Religion, Government and Education," p. 19.

53. If the state must remain neutral, can school officials prevent voluntary prayers in the schools? A United States District Court, in *Stein* v. *Oshinsky,* 224 F. Supp. 757 (1963), ruled that the state cannot interfere. The decision, however, was reversed by a Circuit Court 348 F. 2d. 999 (1965) and the U.S. Supreme Court denied Cert. 34 L.W. 3218 (1965).

54. August W. Steinhilher, "The U.S. Supreme Court and Religion in the Schools," *Theory into Practice,* IV, 1 (February 1965), 11.

opposed to these amendments and in sympathy with the court's decisions.[55] Nevertheless, in some sections of the North, it was as difficult
to enforce this decision as it was to enforce the earlier desegregation
decision in most Southern communities. For example:

A 1964 survey conducted by the Indiana School Boards Association shows
that 17 school districts permit Bible reading by school board vote, and in 62
districts it is the practice although the local board has no policy requiring or
forbidding it. On recitation of the Lord's Prayer, the figures are 17 and 87 respectively.[56]

Indiana seemed to have as much difficulty complying with this decision
as Mississippi had complying with the Brown decision. In both cases,
the court clearly ruled against predominant local sentiment. If, however,
the American nation is a nation of law, then noncompliance with court
decisions seriously undermines the constitutional system of government.

Although the Supreme Court has not ruled on such religious exercises in the public school as are usually associated with Christmas,
Hanukkah, Easter, and baccalaureate, some of these practices are open
to question. To what extent are the purpose and primary effect of these
practices to advance religion? Using the test that the court developed in
the Schempp Case, it seems reasonably certain that there still remain
in the American public school certain practices of questionable constitutionality. In general, it is clear that released-time programs held off
school property but on school time are constitutional, while Bible reading and prayers in the public school, instituted by school authorities, are
not. For the most part, the court has heard cases in which school practices seemed to facilitate religion. There is, however, another set of
cases in which the state's concern for its own survival is at odds with
religious minorities, and once again, the meeting place of conflicting
authority is the classroom.

Nationalism, religious convictions, and education

Can the state require military training at its own public educational
institutions? How far may the state go and what methods and techniques
may it employ within the public educational system to teach patriotism
and achieve loyalty on the part of its citizens? When these requirements,
methods, and practices conflict with the conscience of the individual,
which takes precedence—the authority of the state or the conscience
of the individual? These were but a few of the more difficult issues the
court was called upon to decide.

In 1933, two young conscientious objectors of the Methodist Episcopal Church refused to take the R.O.T.C. training required of all male
students at the University of California.[57] After considerable petitioning,

---

55. See Steinhilher, "U.S. Supreme Court and Religion in the Schools," p. 12.
56. Steinhilher, "U.S. Supreme Court and Religion in the Schools," p. 13.
57. This requirement was a part of the state's attempt to comply with the original intent of the Morrill Act of 1862. See Chapter Four.

the students were suspended. In *Hamilton* v. *Regents of the University of California* (1934), the students charged that, "contrary to the Fourteenth Amendment, their privileges and immunities as citizens of the United States were being abridged and their liberty and property were being denied them without due process of law."[58] They further argued that since the Senate ratified the Kellogg-Briand Peace Pact (1929) and since any treaty ratified by the Senate becomes the supreme law of the land, the state had violated this law by furthering military training. The court concluded that the latter charge required little consideration and went on to consider the central issues. The substantive question was what privileges and immunities were denied the student by the requirement that the student who attends the University of California must take military training. A unanimous court held that since under the Constitution the conscientious objector has no right to refuse to bear arms but only a privilege granted as Congress sees fit, no "privilege and immunities" guaranteed by the Fourteenth Amendment were abridged by the state requirement. The court was clear on this issue. When it came to a conflict of war powers versus individual conscience, the war powers were more important. The Constitution does not protect the conscientious objector on this issue. "The conscientious objector is relieved from the obligation to bear arms in obedience to no constitutional provision, express or implied; but because, and only because, it has accorded with the policy of Congress thus to relieve him."[59]

If the individual does not have a constitutional right to refuse to bear arms, does he have a constitutional right to refuse to salute the flag in an educational institution where the state requires such an action and when such a salute violates his religious conscience? In *Minersville School District* v. *Gobitis* (1940), the court concluded, in an eight-to-one decision, that the state educational authority may require saluting of the flag, in the interest of "national feeling and unity," as a condition of school attendance. In this case, a Jehovah's Witness' religious beliefs were directly opposed to a state practice designed to achieve national unity.[60] By a large majority the court upheld the state's right to inculcate patriotic values through the use of a required flag salute in the schools.

Only three years later, in essentially the same kind of case,[61] *West Virginia State Board of Education* v. *Barnette* (1943), the court reversed itself in a six-to-three decision. What accounted for such a quick reversal? Two new justices joined the court and three justices changed their opinion. It is reasonable to suspect that the latter justices viewed the consequences of the Minersville decision, did not like what they saw, and reversed their earlier opinions on that basis.

58. Spurlock, *Education and the Supreme Court*, p. 97.

59. *Hamilton* v. *Regents of the University of California*, 293 U.S. 245, 55 Sup. Ct. 205 (1934).

60. The Jehovah's Witnesses interpret Exodus 20:4-5 of the Bible literally. While they may respect what the flag stands for, they cannot salute it because such an act is deemed as bowing down before graven images.

61. There were, however, some differences; the Minersville Case of 1940 involved a local board, while the Barnette Case of 1943 involved a state law which carried explicit penalties for those who violated the law.

The consequences of the Minersville decision were immediately apparent. Within one week after the decision was made, hundreds of Jehovah's Witnesses—men, women, and children—were physically attacked and abused in most inhumane ways. Jehovah's Witnesses' meeting places were burned and their leaders driven out of town, usually with the law enforcement agency of the community leading the way. For example:

In one town, the chief of police and the deputy sheriff forced a group of Jehovah's Witnesses to drink large doses of castor oil and then paraded them through the streets tied together with police-department rope. In another, a local judge warned a group of Witnesses that unless they compelled their children to salute the flag he would take the children away from them and place them in an institution where they would be taught to understand what Americanism is.[62]

A wave of religious persecution, fanned by wartime nationalistic fervor, swept the country.[63] These were some of the conditions surrounding the Barnette Case, in which the court made one of the quickest reversals in its history. Objecting to the reversal, Justice Frankfurter argued:

As a member of this Court I am not justified in writing my private notions of policy into the Constitution, no matter how deeply I may cherish them or how mischievous I may deem their disregard. The duty of a judge who must decide which of two claims before the Court shall prevail, that of a State to enact and enforce laws within its general competence or that of an individual to refuse obedience because of the demands of his conscience, is not that of the ordinary person. It can never be emphasized too much that one's own opinion about the wisdom or evil of a law should be excluded altogether when one is doing one's duty on the bench. Most unwillingly, therefore, I must differ from my brethren with regard to legislation like this. I cannot bring my mind to believe that the 'liberty' secured by the Due Process Clause gives this Court authority to deny to the State of West Virginia the attainment of that which we all recognize as a legitimate legislative end, namely, the promotion of good citizenship, by employment of the means here chosen. . . .[64]

---

62. Leo Pfeffer, *The Liberties of an American: The Supreme Court Speaks* (Boston: The Beacon Press, 1963), p. 51.

63. One is reminded, here, that the real test of religious tolerance of a community, like a test of individual character, is not what one does to the powerful individual or group that has the means to fight back but what one does to the weak who cannot defend themselves. The question, then, is not how much freedom the politically powerful religious groups exercise but rather how much freedom the politically weak religious groups have within that society. In the 1830's, it was the Roman Catholic who was in the position of threatening the community and getting his churches burned. A century later, in the 1940's, the Jehovah's Witnesses were in a similar position. The main defense this religious sect has had against local community attacks has been the federal courts. Thus, between 1938 and 1950, the Jehovah's Witnesses have been involved in over twenty major cases concerning religious liberty. See Spurlock, *Education and the Supreme Court*, p. 101. Perhaps the real test of the American sense of religious tolerance is not whether we can elect a Catholic president but rather what we have been doing to the Witnesses within our communities.

64. *West Virginia State Board of Education v. Barnette*, 319 U.S. 624, 63 Sup. Ct. 1189-1190 (1943).

On the other hand, in delivering the majority opinion of the court, Justice Robert Jackson argued that this was not so much a case involving freedom of religion as a case involving freedom of speech, which includes the freedom not to speak. Does the state have the authority to coerce its citizens to say that which they don't believe? While it may be that the national unity which officials foster by persuasion and example is a desirable end, Jackson argued that:

As governmental pressure toward unity becomes greater, so strife becomes more bitter as to whose unity it shall be. Probably no deeper division of our people could proceed from any provocation than from finding it necessary to choose what doctrine and whose program public educational officials shall compel youth to unite in embracing. Ultimate futility of such attempts to compel coherence is the lesson of every such effort from the Roman drive to stamp out Christianity as a disturber of its pagan unity, the Inquisition, as a means to religious and dynastic unity, the Siberian exiles as a means to Russian unity, down to the fast failing efforts of our present totalitarian enemies. Those who begin coercive elimination of dissent soon find themselves exterminating dissenters.[65]

Jackson went on to point out that freedom cannot be limited to only those things which make little difference but must be extended to those things which we view as important.

To believe that patriotism will not flourish if patriotic ceremonies are voluntary and spontaneous instead of a compulsory routine is to make an unflattering estimate of the appeal of our institutions to free minds. We can have intellectual individualism and the rich cultural diversities that we owe to exceptional minds only at the price of occasional eccentricity and abnormal attitudes. When they are so harmless to others or to the State as those we deal with here, the price is not too great. But freedom to differ is not limited to things that do not matter much. That would be a mere shadow of freedom. The test of its substance is the right to differ as to things that touch the heart of the existing order.
    If there is any fixed star in our constitutional constellation, it is that no official, high or petty, can prescribe what shall be orthodox in politics, nationalism, religion, or other matters of opinion or force citizens to confess by word or act their faith therein. If there are any circumstances which permit an exception, they do not now occur to us.[66]

The Barnette decision was based, then, on both freedom of religion and freedom of speech, guaranteed by the First Amendment.[67]

---

65. *West Virginia State Board of Education* v. *Barnette,* pp. 1186-1187.
66. *West Virginia State Board of Education* v. *Barnette,* p. 1187.
67. See Pfeffer, *Liberties of an American,* p. 89; see also Pfeffer, *Church, State and Freedom,* pp. 524-528. This mixture of freedom of speech and freedom of religion has further complicated this issue. Can a state compel a student to salute the flag if he objects on other than religious grounds? New York State has a compulsory flag salute law (Chap. 874-No. 801 and 802 of the N.Y. laws of 1963), which requires a daily flag salute. According to the State's Attorney General, Opinion of Counsel No. 135, April 8, 1964, the school board may coerce all children to salute the flag except those who object on religious grounds. For the way this issue developed in the following years, see Chapter Thirteen.

In reviewing the decisions of the court with respect to religion and education, it is clear that if one's freedoms under the First Amendment made applicable to the states by the Fourteenth Amendment depended solely on the majority's will, many freedoms now valued, from the right of the parochial schools to exist to the right of the Jehovah's Witnesses to refuse to salute the flag, would be lost. One can further sense the difficulty in maintaining religious freedom in a religiously pluralistic society. The problem of maintaining and developing a vital public school system in such a society is made more complicated by the lack of public consensus as to the function of the schools. Because of this lack each interest group places great emphasis on the importance of the public school for fulfilling its own aims. Under these circumstances, it is not surprising to find that those fundamental social issues which segment the American body politic are the same issues which turn the public schools into centers of conflict. We turn now to an equally emotion-laden area of social and educational conflict.

RACE AND EDUCATION

Segregation as a way of life

In 1896, at the Cotton States Exposition in Atlanta, Booker T. Washington received a thunderous ovation from a white Southern audience, unparalleled in the history of the nation. Both Southerners and Northerners seemed to like what they heard. Washington insisted that "the opportunity to earn a dollar . . . was more important to the Negro than the chance to spend it in the opera house."[68] What the Negro needed was a practical education for the practical job of making himself useful to the South.[69] He brought down the house when he concluded that "in all things that are purely social we can be as separate as the fingers, yet one as the hand in all things essential to mutual progress."[70] Clark Howell of *The Atlanta Constitution* wired New York that the speech was one of the most notable that had ever been given to a Southern audience; it was "a revelation, a platform upon which blacks and whites can stand with full justice to each other."[71] The platform to which Howell referred was a segregated platform, one where the Negro knew his place of service to his former white master. Washington's "revelation" was only one reflection of the nation's general acceptance of segregation as a way of life. Behind this growing consensus stood a past of brutal violence, death, destruction, and the more vile demonstrations of man's inhumanity to man. Out of the dark pages of the Reconstruction Era

---

68. Quoted in Merle Curti, *The Social Ideas of American Educators,* rev. ed. (Paterson, N.J.: Littlefield, Adams and Company, 1960), p. 297.

69. In *Slums and Suburbs* (1960), James B. Conant also argued for a practical education for a practical job.

70. Quoted in Curti, *Social Ideas of American Educators,* p. 297.

71. Curti, *Social Ideas of American Educators,* p. 297.

came not only the lynch law of Mississippi, Georgia, and Louisiana but also the Jim Crow laws of Tennessee, Virginia, and Arkansas.[72]

In 1883 the United States Supreme Court held, in *United States* v. *Stanley,* that the Civil Rights Act of 1875 was unconstitutional on the grounds that Congress does not have the power to regulate the social relations of persons, but that the states do have such authority when exercised with reasonable discretion. In general, both the North and the South rapidly came to accept segregation as a way of handling race relations. The court was reflecting that social consensus when, in *Plessy* v. *Ferguson* (1896), the majority of the court concluded that segregated public conveyances made possible by a Louisiana statute are a "reasonable exercise of the police power of a state" and such a practice does not "deprive a colored person of any rights under the 14th Amendment of the Federal Constitution."[73]

In this case, the U.S. Supreme Court went back to a Massachusetts Supreme Court case, *Roberts* v. *City of Boston* (1849), for the original precedent establishing the legal basis for the "separate but equal" doctrine. The Roberts decision involved a young girl who was denied admittance to a Boston public school on the grounds that she was Negro. Charles Sumner argued for the plaintiff that all persons are equal before the law and that the Negro child should be admitted to the public school. Chief Justice Shaw of Massachusetts agreed in principle, but he pointed out that men, women, and children are not "clothed with the same civil and political powers," and he went on to justify "separate but equal" schools for the races.[74]

Justice Henry Brown, in delivering the majority opinion of the court in the Plessy Case (1896), based his argument on precedents derived from the Roberts Case and many other state and federal court decisions, some of which had been made before the enactment of the Fourteenth Amendment. Although Brown agreed that the intent of the Fourteenth Amendment was to establish absolute equality before the law, he did not believe that its intent was to enforce social equality.

Laws permitting and even requiring their separation in places where they are liable to be brought into contact do not necessarily imply the inferiority of either race to the other, and have been generally, if not universally, recognized as within the competency of the state legislatures in the exercise of their police power. The most common instance of this is connected with the establishment of separate schools for white and colored children, which have been held to be a valid exercise of the legislative power even by courts of states where the

---

72. Between 1880 and 1900, there were over two thousand lynchings on record, the worst offenders being Mississippi, Georgia, and Louisiana. See R. Freeman Butts and Lawrence A. Cremin, *A History of Education in American Culture* (New York: Henry Holt and Company, 1953), p. 319. While it was not until the Brown decision of 1954 that federal power was effectively asserted to break segregation laws, federal authority has not even begun to be effectively used to halt lynch law in many Southern communities.

73. *Plessy* v. *Ferguson* 163 U.S. 537, 41 Led. 256 (1896).

74. It is interesting that it was a northern state which set the legal precedent for segregation in the public schools.

political rights of the colored race have been longest and most earnestly enforced.[75]

Even though this case dealt specifically with the question of segregation on public conveyances, the court pointed out that no one had questioned the constitutional right of Congress to operate segregated schools in the District of Columbia. How, then, was it possible to declare the Louisiana statute which segregates the races on public conveyances in violation of the Fourteenth Amendment?[76]

[The problem] reduces itself to the question whether the statute of Louisiana is a reasonable regulation. . . . In determining the question of reasonableness it [the state] is at liberty to act with reference to the established usages, customs, and traditions of the people, and with a view to the promotion of their comfort, and the preservation of the public peace and good order.[77]

The court, in defining *reasonable* as that which is found in "established usages," could not help but find the separate but equal doctrine reasonable. Segregation of the races was an established practice for many communities, both in the North and in the South, at the end of the century. The same year that Booker T. Washington publicly accepted social segregation, the United States Supreme Court legalized it. Justice Brown concluded that:

We consider the underlying fallacy of the plaintiff's argument to consist in the assumption that the enforced separation of the two races stamps the colored race with a badge of inferiority. If this be so, it is not by reason of anything found in the act, but solely because the colored race chooses to put that construction upon it.[78]

Furthermore, Brown concluded that social legislation cannot overcome social prejudice. "If the two races are to meet on terms of social equality, it must be the result of natural affinities, a mutual appreciation of each other's merits and a voluntary consent of individuals. . . . If one race be inferior to the other socially, the Constitution of the United States cannot put them upon the same plane."[79]

There was one lonely voice of dissent. Justice John M. Harlan, with almost prophetic insight, said, "In my opinion the judgment this day rendered will, in time, prove to be quite as pernicious as the decision made by this tribunal in the *Dred Scott Case.*"[80] The net effect of this decision, he reasoned, would be to perpetuate a modified condition of servitude and second-class citizenship. "There would remain a power in

---

75. *Plessy* v. *Ferguson*, p. 258.
76. See *Plessy* v. *Ferguson*, p. 261.
77. *Plessy* v. *Ferguson*, p. 260.
78. *Plessy* v. *Ferguson*, p. 261.
79. *Plessy* v. *Ferguson*, p. 261. It is interesting that this was essentially the same reason given by Barry Goldwater for his vote against the Civil Rights Act of 1964.
80. *Plessy* v. *Ferguson*, p. 264.

the states, by sinister legislation, to interfere with the full enjoyment of the blessings of freedom; to regulate civil rights, common to all citizens, upon the basis of race; and to place in a condition of legal inferiority a large body of American citizens."[81] Harlan argued that one must recognize that "the destinies of the two races in this country are indissolubly linked together, and the interests of both require that the common government of all shall not permit the seeds of race hate to be planted under the sanction of law."[82] The consequence of legal segregation, he argued, is more likely to result in either race conflict or race subjugation. It seemed to Harlan that "we have yet, in some of the states, a dominant race, a superior class of citizens, which assumes to regulate the enjoyment of civil rights, common to all citizens, upon the basis of race."[83] Harlan concluded:

But in view of the Constitution, in the eye of the law, there is in this country no superior, dominant, ruling class of citizens. There is no caste here. Our Constitution is color-blind, and neither knows nor tolerates classes among citizens. In respect of civil rights, all citizens are equal before the law.[84]

For the next half century, the Plessy decision stood as the constitutional cornerstone of the massive social structure of a segregated society. Just as Justice Harlan had predicted, the segregation of the races did produce second-class citizens and second-class opportunities. The separate but equal doctrine for education, in effect, produced a second-class education for second-class citizens. On the average, twice as much money was spent on white pupils as on Negro pupils in the dual Southern segregated system.[85]

Desegregation

During the first half of the twentieth century, America underwent two world wars and emerged as a major world leader and technological giant with a socially fluid population. American attitudes and values with respect to race were rapidly changing. One indication that the Supreme Court was about to reconsider its Plessy decision in light of the changes in American "customs, traditions, and established usages" appeared in *Sweatt* v. *Painter* (1950).[86]

Fifty years after the Plessy Case, a Negro World War II veteran applied to the University of Texas Law School. He was refused admission on the grounds that he was Negro. Since the University of Texas Law School was the only public law school in the state, there were obviously no equal facilities for Negroes. Under the pressure of court action, the

---

81. *Plessy* v. *Ferguson,* p. 265.
82. *Plessy* v. *Ferguson,* p. 264.
83. *Plessy* v. *Ferguson,* p. 264.
84. *Plessy* v. *Ferguson,* p. 263.
85. See Butts and Cremin, *History of Education in American Culture,* p. 579.
86. Precedent for the Sweatt Case, however, had already been set in *Garner v. Canada* 305 U.S. 337 (1938) and in *Signel* v. *Board of Regents of the University of Oklahoma* (1948).

university set up a mock law school off campus to handle Sweatt on a tutorial basis. After reviewing the case, the Supreme Court concluded, "We hold that the Equal Protection Clause of the Fourteenth Amendment requires that petitioner be admitted to the University of Texas Law School." The court, while not questioning the separate but equal doctrine directly, began to question how it was at all possible to have equal schools when one considered "those qualities which are incapable of objective measurements but which make for greatness in a law school."[87] If equal facilities could not be obtained, the doctrine of separate but equal was open to question.

Increasingly, the court was confronted with cases questioning whether the Negro school was, in fact, equal to the white school. By December of 1952, the United States Supreme Court had on its docket five cases involving segregation of public school systems. Between December 1952 and May 1954, the court heard the many-sided arguments involving segregation in the public schools and rendered one of its most significant decisions of the century, *Brown* v. *Board of Education of Topeka.* In attempting to unravel the original intent of the Fourteenth Amendment, the court concluded that the amendment's history was inconclusive. When the amendment was written, the Southern states did not have a public school system, nor was the importance of public education even in the North anywhere near the significance of public education in the twentieth century. Chief Justice Earl Warren, in delivering the unanimous opinion of the court, said in part:

> In approaching this problem, we cannot turn the clock back to 1868 when the Amendment was adopted, or even to 1896 when Plessy *v.* Ferguson was written. We must consider public education in the light of its full development and its present place in American life throughout the Nation. Only in this way can it be determined if segregation in public schools deprives these plaintiffs of the equal protection of the laws.[88]

In reviewing the place of education in modern life, the court concluded that it is "doubtful that any child may reasonably be expected to succeed in life if he is denied the opportunity of an education."[89] The question, then, is whether segregation on the basis of race, even if the "tangible" factors are equal, deprives children of the minority group of equal educational opportunities. Quoting from the opinion of the lower court, the Supreme Court unanimously agreed that: "Segregation of white and colored children in public schools has a detrimental effect upon the colored children. The impact is greater when it has the sanction of the law; for the policy of separating the races is usually interpreted as denoting the inferiority of the Negro group."[90] The court concluded that separate educational facilities are inherently unequal, and therefore

---

87. *Sweatt* v. *Painter,* 339 U.S. 629, 70 Sup. Ct. 850 (1950).
88. *Brown* v. *Board of Education of Topeka (Kansas),* 347 U.S. 483, 74 Sup. Ct. 691 (1954).
89. *Brown* v. *Board of Education of Topeka,* p. 691.
90. *Brown* v. *Board of Education of Topeka (Kansas),* p. 691.

the plaintiffs had been deprived of the equal protection of the laws as guaranteed by the Fourteenth Amendment.

Although the Brown decision reflected the emerging attitude toward race of the nation at large, it was still far ahead of some sections of the country. At the time of the decision, four states permitted and seventeen states required local school districts to operate segregated schools. Because of the extent of segregation, the court kept open the Brown Case in 1955, not to question the principle, but to hear further argument on the relief to be granted. The court concluded that desegregation must proceed "with all deliberate speed" and that the federal courts would retain jurisdiction in all school desegregation cases until that time when segregation is eliminated from the public schools of the nation.

Within the next decade, the United States District Courts, Circuit Courts, and Supreme Court repeatedly became deeply involved in school desegregation cases from Little Rock to New Orleans. In general, the courts have allowed the local school districts considerable time to devise and implement plans for desegregation. Some school boards have used that time in good faith and devised honest programs for desegregation, while others have used the time either to delay action or to create plans to circumvent desegregation. The federal courts have operated flexibly, usually recognizing that there is more than one way to desegregate; and when an educational problem was involved, they have been willing to grant time to work through the difficulty. These same courts, however, have also held firm in the face of public pressure and violence. In *Cooper* v. *Aaron* (1958), the court heard a plea from the Little Rock School Board for a stay of execution of their desegregation plans because of the opposition of the governor and legislature and because of the resulting violence that occurred in and around Central High School in the fall of 1957. A unanimous court refused to grant a delay in the desegregation proceedings on those grounds. Once again, in the fall of 1960, the court, involved in the desegregation of the New Orleans public schools, demonstrated that it was prepared to declare laws passed by the Louisiana Legislature unconstitutional as fast as they could be written if, in fact, the intent of these laws was to circumvent desegregation proceedings.

In the last decade, federal authority has repeatedly confronted state authority with respect to this issue. In the years immediately after the Brown decision was rendered, the court tended to stand alone, receiving little support from the executive and legislative branches of the federal government. Following the Little Rock conflict, the court received belated but increasing support from both branches of government.[91] With this increased support, one might expect more progress in the desegregation of the public schools.[92]

---

91. The National Education Association has been even more reluctant to take a strong stand with respect to this issue.

92. As of 1960, some 2064 Southern school districts continued to operate segregated schools. See G. W. Foster, "1960: Turning Point for Desegregation?" *Saturday Review* (Dec. 17, 1960), 52.

In the process of desegregation thus far, various pupil placement plans have evolved. Some of these plans offered the possibility of only token desegregation, others complete desegregation, and still others appeared as cleverly designed plans to avoid desegregation entirely. For instance, Alabama developed a plan whereby anyone could seek a transfer to the school nearest his home if he scored high enough on objective achievement tests and subjective interviews to determine his cultural background. Under these segregated circumstances, only Negroes took the tests, and the initiative was left to the Negroes, individually exposed to community pressure, to exercise their right.[93]

By 1960, the courts ruled that whatever criteria for pupil placement were used, they must apply equally to all pupils. Baltimore initiated an open enrollment policy in 1954 in which any child could pick whatever school he wanted on a first-come, first-serve basis. Baltimore desegregated at once; since then, however, it has drifted back to a segregated operation because of segregated residential patterns. Tennessee developed what it called a "three-school plan" in which the parent had a choice to send his child to a Negro school, a white school, or a desegregated school. A United States District Court declared this practice unconstitutional on the grounds that it is not up to parents to determine whether or not they can violate the minority groups' right to equal protection of the laws.[94] By 1960, Nashville was using a grade-a-year plan which was based on residence and the neighborhood school, with the provision, however, that if a child found himself in a racial minority in the school to which he was assigned, he could request a transfer. As a consequence, a game of musical chairs was played, with white children and the bulk of Negro children moving back to their respective schools. By 1963, the courts found the racial-minority criterion for transfer unacceptable.

As a result of the desegregation experience, there have emerged certain courses of action that a state may not take. For instance, a state may not withhold state aid to those districts in the process of desegregating their schools; a state may not use public funds for the support of private segregated schools; and a state may not preferentially close its schools which are under court order to desegregate.[95] Many questions, however, remain unanswered. Can a state give up public education entirely?[96] Furthermore, can the state, using the child benefit theory, give all parents direct grants for their child, allowing them to spend the money for the benefit of the child in whatever private segregated school he may choose? Even more difficult is the question of what constitutes a segregated or a desegregated school.

Increasingly, as school desegregation proceeded in the border states, it became apparent that the North was also guilty of operating segre-

---

93. See Foster, "1960: Turning Point for Desegregation?" p. 54.
94. See Foster, "1960: Turning Point for Desegregation?" p. 65.
95. This attempt was made in Little Rock and in Charlottesville, Front Royal, Norfolk, and Prince Edward County, Virginia. In each case, the schools were reopened through court action.
96. By 1967, six states made it possible to legally abandon public education by a mere act of the state legislature; however, by 1986, no state had taken action to do so.

gated schools. To be sure, the basis of segregation in the North was different, but it was nonetheless effective. While the South had directly legislated social segregation, the North had indirectly created an equally segregated condition through its housing developments, zoning ordinances, and informal restrictive housing practices. In short, the more wealthy North seemed to have bought its way into suburban segregated schools, while the less wealthy South had legislated its way toward the same condition of a segregated school for a segregated society.

By 1965, the federal district courts were being flooded with de facto segregation cases originating in Northern urban areas. Although the Supreme Court has refused to grant certiorari in a number of these cases, it seems reasonable to expect that eventually the court will consider the de facto segregation issue.[97] If and when the court accepts a de facto segregation case, it will have to face the arguments that have been used to make a distinction between segregation and racial imbalance.

The distinction, however, is not easily maintained. Some define a racially balanced school as one which reflects the racial cross section of the population of the entire school district.[98] If, however, a school reflects a racial imbalance, when does it become a segregated school? Some courts have maintained that when a school is made up almost entirely of the racial minority, it is a segregated school. What, then, is a segregated school prohibited by the Fourteenth Amendment? Many people have taken the position that when a school board has consciously placed pupils in a school so as to achieve separation of the races, that school is segregated; but when a school board has merely maintained a neighborhood school that is segregated as the result of housing patterns, this school may reflect a racial imbalance, but it is not a segregated school and therefore does not come under the ban of the Fourteenth Amendment. From this point of view, the distinction turns on the intent and conscious action of the school board. If a school board has made no attempt at gerrymandering its attendance areas so as to achieve a segregated effect but merely has maintained neighborhood schools, it could not have deprived anyone of his equal rights under the law.

Opponents of this point of view argue that de facto quickly turns into de jure when one considers that by law the state requires attendance at a neighborhood school which, in effect, is segregated. Since *all* school board action falls under the requirements of the Fourteenth Amendment, isn't it reasonable to assume that inaction falls under the same requirement? If a citizen may bring charges against a board that has

97. While the court has refused to consider the de facto cases, it has remanded to the District Court for evidentiary hearing a case which involves the right to a desegregated faculty as well as a desegregated student body. On November 15, 1965, *Bradley* v. *School Board, Richmond, Virginia;* and *Gilliam* v. *School Board, Hopewell, Virginia,* were remanded to the District Court. See also *Rogers* v. *Paul* 34 L.W. 3200 (12-7-65). What constituted a desegregated student body remained unsettled in 1967. For an update, see Chapter Thirteen.

98. This is essentially the position taken by New York State Education Commissioner's Advisory Committee on Human Relations and Community Tensions. See statement proposed by the Committee, "Guiding Principles for Securing Racial Balance in Public Schools" (State Education Department, Albany, New York, June 17, 1963).

acted to produce segregated schools, why may not a citizen bring charges against a board that refuses to act to avoid the same condition? Refusal to act constitutes a decision not to act. If de facto segregated schools are the result of the board's decision to use its legal authority not to act, then de facto segregation becomes de jure segregation, already banned by the Fourteenth Amendment.

Can the state educational authority be neutral when it comes to the consequences of its educational policies with respect to race? If, as Justice Harlan said, the Constitution is color-blind, under what conditions may a school board take color into account when organizing its school attendance areas? When is a school segregated or only racially imbalanced? If the educational authority has a constitutional duty to desegregate the public schools, does it have a similar duty to correct imbalance in the public schools? Does the state have the authority to correct imbalance by using color as a chief criterion of pupil placement? Is de facto segregation also de jure segregation? On what basis, if any, can one make a distinction between racial imbalance and racial segregation?[99] These are but a few of the difficult questions that the state and federal courts have been considering and that the United States Supreme Court is likely to face in the near future.[100]

It is evident that the increased importance of education in a pluralistic society having deep religious and racial problems resulted in the school becoming the center of social conflict. While many of these issues are resolved by legislative, judicial, or executive action at a local or state level, some of the most fundamental problems arrive on the United States Supreme Court dockets.

The Brown decision of 1954 was far more than an educational decision. This decision sparked a Negro revolution which is presently working its way through every phase and facet of American life. An oppressed people without hope are always a docile people. What the Brown decision did was to give the Negro hope that the next one hundred years can be vastly different from the last one hundred. That decision also gave the Negro faith in the use of organized effort to make progress. An oppressed people with a hope in the future, realistically based on organization as a lever of social action, are a revolutionary people, unwilling to accept their lot as inevitable. While some might argue that the Negro revolution began long before the Brown decision, few would care to deny that the Brown decision was the spark which set off the social dynamite that had accumulated over the decades. The decisions of the court have had profound social, as well as educational,

---

99. One might even question to what extent the neighborhood school adequately serves the needs of a socially fluid, cosmopolitan society and to what extent it tends to serve limited parochial interests. One would suspect that the neighborhood school is an anachronistic institution used by some to maintain racial segregation under another name—racial imbalance. Furthermore, most attempts to desegregate the Northern urban centers do not begin to touch the most segregated Northern communities, namely, the suburbs.

100. For an excellent analysis of the state and federal court decisions on this issue see Leo Pfeffer, "The Courts and De Facto Segregation," *C.L.S.A. Reports,* 34 (February 1, 1964) and 37 (March 15, 1964), published by the Commission on Law and Social Action of the American Jewish Congress, New York.

implications in the areas of religion and race. Although this short review cannot deal with all the Supreme Court cases involving education, there remains another group of Supreme Court cases of vital significance to education—those dealing with the freedom of teachers.

LOYALTY PROGRAMS

One of the major obstacles to the professionalization of the American teacher has been a lack of public consensus as to the function of the public school and the teacher's role in fulfilling that function. The public has come to understand and accept the need for freedom at the university level, based on the concept that in order to produce new knowledge there must be a wide range of freedom of inquiry.[101] That same public, however, has not come to understand or accept the need for academic freedom at the elementary and secondary school level, based on the concept that in order to produce free men there must be a wide range of freedom of inquiry. Lacking such public consensus and support, teachers and administrators are vulnerable to varied community pressure. In one community, a teacher may be fired for teaching evolution, and in another he may be fired for not teaching it. In one community the teacher's loyalty may be seriously questioned if he teaches about the United Nations, and in another it is questioned if he allows his students to become practically involved in current, controversial issues. If a community views its public school teachers as vital instruments of indoctrination, the question is not one of freedom for the teacher or student but one of *whose* values are to be indoctrinated.

Furthermore, America is undergoing a transformation of basic values, given impetus by the social effects of automation and of mass communication. Some citizens interpret this change in basic values as a threat to their values, and they feel excessive doubt and anxiety in the face of this threat. They attempt to resolve their doubts and allay their anxiety by insisting upon conformity with their values—at the cost of the individual freedom of others.

The dilemma of whose values are to be indoctrinated is further reinforced by the fact that a society under real or imagined threat tends to restrict its freedoms. A shrinking world community has brought confusing and unfamiliar problems—including the possibility of total war—to the attention of Americans. As America came under real external threat of annihilation, its social institutions reacted by internalizing that very threat; they encroached upon the freedom of its citizens in the name of security. The fundamental question, then, is: Can a society remain free in the face of constant external threat? And the corollary question is:

---

101. Even here, however, there are exceptions. For instance, on December 16, 1954, a committee of the House of Representatives headed by H. Carroll Reece, which had been investigating foundations, reported that those foundations which support social science research which ignore "our Judeo-Christian moral system" should not be tax-exempt. See Ralph Henry Gabriel, *The Course of American Democratic Thought*, 2nd ed. (New York: The Ronald Press Company, 1956), pp. 458-460.

Can a system of education maintain freedom of inquiry in a society filled with fear? One may argue that the freedom to teach is dependent on the answer to the first question; however, the answer to the first question may very well depend on the second—whether this society can educate a citizenry that is alert enough and that values freedom enough to withstand the erosion of individual liberty in the name of crisis. The resolution of these questions will have serious implications not only for the future of education but for the future of American society.

At present, many of the issues involved are fought out at the local and state levels of legislative and executive action.

For the most part, academic freedom does not even fall within the scope of the legal protection which is available to parties who go to court. . . . Where issues involving academic freedom can be litigated at all, the outcome normally depends on the interpretation of state law by state courts.[102]

Increasingly, however, cases involving certain dimensions of the teacher's freedom are finding their way to the Supreme Court. At present, if a teacher's job has been taken from him arbitrarily or his freedom to teach has been invaded unreasonably he can seek to take the issue to the United States Supreme Court. For the most part, the decisions the court has rendered thus far have dealt with various state laws and school board actions concerning the loyalty of its teachers.

Loyalty oaths

Whenever American society has been threatened, it has usually responded by having teachers take loyalty oaths. Loyalty oaths were first required for teachers during the Revolutionary War, and during the Civil War teachers were again required to take oaths. From World War I to the present, the number of states requiring loyalty oaths for teachers more than doubled. The increased fear of international Communism is reflected in the fact that from 1907 to 1930 only twelve states required loyalty oaths of its teachers, but by 1958, thirty-three states and the District of Columbia required oaths. In eight of these states, the teacher must swear to teach specific aspects of patriotism, and in three of these states the teacher must swear to refrain from teaching specific theories of governments. Even though the oaths teachers take vary from state to state, they all reflect one intent, namely, the loyalty of the teacher.

Even though the Supreme Court has consistently maintained that the state may require loyalty oaths of its teachers, the court has increasingly struck down certain loyalty oaths for their vagueness. In *Connally* v. *General Construction Co.* (1926),[103] the court held that "a statute which either forbids or requires the doing of an act in terms so vague that men of common intelligence must necessarily guess at its meaning and differ as to its application, violates the first essential of due process of law."

102. David Fellman, ed., *The Supreme Court and Education* (New York: Bureau of Publications, Teachers College, Columbia University, 1960), p. xv.
103. 269 U.S. 385, 391.

In *Cramp* v. *Board of Public Instruction of Orange County, Florida* (1961), the court applied this principle to a Florida oath that, in part, required the teachers to swear: ". . . I have not and will not lend my aid, support, advice, counsel or influence to the Communist Party." The court found that this aspect of the oath admitted such wide latitude of interpretation that the oath violated the teachers' right to due process of law.[104] Three years later, in *Baggett* v. *Bullitt* (1964), the court applied essentially the same principle and struck down the State of Washington's oath on the same grounds. The Washington oath read as follows:

I, the undersigned, do solemnly swear (or affirm) that I will support the constitution and laws of the United States of America and of the state of Washington, and will by precept and example promote respect for the flag and the institutions of the United States of America and the state of Washington, reverence for law and order, and undivided allegiance to the government of the United States;

I further certify that I have read the provisions of RCW 9.81.010 (2), (3), and (5); RCW 9.81.060; RCW 9.81.070; and RCW 9.81.083, which are printed on the reverse hereof; that I understand and am familiar with the contents thereof; that I am not a subversive person as therein defined; and

I do solemnly swear (or affirm) that I am not a member of the Communist party or knowingly of any other subversive organization.

I understand that this statement and oath are made subject to the penalties of perjury.[105]

The court pointed out that such terms as *precept, example, institutions, undivided allegiance, subversive person*, etc., were ill-defined and thus unreasonably exposed the individual to unknowingly perjuring himself. Such vagueness violated the first essential of due process of law. The court clearly asserted that if the state wished to pass measures to safeguard the public service from disloyal conduct, such "measures which purport to define disloyalty must allow public servants to know what is and is not disloyal."[106] In the dissenting opinion, Justices Tom Clark and John M. Harlan pointed out that this decision not only strikes down Washington's Oath Law but also puts a number of other state-oath laws in jeopardy, especially Maryland's Ober Law, which was once upheld by the court in *Gerende* v. *Board of Supervisors of Elections* (1951), and the Federal Smith Act, upheld by the court in *Dennis* v. *United States* (1951).

Freedom of association

Baggett v. *Bullitt* made it clear that if the state is going to use loyalty oaths as a means for keeping disloyal teachers out of the classroom, the state must define what it means by *disloyalty*. If the state defines dis-

---

104. See *The United States Law Week*, Washington, D.C., XXX, 22 (December 12, 1961). For example, one interpretation could mean that if you ever voted for Earl Browder when he ran for president of the United States you could not take the oath.
105. *Baggett* v. *Bullitt*, 377 U.S. 360, 84 Sup. Ct. 1316 (1964).
106. *Baggett* v. *Bullitt*, p. 1316.

loyalty as membership in what it lists as subversive organizations, then the statute must also make provision to protect the innocent who join these organizations without knowing their true subversive character. In *Wiemann* v. *Updegraff* (1952), the court struck down an Oklahoma loyalty oath which lacked this provision. That same year, the court upheld the New York State Feinberg Law.

The preamble of the Feinberg Law states that its purpose is to ferret out "subversive groups" which have been infiltrating the public schools of New York State to the point where it "threatens dangerously to become a commonplace in our schools."[107] The law, then, empowers the Board of Regents, after due deliberation and hearing, to make a list of organizations

which it finds advocate, advise, teach or embrace the doctrine that the government should be overthrown by force, violence, or any other unlawful means. The statute then authorized the Board of Regents to provide, by rule, that membership in any listed organization, after notice and hearing, 'shall constitute prima facie evidence for disqualification for appointment to or retention in any office or position in the school system.'[108]

Irving Adler brought suit charging that the law and the board's action abridged his rights as guaranteed by the First Amendment. A divided court upheld the law. Justice Sherman Minton, in delivering the opinion of the court, found no abridgment of freedom of speech or assembly:

It is clear that such persons have the right under our law to assemble, speak, think and believe as they will. . . . It is equally clear that they have no right to work for the state in the school system on their own terms. . . . They may work for the school system upon the reasonable terms laid down by the proper authorities of New York. If they do not choose to work on such terms, they are at liberty to retain their beliefs and associations and go elsewhere.[109] ·

Referring to an earlier case, *Garner* v. *Board of Public Works of Los Angeles,* the court held that a state may inquire into the reasonable fitness of its employees and that "Past conduct may relate to present fitness; past loyalty may have a reasonable relationship to present and future trust."[110] The state, therefore, has the right to inquire into the past associations of its teachers to determine their fitness to teach.[111] Justice Minton went on to point out that the state action was neither arbitrary nor unreasonable. The statute provided for a hearing to determine what

---

107. *Adler* v. *Board of Education* 342 U.S. 485, 72 Sup. Ct. 383 (1952).
108. Fellman, *Supreme Court and Education,* p. 107.
109. *Adler* v. *Board of Education,* pp. 384-385.
110. *Garner* v. *Board of Public Works,* 341 U.S. 720, 71 Sup. Ct. 912 (1951).
111. However, in *Shelton* v. *Tucker* 364 U.S. 479, 81 Sup. Ct. 247 (1960), the court struck down an Arkansas statute which required every teacher, as a condition of employment in a state-supported school, to file annually a listing without limitation of every organization to which he belonged or regularly contributed within the past five years. The statute was held invalid because it deprives teachers of their freedom of association protected by the due-process clause of the Fourteenth Amendment.

groups would appear on the subversive list, and it further provided a hearing for each teacher before dismissal, at which time he could plead ignorance of the organization's subversive character. Justice William O. Douglas, in dissenting, responded: "But innocence in this case turns on knowledge; and when the witch hunt is on, one who must rely on ignorance leans on a feeble reed."[112] This New York State law, Douglas warned:

> . . . proceeds on a principle repugnant to our society—guilt by association. A teacher is disqualified because of her membership in an organization found to be 'subversive.' The finding as to the subversive character of the organization is made in a proceeding to which the teacher is not a party and in which it is not clear that she may even be heard.[113]

The freedom to teach

Douglas also argued that he could not agree with the doctrine that when the citizen joins the public service, he "can be forced to sacrifice his civil rights." He believed that by this act New York State had entered into legal censorship of its teachers which is "certain to raise havoc with academic freedom." Justice Hugo Black agreed:

> This is another of those rapidly multiplying legislative enactments which make it dangerous—this time for school teachers—to think or say anything except what a transient majority happen to approve at the moment. Basically these laws rest on the belief that government should supervise and limit the flow of ideas into the minds of men. The tendency of such governmental policy is to mould people into a common intellectual pattern. Quite a different governmental policy rests on the belief that government should leave the mind and spirit of man absolutely free.[114]

This latter policy of freedom is the high purpose of the First Amendment. Black went on to say: "Because of this policy public officials cannot be constitutionally vested with powers to select the ideas people can think about, censor the public views they can express, or choose the persons or groups people can associate with."[115] Although the teacher does not have any unique rights under the Constitution and his case inevitably turns on his rights as a citizen and not as a teacher, Justice Douglas expressed great concern for the freedom of the teacher to teach and the student to learn in a state public school system which employs such means to gain conformity of ideas.

The law inevitably turns the school system into a spying project. Regular loyalty reports on the teachers must be made out. The principals become detectives; the students, the parents, the community become informers. Ears are cocked for

112. *Adler* v. *Board of Education*, p. 393.
113. *Adler* v. *Board of Education*, p. 383.
114. *Adler* v. *Board of Education*, p. 387.
115. *Adler* v. *Board of Education*, p. 387.

tell-tale signs of disloyalty. The prejudices of the community come into play in searching out disloyalty. This is not the usual type of supervision which checks a teacher's competency; it is a system which searches for hidden meanings in a teacher's utterances. What happens under this law is typical of what happens in a police state. Teachers are under constant surveillance; their pasts are combed for signs of disloyalty; their utterances are watched for clues to dangerous thoughts. A pall is cast over the classrooms. There can be no real academic freedom in that environment. . . . It produces standardized thought, not the pursuit of truth. Yet it was the pursuit of truth which the First Amendment was designed to protect. A system which directly or inevitably has that effect is alien to our system and should be struck down. Its survival is a real threat to our way of life. We need be bold and adventuresome in our thinking to survive. A school system producing students trained as robots threatens to rob a generation of the versatility that has been perhaps our greatest distinction. The Framers knew the danger of dogmatism; they also knew the strength that comes when the mind is free, when ideas may be pursued wherever they lead. We forget these teachings of the First Amendment when we sustain this law.[116]

Implicit in what Justice Douglas was saying was his belief that the function of the school was to maximize freedom of inquiry in its search for truth, and the role of the teacher in fulfilling that function was to act as a "stimulant to adventurous thinking." On the other hand, the majority argued that "A teacher works in a sensitive area in a schoolroom. There he shapes the attitude of young minds toward the society in which they live. In this, the state has a vital concern."[117] Implicit in this argument was the belief that the function of the school was to prepare pupils to fit into the ordered society, and the role of the teacher was to shape the attitudes of the young for that society. At the heart of the different opinions of the justices in the Adler Case was not only the question of the right of the state to determine the fitness of teachers on the basis of past association but also a serious question as to the function of the school in American society and the role of the teacher in fulfilling that function.

Increasingly the justices have introduced in their opinions their concern for the freedom of the teacher. To be sure, these arguments tend to be peripheral, since the teacher, as a teacher, has no unique right under the Constitution; nevertheless, the unique social function of the teacher in American society is gaining recognition before the court. Justice Frankfurter, for example, in *Wiemann* v. *Updegraff* (1952), took a strong position with respect to the function of the teacher.

To regard teachers—in our entire educational systems from the primary grades to the university—as the priests of our democracy is therefore not to indulge in hyperbole. It is the special task of teachers to foster those habits of openmindedness and critical inquiry which alone make for responsible citizens, who, in turn, make possible an enlightened and effective public opinion. Teachers must fulfill their function by precept and practice, by the very atmosphere which

---

116. *Adler* v. *Board of Education*, p. 393.
117. *Adler* v. *Board of Education*, p. 385.

they generate; they must be exemplars of open-mindedness and free inquiry. They cannot carry out their noble task if the conditions for the practice of a responsible and critical mind are denied to them. They must have the freedom of responsible inquiry, by thought and action, into the meaning of social and economic ideas, into the checkered history of social and economic dogma. They must be free to sift evanescent doctrine, qualified by time and circumstance, from that restless, enduring process of extending the bounds of understanding and wisdom, to assure which the freedoms of thought, of speech, of inquiry, of worship are guaranteed by the Constitution of the United States against infraction by national or State government. . . .[118]

In these cases and others,[119] the court became involved in the unresolved issue of academic freedom for elementary and secondary school teachers while examining the constitutionality of various state laws directed at the loyalty of teachers.

Academic freedom

In 1967 the United States Supreme Court, in a far-reaching decision, declared New York's Feinberg Law and a series of other antisubversive laws unconstitutional. In *Keyishian* v. *Board of Regents* (1967), the court dealt explicitly with loyalty programs which infringed on teachers' freedom of speech and association and extended the protection of the First Amendment to the area of academic freedom. In a five-to-four decision, the court applied the criterion of "vagueness" to that part of the New York Feinberg Law which implemented a 1917 New York State law that established grounds for dismissal of teachers for "the utterance of any treasonable or seditious word or words or the doing of any treasonable or seditious act." The Feinberg Law also implemented another 1939 New York statute that disqualified from "employment in the educational system any person who advocates the overthrow of government by force, violence, or any unlawful means, or publishes material advocating such overthrow or organizes or joins any society or group of persons advocating such doctrine." Although teachers were not required to sign a specific oath in this case, they were informed before assuming their duties that the above described laws constituted part of their contract. The court declared this complicated subversive control system unconstitutional on the grounds of "vagueness" that had the practical effect of restricting one's rights of freedom of speech and association as guaranteed by the First Amendment. The court insisted that academic freedom was intimately linked to the First Amendment. Justice Brennan in delivering the majority opinion of the court said:

Our Nation is deeply committed to safeguarding academic freedom, which is of transcendent value to all of us and not merely to the teachers concerned. That

---

118. *Wiemann* v. *Updegraff,* 344 U.S. 183, 73 Sup. Ct. 215 (1952).
119. For example: *Barenblatt* v. *United States* 360 U.S. 109, 79 Sup. Ct. 1081 (1959); *Beilan* v. *Board of Education of Philadelphia* 357 U.S. 399, 78 Sup. Ct. 1317 (1958); and *Sweezy* v. *New Hampshire* 354 U.S. 234, 77 Sup. Ct. 1203 (1957).

freedom is therefore a special concern of the First Amendment, which does not tolerate laws that cast a pall of orthodoxy over the classroom. 'The vigilant protection of constitutional freedoms is nowhere more vital than in the community of American schools.' *Shelton* v. *Tucker,* Supra, at 487.[120]

The court, in *Keyishian* v. *Board of Regents,* had taken a long step toward extending the protection of the First Amendment to elementary and secondary school teachers as well as college teachers. Freedom for the teacher in American society is a "special concern of the First Amendment."

The minority position in the Adler Case became the majority opinion in the Keyishian Case. In reversing its position in the Adler Case, the court insisted that it could no longer adhere to the premise "that public employment, including academic employment, may be conditioned upon the surrender of constitutional rights which could not be abridged by direct government action."[121] Teachers may work in a "sensitive area," but they do not have to relinquish their rights to freedom of speech and association because of public employment. The court went on to say that freedom of association for the citizen has developed further since the Adler Case. In *Aptheker* v. *Secretary of State* (1964) and other decisions, the court squarely faced the problem of "guilt by association." Membership in the Communist party, the court found, does not constitute guilt. The government must show that the individual not only knows of the unlawful purposes of the Party but also tends to further the unlawful aims of the Party.

As Justice Brennan said: "Mere knowing membership without a specific intent to further the unlawful aims of an organization is not a constitutionally adequate basis for exclusion from such positions as those held by appellants."[122]

The court applied this principle to the Feinberg Law which authorized the Board of Regents of New York State to draw up a list of organizations in which membership "shall constitute prima facie evidence for disqualification for appointment to or retention in any office or position in the school system," and it found the New York State law unconstitutional. "Mere knowing membership" is not enough to prove guilt. Intent to further unlawful aims must be proven. Applying the principle of "vagueness" to those strictures of the New York security system which proscribes behavior in teaching and publishing and the principle of "intent" to that which proscribes membership in associations, the court found most of New York State's subversive control laws dealing with education unconstitutional. *Keyishian* v. *Board of Regents* cast serious doubt on the constitutionality of most loyalty oaths and subversive control systems presently in effect in many states.

The court cases, however, reflected only one factor in the developing professionalism of the teacher, who as a professional would know his rights and responsibilities. There were, of course, other major move-

---

120. 35 *The United States Law Week* 4156.
121. 35 *The United States Law Week* 4156.
122. 35 *The United States Law Week* 4157.

ments and forces at work in this process. The increased educational background of teachers, the teachers' demands for stronger and more effective organizations, and, in turn, the increasing development of collective bargaining laws for teachers are all current trends which seem to indicate that the role of the teacher is in the process of being inductively defined and that the teacher may yet achieve professional status in American society.

By 1965, the United States Supreme Court, through its many and varied decisions, was plotting a course not only in the area of academic freedom but also in the areas of race and religion. The court, in effect, had become the major policy maker in those areas which intellectually and emotionally create the deepest fissures within a pluralistic society. Apparent in these decisions are not only the more critical issues of American society and the increased reliance of that society on the judicial process to resolve those issues, but also the increased significance of education. As America moved from a nineteenth-century parochial kind of society to the more cosmopolitan, socially fluid society of the twentieth century, many of the issues which once might have been satisfactorily resolved at the local level now required a national resolution. A pragmatic court, using the past for the benefit of the living present, changed with the changing needs of society. What the principle of separation of Church and State meant in nineteenth-century education was clearly very different from what it has come to mean today. In the current unanswered questions involving the use of public schools for religious purposes and the use of public funds to support religious schools, one can sense something of the future of the principle in the making. With respect to the area of race and equality before the law, it is also clear that the nineteenth-century answer—separate but equal—is not a satisfactory solution for the twentieth century. Again, in the area of de facto segregation, one can sense something of the future meaning of "equality before the law" in the making.

With respect to the problem of academic freedom, it should be clear that, for the most part, the social life of the elementary and secondary teacher in the nineteenth century was so well regulated by local community standards that there was little concern about academic freedom for the public school teacher. While nineteenth-century society hammered out the rationale for academic freedom at the university level, it remains for twentieth-century society to do the same for the elementary and secondary school teacher. As America moved in the twentieth century to a more cosmopolitan perspective and local regulation of teachers' personal lives decreased, the possibility of defining an area of responsible freedom was enhanced. But the threat of international Communism slowed this progress. A society under external threat is reluctant to extend its boundaries of freedom. In the Supreme Court cases, one can sense a real struggle to maintain a free education in the face of a threatened society. If successful here, teachers may yet have the opportunity to prove they are capable of exercising that responsible freedom which alone is at the heart of any profession. The role of the teacher, then, has been changing. Through these decisions, one can also see a pragmatic court repeatedly making judgments not only on the basis of the traditions of the past but, more important, on the expected consequences of these decisions for the present and the future. The Constitution, then, has become a living, changing document, relevant to the major issues of the times. In maintaining the life of the Constitution, the court has, in effect, concurred with the opinion of Oliver Wendell Holmes: "The Constitution is an experiment, as all life is an experiment."

SUGGESTED READINGS

Bickel, Alexander M. *The Least Dangerous Branch.* Indianapolis, The Bobbs-Merrill Company, Inc., 1962.

Blau, Joseph L., ed. *Cornerstones of Religious Freedom in America.* New York, Harper Torchbooks, 1962.

Butler, Henry E., Jr. "Religion, Government and Education," *Wall or Illusion* (pamph.). Report on the 1965 School Law Conference at Miami University, Oxford, Ohio.

Butts, R. Freeman. "Public Funds for Parochial Schools?" *Teachers College Record,* LXII, 1 (1960), 10.

————. *The American Tradition in Religion and Education.* Boston, The Beacon Press, 1950.

Drinan, Robert F. *Religion, the Courts, and Public Policy.* New York, McGraw-Hill Book Company, 1963.

Fellman, David, ed. *The Supreme Court and Education.* New York, Bureau of Publications, Teachers College, Columbia University, 1960.

Foster, G. W. "1960: Turning Point for Desegregation?" *Saturday Review,* December 17, 1960, p. 52.

Freund, Paul A. *The Supreme Court of the United States.* New York, Meridian Books, 1961.

Frommer, Arthur B. *The Bible and the Public Schools.* New York, Affiliated Publishers, 1963.

Hook, Sidney. *The Paradoxes of Freedom.* Berkeley, University of California Press, 1962.

Humphrey, Hubert H., ed. *Integration vs. Segregation.* New York, Thomas Y. Crowell Company, 1964.

La Noue, George R. "Religious Schools and Secular Subjects," *Harvard Educational Review,* XXXII, 3 (1962), 255.

London, Ephraim. *The Law as Literature.* New York, Simon and Schuster, Inc., 1960.

McCloskey, Robert G. *The American Supreme Court.* Chicago, The University of Chicago Press, 1960.

Perry, Richard L., ed. *Sources of Our Liberties.* Chicago: American Bar Association, 1959.

Pfeffer, Leo. *Church, State and Freedom.* Boston, The Beacon Press, 1953.

————. "The Courts and De Facto Segregation," *C. L. S. A. Reports* (pamph.), No. 34 (February 1, 1964) and No. 37 (March 15, 1964). New York, Commission on Law and Social Action of the American Jewish Congress.

————. *The Liberties of an American: The Supreme Court Speaks.* Boston, The Beacon Press, 1963.

Pound, Roscoe. *The Development of Constitutional Guarantees of Liberty.* New Haven, Yale University Press, 1963.

Research Division—National Education Association. "Shared Time Programs: An Exploratory Study," *Research Reports,* 1964, p. 10.

Spurlock, Clark. *Education and The Supreme Court.* Urbana, University of Illinois Press, 1955.

Steinhilher, August W. "The U. S. Supreme Court and Religion in the Schools," *Theory into Practice,* IV, 1 (February 1965), 11.

Treacy, Gerald C., S. J., ed. *Five Great Encyclicals.* New York, The Paulist Press, 1939.

Tussman, Joseph, ed. *The Supreme Court on Church and State.* New York, Oxford University Press, 1962.

CHAPTER 13
The United States
Supreme Court
and education, 1967–1985

Today, education is perhaps the most important function of state and local governments. . . . it is a principal instrument in awakening the child to cultural values, in preparing him for later professional training, and in helping him to adjust normally to his environment. In these days, it is doubtful that any child may reasonably be expected to succeed in life if he is denied the opportunity of an education. Such an opportunity, where the state has undertaken to provide it, is a right which must be made available to all on equal terms.

BROWN V. BOARD OF EDUCATION
347 U.S. 483 at 493, (1954)

Casting a worried eye to the future, Supreme Court Justice Felix Frankfurter, in *Minersville School District* v. *Gobitis* (1940), sharply warned the court of the danger of becoming the "school board for the Nation." Within the next four decades, the court increasingly came to function in just such a capacity. The phenomenal increase in Supreme Court decisions involving education during the past four decades reflects a number of trends which had begun to appear by mid-century. First, formal education was viewed as more important in the life of the average citizen, especially as it was perceived by more and more people as *the* major avenue for social mobility. Second, by mid-century, American society was deeply divided on fundamental issues regarding religion, race, freedom, and loyalty, all of which were reflected in the educational system. Under such circumstances, more and more cases involving education found their way to the United States Supreme Court.[1] Within the past two decades, this trend has intensified to

1. See. p. 368. I am indebted to Professor Paul Thurston and Professor James Anderson for their advice and counsel in developing this chapter.

the point that the court has heard twice as many cases (140) involving education as it had in its entire previous history.

Number of Supreme Court Cases Concerning Education[2]

1789–1808 . . . 0	1849–1868 . . . 1	1909–1928 . . . 5	1966–1984 . . . 140
1809–1828 . . . 1	1869–1888 . . . 0	1929–1948 . . . 14	
1829–1848 . . . 1	1889–1908 . . . 3	1949–1965 . . . 40	

Americans became more and more litigious in the post-World War II period, while the Supreme Court increasingly mirrored the variety of social tensions and conflicts the country experienced during this troubled historic period. As noted in Chapter Eleven, the federal government became more directly involved in education through the legislative process of mandating programs and directly funding educational activities in order to remedy social problems. As a consequence, the court has increasingly been asked not only to interpret the meaning of the Constitution, but, in addition, to interpret the meaning of the new federal legislation involving education. By one count, since 1950, the court has rendered some 31 decisions involving the federal statutes and education, as opposed to 113 decisions involving the Constitution and education. Most of the statutory interpretations involving education occurred, as one might expect, after 1969, when many of the federally mandated programs went into effect.[3]

Many of the questions that remained unanswered by the Supreme Court in 1967 have since been answered. Some questions, however, have not, while still other new and different questions have emerged. In proceeding to find answers to these very difficult questions, the court, in many instances, has charted a delicately sophisticated and complicated course through the very troubled waters in which the American nation finds itself. During this period of time, the court itself has undergone a significant change from the liberal expansionist views of the Warren Court to the more conservative, restricted views of the Burger Court. Thus, in the recent decade, this conservative court, through its decision-making process, has come to reflect the growing conservative trend of the broader American culture.

Although many of the cases which the Supreme Court heard since 1967 readily fell within the older established categories of religion, race, and academic freedom, whole new significant categories of cases have emerged as a consequence of the history of the 1960's and 1970's. Cases involving student rights have developed which assure the right to due process and

2. Ward W. Keesecker, "Supreme Court Decisions Affecting Education," *School Life* (Feb. 1949), p. 4. Keesecker's chart covered only the period until 1948; this author added data on the period 1949-1965 in 1967, and in 1984 added data for 1966-1984.

3. See Paul Thurston and Fred Coombs, eds., *Schools and the Constitution* (in progress), chap. 1 and Introduction.

equal protection under the law. The court has entered the classrooms of the nation in terms of defining freedom of expression and association, as well as in defining the conditions for admission, suspension, punishment, and dismissal. In a parallel area, the court has made teachers' rights more explicit. In a sequence of cases involving loyalty oaths, free association, and free speech, the Supreme Court has charted the boundaries of academic freedom, as well as job security and conditions of employment. By the latter half of the 1970's, the court was adjudicating women's rights, women's conditions of employment, and sex discrimination. At the same time, the court was active in defining the rights of the handicapped and making decisions affecting language policy and school finance.

In the area of race, the Supreme Court has been very active in attempting to implement Brown II (1955). In the area of desegregation and racial balance alone, the court has rendered more than twenty-five decisions since 1967. In addition, new categories of cases have emerged involving racially biased tests, race and private schools, racial discrimination in hiring, promoting, and firing teachers, as well as in areas of affirmative action and admissions programs. In the area of religion and education, some new categories also have emerged, such as freedom of the private schools from federal regulation, limits of compulsory school law, and new and different kinds of practices which have been struck down by the court for using the public schools for religious purposes, in violation of the First Amendment. However, it is clear that the great bulk of cases which the court has heard in this area have involved the use of public funds for religiously supported parochial schools. While the number of cases involving the use of public schools for religious purposes has increased in more recent years, as a consequence of the evangelical religious revival, and can be expected to continue to do so in the future, the increased pressure to gain public funds for parochial schools has been even greater, as evidenced by the markedly disproportionate number of cases that have emerged in this category. Since 1967, the Supreme Court has ruled on approximately four cases involving the use of the public schools for religious purposes, while during the same period, the court has made more than a dozen decisions involving the use of public funds for parochial school aid.

The pressure for aid for parochial schools has come in a variety of ways, forcing the court to establish new guidelines and tests to chart the federal course between making "no law respecting an establishment of religion," on the one hand, and, on the other hand, "not prohibiting the free exercise thereof." Both clauses, the Supreme Court has insisted, are absolute, but either one, carried to its logical extreme, might easily negate the other. Thus, it has not always been easy to find the neutral ground upon which the Constitution might rest. As the court put it in *Lemon* v. *Kurtzman* (1971), "We can only dimly perceive the lines of demarcation in this extraordinarily sensitive area of constitutional law."[4]

---

4. *Lemon* v. *Kurtzman*, 403 U.S. 602 (1971), p. 612.

RELIGION AND EDUCATION

The use of public funds for aiding parochial schools, teachers, children, and parents

In *Everson* v. *Board of Education* (1947), a unanimous Supreme Court defined what the establishment-of-religion clause of the First Amendment meant when it said, in part:

The establishment of religion clause of the First Amendment means at least this: Neither a state nor the federal government can set up a church. Neither can pass laws which aid one religion, aid all religions, or prefer one religion over another. Neither can force nor influence a person to go to or to remain away from church against his will or force him to profess a belief or disbelief in any religion. No person can be punished for entertaining or professing religious beliefs or disbeliefs, for church attendance or non-attendance. No tax in any amount, large or small, can be levied to support any religious activities or institutions, whatever they may be called, or whatever form they may adopt to teach or practice religion. Neither a state nor the federal government can, openly or secretly, participate in the affairs of any religious organization or groups and vice versa. In the words of Jefferson, the clause against establishment of religion by law was intended to erect a wall of separation between Church and State.[5]

While the court unanimously agreed in principle, the justices were in considerable disagreement as to what that principle meant in practice. In a five-to-four decision, the court upheld the New Jersey statute which provided bus transportation for parochial school children. The majority on the court ruled much as they had in the 1930 case of *Cochran* v. *Louisiana State Board of Education*. In that decision, they allowed the state to provide free textbooks for all children of the state, because such a practice benefited the child rather than the school. So, too, in *Everson* v. *Board of Education* (1947), they found that bus transportation, like free textbooks, would benefit the child, not the parochial school. The court went further, concluding that bus transportation was a legitimate exercise of the state's police power to protect the child going to and from school.

If, then, the state could provide free textbooks and transportation for all children of the state, under the assumption that such practices benefit the child, not the school, just how far might the Supreme Court go in allowing other forms of aid without them falling under the ban of the establishment-of-religion clause? Could the state, for example, provide free medical and psychological services, scientific laboratory equipment, teachers' salaries, school construction, direct tuition grants to schools, or tax deductions, in the name of benefiting all children of the state? These and other questions remained unanswered in 1967. However, over the following decades, the court proceeded to find answers to many of them.

Again applying the child benefit theory in *Board of Education* v. *Allen*

---

5. *Everson* v. *Board of Education*, 330 U.S. 1 (1947).

(1968), the court upheld a New York State law which required local school authorities to loan secular textbooks to parochial schools. While those who supported public aid for parochial schools seemed to have gained ground for their cause, the opponents to such aid countered by bringing suit against a practice which they felt was a long-standing violation of the First Amendment; i.e., tax exemption for church property. Even though James Madison, the author of the First Amendment, thought that tax exemption for church property clearly violated the amendment's prohibition against an "establishment of religion," the practice of tax exemption for church property has become a standard part of American tax law.[6]

In *Walz* v. *Tax Commissioner* (1970), the Supreme Court heard arguments challenging the New York State tax law which provided tax exemptions for property used exclusively for religious, educational, or charitable purposes.[7] In their decision, the justices reasoned that the purpose of tax exemption is not "establishing, sponsoring or supporting religion" and that, furthermore, such exemptions create only a "minimal and remote involvement between church and state." In this case, the court saw itself as struggling "to find a neutral course between the two Religion Clauses both of which are cast in absolute terms, and either of which, if expanded to a logical extreme, would tend to clash with the other."[8] The state, they ruled, in providing for the general welfare, could allow tax exemption for religious, charitable, and educational organizations. *Walz* v. *Tax Commissioner* (1970) became one of a number of important precedent-making cases which eventually led the court, in *Mueller* v. *Allen* (1983), to uphold a Minnesota statute which allowed tax deductions for tuition, textbooks, and transportation for all private and public school parents.

However, the route from the Walz Case, tax exemption for church property, to the Mueller Case, tax exemption for tuition, textbooks, and transportation, was tortuous, with a number of sharp turns along the way. A more direct route was attempted by the Pennsylvania and Rhode Island legislatures. Concerned about improving secular instruction in the nonpublic schools, Rhode Island enacted a law which provided direct salary supplements to teachers of secular subjects in nonpublic elementary schools; a Pennsylvania statute authorized the state to reimburse private schools for their actual expenditures of funds for teachers' salaries, textbooks, and instructional materials in secular courses. Both statutes were struck down for creating excessive entanglement between Church and State. In *Lemon* v. *Kurtzman* (1971), the Supreme Court established the following criteria by which a statute might be judged: "a statute must (1) have a secular legislative purpose; (2) have a principal effect which neither advances nor inhibits religion; and (3) not foster 'an excessive government entanglement with religion.'"[9] Thus, both the Rhode Island and

---

6. R. Freeman Butts, *The American Tradition in Religion and Education* (Boston: Beacon Press, 1950), p. 97.

7. *Walz* v. *Tax Commissioner of the City of New York*, 397 U.S. 664 (1970).

8. *Walz* v. *Tax Commissioner of the City of New York*, pp. 668-669.

9. Perry A. Zirkel, ed., *A Digest of Supreme Court Decisions Affecting Education* (Bloomington, Ind.: Phi Delta Kappa, 1978), p. 22.

Pennsylvania laws failed to pass the test. In *Johnson* v. *Sanders* (1970), the court struck down a similar Connecticut statute because it would create excessive entanglement between government and religion.

New York decided to take a different approach by passing a law which reimbursed nonpublic schools for expenses incurred in administering tests. This included not only costs incurred in giving state-required regents' exams, but also costs for *all* other teacher-prepared examinations. The statute did not limit the funds for secular purposes. In *Levitt* v. *Commission for Public and Religious Liberty* (1973), the court found the practice to be a violation of the establishment-of-religion clause of the First Amendment. The State of New York, however, went considerably further in aiding nonpublic schools. It had enacted legislation which provided funds for maintenance of equipment and facilities of nonpublic schools. Another aspect of the statute provided for tuition reimbursement to low-income parents with children in elementary and secondary nonpublic schools, while another provided for a state income tax credit to middle-income parents of children enrolled in nonpublic schools. The court, in the *Committee for Public Education and Religious Liberty* v. *Nyquist* (1973), used the criteria it had established in *Lemon* v. *Kurtzman* (1971), and found that the tax provisions advanced the cause of religion, and that, at the same time, the law led to excessive entanglements between government and religion. Under the circumstances, they ruled the New York law unconstitutional.

The State of Pennsylvania tried still another approach. It attempted to avoid the excessive entanglement issue by passing a law which provided direct state reimbursement to all parents for the secular portion of the tuition paid by them to nonpublic schools. The court, in *Sloan* v. *Lemon* (1973), concluded that such payments to parents encouraged enrollments in parochial schools and, therefore, had a primary effect of advancing the cause of religion in violation of the test laid down in *Lemon* v. *Kurtzman* (1971) and used in the Nyquist Case (1973). Thus, that law, too, was declared unconstitutional.[10]

With President Johnson's "War on Poverty" came the first major general federal aid to education act: the Elementary and Secondary Education Act of 1965. This legislation represented a compromise between the parochial school leaders, who traditionally stood opposed to general federal aid to public education, and the public school leaders, who supported such action. Parochial school leaders were quick to point out that any attempt to use federal aid to help disadvantaged youth in the inner cities must find ways and means of contributing to the education of those youth in parochial schools, since many parochial schools existed in the inner cities and enrolled considerable numbers of disadvantaged youth. The compromise was effected when it was agreed that the new act would contain provisions for remedial programs of "comparable quality, scope and opportunity" for children in the private schools as well as in public schools. Thus, the political logjam which had held up any significant package of federal aid to education for almost four decades now gave way. Just how these programs were to be set up to comply with the various state laws was to be deter-

---

10. Zirkel, *Digest of Supreme Court Decisions Affecting Education*, pp. 25-27.

mined by the states themselves. Not all states readily complied with the spirit of the compromise. In *Wheeler* v. *Barrera* (1974), the Supreme Court ruled that the Missouri use of Title I money in creating programs for private schools as not "identical" but "comparable" to public schools, while in keeping with the Missouri educational code, was well within the mandate of Congress as expressed in the 1965 Act.[11]

In order to facilitate the use of auxiliary services in the parochial schools, the State of Pennsylvania, relying on the child benefit principle, passed a law which provided for counseling, testing, and remedial education for disadvantaged children, to be provided by public school teachers in non-public schools. The state also enacted legislation which provided secular textbooks to be loaned to those schools. In *Meek* v. *Pittenger* (1975), the court upheld the textbook provision but struck down the provision for providing public auxiliary services in the private schools.[12]

Just how, when, and where might auxiliary services for parochial schools be viewed as constitutional by the court? In testing an Ohio law in *Wolman* v. *Walters* (1977), the court concluded that a state may provide:

(1) secular texts which are approved by public school authorities and which are loaned to private schools, students, or their parents, (2) standardized tests and scoring services such as are used in the public schools, provided that nonpublic school personnel are not involved in test drafting or scoring and nonpublic schools are not reimbursed for costs of test administration, (3) diagnostic speech, hearing, and psychological services performed in the nonpublic schools by public school personnel, and (4) therapeutic guidance and remedial services staffed by public school personnel and performed in religiously neutral territory, i.e., not on private school grounds. A state may not constitutionally provide nonpublic schools with instructional equipment and materials or with field trip transportation and services.[13]

Thus, the three-part Lemon (1971) test, requiring a secular purpose, a principal effect of neither advancing nor inhibiting religion, and avoiding excessive entanglements of government and religion, when applied to educational practice, led the court to make some fine-line distinctions as to what was and was not constitutional for private and public elementary and secondary education. This line of separation of Church and State applied only to elementary and secondary education. When it came to expending public funds for religiously affiliated colleges and universities, the court usually found that the secular purpose of those institutions, along with the age of the students and their freedom from the compulsory education laws, all tended to be overriding factors which combined to make public aid for private colleges constitutional.[14]

As the court proceeded to define what was and what was not a violation of the establishment-of-religion clause, it struck down a New Jersey stat-

---

11. Zirkel, *Digest of Supreme Court Decisions Affecting Education*, pp. 27-28.
12. Zirkel, *Digest of Supreme Court Decisions Affecting Education*, pp. 28-29.
13. Zirkel, *Digest of Supreme Court Decisions Affecting Education*, p. 31.
14. For one such ruling, see *Roemer* v. *Board of Public Works*, 426 U.S. 736 (1976).

ute, in *Beggans* v. *Public Funds for Public Schools of New Jersey* (1979), which allowed a tax deduction for parents who sent their children to nonpublic elementary and secondary schools. In this case, the court found the statute similar to that in the Nyquist Case (1973), and, therefore, declared it unconstitutional. The following year, the court, in *Committee for Public Education* v. *Regan* (1980), considered New York's revised statute providing reimbursement to private schools for costs incurred for tests mandated by state law. These tests were not teacher-made but state-prepared, with clear controls to maintain their secular purpose. The law was upheld.

By 1983, in *Mueller* v. *Allen*, a divided court had rendered what promised to be a precedent-setting decision in this area. In this case, the justices upheld a Minnesota law which allowed taxpayers, when computing their state income tax, to deduct expenses incurred in providing tuition, secular textbooks, and transportation for children attending any elementary or secondary school in the state. Secular textbooks included such school supplies as tennis shoes, sweatsuits, camera rental fees, home economics supplies, art supplies, pencils, notebooks, as well as metal and woodworking supplies.[15] The decision included tuition paid not only by parents whose children attended private and parochial schools, but also by those parents who sent their children to public schools outside their school districts, as well as such expenses as summer school fees and special tutoring services.[16]

The majority, in upholding the Minnesota law, reasoned that one fixed principle the court has consistently rejected was that "any program which in some manner aids an institution with a religious affiliation" violates the establishment-of-religion clause. The court noted that in *Walz* v. *Tax Commission* (1971), and other cases, it had held that tax exemption for church property and other charitable and educational institutions was permissible in the name of promoting the general well-being of society. They further noted that transportation, textbooks, and certain auxiliary services for parochial schools were also permissible.[17] On the other hand, the court pointed to the many decisions in which it struck down legislation that violated the establishment-of-religion clause. The court, then, deliberated on which way the Minnesota law was more like the former set of cases rather than the latter. The Nyquist Case, they concluded, was different, in that the New York law provided specific tuition grants for parents whose children attended specific schools. However, in the Mueller Case, the majority argued that the Minnesota law provided for all children of the state, and that the state has a legitimate interest in providing for their general welfare.

With these thoughts in mind, the Supreme Court proceeded to apply the three-part Lemon (1971) test.[18] The justices surmised that a secular purpose was being fulfilled by sectarian private schools, both in relieving

---

15. See *Mueller* v. *Allen*, 103 Sup. Ct. 3062 (1983), p. 3065.
16. *Mueller* v. *Allen*, p. 3065.
17. For example, as they ruled in *Emerson* v. *Board of Education* (1947), and *Board of Education* v. *Allen* (1968).
18. *Mueller* v. *Allen*, p. 3066.

public schools from teaching those students currently enrolled in sectarian schools, as well as in providing a "wholesome" competitive benchmark for the public schools. The state, the court reasoned, has a legitimate secular purpose in assisting parents whose children attend sectarian institutions in "ensuring that the state's citizenry is well educated."[19]

Considering the second test, whether or not the law "advances or inhibits religion," the court relied heavily on the notion that this was a "genuine tax deduction," similar to other tax laws which allowed medical and charitable deductions, including those for churches. Most importantly, those deductions are made available for "all parents" to use or not to use as they so wish. The law does not single out one class of parents to be aided over all others. Furthermore, the court reasoned that in both the Everson Case and the Allen Case, the school children were the beneficiaries; and so, too, in the Mueller Case, the parents and the children were the beneficiaries. Answering their own question, the majority determined that this case was more like the Everson Case than it was like the Nyquist Case.[20] Thus, in providing assistance to parents, the state was fulfilling its secular purpose of providing for the general welfare, while at the same time, the deduction aided all parents directly, rather than the schools.

Those who brought the suit pointed out that public school parents incurred virtually no tax deductible expense, while private school parents did. It was further pointed out that 96 per cent of the children in private schools in Minnesota (1978-1979) attended religiously affiliated institutions and, therefore, the deduction would aid primarily those in religiously affiliated schools. Nevertheless, the court pointed to the broad language of the law which allowed public school parents, under certain limited conditions, to take a tax deduction.

For the most part, the court accepted the notion of the parochial schools performing a secular function, and the right of the state to reimburse parents for that cost through tax deductions in the name of providing for the general welfare. Quoting from the Wolman (1977) decision, Justice Powell expressed much of the majority view in the Mueller Case when he said:

Parochial schools, quite apart from their sectarian purpose, have provided an educational alternative for millions of young Americans; they often afford wholesome competition with our public schools; and in some States they relieve substantially the tax burden incident to the operation of public schools.[21]

Lastly, the court considered the third Lemon (1971) test, and found that the law did not lead to excessive entanglement of government and religion. It rejected the petitioner's claim that the law required the state to designate which textbooks were allowable and, therefore, constituted excessive entanglement.[22]

---

19. *Mueller* v. *Allen*, p. 3067.
20. *Mueller* v. *Allen*, p. 3068.
21. As quoted in *Mueller* v. *Allen*, p. 3070.
22. The court pointed out that no more entanglement was required than what occurred

Even though a minority of four justices vigorously dissented, a major judicial precedent had been established which promised to change the support level for parochial and private schools of the nation. By 1984, in his State of the Union Address, President Reagan recommended to the members of Congress that they enact federal legislation which would allow tax deduction for private and parochial school tuition. After *Mueller* v. *Allen* (1983), such legislation would likely be constitutional.

The court no sooner seemed to relax a bit its stringent application of the Lemon (1971) test in dealing with laws which allowed state taxpayers to deduct expenses incurred in providing tuition, secular textbooks, and transportation for children attending parochial elementary or secondary schools, than it went on to more stringently apply the same test to declare invalid the shared-time programs administered under Title I in Grand Rapids, Michigan, and in New York City. In *Grand Rapids School District* v. *Phyllis Ball* (1985), the court found that the shared-time and community education programs of Grand Rapids had the "primary or principal" effect of advancing religion and therefore violated the establishment-of-religion clause. In reviewing the New York City program in *Aguilar* v. *Felton* (1985), the court found that while the New York City program had administrative practices which helped prevent it from advancing religion, those very practices inevitably led to " excessive entanglements" of Church and State, and therefore the program was in violation of the establishment-of-religion clause. With this application of the Lemon (1971) test, many shared-time programs appeared to be in jeopardy.

The freedom of the private school from federal regulation

While it is clear that the states may not give direct aid to private schools, they do have the authority to "reasonably regulate" and certify these schools in satisfying the compulsory education requirement. Over the years, the Supreme Court has recognized this authority as a legitimate state power.[23] However, in recent years, with the growth of federal bureaucratic power, has come the extension of that power into the private, religious school domain. During the 1970's, the jurisdiction of the National Labor Relations Board was extended to cover private schools and universities. The Board made a distinction between schools which were "completely religious" and those which were just "religiously associated."[24] The N.L.R.B. assumed jurisdiction in the latter type of school, and proceeded to certify unions as bargaining agents in two groups of Catholic high schools in Chicago. In *National Labor Relations Board* v. *Catholic Bishops of Chicago* (1979), the court held that schools operated to teach both religious and secular subjects are not under the jurisdiction of

---

in loaning textbooks, which was approved in *Board of Education* v. *Allen*, 392 U.S. 236 (1968).

23. As in *Meyer* v. *Nebraska*, 43 Sup. Ct. 65 (1923), and in *Pierce* v. *Society of Sisters*, 45 Sup. Ct. 571 (1925).

24. See Perry A. Zirkel, *Supplement to a Digest of Supreme Court Decisions Affecting Education* (Bloomington, Ind.: Phi Delta Kappa, 1982), p. 7.

the N.L.R.B. It based this decision on acts of Congress and not on constitutional grounds.[25] Federal authority was again rolled back in *St. Martin Evangelical Lutheran Church* v. *South Dakota* (1981), when the court interpreted the federal unemployment compensation tax law so as not to apply to church-sponsored Christian day schools, as well as to Lutheran synod secondary schools. This case involved a statutory interpretation rather than a constitutional decision.

Limits of the compulsory school law

Although it is clearly established by both state and federal constitutional law that the state has the power to make and enforce compulsory school laws, a difficult area of interpretation remains as to how far a state may go in exercising that authority when it clashes with a parent's interest in educating the child as expressed through a religious community. In *Wisconsin* v. *Yoder* (1972), the court heard the Old Order Amish claims against the Wisconsin state compulsory education law, which required school attendance until age sixteen. The Amish argued that formal education beyond the grade school level had a detrimental effect on their established way of life, which combines religion and daily work. It was further argued that Amish children did not need a high school education because the larger community provided ample training for self-sufficient adult citizenship.[26] The court agreed, and found the state compulsory education law an infringement of the Amish right to free exercise of their religion, as guaranteed by the First Amendment. The state, the court surmised, showed no compelling reason for such an infringement. The parents, in concert with their religious community, could reasonably carry out the necessary educational functions for teenaged youth. Thus, in this case, the state was required to give way to the authority of the parents, who were acting in concert with the religious community of which they were a part.

The use of public schools for religious purposes

After *Abington School District* v. *Schempp* (1963) and *Murray* v. *Curlett* (1963), in which both the practice of prayer and Bible reading in the public schools were ruled a violation of the Constitution, the court fell relatively silent in this area. The general public reaction, however, was not so silent, as the number of proposed constitutional amendments to counter these decisions reached well into the hundreds. Nevertheless, the strongest support for these court decisions came from the leaders of the traditional churches, who agreed with the court and stood opposed to any constitutional change.[27] However, with the religious revivalism of the past two decades, the growth of the "moral majority," and the corresponding rise of neo-conservative political activity, has come the revived pressure for Bible reading or some form of prayer in the public schools.

---

25. Zirkel, *Supplement to a Digest of Supreme Court Decisions Affecting Education*, p. 7.
26. Zirkel, *Digest of Supreme Court Decisions Affecting Education*, p. 24.
27. See pp. 381-382.

The Supreme Court's ban on prayer in the public schools became, for many, a symbol for whatever peculiar moral and social ailment the country suffered. The pressure had increased to the point that in May of 1982, President Reagan proposed the following amendment to the Constitution: "Nothing in this Constitution shall be construed to prohibit individual or group prayer in public schools or other public institutions. No person shall be required by the United States or by any state to participate in prayer."[28] By the spring of 1984, Congress had debated and failed to muster the necessary votes in order to send the amendment along its procedural path to the states for passage. The following year the court, in *Wallace* v. *Jaffree* (1985), once again applied the Lemon (1971) test and found that an Alabama law which authorized a one-minute period of silence in all public schools, "for meditation or voluntary prayer," had no secular purpose but was, rather, an "effort to return voluntary prayer" to the public schools. The court interpreted this effort as a state "endorsement of religion," and therefore a violation of the First Amendment.[29] This decision, however, did not rule out the right of the public school teacher to call for a moment of silent meditation, and the right of the student to his or her own silent prayers.

The pressure for using the public schools for religious purposes varied with the winds of evangelism which swept the country from time to time, just as the particular purpose and practice varied. One issue which appears to have come and gone over the past century is the teaching of evolution in the schools. By the 1960's, it was once again an issue as the court, in *Epperson* v. *Arkansas* (1968), reviewed the "anti-evolution" statute of Arkansas, which prohibited the teaching of evolution in the public schools and universities in that state, and found it to be a violation of the First Amendment ban against an establishment of religion. The court reasoned that the Arkansas law was not a manifestation of religious neutrality on the part of the state, but was, in fact, a law which served the interest of a particular religious group. "The sole reason for the Arkansas law is that a particular religious group considers the evolution theory to conflict with the account of the origin of man set forth in the Book of Genesis."[30] The court went on to conclude that "a State's right to prescribe the public school curriculum does not include the right to prohibit teaching a scientific theory or doctrine for reasons that run counter to the principles of the First Amendment."[31]

For many religious fundamentalists, the decision represented a victory for "secular humanism," if not Godless-atheism, in the public schools. The growth of fundamentalism was reflected in the political pressure to teach creationism alongside evolution. Legislation to that effect had been introduced during the school year 1980-1981 in fifteen states and enacted

28. As quoted in Stephen B. Thomas, Nelda H. Cambron-McCabe, and Martha M. McCarthy, eds., *Educators and the Law* (New York: Institute for School Law and Finance, 1983), p. 41.

29. See *Wallace* v. *Jaffree*, 53 U.S.L.W. 4665, June 4, 1985.

30. *Epperson* v. *Arkansas*, 393 U.S. 97 (1968), p. 97.

31. *Epperson* v. *Arkansas*, p. 97.

in two states.[32] The argument often presented for having the biblical account of creation taught in the public schools was that it was a "scientific" theory well on par with the "scientific" theory of evolution. However, by 1982, in *McLean* v. *Arkansas*, a federal district judge found the Balanced Treatment for Creation-Science and Evolution-Science Act unconstitutional on the grounds that creation science is religious dogma and as such is "simply and purely an effort to introduce the Biblical version of creation into the public school curricula."[33] It was clearly not the fundamentalists' wish that creationism be taught as simply just another "theory." Nevertheless, as the pressure to teach the biblical account of creation mounts, the Supreme Court is likely to be called on to render a decision in this area. If and when it does, the age-old conflict between science and religion will once again come to the fore. The American Association for the Advancement of Science has already issued a resolution that creationism is "'perverting science education' and has no place in a public school classroom because it is not grounded in any scientific evidence."[34]

Closely akin to the creationist-evolutionist issue are questions involving sex education and value-clarification programs, which many fundamentalists believe are practices in keeping with "secular humanism." Secular humanism, they believe, is the secular religion that has come to pervade the public school curriculum. A case may yet be made to test whether or not secular humanism pervades a particular public school curriculum and whether or not it can be defined as a "religion."

In response to fundamentalist charges that the schools were too secular, the Kentucky legislature passed a law which required the posting of the Ten Commandments in each classroom of the state, with a notation that the "secular" application of the Ten Commandments undergirds the common-law tradition of the United States. The court, in *Stone* v. *Graham* (1980), struck down the law as not having a secular but a religious purpose. Here, as in the Bible reading cases, the court took pains to point out that the Decalogue was a suitable document for study in a course on the history of religion, ethics, or comparative religions, but could not be used as a religious icon to be posted on classroom walls.[35]

While it is clear that the public elementary and secondary school classrooms cannot be used for religious worship or instruction, the question of whether or not a public state university facility might be so used was tested in *Widmar* v. *Vincent* (1981). In that case, the court ruled that the University of Missouri at Kansas City may not exclude groups from its open forum because they teach religion. The justices found that the university's exclusionary policy violated the principle that a state regulation of speech must be content-neutral. They concluded that the State of Missouri had violated the plaintiff's right to free speech while attempting to fulfill its obligation to avoid an establishment of religion. In applying the three-

---

32. See Gerald Caplan, "Evolution and the Biblical Account of Creation: Equal Time," in *School Law in Changing Times*, ed. M. A. McGhehey (Topeka, Kans.: National Organization on Legal Problems of Education, 1982), p. 68.

33. As quoted in Thomas et al., *Educators and the Law*, p. 43.

34. Thomas et al., *Educators and the Law*, p. 44.

35. Zirkel, *Supplement to a Digest of Supreme Court Decisions Affecting Education*, p. 7.

part Lemon (1971) test, the court reasoned that since the university was dealing with adults not bound by the state's compulsory education law, and the university's broader open forum functioned primarily with a secular purpose, the practice of including religious groups would withstand the test against an establishment of religion. Under the circumstances, the university was violating the group's free-speech right by excluding them from participation. Thus, the free speech rights of student religious groups on university campuses were protected.[36] The Widmar (1981) decision, however, may yet prove troublesome.

There are those who might argue that public elementary and secondary school students need their religious expression protected by the free-speech clause equally as much as any college student. The court could be expected to respond as it has done so often in the past, to emphasize the level of maturity of college students and their generally free social condition, as opposed to that of public school students. Those who support free religious expression in the public schools, however, might point to *Tinker* v. *Des Moines* (1969), in which the court found that the free-speech clause of the First Amendment protects the political expression of minor public school students. Under such circumstances, it could be argued that the public school students' right to religious expression needs the protection of the free-speech clause at least as much as does their right to political expression in the same school. At least it might be difficult to explain why political expression should be protected while religious expression should not.[37]

RACE AND EDUCATION

Desegregation and racial balance

No area of judicial action has proved more difficult than the Supreme Court's attempt to fulfill the promise of Brown II to desegregate American public schools "with all deliberate speed." Since 1967, the court has rendered more than twenty-six decisions involving desegregation and racial balance in the schools. The resistance to desegregation in both the South and the North has been massive. It has taken a variety of forms, involving tokenism, delays, and outright subterfuge.

While the Eisenhower administration reluctantly took action at Little Rock,[38] the court, in its solitary stance, faced the violence, and in *Cooper* v. *Aaron* (1958) ruled that public hostility cannot be used to justify postponement of desegregation court orders. In *Goss* v. *Board of Education* (1963), the court struck down a Tennessee school desegregation plan which permitted students who found themselves in a racial minority to transfer back to their segregated schools. Ten years after Brown I, in *Griffin* v. *County School Board* (1964), the justices ordered Prince Edward

---

36. See *Widmar* v. *Vincent*, 102 Sup.Ct. 269 (1981).
37. For a similar line of argument, see Thomas et al., *Educators and the Law*, p. 40.
38. See Chapter Eleven.

County, Virginia, public schools to reopen, and ruled unconstitutional the private school public aid program that they had developed to facilitate the education of white children. The following year, in *Bradley* v. *School Board of City of Richmond* (1965), the court ruled that the assignment of faculty on a nonracial basis must be considered part of any desegregation plan; and in *Rogers* v. *Paul* (1965), it ruled a "grade a year" plan invalid where equal course offerings were not available to black students at the upper grade levels.[39] The patience of the court was beginning to wear thin as it struck down a "freedom of choice" plan in *Green* v. *County School Board* (1968), which, in effect, was designed to maintain segregated schools. A similar "free-transfer" plan was used in Tucson, Arizona, and was struck down in *Monroe* v. *Board of Commissioners* (1968), because it failed to produce effective desegregation results.

Facing a school board that had exhibited a general pattern of delaying tactics for a number of years, the justices, in *United States* v. *Montgomery County Board of Education* (1969), upheld a District Court's use of specific numerical ratios as proper goals and guidelines for desegregation purposes. While the delays continued, many school boards not only were slow to create plans for desegregation and their implementation, but many also created plans which were purposely designed to delay desegregation. In one such situation, the Fifth Court of Appeals approved delaying the implementation of a number of Mississippi desegregation district plans, while the United States Supreme Court, in *Alexander* v. *Holmes County Board of Education* (1969), overturned the decision and called for immediate desegregation.[40]

Even the court system, itself, was used to create delays. In one such case, a District Court had approved plans to change certain attendance zones, which would have created some desegregation; then, it further ordered the school board to create a comprehensive desegregation plan for the entire district. Upon appeal to the Circuit Court, the school board was allowed to drop the attendance zone plan pending the development of a comprehensive plan. In *Dowell* v. *Board of Education* (1969), the Supreme Court reversed the Circuit Court decision and ordered immediate implementation of the original plan, while the more comprehensive plan was being developed.[41] By 1970, though, the patience of the court had clearly run out. The Fifth Circuit Court of Appeals had approved delaying desegregation orders in some sixteen separate cases, involving hundreds of thousands of school children, from mid-year to the beginning of the next fall term. However, in *Carter* v. *West Feliciana Parish School Board* (1970), the Supreme Court reversed the Circuit Court decision and ordered immediate mid-year desegregation, thus allowing only eight weeks for full compliance.[42]

In 1971, the court rendered a major decision in *Swann* v. *Charlotte-Mecklenburg,* in which it ordered a desegregation plan to be implemented which included racial quotas, manipulation and pairing of noncontiguous

39. See Zirkel, *Digest of Supreme Court Decisions Affecting Education*, pp. 82-85.
40. Zirkel, *Digest of Supreme Court Decisions Affecting Education*, pp. 86-87.
41. Zirkel, *Digest of Supreme Court Decisions Affecting Education*, pp. 86-87.
42. Zirkel, *Digest of Supreme Court Decisions Affecting Education*, p. 88.

attendance zones, and the use of extensive busing. The justices explicitly rejected the "racially neutral" plans developed by the school board which failed to desegregate, and in turn approved a District Court's use of numerical quotas as a flexible starting point to shape a remedy. The school board no longer could hide behind the facade of "racial neutrality." The court said:

When school authorities present a district court with a 'loaded game board,' affirmative action in the form of remedial altering of attendance zones is proper to achieve truly nondiscriminatory assignments. In short, an assignment plan is not acceptable simply because it appears to be neutral.[43]

Thus, having passed beyond the point of neutrality, the court was fully prepared to accept the idea of manipulating attendance zones and busing for the purpose of real desegregation. The arguments against busing were rejected, and the court noted that out of all the nation's public school children, "approximately 39% were transported to their schools by bus in 1969-1970 in all parts of the country."[44] Busing, the justices reasoned, was an integral part of the American educational system, and therefore could be used to implement desegregation plans. For the most part, the objections to busing were essentially racially motivated, and therefore were not accepted as valid objections by the court. It did, however, accept certain limitations as legitimate: "An objection to transportation of students may have validity when the time or distance of travel is so great as to either risk the health of the children or significantly impinge on the educational process."[45]

While the courts have used busing as a vehicle of desegregation, the Congress and the chief executive have more often stood opposed. In most cases, the busing issue appears to be only a screen to cover the segregation existing in the neighborhood schools, which was created for social, economic, and racial purposes. As a consequence of that resistance, by 1976, when some 43 per cent of all public school students were bused, only 4 per cent were bused for desegregation purposes, but of the 4 per cent, most were black students.[46]

In the Swann Case, a unanimous Supreme Court set the guidelines for the desegregation of public schools that had been segregated by law. The court clearly saw itself as implementing the 1954 Brown decision. The court approached school districts which had been segregated by law before Brown I in a more direct and decisive way, proclaiming that the dual school system must be changed to a unitary system. Thus, in *Davis* v. *Board of School Commissioners* (1971), the neighborhood school concept of Mobile, Alabama, was ordered to give way to bus transportation and split zoning; and in *McDaniel* v. *Barresi* (1971), the court found that Title IV of the Civil Rights Act, which prohibits discrimination on the basis of race, does not thereby prohibit the court from taking race into account and ordering

43. *Swann* v. *Board of Education*, 402 U.S. 1 (1971), p. 28.
44. *Swann* v. *Board of Education*, p. 29.
45. *Swann* v. *Board of Education*, pp. 30-31.
46. Zirkel, *Digest of Supreme Court Decisions Affecting Education*, p. 75.

the busing of students on the basis of race for desegregation purposes.[47] Thus, by the beginning of the 1970's, the Supreme Court was vigorously acting to overcome de jure segregation in many of the Southern public schools.

The question of what was to be done about the de facto segregated schools of the North, East, and West, and especially those in the heavily segregated Northern urban centers, remained an even more difficult question. In 1967, I made the following argument against de facto segregation:

> Since *all* school board action falls under the requirements of the Fourteenth Amendment, isn't it reasonable to assume that inaction falls under the same requirement? If a citizen may bring charges against a board that has acted to produce segregated schools, why may not a citizen bring charges against a board that refuses to act to avoid the same condition? Refusal to act constitutes a decision not to act. If de facto segregated schools are the result of the board's decision to use its legal authority not to act, then de facto segregation becomes de jure segregation, already banned by the Fourteenth Amendment.[48]

This line of reasoning would have put the court in a position of requiring the desegregation of virtually all segregated Northern urban schools, regardless of what caused the segregation. The justices, however, resisted this line of reasoning. Instead, when they considered the Northern ghetto school question, they stuck close to the "actions" of the school board, and made a distinction between intentional and nonintentional actions by the board which resulted in segregated conditions. In this way, a portion of the responsibility for the segregated condition might be ascribed without having to declare a nonaction a constitutional violation.[49] Thus, the court recognized that a school board, by its actions, may have intended to produce and develop a segregated system of schools, even if no state law requiring such schools ever existed. The court began to take "intent" into account, particularly in *Spencer* v. *Kugler* (1972), when it found a New Jersey State law which created school district boundaries coterminous with the city boundaries as not being segregative in "intent." The preponderance of blacks in many of the schools resulted from housing patterns and population shifts which the school board did not control. The court upheld a lower court ruling that: "A state law establishing a reasonable system of school districting that is not segregative in intent is constitutional even though subsequent population shifts result in *de facto* school segregation under the system so established."[50]

The following year, 1973, the court heard two cases, involving Southern school districts, dealing with the process of designing attendance zones and district boundaries so as to prevent and obstruct desegregation, and it quickly declared the districts' plans in violation of the Constitu-

---

47. Zirkel, *Digest of Supreme Court Decisions Affecting Education*, p. 92.
48. See pp. 393-394.
49. It should be noted, however, that the court did not hesitate to declare a school board's failure to act a legal violation when it was clear that a previous constitutional violation was to be remedied.
50. Zirkel, *Digest of Supreme Court Decisions Affecting Education*, p. 93.

tion.[51] The court also accepted a case involving a Northern city which never had an explicit law mandating or permitting segregation, yet was operating segregated schools. In *Keyes* v. *School District No. 1, Denver, Colorado* (1973), the court concluded that the important element in identifying illegal segregation was the "purpose and intent" of the school board's action. It further held that a system-wide remedy is appropriate when "an intentionally segregative policy is practiced in a meaningful or significant segment of a school system."[52] Thus, once segregative intent was established as having been practiced in one part of a school district, it was not necessary to prove it existed in all other areas of the district in order to require a district-wide remedy. The case was remanded to a lower court to determine if any intentional state action was involved, and if so, to seek a remedy. The litigation has continued at that level. In the Keyes Case, the Supreme Court counted blacks and Hispanics together when assessing the segregated condition of the district.

The following year, in *Milliken* v. *Bradley* (1974), the court ruled that the District Court which ordered an interdistrict desegregation plan for Detroit, including its suburban schools, acted in excess of what was required. The court remanded the case back to the District Court for an intradistrict remedy. In this case, the justices laid down the following rule: " The controlling principle consistently expounded in our holdings is that the scope of the remedy is determined by the nature and extent of the constitutional violation."[53] The implications of this principle can be viewed as restrictive. The court was now requiring that the plaintiff not only had to show "intent" on the part of the school board or the state to segregate the school system, but any resulting remedy required an establishment of the degree to which segregation had occurred as a consequence of official action, as opposed to that which occurred as a result of other social forces. The difficulty in making such determinations was clear. As a consequence of these complications, some began to feel that the court was beginning to retreat from the segregation area.[54] However, the controlling principle can be interpreted more positively by recognizing that the implication of the principle can be as follows: if the state and/or the suburban school districts can be shown to have taken any intentional segregative action with respect to the inner city schools, then an intradistrict remedy would be clearly required. There are some indications that the court was receptive to this latter interpretation.[55]

By the mid-1970's, the court had remanded to the District Courts a number of cases involving the cities of Austin, Omaha, Indianapolis, and Milwaukee, with instructions to the lower courts to consider such factors as official discriminating action, impact of the action, and the legislative

---

51. See *Wright* v. *Council of City of Emporia*, 407 U.S. 451 (1972), and *The United States* v. *Scotland Neck City Board of Education*, 407 U.S. 484 (1972).

52. *Keyes* v. *School District No. 1, Denver, Colorado*, 413 U.S. 189 (1973), pp. 208-209.

53. *Milliken* v. *Bradley*, 418 U.S. 717 (1974), p. 744.

54. For an analysis of the "controlling principle" argument, see Stephen Barrett Kanner, "From Denver to Dayton: The Development of a Theory of Equal Protection Remedies," *Northwestern University Law Review*, LXXII, 3 (1977), 382-406.

55. As shall be discussed with reference to *Dayton Board of Education* v. *Brinkman*, 443 U.S. 526 (1979).

and administrative history of the districts concerned.[56] In *Dayton Board of Education* v. *Brinkman I* (1977), the court remanded a district-wide desegregation plan back to the District Court in order to determine how much segregative effect had occurred. As the Supreme Court put it in Dayton II (1979), the District Court

should have 'determine[d] how much incremental segregative effect these violations had on the racial distribution of the Dayton school population as presently constituted, when that distribution is compared to what it would have been in the absence of such constitutional violations. The remedy must be designed to redress that difference, and only if there has been a system-wide impact may there be a systemwide remedy.'[57]

Armed with such directions, the District Court proceeded to reopen the case. It came to find that various instances of purposeful segregation in the past were evidenced by "an inexcusable history of mistreatment of black students," much of which would be a violation of the equal-protection clause, if it existed today. The District Court, however, went on to conclude:

Plaintiffs had failed to prove that acts of intentional segregation over 20 years old had any current incremental segregative effects. The District Court conceded that the Dayton schools were highly segregated but ruled that the Board's failure to alleviate this condition was not actionable absent sufficient evidence that the racial separation had been caused by the Board's own purposeful discriminatory conduct.[58]

On appeal, the Circuit Court reversed the District Court and found that the evidence indicated that, at the time of Brown I (1954),

The Dayton Board was operating a dual system, that it was constitutionally required to disestablish that system and its effects, that it had failed to discharge this duty, and that the consequences of the dual system, together with the intentionally segregative impact of various practices since 1954, were of systemwide import and an appropriate basis for a systemwide remedy.[59]

The Supreme Court, in *Dayton Board of Education* v. *Brinkman II* (1979), upheld the Circuit Court ruling. In justifying a system-wide remedy, the court went back to *Keyes* (1973) for precedent, as well as to *Columbus Board of Education* v. *Penick* (1979), in which it called for a system-wide desegregation remedy in lieu of the school board's intentional segregative actions before Brown I (1954), and the failure of the board to discharge its constitutional obligation to disestablish the dual system that continued to exist after Brown I.[60]

---

56. Thomas et al., *Educators and the Law*, p. 50.
57. *Dayton Board of Education* v. *Brinkman*, pp. 531-532.
58. *Dayton Board of Education* v. *Brinkman*, p. 532.
59. *Dayton Board of Education* v. *Brinkman*, p. 534.
60. *Dayton Board of Education* v. *Brinkman*, p. 541.

Dayton I (1977) and Dayton II (1979) reveal the extent to which the District Court was, in fact, holding a narrower, more restrictive interpretation of the "controlling principle" than the Supreme Court actually required.[61] In going back to the Keyes Case, the court seemed to allow a somewhat broader interpretation, and thereby set the direction that future cases might be expected to take.

Given intentionally segregated schools in 1954, however, the Court of Appeals was quite right in holding that the Board was thereafter under a continuing duty to eradicate the effects of that system, *Columbus, ante,* at 458, and that the systemwide nature of the violation furnished prima facie proof that current segregation in the Dayton schools was caused at least in part by prior intentionally segregative official acts.[62]

While the Supreme Court has not resolved the questionable distinction between de facto and de jure, it has extended the meaning of de jure segregation to cover those official school or state policies which, in purpose and effect, produce segregated schools. Using the post-Brown I discrepancy test, the court has essentially said that "if school officials are unable to refute evidence that intentional segregation existed in their district prior to 1954, they have a continuing duty to eliminate the effects of such segregation in the school system."[63] Given the direction of the court and the criteria being used, a number of cases at the lower court level have developed which may find their way, in the future, to the Supreme Court.

Using these Supreme Court guidelines, a District Court and a Circuit Court found the State of Missouri and the school board of the City of St. Louis guilty of intentional segregative acts.[64] The State of Missouri maintained a provision in its Constitution for mandating segregated schools until 1976. The state also had been shown to have financed busing black children from the outlying school districts to the City of St. Louis in order to maintain segregated schools. After some ten years of litigation, the District Court found the state and the city school board guilty of segregative actions and began to consider hearings into possible segregative actions on the part of the twenty-three surrounding suburban districts. The District Court threatened that if the suburban districts were found guilty of such acts, they would immediately be incorporated into a unified metropolitan school district, by court order. Before those hearings could be held, a voluntary desegregation plan was agreed upon, whereby each suburban district agreed to accept enough inner-city black transfer students to bring

---

61. This was apparent to some commentators even before the court ruled in Dayton II (1979). See, for example, Louise E. McKinney, "Finding Intent in School Segregation Constitutional Violations," *Case Western Law Review,* XXVIII, 163 (1977), 119.

62. *Dayton Board of Education* v. *Brinkman II* (1979), p. 537.

63. Thomas et al., *Educators and the Law,* p. 52. They also wrote: "The post-Brown test . . . involves a determination of how much incremental segregative effects the violations have on the racial distribution of the school population as presently constituted, when compared with what it would have been in the absence of such constitutional violations" (p. 52).

64. See *Liddell* v. *Board of Education,* 491F Supp. 351 (1980). Also see *Liddell* v. *Board of Education,* 677F.2d 626 (8th Circ.) (1982).

the black student population in each district up to 15 per cent, in exchange for the state covering the costs and the plaintiffs' agreeing not to
subject the district to further litigation.[65] All districts would be subject to
mandatory review in five years, and those districts not reaching their goal
would be subject to further litigation. The St. Louis voluntary desegregation plan also included special education programs, including magnet
schools, to be established in the inner city, the costs of which would be
borne by the City of St. Louis and the State of Missouri. The plan has been
upheld by the Eighth Circuit Court of Appeals and may yet be appealed to
the United States Supreme Court by the State of Missouri, which is required to bear a sizable share of the overall costs. Another case, similar to
the St. Louis case, is currently in progress, involving the State of Missouri
and the Kansas City school system.[66]

What might happen if a district, in good faith, created a unitary system and met its desegregation responsibilities, and then some years later
found itself racially imbalanced because of random population shifts? In
Pasadena City Board of Education v. *Spangler* (1976), the court ruled that
the school district need not remain racially balanced if the forces causing it
were not school-authority related. In effect, it said that a one-race school is
not necessarily a segregated school, and that a particular racial quota does
not have to be maintained. Thus, at the present time, a racially segregated
school may exist because of population shifts and housing pattern changes;
and as such, it cannot be challenged.

Much of the segregation of the races in America is reflected in housing
patterns resulting from racial and class discrimination, which is often rationalized in purely economic terms. When the village board of Arlington
Heights, Illinois, refused to grant a rezoning request from a single-family
to a multiple-family classification, and then was charged with racial discrimination in violation of the Fourteenth Amendment, the board's response was that its decision was motivated by a desire to protect property
values. In *Arlington Heights* v. *Metropolitan Housing Development Corporation*
(1977), the court ruled that a racially disproportionate impact alone was
not enough; discriminatory intent or purposes must also be shown in
order to demonstrate a violation of the Fourteenth Amendment in such
instances. While it is clear, in this case, that property values took precedence over human values, the court pointed out that once a discriminatory
intent is shown, the protection of the Fourteenth Amendment takes precedence over economic values.

While the path from Brown I to Dayton II, and then to Arlington
Heights, was a tortured one, with many turns, it is clear that the court
has come to say that where government action created, and government officials intended to create, segregation of the races, the Fourteenth
Amendment applies. However, where segregation resulted from government action not intended to segregate, in districts not segregated at the
time of Brown I, a judicial remedy is not possible. The problem still re-

---

65. See *Education Daily,* Apr. 1, 1983, p. 1. Also see E. R. Shipp, "Two Court Cases
Watched as Barometers on Integrating Schools," *New York Times,* Dec. 8, 1983, sect. A,
p. 12.
    66. See *Craig Jenkins* v. *State of Missouri,* Case No. 77-0420-CV-W-1-4 (1983).

mains that in a racist society, many sources of segregation, other than governmental, remain operative. The court had taken a major step in extending the meaning of de jure to cover what in part was de facto segregation when it ruled that school districts violated the Fourteenth Amendment when they intentionally acted to segregate, even though no law existed permitting or mandating such action. Nevertheless, some found themselves impatient with the court's emphasis on the source of segregation. Douglas Lewis Abramson enunciated that point of view well:

It is inconsistent that with a Constitution proclaiming equal protection of the laws, and a Court apparently interested in attaining nation-wide unitary school systems, rights of school children to an equal educational opportunity should be based on an artificial distinction between sources of segregation, rather than on the existence of substantial racial imbalance. Although racial imbalance may result from social and economic determinants of private residential choice, such imbalance nonetheless results in the same harm to segregated students which prompted the Court's decision in *Brown* v. *Board of Education.*[67]

In a truly nonracist society, the sources of segregation would be an "artificial distinction." However, in a racist America, where the minority population of approximately 12.5 per cent represents more than two-thirds of the welfare rolls, half the prison inmates, and only government segregated action is prohibited, the source of segregation *is* important.[68] In spite of Brown I and the civil rights movement of the 1960's, America remains fundamentally a racist society. As noted earlier, behind much of the racial imbalance in the public schools exists the racial imbalance in America's housing patterns, which, in themselves, reflect long-standing racial discrimination in the economic arena. These factors, in turn, are partly caused by racial discrimination in the workplace. In attempting to desegregate the public schools since the Brown I decision, the Supreme Court has only begun to expose the sources and extent of this society's racism. In this context, the court cannot solve the larger problem of deep-seated, latent racism in the culture at large. However, it can interpret the laws so that their force does not support racism. This, in fact, is what the court has repeatedly attempted to do. While some might view these attempts as representing a Band-Aid approach to treating a cancer on the body politic, others would be quick to point out that if progress is to be made, then the education of the future generation is an appropriate place to begin.

Desegregation does not automatically result in integration or improved race relations. A phenomenal educational challenge exists in the area of improving race relations, about which public school educators have remained relatively silent. Nevertheless, if this opportunity is ever to present itself, desegregation of the high-percentage white suburban schools needs to come about not only from the standpoint of guaranteeing blacks equal protection under the law, but, even more important, in the opportunity to eliminate the racism which pervades many of those schools.

---

67. Douglas Lewis Abramson, in *Emory Law Journal,* XXIII, 293 (1974), 311.
68. See Chapter Eleven.

Thus far, the court has been cautious in moving toward interdistrict remedies which include suburban schools.[69] In *Milliken* v. *Bradley* (1974), and some of the ensuing cases, the court reflected on conditions which might call for desegregation of suburban schools. One such approach was suggested by Justice Stewart in *Milliken* v. *Bradley* (1974), when he pointed out that a school desegregation order may be appropriate where it can be shown that a state housing authority or a municipal zoning board has intentionally acted to discriminate and segregate neighborhoods.[70] The use of governmental authority to create segregated housing, which in turn creates segregated schools, appears increasingly open to challenge. At present, there exist a number of cases involving such challenges in the lower courts. One might expect to see more school desegregation cases linked to housing discrimination cases in the future.[71]

While the interdistrict remedies may or may not lie in the near judicial future, resistance to intradistrict desegregation continues. On June 30, 1982, in *Washington* v. *Seattle School District No. 1,* the court struck down a State of Washington law, which was adopted through initiative, prohibiting school boards from requiring any student to attend a school other than the school geographically nearest or next nearest to his or her place of residence. The statute contained provisions which permitted deviations from this rule in all cases required by educational policy, except in those of racial desegregation.[72] In a five-to-four decision, the court held that the law violated the equal-protection clause. In that same term, the court, in *Crawford* v. *Board of Education* (1982), upheld a California State constitutional amendment which limited state court-ordered busing for desegregation purposes only to those instances in which a federal court would order busing to remedy a Fourteenth Amendment violation.[73] In other words, the State of California was saying that it would permit desegregation to the extent that it was required by the United States Constitution, but no further. The court obviously could not declare such an enactment in violation of the Constitution.

Desegregation cases were not the only kinds of cases to occupy the Supreme Court's attention with respect to race. New and different categories dealing with racial discrimination had begun to appear.

Tests and racial discrimination

Prior to 1964, the Duke Power Company required a high school diploma and the passing of a professionally prepared aptitude test in the placement of its employees in the higher-paid job categories. In *Griggs* v. *Duke Power Co.* (1971), the court applied Title VII, Section 703(h), of the Civil Rights Act of 1964, and concluded that the Duke Power Company

69. As, for example, *Milliken* v. *Bradley* (1974).

70. See *Milliken* v. *Bradley,* p. 755.

71. For one such analysis, see Robert R. Harding, "Housing Discrimination as a Basis for Interdistrict School Desegregation Remedies," *Yale Law Journal,* XCIII, 2 (Dec. 1983), 340-361.

72. *Washington* v. *Seattle School District No. 1,* 102 Sup.Ct. 3187 (1982).

73. *Crawford* v. *Board of Education,* 102 Sup.Ct. 3211 (1982).

practice was in violation of the law because the company could not show a direct correlation between the diploma required, the skills tested, and the actual job performance required. In a somewhat related case, a suit was brought against the Washington, D.C., police for using "Test 21," a verbal ability civil service test, for its police officers. The suit charged that the test was racially discriminatory, and therefore violated the due-process clause of the Fifth Amendment. In *Washington* v. *Davis* (1976), the court concluded that:

A test that is racially neutral on its face, that is administered without racially discriminatory action or intent, and that is reasonably related to a legitimate state purpose, e.g., that of insuring a minimum level of verbal ability in police recruits is constitutional.[74]

In a similar case, South Carolina's use of the National Teacher Examinations for purposes of certification of teachers was tested in *United States* v. *South Carolina* (1978), and found not in violation of the equal-protection clause of the Fourteenth Amendment, as well as not in violation of Title VII of the Civil Rights Act. In upholding the use of the test, the court essentially found that the plaintiff had failed to establish racial discriminatory intent and, as in the previous case, that a reasonable relationship appeared to exist between the degree of knowledge a teacher possesses and his or her performance in the classroom.[75]

Racial discrimination in the appointment of school board members and teachers

In the case of *Mayor of Philadelphia* v. *Educational Equality League* (1974), the League failed to prove that the mayor had racially discriminated in nominating panel members for selecting board members. In this case, as in so many others like it, the Supreme Court ruled that numerical racial imbalance does not, in itself, prove unconstitutional discrimination. In the *Hazelwood School District* v. *United States* (1977), the court reversed a lower court ruling that the suburban St. Louis school district was in violation of Title VII of the Civil Rights Act because the number of black teachers employed was less than the average for the county, excluding the City of St. Louis. In reversing that decision, the court maintained that the relevant comparison to be made was not to the county average, but rather to the total size of the available black labor pool.[76] Unlike the liability which school boards incurred with respect to correcting their pre-Brown I actions involving segregation, the court was not holding the school boards liable for the hiring practices used by them prior to the passage of the Civil Rights Act of 1964. A decision to do so might have put the court in the position of enforcing an ex post facto law.

By 1979, in the *Board of Education of the City of New York* v. *Harris*

74. Zirkel, *Digest of Supreme Court Decisions Affecting Education*, p. 104.
75. *United States* v. *South Carolina*, 434 U.S. 1026 (1978).
76. Zirkel, *Digest of Supreme Court Decisions Affecting Education*, p. 110.

(1979), the school board sued the Department of Health, Education, and Welfare for withholding funds from New York City due under the Emergency School Aid Act. That 1972 Act required the withholding of funds from those districts that, after the date of the act, continued to engage in discriminatory action with respect to assignment of employees. Based on statistical evidence reflecting the board's hiring practices, the Department of Health, Education, and Welfare concluded that New York City was not eligible for payment under the act. While the city school board argued vigorously that the apparent discrimination resulted from other factors, the court agreed with the defendant's conclusion.[77]

Race and private schools

A response to the court's attempt to desegregate the public schools led those who believed in racial segregation to withdraw from the public schools and create their own private schools. As earlier noted, in *Griffin* v. *County School Board* (1964), when the Supreme Court ordered the reopening of the public schools in Prince Edward County, Virginia, they also ruled that public financial assistance to parents who sent their children to private segregated schools was unconstitutional. If, then, tuition payments were unconstitutional, what other forms of aid might be possible? In *Norwood* v. *Harrison* (1973), the court declared that the Mississippi practice of furnishing free textbooks to private segregated school students was unconstitutional. In 1971, a complaint was brought against the city of Montgomery, Alabama, for permitting racially segregated private schools to use the city park's recreational facilities. In *Gilmore* v. *Montgomery* (1974), the court ruled that only if such a practice can be shown to conflict directly with a district desegregation order, or if the private segregated schools were given exclusive use of the facilities, could such action be held a constitutional violation. Still, following a critical course with respect to private segregated schools in *Runyon* v. *McCrary* (1976), the court ruled that those private schools which advertise through the U.S. mails cannot refuse admission on the basis of race. In this case, the court used Title 42 U.S.C., Section 1981, a post-Civil War act created under the authority of the Thirteenth Amendment, which prohibits private acts of racial discrimination in the offering of contracts to the public.

Perhaps the most far-reaching case involving private segregated schools came when the Internal Revenue Service denied tax-exempt status to those schools on the grounds that they could no longer be considered "charitable" institutions. In *Bob Jones University* v. *United States* (1983), the court "held that nonprofit private schools that prescribe and enforce racially discriminatory admission standards on the basis of religious doctrine do not qualify as tax-exempt organizations under the Internal Revenue Code, nor are contributions to such schools deductible as charitable contributions."[78] This case included the Goldsboro Christian Schools as well as

---

77. Zirkel, *Digest of Supreme Court Decisions Affecting Education*, pp. 31-32.
78. *Bob Jones University* v. *United States*, 103 Sup.Ct. 2017 (1983).

Bob Jones University. The court's conclusion was clear. Irrespective of the religious claims made for segregation of the races, such schools cannot be viewed as conferring a public benefit within the ordinary meaning of "charitable."[79]

Race and affirmative action admissions programs

Recall that on a number of occasions the Supreme Court has ruled that, in desegregation cases, it is constitutionally permissible to use race and statistical ratios as a basis to right the constitutional wrongs that have been committed against blacks.[80] On the other hand, recall further that in *Milliken* v. *Bradley* (1974) and *Dayton Board of Education* v. *Brinkman II* (1979), it was found that the constitutional remedy must be related to the degree of clearly shown legal constitutional violations. Where a constitutional remedy is involved, the court has clearly maintained that the classification of race in student placement matters can be a determining factor in establishing a specific legal remedy. However, the question emerged: Can universities and professional schools, absent any specific legal or constitutional violation, operate special admissions programs for black students, using race as a determining factor, in order to overcome the broader social and racial discrimination that has existed within the professions for centuries? The first case brought to test this question was *Marco De Funis* v. *Charles Odegaard* (1974), in which a divided court ruled the question "moot," since De Funis had already been admitted to the University of Washington Law School and was nearing graduation.

Those opposed to special admissions programs found their case at the University of California Medical School at Davis. In a relatively new program, whereby the school had opened its doors only in 1968 and no history of institutional discrimination could be shown to have existed, Allan Bakke was refused admission because he failed to meet the racial criteria used in the special admissions program. In *Regents of the University of California* v. *Bakke* (1978), over fifty-eight "friends-of-the-court" briefs were filed; more than two-thirds opposed Bakke's admission. The case for preferential admission according to race found support from the attorney general's office, the N.A.A.C.P. Legal Defense and Educational Fund, the American Civil Liberties Union, the Association of American Law Schools, the Association of American Medical Colleges, black law student associations, and numerous other religious and ethnic groups. The case for Bakke was supported by the American Jewish Committee, the Anti-Defamation League of B'nai B'rith, the Chamber of Commerce of the United States, the Fraternal Order of Police, and a variety of other ethnic, religious, and social groups.[81] A large segment of those who opposed the special admissions programs came from the Jewish community. Although today we are increasingly aware of a complex history of conflicts between the Jewish and

79. *Bob Jones University* v. *United States*, p. 2020.
80. For example, see *Swann* v. *Board of Education*, 402 U.S. 1 (1971), p. 25.
81. *University of California Regents* v. *Bakke*, 438 U.S. 265 (1978), pp. 268-269.

black communities in the United States, this support for Bakke's position was in part due to the long history of negative experience the Jewish people had had with quotas being used in the past to exclude them from a variety of occupations, and their possible use against them in the future. Blacks, however, because of the ease with which they can be identified, are invariably under a quota system. The two communities thus had real conflicting interests in the Bakke case, which was highly publicized and resulted in spirited public commentaries.[82]

A divided court made its decision. Six of nine justices wrote separate opinions, but together the court split four-to-four, with Justice Powell making the determining decision. In the opinion of the majority, Title VI was not applicable in this case. The majority went on to conclude that while race may be taken into consideration as *a* factor in admissions, in the interest of maintaining a diverse student body, as Harvard University had done, it could not be used as *the* determining factor, as the University of California at Davis had done in its special medical school admissions program. Finally, the majority directed that Bakke be admitted to the Davis Medical School. Race could be taken into account as a factor in affirmative action programs, but could not be *the* factor in admissions. Thus, the court stood opposed to the development of a racial quota system for higher education.

What, then, made this case of affirmative action using a racial classification so much different from the earlier public school decisions in which racial classification was permissible, such as in *Swann* v. *Charlotte-Mecklenburg Board of Education* (1971)? The answer was to be found in the failure of the University of California at Davis to show that the special medical school admissions program was designed to remedy "clearly determined constitutional violations."[83] Rather, the Davis program was shown to be designed to remedy perceived "societal discriminations," which the court did not find sufficiently legally compelling to justify a dual system.[84] When might the court find compelling reasons to justify using race to affirmatively discriminate? The answer appears to be, only when it can be shown that a clear constitutional violation has existed. In the Bakke case, the Davis Medical School was a new school, relatively free of any history of discrimination, and under the circumstances, the University of California at Davis failed to convince the court adequately that it was, in fact, remedying "clearly determined constitutional violations."[85]

---

82. See McGeorge Bundy, "The Issue Before the Court: Who Gets Ahead in America?" *Atlantic Monthly,* Nov. 1977, pp. 41-54. Also see Nathan Glazer, *Affirmative Discrimination: Ethnic Inequality and Public Policy* (New York: Basic Books, 1975); and Allan P. Sindler, *Bakke, De Funis, and Minority Admissions: The Quest for Equal Opportunity* (New York: Longman, 1978).

83. *University of California Regents* v. *Bakke,* pp. 300-301.

84. In fact, the majority seemed persuaded by the suggestion that the dual Davis system could not substantially increase the number of blacks in the medical profession. See *University of California Regents* v. *Bakke,* p. 311.

85. *University of California Regents* v. *Bakke,* p. 300.

STUDENT RIGHTS

The right to due process

A whole new area of cases emerged after 1967, involving student rights, as a consequence of the Supreme Court's action *In re Gault,* 387 U.S. 1 (1967), which extended the due-process protection of the Fourteenth Amendment to children under eighteen years of age. This case developed when the State of New York sentenced a fifteen-year-old boy to six years in the state school for juvenile delinquents for making an obscene phone call. The same act, in the same state, committed by an adult, would have resulted in a maximum two-month imprisonment and a fifty-dollar fine.[86] The boy was sentenced without advice of legal counsel and the protection of his constitutional right to due process. The court concluded that children under eighteen years of age are protected by the Fifth Amendment right against self-incrimination, as well as the Fourteenth Amendment right to due process. This was the beginning of a series of cases which brought the court directly into the classroom to protect young people's constitutional liberties.

The right to freedom of expression

In Des Moines, Iowa, three public school students were suspended from school for wearing black arm-bands as a symbolic protest against the Vietnam War. The court, in *Tinker* v. *Des Moines Independent Community School District* (1969), found that the wearing of an arm-band did not interfere with or disrupt the school's routine in any way. It further concluded that the action was a peaceful symbolic expression, protected by the free-speech clause of the First Amendment, made applicable to the states by the Fourteenth Amendment.

What followed was a series of cases involving picketing and other forms of protest activities. In *Police Department* v. *Mosley* (1972), the court heard a case in which a lone, peaceful picketer was arrested under an antipicketing ordinance, which prohibited nonlabor picketing during school hours. The court struck down the ordinance as a violation of the equal-protection clause of the Fourteenth Amendment. In *Grayned* v. *City of Rockford* (1972), the court again struck down a similar antipicketing ordinance, but upheld that part of the ordinance which prohibited noisemaking during school hours.[87]

As the conservative backlash against the antiwar movement grew in the 1970's, the court was increasingly called upon to protect students' rights. In *Healy* v. *James* (1972), the court came to the aid of state college students and protected their right to free association by striking down a college administration prohibition against the formation of an S.D.S. chapter on campus.[88] The following year, the justices prohibited a state university

86. Zirkel, *Digest of Supreme Court Decisions Affecting Education,* p. 37.
87. Zirkel, *Digest of Supreme Court Decisions Affecting Education,* pp. 38-39.
88. Zirkel, *Digest of Supreme Court Decisions Affecting Education,* p. 41.

from expelling a graduate student for distributing an "indecent" cartoon with a political message. In *Papish* v. *Board of Curators* (1973), the court ruled that the state could not suppress the student newspaper for violating "conventions of decency" unless it could be shown that such material was legally obscene, or disruptive of the educational process. The First Amendment, the court held, protects students' freedom of speech and press on state college campuses, as it does elsewhere in the general community.[89]

Conditions of punishment

For a complex variety of educational and social reasons, discipline in the schools became more problematic in the 1970's. As it did so, state legislatures responded by passing more stringent laws which they believed might solve the problem. The State of Ohio passed legislation which permitted school principals to suspend students for up to ten days without giving them either notice of the reasons for suspension or the opportunity to give their own explanations for the events which led to the suspension. In *Goss* v. *Lopez* (1975), the court declared the Ohio law in violation of the Fourteenth Amendment, which prohibits the states from impairing a person's life, liberty, or property without due process of law. In this case, the justices found the student's "property" interest in public education and his "liberty" interest in terms of his reputation were being impaired without due process. The Ohio law clearly abrogated those rights. The court went on to set explicitly some practical guidelines for administrators to follow in order to keep within the constitutional rights of the student. It said a student must be told, in oral or written form, of the charges brought against him or her, must be given an explanation of the evidence against him or her, and finally, must be given an opportunity to present his or her view of the incident.[90]

In *Wood* v. *Strickland* (1975), the court laid down the condition under which a school official might be sued for violation of a federal statute which makes state officials liable for violation of a student's constitutional rights. The principal is liable, the court concluded, if he or she acts with malicious intent, and if he or she should have known that the action taken was a violation of the constitutional rights of the student.[91] In *Carey* v. *Piphus* (1978), the court held that in school suspension cases in which due process had been denied, and where actual injury to the student had not been shown, nominal damages could still be awarded in recognition of the student's right to procedural due process.[92] Thus, it made clear that when a principal suspends a student, the principal must act within the limits of the student's constitutional rights. Those limits apply in the area of corporal punishment, as well as in suspensions.

In *Baker* v. *Owen* (1975), the Supreme Court upheld a North Carolina law that permitted corporal punishment. In this case, the justices affirmed a lower court decision that laid down guidelines which included warning

---

89. Zirkel, *Digest of Supreme Court Decisions Affecting Education*, p. 42.
90. Zirkel, *Digest of Supreme Court Decisions Affecting Education*, p. 42.
91. Zirkel, *Digest of Supreme Court Decisions Affecting Education*, p. 44.
92. Zirkel, *Supplement to a Digest of Supreme Court Decisions Affecting Education*, p. 12.

the student ahead of time as to what would occur if the infraction was repeated, and the use of other means to modify the student's behavior. When the punishment is administered, a second school official must be present and informed at the time of punishment as to the reasons for such punishment. Lastly, on parental request, the person administering the punishment must provide a written explanation of the punishment and the name of the official present.[93] In a Florida case in which there occurred exceptionally harsh punishment requiring medical attention, the parents brought suit, in *Ingraham* v. *Wright* (1977), arguing that the paddling received was cruel and unusual punishment, and therefore a violation of the Eighth Amendment, and also deprived the student of his procedural due-process protection under the Fourteenth Amendment. The court concluded that the Eighth Amendment did not apply to discipline in the public schools, and further, that the due-process clause of the Fourteenth Amendment does not require formal notice and hearing prior to imposition of corporal punishment.[94] It determined that the Fourteenth Amendment's requirement of procedural due process was satisfied by Florida's preservation of common-law constraints and remedies, and therefore made the case for additional administrative safeguards significantly less compelling. The court took note of the exceptional harshness in this case, and pointed to the fact that the parents still had the opportunity to bring civil or criminal suit against the school personnel in charge.[95]

While the court has extended the meaning of the Fourteenth Amendment to include cases of suspension and, to a somewhat lesser degree, cases involving corporal punishment, it has been more reluctant to enter the area of academic evaluation. Many institutions have adopted a variety of codes to protect the student against capricious grading on the part of a teacher or a faculty committee making an academic evaluation. The Supreme Court has avoided the academic evaluation area by making a sharp distinction between disciplinary decisions and academic decisions. The latter, the court insists, require far fewer stringent procedural requirements and ought to permit much greater flexibility for expert evaluation to occur.[96] In *Board of Curators of the University of Missouri* v. *Horowitz* (1978), the justices reviewed the case of a student who was dismissed in her last year of medical training. The plaintiff argued that she had been deprived of her liberty without due process because she did not have a final hearing before the school's decision-making body. The court concluded that the plaintiff, given the evaluation process that had occurred, had been accorded all her rights as required by the Fourteenth Amendment. The court said, "Dismissals for academic (as opposed to disciplinary) cause do not necessitate a hearing before the schools' decision-making body."[97] The

---

93. Zirkel, *Digest of Supreme Court Decisions Affecting Education*, p. 45. See also *Baker* v. *Owen*, 395 F.Supp. 294 (1975).

94. Zirkel, *Digest of Supreme Court Decisions Affecting Education*, p. 46.

95. See *Ingraham* v. *Wright*, 430 U.S. 651 (1977), p. 652.

96. See *Board of Curators of the University of Missouri* v. *Horowitz*, 435 U.S. 79 (1978), p. 86.

97. *Board of Curators of the University of Missouri* v. *Horowitz*, p. 79.

plaintiff did not show arbitrariness or capriciousness in the process of evaluation. She, in turn, argued that in *Goss* v. *Lopez* (1975), the court required a hearing. The court responded by making a distinction between disciplinary decisions as opposed to academic decisions, the latter of which, it concluded, did not require a hearing.[98] While it seems fairly clear that an outright capricious grading case could logically be argued as a violation of one's liberty and property interests under the Fourteenth Amendment, it seems equally clear that, up to this point, at least, the Supreme Court has expressed reluctance to enter the academic evaluation arena.

While the court has hesitated in the area of academic evaluation, it also has hesitated to accept a number of other cases involving searches and seizures in public schools. With the increase of drug traffic in the schools, and the corresponding increased attempts to curb that traffic by school authorities, numerous lower court cases involving searches and seizures have emerged. Even though the Supreme Court has sidestepped making some decisions in this area, it was recently pressed into doing so.[99] By January of 1985, the court was ready to render a decision in this area. In *New Jersey* v. *T.L.O.* (1985), the court considered whether or not a school official violated a student's Fourth Amendment rights when he searched her purse for cigarettes and found evidence of drug use as well as drug dealing, and then turned that evidence over to the police. The court ruled that the Fourth Amendment's prohibition against unreasonable searches and seizures does apply to public school officials, and that school children have a legitimate expectation of privacy while in school. However, in balancing the right of the student to privacy with the right of the school official to maintain an environment for learning, the court concluded that such an official need not obtain a search warrant before searching a student, nor must such a search be based on the more stringent rule of "probable cause." Rather, the court ruled that the legality of a search should depend simply on the "reasonableness" of the search, under all circumstances of the search. "Reasonableness" was to be determined by whether the "action was justified at its inception," and secondly, whether the search was "reasonably related in scope" to the circumstances which justified the intrusion in the first place. If the school official has reasonable grounds for suspecting that a search will turn up evidence that the student has or is violating the law or the rules of the school, then a search is justified. In applying these criteria to the case at hand, the court found that the school official had, in fact, carried on a reasonable search, and thus had not violated the student's Fourth Amendment rights.

In *Board of Education, Island Trees Union Free School District* v. *Pico* (1982), the court ruled that the school board had violated a student's First Amendment rights when it removed books from the school library with

---

98. *Board of Curators of the University of Missouri* v. *Horowitz*, p. 80. Justice Marshall, however, in an opinion concurring in part and dissenting in part, suggested that the clinical evaluation appeared to be based on something other than "purely academic reasons" (p. 104).

99. The court had denied cert. in two such cases. See *Doe* v. *Renfrow* (7th Cir. 1980) cert. denied (1981); and *Horton* v. *Goose Creek Independent School District* (1982) cert. denied (1983). However, by 1985, the court heard such a case. See *New Jersey* v. *T.L.O.*, 53 U.S.L.W. 4083, Jan. 15, 1985.

the intent of denying the respondent access to certain ideas the board believed were in conflict with the community values it sought to transmit. While the court did not deny the board's legitimate role in determining library content, they did conclude that it had overstepped its constitutional bounds. The board, in effect, was prescribing an orthodoxy of opinion in matters of politics, nationalism, and religion which the court had earlier ruled, in *West Virginia* v. *Barnette* (1943), was prohibited action.[100]

TEACHERS' RIGHTS

Loyalty oaths and the right to free association and free expression

As a consequence of the cold war, there was an increase in laws requiring loyalty oaths and legislation attempting to control teachers' associations. New York State had enacted a loyalty system which made membership in certain organizations and the utterances of "treasonable" or "seditious" words or acts sufficient grounds for termination of employment. In *Keyishian* v. *Board of Regents* (1967), the court declared New York's loyalty laws unconstitutional. It insisted that for any loyalty system to be valid, it must be limited to only those people who knowingly and actively pursue illegal goals of subversive and illegal organizations. In defending the teacher's right to freedom of speech and free association, the court argued eloquently for the need to preserve academic freedom, which is "a special concern of the First Amendment."[101]

In *Whitehill* v. *Elkins* (1967), and a number of other cases, the Supreme Court struck down loyalty oaths because of "vagueness," and therefore ruled that they violated a teacher's First and Fourteenth Amendment rights. Not until *Cole* v. *Richardson* (1972), when the court found a Massachusetts oath constitutional, did this area of litigation appear settled. The oath was worded:

I do solemnly swear . . . that I will uphold and defend the Constitution of the United States . . . and the Constitution of the Commonwealth of Massachusetts and that I will oppose the overthrow of the government of the United States or this Commonwealth by force, violence or by any illegal or unconstitutional method.[102]

The justices determined that this oath did not violate either First or Fourteenth Amendment rights, but was "simply an acknowledgement of a willingness to abide by constitutional processes of government."[103]

While the issue of loyalty oaths now appeared to be settled, the right of the teacher to speak out on public issues without fear of losing his or her job was not. In *Pickering* v. *Board of Education* (1968), the court heard a

100. *Board of Education, Island Trees Union Free School District No. 26* v. *Steven A. Pico*, 102 Sup.Ct. 2799 (1982).

101. See *Keyishian* v. *Board of Regents*, 385 U.S. 589 (1967), p. 603.

102. Zirkel, *Digest of Supreme Court Decisions Affecting Education*, p. 62.

103. Zirkel, *Digest of Supreme Court Decisions Affecting Education*, p. 63.

case in which an Illinois teacher was dismissed for writing a letter to the local newspaper criticizing the board's allocations of funds between athletic and educational programs. After a full hearing, the board concluded that the teacher's letter was "detrimental to the efficient operation and administration of the schools of the district," and therefore the teacher was dismissed. The teacher brought suit, claiming that the board had violated his freedom of speech as protected by the First Amendment. The court ruled that the teacher's comments regarding matters of public interest were protected, just as the rights of any other member of the general public would be. While it to some extent appreciated the necessity of balancing the right of the employee as a citizen in commenting on matters of public concern against the interest of the state as an employer centrally concerned with promoting efficiency in public service, the court concluded that a public employee does not relinquish First Amendment rights to comment on matters of public interest by virtue of government employment.[104]

In *Perry* v. *Sindermann* (1972), a teacher in a state college was fired for his public criticism of the Board of Regents' policies. In this case, the teacher, though nontenured, claimed to have tenure rights because he had been hired on a one-year contract basis for ten years, and the Texas Faculty Guide explicitly stated that a teacher with seven years of employment in the system was tenured. In this case, the court concluded that where the state created an objective expectation of tenure, it also created a "property" interest on behalf of the employee in continued employment, and that the employee's property interest was protected by the Fourteenth Amendment due-process clause. With respect to the firing, itself, the court found that the regents had violated the teacher's First Amendment rights, and therefore had to reinstate the teacher, irrespective of presence or absence of tenure rights.[105]

The question remained: How far do one's free speech rights go in protecting one from dismissal? If a school board, for example, intended to fire a teacher for legitimate educational competency reasons, but in the course of events violated the teacher's free speech constitutional rights, would the board be required to continue the employment of the teacher? In *Mount Healthy City School District* v. *Doyle* (1977), the court heard a case in which a nontenured teacher who had a previous series of professional difficulties had been fired shortly after phoning a local radio station and reading, on the air, the substance of a principal's memorandum which dealt with a faculty dress code. In this case, the court concluded that the motivating factor in the termination of employment was the call to the radio station, but that the teacher's right to do so was protected by the First Amendment. Therefore, the teacher was entitled to reinstatement with back pay. The court went on to say, however, that if the board could show that they had planned to fire the teacher anyway for other professional reasons, and that the action involving the free-speech question was not the motivating reason for termination, then the board was free to dismiss the teacher. The board's right to hire and/or fire was not at issue; the sole issue was whether

---

104. Zirkel, *Digest of Supreme Court Decisions Affecting Education*, p. 60.
105. Zirkel, *Digest of Supreme Court Decisions Affecting Education*, p. 64.

or not the teacher was being fired for the exercise of his constitutional rights.[106] In *Givhan* v. *Western Line Consolidated School District* (1979), the court held that a teacher could not be dismissed for private expressions of criticism to the principal concerning school board policies, and remanded the case to the lower court for further tests based on the Mount Healthy decision.[107]

The Supreme Court increasingly made a distinction between those expressions of speech which involved the concern of an ordinary citizen, and those issues which were particularly germane to the government as an employer concerned with maintaining operating efficiency. In *Connick* v. *Myers* (1983), the court held that the discharge of a former assistant district attorney did not violate that person's constitutionally protected free speech. Myers had been discharged, in large part, because of an office questionnaire she had distributed which dealt primarily with issues of office management and efficiency. She was told by her employer that this was an act of insubordination. She appealed on the grounds of infringement of her First Amendment constitutional rights. The court, after reviewing the case and carefully examining the questionnaire involved, concluded that the primary issue was not that of concern to the interest of the ordinary citizen, but rather that which concerned the operating efficiency of the particular office. Under such circumstances, the court did not find a constitutional violation.[108]

Job security and conditions of employment

Most teacher tenure contract systems are based on state laws and involve state court interpretation. However, teacher tenure contracts are also protected by Article 1, Section 10 of the United States Constitution, which prohibits the creation of laws impairing contract rights. This was the case in *Indiana ex. rel. Anderson* v. *Brand* (1938), when the Supreme Court struck down the State of Indiana statute which attempted to eliminate, without sufficient justification, township schools from tenure coverage. Nevertheless, most tenure cases, especially those involving financial retrenchment, have usually been confined to the state court system.

The issue of whether Fourteenth Amendment due-process protection extends to nontenured teachers was considered by the court in *Board of Regents* v. *Roth* (1972). It concluded, in that case, that when the teacher involved was dropped from employment, after a year of service, without notice or hearing, his rights were not violated. Without any employer's statement which would damage his reputation, he was not deprived of "liberty"; and without any state language which created an expectation of continued employment, no "property" interest could be said to have existed. Under such circumstances, the Fourteenth Amendment did not apply to the nonrenewal of nontenured teachers' contracts.[109]

Teacher contracts may be written so as to require them to live within the

---

106. Zirkel, *Digest of Supreme Court Decisions Affecting Education*, p. 70.
107. Zirkel, *Supplement to a Digest of Supreme Court Decisions Affecting Education*, p. 20.
108. *Connick* v. *Myers*, 103 Sup.Ct. 1684 (1983).
109. Zirkel, *Digest of Supreme Court Decisions Affecting Education*, pp. 63-64.

city in which they teach. Although the court has never heard a specific case dealing with such a requirement for teachers per se, in *McCarthy v. Philadelphia Civil Service Commission* (1964), it upheld the city of Philadelphia's requirement that all city employees live within the city limits.

With the rise in teachers' unions and collective bargaining units in recent decades have come a number of Supreme Court cases pertaining to teacher organizations and collective bargaining activities. In *Hortonville Joint School District No. 1 v. Hortonville Education Association* (1976), the court upheld the school board's right to terminate illegally striking teachers at the same time that they were negotiating contract questions with them; and in *Madison v. Wisconsin Employment Relations Commission* (1976), the court declared a State Employment Commission order prohibiting nonunion teachers from speaking to the board on collective bargaining issues unconstitutional.[110] In that same year, the court declared the extension of the Federal Fair Labor Standard Act of 1938 (amended in 1974), covering teachers and other state employees, a violation of the Tenth Amendment, and an unnecessary federal intrusion into state authority.

In 1977, the court took up a challenge to an "agency shop" agreement which required all Detroit teachers to pay union dues, whether they belonged to the union or not. Challenge was also made as to the union's expenditure of dues for political and other social activities. In *Abood v. Detroit Board of Education* (1977), the court upheld the school board's right to require all employees to pay union dues, but it also forbade the union to use those funds collected from nonunion members for anything other than collective bargaining purposes.[111]

Challenges with respect to the school board's right to set conditions of employment continue. A tenured teacher in Oklahoma brought suit against the board for refusing to renew her contract because she had failed to meet the board's minimum continuing education requirement. In *Harrah Independent School District v. Martin* (1979), the Supreme Court ruled that the board was well within its rights in linking contract renewal with a continuing education requirement. In that same year, in *Ambach v. Norwick*, the court upheld a New York State law which withheld teaching certification from aliens. The court concluded that the requirement of citizenship for teaching certification bears a rational relationship to a legitimate state interest in having loyal teachers in the classroom.[112]

Women's rights, conditions of employment, and sex discrimination

With the emergence of the women's movement in the 1960's and 1970's came a series of cases dealing with women's rights. One of the early challenges was the right of the state to operate single-sex schools. In *William v. McNair* (1971), the court upheld the right of the State of South Carolina to run a college for females, and reasoned that as long as similar course offerings were available at equally prestigious institutions for

110. Zirkel, *Digest of Supreme Court Decisions Affecting Education*, p. 69.
111. Zirkel, *Digest of Supreme Court Decisions Affecting Education*, p. 72.
112. Zirkel, *Supplement to a Digest of Supreme Court Decisions Affecting Education*, pp. 21-22.

males, no violation of the equal-protection clause had occurred.[113] It is noteworthy that the court did not rule that sex-segregated education was inherently unequal, as they had when considering race segregation in the Brown I decision of 1954. In the South Carolina decision, though, sex was not held to be a suspect classification. The court continued to accept sex-segregated schools as a legitimate educational practice as long as attendance was voluntary and alternative coeducational choices were available. In *Vorcheimer* v. *School District of Philadelphia* (1977), the court upheld the right of the City of Philadelphia to operate two sex-segregated high schools for the academically talented. Here, again, it found these sex-segregated schools not in violation of the equal-protection clause of the Fourteenth Amendment, because students could choose between a comprehensive coeducational school and a sex-segregated, academic, elite school.[114]

By 1982, however, the court had begun to show some signs of change in this matter. In *Mississippi University for Women* v. *Hogan* (1982), the justices heard the case of a male student denied admission to a nursing program at an all-female college. In a five-to-four decision, the majority concluded that the state failed to make clear reasonable government purposes, and further failed to demonstrate how the discriminatory means used were related to those purposes. They ruled that the school's admissions policy perpetuated the stereotype of nursing as being a woman's occupation. The plaintiff was thus denied his right to equal protection under the Fourteenth Amendment, and was therefore ordered admitted.[115]

By the middle of the 1970's, the Supreme Court began to hear cases involving pregnancy. In *Geduldig* v. *Aiello* (1974), the court reviewed a State of California disability insurance system which excluded normal pregnancy from coverage. The charge was brought that the program discriminated against women, and therefore violated the equal-protection clause of the Fourteenth Amendment. The court upheld the California exclusionary practice, concluding that the practice of excluding women from eligibility for benefits due to normal pregnancy is not a sex-based discrimination, and therefore is not barred by the equal-protection clause of the Fourteenth Amendment. It reasoned that the program was not sex-based because:

The program divides potential recipients into two groups—pregnant women and nonpregnant persons. While the first group is exclusively female, the second includes members of both sexes. The fiscal and actuarial benefits of the program thus accrue to members of both sexes.[116]

---

113. Zirkel, *Supplement to a Digest of Supreme Court Decisions Affecting Education*, p. 89.

114. Zirkel, *Supplement to a Digest of Supreme Court Decisions Affecting Education*, pp. 107-108. One might, however, just as easily argue that the choice between the sex-segregated school for academically talented females and the less-talented coeducational school was not a reasonable choice. The appropriate choice should have been with an academically talented coeducational school, which did not exist.

115. In this case, the state further argued that Title IX exempts the single-sex schools from prosecution under that act. The court, however, said that the constitutional violation took precedence over the legislative action.

116. *Geduldig* v. *Aiello*, 417 U.S. 484 (1974), p. 497.

Given the increased burden of costs involved, the majority of the justices argued that the exclusion of normal pregnancy was justifiable. Speaking for the minority, however, Justice Brennan pointed out that the court, in upholding this practice, was allowing the state to clearly discriminate against women, because the same law which prohibited a gender-linked disability such as pregnancy also permitted a gender-linked disability such as operations for prostatectomies.[117]

In that same year, the court, in *Cleveland Board of Education* v. *Lafleur* and in *Cohen* v. *Chesterfield County School Board,* reviewed cases involving a set of mandatory rules governing maternity leave. The Cleveland Board of Education required pregnant teachers to leave work without pay five months before the expected birth, and did not allow them to return until the beginning of the next regular school semester. The Chesterfield County School Board of Virginia used similar rules. The court found both boards' rules arbitrary and in violation of the employees' due-process rights under the Fourteenth Amendment. Pregnancy, the court held, must be treated like any other temporary disability for all job-related purposes.

As the women's movement gained momentum, the court began to hear more cases involving women's rights and sex discrimination. By the late 1970's, it was increasingly being called upon to interpret the new statutes which prohibit sex discrimination. The statutes most frequently interpreted by court ruling were part of Title VII of the Civil Rights Act (1964), which prohibits employers, employment agencies, and labor organizations from discriminating against employees on the basis of race, color, religion, sex, or national origin; the Equal Pay Act, enacted in 1963 as an amendment to the Fair Labor Standard Act of 1938; and Title IX of the Education Amendment of 1972, which prohibits sex discrimination against participants in, or beneficiaries of, educational programs receiving federal funds.

The issue of pregnancy once again appeared in the Supreme Court's interpretation of Title VII in *Nashville Gas Company* v. *Satty* (1977). In this case, the court found the Nashville Gas Company's mandatory maternity leave policy, which deprived the pregnant employee of her accumulated job seniority, a violation of Title VII, which prohibits discrimination against employees based on sex. However, in regard to that same company policy which did not allow sick leave pay for pregnancy, the court upheld the right of the company to do so, on the grounds that pregnancy was not sex-based discrimination as determined in *Geduldig* v. *Aiello* (1974), and as later upheld in *General Electric Company* v. *Gilbert* (1976).[118] Thus, the court so interpreted the meaning of Title VII as to exclude pregnancy. Congress reacted to this interpretation and passed legislation specifically to prohibit discrimination based on pregnancy.[119] In this instance, Congress was clearly ahead of the court in extending women's rights.

---

117. *Geduldig* v. *Aiello,* p. 501.
118. Zirkel, *Supplement to a Digest of Supreme Court Decisions Affecting Education,* pp. 16-17.
119. Pregnancy Disabilities Act, 42 U.S.C.A., Section 2000e(k) (1978). See Thomas et al., *Educators and the Law,* p. 120.

By 1978, the court, in *Los Angeles* v. *Manhart*, found the state pension plan of California, which required larger contributions from females than males because they lived longer, a violation of Title VII. The court has continued to find the use of sex classification in insurance programs and pension plans a violation of Title VII. In the *Board of Trustees of Keene State College* v. *Sweeney* (1978), and a number of other cases,[120] the court has further clarified the procedural process through which sex discrimination cases can and will be heard as they arise from both the private and public employment sectors.

As Title IX began to be used to attack sex discrimination, it, too, required interpretation. In *Cannon* v. *The University of Chicago* (1979), the Supreme Court ruled that, as a consequence of discrimination, not only might federal funds be withheld from the institutional violator, but the individual affected by such discrimination could also bring a private suit.[121] The meaning of Title IX was again open for judicial review when Elaine Dove, a tenured teacher in the North Haven public school system, after having been given a one-year maternity leave, was not rehired. She appealed to the Department of Health, Education, and Welfare, charging a Title IX violation. Section 901(a) of Title IX of the Education Amendment of 1972 provides that "no person," on the basis of sex, shall "be excluded from participation in, be denied the benefits of, or be subjected to discrimination under any education program or activity receiving Federal financial assistance."[122] The North Haven Board contended that this phrase covered students, not employees. The court, however, held that employment discrimination falls within Title IX's purview.

The fear of termination of federal funding due to discriminatory practices proved to be a potent weapon in the battle against institutional discrimination. H.E.W. implemented the law so that, if the institution was found in violation, the penalty would be institution-wide. Under such circumstances, some institutions might pay dearly for a single program violation. In *Grove City College* v. *Terrel H. Bell* (1984), the court ruled that the remedy must be program-specific rather than institution-wide.[123] Thus, while it began restricting Title IX's potential institutional threat, cases involving Title VII, Title IX, and the Equal Pay Act of 1963, concerning work conditions and equal pay, steadily began to mount in the lower courts. Throughout most of these court deliberations, the equal-pay-for-equal-work standard, as enunciated in the Equal Pay Act of 1963, was accepted. No lower court, nor the Supreme Court, has as yet accepted the comparable-work standard. In *The County of Washington* v. *Gunther* (1981), the Supreme Court held that wage differentials for female guards were based on sex discrimination, even though the female guards were shown to have performed work that was not the same as that of the male guards. Although, in this case, the court was explicit in pointing out that

---

120. For example, see *McDonnell Douglas Corp.* v. *Green*, 411 U.S. 792 (1973); and *Furnco Construction Corp.* v. *Waters*, 438 U.S. 567 (1978).
121. Zirkel, *Supplement to a Digest of Supreme Court Decisions Affecting Education*, p. 13.
122. *North Haven Board of Education* v. *Bell*, 102 Sup.Ct. 1912 (1982), p. 1913.
123. See *Grove City College* v. *Terrel H. Bell*, 52 L.W. 4283.

they were not adopting a comparable-work standard in interpreting Title VII, many, especially the dissenting justices, felt the court was dangerously close to doing so.[124]

If the court thus proceeds on its present course, more decisions might be expected involving sex discrimination in terms of hiring, promoting, firing, and improving work conditions, including the controversial equal-pay-for-equal-work standard. Given the increasing number of sexual harrassment cases which have begun to appear in the lower courts, one might reasonably expect that the court may yet be called upon to render a decision in that area as well.

THE RIGHTS OF THE DISABLED

Throughout the twentieth century, it has largely been the case that most of the political efforts in support of education for the handicapped have taken place at the state level. In the 1960's, however, a significant shift to the national level took place, highlighted by the creation of the Bureau of Education for the Handicapped (B.E.H.) in 1966. Strong congressional lobbying on behalf of the handicapped developed, as did successful action at the Federal District Court level on behalf of handicapped people in public education.[125] As the pressure on the Congress mounted, it responded with passage of the Rehabilitation Act of 1973, despite President Nixon's veto. Because of the sweeping nature of the law, three presidents—Nixon, Ford, and Carter—each tended to resist implementing the law. Their primary reason was the extremely high cost of full implementation. The law, especially Section 504, prohibited discrimination against "otherwise qualified handicapped individuals" in all activities and programs receiving federal assistance. In spite of resistance from the executive branch of government, Congress continued to respond to strong lobbying pressure and passed the Developmentally Disabled Assistance and Bill of Rights Act (1975), followed by the Education for All Handicapped Children Act (1975), known as the mainstreaming act.[126] While these acts required the states to respond in significantly different ways with regard to how they institutionalized, as well as educated, the handicapped, in all cases Congress failed to adequately fund the legislation that was passed. Questions involving costs were immediately raised, as were questions of what, in fact, was an "appropriate" education for any given handicapped person. In the absence of adequate congressional funding and executive branch implementation, the judicial branch was called upon to interpret the new laws.

In *Southeastern Community College* v. *Davis* (1979), the Supreme Court heard an appeal from a plaintiff who had been denied admission to a nurs-

---

124. See *County of Washington* v. *Gunther,* 452 U.S. 161 (1981).

125. See *Mills* v. *Board of Education of the District of Columbia,* 348 F.Supp. 866 (D.C. 1972); and *Pennsylvania,* 334 F.Supp. 1257 (1971), 343 F.Supp. 279 (E.D. Pa. 1972).

126. See Erwin L. Levine and Elizabeth M. Wexler, *P.L. 94-142: An Act of Congress* (New York: Macmillan, 1981).

ing program because of a serious hearing disability. She charged that she had been deprived of her Fourteenth Amendment rights and of her rights under Section 504 of the Rehabilitation Act of 1973. The plaintiff argued that she was an "otherwise qualified handicapped individual" who was denied admission to a federally funded program solely for the reason of her handicap. A unanimous court ruled that the school action was not a violation of her Fourteenth Amendment rights, nor was it a violation of Section 504 of the Rehabilitation Act. "Otherwise qualified" persons, the court reasoned, were persons who were able to meet all of the program's requirements *in spite of* their handicaps. Thus, the institution did not have to change its program to meet the needs of the handicapped.[127]

The following year, the court took up a case which required an interpretation of the Developmentally Disabled Assistance and Bill of Rights Act of 1975. In *Pennhurst State School and Hospital* v. *Halderman* (1982), the justices agreed with a lower court ruling that the conditions at the state school at Pennhurst were "dangerous" and unfit for habitation by retarded persons. They did not, however, find that the "bill of rights" section of the act created any substantive—judicially enforceable—rights for the mentally retarded.[128] The court ruled that Section 6010 of the act was not mandatory, but merely advisory. The section says in part:

. . . persons with developmental disabilities have a right to appropriate treatment, services, and habilitation; treatment should be designed to maximize the individual's potential and should be provided in the setting that is least restrictive of the person's liberty; the state and federal government have an obligation to assure that public funds are not provided to institutions or programs that do not provide appropriate treatment, services, and habilitation or do not meet minimum standards of care in six specific respects such as diet, dental care, and the use of force or chemical restraints; and rehabilitation programs should meet standards designed to assure the most favorable possible outcome for patients, and these standards should be appropriate to the needs of those being served, depending on the type of institution involved.[129]

In a six-to-three decision, the court concluded that this was but a policy statement by the Congress, intended to "encourage" rather than "mandate" better services for the developmentally disabled.[130] The court further reasoned that if, in fact, Congress had intended to mandate such programs under the act, then Congress would have provided more funds to defray the costs; it would not have imposed such massive financial obligations on the states. Therefore, the voluntary contract with the states under the act rests, at best, on ambiguous terms.[131] Finally, the majority questioned the right of the plaintiff even to bring the case to trial under this

---

127. Zirkel, *Supplement to a Digest of Supreme Court Decisions Affecting Education*, p. 14.
128. See *Pennhurst State School and Hospital* v. *Halderman*, 451 U.S. 1 (1981), pp. 1-4.
129. As quoted in Thomas et al., *Educators and the Law*, p. 117.
130. *Pennhurst State School and Hospital* v. *Halderman*, p. 19.
131. *Pennhurst State School and Hospital* v. *Halderman*, pp. 16-24.

act, because the Pennhurst School, itself, was not a direct recipient of federal assistance. Using such a narrow definition of "federally funded," the court began to limit the scope of other civil rights legislation as well.[132]

Disappointed supporters of the handicapped observed what appeared to them as clear mandatory federal legislation being transformed by court interpretation into mere legislative policy statements designed only to "encourage" the states to improve conditions for the handicapped. Some saw this interpretation as "A Blow to the Retarded."[133] Those who did so tried to remain hopeful, when on March 23, 1982, the court began to hear arguments involving the Education for All Handicapped Children Act of 1975. In *Board of Education* v. *Rowley* (1982), the justices considered the appeal that when the school district had failed to provide an eight-year-old deaf child with a sign-language interpreter, it had violated the Education for All Handicapped Children Act by not providing a "free appropriate public education" as mandated by the act. In reviewing the facts in the case, the court found that Amy Rowley had already been given special treatment, such as an F.M. hearing aid, speech therapist services for three hours per week, and an "individualized education program." She was doing well in her school work, generally achieving above her grade level. While it was clear to all that a sign-language interpreter might help her do even better, the school did not believe that the interpreter was essential. The court agreed. The majority concluded that the requirements of the act are met when the state provides personalized instruction with sufficient support services to permit the handicapped child to benefit from that instruction. They found that "the Act does not require a state to maximize the potential of each handicapped child commensurate with the opportunity provided nonhandicapped children."[134] Its intent was simply to "open the door of public education to handicapped children,"[135] not to guarantee a substantive level of support. The state met the law's requirement when it provided instruction and support services which comported with the child's grade level and her "I.E.P."[136] Thus, the court, while upholding the right to a free public education for the handicapped, interpreted Congress's intent of mandating an "appropriate education" as essentially that of "being served."

While preserving the mainstreaming law, the Supreme Court significantly reduced the possible claims the handicapped might have made under a broader interpretation of the law. Some legislators and taxpayers viewed the situation as a welcome relief, while parents of handicapped children could not help but be disturbed to find that the law, while mainstreaming their child, did not require the state to provide support services

---

132. Which they did, for example, in *Grove City College* v. *Bell* (1984). For an analysis of *Pennhurst State School and Hospital* v. *Halderman* (1981), see McCarthy's analysis in Thomas et al., *Educators and the Law*, pp. 115-120.

133. See "A Blow to the Retarded," *Newsweek*, May 4, 1981, p. 55.

134. *Board of Education of the Hendrick Hudson Central School District* v. *Amy Rowley, by her parents*, 102 Sup.Ct. 3034, p. 3036.

135. *Board of Education of the Hendrick Hudson Central School District* v. *Amy Rowley, by her parents*, p. 3036.

136. *Board of Education of the Hendrick Hudson Central School District* v. *Amy Rowley, by her parents*, p. 3049. "I.E.P." stands for "individual educational program."

to "maximize the potential of each handicapped child commensurate with the opportunity provided nonhandicapped children." It is clear that while Congress has created far-reaching legislation for the handicapped without funding, the court has restricted the scope of that legislation through interpretation. However one views these actions, it is obvious that there is nothing stopping Congress from making its intentions more explicit with new legislation, if it so chooses.

LANGUAGE, EDUCATION, AND THE LAW

As discussed in Chapter Eleven, there has been a growing need for the development of a federal language policy to assure everyone adequate access to the American cultural mainstream while protecting the individual's ethnic culture. The recent history of bilingual education reflects deep divisions with respect to these matters. At present, there are a number of lower court cases that can be expected eventually to reach the Supreme Court. Lacking any significant consensus regarding a national language policy, litigation can be expected only to increase in this area. Currently, however, the court has considered only one major case. In *Lau* v. *Nichols* (1974), it heard a class action suit brought on behalf of 1800 students of Chinese ancestry, who did not speak English, against the San Francisco school system for practices the plaintiffs believed violated Section 601 of the Civil Rights Act of 1964, which bans discrimination on the grounds of race, color, or national origin. As a result of a federal court decree, the San Francisco school system was desegregated in 1971, and as a consequence of that action, a large number of Chinese-speaking students found themselves in schools where English was the language of instruction. While the school district took no action to remedy the situation, the students and their parents, caught in such an untenable educational situation, appealed to the Supreme Court for help. The justices understood the complaint to mean that

No specific remedy is urged upon us. Teaching English to the students of Chinese ancestry who do not speak the language is one choice. Giving instruction to this group in Chinese is another. There may be others. Petitioners ask only that the Board of Education be directed to apply its expertise to the problem and rectify the situation.[137]

The Circuit Court of Appeals, which had turned down the students' complaint, reasoned that every student comes to the starting line of his or her educational career with different social, economic, and cultural advantages and disadvantages, and therefore it was not the responsibility of the courts to equalize such advantages or disadvantages. In hearing the case, the Supreme Court pointed out that the California Educational Code explicitly required that "English shall be the basic language of instruction in all schools." That section also made it clear that it was state policy to en-

---

137. *Lau* v. *Nichols*, 414 U.S. 563 (1974), pp. 564-565.

sure "the mastery of English by all pupils in the schools." Bilingual instruction was authorized by the state educational code "to the extent that it does not interfere with the systematic sequential and regular instruction of all pupils in the English language."[138] The court further pointed out that by state code a student could not graduate from grade twelve without meeting standards of proficiency in English.

Under these circumstances, if special assistance was not given, the court concluded, the non-English-speaking student would be effectively foreclosed from any meaningful instruction. Thus, it found the school district in violation of Section 601 of the Civil Rights Act of 1964, which bans discrimination "on the grounds of race, color, or national origin, in any program or activity receiving Federal financial assistance."[139] While reversing the Circuit Court decision, it remanded the case back to the lower court for relief. Some justices, in concurring briefs, worried about H.E.W. interpreting the decision in such a way as to warrant affirmative action to overcome every language deficiency which occurs in the schools. This, they believed, would go beyond the scope of Section 601, as they interpreted it. Justice Stewart, with the Chief Justice and Justice Blackmun concurring, warned:

I merely wish to make plain that when, in another case, we are concerned with a very few youngsters, or with just a single child who speaks only German or Polish or Spanish or any language other than English, I would not regard today's decision, or the separate concurrence, as conclusive upon the issue whether the statute and the guidelines require the funded school district to provide special instruction. For me, numbers are at the heart of this case and my concurrence is to be understood accordingly.[140]

The implications of the Lau Case thus remain an open question, as do so many other questions involving minority rights and language policy in the public schools. This is reflected in the increasing numbers of lower court cases developing in this area.

FINANCING PUBLIC EDUCATION

The question of school financing has understandably been the subject of concern and litigation for many years. However, during the 1970's, the heightened concern for equal educational opportunity began to have an effect on the unequal way the nation's schools were financed. Primarily controlled by local boards, and heavily financed by local property taxes, the American public school's per pupil costs varied markedly, not only by regions of the country, but also to extremes within the states themselves. While most states have established, through their state aid formulas, some minimum standard below which the poorer school districts cannot fall, the difference between the per pupil expenditure in rich districts as op-

---

138. *Lau* v. *Nichols,* p. 565.
139. *Lau* v. *Nichols,* p. 563.
140. *Lau* v. *Nichols,* p. 572.

posed to that in poor districts in any given state is significant. Responding to this problem of disparity, suits challenging state school financing systems were brought in over half the states during the 1970's.[141] Beginning with *Serrano* v. *Priest* (1971), when the State Supreme Court of California declared the financing system in violation of the state constitution, the Supreme Courts of New Jersey, Connecticut, and Washington have also found their respective systems in violation of their state constitution.[142]

The battle for equal financing of the schools continues largely at the state level. Challenge has usually not been made at the federal level, but when it has been, the Supreme Court usually has upheld the state system of financing. For example, in *McInnis* v. *Ogilvie* (1969), the court upheld the Illinois system of financing based on property tax, with state grants to assure a minimum per pupil expenditure. In this case, it not only found that the Fourteenth Amendment was not violated, but that there was no constitutional right to equal per pupil costs.[143] After the State Supreme Court of California found their school financing system in violation of the equal-protection principles embedded in the state constitution in *Serrano* v. *Priest* (1971), another case testing the widely used traditional, unequal system of Texas was appealed to the United States Supreme Court. In *San Antonio Independent School District* v. *Rodriguez* (1973), the people from the poorer school districts brought suit charging that the state financing system represented a violation of the equal-protection clause of the Fourteenth Amendment. In a five-to-four decision, the justices upheld the Texas practice. The majority reiterated their position that the equal-protection clause of the Fourteenth Amendment does not require states to expend equal financial resources on the education of each child. They noted, however, that the state constitutions may require stricter rules and conditions than does the federal Constitution, as a number of state constitutions do.

Since *San Antonio* v. *Rodriguez* (1973), the court has not been called upon to render any further decisions in this area. The problem of unequal expenditures for public school children remains a fundamental one, and throws into serious question any claim to equal educational opportunity in American public schools.

Just two years after the Rodriguez Case (1973), when a divided court upheld the right of the State of Texas to unequally fund its public schools, that state proceeded to enact another law which withheld from all local school districts any state funds to be used for the education of illegal alien children. In *Plyer* v. *Doe* (1982), the Supreme Court heard the State of Texas argue that the law did not violate the Fourteenth Amendment, which said in part that "No State shall . . . deny to any person within its jurisdiction the equal protection of the law," because undocumented alien children were not "persons within the jurisdiction" of the state, and therefore did not come under the equal-protection clause. The nonperson argument, which in effect would produce a discrete class of people against which the state might freely discriminate, was rejected, as was the argu-

---

141. See Thomas et al., *Educators and the Law*, p. 96.
142. Thomas et al., *Educators and the Law*, p. 97.
143. Zirkel, *Digest of Supreme Court Decisions Affecting Education*, p. 9.

ment that these undocumented children did not come under the state's jurisdiction. Thus, the court, in a five-to-four decision, found that the Texas law violated the equal-protection clause of the Fourteenth Amendment, and was therefore null and void.[144]

A NOTE IN RETROSPECT

In the past twenty years the Supreme Court has heard more than twice as many cases involving education as it had in its entire previous history. Education has clearly become a battleground on which many of the fundamental issues dividing this society have emerged. This increase in the number of cases results not only from the fact that Americans have become more litigious, but also from the fact that the federal government has become more involved in education at a time when the country has grown more deeply divided. The court, in many ways, is a barometer of social conflict, and in no small way reflects the perilous storm through which the nation is moving. Throughout the religion cases heard by the court, one could sense the difficulty in maintaining a religiously neutral public school system, as the court tenuously seemed to try to find its way between the ban against an establishment of religion and guarantees for the free exercise thereof.

Equally obvious is the court's difficulty in desegregating American institutions and eliminating racism and sexism from the laws of a society that remains both sexist and racist. Increasingly, as the powers of government have grown, so, too, has the need of the court to protect the rights of teachers, students, women, minorities, and the handicapped. In these cases, it has interpreted both the Constitution and the federal statutes dealing mainly with civil rights. As it has interpreted some cases, it has extended and broadened the meaning of the law, while in other cases it has contracted and narrowed the law's meaning. In doing so, it has expanded and contracted the freedom of individuals and groups within American society. Across the spectrum of decision making, one can sense the direction the court is moving in, and thereby sense as well the direction American education is moving in within the context of a broader set of social and historical determinants.

While some might look back on all these cases and see signs of national disintegration or evidence of a nation at war with itself, others might just as easily point to the fact that conflict in the courtroom is to be preferred over conflict in the streets, reminding us of John Locke's wise observation: "Wherever Law ends, Tyranny begins." There are those, too, who might justly argue that all of these cases reflect real signs of progress. Many of America's basic social problems, such as racism and sexism, are just now beginning to be seriously confronted. Increased litigation, under such circumstances, can be viewed as the inevitable price of social progress.

---

144. *Plyer* v. *Doe*, 102 Sup.Ct. 2382 (1982).

However one tends to interpret this phenomenal growth of court activity in education, most would agree that this nation is in a state of transition. And a fundamental part of that transition, as it appears in education, is reflected by the United States Supreme Court serving as a school board for the nation.

SUGGESTED READINGS

Abraham, Henry J. *Justices and Presidents: A Political History of Appointments to the Supreme Court,* New York, Oxford University Press, 1974.

Bickel, Alexander M. *The Supreme Court and the Idea of Progress,* New York, Harper & Row, 1970.

Bundy, McGeorge. "The Issue Before the Court: Who Gets Ahead in America?" *Atlantic Monthly,* November 1977, pp. 41-54.

Chafe, William H. *Civilities and Civil Rights,* New York, Oxford University Press, 1980.

Cross, Robert D. *The Emergence of Liberal Catholicism in America,* Cambridge, Mass., Harvard University Press, 1967.

Glazer, Nathan. *Affirmative Discrimination: Ethnic Inequality and Public Policy,* New York, Longman, 1978.

Hahn, George. "Creation-Science and Education," *Phi Delta Kappan,* LXIII (April 1982), 553-555.

Harding, Robert R. "Housing Discrimination as a Basis for Interdistrict School Desegregation Remedies," *Yale Law Journal,* XCIII, 2 (December 1983), 340-361.

Kanner, Barrett Stephen. "From Denver to Dayton: The Development of a Theory of Equal Protection Remedies," *Northwestern University Law Review,* LXXII, 3 (1977), 382-406.

Kluger, Richard. *Simple Justice,* New York, Random House, 1975.

McCarthy, Martha M. *A Delicate Balance: Church, State, and the Schools,* Bloomington, Ind., Phi Delta Kappan, 1983.

McKinney, Louise E. "Finding Intent in School Segregation Constitutional Violations," *Case Western Law Review,* XXVIII, 163 (1977), 119.

Sindler, Allan P. *Bakke, DeFunis, and Minority Admissions: The Quest for Equal Opportunity,* New York, Longman, 1978.

Teitelbaum, Herbert, and Richard J. Hiller. "Bilingual Education: The Legal Mandate," *Harvard Educational Review,* XLVII, 2 (May 1977), 138-169.

Thomas, Stephen B., Nelda H. McCabe, and Martha M. McCarthy. *Educators and the Law,* Elmont, N.Y., Institute for School Law and Finance, 1983.

Valente, William D. *Law in the Schools,* Columbus, Ohio, Charles E. Merrill Company, 1980.

Washby, Stephen L., Anthony A. D'Amato, and Rosemary Metrailer. *Desegregation from Brown to Alexander,* Carbondale, Southern Illinois University Press, 1977.

Wilkinson III, J. Harvie. *Serving Justice: A Supreme Court Clerk's View,* New York, Charterhouse, 1974.

————. *From Brown to Bakke,* New York, Oxford University Press, 1979.
Zirkel, Perry A. *A Digest of Supreme Court Decisions Affecting Education,* Bloomington, Ind., Phi Delta Kappa, 1978.
————. *Supplement to a Digest of Supreme Court Decisions Affecting Education,* Bloomington, Ind., Phi Delta Kappa, 1982.

Index

Note on the Author

CLARENCE J. KARIER is a professor of the history of education and chairperson of the Department of Educational Policy Studies at the University of Illinois, Urbana-Champaign. He received a Ph.D. in the history of American education in 1960 from the University of Wisconsin, Madison, and taught for several years at the University of Rochester, where he held a joint appointment in the Department of History and the College of Education, before moving to Illinois. He is a coauthor of *Roots of Crisis: American Education in the Twentieth Century* (1973) and author of *Shaping the Educational State: 1900 to the Present* (1975) and *Scientists of the Mind: Intellectual Founders of Modern Psychology,* published in 1986 by the University of Illinois Press.